British Car Advertising of the 1960s

British Car Advertising of the 1960s

Heon Stevenson

McFarland & Company, Inc., Publishers

Jefferson, North Carolina, and London

LIBRARY OF CONGRESS CATALOGUING-IN-PUBLICATION DATA

Stevenson, Heon, 1966–
British car advertising of the 1960s / Heon Stevenson.
p.   cm.
Includes bibliographical references and index.

ISBN 0-7864-1985-7 (illustrated case binding : 50# and 70# alkaline papers)

1. Advertising — Automobiles — Great Britain.   I. Title.
HF6161.A9S75   2005   659.19'629222'094109046 — dc22   2004020957

British Library cataloguing data are available

On the cover: Ad for the 1962 Vauxhall Cresta Hydra-matic (PA) (*Country Life*, March 8, 1962).
Accompanying copy reads, "Slave driver! — all that restless horse-power meekly
submissive to you. You whisper through traffic, you surge along the open road, you
arrive in style. Mistress of the machine, is it your genius — or is it your new Cresta, with
Hydra-matic to do all the gear-changing for you?"

Manufactured in the United States of America

*McFarland & Company, Inc., Publishers
Box 611, Jefferson, North Carolina 28640
www.mcfarlandpub.com*

Acknowledgments

I would like to thank all of the British car manufacturers, importers and others who have expressed interest in this book and who have allowed their advertisements to be reproduced, in particular Aston Martin Lagonda Ltd., the Ford Motor Co. Ltd., Jaguar Cars Ltd., the Jensen Car Company Ltd., Lotus Cars Ltd., the Peugeot Talbot Motor Co. Ltd., The Reliant Group plc, Renault UK Ltd., Rolls-Royce Motor Cars Ltd., Rover Cars, Vauxhall Motors Ltd., and *Autocar* (Morris Minor, Triumph 2000 and Triumph Vitesse).

I would also like to thank the late Graham Lee and colleagues at the famous Adversane Vehicle Breakers in West Sussex for allowing the yard's rarer 1960s stock to be studied and photographed at leisure. Many of these cars have since been acquired by enthusiasts for restoration. My sincere thanks, too, to Paul Veysey for providing numerous examples of pre-war advertisements for background research (a few of which accompany the Introduction to this book) together with information on the 1967–72 Vauxhall Victor (FD); to Paul Martin for several of the post-war advertisements shown in the book; to Derek Andrews of the Morris Cowley and Oxford Owners' Club for information on the Morris Oxford and Isis Travellers of the mid-1950s; to John Terry of the Singer Owners' Club for detailed information on the Singer SM1500 and Hunter; to Hector Mackenzie-Wintle, archivist of the Renault Owners' Club, for information on the Renault Dauphine; to Lavinia Wellicome, Curator at Woburn Abbey, for information provided by kind permission of the Duke of Bedford and the Trustees of the Bedford Estates during research into Ford's "Three Graces" campaign of 1956; to Malcolm Parsons, Reference Library and Library Archive Manager at the National Motor Museum, Beaulieu, for guidance in the course of research; to Yvonne Jones of the Vehicle Policy Group at the Driver and Vehicle Licensing Agency in Swansea for information about number plates in the 1960s; to Chloe Veale, curator, and Margaret Rose, general manager, of the History of Advertising Trust (HAT Archive) at Raveningham, Norfolk, for their help during research into the period's advertising; and to the librarians at Cambridge University Library for their great help throughout the research for this book, not least in making available long runs of those redoubtable journals of automotive record, *Automobile Engineer*, *The Autocar* (later, *Autocar*), *The Motor* (later, *Motor*), *Small Car* (later, *Car*), and the society of Motor Manufacturers and Traders' annual, *The Motor Industry of Great Britain*, together with similar runs of *Country Life*, *The Illustrated London News* and *Punch*, and issues of *(Thoroughbred &) Classic Cars* and *Classic and Sports Car* missing from my own files.

In addition, I am most grateful to the many enthusiastic owners of cars from the 1950s and 1960s who have given so freely of their time and knowledge in conversation during the last few years. Many of these cars are rare — in some cases, sole — survivors, kept and restored in order to preserve motoring history that would otherwise have been lost, and they yield the kind of detailed information that can only be acquired by experiencing a car first-hand.

It is a cliché, but no less true for being so, that anyone writing about the history of a subject stands on the shoulders of others, and in the case of this book those others are identified as often as possible in the notes, appendices and bibliography. Although many individual books and issues of magazines and journals mentioned are now out of print, copies of most remain in circulation or in preservation and, given time, can be found through motoring museums and their libraries, inter-library loan schemes, car clubs, autojumbles, the Internet, surviving magazine publishers' own back-number services and the specialists in motoring literature who advertise in the classic car press. At the time of writing, clubs for individual marques and models are listed each month in *Practical Classics* magazine. The contemporary road tests and other articles mentioned in the text and footnotes are cited directly from their original sources, but excellent retrospective compilations for individual marques and models have been published. Information on many specialist luxury and sports cars that were advertised only sparsely when in production is now widely available.

Finally, my thanks to Michael Worthington-Williams, chairman of the Society of Automotive Historians in Britain, for help and encouragement over many years; to Jeremy Kendall, Patrick Timperley, Clare Langan and George Home-Cook for suggestions and sustenance; and to Claire Masson, who read part of the draft manuscript and excised stylistic howlers. Any that remain are mine.

Contents

————————— *Between pages 276 and 277 are 8 color plates* —————————

Part Three — Imported Marques: Britain Embraces the World

Appendices

Preface

During the 1960s, the automobile finally secured its position as an indispensable component of daily life in Britain. Car ownership more than doubled from approximately one for every ten people in 1960 to one for every 4.8 people by 1970. Advertisers, who had once needed to promote the joys of motoring as well as the particular pleasures of the individual product, no longer needed to wonder whether the potential consumer, let alone society at large, might be content with no car at all. The question was not "Do we need a car?" but rather, "What car shall we have?" The car became all but universal, and most potential buyers were neither unusually prosperous nor unusually devoted to motoring. A new generation, mostly of men aged between thirty-five and fifty-five, bought new cars for the first time, and an even larger generation twenty years younger drove them second-hand in the 1970s. As in America in the 1920s, so in Britain forty years later.

Yet surprisingly few books have been published on British cars of the 1960s, considered together. Individual—particularly sporting—marques and models have attracted learned and popular monographs, many of which are listed in the Bibliography to this book. Cars of the 1960s, in combination with those of other decades, have been described in encyclopedias, general motoring histories and A–Z guides. But the reader new to the subject, and the restorer seeking an overview with which to recuperate from the benign tunnel vision enforced by the demands of a particular project, are comparatively under-served. Moreover, it is difficult for the present-day enthusiast to discover quickly what has, or has not, been published on a particular car in the classic car magazines over the years, and, as a result, many historical articles and interviews with designers remain unread by those who would most enjoy them today.

For this reason, extended references are given in the endnotes. Space has not allowed everything to be listed, but what is given will, I hope, provide a useful starting point for research.

What of the advertising? Of the narrative accounts of car advertising so far published, only Michael Frostick's *Advertising and the Motor-car* (1970), itself now a period piece, includes British cars from the 1960s, and histories of British advertising as a whole are scarcely more numerous. This might be because, as a subject, general advertising history still falls between several academic stools and is not easily researched within the boundaries of a single university town or city. Fortunately T.R. Nevett's detailed and scholarly *Advertising in Britain: A History*, although first published more than twenty years ago, is at the time of writing still available (from the History of Advertising Trust in Raveningham, Norfolk, at *www.hatads.org.uk*); and *Inside Collett Dickenson Pearce* (2000), edited by John Salmon and John Ritchie with numerous contributions from past and present members of that agency, is as fascinating an account of an agency's work over forty years as it is unusual. It includes some Ford advertisements of 1968–69.

The comparative scarcity of material on British advertising history might also be explained by a traditionally British intellectual disdain for commerce which every now and again expresses itself, on social or environmental grounds, as an objection to advertising *tout court*. This debate has been going on for a long time, and was never fiercer than during the early years of commercial television in 1955–60. Then, as now, the objectors were a vocal minority, and the exact grounds of their objections were often vague. Discovering how over fifty million Britons[1] might individually be affected by this or that strain of advertising always threatened to be difficult, and when researchers advanced with notebooks and propelling pencils the public made the most of the opportunity to diverge one from another, to guess their own motivations mistakenly, and, no doubt, occasionally to send the researchers up.

The copywriters survived, however: Ford and BMC quickly adopted television advertising, as did Vauxhall intermittently; Hillman and Standard followed; and Renault spent more than anyone in the early months of 1960. In the following years car manufacturers agreed privately amongst themselves not to compete through the new medium, although this did not prevent Ford from announcing the new Cortina in September 1962 with a flourish of an estimated £35,000 (though probably in fact about £25,000: see Appendix 11) before disappearing beneath the parapet with everyone else. A year later Ford's agency of the time analyzed the respective advantages of press and television advertising (see Appendix 12) and concluded that each had its distinctive merits. The printed advertisement remained car manufacturers' most useful medium throughout the 1960s, as contemporary estimates of television and press advertising expenditures reveal (see Appendix 11). It continued to thrive after the advent of commercial colour television in November 1969.

Within this book, Part One considers the advertising of Britain's eight family marques of the 1960s: Austin, Ford, Hillman, Morris, Reliant, Singer, Standard and Vauxhall. Part Two opens with a chapter on the sports and luxury specialists Bristol, AC, Alvis, Armstrong Siddeley, Morgan, Austin-Healey, Lotus, Gilbern and Bond (all of whom advertised comparatively infrequently), and discusses the advertising of the fifteen major sports and luxury marques of Aston Martin (including Lagonda), Bentley, Daimler, Humber, Jaguar, Jensen, MG, Riley, Rolls-Royce, Rover, Scimitar (built by Reliant but advertised separately from the firm's three-wheelers), Sunbeam, Triumph, Vanden Plas and Wolseley. Finally, the advertisements of twenty-four imported marques, whose products together made up between about 2 percent (1958) and 14 percent (1970) of cars sold in Britain (see Appendices 5 and 6) are analyzed in Part Three. As in the United States, Britain's most popular imported family cars in the early 1960s were the Volkswagen and the Renault Dauphine, whilst various models from Citroën, Lancia, Mercedes-Benz, Alfa Romeo and BMW attracted attention from enthusiasts out of all proportion to the small numbers actually imported. The advertising agencies of domestic and imported marques known to have advertised in British newspapers and magazines between 1958 and 1970 are given in Appendix 10. For collectors and readers wishing to carry out further research, approximately 2400 references to about 1200 representative magazine advertisements of the period are listed by marque in the Bibliography.

Each section on the advertising of an individual marque gives relevant historical background to the cars built in the 1960s, describes the models advertised and the themes employed in advertisements, makes comparisons with rival products and their advertising and includes quotations from contemporary road tests and, in many cases, recollections of the cars' designers. Many marques and models were related, with a family marque being the parent of sports and luxury models within the same corporate group. Thus while Ford, Vauxhall, Jensen, Reliant and Rover sailed alone (although Rover merged with Alvis in 1965 and became part of the Leyland group in 1966), the story of Triumph in the 1960s is inseparable from that of Standard; the development of Austin, as the British Motor Corporation's senior marque, provides necessary context for the stories of Morris, MG, Riley, Vanden Plas and Wolseley; Daimler was efficiently subsumed within Jaguar in the course of the decade; Rolls-Royce and Bentley offered very slightly different versions of the same cars with individual campaigns being devised for each; and Hillman, as the Rootes Group's principal marque, made possible the decade's more specialized and aspirational Humbers, Singers and Sunbeams. The sections on connected marques can be read individually or in sequence, and the treatments of related models within different marque ranges are intended to complement each other.

The influence of American trends on British car design and advertising is immediately apparent, and striking. Far from being confined to Ford and to General Motors' British subsidiary, Vauxhall, American inspiration also gave life to products of the British Motor Corporation, Standard-Triumph, the Rootes Group (even in pre–Chrysler days) and Rover. Designers familiar to American automotive historians, such as Roy Brown, Elwood Engel, Clare Hodgman, Bob Koto, Raymond Loewy, Tucker Madawick, Carl Otto and George Walker, all worked on or affected the shapes of post-war British cars. The 1947 Studebaker by Raymond Loewy and Virgil Exner is well known as the inspiration behind the 1949 Rover 75, and Howard Darrin's 1947 Frazer and Kaiser inspired Singer's Leo Shorter to create the SM1500, whose engine was used in the first Singer Gazelles. Advertising themes crossed the Atlantic, too: even the most British of saloons, when posed artistically in front of suburban houses and shopping centres, maintained a pre-war American visual tradition. Some advertisements had direct American precedents, as with copy for "England's Thunderbird," the Ford Consul Capri, in 1962. This trend reflected a wider influx of American styles and methods into British advertising in the early 1960s which diminished towards the end of the decade. Many agencies retained by British car manufacturers (see Appendix 10) had American origins or connections.

Between three and four hundred domestically produced and imported models were sold in Britain between 1960 and 1970 (the number depending on when different marks or series of a car are said to constitute different models) in addition to kit cars, one-offs and specialized sports machines rarely seen on the road. Almost all series-produced cars were advertised, many of them extensively. Not that anyone will ever know *exactly* how many different advertisements were published by British car manufacturers and importers during the 1960s—in many cases, at forty years' distance, it is impossible to complete a definitive account of the copy deployed, regionally and nationally, to promote even an individual model. A few cars, on the other hand, were barely advertised at all, their reputations, for good or ill, passing largely by word of mouth.

The advertisements shown in this book, chosen for their graphic interest and variety and as being representative of the marques and models of the period, come from a much larger collection gathered over the last twenty years, beginning with magazines passed down through my own family and augmented with discarded material found in second-hand bookshops, roadside junk and charity stalls and through fellow enthusiasts. Many first appeared in *The Field*, a slim, high-quality weekly magazine for countrymen and women whose market overlapped with that for the more self-consciously aspirational *Country Life*, which carried many—but by no means all—of the same advertisements. Other illustrations appeared in the more metropolitan *Sphere*, the long-lived humorous *Punch*, *The Illustrated London News*, *The Geographical* and *Country Fair*, among others. All were respectable papers for the middle-class readers who made up the majority of new car buyers of the time, and numerous advertisements placed in these magazines appeared in contemporary newspapers including, as the decade progressed, their weekend colour supplements. Also included are a few advertisements for British cars from English-speaking export markets, along with occasional advertisements for non-automotive products which used automobiles as backdrops. The pre–1960 advertisements

which accompany the Introduction, including several for immediate ancestors of popular models of the 1960s, illustrate the background in car design and advertising against which advertisements of 1960–1970 appeared, while a small selection of advertisements from the 1970–1980 period is shown with the Conclusion.

American readers should note that engine capacities are given in cubic centimetres (cc) and fuel consumption figures in UK gallons. Conversions: 1 cu. in = 16.39cc; 1 UK gallon = 4.55 litres; 1 US gallon = 3.79 litres.

Many British car advertisements of the 1960s belong in spirit to an earlier period, while others from the last years of the decade will be seen to anticipate the styles and preoccupations of the 1970s. Yet there are trends, visual approaches and consumer fetishes that are quintessentially "sixties" in flavour, recognizable as such forty years later, and celebrated by the mythology that has grown up around a period that continues to fascinate. Such is the transitory nature of advertising, and of the magazines and papers in which it appeared, that car advertisements for the 1960s are now rare—as indeed are most of the cars. I hope that the selection reviewed in this book will bring a representative sample of that copy to a wider audience once again, whether of automobile enthusiasts and restorers, designers seeking retrospective references and themes, students of automotive, social and advertising history, or those for whom these advertisements were the first point of contact with cars that became an integral part of personal, social and commercial life.

Heon Stevenson
Cambridge, England, Fall 2004

Introduction

"I think this is an awfully immoral job of ours. I do, really. Think how we spoil the digestions of the public."

"Ah, yes — but think how earnestly we strive to put them right again. We undermine 'em with one hand and build 'em up with the other. The vitamins we destroy in the canning, we restore in Revito, the roughage we remove from Peabody's Piper Parritch we made up into a package and market as Bunbury's Breakfast Bran; the stomachs we ruin with Pompayne, we re-line with Peplets to aid digestion. And by forcing the damn-fool public to pay twice over — once to have its food emasculated and once to have the vitality put back again, we keep the wheels of commerce turning and give employment to thousands — including you and me."

"This wonderful world!" Bredon sighed ecstatically.

— Dorothy L. Sayers, *Murder Must Advertise*, 1933.

"Set the style — make the pace." Was this a new kind of running shoe? Or the slogan of a political party? No: it was the "all new Consul Classic 315," one of Ford's more stylish, if less successful, products of the 1960s. In many ways this advertisement set the agenda for the decade. A large colour photograph showed a blue Classic in a lush field, with a young family playing in the background. Youth, vigour, style, affluence — these were the themes that dominated British car advertising in the ten years that followed.

In the 1960s, the mass-produced family car came to be portrayed not simply as a tool for transporting people, but as an integral part of a desirable lifestyle. The austerity and restrictions which had overshadowed all but the last years of the 1950s had retreated, and advertisers exploited a new sense of freedom and promise. The Ford Consul Classic, though designed in the late 1950s, was, with its "motorway pace," essentially a creature of the 1960s.

This advertisement exemplified not only the changing way in which products were described in copy, but also the way in which they were illustrated. The colour photograph, widely adopted by 1961 after several decades of occasional use by advertisers, marked a permanent move away from the exaggerated, painted portraits which had been so common in the 1950s towards more realistic depiction on film.

Early colour photographs had tended to be drab, if undoubtedly realistic, and in the immediate post-war years it was often easier and less expensive to conjure up the desired effect by means of a painting, or even a line drawing, not least because so few early photographs showed cars in motion. While some painted portraits were almost as accurate as posed photographs, the majority were deliberately atmospheric, showing, for instance, a rally car speeding across the countryside, or a new model parked outside an upmarket hotel or club with staff and guests gratifyingly, if implausibly, obsequious.

In the early part of the decade, Hillman, with the Imp, and Jaguar, with a wide variety of models, perpetuated the old idiom, but they were in the minority. Even Wolseley's paintings exaggerated the proportions of the 16/60 and 1500 only a little. Most advertisers eschewed the paintbrush in favour of the newer medium, as a good colour photograph made its subject appear glamorous while retaining dimensional realism, rendering it both plausible and attractive. This change was generally welcomed by the buying public, who came to associate the old, exaggerated paintings with an earlier era. Such an association could be fatal, unless a nostalgic effect was sought, whatever the artistic merits of the earlier medium.

1

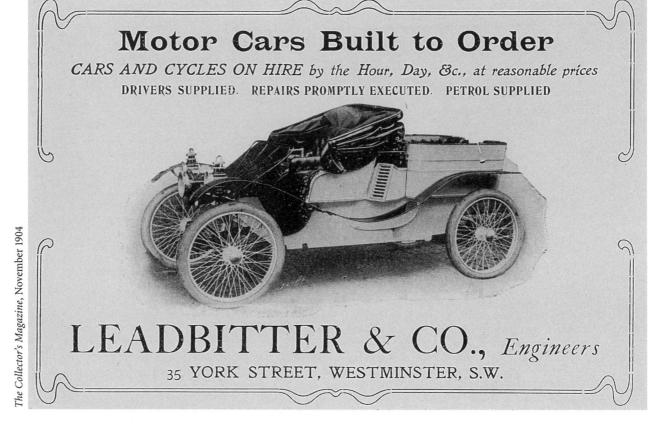

Motor Cars Built to Order

CARS AND CYCLES ON HIRE by the Hour, Day, &c., at reasonable prices

DRIVERS SUPPLIED.   REPAIRS PROMPTLY EXECUTED.   PETROL SUPPLIED

LEADBITTER & CO., Engineers
35 YORK STREET, WESTMINSTER, S.W.

1904 Leadbitter. A simple beginning: the decorative border, multiple serif typefaces and natural-looking photograph are typical of many advertisements from motoring's pioneer years. In 1904 the automobile was little more than a rich man's plaything, and was generally seen as at best a curiosity and at worst a public nuisance. Nevertheless, its potential was already apparent to thoughtful commentators.

1906 Humber. Reliability trials, owner-testimonials and simple line drawings were all popular at the beginning of the century; this piece, in effect, combines three advertisements in one. Humber was Britain's best-selling marque by the end of 1906, with approximately 1000 cars sold during the year. Production continued at the Coventry and Beeston factories (about fifty miles apart) until 1908, when expansion in the Coventry area and an industry-wide recession dictated the closure of Beeston and financial rescue in 1909 by Humber shareholder Earl Russell. During 1927-28 the Rootes brothers gained control of the company, securing this respected marque's survival during the depression years from 1929.

As illustrations became more lifelike, advertising copy shed much of its earlier restraint. While Humber, in 1949, had offered a car that was "ideal for the family, roomy but compact, powerful but economical," and the Nuffield Organization had boasted in 1950 that "the modern Morris [Six] is so much in advance of its predecessors that it creates an entirely new class of motoring," their successors were brisk and energetic. According to Vauxhall, uncharacteristically skittish in 1967, "Cresta jets you to 50mph in 7.8 secs. On 8-inch upholstery. And you feel thunderpower." The reader also felt the impact of some nauseating puns, of a kind which have proved remarkably enduring. "Vauxhall announce the new K cars," in 1971, when K registrations began, hovered in that no man's land between wit, brevity and matiness from which advertisers of executive cars have never quite escaped, and several variations on the "country estate" theme within a few short years suggested that promoters of station wagons did not always read each other's copy. Or perhaps that they did.

Some copywriters managed to combine genuine humour with the hype, and there was the usual crop of *double entendres*. While the 1950s had spawned the "Gay Look" Hillman Minx and, in American copy, "Let's take the Austin — the car that is always at home" (at a time when servicing British cars abroad was a notoriously hit-and-miss affair), it was revealed in 1960, to the amusement of cynics, that "Everyone drives better in a Vauxhall." The riposte was predictable, as older drivers recalled the bad old days of 'Dubonnet knees' and the infamous Vauxhall reverse-curtsey. With irony that may or may not have been intended, a well-known oil company proclaimed that "Getaway people get Super National," showing that archetypal getaway car, the Jaguar E-type. And then there was Riley's foray into liberality: "She's gay, she's safe, she's unashamedly fast" said one copywriter about the new Elf and, by implication, about the girl who drove it. She was shown getting into the car with the help of a hotel doorman who looked remarkably like Josef Stalin, and whose deferential smile could be mistaken for a leer. The theme was not perpetuated. The MG buyer, meanwhile, was invited in 1966 to follow his "restless, driving, nagging, yearning, longing" for a sports car, and to "proceed immediately" to a BMC showroom for satiation. The copy may have lurched from the purple to the bufferishly jocular, but the punchline was direct: "MG drivers never travel alone."

Copywriters frequently went overboard in their efforts to convince motorists that needs they never knew they had could be fulfilled completely by the new car. The reader was not supposed to observe sardonically from the sidelines, but to enter into the spirit of the copy. It was not always clear whether advertiser and reader shared the same joke. "Fanfare! Roll away the work-a-day! Enter the swish new Anglia Estate" gushed Ford in 1961. A more workaday conveyance, vans excepted, was hard to imagine. Hillman tried the Joyce

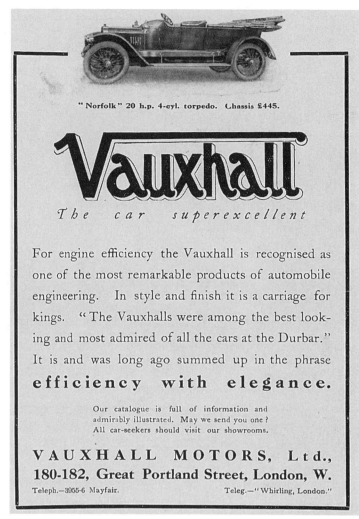

"Norfolk" 20 h.p. 4-cyl. torpedo. Chassis £445.

Vauxhall

The car superexcellent

For engine efficiency the Vauxhall is recognised as one of the most remarkable products of automobile engineering. In style and finish it is a carriage for kings. "The Vauxhalls were among the best looking and most admired of all the cars at the Durbar." It is and was long ago summed up in the phrase **efficiency with elegance.**

Our catalogue is full of information and admirably illustrated. May we send you one? All car-seekers should visit our showrooms.

VAUXHALL MOTORS, Ltd., 180-182, Great Portland Street, London, W.

Teleph.—3955-6 Mayfair.   Teleg.—"Whirling, London."

Country Life, 1912 (With thanks to Paul Veysey)

1912 Vauxhall 20hp. Modest advertising from a maker of high-quality, quite specialized cars in 1912. The emphasis, understandably in an era when reliability could not be taken for granted, was on mechanism, which was a matter of prestige at much as utility. Style, in this context, was quite different from the decorative styling which advertisers of mass-produced cars would highlight in the 1930s, and the quotation is unattributed — forgiveable when describing subjective impressions, perhaps, and more so given that many potential buyers would move in overlapping social circles and be likely to know, or know of, each other.

Grenfell touch in 1960: "You'll thrill to the elegant sweeping lines of the Hillman Estate Car." This, too, was not a car to set the blood racing, as most new car buyers were used to post-war standards of power and styling by the end of the 1950s. More measured was the assurance a year later that the Super Minx had "all the qualities this age demands." It was an earnest recommendation, the very antithesis of Ford's hyperbole, and there were no exclamation marks, which was some achievement for 1961.

As the decade advanced, copy became polarized between the factual and the inspirational, the latter providing much of the atmosphere which had once been captured by the illustrator. In many cases an escapist or glamorous pic-

WOLSELEY

"The Car for Durability and Reliability."

W   W

A WOLSELEY 24-30 h.p. LIMOUSINE LANDAULETTE.

Send for Catalogue No. 46, Post Free.

THE WOLSELEY TOOL AND MOTOR CAR CO., Ltd.,

LONDON DEPOT: YORK STREET, WESTMINSTER. Telegrams: "Autovent, Vic, London." Telephone: 6220 Victoria.

Telegrams "EXACTITUDE, BIRMINGHAM." ADDERLEY PARK, BIRMINGHAM. Telephone 6153 CENTRAL.

Proprietors : VICKERS, LIMITED.

MARINE DEPT.: COLUMBINE YARD, EAST COWES, I.O.W Telegrams: "Wolseley, Cowes." Telephone : 493 Cowes.

1913 Wolseley 24–30hp. The elaborate border of this piece was slightly old-fashioned by 1913, even for a formal carraige, but luxury cars would be shown against palatial and country-house backdrops until well into the 1960s and beyond, even if a formal or aristocratic lifestyle — as distinct from the country house itself — was not something every luxury car buyer aspired to in later years.

Left: **1916 Standard Light Car.** None simpler — or smaller, as this wartime piece originally occupied a 2" × 2" space within a 16" × 11.5" magazine page. It contains the absolute minimum of information needed in a car advertisement.

Opposite: **1926 Fiat 10/15 hp.** In the 1960s, commentators wondered how much of the British market would eventually be taken by imported cars, but the challenge was not new and the McKenna tariff, an import duty of 33⅓ percent, was imposed in 1915. It lasted until 1956 with a brief suspension during 1925, for which Fiat were just too late with this advertisement, published early in January 1926. Meanwhile closed bodies were rapidly supplanting open tourers, elaborate borders were almost banished from advertising, copywriters were describing individual features in greater detail than before, and the typical backdrop was a bustling scene rather than a frozen tableau.

The Car of International Reputation

The Wisest Step

to take when contemplating the
purchase of an enclosed car is to
select the 10/15 h.p. FIAT Saloon

The years of economical service for which this Model
is famous will best illustrate the wisdom of your choice

The appointments are of the highest grade and in exquisite taste. The
coachwork is of the de luxe type. Upholstered in Bedford Cloth and the
cabinet work inlaid. All six windows lowered at will. Four speeds
forward and reverse ensuring a delightfully smooth and easy change.

Standard equipment for touring car and chassis
includes : Electric lighting set and starter,
5 lamps, clock, speedometer, spare wheel and
5 tyres. Any type of coachwork supplied.

RANGE OF MODELS include :
7 h.p., 10/15 h.p., 15/20 h.p.,
20/30 h.p. (6 cyl.), 40 h.p. (6 cyl.)

LET YOUR NEW CAR BE A FIAT
which for value and road service is unequalled

FIAT (England) LIMITED

—WARNING—
With every Fiat Car a full
guarantee is issued by this
Company. Every purchaser
should obtain this guarantee
and see that it bears the chassis
and engine numbers of the
machine purchased. The public is warned not to purchase
a car without this guarantee.

FIAT

10/15 h.p. Saloon
£375 Tax £11 ; Front Wheel
       Brakes £15 extra

Registered Offices and Showrooms :

43-44, Albemarle Street,
London, W.1

Telephone: Gerrard 7947 (4 lines).
Wires: "Fiatism, Piccy, London."
Works : WEMBLEY, MIDDLESEX.

Country Life, January 9, 1926 (With thanks to Paul Veysey)

. . . why don't *you* get a CHRYSLER?

YES, why don't *you* get a Chrysler? Expensive? Not to-day. You can own one of these swift, silent, arrogant-looking cars for as little as £299. Never before has even a Chrysler offered so much in speed and luxury. Smoothness? Ride behind Floating Power and see. See how the automatic clutch and easychange gearbox make racing changes, dead silent, at all speeds. Feel the terrific acceleration—with *all* gears silent as top. Realise the impregnable safety of Chrysler all-steel bodies —the titanic stopping power of Chrysler hydraulic brakes.

Now with the best selling season before him, your dealer can allow top price for your present car. Why *don't* you get one of these Chryslers?

Chrysler Kew Six	from £299
Chrysler Wimbledon Six	from £425
Chrysler Richmond Six	from £455
Chrysler Kingston Six	from £495
Chrysler Royal Eight	from £585

Chrysler Motors Ltd., Mortlake Road, Kew, Surrey. 'Phone: Prospect 3456

ture could be combined with technical details, but it was never easy to persuade the casual reader to wade through specifications as he would a brochure. The most memorable pieces highlighted noteworthy features and left the recirculatory heaters and back axle ratios to the devotee. But this caution was not universal. A 1961 advertisement for the last of Vauxhall's F-type Victors included a series of diagrams of mundane features such as "all round vision" and "complete proof against dust, draughts and water"—which was admittedly more than could be said of the 1957 original. "Own a wonderful world! Own a Vauxhall" sounded desperate, and the copywriter appeared to be mocking the car on its deathbed with an embarrassing rehearsal of uncompelling detail virtues. It was a tactful obituary for a car that had improved greatly since its early days, and the FB model which followed later in the year could fairly claim to embody the "clean line of good design," even in the two-tone pink in which it was shown in advertisements.

Others were more light-hearted, playing down worthy virtues in favour of less tangible inducements. Escapism, in particular, gained ground during the early 1960s. Favourite among escapist motifs was the deserted beach, closely paralleled by the deserted wood. Ford used both, showing a Zephyr 6 speeding along the sand in 1962, with "all the zest in the world" and with a slogan, "Why come second when you can be first?" which was calculated to kindle executive paranoia. The 1963 Consul Corsair, with "flair everywhere," appeared at a similar venue, tended by a carefree young(ish) couple who tossed slices of watermelon to each other as the Cyprian tide lapped at the white stripe tyres. Romance featured, Thunderbird-style, with a new "personal car." "Let go with the new Consul Capri" ran a headline below a photograph of a white coupe parked in a wood with an exotically

Right: **1933 Vauxhall Cadet.** Contented-ordinary-used testimonials featured in both American and British car advertising during the 1930s, and this piece is very much in the American photo-realist style. In 1925 Vauxhall, formerly an upmarket specialist, became a wholly owned subsidiary of General Motors, and entered the mainstream family car market with this car in 1930. In 1931 the Cadet was fitted with synchromesh—a first in Britain. Painless motoring became widespread theme in British family car advertising as the new middle-class motorists could not be relied upon to be enthusiastic about machinery or mechanically sensitive. The theme would be revived with automatic transmissions, not least Vauxhall's own Hydra-matic, in the 1960s.

Opposite: **1933 Chrysler.** American cars were highly regarded in Britain during the 1930s, particularly among business motorists covering high mileages, and the foundations of this reputation were laid by Chrysler, whose advertising by W.S. Crawford Ltd. in the late 1920s employed a novel, Bauhaus-influenced dynamic impressionism which suited this fast and well-braked marque. Crawfords' approach continued to influence Chrysler advertising after the agency gave up the Chrysler account and their style inspired many other advertisers during the 1930s and early post-war period. It was detectable in Jaguar and Daimler advertising as late as 1965.

 "*A car like this doubles the pleasure of my driving*"

" After a decade of varied experience with other cars, my Vauxhall Cadet is all the more convincing," writes this happy owner. "*A car like this doubles the pleasure of my driving*. The controls, and in particular the Synchro-Mesh gearing, are so simple and effective, one feels complete confidence in manipulating traffic, awkward bends, and, in fact, any situation demanding quick decision."

This is just one opinion of hundreds. All Vauxhall Cadet owners find that they use their gears as *they should*, becoming better drivers. Gear changing with Synchro-Mesh is so easy that it gives you confidence. Just move the lever across for a perfect change—no pausing in neutral, no clashing.

The smooth six-cylinder engine gives ample power for any driving contingency. Steering, braking, acceleration are superb, owners say, and petrol consumption is surprisingly low. Springing is smooth, upholstery luxurious, the equipment for comfort and convenience splendidly complete. Truly the Cadet is ideally satisfying as a loyal friend, and stylish as only a Vauxhall can be.

Any Vauxhall dealer will provide a car for *your own* test of these statements.

17 h.p. six-cylinder VAUXHALL CADET. 4-door Saloon —£295. Grosvenor Saloon de luxe—£325. Fixed-Head Coupe (2 or 4 light)—£295. (Sliding roof on Saloons and Fixed-Head Coupe models.) Romney 2-seater Drop-Head Coupe—£325. Denton 4-seater Drop-Head Coupe—£335. Tickford All-Weather Saloon—£335. (All prices ex-Works.)

Complete range on view at 174-182, Great Portland Street, W.1. *Vauxhall Motors Ltd., Edgware Road, London, N.W.9*

SYNCHRO MESH **FAULTLESS GEAR CHANGE**

VAUXHALL CADET
THE CAR WITH THE SILKY PERFORMANCE

Country Life, June 3, 1933 (With thanks to Paul Veysey)

Country Life, June 3, 1933 (With thanks to Paul Veysey)

Within the advertisement:

ROVER

ROVER SPEED MODEL (14 H.P.)
HASTINGS COUPE £395

"It can now be seen that of the 15 Rovers which started, 14 finished without loss of marks, securing three Class prizes and three Town prizes in the Rally and two Coachwork prizes, including the Championship in the Coachwork Competition, while Rover cars made the best time in the acceleration and braking tests in both Class 1 and Class 2."

The Motor—28.3.33

"During the Hastings Rally I used a Rover Pilot with freewheel and enjoyed every minute of it. It has one of the quietest engines...and the springing comfort would satisfy faddy old ladies. The freewheel provides new sensations in motoring— long and gentle descents at speed without any sound give a thrill which has to be experienced to be realised."

"The Scribe" in the Autocar—31.3.33

10/25 from - £195	Meteor 16 - £395
Pilot 14 - £258	Meteor 20 - £445
Speed Model	Speed Chassis
(14 h.p.) from £330	(20 h.p.).- £395

The ROVER CO. Ltd., COVENTRY
London Distributors: HENLYS LTD.
Henly House, Euston Road, N.W.1

ROVER "FOURTEEN" £258

cvs— 46

1933 Rover 14hp. Side views showing different body types, sometimes with exaggeratedly long bonnets and low roofs, were common between 1930 and 1935, less common after 1936, and rare after the war as the style did not suit the full-width post-war bodies; its use with Jensen's 1947 Nash-engined Straight-Eight was probably the last. Simple elongation, however, remained widespread until the late 1950s. Advertisers quoted the motoring journals at all levels of the market and, as tests became more objective during the 1950s, their increasing emphasis on facts and figures was reflected in the quotations chosen.

dressed couple *en route* from a sophisticated party. It was a mild precursor of MG's more risqué use of the same theme in the 1970s. The wood also provided a surprising setting for two new executive expresses, the Jensen C-V8 and Rover's 3-Litre Mk II.

Copywriters and photographers were quick to see the potential of exotic settings, and as more people decided to forego the annual excursion to Brighton or Bridlington and go to Europe instead, they took their cars with them, in advertising as in life. The presence of the car abroad showed that it could get there without breaking down, that it attracted the admiration of Europeans as well as Britons and, above all, that it was favoured by the kind of people who

could afford to go abroad for their holidays. Ford Consul Classics, Hillman Super Minxes and Rovers were sent across the Channel to be identified by mainland Europeans as "style setters," as Hillman put it, as well as worthy accessories to the daily grind.

Social sophistication, as imagined by copywriters, evolved steadily, and the old order of the 1950s underwent much modification. Image and glamour were, as ever, imputed to the most unlikely cars, but were suggested in new ways. Snobbery became more meritocratic than aristocratic, and young people who were rich enough to buy new cars no longer slavishly followed the older generation. New models ceased to be defined socially by what their buyers "were," and

Opposite: **1935 Austin Ten-Four.** Austin's natural photographs contrasted markedly with Chrysler's dynamic impressionism, and suited the down-to-earth, practical tenor of much Austin advertising during the 1930s. Investment and dependability were longstanding Austin themes which lasted into the 1960s. Like Plymouth with solid family cars in America, Austin based many pre-war advertisements on ordinary-user testimonials. The theme of practical realism largely continued after 1945, with a new emphasis on modernity and style arriving in the late 1950s.

─── BRITAIN'S DEPENDABLE CAR ───

The car illustrated above is the Ten-Four Colwyn Cabriolet, price £178

what AUSTIN OWNERS say about INVESTING

"I IMAGINED THAT I HAD ACQUIRED A CAR THAT WOULD COST ME NOTHING FOR REPAIRS, BUT . . .

Report No. 560.   Reg. No. UL.4038

I found when I disposed of it after six years of hard use, that I had spent *fourpence* for replacements during that period. That is what it cost me for a new pin for the timing chain. I have just bought a new Austin Sixteen which I hope . . . will not cost me so much for repairs as the old one."

The York Saloon with 18 h.p. (Tax £13.10.0) or with 16 h.p. (Tax £12) six-cylinder engine. Synchromesh on top, third and second gears. Deep, comfortable and adjustable seats upholstered in Vaumôl hide. Dunlop tyres. Prices at works. £328
CHALFONT SALOON (with division) £338
WESTMINSTER SALOON . . £348
HERTFORD SALOON . . . £318
Hayes Self-Selector Transmission £40 extra.

* * *

Could motorists and intending motorists have stronger evidence of dependability and running economy than this? The very people who form the motoring public confirm the solid truth behind the slogan :

You buy a car—but you INVEST in an AUSTIN

Read the Austin Magazine: 4d. every month.

The Austin Motor Company Limited, Birmingham and 479 Oxford Street, London.   London Service Depots   12, 16 and 20 h.p., Holland Park, W.11.   7 and 10 h.p., North Row, W.1.   Export Dept.: Birmingham.

─── BUY A CAR MADE IN THE UNITED KINGDOM ───

Country Life, May 4, 1935 (With thanks to Paul Veysey)

The Sketch, February 24, 1937 (With thanks to Paul Veysey)

whose organisation handles our publicity, has prevailed on me to give a series of personal messages in our advertisements.

For instance, so many people who do not know, ask "What do the letters M.G. stand for?"

They don't stand for "More Ginger" though that would be applicable. They were given as a compliment to Lord Nuffield, being the initial letters of the Morris Garages which was his original business, and from which the M.G. in particular and all his other vast enterprises have sprung.

Cecil Kimber
MANAGING DIRECTOR

"BRITISH CARS ARE BETTER BUILT — BRITISH CARS LAST LONGER"

M.G. *Midget Series* T £222 • M.G. 1½-*Litre from* £280

M.G. *Two-Litre from* £389 • *Prices ex works. Dunlop, Triplex*

THE M.G. COMPANY LIMITED · ABINGDON-ON-THAMES · BERKSHIRE · SOLE EXPORTERS — M.I.E. LIMITED · COWLEY · OXFORD · ENGLAND

Punch, February 23, 1938 (With thanks to Paul Veysey)

1938 M.G. Sir William Crawford had become well known for his Chrysler advertising, but the agency took on other makes, too. Here, M.G.'s connection with Morris is displayed proudly — neatly spiking the guns of detractors who claimed that M.G.s were "only fancy Morrises you know" and the worse for it. (The Two-Litre, or SA, announced in September 1935 and slow to reach production, had attracted anxiety on the point.) This One-and-a-Half-Litre, or VA, was announced in October 1936 under the slogan "For space … for grace … for pace…" which, slightly modified, was used by Jaguar after the war. The VA was a personal favourite of M.G.'s founder, Cecil Kimber, who guarded the marque's distinctiveness ferociously. Post-war M.G. advertising, especially for the 1959–68 Magnettes, would shamelessly tap into this heritage. From the late 1960s onwards, the M.G. name was generally written as MG, without stops.

instead became tied into what they did — for work, for fun, and in their leisure time. For aspirational graduates, status was no longer an adequate substitute for fun, and portraits of position within the established order were superseded by images of action.

Thus the equivocal virtue of class came to be supplanted by the unequivocal virtues of speed, power and technical prowess. Snobbery remained important, but it was expressed less by assertions of breeding and more by acquisition and tangible prosperity. If a car was good, it was worth buying; if dynamically feeble, it was best left to the old guard who knew no better. The 1965 Daimlers, for instance, were sold primarily on their technical features, rather than as props to help their owners in their ascent of the social pecking order. Among the middle classes (if not at the very top of the social scale), old snobberies became self-conscious and defensive where they persisted — surviving as a source of private reassurance rather than public hegemony — and, while they never disappeared entirely, advertisers could no longer rely on them to sustain sales.

Competition among copywriters consequently became more aggressive. In earlier years, the disdain of domestic buyers for a car was no handicap if export markets loved it, but by the early 1960s Britain was no longer a general provider to the world, particularly as Fiat, Opel, Volkswagen and Renault were more than capable of satisfying their

Opposite: **1937 Wolseley 18/80.** Stylish advertising from the art deco era promoted the upper-middle-class Wolseley in 1937. Social pretension was much less evident in this piece than in some others from the marque at the time, although success in concours competitions, a 1930s fad, is mentioned. The "18" of 18/80 represents the car's RAC-rated, annually taxable horsepower, calculated according to the cylinder bore and the number of cylinders. The "80" represents the claimed power output in brake horsepower. The tax was abolished in 1947, but Wolseley continued to use model names of this pattern in the 1960s, with the first number reflecting the number of cylinders or the cubic capacity of the engine.

The Autocar, November 11, 1938 (With thanks to Paul Veysey)

1938 Opel Olympia. You impose a tariff; we'll subsidize — heavily in the case of the Opel Cadet (Kadett in its native land) and the larger but similar-looking Olympia (seen here), which arrived from Nazi Germany in the late 1930s, giving rise to complaints of dumping. This advertisement looks uninspired, perhaps even slightly sinister, and the use of several blocks of print in different typefaces is typical of a certain late-1930s school which did not long survive the war. But the austere Cadet was also light, lively, technically ahead of several British competitors and able to cruise at 55–60mph. Many British advertisers, from Austin to Rolls-Royce, urged motorists to "buy a car made in the United Kingdom," and the theme became an industry campaign in its own right. One 1936 advertisement showed a city type standing beside the streamlined tail of an unidentified but Teutonic-looking car, remarking to his friend, "Surprised at a man like Charles running a foreign car." *The Advertising World*, reviewing the campaign in December 1936, responded briskly: "If two avowed pro-British Britishers are mealy-mouthed enough to stand near a friend's car and to whisper in accepted mothers' meeting parlance…then the immediate reaction is more in the favour of the unseen Charles and his car than it is towards these two city magnates…. We have to see two people sneering covertly in almost every one of the series. And we are expected to feel a wave of indignation against the owner of the foreign car. Which…is absurd." Nevertheless, few British motorists willingly drove prewar Opels after 1945, and they were rarely seen among the native Fords, Morrises, Singers and Austins.

Opposite: **1936 Ford 8hp, 1936 Ford V-8 "22," 1938 Ford Eight, and 1939 Ford Prefect.** One make, but four very different approaches within the value-for-money theme that would dominate Ford advertising until the late 1950s and remain prominent during the 1960s. According to its historian Ralph M. Hower, Ford's advertising agency, N.W. Ayer & Son, found in 1928 that "American-made advertising and selling methods could not be successfully transplanted to England", with the result that the agency "decided to have a British staff under an American manager…[who], until all phases of operation were well in hand…was assisted by three other men from the Philadelphia staff." The manager, Douglas Meldrum, stayed until 1939 and the agency kept the Ford account until Rumble, Crowther & Nicholas Ltd. took over at the end of 1946.

Among British Fords the Dearborn-designed 8hp Model Y, uniquely for a four-seater saloon in Britain, was sold at £100 from October 1935. It was also unusual in being advertised as available on hire purchase at a time when the possibility was rarely mentioned in car advertising. Although hire purchase had been available since 1912, many more people bought cars this way than ever admitted it. Some advertisements for the £100 Model Y referred to the car as the Popular Ford; everyone else called it a Ford Popular. The illustrations here are realistic: the dimensions of the V-8 "22" (Model 62, announced in June 1936) are exaggerated only a little and those of the Essex-designed Eight (Model 7Y, introduced in August 1937) not at all. The V-8 "22," with a body almost identical to that of the French Matford, proved more popular in Britain than successive editions of the larger V-8 "30."

Socially speaking, Ford copy of the period occasionally exhibited a certain nervousness as well as aspiration — possibly because middle-class owners of Morrises, Austins and Singers often looked down on Ford drivers as poverty-motorists or cheapskates — and it is not obvious whether the portentous style is meant to be taken seriously or tongue-in-cheek. The 1939 advertisement shown here, for the new Prefect (Model E93A), was one of a series that used humour and more than a little wishful thinking to created vignettes of upper-middle-class life around the product. The privilege alluded to in the headline was the Benefit of Clergy of the Middle Ages, under which a clergyman charged with a felony was exempt from trial in a secular court — a reference that was a little contrived even in 1939, when churchgoing was much more widespread in Britain than it is today. Ironically, the smaller, two-door Fords were thought by many to have a rather ecclesiastical look. The last small Ford in the pre-war style was the austere Popular (103E), made from 1953-59, Britain's cheapest conventional car at a little under £400 but, like its pre-war counterparts, liable to tip over if cornered clumsily with worn suspension and a full load. By the early 1960s Ford could capitalize on a reputation for good value, but still had to work hard to convince middle-class motorists that the company's cars were in any way sophisticated.

THE UNIVERSAL CAR

As Illustrated £100.   Double-Entrance Saloon £112 10s.   Hide Upholstery and Sliding Roof, £10 Extra, on either model.

The £100 FORD
(£6 TAX) Saloon

£25 DOWN taxed and insured

Manufactured and built entirely at Dagenham, Essex, has by sheer efficiency sold itself more numerously than any other British example of motor engineering in a given period.

Inexpensive to buy, tax, insure, run and maintain, amply powered, adequately roomy, gratifyingly comfortable when fully occupied,

very completely equipped, nicely finished, inside and out, from its introduction, it is more than ever popular at the price effective from October last. Only its elegant appearance prevents its being an incessant offence in the eyes of busy British roadfarers. Count the £100 Ford Saloons you meet tomorrow. See how they run!

THE LOCAL FORD DEALER CAN DELIVER THE £100 FORD SALOON, TAXED AND INSURED, ON AN INITIAL PAYMENT OF £25. 18-MONTH AND 24-MONTH TRANSACTIONS CAN BE ARRANGED WITH SLIGHTLY HIGHER INITIAL PAYMENTS : : Literature on Request : : All Prices at Works

FORD MOTOR COMPANY LIMITED, DAGENHAM, ESSEX. London Showrooms: 88 REGENT STREET, W.1.

FORD CARS, FORDSON VANS AND TRUCKS—PROVED BY THE PAST—IMPROVED FOR THE FUTURE!

COMPLETELY EQUIPPED, AS ILLUSTRATED, £210, AT WORKS

The new FORD V-8 (£16 10s. Tax)

For a generation the word "Ford" has meant utility, efficiency, economy harnessed. Curious, then, that it should have been left to Ford to create the super-luxury, multi-cylinder car ; but just as well, because a long, arduous apprenticeship devoted to utility has given to this New Dagenham-built V-8 all the dependability and inexpensiveness of purchase, running and maintenance, associated with the name of Ford through thirty years and more. In the result we find a car of brilliant acceleration, high average speeds without excessive maxima, faultless performance all-round, plus extreme lowness of cost in every way. You have to see, examine at close range, test on the road, this New Ford V-8, to realise how fine, handsome, dependable—and, above all, how *economical* a car it is.

Do that ; weigh it in the balance. You will not find it wanting, and every Authorised Ford Dealer simply loves to watch your amazement, hear your praise, of something entirely new in motor cars.

"There is no comparison !   More miles per gallon is good :   Fewer pence per mile is better !"

Be sure to visit the Ford Motor Exhibition, Royal Albert Hall, Kensington, London, W., October 15-24 next, 10 a.m. to 10 p.m. Daily ; Admission, 1/3, inc. Entertainment Tax.

FORD MOTOR COMPANY LIMITED, DAGENHAM, ESSEX.   LONDON SHOWROOMS: 88 REGENT ST., W.1.

THE FORD "EIGHT"
(Develops over 23 B.H.P., £6 Tax)

EFFORTLESS CONTROL — AMPLE POWER — DEPENDABLE SMOOTH BRAKES — BRILLIANT ACCELERATION — PERMANENTLY WEATHER-PROOF FINISH — MATCHLESS ECONOMY OF OPERATION — LOW FIRST-COST, RUNNING & MAINTENANCE

Excels, above every other car in its price-class, on a number of points, each of which makes it a perfect selection for the *thinking* motorist, "buying for keeps," tired of costly, tedious experiment.

It embodies more solid value than anything else of comparable price manufactured and built in the British Isles. Catalogue on application, or from the Local Ford Dealer, who will gladly demonstrate every claim advanced on behalf of any Ford product.

Overseas Deliveries of any Ford Car will be arranged on request by any Ford Dealer or through our London Showrooms.

FORD EIGHT SALOON £117-10-0
SALOON DE LUXE, £127-10-0

FORD MOTOR COMPANY LIMITED, Dagenham, Essex. London Showrooms: 88 Regent St., W.1

iii

Privilege of Clergy

"Have a look at the car clock, Peter. I always set my watch by the clock in the car."

*   *   *   *

They had finished lunch. Smoke from the vicar's best cigars hung in three fragrant clouds over the table.

"I have one, too," the bishop was saying, ". . . . a Ford, I mean. Mine is open, as cool as yours is snug. In Africa we have to take our motoring seriously. I think nothing of driving two hundred miles to a mission service."

WELL, they'd have to have the garden party in the church hall. It had been raining since early morning, and the vicarage lawns were sodden.

The vicar looked out of his study window and waited for the crunch of tyres on his gravel drive. They should be back from the station by now, his curate, Peter, and the African bishop who was arriving on a visit on the 12.45.

"No need to 'phone for the taxi, Peter," he had said. "You'll manage in the 'Prefect.' The key of the ignition fits the luggage compartment. There'll be lots of room for the bishop's suitcases in there out of the rain."

Peter had scratched his head. "How about the bishop ?"

"Lots of room for him. Don't forget I brought Mr. and Mrs. Tukle and their two children from Abbot's Farm the other day. If the 'Prefect' fits *them*, it will fit any bishop born of man."

"True enough ! I'd better start."

"I doubt if you use your Ford more than I do," replied the vicar urbanely. "After all, we use it continuously—all day long—not all in the same direction, of course, but it travels just as far."

"Have you ever driven on African roads ? They test *any* springing, I can tell you."

"Have you ever seen the lane to Abbot's Farm in wet weather, my lord," interposed the curate, " or tried to negotiate the left-hand bend on the hill outside Miss Raughton's place ? "

"Of course I haven't," said the bishop, with a touch of asperity, "and your Ford hasn't climbed the Wemba Pass in top like mine has." He blew out his cheeks.

"Quite," said the vicar hastily. "Some more coffee, my lord ? " He looked at the clock. "Peter," he added, " you'd better go now

and fetch Miss Raughton. She isn't nervous in the 'Prefect.' On the way back, collect the flowers at the Cedars and then tell the Websters that the party's at the hall. They haven't a 'phone. Pick up Lady Louding, too. She has rheumatism and says her own car jolts her too much. You should be back for us in half an hour."

"Argumentative young man," said the bishop when the door had closed.

"Well, you see, we do use our Ford a lot in the parish. It's the taxi, the children's bus, the ambulance, the delivery van, all in one. And now even Lady Louding prefers it to her own car. . . . Anyway, I think the three of us are agreed on one thing, that Ford cars are the finest value for money in the world."

THE "PREFECT" the Ten Ahead of its Class. SALOON £145
Double-Entrance Saloon £152 - 10. Touring Car £155.
Prices at Works.

• FORD OWNERS WILL TELL YOU •
Make a close examination of the "Prefect" at any Ford Dealers, or at the Ford Showrooms, 88 Regent St., London, W.1. Catalogue from Ford Dealers, Everywhere.
FORD MOTOR COMPANY LIMITED, DAGENHAM, ESSEX. LONDON SHOWROOMS : 88 REGENT STREET, W.1

vii

Change to HILLMAN and keep the CHANGE

Hillman owners know the truth of this statement — here is a typical letter :

"*I saved quite a lot when I bought a Hillman. I found that to get a car anything like as good would have cost me from ten to fifty pounds more — incidentally she is very reasonable on maintenance, and better than most for comfort.*"—*J.H., Tulse Hill, S.W.*

MINX SALOON £163   **'14' SALOON £239**

BUY HILLMAN AND SAVE

THE HILLMAN MOTOR CAR CO. LTD., COVENTRY   *London Showrooms & Export Div.*: ROOTES LTD. DEVONSHIRE HOUSE, PICCADILLY W.I

own and nearby markets, and competed directly with Britain in America and in former British colonies. Moreover, foreign cars were becoming a frequent sight on British roads, most of them imported into Britain complete, rather than built up from assembled parts in the manner of the Citroën DS or Renault Dauphine in their early years. Failings in domestic products that had been tolerated for want of alternative or comparison in the sellers' market of the 1950s were no longer suffered. Even while actual sales of continental cars remained low (amounting to about 3 percent of new car registrations in 1961), advertisements by their importers proliferated in newspapers and magazines, reminding the conservative buyer of a British family car of what he was missing. And who could blame the newly affluent suburbanite if, indirectly persuaded by advertising for British cars that everything European was chic, he determined to buy foreign the next time he changed his car?

Those who did buy foreign cars often discovered that spare parts could be expensive or their availability erratic; some motorists, bitten hard by depreciation and ham-fisted local mechanics, returned shyly to the domestic fold. Advertising for most imported continental and American cars was modest. Tight budgets, particularly in the early 1960s, precluded elaborate colour photography and potential buyers were too diverse in their tastes to be targeted systematically. Moreover, middle-class individualists who could afford to take a risk often reacted badly to overstrenuous attempts at persuasion. BMW's 1964 copy for the rear-engined 700-LS, promising "spirited performance, distinctive styling and

Until then ...

Skating by carlight is just one of the pleasures we have had to give up for the duration ... like the pleasure of having a new Ford Car and being able to run it without restriction. But we willingly forego these things for the sake of speeding the day of Victory and the return of the good life, not just for ourselves, but for people all over the world. Until then, Ford marches on ... even under to day's difficult conditions, Ford Dealers' Service Facilities remain ready and able to meet the situation, especially in the case of vehicles on work of national importance.

FORD MOTOR COMPANY LIMITED, DAGENHAM, ESSEX. LONDON SHOWROOMS : 88 REGENT STREET, W.1

vi

The Geograhpicl Magazine, January 1942

1942 Ford. Passenger car production stopped almost completely during the war, with only a few cars, of a limited range of types, being made for military and other essential uses. Fuel was rationed from September 1939 until May 1950, pleasure motoring ceased, signposts were taken down — and then there was the blackout, designed to prevent light from the ground inadvertently guiding bombers to their targets. Black curtains were fitted in houses and car headlamps were heavily masked, while bumpers and mudguard edges were painted white. The accident rate was horrendous. But Ford approached Chrysler's old agency, Crawfords, who devised, as part of an imaginative prestige campaign, a series of famous, morale-boosting advertisements which included a mini-series of 1941–42 showing night-time pleasures involving light that had been given up for the duration. Subjects included fireworks in November 1941, the illuminated Christmas tree outside St. Paul's Cathedral in December, and ice-skating by carlight in January 1942. After 1945, Ford advertisements showed Prefects in workshops and reminded readers to maintain them, as only in the mid–1950s did new cars become more or less freely available.

Opposite: **1939 Hillman Minx and Fourteen.** Stylish, American-influenced photography from the highly market-conscious Rootes Group in 1939. The Minx was a great success from its introduction in 1931-32 and was regularly updated. The body style shown here was introduced in 1935 and improved in mid–1937. Until the mid–1960s, the Minx succeeded by offering a little bit extra to motorists for relatively little more money — hence the theme of this owner-testimonial. Atmospheric, ground-level, front-three-quarter shots were popular in American advertisng of the time, especially with Buick in 1936 and 1939. Although brand loyalty was encouraged by a marque "look," the Fourteen sold poorly, not so much illuminated by the Minx's aura as hidden in its shadow. After the war a developed version was revived as the Humber Hawk.

CARS FOR BREAD

Britain is bartering her manufacturing skill for her daily bread. Her finest products are going abroad, including the famous cars and commercial vehicles made by firms of the Nuffield Organization, to be exchanged for wheat and other vital foods. The export figures for Nuffield products are reaching new high records, thanks to the endeavours of the 25,000 Nuffield workers. It is such willing and sustained effort on the part of all of us which will overcome the present crisis.

MORRIS · WOLSELEY

RILEY · M.G.

MORRIS - COMMERCIAL

THE NUFFIELD ORGANIZATION

THE FIELD, with which is incorporated *Land and Water* and *The County Gentleman*, is published every Friday, price 1/6, by THE FIELD PRESS LTD., 8, Stratton Street, London, W.1, and at 41, Southgate Street, Winchester, in the County of Southampton. Saturday, March 27, 1948. Printed by SIR JOSEPH CAUSTON & SONS, LTD., 72, Fleet Street, London, E.C.4, and Eastleigh, Hants. PRINTED IN GREAT BRITAIN and entered as second class matter at the Post Office, New York, N.Y., March 1897. Registered at G.P.O. as a newspaper.

unusual roominess, seating four or when necessary five adults in comfort and providing ample space for holiday luggage," could have been written about any small or medium-sized saloon from around 1935 onwards. Yet by 1970 the 700 was long forgotten, and BMW was well on the way to establishing its later niche.

Fortunately there were exceptions to the low-key continental norm. Alfa Romeo showed light-coloured coupes at speed or posed dramatically against black backdrops with headlines ("Take a test drive for two—you and your ego"; "Alas! It does 55mph more than the law allows!") that appealed to potential buyer and wistful onlooker alike, though few people could afford a "hand-built…and decidedly expensive" streamlined Giulia SS at nearly £2400. Renault, too, were ahead of their time, using arresting colour photography for glamorous Floride advertisements at the beginning of the decade and for imaginative portraits of the R4, shown fully laden but *sans* bodywork, in 1966. By contrast, advertisements for the earliest Japanese imports of 1965 are worth recalling for what they presaged rather than for what they were; as advertising they were unremarkable. A few imports sank without trace, their appeal too specialized or obscure. But where the cars were good and had wider appeal, they stayed. It was a conservative private motorist who, having sampled a new Renault 16 for £868 in 1966, would willingly return to its fading British contemporary, the £893 Vauxhall Victor 101 de Luxe Estate Car.

As old marque loyalties disintegrated, many British makes vanished, among them Armstrong Siddeley from the top of the market and Standard from the middle ranks. The latter, in particular, was an early example of an old moniker sacrificed at the altar of marketing expediency. As a word, the name was less likely to be associated with something to be admired than with a basic product, and its solid qualities were too readily seen as default virtues—characteristics worth emphasizing only in the absence of anything interesting, original or advanced. "Triumph" was in every way less ambiguous, and was adopted for all

The Field, February 21, 1948

1948 Humber Super Snipe Mk I. In the 1930s advertisers and their critics argued with surprising vigour about whether photography or painted illustrations were most effective in advertising. Photography, it was argued, did not mislead the consumer and demonstrated confidence in the product. But paintings achieved atmosphere—a sense of the totality of the automotive experience—that eluded photographic realists; was not this totality the true reality of the product? For that matter, could a photograph be truly objective when the choice of what to photograph, and how, could be as contentious as any illustrator's caprice? And if this were a good rather than a bad thing, might not a talented photographer achieve atmosphere as easily as the artist, making the latter redundant? Eventually the photographers won—1958 was the deciding year in Britain—and paintings were rare by 1970, but some earlier illustrations had been very good indeed. A Prefect by Terence Cuneo graced Ford's 1948 prestige advertising, and this Humber Super Snipe Mk I by wartime aviation (and official RAF) artist Frank Wootton, who painted a number of advertising illustrations for Rootes in the 1940s and 1950s, was arguably one of the best. Wootton's work had featured in de Havilland aircraft advertisements before the war, and the Humber itself had a distinguished war record, crowned by Field Marshal Montgomery's own "Old Faithful."

Opposite: **Nuffield Organization, 1948.** Export or die—or how post-war conditions brought a different kind of prestige advertising from Nuffield, who, like everyone else, exported as many cars as possible in order to earn foreign currency. The government allocated steel according to the proportion of production exported, and in 1950 Britain exported 75 percent of its cars. During 1952–53 Nuffield showed M.G.s and Morris Minors among the skyscrapers of New York ("We're part of the American scene, too!") and emphasized durability with paintings of Morris Oxfords emerging triumphant from potholed tracks and sandstorms. The Organization (which included the M.G., Morris, Riley and Wolseley passenger car marques) merged with Austin to form the British Motor Corporation (BMC) on March 31, 1952.

CONTINUING 16 YEARS OF LEADERSHIP...THE

Magnificent new Minx !

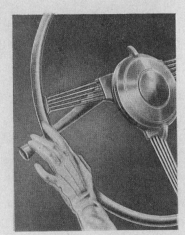

WITH SYNCHROMATIC FINGER-TIP GEAR CHANGE
in conjunction with
new fully proved, 4-speed smooth action crash-proof Synchromesh Gearbox

Distinguished new appearance
Lockheed hydraulic 2 leading shoe brakes
Everything—bonnet, interior, luggage—under lock and key
Exceptional enclosed luggage accommodation
Long beam sealed reflector headlamps
Powered by the famous fully proved Hillman Minx engine
Attractive strong vee-section bumpers at front and rear
Easi-clean disc wheels

Highly attractive interior design with stylish facia panel in jewellescent grey
New 3-spoke spring steering wheel provides clear view of instrument panel
Easi-lift safety bonnet unlocked from inside car
Wide arc safety vision dual screen wipers with single master control
Quick action positive location, 4 corner jacking system
Driving seat fully adjustable for height and leg room

*Plus the reliability, performance, economy and comfort resulting
from 16 years' continuous development*

HILLMAN MINX

A car with a great past . . . and a great future

A PRODUCT OF THE ROOTES GROUP

The Field, January 31, 1948

Holiday, June 1948

1948 Austin Devon. Contrast of styles, or how the same product can mean very different things to different markets. For a short while Austin's first true post-war model, launched late in 1947, was America's favourite imported car, and 11,740 were sold in the US sellers' market of 1948. But like many imports it was mainly a novelty, if an economical one — a junior car for Junior who, if truth be told, would probably have preferred an older Ford V-8 convertible or even, if Dad were incurably Anglophile, an M.G. In Britain the Devon was a desirable family car, well beyond the means of most people even at £416.0.6. The two-door Dorset, originally intended to be 4" narrower than the Devon and unsuccessful even as eventually produced, was made for export only from September 1948 and discontinued in October 1949. Elongated, painted portraits, an advertising staple of the period, would feature in Austin advertising until 1957–8, and the Devon would be replaced in 1952 by the Somerset, for which David Ogilvy, later to become famous for his "ticking clock" Rolls-Royce advertisements, wrote copy in America.

its maker's cars: the Herald replaced the Standard Ten in 1959, and the Triumph 2000 succeeded the Standard Vignale Vanguard four years later. Testing a 2000 for *The Field* in 1964, S.C.H. Davis recalled the day that "someone stated publicly that the name Darracq, carried by one of France's famous cars, meant 'scrap' in Russian. Immediately sales dropped."

Badge engineering, that time-honoured ruse of mar-

keting and product planning departments, gained a new lease of life in the 1960s. The sharing of components between related marques was nothing new, and had continued apace since the early 1950s. Wolseleys, Morrises and MGs had been visibly related since pre–BMC days, and the merger of the Nuffield Organization with Austin in 1952 to create the British Motor Corporation merely added complication. Corporate planning at Rootes had dictated that the 1954

Opposite: **1948 Hillman Minx Phase II.** Prestige advertising, but of a subtle kind. In 1948 it would not have mattered if the gear lever had come out of the exhaust pipe, as in the sellers' market of 1948–54 the Rootes Group could sell every car it made. In July 1950, recalls Geoff Owen, who sold cars in London at the time, a *used* Hillman Minx with an original price of £505 was valued by *Glass's Guide* at £735, and something like the usual order of things only began to return in 1953. Priority users could obtain new cars, but in March 1946, with enterprising doctors and others buying and reselling at a large profit, the British Motor Trades Association, together with the Society of Motor Manufacturers and Traders, instituted a rigorously-enforced covenant scheme which prevented resale of a new car other than at an agreed price within six months, a period extended to a year in March 1947 and in December 1950 to two years. The scheme was relaxed on some models in July 1952, its period was reduced to one year four months later, and it was abolished completely in January 1953. This Minx, an updated version of the 1939–42 Phase I which had featured Hillman's first essay in unitary construction, was replaced in 1949 by a full-width Phase III model heavily influenced by design consultant Raymond Loewy's famous 1947 Studebaker. The craze for column-changes reached its zenith in Britain in the early 1950s and gradually declined during the following ten years.

1949 Morris Minor. Only the most subtle of elongations (between the front wheelarch and door) was used in this very early advertisement for the star of the Earls Court Motor Show, where it was launched in October 1948. The slogan and illustrations were carried over to catalogues and other publicity material in an integrated campaign of a kind far from universal at the time. American awareness began slowly, with approximately 440 cars sold in the U.S. in 1949, but sales rose gradually during the 1950s to 10,000 or so in 1960 as the car's superb handling became known to enthusiasts, before declining in the 1960s. In Britain the Minor was heavily advertised within the overall scheme of Morris publicity during the 1950s but less so after the millionth had been celebrated in 1961. It nevertheless continued in production for another decade.

COUNTRY LIFE—SEPTEMBER 30, 1949

EXPORT MODEL
With its many new features and refinements the 1950
Standard Vanguard offers the finest car value in the world.
See it at
STAND 144
MOTOR SHOW   EARLS COURT

THE STANDARD MOTOR CO. LTD., COVENTRY.   LONDON: 37 DAVIES STREET, GROSVENOR SQUARE, W.1.   TEL: MAY. 5011
STANDARD CARS · STANDARD COMMERCIAL VEHICLES · FERGUSON TRACTORS · TRIUMPH CARS

STANDARD
VANGUARD

Country Life, September 30, 1949

1949 Standard Vanguard Phase I. British advertisers occasionally used realistic colour photographs in the 1930s, but the medium remained rare until 1957–58. Standard-Triumph, however, produced several colour series between 1948 and 1952 showing Vanguards and Triumph saloons against backdrops typical of England or of targeted export territories. The first full-width saloon to be sold in Britain, the Vanguard was stylist Walter Belgrove's interpetation of the 1942 Plymouth, suitably filled out. Freelance stylist George Walker (later of Ford in Dearborn) thought the original proposal "as high as a haystack" when he visited England in 1946 and the final version was lower. It was an export success in the car-starved world of 1948–50, but teething troubles included weak front suspensions, related chassis cracking, and poor dust sealing, the very earliest bodies lacking all-round door sealing as designers had forgotten to leave room for it. This kind of thing weakened British cars' reputation and, cumulatively, made potential buyers more willing to switch to continental and Japanese makes in the 1960s. America imported only a handful of Vanguards (Canada and Australia took many more) but the engine would power the Triumph TR2, first of a long and successful line of sports cars.

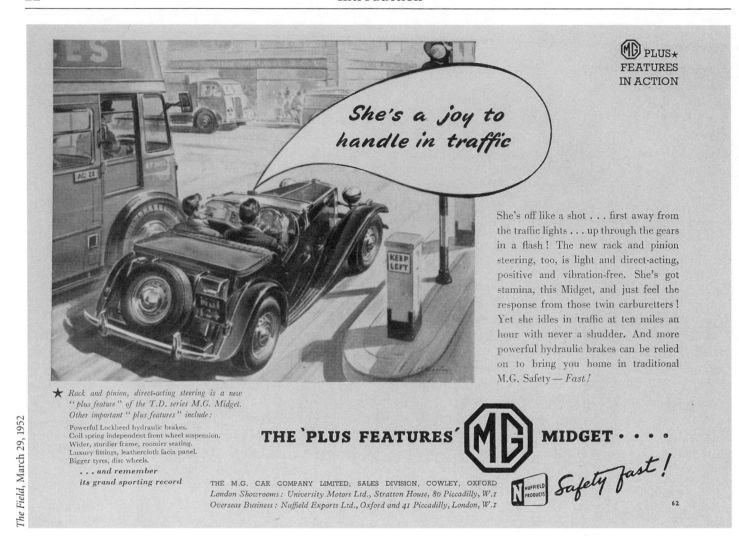

This page and opposite: **1952 M.G. TD and 1954 Riley 1½ litre RME.** Pre-war copy styles for cars of pre-war conception that provided the heritage memory on which copywriters for later badge-engineered M.G.s and Rileys relied. This saloon — last of a line first produced in 1946 — provided fine handling and quality to an upper-middle-class clientele unenamoured of full-width bodies or soft suspensions. It became known as the "last proper Riley" and was made until 1955. M.G., by contrast, are gung-ho in a kind of exaggerated English style that could, mishandled, congeal into an unappealing golf-club bufferism, but which is intended light-heartedly here. Getting hold of a new M.G. would remain difficult even when the general sellers' market subsided, as most sports cars went for export; for early delivery it was best to choose an orphan saloon (a Jowett Javelin, say, or a Singer SM1500). As late as the 1960s, a buyer wanting a particular specification of Triumph or MG sometimes had to wait for several months.

Humber Hawk should share an engine with the Sunbeam-Talbot, and that the larger 1952 Super Snipe should use the "Blue Riband" Commer engine. A 1956 Hillman Minx could be bought as a Singer Gazelle compact-luxury saloon (with a Singer engine until 1958) or as a Sunbeam Rapier coupe. All three models survived into the 1960s, mildly modified.

Standardization of components increased further in the 1960s, with BMC in particular offering several ranges, each in a number of badge-engineered variants. Buyers of the 1½ litre "Farina" saloon were urged to "Get the power to go places" in an Austin Cambridge. If they were "men who like finer things in life" they could choose a Riley version; the less sybaritic could "buy wisely" and "buy Wolseley" — at a modest premium over the Austin, of course. And for those who always bought Morris or MG, there were versions with those

badges, too. Differences between the models were confined to exterior and interior trim, a few body panels and minor mechanical items, chiefly the number of carburettors. It was an inexpensive way of covering all corners of the potential market and of satisfying the demands of dealers, while avoiding the need to tool up for genuinely different products. As a distillation of what had gone before, the "Farina" range was far from extravagant.

In this case, as in others, the different versions were advertised separately. In the case of the upmarket Riley, Wolseley and MG variants, attention was drawn to the values or heritage of the marque represented and to equipment exclusive to the particular type. The MG Magnette Mk IV was illustrated with the pre-war sports car of that name, and the Wolseley's special grille was shown in preference to the tail,

The Field, January 28, 1954

which all but the knowledgeable would mistake for that of a Morris Oxford. Similar juggling was employed for the Mini and 1100 ranges and, albeit with special bodywork and 1½ litre engines, for the Wolseley 1500 and Riley One-Point-Five derivatives of the Morris Minor. On the most cynical interpretation, badge engineering was a cheap way of satisfying those motoring die-hards whose limited budgets and dwindling numbers did not justify greater indulgence, but that is not the whole story. The younger motorist who had no long-standing interest in a particular marque, but who wanted a car that was a little out of the ordinary, luxuriously trimmed yet easy to service, could also be accommodated.

If traditionalism retained a limited rôle in the new car market of the 1960s, there were other influences at work. It was a period in which American styling changed dramatically, while, at the same time, fashion-conscious British motorists looked increasingly to Europe, rather than to America, for the stylistic lead. At the beginning of the decade, American ideas still had a strong hold on British car design. Sometimes, as with Dagenham-built Fords and General Motors' Vauxhalls, this was the result of consultation with American designers, even of American corporate *diktat*. But in several cases an American look was deliberately contrived by British stylists in order to make the product acceptable to American and more distant export markets, even though the worst of the parodies that resulted from this approach were obsolete by 1962.

In the case of the BMC "Farina" saloons, Italian and British influences were mixed in with the American, and what the designers of the Hillman Super Minx gave with one hand (fins, wraparound rear window and a metallic-painted dashboard) they took away with the other when they added a traditional British grille and a wooden dashboard to its compact-luxury derivative, the Singer Vogue. The Humber Sceptre, most sporting of the range, inclined towards Chevrolet (1958) in its rear styling but was more British than American inside, even if one wondered whether the car's round instruments represented naive convention or pastiche traditionalism re-imported. The tail fin, that most characteristic of American motifs, was on its way out by 1961, but had a few years to run elsewhere, if only because body styles changed less frequently in Europe. America had grown tired of Harley Earl's excesses and Britain's commercial travellers, too, eventually looked for something less brazen.

Where America withdrew, Italy advanced. From 1958 onwards, increasing numbers of British cars were designed by, or along lines inspired by, the Italian styling houses, and where the new, finless American idiom persisted, it did so unobtrusively, its influence being seen more in shape than

The Field, December 13, 1952

The Field, February 18, 1954

This page and opposite: **1952 Ford Zephyr Six (Mk I), 1954 Vauxhall Velox and Wyvern (E-type), 1950 Singer SM1500, and 1956 Singer Hunter.** This kind of illustration, used for several marques between 1947 and 1957, had the advantage of being dramatic yet tailor-made for black and white reproduction, as it was not sensitive to print or paper quality. Moreover, a single illustration could be doctored or updated to represent a slightly different model—here a Vauxhall Wyvern receives bonnet and side badges, side flash and number plate to turn it into a Velox within the same advertisement. If the uphill-speeding theme and distinctive combination of typefaces recall European Chrysler advertising of 1928–29, that is no accident: W.S. Crawford Ltd. had succeeded J. Walter Thompson as Vauxhall's agents in 1933, and would stay until late 1966. Ford's approach for the Velox's main rival is interesting: driver's-eye views were always rare and this one, showing the Zephyr's restyled dashboard, is dead-accurate and fascinating in its creation of shadow and texture. Rootes, meanwhile, completed their takeover of Singer in January 1956 and continued to produce diminishing numbers of Hunters until the summer. The Hunter was a tough car of good quality, but it was expensive without being luxurious and, although it sold well in Australia and New Zealand, the home market did not want the surplus when those territories imposed import restrictions. As an independent make, Singer had used a very different, slightly whimsical style of copy for the Hunter; the emphasis here on detailed equipment is characteristic of Rootes, although the illustration was carried over from a 1955 advertisement for the still-born Hunter 75. Like several British cars whose shapes had become outmoded, the Hunter was a traditionalized version of an earlier modernist style. With its simple, horizontal grille, slab sides and small windows, the original Kaiser-inspired SM1500 of 1948 had looked surreally like a toy car blown up to life size—something which the London Press Exchange's 1950 advertisement does nothing to alleviate; one wonders if the incongruous border, carried over from earlier Singer advertising, was retained in a spirit of gentle mischief or in desperation. But the design's essential quality and roadability meant that the Singer name would still be worth using for upmarket Minxes in the 1960s.

in decoration. The styling of British luxury cars became less conservative, and there was a general convergence in design. In 1955 there had been distinct schools of utility, luxury and pseudo–American styling; by 1965 there was comparative uniformity. Razor edges, panoramic windscreens and blobular little monocoques had all had their day.

The early 1960s were therefore years of transition, in which copywriters had to sell the remaining examples of a transatlantic style whose parent idiom had been superseded in its homeland long before the imitant model could be discontinued in Britain. The Humber Hawk, for example, which loosely resembled a 1955 Chevrolet, had a traditional wood and leather interior, and with sober colour schemes and modified front, rear and side windows, it looked relatively modern until 1964–65. The Vauxhall PA Cresta had acquired single-tone seats and mock-walnut door cappings by

The Illustrated London News, January 7, 1950 (With thanks to Paul Martin)

The Field, April 5, 1956

its last year (1962), and later advertisements for the PA played down — or at least endeavoured not to play up — the car's outdated appearance. Such adjectives as "distinguished" were employed in an effort to lend a sense of dignity and substance to an essentially flamboyant design. The translation from flashy upstart to respectable pillar of motordom was sometimes successful and, in the case of the big Humbers, modest styling changes were combined with sober copy to effect a change in image that was at least adequately convincing to the conservative buyer who would chose 1957's shape in 1967. Not that Vauxhall were so lucky. In 1971, the writer Kenneth Ullyett recalled that "a respected friend of mine in the judiciary has a certain prejudice against [black Vauxhall PAs, and] believes that they now largely fall into the hands of impecunious, reckless drivers, so whenever a careless-driving case comes into his court he scans the charge sheet. 'Ah', he will venture on occasions, 'I'll wager the defendant was driving an old black Vauxhall'."

The new car buyer of the 1960s demanded not only the latest styling, but comfort and the latest features, too. His counterpart of 1955 had generally looked out over a painted metal dashboard containing a stylized speedometer and one or two other instruments, a glovebox (with or without lid),

a motley collection of warning lights and black or cream knobs scattered almost anywhere. Relief had been given by attractive detailing: Ford's 1955 Prefect had a silver-painted central fascia panel and a pleasing steering wheel medallion in gold, chrome and black, while Alec Issigonis's 1948–54 Morris Oxford MO (a contemporary of the Minor) displayed the touch of a master in its deep bronze instrument panel containing cream and black dials with red needles. With the succeeding model, Issigonis settled on an open-cubbied minimalism which found its most attractive (and natural) expression in the 1959 Mini, even if it smacked of penny-pinching elsewhere. It was largely abandoned by 1970. Other techniques had been tried, too: Singer mitigated the heavy-pillared austerity of its SM1500 with an attractive mock-wood finish painted onto metal, and that Vauxhall PA, in 1957 Velox form, could be ordered with cream quilted door trims with black inserts (each diamond of the cream quilt containing pale green flashes), together with red seats and black quilted dashboard top. The car's speedometer, which combined gold and chrome decoration with a rotating orange band and various shades of blue for the figures and instrument face, looked almost restrained by comparison. But such details could not make up for the surrounding bare-

The Wolseley Four-Fortyfour has a 4 cyl. o.h.v. engine of 1250 c.c. Excellent suspension and road-holding. Real English leather upholstery, pile carpets. Safety glass all round.

Noblesse is obliged to

If one is very rich, choosing a car is easy. The trick is to coincide expensive and discriminating tastes with a moderate income. This the Wolseley Four-Fortyfour is doing very successfully for many people who want something better than a multi-production model without having to pay a lot for it. It gives you about as good a performance as you can use on our roads, its superb comfort, suspension and visibility are quite remarkable in a 1¼ litre and above all it looks what it is—a car of unmistakable character and distinction. Noblesse ought to be very obliged to Wolseley . . .

The Wolseley Six-Ninety
Basic Price £750
Plus Purchase Tax £376 7 0

The Wolseley Four-Fortyfour
Basic Price £595
Plus Purchase Tax £298 17 0

Polished walnut panel. Instruments and controls neatly and conveniently grouped.

Exceptionally wide and deep luggage locker. Built-in heating, demisting and ventilation unit.

Buy wisely—buy

WOLSELEY
Four-Fortyfour

REMEMBER. Quality and dependability are guaranteed by the B.M.C. Used-Car Warranty and you are certain of a good deal when you sell.

WOLSELEY MOTORS LTD, COWLEY, OXFORD
London Showrooms: 12 Berkeley Street, W.1. *Overseas Business:* Nuffield Exports Ltd, Oxford and 41 Piccadilly, London, W.1.

155

1956 Wolseley 4/44. It was no surprise that Wolseley, of all makes, should use as a headline the title under which Nancy Mitford's controversial, teasing 1955 essay on aristocratic manners, first printed in *Encounter* in 1955, reached a wide audience in 1956. Wolseley occupied a unique but slightly unstable middle-class niche in the home market of the 1950s, its Britishness self-conscious, edgy and business-orientated: Copy lines such as "I thought, somehow, you'd have a Wolseley"; "No one of their possessions places them so accurately as their Wolseley Four-Fortyfour"; "It has the quiet unassuming purposefulness of a man…who is proud of his Company and of himself"; and "Your successful man, though he 'lose' the game and a fiver at the 18th can still win a £5,000 contract at the 19th" appealed to men preoccupied much more with public image than with private comfort. To the Riley or Rover driver, it was too obviously effortful, and, stripped of deliberate anglicisms, Wolseley copy was at times surprisingly similar to Cadillac's. The danger with such a specific appeal is that the product can be left high and dry when society moves on, and after 1960 Wolseley copy would concentrate much more on the features of the cars themselves.

Sport & Country, October 3, 1956 (With thanks to Paul Martin)

1956 Hillman Minx Series I. In 1956 Hillman, unusually for a car maker, tapped into a graphic vernacular more often encountered in advertising for popular luxury foods and other non-automotive products. It worked as well in black and white as in colour, and its influence could still be seen in Rootes advertising in the early 1960s. The new Minx was produced until 1959 with only minor changes and formed the basis of updated Minxes, Husky wagons, Sunbeam Rapiers and Singer Gazelles until 1967. The body was designed in England in 1953 by Clare Hodgman and Holden ("Bob") Koto of the American design house Raymond Loewy Associates; interviewed by historian Barney Sharratt in the 1980s, Koto recalled that "the production model was exactly the same as our full-sized model." The influence of the 1953 Studebaker can be clearly seen.

Country Fair, November 1955

Punch, March 19, 1958

1955 Austin A30 Countryman and 1958 Vauxhall Victor F-type Series I estate car. The late 1950s saw the arrival of the modern station wagon (or estate car, or shooting brake) that would take an expanding share of the market after 1960. Early post-war wagons had almost always been adapted vans (Hillman, Austin A40, Ford Squire and Escort) or wooden-bodied adaptations of existing saloons (Alvis, Lea-Francis, Riley, Austin A70), devised in many cases by independent coachbuilders. Morris compromised with a wooden-framed Minor (produced until 1971) and a similar Oxford that was succeeded in 1954 by metal-bodied Oxford Series II and Isis Travellers that looked, with wood trim that was almost entirely decorative and van-type doors except on occasional split-tailgate conversions, as if they should have been gentrified vans, but weren't. More advanced were Abbot of Farnham's conversions of the larger Fords of 1954–62 with side-opening tailgates in the continental style, and almost modern were Humber's Hawk Mk VI of 1955; the Austin A95 Countryman and Standard Vanguard Phase III of 1956; the Hillman Minx and Morris Oxford Series IV of 1957; and independent conversions of Vauxhall's E-type Velox by Grosvenor (Swansong) and Martin Walter (Dormobile), the latter offered on customers' cars in 1956 and as a new car in 1957. Of these, only the Dormobile offered a modern full-length tailgate (made of plastic, and intended to serve as a makeshift tent roof when camping, with the seats folded down into a bed inside) while the Oxford had an unusual three-quarter length tailgate with a separate hatch below for the spare wheel.

Among the last factory-produced wagons in the converted-van style was this Austin A30 of 1954–56. Advertised in country-oriented magazines as a working car rather than as a lifestyle accessory, it was distinguished by mock-wood painted panels that drew the eye from a utilitarian shape but which were discontinued (though the panels themselves remained slightly recessed) when the model was updated in 1956 to become the A35 Countryman, in which form it lasted until 1962. By contrast, the Vauxhall Victor of 1958, factory-built with a full-length, counterbalanced steel tailgate and unrelated stylistically to any van, was Britain's first truly modern estate car. In both original (as here) and later Series 2 forms it was promoted on its styling (which was controversial) as well as its practicality, and if it was relatively expensive at $2400 in the U.S., where only 17,365 Victor saloons and estates were sold (by Pontiac dealers) during 1958, it was more successful in other markets and set the pattern for the Cortinas, Anglias, Hunters—and subsequent Victors—of the 1960s.

ness, and the ghost of austerity would not be wholly exorcized while painted metal remained.

Exotically coloured speedometers and chromium scripts became less common in the 1960s, and their loss was compensated by the adoption of former luxuries, such as screenwashers (by law), radios and cigarette lighters. Practical features, often of continental origin, became widespread — they included such gadgets as reclining seat backs,

stalk-operated indicators and lights, childproof door locks and oddly shaped switches identifiable by symbols in the daytime and by feel at night. Here, Rover and Triumph — and in advertisements, photographic realism — excelled. Buyers occasionally claimed to detect parsimony, and sometimes they were right. The chromed plastic used for some instrument bezels and ventilator knobs discoloured and wore off, doing nothing for second-hand values, as Ford and

Vauxhall discovered. Yet it took a practised eye to distinguish a good plastic-and-paint hubcap medallion from a chrome-and-enamel one, and perhaps a certain obsessiveness to want to.

Safety padding, which had appeared on dash tops in rudimentary form in 1957, became almost universal by 1970. Used clumsily, it could seem plasticky, but it could also be smart and sporty, particularly when covered with the black vinyl that became popular after 1965. The latter was a boon for advertisers because it photographed well, and for cost accountants because it went with any exterior colour — or, indeed, with a vinyl roof. It was inexpensive, easily heat-moulded to complicated shapes and could incorporate fake stitching and a mock leather finish. Its disadvantages were minor: it became hot in summer, it could look sombre in a car with smaller than average windows, it lacked the cosiness sought by some older buyers of small saloons, and it could smell uninviting. But it banished painted-metal austerity for good.

In the 1960s, advertisers popularized engineering innovation. BMC's was as advanced as any, though it was sometimes promoted with surprising modesty and made them little money; Ford, more conservative and cost-conscious, and with brasher copywriters, were more successful long-term, and their cars were more reliable. Many early post-war cars disintegrated on motorways for which they had not been designed, and a few, such as that 1930s throwback, the "sit-up-and-beg" Ford Popular, turned over. Engines consequently became more robust, and independent rear suspension displaced old-fashioned leaf springs on sports and luxury models, not least because fewer of them had to cope with the vicious roads of their predecessors' export markets. Front-wheel drive advanced steadily; rear engines were tried, found perilous on ice, and usually abandoned at the prototype stage. The aluminium-engined Hillman Imp was an exception — but not a reliable one. Disc brakes quickly became popular and aftermarket bumper stickers warned drum-braked boot-huggers who tempted fate. Speed and handling featured more than ever in advertisements during 1966–69.

The opening of the M1 in 1959 rekindled the industry's fluctuating preoccupation with gearboxes. Synchromesh was considered a necessity on all gears by 1970, as, for most people, were four forward speeds. Fords and Vauxhalls were famous for their three speeds, and Austin, Humber, and Standard had also considered them adequate for six-cylinder cars in 1960, but Vauxhall alone offered them ten years later. The column-shift declined, too; both Ford and Vauxhall made their last in 1972, with four and three speeds respectively, although the type lingered on the continent for another five years or so. Automatic gearboxes made headway, albeit more slowly than almost anyone expected in 1960. BMC's 1100 automatic was unusual, in that one could select "D" and let the gears change themselves or choose any gear from 1 to 4 and stay in it, even to a dead stop. It was a true manual override long before such things were common. But the conventional automatic never became really popular; although for the most part dependable mechanically, it had the annoying habit of changing into top when one wanted to stay in second unless one held it there, and many who might have enjoyed it said that they "liked the feeling of control" that a manual gave, and feared skidding on slippery bends or shooting off in reverse by mistake. Vauxhall made much of Hydra-matic in 1961–62, and others mentioned automatic gears boldly when they became available, but advertisers usually offered the option and left it at that.

Overall, copywriters had much to crow about in the 1960s. Bold photographs, punchy copy and a kind of intensified realism made their best pieces memorable. Some, such as Super National's E-type, were remembered for years after they appeared. There were horrors, too: the booby prize must go to Singer for "Luxury — Performance — Economy is [*sic*] yours when you buy a Singer Gazelle" — not so much for the syntactical gremlin as for an uninspired layout and an illustration that made the neat, colourful little Gazelle look about as fleet-footed as a heifer in a peat bog.

Much car advertising of the 1960s can be seen to mark a transition between the unselfconscious confidence of the late 1950s and the doubts and tribulations of the 1970s. Yet there was more confidence than doubt, and the tone of the period's copy reflected an optimistic sense of newfound freedom and faith in progress, of an infinity of possibility and social advancement which today seems poignantly naïve, but which at the time was a natural concomitant of rapid consumer growth. Looking back, the extrovertism of the late 1960s can be seen as the public face of an industry in retreat; progress, though real, was finite, and, through the haze of excitement, its boundaries came into view. That is the paradox of the period. Yet none of this was immediately obvious to the new car buyer of the time, and many who responded to these advertisements were the first in their families ever to own a car. The best copywriters not only stimulated their excitement but shared it, too. Their enthusiasm is still infectious.

◆

PART ONE

Family Marques

Engines of an Industry

◆

Economy being the mother of automobile invention, the Corncrake relies on only two speeds, yet so shrewdly chosen are the ratios that four inmates of the box would seem superfluous. Reverse gear has been daringly but effectively abolished — thereby greatly reducing production costs — since the machine is easily pushed backwards by four average adults by virtue of its low (dry) weight of 30cwt.

—Ronald Collier, "The Motocar Road Test No. NVG/99, Cootemaster Corncrake," *Punch*, October 20, 1954.

1

Austin

"*You* invest *in an Austin*"

The majority of car advertising created in the 1960s was for family cars, and between them the British Motor Corporation (BMC), the Rootes Group, Standard-Triumph, Ford and Vauxhall accounted for most advertisements. Ford's advertising budget was generally the highest while BMC, as the parent corporation of Austin, Austin-Healey, Morris, MG, Riley, Vanden Plas and Wolseley, combined the greatest number of marques, some of which had been mutual competitors before merging and remained so afterwards. Each had its own its own heritage and traditions and so, consequently, its special place in the affections of the British public. With products whose specifications and prices made them potential rivals, discrete brand identities were essential, and public affection was nurtured most effectively with advertising specific to each marque. If one artist painted Wolseleys, another should paint the equivalent Rileys, unless he were unusually versatile. Copy styles should differ; unique heritage should be emphasized; above all, advertising for one marque should look like advertising for no other. At first this could be achieved with different layouts and styles of illustration, but as layouts in mainstream car advertising converged in the late 1960s and photography reduced the scope for graphic individuality, distinctive marque-wide campaigns gained ground. An advertisement for a Riley 4/Seventy-Two looked very like a parallel advertisement for the Riley Elf and not at all like publicity for its sister car in a similar market, the Wolseley 16/60.

The resulting identities were increasingly superficial and by the mid-1960s almost entirely synthetic. As the public became more value-conscious and new models more expensive to develop, sisterhood burgeoned under disparate skins. When Austin and the Nuffield Organization merged in 1952 to create the British Motor Corporation, a period of badge-engineering began in Britain's motor industry that made General Motors' artful juggling of "A," "B," "C" and "D" bodies during the late 1940s and early 1950s look like a Saturday morning *jeu d'esprit*.[1] Yet BMC's ranges of the 1960s included many models unique to individual marques, and four were unique to Austin. These were the 1958–67 A40 Farina (so called, semi-officially, to distinguish it from its Devon, Dorset, Somerset and Cambridge A40 predecessors of 1947–57); the 3-Litre of 1967–71; the Maxi of 1969–81; and the large Princesses, which were advertised as Austins until mid-1957, then under the "Princess" name until mid-1960, and subsequently under the marque name of Vanden Plas. As with Chrysler and Imperial, however, the public always thought of Princesses as ultra-luxurious Austins, and even the 4-litre limousine, which combined the official demeanour of the earlier Humber Pullman and Imperial with some of the grandeur of Daimler and Rolls-Royce, never completely shook off its original appellation — or needed to, such was the respectability of the Austin name.

In the 1920s and 1930s Austin (founded by Herbert Austin in 1905) and Morris (founded by William Morris, later Lord Nuffield, in 1913) had been Britain's best-selling marques, producing complete ranges from the popular Austin Seven (1922–39) and Morris Minor and Eight (1928–48) to big, six-cylinder saloons and limousines which competed with American cars on the British home market and in Britain's colonial territories. Morris was easily Britain's best selling marque in 1939, with Austin immediately behind. Loyalty to these marques remained strong throughout the 1960s, not only amongst the comparative few who had bought new cars before 1939 or had a family connection with one or other factory, but also across generations within families who had no particular interest in cars at all.

Thousands of potential buyers were loyal, with varying degrees of intensity, to Morris or to Austin. It was true that a few people did not realize how much different derivatives of a given design had in common, whilst others, out of a residual snobbery, pretended to innocence as they chose an MG, Riley or Wolseley. Some dealers, too, liked to exaggerate the number of sales made through buyers' apparent ignorance of commonality in order to promote their particular marque franchises as continuing to be indispensable to overall BMC sales—but it was not ignorance as much as politeness combined with a certain light-hearted conspiratorial spirit which led most buyers to stay quiet about the opposition when talking with salesmen. *Small Car* magazine, ever the iconoclast, enjoyed lining up equivalent cars grille to grille and testing them against each other.[2]

Of BMC's ranges which included Austin variants, the Mini (August 1959—October 2000) appeared under the Austin and Morris marque names until 1969 and subsequently under the "pure" marque name of "Mini," as did the Mini Cooper, which was either an Austin or a Morris until 1969 and a pure Mini thereafter until 1971, when it was discontinued. By contrast, the Mini's upmarket derivatives, the Riley Elf and Wolseley Hornet of 1961–69, were advertised under their original marque names within the overall schemes of Riley and Wolseley advertising. An MG Mini was considered but did not enter production.[3] In July 1966, BMC merged with Jaguar to become British Motor Holdings (BMH), and in May 1968 BMH merged with Leyland (which included Standard-Triumph cars and Leyland trucks and, from 1966, Rover cars) to create the British Leyland Motor Corporation (BL), and it was from the re-organization prompted by this merger that "Mini" arose as a pure marque name in its own right in 1969.

The compact, front-wheel-drive Austin 1100 (1963–74) and larger-engined 1300 (1967–74), were accompanied by Morris (1962–73), MG (1962–73), Riley (1965–69), Wolseley (1965–73) and Vanden Plas (1963–74) versions of the same design, while the mid-sized 1800 (1964–75), also with front-wheel drive, was made as an Austin from 1964, as a Morris from 1966, and as a Wolseley from 1967. Riley and Vanden Plas versions were contemplated but not produced. The 1489cc, four-cylinder Austin A55 Cambridge, produced from January 1959 until late 1961, was developed alongside Morris Oxford Series V, MG Magnette Mk III, Riley 4/Sixty Eight and Wolseley 15/60 sisters which were announced in March, February and May 1959 and December 1958 respectively. With the updated, 1622cc, Austin A60 Cambridge of 1961–69, they became the Oxford Series VI (to 1971), Magnette Mk IV (to 1968), Riley 4/Seventy-Two (to 1969) and Wolseley 16/60 (to 1971). Sister cars of the 2912cc, six-cylinder 1959–61 Austin A99 Westminster (A110 from 1961–68) were the Wolseley 6–99 (6/110 from 1961–68) and the Vanden Plas 3-litre (3-litre Mk II from 1961–64 and 4-litre R from 1964–68).

Many other BMC models not produced as Austins had parts—particularly engines—in common with Austins: the Austin A40 shared its "A" series engine with the Morris Minor, which had adopted it in earlier, 803cc form from the Austin A30 in 1952; and the Riley One-Point-Five and Wolseley 1500 of 1957–65 used the same ("B" series) engine as the 1959–61 Austin Cambridge and its sisters[4] in a body developed from a proposed replacement for the Morris Minor that also spawned the Australian Austin Lancer and Morris Major[5]. A version of the A55 Cambridge, with the larger fins of its Riley and MG derivatives and with a locally-developed six-cylinder engine, was introduced in Australia in 1962. Called the Austin Freeway, it was sold alongside a companion model called the Wolseley 24/80. A variant of the British Wolseley 1500 for the Republic of Ireland (Eire) was fitted with an engine of exactly 1200cc, inherited from the 1954–56 Austin A40 Cambridge. The six-cylinder "C" series engine fitted in the Westminster and in the large Austin-Healeys from 1956–67 (and to a final Austin-Healey in March 1968) was designed by Morris Engines in Coventry and first seen in 2639cc form in the low-production Wolseley 6/90 of 1954–59 and Morris Isis of 1955–58. The Isis was the last six-cylinder car of specifically Morris design, the only subsequent Morris "six" being the 1800-derived 2200 of 1972–75, which was accompanied by equivalent models from Austin (2200) and Wolseley (Six). The Austin 3-Litre (1967–71) shared its engine with the MGC (1967–69); and the corporation devised many other inter-marque commonalities, too.

This was cross-fertilization of unprecedented fecundity, beyond anything attempted even by the Rootes Group with Hillman, Humber, Singer and Sunbeam. It was justified not only by comparison with the diversity that had gone before (which would have been ruinously expensive and pointless to maintain), but also by the need to provide cars for established and rival dealers who sold either Austins or cars of the former Nuffield marques, but not both. The dealers in turn supplied customers who, in many cases, however irrationally (and however knowingly and cheerfully so), would have strayed outside the BMC fold if deprived of a desired model in the livery of their favourite marque.

During the 1960s most BMC advertisements, for Austin as for other marques, were therefore for individual makes and models. But there was some overlap between marque, model and corporate advertising, as from the early 1960s many advertisements promoted Austin and Morris versions of the Mini together (latterly under the combined informal name of "Austin/Morris") while others showed Minis with Austin and Morris 1100s as complementary ranges. The front-wheel-drive cars in particular were highlighted under BMC's "Creative Engineering" slogan and campaign of 1967,[6] which augmented conventional corporate prestige advertising for BMC's whole car range. One October 1965 advertisement lined up 41 different BMC cars in formation, ranging from a £469 15s 10d Austin Mini to a Vanden Plas Princess Limousine at £3082 16s 3d. By this time, Alec Issigonis, creator of the Morris Minor and of the Mini, and the leading mind behind BMC's other front-wheel-drive cars, had become famous in engineering and motoring circles across the world and a nationally known figure in Britain.[7]

In September 1958, however, Austin announced a small, 948cc saloon that would be produced under no other marque name. Called the A40 and costing £676 7s or £689 2s for a De luxe, it was first shown to Britons at the Earls Court Motor Show in October following an initial public appearance in Paris, and it marked a turning point for Austin. The company's early post-war cars had been homely and, until the A40/A50 Cambridge and A90 Six Westminster of 1954, bulbous. Their conservatism was reflected in advertising which was equally conventional, even if the colour photographs increasingly used during 1955–58 were modern for their time. The former racing driver Kay Petre had persuaded BMC's chairman, Leonard Lord, that Austins were dull and was employed as a colour consultant for the 1954–56 Cambridge, which allowed an off-white and black car to be photographed in advertising among multi-coloured fabric samples above the unimpeachably modest headline, "Woman consultant chooses materials and colours for new Austin Cambridge." But she faced an uphill struggle. "Kay's ideas were too advanced for the day; she wanted pinks and blues as opposed to our blacks and browns…," recalled Austin works manager Joe Edwards; and according to Dan Warren of BMC Service, "She certainly brightened up the cars, and did some excellent work on trim co-ordination. But she came unstuck when she followed the fashion of the time that had gone barmy on rust colours. Her proposed rust-coloured A30 didn't go down well at all. She didn't last long after that."[8] Austin's two-tone paint schemes of 1957–58 were much less adventurous than those from Ford or Vauxhall.

But the colours of the new A40[9], particularly when combined with the black roof of the De luxe, heralded a new era for Austin, as did the design of the car itself. In December 1955, the Duke of Edinburgh, a keen motorist with considerable knowledge of the industry, visited the Austin factory at Longbridge, near Birmingham, and looked at the proposals from Ricardo (Dick) Burzi, Austin's stylist since 1929. Formerly with Lancia, Burzi been compelled to leave Italy for Vincenzo Lancia's Paris coachbuilding firm after lampooning Mussolini in newspaper cartoons, and Lancia recommended him to Herbert Austin when the two happened to meet *en route* to America aboard the Queen Mary.[10] Remembering the Duke's 1955 visit, Joe Edwards told Austin historian Barney Sharratt, "[after lunch Leonard Lord] said, 'Let's go and have a look at the models below in Burzi's studio.'…and after Len had shown him the models the Duke said, 'Sir Leonard, I think you ought to have another look at things because I'm not sure these are up to the foreign competition.' Old Len just didn't know where he was. Eventually Edinburgh went and the next day Len sent for Farina…. He flew in one morning and went away that night with an £84,000 contract for designing our first Farina cars. Not many people know that but I assure you that it was the Duke of Edinburgh's comments which brought it all about."[11] Burzi, however, remained widely respected and Austins of the 1958–64 period between them combined the ideas of Burzi, Pinin Farina and Alec Issigonis in differing proportions. The Mini was pure Issigonis; the Cambridge Mk II and its derivatives were Pinin Farina with refinement by Burzi and badge-engineered variants by the former Morris chief stylist at Cowley, Sid Goble; the 1100 was lightly modified Farina with accentuated wheel-arches and sills in the earlier Morris style; and the 1800 was by Issigonis and Sergio Pininfarina (son of the design house's founder, Battista Pinin Farina) working together around proportions and wheel positions determined by Issigonis.

Burzi's designs had often been compromised by modifications made at the insistence of Leonard Lord, who had previously dismissed the idea of consulting Pinin Farina. But the design for the A40 went into production without significant alternation, the most noticeable difference between the prototype and the production car being in the thickness of the window pillars, which was needed for strength and ease of production. Although the A40 inherited the drivetrain of the 1956–59 A35, its "two-box" body represented a genuine innovation which reached its full potential in September 1959 with the Countryman, a version which had a split tailgate to make the most of the existing, folding, rear seat, and which used a name which had become familiar on Austin estate cars since the days of the original, van-like A40 (Devon) Countryman of 1948. When Innocenti began building A40s in Milan in November 1960, a version with a true hatchback, called the Combinata, was built alongside the equivalent saloon. An A40 Mk II, with a lengthened wheelbase, improved brakes and trim, an enlarged (1098cc) engine from 1962 and updated interior from 1964, was built until November 1967. Never a best-seller (sales of 342,162 were only respectable), the A40 was always squeezed between BMC's other mechanically traditional cars such as the Morris Minor and the corporation's more adventurous 1100s — not to mention the Ford Anglia (from 1959), Triumph Herald (also from 1959) and Vauxhall Viva (from 1963). But it paved the way for the Pinin Farina's subsequent, best-selling 1100 — which, of course, relied on the A40's having been commissioned in the first place — and the 1959 Countryman was the ancestor of the modern hatchback.

With the A40, Austin advertising broke away from the homely themes which had suited the A35. ("Life's more fun with an Austin A.35…Like all fishermen, Gerald and Keith are reflective types. They had a lot of questions to ask before they let their father get a new A35…") Copy lines such as November 1958's "Cyclorama view... No small car has ever given you the perfect visibility you get driving the new A.40" were practical, and "The looking-ahead look... Designed by world famous stylist Pinin Farina, the A.40 presents a glimpse into the future of small car styling" was truer than the copywriter knew.

The trade, meanwhile, advertised the advertising. As press advertisements appeared with the "latest expression of the Austin line" speeding over the imaginary bridge of a future motorway in an echo of America's highway fantasies of the late 1930s, *Motor Trader* showed the same picture above the headline, "Austin make news — and so can you.... Austin will steal the limelight at this year's Motor Show.... And this is the moment when Austin advertising hits peak revs. At Motor Show time, outsize ads for Austin will appear in all the top newspapers and magazines, carrying the dramatic message of Austin's world leadership in design.... Here's how you can slip-stream! Spend a little yourself on advertising *now* and you catch all the power behind the Austin national campaign. There's material in abundance for you — and it's all free. Press advertisements, showroom posters, mailing leaflets...all tying in with the Austin 'view of the future' theme. It's ready and waiting — order *now*."

By the spring of 1959 the A40 could be photographed outside a theatre at night for a fashionable respectability, with the headline, "The Austin A40 moves in dress circles," followed by copy which made the most of the A40's novelty: "Here's one car that does NOT have to be big to be impressive...." November 1958's "Looking ahead" copy line turned out to prefigure an entire campaign, for in February 1959 the slogan, "Austin looks years ahead" began to appear at the bottom of A40 advertising. It would become a marque-wide slogan in a unique and cleverly arranged 1960 colour campaign that used dramatic photographs of all Austin cars — A40s, Minis, Cambridges, Westminsters and Austin-Healeys — in advertisements which were designed to be published individually or combined in double-page spreads.[12]

1961's marque-wide "Get into an Austin and out of the ordinary!" campaign made the most of the new Pinin Farina look, which by now was shared with the A55 Cambridge and A99 Westminster; and humour, always useful with a small car, was used in an interpretation of the two-cars-in-one theme to which the A40 naturally lent itself. "You and your other self agree on the Austin A40," said a mid-1961 advertisement. The picture showed a red A40 with its owner on one side dressed in a morning suit and on the other in flippers and diving gear with a newly caught flatfish that looked to the casual reader as if the A40 had just run over it. During 1962–64 the pre-war Austin slogan, "You *invest* in an Austin" was revived, implicitly emphasizing the reliability of Austin's rear-wheel-drive ranges, and it worked well with the high-quality, realistic photographs of interior details such as carpets, dashboards and seats that became a feature of advertising for A40s and other Austins during 1962–66.

This imaginative use of photography also anticipated 1968's dramatic photographs of front-wheel-drive Austin and Morris cars in motion, which combined practical realism and engineering competitiveness with slogans such as "BMC make the cars that hold the road" and "BMC make the cars that fit where others can't." For the A40, headlines such as 1965's "Some cars are rounded off at the corners. The Austin A40 is elegantly squared off at the corners. Square cars carry more than round cars" usefully emphasized the essential practicality of the car. By 1965 the A40 was less fashionable than the 1100 but, with its folding rear seat, it could take large objects, like the sheet of timber shown, that were beyond the 1100 despite the latter's greater overall cabin space. 1966's "You don't happen to own a cello yourself? But ask yourself what ordinary car carries awkward objects as harmoniously as the Austin A40" made the same point to the kind of middle-class buyer who might otherwise choose an 1100. To outsiders, the internal competition between different BMC designs was striking: Ford's Consul Classic (1961–63) was sold alongside the overlapping 1962 Consul Cortina for only a year.

The "Austin looks years ahead" slogan, with its useful double meaning, suited the A55 Mk II of 1959[13] as much as it did the A40, and the new Cambridge was photographed in bright, two-tone colour schemes such as white and pinkish red, white and green, grey and black — and, in one March 1960 piece, turquoise and lilac, although this was admittedly a left-hand-drive car. The copywriter played his part, too, machine-gunning his way through the period's favourite selling-points with exemplary efficiency: "Kitzbühel, January 1960. When the family look back at this photograph in their album, they will have to guess its date by the size of the children. There are no other clues: ski clothes change little from year to year, and the car gives nothing away. For the car is an Austin A55. And as it's an Austin it will be their car next year, and many years after. The point being, of course, that Austins are famously faithful cars. You just top up with petrol, oil, and two kinds of water; you go in for punctual services at regular intervals; and that's the end of your responsibility. In the old days people used to say: 'Austin — you can depend on it.' Today it's the same thing, but more so." Continental sophistication (foreign-registered car), snob-

Opposite: **Austin A40 Mk II.** Detailed, close-up photography at its best showed the one major feature that the A40 enjoyed over the more adventurous 1100. The slogan at the foot of the page had a long history, appearing in pre-war copy for Austins of all kinds. The A40 was a sturdy car, but the driving position, with a rather low-set steering wheel, did not suit everyone. A Countryman version had a drop-down bootlid for long loads and a lift-up rear window, too, giving it a split hatchback of a kind revived in the 1990s on the Honda Civic. A one-piece tailgate was fitted to the Countryman's Italian-built sister car, the Innocenti A40S Combinata of 1962.

THE AUSTIN A40

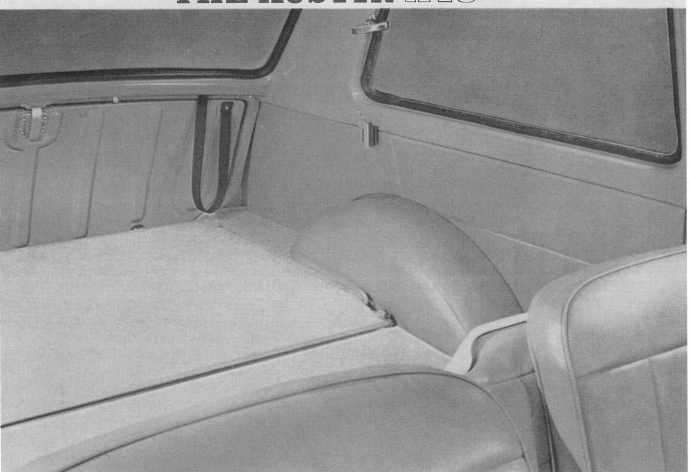

The shape isn't just for fun...
it gives you space you can double

THAT MAKES SENSE

It's a distinctive shape, the A40. But not just to be different. That shape was designed for the best and simplest of reasons: it makes sense! Look inside. You get more than just four-up comfort. Get inside and move the fully folding back seat down—and there's extra space for a mountain of luggage. And that's not all.

With the back seat up, you get a normal-sized boot that's *inside* the car. Perfect for carrycot, or sudden-shower picnics. Then feel the performance of the 1098 c.c. engine; make friends with the fuel gauge; and check the price; £460 plus £96.7.11 P.T. . . . £556.7.11. It makes sense to invest yourself with an Austin A40.

THE AUSTIN MOTOR COMPANY LIMITED · LONGBRIDGE · BIRMINGHAM   PERSONAL EXPORTS DIVISION · 41-46 PICCADILLY · LONDON W1

you invest in an AUSTIN

value (skiing), affluence (the venue), escapism (the venue again), fashionability (the colours), styling (well known, by 1960, to be from Pinin Farina), family utility, reliability, durability, and marque heritage — all were felled in not many more than a hundred words. The people who used to say "Austin — you can depend on it" were, of course, earlier copywriters, but thousands of pre-war Austins were still on the road in 1960, and surprising numbers would see out the decade.

Like Nash in the early 1950s, Austin made much of the Pinin Farina name in early copy for the A55 Mk II, even if the designer's original proposal for the car had looked un-characterisically overdone and was toned down for produc-tion by incorporating ideas from Dick Burzi. Sid Goble, meanwhile, devised distinctive panels and trim for the other marque variants. As he later recalled, the task required in-genuity: "From Farina's design for the Cambridge [£801 10s 10d; De luxe: £829 17s 6d] I had to develop designs in as-cending order of price for the Morris Oxford [£815 14s 2d; De luxe: £844 0s 10d], Wolseley 15/60 [£936 2s 6d], MG Magnette [£1012 12s 6d], and Riley 4/68 [£1028 4s 2d]. I was only allowed to alter the bonnets and grilles of each car and had to produce any further differentiation by playing about with the trim, fascias and paintwork. Although there were different sidelights I got away with the same pressings for the front wings. One draw die could produce all the rear wings [of two basic types for the Cambridge, Oxford and Wolse-ley on the one hand, and for the MG and Riley on the other] because we simply used a different clipping tool to produce the variations for each model. Farina wasn't involved with these variants at all."[14]

In October 1961, the A55 Mk II was updated to become the A60. The Mk II had always been comparatively long, tall and narrow, with a substantial rear overhang, as it inherited the wheelbase, much of the drivetrain and, in all but frac-tions of an inch, the front and rear tracks of the 1957–58 A55 Mk I. For the A60 the wheelbase and tracks were in-creased along with the engine capacity while performance and handling — never very good — both improved. The orig-inal "wasp tail" rear lights, with chrome bands between the individual lamps and ribbed decoration below, survived only on the A60 and Morris Oxford station wagons, the saloon's fins were cropped and, like the more specialized Vauxhall VX 4/90 announced (if not actually produced) at the same time, the A60 De luxe gained a side flash in a contrasting colour. The A55 Mk II's light grey painted dashboard was replaced by a plusher looking panel with a surprisingly tasteful mock wood finish. Copy continued to promote the car's styling

("Get the style to go places") but showed the car against re-alistic, day-to-day backdrops and reverted mainly to tradi-tional Austin virtues. By 1966 the design was beginning to look old-fashioned, and practical virtue triumphed: "How to make the pennies count when you're in the market for a new car? Take a tip from your wife. Shop around. Then take a cool look at the Austin A60." It offered unusual solidity and a general air of prosperity from a modest £854 in 1961, and, following purchase tax reductions from which the whole industry benefited, from £736 16s 8d in January 1966. The model lasted until 1969, by which time more than 425,000 had been built since 1959.[15]

In July 1959 the Cambridge was joined by the similar-looking but larger Austin A99, and campaigns for the two cars ran in parallel. A99 advertisements were included in the matched pairs chosen for the "Austin looks years ahead" campaign of 1960, although one piece showing a big new car outside a luxury hotel looked a little incongruous beside its "pair," in which the owner of an A40 picked mushrooms in a forest. At £1149, the A99 competed with that odd mix-ture of trans-Atlantic glitz and clubroom luxury, the 3-litre Humber Super Snipe, and — alongside its better-trimmed Wolseley 6–99 sister at £1255 — with the more straightfor-wardly patrician Rover 3-Litre, both newcomers of the pre-vious year.[16] Like the Humber, the Austin at first hovered be-tween affluent glamour and sober respectability: with a three-speed gearbox (albeit with Porsche-type synchromesh and standard overdrive), two-tone paint, brightly coloured two-tone interior trim and a painted metal dashboard (though a tasteful one) it was not yet quite aloof from the big Fords and Vauxhalls, and only when developed into the A110 in 1961 did it really find its feet as a sober semi-luxury car for businessmen. 1962's advertising reflected this matu-ration, and headlines such as "This man gets high power...," "This man gets sports car response..." and "This man gets style...," each finished with "...but not at any price," made a straightforward — and very Austin-like — appeal to sober judgment. "Sports car response" was to the accelerator rather than to the enormous steering wheel, which needed strong arms to manoevre the 3400 lb. car before power steering ar-rived as an option in July 1962. The A110 was advertised sparingly in its last years, and in 1968 made way for the much less successful Austin 3-Litre.

The Mini was a completely different proposition. Yet for all the novelty of the car itself, little was truly unusual in ad-vertising for the Austin version ("From Austin — a new breed of small car!") except that 1959's announcement ad-vertising used a labelled cutaway diagram to point out the

---

Opposite: **Austin A55 Cambridge Mk II.** Austin used both paintings and photographs for its colour adverstisements during the 1950s, but by 1959 the photographers had won. They showed two-tone A55s to dramatic effect in both black and white and colour pieces — even if 1960's turquoise and lilac car was Swiss-registered. In the 1950s British styling had been characterized by distinct mini-American, razor edge, full-width "blobular," and Italian-plus-British-grille schools, but Pinin Farina brought many elements together in a style only lightly anglicized by BMC, and which had much in common with his Fiat 1800 and 2100 (1959) and Peugeot 404 (1960). Surprisingly, air travel had been an Austin adver-tising theme with the 1958 A55 Mk I and A95, too.

New swift line, new uncrowded comfort

"THAT'S A NICE CAR YOU'RE WEARING," her husband remarked. Indeed, they both enthuse about the looks of their new Austin A55 Cambridge Mk II — and they know its looks stem from strictly practical considerations. **PININ FARINA,** who designed the car, always works from the inside outwards, which means that every line of the modern styling is justified by functional advantages like the following:

FAMILY SIZE: added inches everywhere to give big-car comfort for a medium-car price. Huge 19 cu. ft boot with counterbalanced lid. **RELAXED DRIVING:** unrestricted view all round with 22 sq. ft of safety glass. Raked steering wheel for greater ease. 4-speed gearbox with either floor or steering column change. **PERFORMANCE:** lively BMC 1½ litre, 4-cylinder engine chalks up 39 mpg at a steady 40 mph.

Top speed: in the upper 70s.
FACTS ARE IMPORTANT, but to know the character, the *feel* of the A55, visit your Austin dealer. Go over the car inch by inch. Then drive it — you'll like it! Arrange for a test drive today.
EUROPEAN TOURING SERVICE. Ask your dealer about the BMC Service Vouchers. Bought in Britain with sterling, they are valid throughout Europe.

AUSTIN A55

By Appointment to
Her Majesty The Queen
Motor Car Manufacturers
The Austin Motor
Company Limited

Backed by
BMC 12-month
warranty
and BMC
service

AUSTIN LOOKS YEARS AHEAD

THE AUSTIN MOTOR COMPANY LTD · LONGBRIDGE · BIRMINGHAM

Austin A60. Déjà vu. This improbable Rhodesian advertisement for a locally assembled product (distinguished by its white front reflectors) prefigured a much better known BMW piece of the 1970s (inset)—which was ironic, given that British manufacturers faced increasing competition from European marques in the late 1960s. English advertisements showed the A60 in realistic settings with copy to match; one, in particular, was happy to admit that it was definitely not the car for the young man "enjoying his last fling before marriage," and showed the car outside one of the new supermarkets.

car's genuinely interesting features.[17] Cutaways were normally confined to sales brochures and were uncommon in British car advertising, but the 848cc, 1260 lb. Mini (or Se7en and Mini-Minor as the Austin and Morris versions were initially called), at ten feet long without bumper overriders and four feet, seven inches wide on a wheelbase of six feet, eight inches, was so different from other cars that it justified a departure from convention—in this, as in much else. Elements of the Mini's design were traceable not only to earlier Issigonis design studies of various sizes, but also—and this was particularly true of the spartan dashboard, rounded tail and gently curved front wings and bonnet—to the Morris Oxford, Cowley and Isis production cars of 1954–56. But although the Mini shared with those cars a certain functionalism, its character was unique. It was also cheap: sold—unprofitably to BMC—at £497 in 1959, the standard Se7en and Mini-Minor were undercut in Britain only by the basic Ford Popular at £494. The Austin Seven Countryman estate car of September 1960 (at £641 in November 1961 compared to £526, by then, for the standard Seven and £568 for the De luxe) was, with its identically priced Morris Mini-Traveller sibling, Britain's cheapest four-wheeled estate car. In March 1961, motorists were invited to "Just try to find the 'ordinary' in an Austin Seven" with the help of eight young musicians who clambered in and over a bright blue car, unconsciously anticipating the "How many people can we fit in a Mini?" competitions gleefully devised by students in the 1960s. From September 1961, a Super Seven ("How luxurious can an Austin Seven

get?") appealed to the increasing proportion of the Mini's constituency who bought the car because they liked it rather than simply because it was cheap. They happily paid £591 17s 3d for a car with better sound insulation and trim.

At the beginning of 1962, the Sevens were renamed

Austin A110 Westminster Mk I. 1962's powerbroker suddenly realizes that he left the handbrake off. That archetypal venue of the period, the deserted beach, suggested glamour and escape, and provided an uncluttered backdrop for the car—not to mention good light levels, unlike the country-house-at-night locations intermittently popular with Austin and others in the late 1950s. With post-war rationing a receding memory by 1962, extravagance was no longer a dirty word. Austin's absent-minded individualist is much younger than his pipe-smoking, A70 Hereford-driving counterpart of ten years earlier. They could (just) have been father and son.

"Austin Minis." In October the Super made way for a Super De Luxe, and the trend away from austerity reached its height with the Radford Mini de Ville, announced in May 1963 and anticipated by a car built by Hooper Motor Services Ltd. for the actor Peter Sellers.[18] At the time, Harold Radford were coachbuilders best known for their "Countryman" conversions of the post-war Bentleys and Rolls-Royces. According to Harold Radford, "After driving [a Mini], I could see that it was ideal for running around town. I then began to hear through my clients that there was a market for a small runabout which was different from the average volume manufactured car. That gave me the idea for the Radford Mini. It was designed to match the customer's Rolls or Bentley in both paintwork and trim. Then I had the idea of the lifting tailgate (which preceded the hatchback trend by nearly ten years) and designed a divided rear seat, one third/two thirds, which could be tipped forward individually…. At the peak of the Rolls-Mini era I was building…five Minis per week."[19] In 1986 Radford remembered, "I held the patents for the…rear seat…and when my company was sold in 1963, the renewal fee was so high for re-signing the patents that I let it lapse. If I had kept it on, I think I should be a millionaire by now!"[20] Not every Radford Mini had the patented seats: cars were equipped to customers' individual specifications and in some the rear seat space was converted into a padded luggage shelf. The cost of what the company described in a May 1963 advertisement as "the most luxu-

Austin Gipsy. "It would help if the machine looked quite different from its world-famous rival" said S.C.H. Davis in a contemporary test of the 1958–68 Gipsy, which was destined to remain forever in the Land-Rover's shadow. Testimonials were rare in automobile advertising by the late 1950s — most tended to be earnest, which was not always desirable. But this one suits a working vehicle, as Godfrey Baseley, who appeared in a short series of pieces for Gipsy, was better known as the creator of a more long-lived and successful venture, *The Archers* radio serial.

rious small car ever offered for prestige motoring in busy town traffic" was about £1500, and *Small Car* found that even without the optional imitation (originally real) basketweave wickerwork side panels the de Ville attracted an unexpected amount of attention from passersby.[21]

When Austin introduced its 1100[22] in September 1963, a little over 12 months after the arrival of its sister, the Morris 1100, the marque re-entered the mainstream small family car market. Considered as a single model, BMC's 1100/1300 was Britain's best-selling car in every year from 1963 to 1971 except 1967, when the new Ford Cortina Mk II edged ahead, and the 1100's success was achieved without any significant updating; the 1100 Mk III of 1971–74 looked the same, except in minor details, as the Mk I of 1962–67, while by 1974 the Cortina was four years into its third style. British Leyland's successor for the 1100, the much-ridiculed Austin Allegro of 1973–84, was a much less coherent design made worse by the gratuitously organic browns in which many were painted. The 1100 was particu-

ENORMOUS ECONOMY

THE NEW AUSTIN seven COUNTRYMAN

Meet a spacious new estate car—The Austin Seven Countryman. As an estate car it will take four passengers, a dog or two, and ample luggage; fold rear seat forward and you've still more room for cargo. And as an Austin Seven it has all the virtues of this new breed of small car.

To list them: *Enormous economy at around 50 mpg.* Top speed over 70 mph.

Independent rubber suspension (no maintenance needed) on all wheels. Front-wheel drive for sports-car cornering. Manoeuvrability in dense traffic, parkability in tiny spaces. Four forward gears. All at a price that's never been matched for estate-car motoring; and a price which makes it a magnificent business proposition as a strictly business car.

By Appointment to Her Majesty The Queen Motor Car Manufacturers The Austin Motor Company Limited

Backed by BMC 12-month warranty and BMC service

AUSTIN LOOKS YEARS AHEAD

THE AUSTIN MOTOR COMPANY LIMITED · LONGBRIDGE · BIRMINGHAM

6

Austin Seven Countryman. Austin adopted Morris's station wagon heritage when the tiny, 848cc Austin Seven Countryman and Morris Mini-Traveller were launched in September 1960. On a wheelbase almost four inches longer than the saloon's, it looked like a miniature Oxford Series II or Isis. The wood trim was entirely decorative and endeared the model to a middle-class market whose loyalty to the Mini concept was not yet assured, and early advertising prudently emphasized the car's practical and business benefits. Versions without wood became available in October 1962, while the van could be turned into a four-seater with a £15 conversion kit, claustrophobia being compensated by the Purchase Tax saved on what, lacking windows, was still deemed a commercial vehicle. As affection for the Countryman and Traveller grew, Meccano Ltd. tapped into parental marque loyalty by producing Dinky Toys of both.

YOUR TOWN CAR SIR...

ANNOUNCING THE
Mini de Ville

Harold Radford Coachbuilt

THE MOST LUXURIOUS SMALL CAR EVER OFFERED FOR PRESTIGE MOTORING IN BUSY TOWN TRAFFIC.

As one of the few remaining craftsmen coachbuilders we have developed three super luxury versions of the amazing Mini range. We have fitted these cars with every imaginable extra and retrimmed them to the very highest standards of comfort and luxury.

MINI de VILLE "GRANDE LUXE" ON AUSTIN OR MINI COOPER £1,088.

MINI de VILLE BEL AIR. Slightly reduced specification but retaining all the most desirable adaptations. Car plus £223 (And all Mini models).

MINI de VILLE—De Luxe. This car has the accent on limousine comfort, but retains most outward features of the ordinary Mini. Car plus £87 . 10 . 0 (And all Mini models).

Modified cars can be supplied based on any one of the Mini-range or customers' own cars modified to specification or personal requirements.

Basketwork optional on all models.

HAROLD RADFORD (COACHBUILDERS) LTD
124 KING STREET, LONDON, W.6. Telephone: RIVerside 8831
Officially appointed Specialist Coachbuilders to Rolls-Royce and Bentley (A proud Member of the Swain Group)

Our Sister Company
H. R. Owen LTD
At MELTON COURT, SOUTH KENSINGTON, LONDON, S.W.7
Would be pleased to supply cars suitable for any of our conversions

Austin Mini de Ville (Radford). This was one of the better known of the many cars which Harold Radford adapted during the 1960s. Others included the Bentley 'S' Series (Countryman), Aston Martin DB5 (station wagon), Vauxhall PB Cresta (limousine) and Volvo P1800 (convertible). This advertisement shows how acceptable the Mini — ostensibly a utility car — had become amongst the trend-setters of affluent London. It is nevertheless implied — as Harold Radford himself intended — that Sir has another, more substantial car for long distance work.

larly popular with private buyers, whereas a higher proportion of Cortina drivers had the car chosen for them in the course of working life. With front-wheel drive and Hydrolastic suspension, standard disc brakes and uniquely spacious accommodation for its length (augmented by curved side windows, then a novelty), the 1100 was an enthusiast's car to handle and one of the best-looking small cars of its

generation. The first Cortina's attraction was more ephemeral; by 1966, it looked old-fashioned.

Yet the 1100's timeless quality did not arise from a masterly design produced without compromise. Pinin Farina's first (1959) proposal was similar to the eventual car in its essentials and visibly evolved from the A40, but it featured a bluff, wind-resisting front with headlamp peaks, its outline traced with a chrome strip in the manner of the Fiat 1800 and 2100. Farina's actual grille, similar to that of the A40, was accepted, but Issigonis and BMC's body engineers refined the surrounding bodywork so that the front panel and head-lamps merged gently into the wings.[23]

To some extent the Austin version of the 1100 always rested in the shadow of the Morris, which had been announced with much more extensive publicity; the non-owner who saw an 1100 on the road would usually think of it as a "Morris 1100" unless he happened to notice, and recognize, the wavy Austin grille bars. But few BMC sales are likely to have been lost by the confusion, as a marque devotee partisan enough to buy one but refuse the other in favour of a Ford would know that both Austin and Morris 1100s existed and be able to tell the difference; and a true die-hard would see the marque-specific hubcaps and bootlid handle, too. The only significant alteration was inside the car, where a narrow dashboard panel, to a design favoured by Issigonis but not quite as narrow as he originally wished (that wish would be granted with the 1800) contrasted with a slightly crude-looking binnacle in the Morris. Advertising for the Austin 1100 was comparatively low-key, although the car received a boost when automatic transmission became available in 1966. Because the 1100 was a compact car in its essentials as well as in its price, this was somehow more of an event than the Cortina's becoming available with a three-speed Borg-Warner early in 1964. Much was made of front-wheel drive, even when it was well known. The headline "Reindeer with front-wheel drive: the go-anywhere Austin 1100," at Christmas in 1965, highlighted a definite advantage of the layout. The 1100's front-heavy weight distribution gave it good traction in snow, and if the wheels did still spin the car would not swing its tail sideways into traffic.

Despite its success, the car did have faults. Warranty claims were often high although nothing about the 1100 was inherently unreliable; the boot space was greater than seemed likely from outside the car but was still limited; the body was prone to structural rust around suspension sub-frames and sills (a lifespan of six years was common in hard use)—and it was scarcely profitable, particularly in its early years, notwithstanding high production levels. Lower average running costs and greater reliability made the Cortina the natural choice for the fleet buyer while its larger boot was necessary for some fleet drivers, too. The Cortina was sold at the highest price its market could stand without contracting and extracted the maximum (considerable) profit from established thinking. But the 1100 anticipated the way small car design would develop during the following 40 years and by a small margin won the immediate sales battle; approximately 2.1 million 1100s and 1300s of all marques were built between 1962 and 1974. Austin and Morris 1300GT variants were introduced in 1969 and a two-door 1300 called the Austin America was developed for sale in the United States to replace the less robust MG (1100) Sports Sedan im-ported since 1963. Introduced in March 1968, this new model impressed *Road & Track*: "The new Austin America is some keen thing. Great fun to drive, superb ride and handling, outstanding space utilization and the dandiest automatic transmission we've encountered in a small car. We're sufficiently impressed by it that we're going to say that its under-$1900 price tag makes it the biggest bargain in today's imported car market."[24] Only later did the transmission reveal itself as rather fragile in everyday use.

In February 1968, motorists read an apparently irresistible offer: "This is a revolution on wheels. It is a radically new approach to power, combined with passenger safety and comfort. It has the finest suspension system on the road today." This had to be a Citroën DS with a Wankel rotary engine, surely? Or a Mercedes-Benz with air suspension? Or perhaps a gas turbine car from Chrysler or Rover finally put into full production? It had to be—but it wasn't (although it did inspire a Pininfarina prototype that, with a similar 1100, anticipated the styles of later Citroëns).[25] The car was "called the Austin 1800. To you, £923.11.11 (de luxe) (including £173.11.11 purchase tax.) New interior luxury. Power steering optional." Announced as an Austin in 1964 and as a Morris in 1966, by 1968 it had been called many things, not all of them polite. Unreliable when first introduced, its comparatively wide and short proportions invited the nickname "Landcrab" which stayed with it ever after. A subsequent journalist's red Austin 3-Litre, a longer car which shared the 1800's doors and general demeanour, naturally came to be called the "Landlobster."[26]

The 1800 was intended as a replacement for the A60 Cambridge and equivalent Morris Oxford Series VI, but although it won welcome publicity when voted *Car of the Year* in 1964, and was planned for production at 4500 a week, it did not sell in the numbers hoped for and weekly production never exceeded 1500–1800 copies.[27] The 1800's strengths were low-key: its body was one of the strongest ever built, particularly in torsion; like the 1100 it was uniquely spacious for its length, especially in the rear; it incorporated the remarkable Hydrolastic suspension, front-wheel drive and engine layout of the Mini and 1100; and, once early faults with engines and drivetrains had been corrected, it proved durable, particularly as a Mk II from May 1968, a year in which sales began to improve. It joined Britain's top ten best-sellers in 1969 and moved up to ninth position in 1970. An aftermarket hatchback conversion by Crayford Auto Developments of Westerham in Kent (costing £180 in 1969) added further practicality and anticipated the Austin Maxi. What the 1800 lacked was sales appeal: its styling, whilst inoffensive, was dull, even in the form originally proposed by Pinin Farina in 1960; the cable-operated gear-change could be recalcitrant (though less so than an early proposal for a hydraulic control in the driver's door pocket); the steering was insufficiently responsive for the available roadholding; and the interior, although inspired in its layout, was austere and cheap-looking in its execution. The 1800 appealed to a certain cast of mind for its thoughtful design and outstanding roadability, but for many drivers to admire was not to buy; first and foremost, a car had to be reliable and easily serviced. The owner who found that his clutch was slipping wanted it to be replaced quickly; he found it disconcerting if, as he approached the dealership, staff recognized the noise and hid. Issigonis's engineering introduced more small children to more rude words than anyone had imagined possible. Advertising wisely emphasized features and solidity, as in July 1966 when a white 1800 was seen overtaking a Security Express van: "There are two kinds of Security Express on the road these days. The Austin 1800 comes in a wider range of colours.... The 'express' part of it? An 84 bhp, 1798-cc power plant takes care of that!"

Part of the 1800 gained an extra lease of life at the Motor Show in 1967 when Austin announced a replacement for the A110 Westminster and its Wolseley and Vanden Plas derivatives. The Austin 3-Litre had been initiated by BMC's chaiman since 1961, George Harriman, and used the centre section of the 1800 with an engine developed from the Westminster's, whose capacity (2912cc) it retained. But the new engines shared few actual parts with the old and offered only a little more power (124 bhp against 120 bhp). At the rear, the 3-Litre's styling was inoffensively European-generic, with a curved bootlid and forward-leaning, vertical tail-lamps; but the front, with four headlamps in prominent wings and a

Discover the front-wheel-drive Austin 1100 the way it's meant to be discovered. On any rough mountain road like this one in Wales.

One good way to find out about the Austin 1100: stop at any Austin showroom. Take an 1100 out for a free trial run.

A more exciting, more *revealing* method (some thoughtful motorists choose all their new cars this way) is to hire one for a weekend, and point it in the direction of the nearest mountain. There, as quickly as you can find a rough track cut at all the wrong angles into the side of a cliff, you will come to a real

appreciation of the 1100's most remarkable qualities.

Front-wheel-drive, first and foremost, supplies the cling, especially on the way up a series of hairpin bends. Hydrolastic® Suspension supplies the ride. And it's never smoother than when the going is rocky.

The benefits of the transverse engine are evident long before you reach the mountain. Now, for a change, there's room to stretch your legs, front and

back. Austin believe in putting engines in their place—sideways—for the sake of your comfort.

NEW AUTOMATIC TRANSMISSION
Latest luxury feature: an automatic transmission with over-riding manual gear change. Takes the work out of driving without sacrificing your own selective control. First try the automatic in heavy traffic to test the luxury of no-change motoring. Then drive it into the mountains to discover the fun!

AUSTIN

An Appointment to
Her Majesty The Queen
Motor Car Manufacturers
The Austin Motor
Company Limited

THE **BRITISH** MOTOR
CORPORATION LTD.

*Austin 1100 Saloon (including £107.3.9 P.T.) - £614.3.9.
Automatic transmission (including £15.12.6 P.T.) - £90.12.6 extra.*

BACKED BY BMC SERVICE — EXPRESS, EXPERT, EVERYWHERE
THE AUSTIN MOTOR CO. LTD., LONGBRIDGE, BIRMINGHAM, BMC EXPORT SALES LTD., BIRMINGHAM AND 41-46 PICCADILLY, LONDON, W.1

Austin 1100 Mk I. By 1966, automatic transmission was finding its way into small cars such as the BMC 1100, whose version was much praised. The car itself proved a revelation to motorists reared on a diet of Somersets and A30s, with ride, handling and accommodation that could at last give the continental opposition food for thought. It was, however, prone to rust: most expired after six to eight years. The copy here is unpretentious; it is rational without pedantry, and the technical features are not surrounded by jargon. An unusually good balance is struck between simple description, excitement and escapism.

huge, almost full-width grille, looked like a Japanese amalgam of Humber Super Snipe Series III and 1957 Hudson, *circa* 1964. Issigonis had little interest in the car, which was developed without enthusiasm for a market amply covered by Ford, Vauxhall and Rover, and already squeezed by two-litre models from Rover and Triumph. A Vanden Plas version was contemplated whose grille, unusually for a "traditionalized" version of a mainstream car, looked better than the Austin original, but the model did not reach production. With rear-wheel-drive and a Hydrolastic suspension that proved difficult to adapt to such a heavy new body (self-levelling was eventually used), the 3369 lb. 3-Litre lacked the smaller Austins' innovative engineering and looked contrived. It needed all the marketing it could get. Yet, for once, BMC decided to introduce the car only once it had been thoroughly tested. The first one hundred cars went discreetly to selected customers, and full production — significantly with an improved interior, as the original, while better than the 1800's, was still much too austere for the 3-Litre's intended market — began only in October 1968. The car was never properly launched at all, and, as road testers remarked in 1968 and 1969, the car remained comparatively unknown. Its virtues of good handling and ride, solid build, spaciousness and a surprising speed, point-to-point, were consequently under-appreciated.[28]

By 1969 it was apparent

The Maxi is no ordinary car. It's a very comfortable five seater saloon when you want a saloon.

In fact, it's a lot more comfortable than most, with standard features like fully adjustable and reclining front seats and fitted carpeting throughout.

The Maxi is an estate when you want an estate. Simply fold the rear seats forward and there's 44·5 cu. ft. of load space behind you.

The Maxi combines fast lane motorway performance (the fifth gear keeps the revs. and petrol consumption down) with rally class roadholding – front wheel drive and radial tyres keep it firmly on the road.

The Maxi does so much more.

Your life is full of surprising variety. Your car should be the same.

Austin Maxi

Maxi. It goes with a way of life.

Maxi prices from £1,397.83 inclusive of car tax and VAT (seat belts, delivery charges and number plates extra). Automatic transmission available as an optional extra on the 1750 only.
Prices correct at time of going to press.

Austin Maxi. First conceived under BMC in 1964–65, and using doors from the Austin and Morris 1800, the Maxi was introduced in April 1969, fifteen months after the merger between BMH (created from BMC and Jaguar-Daimler) and Leyland (incorporating Standard-Triumph and Rover) that produced the British Leyland Motor Corporation. The last Issigonis design to reach production and Britain's first family hatchback, it was if anything under-promoted in announcement advertising. Copywriters' initial down-to-earth appeal — "Will you like the Maxi? We haven't got a clue. But go long to any Austin dealer and try it" — although intended to reassure the reader that no-one was trying to pull the wool over his eyes, suggested a neglect of market research that no other company would have admitted, even in jest. The detail design and reliability of early Maxis were lamentable, making the slogan here risky, but the car eventually achieved steady sales to the practically minded. The copy in this 1974 advertisement is brief, to the point, and informal. In its layout, style and photography it indicates the eventual destination of much family car advertising of the late 1960s.

that the 3-Litre would never meet its original sales target of 10,000 cars a year, but British Leyland advertised the car heavily during 1969–70. Under the slogan, "Austin 3-Litre, built like a thoroughbred," it was shown in forests with gundogs ("All the best thoroughbreds expect exercise at dawn"), at the races ("You can judge a car by the company it keeps… They'd called you in at the last moment. 'You'll be a steward, of course', they'd said…") and as the car for the country solicitor ("Possession is nine points of the law. They know you round here. They know you have done well out of them. But they respect you for it. You do your bit for the country. You take a personal interest in your clients…"). It was all a little too esoteric, however, and the copy fell into the trap of much upmarket slice-of-life copy: the lifestyles shown were too difficult to break into if you were not already there (at the age of potential 3-Litre ownership you were either a country solicitor or you weren't) while those already there found their portraits unconvincing. "They know you have done well out of them" was much too brutal for the kind of man who would choose this, the least pretentious of large cars. The Austin 1800 had become popular with farmers, but the 3-Litre was a city car at heart, as 1970's campaign acknowledged. "O.H.M.S." began an April 1970 piece, with a headline to startle any electrician whether on Her Majesty's service or not: "When a government decides the time has come to buy new cars for its members, it has to be careful. Because, of course, its's our money they're spending. And yet at the same time, they can't afford to look cheap in public.

That's why the British Government has now settled on Austin 3-Litres for its senior civil servants…You see, the 3-Litre looks very much a part of the Establishment… Because it's hardly what you'd call an 'executive' car. And it isn't flashy either."

Exactly. But if this was worthy copy, it was also a little dull, and not everyone wanted to be mistaken for a civil servant or official of any kind. A few months later the copywriters decided to have some fun. "Liz Wilcox gained a lot of experience in the back of a 3-Litre" announced a June 1970 headline. "Like any good secretary, Liz will do almost anything for her boss…there's space to sit back and, say, take notes." The reader might just have chided himself for finding a *double-entendre* where none was intended but for the fact that Liz Wilcox, perched on the 3-Litre's back seat with notepad and ambiguous grin, was all too obviously a man dressed as a woman in drag-act style. It was funny—but would it persuade late-middle-aged, upper-middle-class luxury motorists to spend £1745 on a 3-Litre? On the evidence of the car's sales, it didn't, and in April 1971 the model was quietly discontinued after 9992 had been built. It deserved a better fate. But by this time Austin had innovated once again, with the initially troublesome but eventually respected Maxi hatchback. Planned by BMC in the mid-1960s and, like the 3-Litre, using doors from the 1800, the Maxi was Britain's first production car with a five-speed gearbox and was introduced in April 1969. Ancestry notwithstanding, however, this was really a car of the 1970s.

2

Ford

"Made with care by Ford of Britain"

Ford was arguably the most successful of Britain's car manufacturers in the 1960s. It did not have the largest market share: that honour went to the British Motor Corporation (BMC), whose marques included two of the country's biggest, Austin and Morris, as well as the more specialized Austin-Healey, MG, Riley, Wolseley and Vanden Plas, all of which used components from the mainstream Austin and Morris lines. But in combining market share, coverage and leadership with profitability, Ford, despite some difficulties of its own and a fair share of industrial disputes, was unrivalled among British car manufacturers.[1] The company also enjoyed an enviably low ratio of unsuccessful to successful models: those which sold more slowly than intended were greatly outnumbered by those which sold in much larger numbers than anticipated.

Throughout the 1960s, the designs and specifications of Ford cars were intimately bound up with marketing and sales strategies to a degree which was unusual in Britain and was approached in spirit (though not in sophistication) only by Vauxhall, a smaller company selling fewer cars of a more limited range of types. The story of Ford's advertising is therefore inextricably intertwined with the stories of its products.

Ford secured much of its comparative success in the 1960s by deciding, from the early 1950s and with prompting from the parent company in Dearborn, to employ university graduates as product planners and accountants at a time when many British manufacturers disdained all three. But Ford's American epiphany had come in the late 1940s, when Henry Ford II's ex-army, ex-business-school Whiz Kids had brought cost controls and statistical analysis to a company in which one department had been found to estimate its

costs by weighing its invoices, whose average value per pound had once, long ago, been calculated. The graduate mind, artfully deployed, could give a company stability. Traditional "try it, hope, and if it doesn't work don't repeat it" approaches to market penetration were increasingly expensive and market share, once lost, was not easily regained. It was in developing general principles and procedures, while analyzing their potential long-term applications at some distance from immediate events, that many graduates excelled. Ford benefited from being able to quantify and avoid many potential problems, and by anticipating many of the ways in which competitors might react to its own innovations.

BMC, by contrast, costed its 1959 Mini against a Ford Anglia (100E) produced since 1953[2] which, even when the Mini was authorized in 1957, appeared likely to overlap it in production only by a year or two at most.[3] When the Mini appeared, Ford bought one, "stripped it down to its spot welds, and subjected it to a minute cost analysis. The results of this investigation were astonishing for the team found that on their costings, which they knew to be superior to BMC's, the Corporation was losing around £30 on every Mini it sold, 'though I could see ways in which we could have taken costs out of it without in any way reducing its sales appeal,' recalls [Ford's Product Planning General Manager from 1955 to 1963] Terence Beckett. They concluded that the car was not so much over engineered but its materials were over specified; in short they were too good for such a cheap car. Furthermore Ford concluded that if the car had been priced at £30 more it would hardly have affected the model's sales. These conclusions were subsequently confirmed by close scrutiny of BMC's published accounts."[4] As is now well known, "Dagenham's joint managing director Allen Barke called on BMC managing director George Harriman at his London office for an off-the-record meeting: 'Look here, George,' he said, 'We've costed your new Mini and you can't possibly be making any money on it. If you raise your price so you're making a profit, we'll raise the price of the Anglia [105E] by the same amount.' But Harriman was adamant: 'The product will push the price,' was his gnomic response. Loosely translated, this signified: 'Sell enough cars and the profits will take care of themselves.' History was to prove him sadly wrong...."[5]

Ford also succeeded by advertising heavily and imaginatively, with advertisements that drew potential buyers' attention to features which extracted maximum sales appeal from the minimum production cost. In 1962, Sir Patrick Hennessy, Ford of Britain's general manager since 1939, managing director since 1948 and chairman since 1956, recruited Walter Hayes, a past editor of the *Sunday Dispatch* and former associate editor of the *Daily Mail*, to replace the longstanding Maurice Buckmaster as Ford's director of public affairs.[6] Hayes, later Vice-Chairman of Ford of Europe, recalled in 1995: "The first thing that [Hennessy] said to me was, 'We are going to reorganize the company. We're going to put in things called profit centres; we're going to have a new management organization and you're going to have to explain it to everybody.'"[7] During 1960–61 the London Press Exchange Ltd. took over as Ford's advertising agency from Rumble, Crowther & Nicholas Ltd., who had been the company's agents since 1946, and Ford's advertising expenditure was usually the highest of all marques in Britain during the 1960s.[8]

The period's failures were relatively incidental. The Consul Classic 315, planned for 1960 but eventually introduced in May 1961 owing to the success and consequent production demands of the 1959 Anglia (105E), had been developed from a proposed replacement for the previous Prefect and Anglia in the 1950s. It was already well on the way to production when planning for the Cortina began, and Ford knew that the Cortina, whose success was much more important for the company's long-term future, would steal much of the Classic's potential market. Body panels for the Classic and its hardtop derivative, the Consul Capri, were consequently "produced on short-life 'Kirksite' dies rather than the steel ones used for long production runs."[9] The only true failure was the Zephyr and Zodiac Mk IV range of 1966–71: "Initially its sales rate was only a tenth of the planned production rate and it never did as well as the cheaper model which it replaced. Sales executives blamed the Ford image for this failure; the public failed to realize how much quality was offered in this car and had merely thought it expensive for a Ford."[10] The Cortina (1962), Escort (1968) and Capri (1969) were resounding successes. The Cortina's stylist, Roy Brown, also responsible for the Edsel, said of the Cortina, "we had a wonderful time with that little car. It was nice to see it become such a success,"[11] adding

that it "made more money for Ford than the Edsel ever lost."[12]

The quest to offer value for money had accompanied Ford throughout its history. The first Ford ever assembled in Britain was a Model T, which left the factory taken over by Ford at Trafford Park, south of Manchester, on October 23, 1911.[13] By 1914, "annual production was 8,300 cars and the Model T outsold the next five biggest British marques combined."[14] But in 1920 the introduction of a protectionist horsepower tax (calculated according to the combined bore of a car's cylinders) hit Ford sales badly, and in 1924 Morris overtook Ford to become Britain's market leader. In 1927 the Model T ceased production and was replaced by the Model A. Like the Model T, the Model A was a large car, and from 1929 the horsepower tax combined with economic depression to reduce its sales drastically,[15] despite its acknowledged abilities and modest price of £185.

In 1928, however, Henry Ford decided to expand the company's European operations and to make the new company as self-sufficient as possible, and in May 1929 work began on a new factory complex at Dagenham. Briggs Motor Bodies built a plant nearby, as did the Kelsey-Hayes Wheel Company, both of which would supply Ford, who took over the English Briggs Company in 1953.[16] In October 1931 the first Dagenham-produced Ford, a Model AA truck, left the new production line, but production of the Model A and smaller-engined model AF continued to decline. Between October 1931 and July 1932, only five Model A and AF cars were made. On October 19, 1931, therefore, work began in Dearborn on the car that would secure Ford's future. With a suspension layout based on that of the Model T and Model A, but attractively styled by Eugene Gregorie, the 8hp Model Y entered production on August 10, 1932.

The car was an immediate success, and famously became available from October 1935 until June 1937 for £100, in a marketing coup that was never matched by rivals and which increased Ford's share of the 8hp market from 22 percent in 1935 to 41 percent in 1936.[17] "Only its elegant appearance prevents its being an incessant offence in the eyes of busy British roadfarers," crowed an August 1936 advertisement, "Count the £100 Ford Saloons you meet tomorrow. See how they run!" In October 1934, the Model Y was joined by a Dearborn-designed 10hp Model C, and new Dagenham-styled 10hp and 8hp models (7W and 7Y) arrived in 1937. These were developed into the post-war Prefect and Anglia of 1945–53 and Popular 103E of 1953–59, which was Britain's cheapest conventional car at £443 17s in 1959. Although sturdily built from sound materials, the Popular was a "mechanised coelacanth"[18] which by 1959 was not very safe in the hands of a new generation of post-war motorists, let alone on the new M1. It embodied, inimitably, Ford's reputation for providing value for money — a reputation that would help sales of Anglias and Cortinas in the 1960s — but it also ensured that no-one seeking a "snob" purchase would choose a Ford. If a Ford ever *failed* to offer unbeatable value for money in its class, it would sell, at best, indifferently, as in the case of the Consul Classic and, to a lesser extent, with the Corsair of 1963–70. For the most part, Ford accepted this deal: with non-utility products, "non-snob" desirability, such as obvious glamour, would have to be achieved instead, as with the 1969 Capri.

The small Fords of 1932–40 were supplemented by modest numbers of V-8s, imported complete during 1932–34 and assembled at Dagenham from 1935 onwards. Beautifully advertised in colour by N.W. Ayer & Son in up-market magazines—as was the imported Lincoln-Zephyr—they offered unmatched performance for their prices. But in Britain in the late 1930s, motoring was still mainly an upper-middle-class activity and large cars, however inexpensive for the performance offered (£210 for a small V-8 "22" in 1936; £280 for a 30hp Saloon de Luxe in 1939), still demanded upper-middle-class incomes to fuel, service and tax, even when the car itself offered good value. Many British motorists able to afford the V8's running costs preferred commensurate styling and furnishings, too, and were prepared to pay extra for them. This was implicitly accepted in 1947, when the larger V-8 engine was put in a "traditional-ized" version of the smaller V-8 body to produce the Pilot, a tough and well-regarded luxury model produced—with what was said to be the world's largest Bakelite plastic moulding as its dashboard—until 1951.

In October 1950, Ford announced its first post-war models, the four-cylinder Consul and six-cylinder Zephyr, designed in Dearborn with a strut-and-coil-spring front suspension by Earle S. MacPherson which, from the late 1960s onward, began to appear on a multitude of cars and which had first been fitted on the stillborn Chevrolet Cadet compact car prototype of 1948. The low periodicity of the springs gave a comfortable ride and hydraulic dampers were built into the struts; nose-dive under braking was limited by built-in "stiction." The new models were advertised as the "Five-Star" cars. The stars—which were reproduced instead of dots beneath the figures 30–70 on the speedometer—represented the features of monocoque construction (a first among Fords worldwide); inter-axial seating; oversquare cylinder dimensions; overhead valves; and hydraulic clutch and brakes, operated by pendant pedals.

The 1953 Monte Carlo Rally was won in a Zephyr by the Dutch rally driver Maurice Gatsonides, who later invented the "Gatso" speed camera[19], and in October 1953 the range was joined by the luxurious Zephyr Zodiac and by Consul and Zephyr convertibles built by Carbodies in Coventry. (A single Zodiac convertible was made for Mrs. Benson Ford.) A power top, assisted to a half-way, "de ville" position, was standard (though not compulsory) on the Zephyr and optional on the Consul. In October 1954, estate car conversions of the saloons, approved by Ford although not included in the company's catalogue, became available from coach-builders E.D. Abbott Ltd. of Farnham, Surrey. A conversion cost £217 10s, including purchase tax, on a completed car and £145, tax-free, on a car already in use. Meanwhile, in September 1953 the pre-war style of Prefect and Anglia was replaced by a new, full-width design which was supplemented in 1955 by a two-door (Escort or better-trimmed Squire) estate car, based on the Ford Thames van.

By 1956, having taken over Briggs in England, Ford had acquired its own styling studio, where Colin Neale and his team designed the highly successful[20] new Consul, Zephyr and Zodiac Mk II. These resembled the company's 1955–56 American models in overall outline and proportion but not in character or decoration, even if the tail of the Zodiac reflected that of the 1956 Lincoln, and the Consul, when all three models were updated early in 1959, acquired tail-lights similar to those of the 1955 American Ford. The new models were announced in February 1956 as "The Three Graces." In its reference to Antonio Canova's famous sculpture, the slogan implicitly aimed the cars upmarket, but although Woburn Abbey in Bedfordshire, which housed the original *Three Graces*, had opened to the public in 1955, the sculpture could not then be seen by the public and was not referred to in Ford's—or the Abbey's—publicity.[21] The new cars had been tested in Germany and Kenya as well as at Ford's Dagenham proving ground, and were immediately in demand. Americans first saw them at the 1956 New York International Motor Show and imported a few thousand a year, most of them Zodiacs, during the late 1950s. More than 50 percent of early production was exported. High-performance Z115 saloon and stylish hardtop Zodiacs were contemplated during 1956–57, but did not reach production.

Later in 1956 the large Fords joined the Anglia and Prefect 100E in Ford's "Now, more than ever" campaign which showed the cars in dramatic front three-quarter photographs, taken at ground level. In 1957 a new campaign, "I've a Ford in mind…" promoted each car by analogy with the lives of race-goers ("I'll back a car with staying-power"), female doctors ("The remedy for my 'travel-itis' is a car to carry me safely and surely…") and others who were shown at the top of each advertisement with a painting of a car against a plain background, above the modest slogan, "'5-star' motoring—the best at lowest cost." In 1958 the Zodiac featured in *Vogue* advertisements which emphasized its colours ("Ford sets the fashion—in Coffee and Cream") while the Zodiac convertible, one of a line of convertibles "included in the range because Sir Patrick Hennessy…liked them"[22], was shown with a steeple-chaser in an advertisement that was as much for the marque as for this specialized model: "Ford—Nationally Grand! Ford motoring, even in the luxury Zodiac class, is supremely economical…" The copy concluded with the slogan, "Ford fine cars—and World-wide Ford Service, too!," the latter a Ford selling-point since well before the Second World War, when exchange engines were available at a time when many motorists had to wait for their original engines to be overhauled before refitting.

Other 1958 advertisements showed rowers on a river with a Consul ("Lengths ahead!"), an attractive female tennis player with a Zephyr ("Game, set and match!"), and the headline, "Beauty and balance," with a ballet dancer and another Consul, echoed an analogy made by Daimler in 1952. "Meet the champion!" referred not only to a boxer but also to the Zephyr: "You'll be thrilled by its fighting-fit power and all-round ability...." Female readers of upmarket magazines were enticed with a Zodiac, shown beneath a photograph of an earnest, dinner-jacketed suitor with a cigarette in one hand and the wrist of an undecided-looking woman in the other: "Falling in love... They've discovered each other, and they're wonderfully happy...as you will be, when you discover the Zodiac. Let your eye linger on elegant lines...the sumptuous interior, with soft leather seating, rich astrakhan carpets... You'll know...you and the Zodiac are made for each other!" Assuming, of course, that the lovers could find £1013 17s between them.

1959's campaign adopted a similar theme for the improved, "lowline," "Three New Graces," and in 1960 the cars were photographed in studio poses of freeze-framed jollity. A Zodiac was shown on a chequered floor: "White queen wins... She's set her heart on a Zodiac and at last the Black King is in check! Move by brilliant move she's countered his resistance and now he nods approvingly!" A February 1960 advertisement showed a white Consul Convertible and anticipated the "continental" theme of much car advertising of the following few years: "Not all roads lead to Rome... Wherever you plan your own run this summer — be it Portofino or Polperro, Innsbruck or Inverness — your Consul Convertible will carry you there in swift, sure luxury...." In December, the Consul saloon was a companion on a "voyage of discovery... Wind favourable...position plotted ...everything set very fair... Their means of transport? Consul of course...!" And in January 1962, three months before the end of the Mk II's run, an immaculate and sober-looking dark blue Zephyr was, in a very different style, "a *motorist's* car, brilliantly designed and brilliantly built to give any-road, any-conditions satisfaction." "Competitor and spectator alike are proud to own Ford's splendid Zephyr," said the copy. For the truly competitive there was always, as on the retrospectively named Mk I, a Raymond Mays engine conversion.[23]

In April 1955, the journal *Automobile Engineer*[24] described a number of recent designs by Italian coachbuilders. These included a Fiat 600 for which Pinin Farina had devised a small, two-door body with interchangeable (rear-hinged)

door pressings and a reverse-raked rear window. A dozen potential advantages of the window design were listed, including ease and cheapness of production; increased headroom, if desired, without disadvantage to the car's styling (which was already established, for good or ill, by the existence of the window in the first place); and improved rear vision in rain. Potential disadvantages were that it was "a difficult feature to incorporate in the styling of the vehicle" and that air turbulence behind the window might render it unsuitable for fast cars. In other respects Pinin Farina's style was demurely conventional.

Meanwhile, in 1954 Terence Beckett had been appointed styling manager at Briggs. As Ford historian David Burgess-Wise recalls, "Beckett instituted a three-pronged approach, with separate departments planning small, medium and large cars. Dagenham's studio—familiarly known as 'the Odeon'—became a sought-after centre of design skills: Colin Chapman...recruited three gifted designers from Ford...They were John Frayling, who translated accountant Peter Kirwan-Taylor's design for the Lotus Elite into a three-dimensional model...interior designer Peter Cambridge and South African Ron Hickman, who had worked for Colin Neale as a clay modeller before training as a designer. Famed for his invention of that brilliant DIY aid, the Workmate, Hickman was design director at Lotus from 1958–67. Then there was Tom Karen...whose post-Ford portfolio at Ogle Design includes the Daimler SX250 prototype[25], the Reliant Scimitar and the futuristic Bond Bug three-wheeler."[26]

Later in the year, Beckett asked a Briggs designer, Colin MacGregor, to work at Ford's research centre at Lodge Road, Birmingham on a replacement for the Popular 103E. The car, which came to be known within Ford as the "New Popular," had to be cheap to produce, and, in March 1955, Sir Patrick Hennessy saw Pinin Farina's Fiat at the Geneva motor show and suggested adopting its window design for the new car.[27] This was done and MacGregor's project, originally conceived as an austere utility model, was "re-engineered under [Executive Engineer, Light Cars] Fred Hart's supervision to become the 105E Anglia, which was styled with the aid of a wind tunnel by Elwood Engel, a regular visitor from Dearborn. The [other] cost-cutting features were shelved...."[28] The rear window was marketed as a styling feature ("the look of tomorrow"), and was not obviously the result of production economies. As *The Autocar* later reported, "The rear window treatment is a striking breakaway, and attracts such attention that that car cannot (at present) be parked for long without drawing a crowd."[29] On September 30, 1959, the Anglia was launched as "the world's most exciting light car!"

Opposite: **Ford Zodiac Mk II.** Ford courted the fashion-conscious female motorist in 1960. The frozen jollity of this studio shot was typical of a light-hearted, humorous school of advertising which was gaining ground, and the copy is appropriately gushing, in the American style. Nothing ironic was intended in the opening line, "fashion tirelessly in search of fashion," which forty years later might be interpreted as a jaundiced critique of modern consumerism. The Zodiac itself was a successful product, and remained so until the end of its life in 1962.

west-end safari

The hunt is on—fashion tirelessly in search of fashion. Location? Knightsbridge, Bond Street, Piccadilly . . .
wherever there's a flair for dashing femininity. Transport? Ford Zodiac of course. The car with high fashion ideas
and plenty of them; high fashion colours and many to choose from. The car that's easy to handle,
blissful to drive. That rounds off its care for comfort and sun-lounge splendour, with safari-like stamina
for country-wide treks and short hops to town. And offers the completest luxury of all for never-so-easy driving—
fully automatic transmission—as an optional extra! So—if your mind's on any sort of smooth-going
expedition, automatic or otherwise, fly straight to your nearest
Ford Dealer and book seats (first-class all six of them)
in the first Zodiac you can get your hands on!

BY APPOINTMENT
TO HER MAJESTY THE QUEEN
MOTOR VEHICLE MANUFACTURERS
FORD MOTOR COMPANY LTD.

ZODIAC £675 plus £282.7.6 P.T. = £957.7.6   UNIQUE WORLD-WIDE **FORD** SERVICE TOO!

Motor Trader gushed, "Quite how Ford manage to produce an Anglia to sell at £589 inclusive, or £610 in its de luxe form, is a mystery to which only they hold the key."[30]

Essentially conventional, the new Anglia embodied several advances over previous small Fords, such as electric rather than vacuum-operated windscreen wipers, a four-speed gearbox and, in particular, a new 997cc overhead-valve engine with the remarkable bore-to-stoke ratio of 0.6 to 1, by far the lowest then in production. *Small Car* reported in 1963: "Every owner [of at least a dozen encountered in conversation] was adamant about one prime virtue...it was the Anglia's thoroughly remarkable aptitude for economical and even peaceful high-speed cruising. Both [a taxi driver and an advertising salesman spoken to] are northerners and make frequent trips home at weekends. Both say, and quite categorically too, that they can't consider buying any other car until more manufacturers realize that fast roads (and Britain's trunk roads *are* getting faster) mean cars that cruise fast."[31] The only disadvantages were a need for more gear-changing in town as a consequence of the car's high gearing and the engine's comparative lack of low-speed torque.

"Excitement"—usually with an exclamation mark or two—was chosen as the theme for early Anglia advertising. If it seemed to be overdone, it was no less compelling than BMC's "Wizardry on Wheels!" for the Morris version of the Mini or Standard-Triumph's "It's a new experience in motoring!" for the Herald. Themes for small car advertising had to be general; to be over-specific was to exclude some potential buyers, and "excitement" was an uncontroversial and democratic theme. Announcement advertising showed the car in side view in the usual elongated paintings while photography took over in 1960—strikingly in the case of several advertisements for English-speaking export markets—and settings were glamorous. "Eccitantissima!" exclaimed an April 1961 piece, "In Italy, as in Britain, they've fallen for the Anglia. There it's the best-selling imported car... Why? Because the Anglia's such a stimulating car to drive... The world's most exciting light car." The reader could only wonder whether the horse-drawn vehicle alongside was part of the exotic scenery or a trade-in. English settings were used too, in 1961—from studio shots of a blue and grey de Luxe with racing cars ("Sporting spirit... Car for enthusiasts, for pace setters, for men who really *know* performance") to gravel tracks ("Exciting in, Exciting out—The Anglia makes adventurers of us all. Light and lively,

swift and sturdy, it urges you to point its nose towards far-away places with exciting possibilities.")

The Anglia did have an eager character (with an engine that lent itself to tuning), and if the grille in combination with the name reminded some 1959 motorists of the least edible of marine scavengers, its appearance was soon forgotten when the car became familiar on British roads. Later advertisements emphasized its value for money: "Save money with a £479 Anglia...and enjoy life more!" said a June 1965 advertisement, "Anglia's the success of the sixties; and it's here to stay. Why? Because the Anglia saves you money all the way...."[32] Anglia-based Thames 5cwt and 7cwt vans arrived in June 1961, of which Kenex Coachwork Ltd. of Dover in Kent offered pick-up conversions at £45, while the model would also form the basis of an ice cream van. In late 1961 a simple, elegant and practical estate car appeared, the first design for Ford of Britain by Roy Brown, the former General Motors stylist who had joined Ford in 1953 and moved to England from Dearborn in 1959.[33] At first it was advertised in the style of the saloon: "Enter...the new shape of excitement!," but by its last year it was sold with cheerful practicality as one of a range of estate cars, as in February 1967: "Ford estate cars have a way of making mountains into molehills... The Anglia estate car de luxe. The smallest of the Ford Estate Car Range—if you can call a big 39 cubic feet of loadspace small!... Tried, tested, still going strong Anglia...and with Ford there's no charge for delivery." This sturdy and characterful car was ideal for the small businessman as well as for country families needing space in the rear, and many found it more attractive than the saloon. The car sold steadily in saloon and estate forms until November 1967, when production ended with a special edition of about five hundred 1200 Super saloons, finished in gold or metallic blue.

The Anglia was accompanied in its first three years by updated versions of its predecessors. A revised Prefect (107E) with the new Anglia's gearbox and engine was introduced in October 1959 at the same price as the earlier model—£621 12s 6d—and was made until 1961, while the two-door 100E continued as the Popular at £494 and Popular de luxe at £515, undercutting BMC's Mini and Mini de luxe by £3 and £22 respectively. The basic Popular was very austere: in a de luxe the buyer gained oil and main beam warning lights, three ash trays (rather than none), door pulls (the window winders otherwise sufficing), an interior light, two sun vi-

Opposite: **Ford Anglia (105E).** If not really "the world's most exciting light car" on its launch in 1959, it was certainly Ford's with a high-revving overhead valve engine, electric wipers, four-speed gearbox—and that reverse-rake rear window, inspired in 1955 by a Pinin Farina-bodied Fiat 600. Allowing a simple roof pressing and small, flat window, it reduced production costs and gave a large boot opening, though rear passengers could receive a crack on the back of the head if the car were struck from behind. The feature also appeared on the 1958 season's Lincoln Continental (1957), Flaminio Bertoni's Citroën Ami 6 (1961), the Reliant Regal (1962), Ford's own Consul Classic (1961), and on several design studies and prototypes from other manufacturers. But Abbott disdained it in their Friary Motors hatchback ("Touring") conversion of the Anglia, as did Michelotti with the Torino, an Anglia heavily restyled for Ford-Italy, Italians not being quite so artlessly devoted to the standard type as suggested here. Advertisements showed Anglias in many attractive European locations, and it was a genuine—and profitable—home and export success.

FANFARE! Roll away the work-a-day! Enter the *swish* new Anglia Estate. Is it exciting? You never saw an estate car so excitingly good-looking. Or sat in one so excitingly comfortable. Or drove one so excitingly energetic. That's because Ford said: Give the new estate car all the excitement of the de luxe Anglia Saloon ... *but in an entirely new estate-car shape.*

So you get saloon-bred elegance, with luxury comfort for four adults. You get the rally-proved, highly-praised Anglia engine. That joy of a gear stick. And terrific cycloramic vision (thanks to vast all-round windows and *low* loading floor).

What else? Traditional Ford operating economy. 70-plus top speed. Separate front seats. Padded arm rests. And those wonderful Ford specials—easy hp, low insurance rates, fixed-cost country-wide service. See your Ford dealer *today.*

ENTER··· THE NEW SHAPE OF

excitement!

THE NEW ANGLIA ESTATE CAR

De luxe model illustrated

Integral construction of body and chassis gives great strength and durability throughout. Safety glass all-round. Soft padded sun visors.
Back seat folds down in a wink when you want, to give any amount of low and therefore safe storage space. The floor is neatly linoleum-covered and completely flat.

Ex-works from

£679.7.3

(£465 + £214.7.3 p.t.)
Over-riders optional extra.

WORLD'S MOST <u>EXCITING</u> ESTATE CAR FROM **FORD** OF BRITAIN

sors, opening vent windows, an engine air cleaner (!), a handle on the boot instead of a carriage lock and chromium on window surround trims and windscreen wipers. As with many small cars, a heater was an optional extra on either model.[34]

Most private buyers preferred the Popular de luxe, but to make a standard model available represented canny marketing. By doing so, Ford maintained its unique reputation for offering Britain's cheapest mainstream car; it undercut BMC; and it attracted people who would seriously consider a new car if the price were less than £500, and who, once committed to the idea, would not mind too much if the eventual cost crept up. Would the dream, now dreamt, be shattered for a mere £21? What husband would deny his wife door pulls and a boot handle? (What wife would let him, in a year when "Most of our people have never had it so good"?[35]) Announcement advertising for the Popular showed it outside a low-built suburban house (of a kind also used in BMC's 1958 corporate advertising) as two women and a boy looked proudly on: "Lowest-priced family car! Ideal as a first or second family car, ideal for the representative too, has millions of miles of *proven* reliability too!" In the summer of 1960 a Popular appeared in a studio pose in a striking lime green, its owner holding up a tennis cup defiantly. The reader didn't have to be a tennis player to "realize what a difference two-Ford freedom could make to your life…" The two-Ford family was a venerable institution in British and American Ford advertising, and at the foot of the page the car was shown beside a Zodiac. The last Popular 100E was made in June 1962.

While the utilitarian "New Popular" and future Anglia 105E was being conceived in Birmingham, a replacement for the existing Prefect and Anglia 100E, approved in the autumn of 1956, was under development at Dagenham. This car, codenamed "Sunbird," was expected to beat the Birmingham project into production but as the designs progressed the Birmingham car seemed likely to be completed first, so Ford decided that the "New Popular" should become the much-needed new Anglia while the Dagenham "Sunbird" design would become the Consul Classic (and Capri) and be introduced in mid-1960 to fill the gap between the Anglia and the existing Consul. It would be developed as a rugged design with as much potential as possible for export to difficult territories, and, like the Anglia, it would adopt the Fiat-inspired rear window. The front of the first full-size clay model looked like a simplified version of the 1957 Packard Clipper with its grille reduced in size and separated from the side-lights by bodywork; its windscreen profile and front door, with a flush handle, resembled those of 1957 Chrysler Corporation cars while the rear fin treatment, seen in front three-quarter view, anticipated the 1960–61 Ramblers. A prototype was running by January 1958, and the car was styled at the height of the craze for fins and sculpted body sides by Colin Neale, who later in 1958 moved to Dearborn to work on the 1961 Lincoln Continental and Ford Thunderbird. Neale eventually became second-in-command of styling at Chrysler Corporation and, on a visit from Chrysler to Rootes in the 1960s, influenced the design of the 1967 Sunbeam Stiletto.[36]

In 1957 Ford in America asked the British and German companies to submit designs for a subcompact sedan that could be sold in Europe and in America. In Cologne, ex-Borgward designer August Momberger devised a V4-engined car with front-wheel drive and called it "Cardinal," after the small North American bird. Ford decided to produce this design in both Cologne and Louisville, Kentucky. In the American market it would rival imported subcompacts like the Volkswagen, and in Germany it would replace the existing, elderly, side-valve, Taunus 12M. American and European versions would have 1.5 and 1.2 litre engines respectively, and it would be launched in September 1962. Such was the plan. But during a visit to Dearborn in the spring of 1960, Sir Patrick Hennessy saw the prototype Cardinal and it was suggested to him that Ford of Britain might like to become involved in the project. He declined the offer, but back in England decided to produce a design of similar conception, offering a medium-sized sedan for the price of a small one. There was enough time, said Fred Hart, only if the car's layout were conventional, with rear-wheel drive. The Cardinal's British rival, codenamed "Archbishop" (competitively, rather than through ornithological innocence) would become the Cortina.[37]

The existing product plan was consequently discarded and the Consul Classic became a stop-gap model. Finally announced in May 1961 as the Consul Classic 315[38] for the British market and as the Consul 315 in many export markets, the new car was available in British Ford showrooms from June 17, 1961. The 1956-style "pure" Consul was redesignated Consul 375. This complex nomenclature inadvertently reflected the rather uncertain image of the Classic, which, at £801 10s 10d for a four-door de luxe, was not Ford-cheap for its size (14' 2" × 5' 5" on a 99" wheelbase) or engine capacity. Even in 1960 Ford knew that the 1340cc engine, a long-stroke version of that fitted to the Anglia, would

Opposite: **Ford Anglia Estate Car (105E).** Shout it loud enough and they'll believe you — the words "exciting," "excitingly" and "excitement" appeared seven times in this piece, which was possibly a record. Ford were among those who realized the potential of rain at night to create a moody picture, but it only worked when the owners were young and carefree — Rover and Wolseley declined to show bedraggled pensioners in raincoats. Among the car's features, "cycloramic vision" was nothing remarkable and "separate front seats" had been fitted to Anglias since the Dark Ages, some export cars excepted. The 105E's seats were comfortable for anyone who resembled "Oscar," the mannequin devised by Ford in America around the average (5'10", 170lb) body measurements of 68,000 American troops, but they proved uncomfortable for many other people, for whom osteopaths rather than copywriters had the last word.

be uncompetitive, and a much better five-bearing, 1498cc engine arrived in August 1962. The Classic was more controversially, and heavily, styled than any of its predecessors. Its individual features were modern — the four headlamps were excellent and an innovation in the car's class, as were the equally good disc brakes, and the boot capacity of 21 cubic feet, demonstrated in publicity photographs by a girl in a deckchair sitting in it, was useful. Variable-speed windscreen wipers were standard as was a four-speed gearbox with a floor lever; a column change, good of its type for a four-speed, was optional. The metallic-lustre two-tone pvc upholstery of the de luxe was fashionable and a first in Britain, while leather on wearing surfaces was optional at £19 5s 3d.

Yet, in truth, the car already looked out of date when it was launched and within four months Vauxhall's new Victor FB appeared with a new, four-door-only but largely gimmick-free style at £745 (standard model), £781 (Super) and £847 (De Luxe). By contrast, the Classic's fins, rear window, grey strip speedometer with white figures, oval door release buttons, ribbed chrome seat adjustment levers and dimpled interior door handle bases were too end-of-last-decade. The five stars in the grille — ingeniously devised by Ron Hickman[39]— embodied an advertising theme, albeit one familiar on the badges of various Fords, from the *beginning* of the previous decade. It didn't help that the Classic's three-bearing 1340cc engine proved to be prone, *in extremis*, to crankshaft failure or that the tail sometimes skittered out in rain or on bumps; one journalist even turned over a car at the launch. But the occasional journalist in 1961 could overturn an armchair just by sitting in it, and for its period the Classic was not a notably ill-handling car.

Early advertisements for the Classic concentrated on its style and, cunningly, its "pace" — a word which suggested performance while not actually promising it. The car — invariably a four-door De luxe, usually in white or blue, occasionally in turquoise — was beautifully photographed: "Set the style — make the pace — with the all-new Classic…This is the new look of British motoring. The clean look. The classic look. The long low look that makes your new Classic the stylesetting pacemaker on the roads today." Copy changed slightly from advertisement to advertisement, and was greatly extended in a four-page launch in *The Autocar* of June 23 which included the cover of the magazine (which habitually carried advertising). One setting was quite modest, with a blue car shown in front-three quarter view in a field and a young family playing in the background. Curiously, the page of *The Autocar*'s advertisement which carried

most of the copy showed the same car from behind, and with the family now behind the camera the Classic looked as if it had been abandoned while its owners went to lunch. But most settings were holiday destinations, usually in southern Europe, where the light suited a white car and where proud owners could be seen at the quayside or near modern skyscrapers, in atmospheric back streets or parked on cliff-top roads with fishing boats below. "Ford holidays are so much more so than others," said a February 1962 piece, which used the Classic as a springboard for a general promotion. "Some people holiday the rough-and-tumble way. Some scramble across the map. Others head straight for sunbaked sands to laze through their vacation….Driving is delightful, touring is trouble-free, you've room for all your luggage, and there's Ford Service to look after your car wherever you go (our Man in Havana stocks the same spares as our man on the Kingston By-Pass!)" A promotional film shot by the Ford Film Unit was called "Classic Holiday."[40]

When the new, 1498cc engine arrived in August 1962, Classic advertising showed a white car in side view, speeding along a main road in a dramatic "motion" photograph. The copy was down to earth, and it did not take advanced hermeneutical skills to guess how the 1340cc engine had been received: "New Consul Classic 1½ Litre for extra pace — at no extra cost! We had a pacemaker — a fine car whose stylesetting design and pacemaking performance had won it the applause of the world. We gave it an improved engine — with an added 160cc of heart for extra power, and with a five-bearing crankshaft for extra smoothness. We gave it an improved gearbox — now with full synchromesh on all four gears. We gave it lifetime lubrication, 5,000 miles or twice a year servicing, and backed it with a 12 months/12,000 miles warranty…." *Now* will you buy the wretched thing? But many car buyers had already been enticed away by Rootes' new Hillman Minx 1600 and Super Minx, and by the Vauxhall Victor. Even natural Ford buyers were still unconvinced, especially after January 1963, when the new engine became available in a four-door Cortina (called the Super). In September 1963, Classic production discreetly stopped.

But this was not quite the end of the story, for in September 1961 the Classic was joined by a derivative called the Consul Capri, a hardtop coupe with fully retracting side windows that echoed the Ford Thunderbird and would outlast the Classic to survive in GT form until July 1964. The name, though borrowed from Lincoln, was still associated by Britons mainly with the island. A personal project of Sir Patrick Hennessy,[41] the Capri was "instigated by Horace Denne, Ford's Export Director, who wanted a 'co-respon-

Oppposite: **Ford Consul Classic 315.** Four speeds, four headlamps, disc brakes and MacPherson strut front suspension identified, in combination, a car of the 1960s, even if the "new look of British motoring" was in fact 1959's look, as seen on Fords and Mercurys of that period. The Classic was a solid car, with doors a handspan thick, but the reverse-rake rear window made it seem dark and cramped inside compared with its rivals from late 1961 onwards, the Hillman Super Minx and Vauxhall Victor FB (also from £745). Little was wrong with the Classic, particularly in later, more durable, 1497cc form, but the styling was controversial and it sold poorly, not least because the Cortina, similarly sized yet 300lb lighter and £105 cheaper, stole much of its market a year later.

SET THE STYLE—MAKE THE PACE—WITH THE ALL-NEW CLASSIC

This is the new look of British motoring. The clean look. The classic look. The long low look that makes your new Classic the stylesetting pacemaker on the roads today. Motorway pace (steady as a rock at speeds into the 80's) country-lane control (wonderful road-holding, front-wheel disc brakes standard) and all kept safe, smooth and stylish by quality Ford Service. Ask your Ford dealer to give you a test drive in the Classic.

THE ALL-NEW CONSUL CLASSIC 315

Ex-works from ✳
£744.17.6
(£525 + £219.17.6 purchase tax)

✳ 2-door Standard model £744.17.6 (£525 + £219.17.6 p.t.) 4-door Standard model £773.4.2 (£545 + £228.4.2 p.t.) 2-door De luxe model £773.4.2 p.t. (£545 + £228.4.2 p.t.) 4-door De luxe model £801.10.10 (£565 + £236.10.10 p.t.)

FROM ⬡ FORD ⬡ OF BRITAIN

dent's car' to add a little glamour to the Ford line in export markets."[42] When it was announced, *Motor Trader* commented, "We understand that this car will go first to the American market..."[43]— where in 1962 it cost $2331 at port of entry, rising to $2210 in 1963–64 with the GT costing $2800 in the latter year. (The four-door Classic De luxe cost $2120 in 1962 and $2130 in 1963.)[44] Once fitted with the larger engine, the Capri also pleased Ford in Germany, where it was the only British Ford sold alongside the German product, there being no equivalent Taunus.[45] The nearest British equivalent had been the original 1390cc Sunbeam Rapier of 1955, but that car was always a four-seater, and by September 1961 had gained a more rugged, sporting character and a 1592cc engine.

The Capri was the same length as the Classic and essentially a two-seater, although thin cushions were available for a shelf behind the front seats normally intended for luggage that would not fit in the boot — a boot already six inches longer internally than that of the Classic, and huge. Late in the Capri's development, Hennessy ordered the roofline, originally the same height as the Classic's, to be lowered by two inches to improve the car's appearance,[46] but it remained a two-seater. Roy Haynes, who would style the Cortina Mk II, recalled: "The Capri could have had proper back seats if Ford had been willing to re-tool the boot lid so that it didn't take up as much space — but they weren't."[47] Unexpectedly, there proved to be a worthwhile demand for the car from the home market despite its relatively high price of £915 12s 3d and low power of 54 bhp net, which gave acceleration of 0–60 mph in 23 seconds and a top speed of just 80mph. The Capri therefore became available in Britain during the first week of 1962. The 1498cc engine arrived in August, and in February 1963 Ford announced a Capri GT with a Cosworth-developed, 78 bhp twin-carburettor version of this engine which gave 90–95 mph performance and was later adopted by the Cortina GT of April 1963. The Capri GT was also distinguished by a brake servo, improved trim, extra instruments and a remote-control gear lever — the original, long, black-ball-on-a-rod affair had always looked incongruous in such stylized surroundings. A few Capris, including some GTs, were built with a Westinghouse-Hobbs Mechamatic automatic transmission, identified by a "Westinghouse Automatic" badge.[48]

From September 1962 the Capri buyer seeking something truly exclusive was offered, for about £500 on top of the standard car's price, a super-luxury conversion by the famous coachbuilders, Hooper (as Hooper Motor Services Ltd.) of Kilburn, West London. Overriders were added and special tail-lights with reversing lamps were substituted for the originals; the decorative aluminium panel on the standard car's tail was replaced by a simple chrome border; a plain chrome bar replaced the five stars in the grille; and the body was hand-finished with 14 coats of paint. But the real point of the car was the interior, which was fitted with a walnut veneer dashboard, high-quality carpets, Reutter reclining seats covered with Vaumol leather from Connolly and augmented by occasional seats in the rear, new door trims with pockets, extra trim and fittings in the boot, and other equipment as required. About 90 Hooper Capris were eventually made.[49]

The market for the Consul Capri in Britain was specialized and new to Ford, and early advertising echoed that for the Thunderbird in America. In January 1962, the "First personal car from Ford of Britain," was seen, Thunderbird style, in moody evening and woodland settings. "Let go with the new Consul Capri!" said the copy in January 1962, with a whitewall-tyred Capri in the moonlight, its owners in evening dress, "This car is very personal property; once you get the feel of it, you won't want to hold back. Behind the wheel a man feels power — and a woman feels freedom. Turn the key and feel the Capri spring to life, gliding like a panther, hugging the road, clinging to the curves...a sleek and elegant extension of your own personality." Later in the month a light yellow car with a white roof rested beside a lake, its owners looking out into the evening mist. In July, the same Capri, seen in rear-three-quarter view to show off its fins, was "Newest personal car from Ford of Britain," the yellow and white paint glowing in dappled early morning sunlight, its owner still in evening dress, sitting on the low branch of a nearby tree: "It's a little big for me, but I don't like to be crowded. It does go rather fast, but sometimes it's nice to get somewhere in a hurry. The disc brakes do stop me quickly, but I prefer to be safe. Extravagant? Well, its not a car for everybody. Let's go — in my Consul Capri." For Christmas, a white Capri was photographed at night in a conventional, front-three-quarter view at ground-level, the surrounding forest dreamily out of focus, the whole ensemble infused with a faint haze of mauve: "On the first day of Christmas my true love gave to me... One new Capri (He can keep the partridge)." Who could not smile? The price was not mentioned. The car was "Different. Special."

By 1962, the Consul, Zephyr and Zodiac Mk II were six years old, and designing successors did not prove easy. In 1955 Colin Neale had asked a young apprentice draughtsman who was training in modern car manufacture at Briggs, Charles Thompson, whether he would like to join the styling studio rather than become an engineer, and he immediately agreed. National Service in the RAF intervened during

Opposite: **Ford Consul Capri.** A low-production foray into niche marketing with a mini-Thunderbird and American-inspired advertising to suit. The 1969 Capri (no "Consul"), the "car you always promised yourself," was a much more successful venture, promoted with press and television advertising which emphasized fun rather than dinner-jacketed glamour. Yet this car was arguably better built, and its only hardtop rival, the Sunbeam Rapier, was an older design which looked it — and it cost over £100 more. Annual sales of the two types (the Consul Capri running from 1961–64) were comparable.

LET GO
WITH THE NEW CONSUL
CAPRI !

This car is very personal property; once you get the feel of it, you won't want to hold back. Behind the wheel a man feels power—and a woman feels freedom. Turn the key and feel the Capri spring to life, gliding like a panther, hugging the road, clinging to the curves, responding instantly . . . a sleek and elegant extension of your own personality. The Consul Capri is a luxury two-seater version of the dynamic new Consul Classic, superbly built to perform with ease, grace and economy. It's got rally-proved disc brakes and twin sealed-beam headlamps that mean maximum safety at speed. Plenty of luxury: soft bucket seats to sink into, room to spread out, space behind if you need it and a huge boot for luggage. Panoramic visibility—all four windows, back and front, wind down out of sight. For £915.12.3 (£627 + £288.12.3 p.t.) you get all this—*and* the blessing of world-wide quality Ford Service. Now at your Ford Dealer—get the feel of the fabulous Capri for yourself.

FIRST PERSONAL CAR FROM OF BRITAIN

1956–57, but later that year Thompson returned to what was now Ford's styling studio and, as a junior stylist under Neale, began work on proposals for Mk III versions of the Consul, Zephyr and Zodiac.[50] His earliest sketches show a style with plain bumpers, modest, forward-leaning fins that emerge from sculpted body sides and an overall appearance astonishingly like that of the future 1961 Pontiac Tempest[51]. The first Mk III design clay employed very different, larger, horizontal fins, similar to those of the large Dearborn Fords of 1960, while a full-size 1958 mock-up by Colin Neale abandoned fins and included flush door handles and rear side sculpture which anticipated the full-size American Ford line of 1964. This design proved more or less a dead-end, although its flat bonnet with curved edges and slightly raised centre section would, essentially, survive.[52] The styling studio's proposals were, however, rejected and for a short period Neale returned to Dagenham with American stylist Elwood Engel, although their ideas were rejected, too, as being "too American." "We're still in trouble with our Mark III," wrote Hennessy to Neale when the latter was back in America with Engel, "For one thing it seems difficult to marry the Galaxie type of roof to the design below the belt line. We have tried a number of variants, yet are not happy."[53]

Ford sought help from Pietro Frua in Italy, who produced a design in 1959. In its overall proportions, and in details such as canted fins, rear door line and rear quarter windows, Frua's suggestion was quite similar to the final car, but it had a more delicate glasshouse, slanted headlamps and overriders, and a general air of being the best possible interpretation of a restrictive design brief.[54] Frua's curved side windows would, however, be adopted on the production car, as would his fins[55]. Charles Thompson then developed Frua's grille on paper and considered incorporating into it some of Elwood Engel's ideas, but Dearborn accepted only a few elements of Frua's style while rejecting it as a complete car because it diverged too far from Ford's intended house style. Meanwhile, the final departure of Colin Neale for Dearborn left the styling studio without strong leadership and the project threatened to languish.

Help for the Mk III came, indirectly, from the hundreds of thousands of mid-range American car buyers who declined to buy Edsels. In November 1959, the Ford Foundation in Dearborn wished to sell two million shares of its Ford stock, and in order to do so was required by law to issue a prospectus stating the future plans of the company. The prospectus listed the company's brands as Ford, Mercury and Lincoln and only in a footnote referred to the Edsel, which, it said, was "introduced in September, 1957, and discontinued in November, 1959." The Edsel's discontinuation had not yet been made public and the American press were immediately curious. The final decision to abandon the Edsel marque had to be made, and was announced shortly afterwards.[56] This left the future of the Edsel's designer, Roy Brown, uncertain to say the least. But George Walker, Ford's Vice President of Design (and creator as outside consultant of the 1949 Fords that had inspired Britain's first Consul and Zephyr) admired Brown's work and approach. "Roy," said Walker to Brown, "I said this before, when that Edsel went down the tubes—for two days you were crying in your beer. After that you were your old self again, whistling down the hallway." Meanwhile Sir Patrick Hennessy had told Walker, "I want a designer with a lot of enthusiasm to come over here and build us the finest design department in Europe."[57]

Shortly afterwards, Roy Brown crossed the Atlantic,[58] and his first major project was to mastermind the Mk III and to develop Frua's design into not just a good car, but a good Ford. He involved Charles Thompson, who, at the suggestion of Sir Patrick Hennessy, included a shallow top section of vertical bars in the grille of the proposed Zodiac version in order to establish continuity with the earlier Mk II. Mockups began to resemble the final car closely, although one early design in particular, with wide, turned-up bumpers and flush door handles, would have been mistaken by anyone for a small Chrysler. And without Sir Patrick Hennessy's vertically-barred top section, the concave, full-width grille of the later Zodiac prototypes, with four integral headlamps and side-lights incorporated into the bumper ends, would have looked exactly like that of the full-size 1961 Dodge. How the cars would be badged and marketed was still being debated in 1961. "Consul" was now associated with the Consul Classic and with the Consul Cortina to come, although that car was planned as a "Prefect" in March 1961, had been promoted to "Consul" by December and was not yet a Cortina. For the large car, "Consul" was dropped and it was decided that the "Zephyr 4" and "Zephyr 6" would inherit the four and six-cylinder engines of the existing Consul 375 and Zephyr.

Zodiac prototypes had been built in six-window and four-window styles, the latter following the line of the Zephyrs, but Ford settled on the six-window style to distinguish the Zodiac from the other models. The Zodiac was announced on April 13, 1962, with the Zephyr 4 and Zephyr 6 following two weeks later. For the Motor Show in October, the cars' rear track was widened and the seat was moved backwards to release two extra inches of kneeroom. The Zephyr 4's trim was improved and estate cars by Abbott of Farnham were announced at the same time. A super-luxury Zodiac, of which fewer than one hundred would be built, was introduced by Hooper Motor Services Ltd. on October 17. In January 1965 Ford introduced its own super-luxury model, the Zodiac Executive, which incorporated all normal Zodiac extras along with extra equipment to provide the maximum of luxury and quietness. The "Executive" name, recalled Graham Arnold, then of Harold Radford (Coachbuilders) Ltd. and later to become sales director at Lotus, was first used by Radford for a super-luxury version of the Vauxhall Cresta.[59] Notionally at least, the Zodiac Executive rivalled the Wolseley 6/110 Mk II. But few people who bought Wolseleys would buy Fords, and only about two hundred Zodiac Executives were made. The Mk IIIs never really lost their "compact Chrysler" look, but as production cars they did not look like any *particular* Chryslers. It was ironic that a design which Dearborn wished above all to be recognizable as a Ford should look as a 1960 Valiant might have done, had Chrysler chosen to miniaturize the original Forward Look in the economical spirit of the Falcon, yet the Mk IIIs were easily identifiable as Fords to the British motorists who bought them.

"With a flourish of trumpets, in the glare of the spotlights, the new Ford Zodiac was unveiled recently in London's Grosvenor House Hotel. The new model was seen at once to have the simple lines and elegant appointments of a potential 'winner' in world sales markets," announced *Motor Trader* in April, 1962.[60] Local dealers entered into the spirit of the occasion. In Redcar, North Yorkshire, Cleveland Motor Service Ltd. and its local advertising agent planned a party. The idea, recalled the (privately sceptical) new sales manager, Geoff Owen, was "that the party should begin at around 10.30pm and the Zodiac kept covered under a dustsheet in the centre of the showroom. At midnight precisely all lights were to be extinguished without warning, a brief announcement would be made, the cover whipped off and the lights switched on — to suitable gasps of admiration." Tape recorded music rose gradually in volume as 500 guests arrived and grew steadily merrier. "At dead on midnight, offering a silent prayer, I hit the switch. The music stopped and out went the lights. You could have heard a pin drop, the abrupt silence so completely astonishing that I nearly forgot my lines: 'Ladies and gentlemen — the directors and staff of Cleveland Motor Service are proud to announce the all-new Ford Zodiac Mk. III.' This was the cue for the cover to be whipped off. There was a whispered, 'Ready, Joe' from Mike, followed by a piercing female shriek, the crash of breaking glass, then all the lights came on…some idiot had parked the best part of a pint of beer on the roof of the car which had shot off with the dust cover and soaked a lady guest."

This proved no more than a minor diversion and the guest was quickly mollified, but "with what had been consumed in food and drink, plus a crate of scotch that vanished without trace, the evening had cost a fortune. We didn't sell a single car." In due course, however, the Zodiac did sell, as did the Zephyrs and the Cortina. Inadequately bribed with only a promise of coffee and sandwiches, the official invitees stayed away from the Cortina launch, but cheerful passersby, on their way home from the pub, ordered four cars between them.[61]

In April 1962, English-language export advertisements promoted the three new cars together as "Three fabulous new Fords." Home market advertising, however, kept much of the export copy's flavour for the Zodiac but showed the Zephyr 4 and Zephyr 6 together in very different advertisements which used Libyan desert scenes that inaugurated a long line of "deserted-beach" advertisements from British car makers. Zodiac announcement advertising showed a painting of a dark green car in side profile, while the headline emphasized its claimed 100 mph top speed (which was confirmed — just — in independent tests). The copy wavered uneasily between the mechanical and the aspirational, surging occasionally into Jaguar-ese: "A new concept in Ford motoring — The new luxurious 100 m.p.h. Zodiac Mk. III…The Zodiac Mk. III is powered by a newly-developed 2553cc unit, designed with twin exhausts to deliver 112 bhp. The four-speed gear box has synchromesh on all four gears….The road holding is superlative in any circumstance….With all this goes the quietness, comfort and security of a prestige limousine….Foam rubber seating trimmed with new Cirrus 500 and optional extra of fully reclining adjustable-rake separate front seats….And everywhere everything finished and polished at it should be, as *you* want it, in 1962's top car. *Invitation.* The Zodiac Mk. III is now available at your Ford showroom. You are cordially invited to inspect it and, if you wish, to test-drive it." But did upmarket car buyers call their engines "units"? Would they know what Cirrus 500 was, or be interested when they found out?

In June, with essentially the same advertisement (the painting was reversed, to point to the right), the copywriter tried again: "Men who enjoy power…enjoy the new luxurious 100 m.p.h. Zodiac Mk. III…Take a newly-developed 2553cc engine. Have it designed with twin exhausts (and 4-speed synchromesh gear box) to deliver 112 bhp…Specify…extravagantly safe road holding…Next, insist on armchair relaxation for six big people. With foam rubber seating trimmed with new Cirrus 500. Fully reclining, adjustable-rake, separate front seats….Then as a final perfect touch, clothe it all in an entirely new motor car shape of consummate elegance and freshness. What you have then is 1962's top car…the new luxurious 100 mph Zodiac Mk III. See it today at your Ford dealer." Only rarely was an advertisement revisited in this way.

By 1963, the car was selling steadily and could be photographed in a glamorous studio pose: "Shooting star…This Zodiac Mk III has star quality. Flashing acceleration. Up to 100 mph. Disc brakes. Gleaming wheel trims…All this costs only £970–17–11…the Zodiac Mk III can give you *everything.*" The Zephyrs (with narrow whitewall tyres in export advertising and standard tyres in Britain, where whitewalls were a minority taste and were quickly made grey by the weather), were more openly promoted as the Mk II's successors: "Two new Zephyrs! Zephyr 4 — takes over from famous Consul 375. Zephyr 6 — crispest-ever statement of the Zephyr formula!" With the Zephyr 4, "only the price is pocket-sized." At £846 12s 6d for a 22.5 cwt car, fifteen feet long and five feet nine inches wide on a 107" wheelbase, the

The Field, May 16, 1963

SHOOTING STAR This Zodiac Mk III has star quality. Flashing acceleration. Up to 100 mph. Disc brakes. Gleaming wheel trims. Twin headlamps. Fitted pile carpets. The very latest heating and ventilation. All this costs only £970-17-1. But pay a little extra and you can also have... white sidewall tyres... individual fully-reclining front seats... crushed hide upholstery... all transistorised radio... and the best automatic transmission in the world. In other words, for a very little more, the Zodiac Mk III can give you *everything.*

ZODIAC
MKIII

MADE WITH CARE BY FORD OF BRITAIN *Ford*

919

Ford Zodiac Mk III. In the early 1960s, Ford used a combination of outdoor and studio settings for its advertising, tending towards cheerful, natural scenes with small cars and more studied glamour pieces with expensive models, 1962 announcement advertising for this Zodiac (curiously) excepted. So there was nothing really anomalous about this piece, whose layout had much in common with that for the Zephyr 6 of a few weeks earlier. Yet somehow it seemed a throwback to an earlier school, an impression increased by the "if we must" expression of a dinner-jacketed driver for whom formal parties were presumably a chore. The car itself boasted a six-light window treatment exclusive to the model, and the grille neatly acknowledged that of the earlier Mk II, which in turn had been inspired by the Aston Martin DB3.

Antler 'Airlight' companion case, £5. 5s.

To match the luxury of the Executive Zodiac... the graceful elegance of antler luggage, of course

Every feature of the Executive Zodiac has been chosen to reflect the highest standards of comfort and performance —from the automatic transmission to the individual reclining front seats and real leather upholstery. Antler luggage fits perfectly into this world of first-class motoring —as only the best can do.

antler LUGGAGE

Antler 'Airstream' suitcases and Pakswell from £10. 10s. to £15. 15s.

Ford

Ford Zodiac Executive Mk III. By 1965, "parasitic" advertising, in which advertisers of non-automotive goods capitalized on the image of the "host" product, was not unusual, but this piece, which promotes the luggage on more or less equal terms with the car, bucked the general trend. This car marked the emergence of the executive as a marketing concept in Ford's advertising. By the 1990s, it had changed its meaning, coming to signify a salesman or clerk in many contexts, so its use as a car name could be perilous. Chrome strips were fitted to black vinyl door trims for another ten years by Ford and others. From the rear this car resembled not only a Forward Look Chrysler or DeSoto, but also, with chrome ribbing not fitted to Zephyrs, a 1957 styling proposal for the French Simca (née Ford) Vedette.

Ignore the could-be-better! Choose the can't-be-beaten! The enviable Zephyr 6. Top speeds in the high nineties. Acceleration to match. Disc brakes. Surefooted road holding. Sumptuous luxury. Every desirable extra. And all the zest in the world! From only £836.14.7 (tax paid).

ZEPHYR 6

 MADE WITH CARE BY FORD OF BRITAIN

Zephyr 4 offered unmatched value for money. Even its 1703cc engine (giving acceleration of 0–60 in 22.8 seconds) was adequate. No Vauxhall was equivalent to the Zephyr 4, as the Velox was a "six,"[62] whose natural rival was the Zephyr 6. A year after its launch, that car was shown in a sober maroon, speeding along the beach in an advertisement which sailed deftly between the Scylla of aspiration and the Charybdis of value for money: "Why come second when you can be first?...Every desirable extra. And all the zest in the world! From only £836.14.7 (tax paid)."

Early in 1961, meanwhile, "Archbishop" received a boost. In 1960, Robert McNamara, one of Henry Ford II's post-war Whiz Kids and from 1955 head of the Ford Division of Ford Motor Company in Dearborn, had replaced Ernest Breech as president of the company. His place was taken by Lee Iacocca, who was convinced that Ford should cultivate a sporty image and who decided that the definitely unsporting Cardinal would not be produced in the United States. Thus the Cardinal and Archbishop became purely European rivals, and Sir Patrick Hennessy and Terence Beckett were determined that the Archbishop would beat the Cardinal on cost-effectiveness and eventual sales appeal. The Archbishop had to be produced inexpensively if it were to be sold profitably in competition with BMC's forthcoming 1100, and its development was controlled by "the introduction of Dearborn's 'Red Book', which laid down at the outset of a programme its projected cost — by costing to the last cent...500 key items in the car...and also [laid down] the date for 'Job One', the first production example of the new model. The 'Red Book' brought a new discipline to Dagenham [and to Britain]: henceforth, new cars would have to be ready for launch, as opposed to being launched when ready."[63]

Roy Brown and his styling team prepared five mockups to a very detailed prior specification during 1960. Terence Beckett was attracted by one mock-up in particular, in which each body side had a tapering, concave side flute that grew wider towards the rear of the car, giving strength, an appearance of length and just the hint of a fin. The flute merged into a gently downward-pointing triangular taillight, like that of the 1957 Mercury but completely integrated into the simple overall shape of the rear.[64] This design was authorized for production in November 1960, although the tail-lights did not survive. John Bugas, head of Dearborn's International Division, demanded circular taillights in the Ford tradition[65]: "The three-pointed star shape and the outer ring were intended to be a stylish sharp-edged casting, but while Charles [Thompson] was off ill...the accountants got to it and changed it" into an alloy pressing.[66] This made it look cheap, but the lights' division into stop/tail, indicator and reflector sections gave the car character.

The Archbishop was also light: Ford's chief body engineer, Don Ward, had recruited from Briggs a man who had worked for Ford in the early 1950s but later joined Bristol until 1957, and who was therefore an automobile engineer and an aircraft stressman. Dennis Roberts produced a design more than strong enough for most markets with as little metal as possible and the minimum of spot-welds. An alternative, tougher, shell was developed for the Australian market and shared with the British Cortina GT of 1963. The car's engine would be an 1198cc engine version of the Anglia's, which would also be used in the Anglia Super to announced at the same time. All that remained to be decided was a name, and after Sir Patrick Hennessy's suggestion of "Caprino" was found to mean "goat dung" in Italian, the more invitingly Italian "Cortina" was suggested by Terence Beckett, after Cortina d'Ampezzo, the alpine venue of the 1960 Winter Olympics, in the spring of 1962. "I wanted to give the car a European flavour as Britain was negotiating for membership of the Common Market and the name would also provide a sporting image," recalled Beckett in 1983[67]. The name also meant "kettle" in Latin, but any pedantic analogy *via* tin and utility was much too strained to matter. At a pre-launch marketing conference at the Montlhéry race track near Paris in June 1962, where Henry Ford II and other Ford executives tested and appraised both models, the Cortina trounced the Taunus 12M and Henry Ford II enthusiastically authorized the heavier GT.[68]

The regular Cortina was launched at the Grosvenor House Hotel in London on September 21, 1962 in Standard and better-equipped de Luxe two-door versions costing £639 0s 3d and £666 10s 3d respectively. In size and performance they were directly comparable with the Morris 1100 (from £675), the Hillman Minx 1600 (from £702), and the Vauxhall Victor (also from £702), while being slightly faster to 60 mph than either of the latter, longer than all but the Victor (which was 3.7cwt heavier), and cheaper than any of them, though the Standard Cortina was admittedly very basic indeed.[69] Slightly more expensive four-door Cortinas followed in November, and 1498cc Super variants arrived in January 1963 alongside the now famously successful Cortina Lotus,

---

Opposite: **Ford Zephyr 6 Mk III.** "Every desirable extra" in a car that became popular with police forces all over Britain and so was adopted by BBC Television for its police drama series, *Z Cars*, which brought welcome publicity to the model and to Ford. The deserted beach, an established advertising motif by 1963, suited the emphasis in this and similar advertisements on escape, individualism and achievement-orientated social success. The car itself looked slightly old-fashioned when compared with rival Vauxhalls, as the tail fins and concave grille were Chrysler Corporation features from 1957 and 1961 respectively. The whole creation, although developed by stylist Roy Brown from a 1959 proposal by Frua, had a compact Forward Look about it, especially in early mock-up form with flush door handles and more elaborate bumpers. The back of the production car was very slightly wider than the front, which caught out a few new owners who were used to earlier models, but the new car, unlike them, had four forward gears. A single real Zephyr 6 police car survives.

which everyone called the Lotus Cortina, and which was advertised in the United States by by Imported Vehicles, Ford Division as "the same exciting sedan Colin Chapman modifies for Jim Clark." British advertising photographed the car on a wide road in characteristic white paint with a green stripe beside the headline, "High speed performer from Ford…with about-town manners!!" and described the car as the "Cortina developed by Lotus." Estate cars followed in March, the GT arrived in April, the dashboard was updated in October 1963, and a Borg-Warner automatic followed in January 1964.

The £748 10s 5d Cortina GT, with its 78 bhp and top speed of over 90 mph, was a great image-booster for mainstream Fords, though its name was not the result of conventional product planning. "[W]e sent somebody to Halfords to find the prettiest badge to put on it. The prettiest badge he could find had 'GT' on it, so we bought one…It was an enormous success. This splendid performance sedan was a new concept in the marketplace, but…a 'super GT' was obviously needed because the competitors were beginning to nibble at us"[70], recalled Walter Hayes. GTs for a time accounted for a quarter of Cortinas built, the model was a race and rally success (a GT won the 1964 East African Safari Rally) and the "super GT" eventually beat the GT to production as the Lotus Cortina.

The Consul Cortina was launched with heavy national and local advertising, and early publicity which announced the car in September 1962 as "The small car with a big difference!…Making small-car history" hovered between American and European idioms. The studio shot of a maroon de Luxe against a maroon background looked American (although it had no direct equivalent in American Ford publicity), while the catalogue showed the car in mainland Europe, implied to be at home on the road full of Renault Dauphines and Citroëns seen in aerial view. Only the interior looked unappetizing, photographed in plasticky grey, and the woman who approached with her shopping, although obviously photographed somewhere else and pasted in, looked doubtful. Other advertisements showed cars in lighter colours, and in April 1963 a four-door was shown in bright blue with a full complement of happy passengers and white-stripe tyres: "Buy big-car everything—at small-car costs! This is a tough car. A big five-seater car. A fast 78 mph car…Big-car ride. Big-car pride." The mechanical features were listed in very small print above the prices, so as not to bring the main body copy too heavily down to earth. Export advertising—in which the Cortina competed with the Taunus 12M—was less excitable ("Ford presents the big difference in economy cars…Consul Cortina") but used the same theme.

For the estate cars' announcement, the London Press Exchange Ltd. produced two parallel advertisements with almost identical copy. One showed the de Luxe in the main picture, described it as the Cortina Estate, and included a small picture of the Super below, while in the other the pictures were transposed and "Super" added between "Cortina" and "Estate" in the copy. The Super Estate was highly distinctive in bright blue (then a favourite colour in Ford advertising) with Roy Brown's Di-Noc side and tailgate trim bordered by glass-fibre mock-wood strips. But although the estate car was a success the trim, in the style of Dearborn's Ford Country Squire and Mercury Colony Park wagons was not; like the Classic's fins, it looked overdone on a small European car and was discontinued for 1965. The Super was the most expensive estate at £785 19s 7d, but the £683 5s 5d de Luxe, with a white side flash bordered by stainless trim, *looked* more expensive. Late in 1964, for the 1965 model year, the "Consul" moniker was dropped and the range was updated with a new grille and a pioneering ventilation system called Aeroflow, with adjustable dashboard outlets and efficient extractor vents in the rear pillars. Except briefly with the Cortina Mk II in 1967, the Cortina never managed to beat BMC's 1100 as Britain's best-seller, but that car was not nearly as profitable to produce, and the millionth Cortina was sold in September 1966. The Mk 1 Cortinas were discontinued during October and November to make way for the Mk II.[71]

Ford's next two lines—the Corsairs of 1963–70 and the Zephyrs and Zodiacs of 1966–71 were not true successes[72], but only the latter range was really a failure, even if the Corsair cost much more to develop than Ford expected. The Consul Corsair arrived on October 2, 1963 as a replacement for the Consul Classic, and was said to have been designed as a result of a two-year pan-European survey of potential customers' preferences. It was meticulously styled under Roy Brown and stylist John Fallis by Charles Thompson, who produced a distinctive shape using the Cortina's floorpan, track, internal body structure and door shells. Thompson later named it as his favourite design.[73] In some respects it reflected the 1961–63 Ford Thunderbird while in others it echoed existing and future Taunus models from Germany. Considerable attention was paid to quietness and refinement, and the instruments used Britain's first printed-circuit wiring. The Corsair employed much of the Cortina's drivetrain and, until 1965, its 1498cc engine; it was introduced in standard, de Luxe and GT forms, each with two or four doors. Few standard Corsairs were built, however, and the two-door models were virtually discontinued when the

---

Opposite: **Ford Consul Cortina Super Estate Car.** S.C.H. Davis called the Di-Noc fake wood trim "perfectly horrible," and enough people agreed for it to be dropped in 1964. Cortina estates became popular with business motorists, and this model was upgraded alongside the saloon. This static, posed shot is typical of Ford advertising of the time, although later in the year larger Fords would be shown in motion, and in more natural surroundings—a trend continued into the 1970s.

THE FIELD, *March 21 1963*

NEW CONSUL
CORTINA
ESTATE CAR

Largest in its class—smallest in its costs!

No other estate car in this price range gives so much usable rear space as this beautiful Cortina Super Estate! You can sleep in it—it's over six foot long. You can practically live in it. You can carry a rowing boat if you want. And you've got power too—from a brawny 1500cc unit which makes light work of any load and quick work of any road. Yet the Cortina Super Estate is not an expensive car. Look at the price... the running costs! The same inspired engineering which makes the amazing Cortina Saloon such a superbly practical proposition has succeeded again, brilliantly! Your Ford dealer will gladly arrange a test drive! Super from only **£785.19.7** (tax paid.)

Seats 5 in comfort. 4 doors, plus counter-balanced tail-gate. 56 cu. ft. rear loading space. Solid uni-construction. Steel rear floor. Heavy-duty suspension. 4-speed all-synchro gear box. Immense window area for all-round visibility—and for sun!

AND THE NEW CORTINA DE LUXE ESTATE CAR. Same space! Same toughness! Even more economy. Choice of 1200cc or 1500cc engine. Rim embellishers optional extra. From only **£683.5.5** (tax paid).

MADE WITH CARE
BY FORD OF BRITAIN

"Consul" name was dropped in October 1965, when the range received new 1996cc V4 engines.

"Corsair" was an inspired name, well suited to a car with a sharp, streamlined-looking prow and, said Ford ingeniously, an echo of the original corsairs who once pirated the coastal waters close to the car's new factory at Halewood, near Liverpool, the most promising of the locations which had been permitted by the Government. "Corsair" also rhymed with "flair," the dominant word in early Corsair advertising, and with "fanfare." Devising the announcement headline, "Fanfare for the flair-everywhere Consul Corsair!" was therefore easy. The car was most striking in the side profile chosen for much early advertising, while white paint was fashionable and allowed cars to be shown not only on the beach, as in 1963–64, but also at night when the new V4 was announced for 1966.

The V4 engine, however, which seemed to bring the Corsair into the expanding and aspirational two-litre class, was— at least in its early form — a mistake. In theory more powerful than the in-line "1500," it was slower in some circumstances and also heavier, noisy, rough, thirsty and prone to oiling its plugs. Undaunted, Ford boldly claimed smoothness— at least at first. The headline of late 1965, "We've got a V in our bonnet!" was followed in the spring of 1966 by: "The car that's seen but not heard. Smooth, silent, V-power. Simply turn the key in your new Corsair V4 and you have started a quiet revolution." But by the middle of the year anyone living on a hill knew it to be a noisy beast. In March 1966, a luxury estate car by Abbott of Farnham was announced under the same headline, while in the same month Crayford Auto Developments introduced a Corsair convertible based on the two-door body shell which, by then, was otherwise available only for export, to fleet owners and to special bulk order. Advertised by its dealer, Phillips Motors in London, as "Fun in the sun…cosy in the rain," it cost £1026 19s 2d and was sold alongside an equivalent Cortina until 1968. About one hundred were made.

In January 1967, Ford introduced the Corsair 2000E (for "Executive"), with a new camshaft, improved carburation and, in particular, luxury trim and fittings. These were emphasized in advertising by Ford's new agents, Collett Dickenson Pearce: "Slip into something elegant..The elegant new Corsair 2000E, distinguished by its black vinyl roof and unique grille packs all the power of the 2-litre performance package…" invited the copy, which emphasized features and performance (which had greatly improved) rather than mechanical refinement. Corsair advertising in the model's last years used dramatic photography while highlighting its low

price for a two-litre car; the range continued, with minor improvements, until June 1970.[74]

In January 1961, the Ford Motor Company in America paid nearly £130 million for all remaining independently owned shares in Ford of Britain. The British company thus became a wholly owned subsidiary of its Dearborn parent, and Dearborn's increasing influence was nowhere more apparent than in the design of the Mk IV Zephyrs and Zodiacs of 1966–71. These were the last Fords designed in Britain under Roy Brown, the last styled by Charles Thompson and, to British eyes, the most thoroughly American in conception — even if they were more European than they looked in many individual details and more sophisticated, in theory, than equivalent Vauxhalls. The design achieved Mustang proportions with adequate accommodation by innovation: the air intake was under the front bumper, allowing the spare wheel to be placed in front of the engine to release space in the boot, so that the car's cabin could be moved backwards relative to the wheel centres. Ford's Product Planning Committee approved the Mk IV ("Panda") project in May 1961, and the final scheme of the car was conceived after extensive consultation with the export sales and marketing strategists, from whose recommendations 20 alternative packages were devised. One of them, using "V" engines, seemed by far the most promising and was chosen for development.

Late in 1962, however, the company gained a new Director of Engineering, Harley Copp, who had been chief engineer at Lincoln Division and who decided that the Mk IV should be a car for Britain in the Lincoln "fine car" tradition. Not that British motorists knew much about Lincolns, or spoke of the "fine car tradition." If anything, the expression recalled the Rover, long advertised as "one of Britain's fine cars." Roy Brown later found himself caught between two motoring cultures: "We'd had five successes in a row, but with the Mk IV Zodiac, we wanted to do something very different. We wanted something with a long front end and a short deck. It was a very simple design. I did five models. Mr. Ford and everybody who came over from America loved what we had done. The new chairman of Ford, who replaced Sir Patrick, said, 'I don't want this. This is an American-looking design and I don't want the damn thing.' He started shooting guns at me. Finally, Mr. Ford said [to Gene Bordinat, George Walker's successor], 'Bring Roy back to America before the sonovabitch crucifies him.'"[75]

Introduced on April 20, 1966, the Mk IV range consisted of Zephyrs with 2 litre V4 and 2.5 litre V6 engines, a Zodiac with 3 litre V6 and, from October, a 3 litre Executive and what would be the last estate car design by Abbott

Opposite: **Ford Consul Corsair.** Inevitable alliteration announces the Classic's replacement in October 1963. Much of the car (whose name was taken from a version of the Edsel) was based on the Cortina, underneath a cigar-shaped body that resembled the 1961 Ford Thunderbird. Early Corsairs came with American-style colour co-ordinated interiors. With green and cream bodywork, for instance, the buyer could have a metallic green vinyl interior with green carpets, dashboard, seats and steering wheel, the latter with a ribbed oblong horn ring. "Lube for life" was a relief for home mechanics, but some older buyers were suspicious as, with very regular greasing, the older type of suspension joint could be made to last a long time. Note the new-style white stripe, rather than whitewall, tyres.

NEW FROM **FORD!**
CONSUL **CORSAIR** RANGE

FLAIR EVERYWHERE!!!

Fanfare for the flair-everywhere Consul Corsair! Motorists everywhere applaud Corsair's new high quality and inspired blend of comfort, power, style and economy. *You* must try Corsair. For a no-obligation test drive, phone your Ford dealer now.

FLAIR IN DESIGN AND FINISH! From their colourful trend-setting profile, to the smallest detail of interior craftsmanship, Corsairs have a look which says "Quality Car"! Exacting new standards of workmanship backed by Europe's most modern car-making plant give Corsair owners enviable advantages.

FLAIR IN POWER! Relish the Corsair's race and rally proven 1500 cc 4 cylinder unit, brilliantly developed to deliver sizzling top speeds into the 80s and zippy 0-60 mph take-offs in under 21 secs. Corsairs have self-adjusting front-wheel disc brakes and magnificent roadholding capabilities. Automatic transmission available.

FLAIR IN COMFORT! Imaginative interior styling gives the Corsairs spacious seating for five and more rear leg room than similar cars. You can have all the extra luxury and equipment you demand. Corsairs add still more to your comfort by achieving an incomparably smooth and quiet ride.

FLAIR IN VALUE! These magnificent newcomers can do up to 32 mpg. And in spite of their expensive finish and many luxury fittings they cost less to buy and less to run than comparable cars. Bucket seats, remote floor shift come at very little extra.

ADDED SAFEGUARDS FOR YOUR INVESTMENT. 12 months/12,000 miles warranty. 5,000 miles/twice a year servicing. No greasing – Lube-for-Life. Low-cost fixed price Ford service and genuine FoMoCo parts everywhere. Attractive hp/insurance rates.

and Flair

MADE WITH CARE BY FORD OF BRITAIN

Ever seen a G.T. Estate Car?

Take a look at the Corsair V4 G.T. Estate Car.
The one that's seen but not heard.

At last the perfect answer for the many discriminating people who've long been waiting for a good-looking estate car that goes as well as it looks. From its stylish bonnet to its upward swinging tailgate, the Corsair GT Estate Car is a compliment to your good taste. It goes smoothly and quietly on a country road, looks beautiful in front of a country house.

And this car is meant for big things. Simply load up the fully carpeted load space, slide into the luxuriously comfortable, individual front seats, then start the V4 GT engine. Smooth, silent V-power carries you and whatever you want to take with you in great style, with a 0—60 acceleration in only 14 seconds!

Corsair V4 GT performance . . stylish lines . . luxury interior . . Aeroflow ventilation . . vast space. See your Ford Dealer today. *Recommended delivered price, inclusive of tax, £1,130.*

CORSAIR V4
GT Estate Car Ford

of Farnham. The Mk IV was approximately Fairlane-sized, at fifteen feet six inches long and five feet eleven inches wide on a wheelbase of 115.5 inches, and it was Ford's first car in Britain with independent rear suspension and disc brakes on all four wheels. Early advertising showed a silver Zodiac against a deep blue background as the "mark of distinction," accompanied by a lethal-looking "symbol in fine silver" whose significance remained a mystery to readers. In October, however, advertisements for the Executive showed an interior that was invitingly lavish (if one liked olive green) and made a feature of real leather: "Leather is as luxurious as it looks in The Executive... In the world of The Executive, luxury can truly be taken for granted." The Executive was a success within its limited market... much more so than the earlier Zodiac Executive Mk III — but by the end of 1968 Ford knew what the public thought about the range as a whole, and bravely challenged preconceptions with the Zephyr V6 de luxe: "Don't let its size make you shrink from a test drive." In another advertisement the Zodiac's power steering was promoted in stream-of-consciousness copy by Charles Saatchi which concluded, after an exhausted motorist had extracted an unassisted car, "...then finally, you're out, and feeling just marvellous, when a little old lady in a big new Zodiac tries getting into your space, and she's spinning the steering-wheel with one finger, and for Pete's sake, she glides in in one go and you wish you were dead." It was modern, clever, and memorable.

Yet advertising could only do so much for a range which, from the outset, suffered certain handicaps. The new cars were really too large and unwieldy for British driving styles and conditions. By the time the owner of an understeering 1968 Zephyr V4 de luxe had turned the wheel through the 3.2 turns needed from *straight ahead* to full lock he would have hit whatever he was trying to avoid. Secondly, the Mk IV looked American, which was a potential disadvantage in a luxury model as traditional Britishness was still a calling card in much of middle-class business and social life. This was one reason why, as James Ensor, in a *Financial Times* publication of 1971, put it: "The market for Ford cars in Europe seemed to be artificially limited to a class of Ford buyer.... When the company produced an expensive car, offering more luxury than the rest of the range, existing Ford owners tended to think it was too expensive, while owners of other makes merely thought of it as another Ford."[76] Professional people who bought privately in the two-litre class without any work-related reason to choose a particular make generally chose a Rover or Triumph — or something smaller.

Thirdly, the Mk IV was developed inadequately and with too many visible economies owing to an over-rigorous application, for a British luxury car, of the Product Timing Plan and Red Book, which sapped engineers' enthusiasm and in cumulative small ways diminished the quality of the finished product. Fourthly, the novel independent rear suspension, with fixed-length half-shafts and semi-trailing wishbones, jacked up when lightly laden, slewing the car sideways and spinning the inside rear wheel. The Mk IV was no Corvair — but the Goodyear G8 tyres of some early cars brought out the worst in it and only in 1969 was the design substantially improved.[77]

Finally, the new engines were not as smooth or reliable as the earlier in-line four and six, and some other details were skimpily engineered. *Car* found the column-change of the Zephyr V6 "appalling." One kind of breakdown was even caused by the Mk IV's styling: the back of the engine was difficult to reach over the front of the car, so that mechanics often did not tighten rear cylinder head nuts as required during early servicing. One or both head gaskets would then fail and, in some cases, consequent overheating weakened the fibre timing wheel, which would disintegrate later without warning and destroy the engine. Yet many examples *were* reliable, and by 1970 the Mk IV was in many ways a good car for its price. According to Ensor, "Zephyr sales did recover substantially after design modifications and a switch to radial ply tyres, but continued to lag behind both Rover and Triumph."[78]

Ford's last three major designs of the decade were all successes. The Cortina Mk II of 1966–70, like its predecessor, sold just over a million in four years (1,027,869 to the Mk 1's 1,013,391) and was styled in a restrained idiom with a grille like that of the Falcon but which appealed to buyers on both sides of the Atlantic.[79] Nearly 1,100,000 British-built Escorts were sold seven years from the beginning of 1968 to December 1974, while Germany built more of its own; and the creation of Ford Europe by Henry Ford II in mid-1967, which had made the Escort a co-operative effort, also spawned the Anglo-German Capri, of which 374,700 were made in Britain. The Capri was an even greater success in Germany, traditionally a strong market for two-door medium-sized sedans and coupes, and Lincoln-Mercury dealers sold several hundred thousand in the United States, including over 113,000 in the car's peak year of 1973. British and German cars used different, indigenous, engines, although cars for the American market were hybrids, being built in Germany with engines shipped from England.

Opposite: **Ford Corsair G.T. Estate Car.** If there was one car that could be heard before it was seen, it was a rough old V4 Corsair, but the target market for this low-production special edition would not necessarily have experience of Corsairs or know people who drove them. And it was a handsome car of its type, a cut above the Cortina estate to which it was related, and better-trimmed than the average carpet salesman's hack. No secret was made of its origin: a discreet badge was fitted below the tailgate window containing the legend, "Abbott Farnham" within a crimson-enamelled shield surmounted by a representation of a coach, or berline, of horse-drawn type, the company having begun as traditional coachbuilders shortly before the First World War. Ford approached the borders of exclusivity with this model, which was a spiritual ancestor of the "lifestyle estates" of the 1990s.

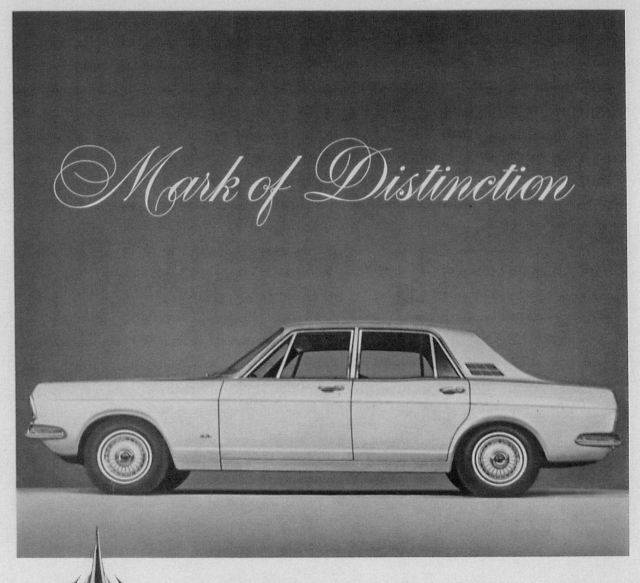

Mark of Distinction

To mark the announcement of two distinguished new cars, Zodiac and Zephyr, this symbol in fine silver was commissioned by Ford of Britain. It reflects their particular blend of dignity, craftsmanship and advanced engineering. Many features combine to lend distinction to these fine cars; some of them are listed below. But to appreciate the Zodiac and Zephyr to the full, you should examine and drive them yourself.

ZEPHYR Available in two forms: Zephyr V6 with a 2½-litre V6 engine, and Zephyr with a 2-litre V4 engine □ Both cars are equipped with: 4-wheel independent suspension □ Power assisted disc brakes on all four wheels □ Aeroflow ventilation system □ Adjustable-rake steering column □ Options include automatic transmission, or overdrive with manual gearbox on the V6 engine.

ZODIAC Further refinements and luxury features exclusive to the Zodiac: 3-litre V6 engine □ Twin head-lamps and built-in reversing lamps □ Fully reclining individual front seats with centre console and floor gear shift □ Distinctive facia with comprehensive instrumentation □ Luxurious interior appointments and upholstery.

 **ZODIAC**  *Ford* **Zephyr**

The Cortina Mk II, designed around the floorpan of the Mk 1, was introduced in October 1966 with two or four doors as a (5-bearing, 1297cc) 1300 or 1500 De Luxe, a 1500 Super and a 1500 GT. Equivalent estate cars arrived in February 1967, a twin-cam Cortina Lotus appeared in March, and in September the 1498cc engine was replaced by one of 1599cc, both it and the 1300 gaining "crossflow" cylinder heads. In October 1967 the range was joined by the 1600E, a four-door sports-luxury development of the Corsair's 2000E concept. This car, at £982 2s 1d less than £100 more expensive than the 1600GT (£890) and much cheaper than the more specialized Cortina Lotus (£1080), caught the public imagination with metallic paint, a vinyl roof, lowered and stiffened suspension and Rostyle wheels and radial ply tyres—not to mention a wooden dashboard, extra instruments, sports seats, console and steering wheel. The model was updated in 1969 with an improved gearbox and interior, and a two-door version became available in some export markets. "Our best advertisement yet," said a December 1969 headline below a photograph of a gold four-door, "So far, we haven't succeeded in producing a better advertisement for the Cortina 1600E than the 1600E itself. E, by the way, stands for Executive. But as 'Motor' magazine pointed out, it can also stand for Enthusiast or Extrovert.... Altogether it's quite a car. It would be hard for us to find a better advertisement. And just as hard for you to find a better car."

1600E sales were much greater than anticipated, and had not declined when the Mk II range was discontinued in September 1970.[80] Profitable in its own right, the 1600E boosted the image of the Mk II range and that of Ford. Some Cortina models were rare, such as the GT estate car and Crayford's convertible, of which approximately 400 were built, including perhaps 40 of the Cortina Lotus.[81] The "Savage," a 1968 Cortina fitted with a 144 bhp version of the Zodiac's 3-litre V6 engine by Race Proved Performance in Hanwell, west London, was one of several high-performance Cortinas produced in small numbers by independent specialists.[82] Ford itself aimed for a measure of individuality with production models. In a theme which would be much further developed with the Capri, the company showed a row of six identical-looking Cortinas in April 1968 and boasted, "Out of a million Ford cars, only six need be the same.... We'd like you to know we just don't churn out cars and hope somebody will buy one. We make them to order too. Take Ernie Hambleton of Peckham. He ordered a saluki bronze Zodiac with bucket seats. So we went ahead and made him one..."—no doubt with a profound sense of joy and gratitude, given the Mk IV's low sales: a particular

specification of a high-selling model was not always easy to obtain, especially during industrial action.

This copy was typical of the new realism which came to Ford advertising in 1968: a down-to-earth, man-to-man approach worked well with many mainstream buyers who distrusted pretension and found the glamour of earlier advertising unconvincing when the mud-spattered product could be seen on every street corner.[83] If some buyers found the style patronizing, as if the advertiser was trying, falsely, to be "one of us," most car buyers just compared figures and made up their minds. Some of the best headlines appeared in advertisements aimed at enthusiasts who read motoring magazines: "They appear the same but disappear differently," under a 1968 Cortina 1600 overtaking a 1967 Cortina 1500, allowed Ford to give acceleration figures, describe the new engine and conclude: "...This way you get...more poke. So put your foot down. Get one." A 1967 advertisement stressed the car's competitiveness against foreign competition: if people abroad bought Cortinas, why should Britons buy Fiats, Renaults and Volkswagens? "This is the snazzy, unusual, foreign car people are going wild about, in France, Italy.... Denmark etc, etc.... Those foreigners are a shrewd lot. They know a thing or two about motor cars. That's why they choose British Fords: 200,000 of them last year.... They don't go in for useless ironmongery like nostalgic radiator grilles. Or flashy statuettes.... They're realists. They want a car to be a car. And that's just what we give them."

In the United States the car was promoted on its British roots and often bought as a second car by people who liked British cars and wanted something individual that could be serviced locally, but who did not want anything like the wheezing utilitarian miniatures which had arrived by the boat-load during 1947–52 and 1958–60 and had mostly been scrapped by 1965. "Go window shopping," said one headline above a gold Cortina two-door with a girl wearing a quietly happy smile and a bowler hat with British flag attached. There was no conventional copy—just a computerized specification sheet with the price—$1849—at the top and a list of features with "no charge" written alongside each. Some, like "cold start equipment" (a manual choke) were not really features; others, like "fused electrical circuits" suggested thorough build but no more. But "front disc brakes," "head restraints" and "Aeroflow ventilation" were worth having, and the large doors of the two-door gave it a big-car feel.

Announcement advertising for the Escort, introduced in January 1968 with 1098cc and 1298cc engines, was a world away from Anglia copy of eight or nine years earlier. The car was shown on tarmac, beside a child's pedal car; "The new

Opposite: **Ford Zodiac Mk IV.** Built down to a price and rather hurriedly developed, the Mk IV was not as successful as its predecessors, but it did have to face stiff competition from Triumph and Rover, and from two ranges of Vauxhall sixes after 1968. It was a mystery what the "symbol in fine silver" actually symbolized, except perhaps a faint hint of the Lincoln Continental's bonnet emblem and an obscure kind of self-congratulation. A long, flat bonnet (which housed the spare wheel as well as a V6 engine), a full-width rear reflector panel and a vinyl-and-plastic-chrome interior completed the American feel. The hubcaps, oddly, proved popular, and often turned up on other cars, not all of them Fords.

NEW CORTINA ESTATE
Space to take a whole holiday of luggage! Anything, everything—except your elephant!

The New Cortina Estate was designed to give you more stow-away space, more pull-away power. And it does. But we had to draw the line at elephants. Still, when you swing open the tailgate of the New Cortina Estate you'll find all of 70.5 cubic feet of stowage space. Cortina packs away stacks of luggage, furniture, sports equipment—in fact anything you care to carry except an elephant. With the rear seat folded flat the loading platform is 76.5 inches long. Even with the rear seats in use there's still a lengthy 43.3 inches (36.2 cubic feet) to work with. As well as more space at the back, the New Cortina Estate has all the other great features of New Cortina. The De Luxe has the new 1300 cc engine with the 1500 cc engine available as an optional extra. The Super has a 1500 cc engine and exclusive interior trim for people who want power with extra comfort.

New Cortina Estate Cars have more room, more comfort, more style. In fact more of everything that makes New Cortina More Cortina!

CORTINA ESTATE CARS 

Ford Escort. The small car that isn't." The theme was the same as for the 1962 Cortina: "The new Escort might appear to be a small car. It has a price like a small car price. It parks in a small car space. It will cost you as much to run as a small car does. But otherwise, a small car the Escort isn't." Ford in Germany were convinced that the Anglia name would lose the company sales to people who remembered the American and British bombers who flew from East Anglia in the east of England during the Second World War, so in 1967 Ford Europe had abandoned the old name and adopted "Escort" from the long-forgotten estate car version of the mid-1950s Anglia 100E. The Escort's concept, however, was inspired by the success of General Motors in Britain with the Viva and in Germany with the Opel Kadett, which had easily outsold the "Cardinal" Taunus 12M.

The Escort was previewed by journalists in Morocco, and the launch itself made headlines worldwide. The models available ranged from a standard car (for fleets) *via* De Luxe, Super, GT and Twin Cam variants, the latter the first of a distinguished line of rally-winning sports Escorts which would expand in the 1970s.[84] The Escort was praised in particular for its gearbox, which had been designed in Germany and was built in Britain. The car as a whole was described by *Car* magazine in February 1968 as "better than it ought to be — and far better than you expect it to be. You may not like the name, you may not like certain aspects of the styling, but you are very quickly going to get used to both. For this will undoubtedly be a best-seller." The grille's distinctive shape (called "twin-spatula" by Ford and "dog-bone" by everybody else who stopped to look) added character. Launch advertising cost well over £100,000 and the development bill — which included large presses for one-piece body sides — exceeded £20 million, the largest yet for any European Ford. The car was carefully styled — early upmarket versions had rectangular headlights which were *less* efficient than the round lights of cheaper models — but it was not over-styled in the manner of the Consul Classic.

Estate cars arrived in March 1967, and were advertised on their practicality with a dose of the family-orientated whimsy that would sell many such cars in the 1970s and reappear with people carriers twenty years later. "The new Escort Estate has plenty of room for children. And your children's children" in May 1968 was typical. "We give you the elastic sided boot" in June 1969 was nothing if not unglamorous, although the garden furniture and plants with which the car was loaded in a series of eight "stills" suggested an affluent lifestyle — as did a large detached house behind the children in the earlier piece. The "quid" of "And all for just a few quid more than you'd pay for some family saloons…" lent the necessary down-to-earth touch, and "A big rear end is nothing to be ashamed of" added humour in April 1968. A very modern kind of almost-guilt was induced in the family man in October 1969, with the headline, "Don't you think the family ought to get out more often?" above a new four-door saloon: "We're pleased to announce there is now a 4-door Escort…just the thing for getting the family out and about." But so, by 1969, was a Capri…

The Capri was nothing if not carefully planned. The lesson taught by the Edsel was not that market research was a lost cause, but that it should be thorough, and that the resulting product should appeal to as many people as possible. People differed, of course — but the way to accommodate them was not to produce different product lines or marques, but rather to make many different versions of essentially the same car. With sporting cars, moreover, the essentials — rakish styling, a low roofline, the availability of powerful engines — were agreed upon by almost everyone. A car made by Ford could combine all of these things with untemperamental performance from existing engines and the assurance of easy servicing given by the Ford name. There was a certain kind of sports car buyer who would deliberately refuse to buy any car obviously marketed to him; he enjoyed discovering the esoteric; if the last remaining spare carburettor were found propping open the door of a bakery in Turin, he was ecstatic. But he was in a minority. The Capri would cater to the majority. Superficially daring, it was, in the final analysis, safe and unadventurous: it offered nonconformity-lite to conservative, me-too suburbia. And suburbia loved it.

The first drawings of the new car, codenamed "Colt," were completed at the end of 1964[85], following the success of the Mustang's launch earlier in the year. In 1965 Allen Barke, the joint managing director of Ford of Britain who was expected to take over as chairman from Sir Patrick Hennessy, fell ill and was replaced by an American, Stanley Gillen, "trained in Detroit and later sent to England, who was [so far as such a corporate project can be attributed to one man], responsible for [the Capri] being what it is. He wanted to offer European buyers a large-volume model embodying sporty styling and personal-car flair and yet within a practical family package; and he personally saw to it that the finished product retained this character."[86] By the end of

---

Opposite: **Ford Cortina Mk II Estate.** Family whimsy was an occasional theme in advertising for mainstream saloons and estates cars during the late 1960s and 1970s, and it suited the informal copy styles which became popular with Ford and others at the same time. It also had the advantage of being realistic: no-one *desired* an estate car as one might a sports car or coupe, but the consumer might still be persuaded to buy a Cortina rather than a Hunter or Victor. To a much greater extent than with the Mk I, copywriters aimed different versions of the Mk II at different markets while also using the car in prestige advertising to illustrate paint finishes (though without mentioning the notorious flaking metallics) and the wide choice of specifications and options. In 1968 Ford boasted that "out of a million Ford cars only six need be the same." Immediate, fault-free delivery was a different matter, but the straightforward qualities of the Mk II were missed by many when the Mk III, with its mini-Mercury looks, arrived in 1970.

KOO 632K

When it was first suggested we make 12 of these cars a day, some of us felt it was 11 too many.

It took us two long years to build the winner of the London to Mexico Rally.

Then we were asked to build 12 winners a day.

No wonder some of us at Ford's Advanced Vehicle Operations were worried.

But Ford management isn't stupid. If they thought we could turn out 12 cars virtually identical to the first Mexico, who are we to argue?

Exactly.

Each Escort Mexico has a 1600 GT engine uprated to 86 bhp at 5,500 rpm, close ratio gearbox, stiffened and lowered suspension, servo assisted brakes, 5½" J wheels with radius arms, stone deflector plate, heavy duty body, the ability to reach 60 in 10.5 seconds and 100 easily.

A Ford Rallye Sport dealer will sell you a Mexico for only £1179.

He'll also service, tune, and, at your request, run your Mexico through his diagnostic testing equipment. And he'll explain the race/rally parts and options you can have which include the Clubman Pack for competition and the Custom Pack for luxury (special seats with cloth trim, etc).

There are 66 Ford Rallye Sport dealers in Britain. One of them is yours. To get his name and address, see below.

As for those of us at AVO who didn't exactly agree with the policy of making 12 Mexicos a day, the experience has proved rewarding.

So rewarding, we're now making almost twice as many.

 **Rallye Sport**

Send your name & address freepost (no stamp needed) to Ford Motor Co. Ltd, (F2) Advanced Vehicle Operations, 24/801 Freepost, South Ockendon, Essex, RM15 1BR

1966, £20 million had been allocated for the car's development and two prototypes, called "GBX" and "Flowline"[87] had been built and were shown to the public at styling clinics in Amsterdam, Brussels, Cologne, Geneva, Hamburg, London and Milan. Stanley Gillen, encouraged by the results, authorized a new model programme based on "GBX." By the summer of 1967, prototypes very like the eventual production car were under test, but the proposed rear side window — with a backward-slanting rear edge like that of the 1971 Renault R17 — caused rear seat passengers to feel claustrophobic (as it would do in the Renault), and was altered in October 1967. In November the car was named "Capri," as Mitsubishi owned the world copyright for Colt. "Eventually Capri was chosen, despite the fact that [the] earlier Capri had been a failure. The marketing staff felt that the advertising campaign for the new car would be powerful enough to obliterate harmful connotations of the previous model."[88]

Choosing a slogan was far from simple. "There were two views within Ford as to how the Capri should be presented which could be represented in the slogans 'the sports car with space for the family' or 'the family sized car with sporting appeal'…. Another product clinic was staged with members of the public divided into three groups. One was shown the car directly and the other two after watching television commercials based on the two alternative themes. Questions afterwards showed conclusively that the 'sporty appeal' was superior to the 'family car' approach"[89], and it also revealed that the car appealed not only to young drivers, but to middle-aged family men as well. This was crucial in Europe where — as was not the case with American college students and the Mustang — few people could afford new cars until well into middle age, when they already had children. "Eventually the marketing staff sidestepped this point cunningly by tagging it, 'the car you always promised yourself', [a slogan which Walter Hayes later recalled as having been suggested by J. Walter Thompson,[90] and which] suggested a sports car without actually calling it one."[91] Such a slogan, moreover, would not goad insurance companies into rating the car prohibitively.

During 1968, 100,000 photographs for launch advertising were taken during a two-month trip to Portugal, where six cars were accompanied by public relations staff and fashion models as well as by Ford's own engineers.[92] In January 1969, journalists were introduced to the new car for the first time at a ball at the London Hilton with David Frost and world champion Graham Hill. Later, 250 of Europe's most prominent motoring journalists tried out the car in Cyprus, while Ford's major European dealers tested it in Malta. The car was introduced to the European public at the Brussels Show, and in the first week of February the Capri was launched in Britain with three weeks of advertising at a cost estimated by the *Advertising Statistical Review* at well over £200,000, which included television advertising worth at least £80,000.[93] In 1971 the Capri was described as having had "one of the heaviest advertising budgets of any European car, including the use of television commercials, at that time still a novelty in car launches. Capris were on display at every Ford showroom and at most of the major railway stations in Britain. The launch was accompanied by a plethora of special Capri products produced by manufacturers of perfumes, sunglasses, cosmetics and clothes with Ford's encouragement."[94] Although some newspapers thought the car over-exposed, Ford's own research discovered that, by the time that the campaign was over, 98 percent of British people who owned cars knew about the Capri.[95] The impact of the campaign, with advertising that used stylized, moody waterside shots in the style of Mustang and Thunderbird advertising in America, was implicitly acknowledged by the question which *Car* chose for its front cover in February 1969: "Well, is it what you've promised yourself?"

For a great many motorists, it was. *Car* magazine found the Capris much quieter and more stable than equivalent Cortinas, and noticed that the comparative difference in size between the largest and smallest projected engines for the Capri (2994cc and 1298cc, a ratio of 2.32:1) was actually greater than the equivalent difference within the Mustang range (7003cc and 3272cc, a ratio of 2.14:1) — athough the planned 2994cc model had not yet been finalized (it would appear as the 3000GT in September). In the meantime two 1599cc (1600 and 1600GT) models accompanied the 1300 and 1300GT, and a 2000GT arrived in March with the 1996cc V4. "[W]e got the impression that the Escort 1300-engined car is regarded very much as a loss leader, the £890 [7s 6d] price tag tempting us into the showroom where the salesman will try to make sure you drive out with a £1041 1600 or a £1087 V4 two-litre…. Just as in America nobody ever actually buys the basic Mustang, so Ford must be hoping that few people will take a fancy to the smallest Capri," said *Car*.[96] *Homes and Gardens* remarked of the 1600GT, "This motor, by Ford, out of Market Research, has a lovely gearbox and a heavy clutch; good brakes, and unconvincing road holding…. It is…the first British built car to adopt the American custom plan system, whereby a vehicle can be embell-

---

Opposite: **Ford Escort Mexico.** One of the oldest themes in car advertising, sporting success was used by Ford as the *raison d'être* of a model that was reassuringly conservative and mainstream in its essentials, but distinguished by a genuinely sporting image and its sale through specialist dealers. The first Escort of 1955 had been utilitarian estate car, but Ford revived the name when replacing the Anglia in 1968. Announced — in an echo of the Cortina Mk I's introduction six years earlier — as "the small car that isn't," the Escort was built in both Britain and Germany. This advertisement, in its use of white text on a black background, adopts a style popular for sporting cars on both sides of the Atlantic. Research had shown, however, that, other things being equal, black-on-white print was easier to read, so the simple layout and clear fonts of this piece were wisely chosen.

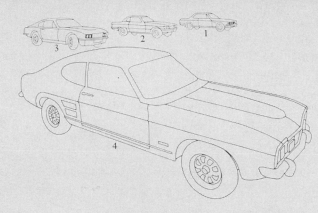

1 **BMW 3.0 CS Coupe**
  2985 cc. Top speed approx. 131 m.p.h. 0-60 in 8 seconds.   Price : £5,118

2 **Mercedes Benz 350 SL Coupe**
  3499 cc. Top speed approx. 126 m.p.h. 0-60 in 9.3 seconds.   Price : £5,601

3 **Aston Martin DBS V8**
  5340 cc. Top speed approx. 162 m.p.h. 0-60 in 6 seconds.   Price : £8,749

4 **Ford Capri 3000 E**
  2994 cc. Top speed approx. 122 m.p.h. 0-60 in 8.4 seconds.   Price : £1,721*

Performance figures from Autocar Road Tests.
*Seat belts and licence plates to your choice at extra cost.
Prices correct at time of going to press.

FORD CAPRI  ...leads the way.

ished…by the addition of one of several packages offered by the manufacturer."[97] With "X" ("major interior kit"), "L" (exterior embellishment) and "R" packages, (the latter being sports equipment for GT models only) that could be fitted individually or in combination, 26 basic derivatives of the car were available when it was launched.[98] A Capri Mk II arrived in 1974, a Mk III in 1978, and the last Capri—number 1,886,647—was produced as late as December, 1986. In its final year the car was built in Cologne exclusively in right hand drive, and sold only in Britain. The advertising, combined with the economies of scale allowed by shared componentry that secured the car's profitability, had worked.

There was one Ford, however, for which the advertising almost certainly gained the model no extra sales whatever while nevertheless being a resounding image-builder for the brand. Only 31 roadgoing examples were built, individually, during 1966–68. "Would you let your daughter marry a Ford owner?" asked the caption to a double-page photograph showing a blood-red car parked at the kerb. "The Ford GT 40. £7540. 0–60 mph: 6 secs. 1st gear: 58 mph. Top gear: 164 mph. Boot space: laughable. Petrol consumption: wicked. If you're a bit worried about your future son-in-law just ponder over the trade-in value: 5 Escorts, plus 3 Cortina Estates, plus a Corsair 2000. You could become the first 9 car family in your road."[99]

Opposite: **Ford Capri 3000E.** The "car you always promised yourself," launched in February 1969 with a three-week press and television advertising campaign at a cost of over £200,000, brought Mustang-type marketing methods, as well as Mustang style, to the British market. So many combinations of options were possible that even the factory got confused: two of a set of four test cars supplied to *Motoring Which?* had the wrong gearboxes fitted, one of them with a missing bolt which had allowed the oil to run out! This advertisement for a luxury V6 model is interesting not only for the disappearance of the famous slogan (it later reappeared as "more than ever the car you promised yourself") but also for the comparison with named contemporaries. Triumph, promoting the Stag two years later, used a similar trick with a country house of a different period and Citroën SM, Mercedes saloon and Porsche 911 "rivals."

3

Hillman

"A better buy because it's better built!"

Between 1927 and 1928, the Rootes Group, an expanding car sales business founded by the brothers William (Billy) and Reginald Rootes in 1918, gained control of Hillman and Humber, two Coventry car makers with adjacent factories who each produced fewer than 5000 cars a year.[1] Both were originally bicycle manufacturers, and had their origins in the great expansion of leisure cycling which took place during the last three decades of the nineteenth century. Thomas Humber issued his first bicycle catalogue in 1873, produced Léon Bollée three-wheelers under licence in 1896, and began production of Humber cars in 1901. Later that year he recruited as chief engineer the French car designer Louis Coatalen, who had previously worked for Panhard, Clement and De Dion-Bouton successively. In 1907 Coatalen arranged to join Hillman, who diversified from bicycle manufacture into car production by forming the Hillman-Coatalen Motor Co. Ltd. Humber, meanwhile, went on to become a respected manufacturer of well-built, conservative, middle-class cars. Had Rootes not intervened, however, both Hillman and Humber would almost certainly have been put out of business by the depression which began in 1929.

The Rootes family began with bicycles, too. When the brothers were born (William in 1894, Reginald in 1896) their father was running a cycle shop in Hawkhurst, Kent. He later set up a motor agency which, by 1914, sold cars of many makes including Humber, Singer and Sunbeam. Leaving his private school at the age of 15 in 1909, William went to Coventry to join Singer, who had begun making bicycles in 1876 and cars in 1904. In 1913, however, enthused by the car business and convinced of its potential, he returned to Kent to run a branch of his father's business in Maidstone. In

1917, with capital from their father, Billy and Reginald Rootes started their own Maidstone company, called Rootes Ltd., which grew rapidly. The Rootes Group owed much of its subsequent success to the complementarity of the two Rootes brothers: "I am the [innovating and sales-orientated] engine and Reginald is the [administrative] steering and brakes of the business," said Billy, famously.[2] In 1919, Billy Rootes made his first trip to the United States, and throughout the 1920s took a great interest in the ways in which American automobile manufacturers made and sold their cars. Impressed by Alfred Sloan's organization of General Motors, and having gained control of Hillman and Humber, he wondered whether the Rootes Group might become a similar organization in England.

The dream came closer to reality when, in 1934, Sunbeam-Talbot-Darracq, a company based in France which made Talbots (profitably) in London and Sunbeams (unprofitably) in Wolverhampton, went into receivership. The Rootes Group bought Clement Talbot Ltd. from the receiver in January 1935, and in July the Group also bought Sunbeam, despite bids from the Coventry machine-tool producer Alfred Herbert Ltd. and from S.S. Cars—makers of S.S. Jaguars—who until a very late stage had expected to take over the concern. But Billy Rootes did not intend to continue producing Talbots and Sunbeams as they had been developed hitherto; what he needed was the marque names, and their acquisition allowed the creation of the entirely synthetic Sunbeam-Talbot marque in 1938. As Rootes historian Graham Robson recalls, "It was a very real surprise to learn that all future products from [the Talbot factory in London] were to be called Sunbeam-Talbot and even more so to discover that there was very little Talbot and no Sunbeam heritage in the new cars!"[3] With the exception of some export cars, there were no "pure" Sunbeams until the first Alpine, based on the 1948–54 Sunbeam-Talbot 90, was announced in 1953, and Sunbeam-Talbot continued as a marque name for the 1948-style saloons until the last of them, called the Sunbeam Mk III, was launched in 1954. The name of Sunbeam-Talbot Ltd. continued to appear in small print at the bottom of advertisements until 1962–63. Finally, in January 1956 the Rootes Group took over Singer, whose dependable but stolid 1948 SM1500 saloon, though initially a brisk seller and favoured by provincial taxi drivers and some police forces, had not proved attractive to buyers in the longer term.

Whilst BMC's model ranges contained many marques and models that competed with each other, the marques of the Rootes Group were complementary, and their advertising styles could therefore overlap without undermining each other. Humbers were luxurious, Hillmans were reliable cars for families and Sunbeams were sporting. Under Rootes, the Singer marque, potentially the weakest, was always— and only— an upmarket Hillman. And from 1945 until 1963 the Hillman was always (and only) a Minx or Minx derivative such as a Husky, Californian, Estate Car or Super Minx. Throughout the post-war period until the early 1960s, Rootes' advertising for Hillman and Humber, occasionally interspersed with full-range prestige advertisements for the Group itself, could be mistaken for no other. All were under Basil Butler Co. from 1946 until early 1962. Singer's advertising, under S.D. Toon and Heath from late 1954 to mid-1961 and subsequently under Erwin Wasey, Ruthrauff and Ryan (and its successors), retained a Rootes look, as did publicity for Sunbeam by the same agency, who had taken on Sunbeam advertising in 1953 and kept it until 1967 or 1968. The name of the Rootes Group was always displayed prominently in advertising for all of its marques.

The Group's great period of overt badge engineering began in 1955. Variants of the same, Loewy-styled car would be produced as the Sunbeam Rapier from 1955 and as the Hillman Minx and Singer Gazelle from 1956, with all three lasting until 1967. The Hillman Super Minx (1961–67) spawned a parallel Singer Vogue and the more extensively redesigned Humber Sceptre of 1963 which, until a very late stage, was planned as a Sunbeam Rapier. The Hillman Imp was produced under the Singer (Chamois and Chamois Sport) and Sunbeam (Stiletto) marque names, while the Hillman Hunter (1966–79) and its less lavishly trimmed Minx derivative (1967–70) were joined by a new Singer Vogue (1966–70) and Gazelle (1967–70) before the Singer marque was abandoned entirely in 1970. The last few Vogues were badged as Sunbeams. The small station wagon version of the Hillman Minx, called the Husky (1958–65), lent its floorpan to the Sunbeam Alpine sports car, and there was much sharing of engines and other components throughout the Group. All production Humbers, Singers, Sunbeams,

and Hillmans except the Imp and its derivatives of 1963–76, would be mechanically conventional.

A consequence of the Group's early history was that, from the 1930s onwards, Hillmans were designed by a company whose origins and founding orientation were not in engineering or in the processes of mass-production, but in sales. Hillmans were never the cheapest cars of their kind, but were sold on comfort, build quality, features, attractive extras and a keen but respectable fashionability. Hillman buyers paid a little bit extra and received a little extra solidity and style. It was a sound strategy for a company whose production levels could not compete with those of BMC or Ford, but which was ahead of Vauxhall before 1960 and comparable with that manufacturer until the mid-1960s.

In 1931, for the Group's first new design, Rootes planned one of Britain's first modern car launches. The medium-sized Hillman Wizard was developed with a choice of engines of approximately 16hp and 21hp for the home and export markets respectively, and with knowledge, provided by Edward Budd of the Edward G. Budd Manufacturing Company in Philadelphia, of some of the latest American developments in closed body construction. Budd's company already had a controlling interest in the Pressed Steel Company at Cowley, which it created in 1925 with William Morris and supportive merchant bankers, and which, once William Morris withdrew his interest in 1930, could secure sufficient work from Morris's competitors to be profitable. Pressed Steel would provide bodies for the Wizard and Minx. To prepare for the Wizard's launch, Hillman's sales manager met the marque's British dealers and gave each of them full details not of the car itself, but of the launch campaign and their own expected roles in it. Dealers would pay most of the local launch costs themselves and were given an illustrated "campaign book" which included a requisition form with which to order sales materials on the spot. A work plan gave day-by-day instructions about mundane arrangements such as "April 18 (Saturday)— Set up Window Display (1st stage) No banners. Supply of handbills will arrive. "Teaser" Press advertisements (2nd day)." The dealers dutifully ordered 1,182,335 folders and leaflets, 530,735 direct mail pieces and 2,112 stereos of press advertisements for local advertising. About 250,000 people were canvassed by direct mail, slides were dispatched for use in local cinemas,[4] and Dudley Noble, Harold Pemberton and George Bedford (named "technician" rather than "mechanic" to preclude any suggestion of unreliability) drove a car to North Africa in a trip that would be serialized in the *Daily Express* once the car had been announced in May. Simultaneous campaigns were arranged by dealers in export markets, and Reginald Rootes personally supervised the South American launch at the British Exhibition in Buenos Aires, which was opened by the Prince of Wales.[5] On April 27, the Wizard was revealed at the Albert Hall in London. Over 1000 people ate lunch to a table plan devised by Billy Rootes so that, as far as possible, people with common interests sat next to each other. Popular tunes were played on the Hall's organ, a twenty-minute film of the car's North African adventure was shown, and the guests "consumed 278 bottles of champagne, 199 bottles of hock, 104 bottles of sherry and 30 bottles of spirits, and smoked a total of 2000 cigarettes and 2000 cigars.... One [guest] was seen with a bottle of champagne which exploded in his pocket...."[6]

At first the campaign seemed to work, but in due course the Wizard was revealed to be a slow and unremarkable car by comparison with rivals, and it was a flop, particularly on the British home market. It was nothing if not hyped, as in a catalogue quoted by Graham Robson: "The voice of the modern world can be heard on all sides calling out for still finer achievements at the hands of man—the strivings of the modern world towards still greater beauty, towards still greater comfort and luxury in living—can be seen in all these great works of iron and steel."[7] Surprisingly, this kind of copy survived in upper-middle-class car advertising until the early 1950s, but Rootes quickly abandoned it along with the Wizard, which even in improved form was discontinued in 1935.

Rootes would not make the same mistake again, and in October 1931 announced the 10hp Minx. It became available early in 1932 and was an immediate success. Simple in design, with an anonymous-looking saloon body by Pressed Steel that was shared with cars from several other manufacturers, it was regularly updated and gained the Group useful publicity when the Melody Minx was launched in the spring of 1934 with Britain's first standard car radio, made by Philco. In September 1948, Hillman brought new, full-width American styling across the Atlantic in the first of two series of Minx (the Mk III-VIIIA of 1948–56, and the Series I-VI of 1956–67) designed by the studios of Raymond Loewy. The 1948 design—like that of the parallel Humber Hawk Mk III—reflected the 1947 Studebakers introduced in April 1946, while its successor, announced in May 1956, looked like the 1953 Studebaker. In 1958 the Sunbeam Rapier, with fins and a mock-traditional grille added by the youthful co-creator of the future Hillman Imp, Tim Fry,[8] gained something of the look of Studebaker's (pillarless) Golden Hawk and (pillared) Silver Hawk of 1957. With the Hillman Californian of 1953, Rootes had produced Britain's first modern hardtop (the Humber Vogue of 1933 qualified in pillarless fact, although not in spirit) and small annual changes, combined with 21st and 25th anniversaries for the Minx line in 1953 and 1958 (the Series II of the latter year being called the "Jubilee Minx"), provided opportunities for publicity. The 1956 Minx design, given a new Series number annually in

its early years, was updated significantly with the Series IIIA of 1959, when it acquired small, wrapped-over tail fins; with the Series V of 1963 it adopted a modernized roofline and tail treatment. The Series V took over directly from the Series IIIC of 1961–63 as the designation "Series IV" had originally been reserved for the British-styled Super Minx before the weight and cost of that car, originally based on the regular Minx and much remodelled during its development, led it to be introduced in October 1961 as a companion model rather than replacement for the existing "Loewy" Minx line.

Not that the Super Minx escaped American influence. According to Roy Axe, who in the 1950s was the most junior of Rootes' six-man styling team under Ted White and his assistant Ted Green, and who later became chief stylist in Rootes' design department when Chrysler took over in 1967, "Billy Rootes had the ability to go to the States and pick features off their cars that could be adapted to suit his own.... In the fifties Plymouths and Chryslers developed a double headlight configuration so they decided to use those in designing the new Hillman Super Minx [and equivalent Singer and Humber] range launched in 1961.... The double headlights weren't too bad on the Humber Sceptre and Singer [Vogue], with their small central grilles, but on the proposed Super Minx it looked ridiculous.... When it was shown to Lord Rootes, he told them...that it was a pile of rubbish and that they had to change it immediately. That's how the Hillman Super Minx got those little half moon [indicator] lights and the long grille. The final re-design was done by Tom Firth...."[9]

From the beginning of November 1962 the Super Minx was assembled in Italy by Touring of Milan, who also assembled Sunbeam Alpines for sale in mainland Europe, together with a specialized coupe built with *Superleggera* Touring bodywork on a Humber Sceptre floorpan and called the Sunbeam Venezia. The Italian Super Minx was identical to the British car except for the addition of a glovebox and armrests and the use of some Italian materials in its construction, but none of these ventures was successful. Italians had little use for a car like the Super Minx and Touring closed down in 1966. Hillmans remained quintessentially British except for a version of the Imp by Zagato, who devised a style which looked almost identical to its earlier interpretation of the Mini, which had been built on a Mini Traveller floorpan and displayed at Olympia by British Zagato Ltd. in 1961. The Hillman prototype, called the Zimp, was constructed by the same company in Dorchester,[10] and Rootes examined it although they did not eventually take it up. Three Zimps were made, of which two are known to survive, as does the Zagato Mini.[11]

Opposite: **Hillman Minx Series IIIB Estate Car.** Suddenly it's 1955 again, in a momentary retreat from the exuberance of 1956–59. The elongated car, multiple typefaces and chunks of descriptive copy were all staples of the 1952–57 period as, on the car itself, were those evergreen extras of whitewall tyres, overriders and "rimbellishers." New estate cars from Ford, BMC and Vauxhall made this model, based on a mid-1950s shape, seem old-fashioned by 1960, but Rootes took advantage of an expanding market for station wagons as the decade progressed.

A town-bred car built for country-size loads!

The HILLMAN Estate Car

£605 plus p.t. £253.4.2. *Sports-type floor gear shift standard. Option of steering column shift if desired. Whitewall tyres and over-riders available as extras.*

lovelier looks
livelier performance
sturdy reliability

· · · · · · · · · · ·

You'll thrill to the elegant sweeping lines of the Hillman Estate Car ... to its eager-to-go acceleration ... lively, sustained power ... extra roominess and comfort—plus those fine qualities which have already made it famous; reliability, economy and practicability. See, try this handsome town-bred saloon which is quickly converted to take your country-size loads the moment you require it!

'Easidrive' fully automatic transmission

takes the strain out of traffic driving and gives a new thrill on the open road. Safer, smoother, simpler, less tiring. Price £88 plus purchase tax £36.13.4.

A product of **ROOTES MOTORS LIMITED**

Hillman Motor Car Company Ltd · Division of Rootes Motors Ltd · London Showrooms and Export Division: Rootes Ltd · Devonshire House · Piccadilly · London W.1

International
Style setter...

THE ISLAND OF MYKONOS (PHOTOGRAPH COURTESY GREEK NATIONAL TOURIST ORGANISATION)

The Hillman Super Minx has all the qualities this age demands. This elegant, superbly fitted car is as modern as next New Year and its air of assured sophistication guarantees head-turning from Copacabana Beach to the Cote d'Azur. Nothing's been left out of it. Built-in heater, windscreen washers, deep carpeting, wide luxurious seating—they're all there—plus speed topping 80 m.p.h. from a powerful 1·6 litre engine plus superb built-in safety, with padded facia, dished steering wheel and safety-belt anchor points. Going places? Show your paces in this superb car. Fully-automatic transmission available as an extra. **Price £585 plus p.t. £220.7.9.**

HILLMAN
SUPER MINX

5385 RW

A product of
ROOTES MOTORS LIMITED LONDON SHOWROOMS & EXPORT DIVISION · ROOTES LTD · DEVONSHIRE HOUSE · PICCADILLY · W1

Hillman Super Minx Series I. Only 20 months separate this piece from 1960's estate car, yet the style has changed completely. This is a good example of the status-through-travel school of copywriting that became popular in the early 1960s, and "assured sophistication" was one of a new breed of clichés resonant with lack of meaning. Unlike many such pieces, this advertisement shows the car and the exotic venue separately, but a studio pose and a photograph of Mykonos from the Greek National Tourist Organization were cheaper than a picture taken on location. The car was solid and well built, and its doors shut with a nice "coachbuilt" click.

THE FIELD, *June 30 1966*

so much _more_ from the start
HILLMAN
Super Minx Estate Car

so much more for the load.
The Super Minx estate car is a big one. Carries a 700 lb load. Yet is as quietly luxurious as a limousine.

so much more inside.
More luxury touches. Like reclining front seats. Thorough soundproofing. Excellent heating and ventilation. Dimmable warning lights. And lockable front quarter vents.

so much more pep.
Super Minx gives you 70 bhp from its 1725 cc engine, acceleration that's really something.

so much more for safety.
Super Minx is designed for today's crowded roads. Disc brakes at the front, big drums at the rear. Padded facia surround childproof doorlocks. Seat belt anchorages, of course.

so much more reliability.
Hillman engineering gives you a five bearing crankshaft for long engine life. A tough, thick-gauge steel body, fully painted and rustproofed. And service intervals of 6000 miles.

Get so much more for the load. See your Rootes dealer today. Recommended price: £844.18.7 inc. p.t.
Fully-automatic transmission, overdrive or whitewall tyres available at extra cost

Hillman Super Minx—so much more to rely on

 ROOTES MOTORS LIMITED

London Showrooms and Overseas Division · Devonshire House Piccadilly · London · W1

Hillman Super Minx Series IV Estate Car. On location this time, but inexpensively. Fruit-picking was a cleverly chose theme, as it lent an element of fun which was useful when selling a utility car to private buyers, while also showing that it could carry heavy loads, that it rode well enough to protect delicate produce and that it fitted into a relaxed and affluent lifestyle. The Super Minx gained a reputation for durability, and thousands were still in use in the 1970s.

From the Minx's inception in 1932 to the last of the line—a Hunter in all but name—of 1970, Hillman advertising concentrated on style and features. In the late 1950s, illustrations were glamorous, tension was created by headlines colour-keyed with the accompanying pictures and by multiple typefaces, and copy reflected American styles: "GO one better with a [1957] Hillman Minx Convertible. Revel in the sunshine, laugh at the rain with the three-position Minx Convertible. The smartest, fastest and most comfortable in its class—and so economical too! Phone your local dealer for a test run NOW!" In 1958 the "New Hillman [Minx] Estate Car!" was "the country car you can take to town!… Only Hillman gives you superb passenger comfort—with up to 700 lbs load capacity. Only the new Hillman 1494 c.c. engine leaps away with such sprightly yet thrifty vigour. Only Hillman could imbue a car with such robustness (unit construction) utter reliability and big-brake safety…new design of front end and facia panel completes a car which will shine in any company!" In 1960 a more British copy style took over, as with the Minx Series IIIB in October: "Hillman—the liveliest, most comfortable and reliable family car on the market…. Continuous development has produced the best in reliability and sheer value for money." In February 1965 the Series V was "Family showpiece. Pleasure. Safety. Beauty. Value. What more could you ask from a fine family car?" The advertisement also boasted of "New features like an all-synchromesh gearbox"—even though such a gearbox had been fitted to the Minx from September 1934, only to be dropped in 1938. But who would remember, or, if they remembered, care?[12]

The Super Minx was too expensive yet too similar to the Minx to be a real success in its own right and, unusually for Rootes, its virtues—mainly of solid durability—were too well hidden. A convertible version of 1962–64, "the family car with the fresh sporting air" at £960 15s 3d, had an exceptionally neat soft top offset by frightening body shake on rough roads, while a robust estate car, "loaded heavily in your favour" and built by Carbodies of Coventry alongside a similar version of the Singer Vogue, was later advertised, in traditional station-wagon style, as the car for "Up country" and "Down town." In 1966 (Mk IV) form, it was promoted as offering "so much more from the start" for £844 19s 7d.[13] Super Minx advertising continued to combine the theme of value for money with realistic, genteel slice-of-life photography until the saloon was discontinued until the end of 1966 and the estate car ceased production in the spring of 1967.[14]

In April 1963, *Small Car* carried a scoop: "Exclusive! First facts and pictures!" shouted the cover, which showed the first colour picture ever published of a small car that looked like a miniaturized Chevrolet Corvair—or an updated NSU Prinz. Admittedly it didn't look its best, standing in the snow, sporting a rickety-looking roof-rack and covered in mud, momentarily abandoned by a guardian answering the call of nature.[15] The car's existence had been an open secret for some time. The motoring historian Michael Sedgwick, testing a pre-release Hillman Imp at night in the winter of 1962–63, had contacted a dealer to cure a minor ailment, whereupon "a huge sheet was thrown over the car while it was still manoevring into a corner of the workshop. Though the Imp was flashed up by several NSU owners who had mistaken the shape, one also has clear memories of seeking the dimmest filling-station in the wilds of the Wiltshire Downs to top up the tank. 'Would it be Apex?' enquired the pump attendant, and this at a time when the code-name was almost as secret as the car."[16]

Originally nick-named "The Slug," the future Imp had a long gestation. It was first conceived in 1955 by Tim Fry and Mike Parkes, both in their early twenties and working in Humber's design department. It was to be "a car with four seats, as small as possible and cheaper than that of any other British manufacturer."[17] The first proposal was tiny and rotund, more bubble than car, and in 1956 was hastily sent by Rootes' directors to be restyled by the Group's styling department, whence it emerged, according to Parkes, looking "very much like the sort of horror you would imagine a typical contemporary stylist would produce."[18] The stylist was Bob Saward, who in 1958 joined Rootes from Ford as assistant to the Group's chief stylist, Ted White, who passed the Imp project to him. Interviewed in 1993, Saward willingly admitted to having been influenced by the Chevrolet Corvair: "We tried to keep the lines sharp to make the Imp look bigger than it really was and I think it did the trick…it was a nice little job to be given and I enjoyed the opportunity of carrying the design right through from the paper to the three-dimensional models. It just doesn't happen like that any more."[19]

The Imp was more sophisticated than any of the small rear-engined cars sold by Fiat, Renault, Simca, NSU, BMW, Volkswagen and Goggomobil in the late 1950s and early 1960s. Its 875cc four-cylinder, overhead-camshaft aluminium engine (with an unusually high compression ratio of 10:1) was ultimately derived from a lowly Coventry-Climax fire-pump but really much more closely related to the racing engines which the company had been developing since the early 1950s, and it was the first light-alloy engine mass-produced for a British production car. This feature, combined with an opening rear window for luggage, numerous advanced touches such as rear suspension by semi-trailing arms, together with carefully arranged controls, made the Imp enjoyable to drive as well as practical. The final decision to produce the car was made in 1960, but Fry and Parkes had known about its main potential rival for some time before the Mini went into production. "Once a month or so, they would have supper with Issigonis and Alex Moulton…. Since both pairs were sworn to secrecy by their respective employers (or, as Tim Fry put it, 'we all wanted to talk about cars but we knew we couldn't say very much!')

there was no question of discussing the finer details of the two prototype small cars…"[20] Years later, shortly before the Imp was announced, Tim Fry gave Alec Issigonis a turn at the wheel. As Fry recalled, "'Absolutely brilliant', [Issigonis] said on his return. 'But you've got it the wrong way round.' We used to have quite strong arguments, and one of Issigonis' classic remarks was that a dart had the weight up front and so went straight. My answer was that a dart wouldn't go round corners."[21] But the Mini certainly did go round corners—in the wet, more controllably than the Imp, good though the Imp was in most conditions and with correct tyre pressures. Nevertheless, at eleven feet seven inches long and just over five feet wide, on a wheelbase of 82 inches, the Imp was not strictly comparable with the Mini, and the experience it offered was quite different.

The Imp was officially launched on May 2, 1963, when the Duke of Edinburgh announced the car and at the same time opened the new plant in Linwood, to the south-west of Glasgow, where it would be built. Linwood was Scotland's only car factory, and, other things being equal, Rootes would have much preferred to build the car in an area close to its existing factories and where experienced labour was available. But there was already some industrial development in the new area, unemployment there was high, and the British government would provide almost half of the necessary investment. The Imp's production target was 150,000 cars a year. "An inspiration in light car design," crowed the first advertisements, "Rootes make motoring history with the new Hillman Imp. There's so much that's revolutionary about Imp that it's difficult to know where to begin. Logically, let's start with the engine…."—and the engine was described and illustrated in a cutaway diagram, acceleration of 0–50 in 15.5 seconds was promised, and convenience features were listed. Basic and De luxe models cost £508 1s 3d and £532 4s 7d respectively. *The Motor* managed 0–50 in 14.9 seconds with a top speed of 78.4 mph and suggested that, while some improvements could be made, the Imp "should on its present merits rise right to the first rank amongst the small cars of the world."[22]

Later advertisements—some with colour photography, others with paintings—showed a blue car speeding through snow and slush, and, as in 1963, called the car "Imp," as if it were a personal friend, rather than "the Imp"—a trick that would be used by many advertisers of small cars in decades to come. "The power behind Imp puts it way out in front," said one piece; "World-Beater!" announced another; "Designed for this modern motoring world" declaimed a third, while a fourth showed the rear window open, offering "Room for the crew and the stowaways too"—the stowaways being four suitcases, a large cuddly toy and a dog. In March 1966 close-up photographs of the more expensively trimmed Super Imp (a newcomer in 1965) displayed the interior ("Pretty Practical!"), engine ("Accent on Action!"), rear luggage space (Hold-all!") and facia ("Dishy dashboard!").

Parked beside a lake, it was a "Shore winner!" The most original advertisement used cartoons to illustrate an imaginary conversation between husband and wife. "Darling." "What?" "Can we have a second car?" "NO." "Oh please." "NO." "I WANT ONE" "Oh? What sort?" "An Imp—a lovely, lovely, lovely Hillman Imp with its super, super 875c.c. aluminium rear-engine and its quite fantastic road-holding and its money-saving economy and its estate car facilities and its gorgeous amount of room and its…" "All right I'll buy you one." "Thank you darling!" In 1967 the new Imp Californian—a coupe version with a more steeply sloping, fixed, rear window was captioned "Hallo Beautiful" with copy that signed off, optimistically, "Envious glances are standard."

Sadly, the Imp was not reliable even after early features such as an ultra-sensitive pneumatic throttle had been discarded, and only 489,830 Hillman and Singer versions, together with an estimated 20,000 Sunbeams, were built in thirteen years.[23] As Graham Robson sums up: "If the Imp had been reliable and well-built, right from the start, it might have succeeded. If it had been cheaper, it might have succeeded. If it had had front-wheel drive, it might have been a true head-to-head competitor to the Mini. If Rootes had not been forced to settle in Scotland, instead of expanding in Warwickshire, it might have worked. If Rootes had not had to borrow and invest to finance this, it might have worked. If, if, if…"[24] Occasionally the ingenious spirit of the car rubbed off on those building it: extremely rapid wear of some gear selector forks was eventually found to be caused by cooling water, in which they were supposed to be hardened, being turned off during the night shift at Linwood, "the rumour being that this had something to do with making tea…."[25] Fortunately, Hillman's next new car would be much more conventional.

"Call off the search—Here at Last! The complete family car!… New Hillman Hunter…complete in every detail. That's Hunter. Safe—for today's crowded roads. Reliable—for today's family motoring. New Hunter is made for more comfort, more economy. Made modern with the long, low, line of today. Made to be the complete family car." It was bland copy, but with the "Arrow" range, led by the Hunter, Rootes gave up major innovation. The white car with a red interior shown against a deep blue background looked like a Ford in all but name—even to the rear door line, which passed the wheelarch at an angle rather than meeting it and following its profile. As Graham Robson recalls, "Arrow was…intended to take over from every existing Minx, Super Minx, Rapier and Sceptre model. It was, in every way, a pure Rootes design, styled by Rex Fleming [under the direction of Ted White]…and virtually unaffected by Chrysler input…. By any standards this was a great and lasting success…."[26] White had styled the pre-war Sunbeam-Talbot Ten and, with his colleague at Talbot of more than 20 years, Ted Green, the post-war 80 and 90. He allowed his team

**Clever people know all the best places.
Know how to get there in style and comfort.
With real economy. 40 to 45 m.p.g.
Clever people understand engine performance.
Accelerate away with a rear-mounted engine.
Pack bags of baggage on the folding back seat.
Clever people go for economy. Go HILLMAN SUPER IMP**

Imp range recommended prices
start at £549, tax paid.

HILLMAN ★ ROOTES

LONDON SHOWROOMS AND OVERSEAS DIVISION:
DEVONSHIRE HOUSE · LONDON · W1

freedom to develop their ideas. According to Bob Saward, "Ted White used to come out of his office and give his opinion now and then but he never interfered. Viewings were organized at the various stages and the management would tell us what they did or didn't like."[27] The Hunter's style did not date rapidly and with only minor changes survived the introductions of two later Cortinas (the Mk III of 1970 and the Mk IV of 1976) and continued until 1979. The upmarket Singer (Vogue and Gazelle) and Humber (Sceptre Mk III) variants had no Ford equivalents as the Cortina 1600E had an altogether brasher appeal, and the "Arrow" floorpan was used for the Sunbeam Rapier, also styled by Rex Fleming, which was introduced in 1967. This car was notionally a rival to the Capri after 1969 but it sold in much smaller numbers and generally appealed to a rather different market. Hunter kits were built up in Iran to create the Peykan, a car that appeared in the annual guides to world cars long after the domestic model had been discontinued, and that car received an unlikely boost in 1968 when a Hunter — a much more agile car than the heavily engineered Super Minx — won the Daily Express London-Sydney Marathon.[28] Approximately 595,000 "Arrow" saloons and estate cars of all marques were built.[29]

At £837 11s 1d and with a 1725cc engine, the Hunter was not a basic car, and in January 1967 it was joined by a new Minx based on the same bodyshell. With a 1496cc engine (except in automatics and some estate cars from late 1968), and with less lavish interior and exterior trim, the £733 Minx was significantly cheaper than the Hunter. As an inexpensive edition of an existing model, it was not a direct replacement for the old Minx Series VI, and some traditionalists resented the demotion. Not that Rootes minded, for the new model, with MacPherson strut front suspension and bodywork that was straightforward to build, was a much more modern and viable proposition for the late 1960s. It was not, in fact, truly austere in the style of a basic Cortina or Vauxhall Victor, even if the influence of Ford's Aeroflow ventilation system was apparent in the fresh-air outlets at the ends of the dashboard. "New Minx is the big one!" crowed announcement copy, "Minx — world's most trusted car goes excitingly big. 35 years of Minx development bring you the new Minx. The Big one. With the crisp new international styling of the 70s." Later in 1967 a "Hillman Estate Car" was announced. The copy began with a prominent quote from *Car* magazine: "If the secret of a successful estate car lies in striking a balance between good looks and capacious accommodation, then the Hillman Estate at its astonishingly low price [£868] is the one to beat." Officially neither Hunter nor Minx, the estate car was a Minx in all but name. Ac-

cording to *Motor*, the saloon version was "one of those sound, unexciting family cars that does most things quite well and nothing particularly badly" — praise too faint to be quoted in advertising.[30]

In export markets the new car was sold by Chrysler with the 1725cc engine and called the Sunbeam Arrow, using the one Rootes marque name which did not — except briefly when the Singer marque disappeared in 1970 — appear on the car in Britain. But as a marque name Sunbeam had become well known in the United States and other export markets through the Alpine and Tiger sports cars. "New Sunbeam Arrow, from the Chrysler people: Britain's posh $2200 family car for unabashed sports car lovers. Temper the fast, sure feel of our Tiger with baby-limousine comforts — add our inimitable 5-year/50,000-mile power train warranty — what happens is pretty exotic. And practical" argued a 1967 advertisement. Much 1967 Chrysler advertising consisted of extended arguments for the Corporation's cars which were presented in long copy and illustrated with semi-technical line drawings of features such as the Arrow's MacPherson strut front suspension. Copy for the subcompact sedan emphasized its heritage as, across the Atlantic, a small car was not mere poverty transport: "Arrow could happen only in Britain — where elegance isn't measured by size, and even limousines must be a little nimble." The copy went on to emphasize commonalities between the Arrow and the $2600 Alpine sports car, such as its 1725cc engine (albeit in 73 bhp rather than 100 bhp Alpine form) and four-speed gearbox. The warranty was described in several hundred words of very small print.

In the last years of the decade, Rootes' home market advertising became more aggressive, and the fashion for grittier slices of life and dramatic photography, already apparent in rival advertising from Ford, Austin and Morris, caught up with the Minx under the Group's slogan, "The myth exploders." Copy was competitive, as in November 1968: "Myth: For the money, there are about three good alternatives to the Minx. Any reasonable person would think that if you've got, say around £850, to spend on a new car, you could look around. Go ahead. We at Rootes would be interested to see what car dealers you'd look at. Please, try to find a new car that gives you the performance and quality features the new '69 Minx gives you...." The rest of the copy listed features and mentioned the Minx de luxe whose modest £873 compared well with the basic car's £828 ("...at one time we toyed with the idea of calling it the de luxe de luxe, but that sounds stupid"). Nevertheless the Minx was dropped in 1970 as the Hunter range diversified from a simple de luxe saloon to the Hillman GT, "100 mph and very

---

Opposite: **Hillman Super Imp.** By 1966 it was clear that the Imp was never going to be a best-seller, so it was targeted towards the buyer who wanted something other than the norm. The point is made boldly, and the implication is that only the ignorant and dull will choose a conventional small car while the Imp is on offer. This Super version fitted between the Imp Deluxe (which was by now the least expensive model) and the Singer Chamois. Only two years separate this advertisement from the earlier piece (see color section), but the style could not be more different — and the deserted beach still has a few years to run as an advertising motif.

hairy," in which one page of a double-spread showed the car at the kerb while the other page illustrated the sporty equipment included, such as "Optional High-back seats," "Matt black grille" and "Twin carbs." This technique was usually left to accessory catalogues, but 1968's headline for the standard model, "Slip into something hot this summer," must have had sports car manufacturers kicking themselves.

In the long term, however, no amount of ingenuity on the part of advertisers could save the Rootes Group, or Hillman. The Group's weakness from 1964–5 onwards lay in fact that its models, being mainly Minx-derived, were too heavily concentrated in the middle of the market and too old-fashioned in their engineering. The 1592cc Hillman Super Minx, originally intended to replace the "Loewy" Minx of 1956, proved too large and expensive to take the earlier car's place. The little bit extra it offered was too little for the quite a bit extra it cost (£854 in November 1961) compared with a Vauxhall Victor Super (£781) or four-door Ford Consul Classic de Luxe (£826), neither of which was marketed or perceived as a development of an essentially smaller car. The Austin A60 Cambridge, comparable with the Super Minx by virtue of its 1622cc engine, was nearly a foot longer and if anything looked more expensively trimmed than the Hillman, yet it cost the same £854. The genius of the original Minx was that it was much better than many other small cars; considered (and priced) as a medium-sized car, it was less attractive.

By contrast, the big Humbers and the small Imps lost sales as a consequence of obsolescent engineering on the one hand and an unreliable interpretation of an outdated layout on the other. The Imp was the most sophisticated of Europe's rear-engined cars—but it was still a rear-engined car. It handled better than others of its kind but, often as the end result of industrial circumstances not of Rootes' own making, it broke down more often. The car buyer increasingly demanded a car that didn't put him in the ditch and didn't leave him stranded at home. The layout of the design that would become the Imp was modern when first mooted in 1955, but by 1963 its time had passed. Morever, whilst the characteristic styling motifs of economy, family and luxury cars generally converged in the 1960s, their engineering diverged—in particular towards front-wheel drive in small cars and independent rear suspension in luxury models. A single conventional layout could no longer be adapted upwards and downwards to cover most of the market unless it were sold inexpensively by comparison with rivals, and this, with modest production levels, Rootes could not manage. Car buyers sought designed-in engineering, and neither elegant metal and plastic trimmings nor a dealer network acknowledged to be excellent were sufficient.

In 1964, with the Rootes Group making substantial losses and the Imp selling at no more than a third of the rate hoped for, Sir Patrick Hennessy of Ford considered buying the company. He consulted Ford in America and "Dearborn's top finance man Arjay Miller and his team moved into Ford's company flat in Grosvenor House in Park Lane. At first, their analysis seemed favourable to the deal. But the night before Henry Ford II was to meet Lord [Billy] Rootes and conclude the deal, Miller realized that buying Rootes, with its poor management and huge overdraft, would be a risky decision…. While Ford was shaving, Miller convinced him to call off the deal."[31] In June 1964, Chrysler bought 30 percent of the voting and 50 percent of the non-voting capital in what had previously been an entirely British-owned business, three Chrysler directors joined the board, and Lord Rootes retired.[32] The Chrysler "pentastar," though not the Chrysler name, appeared with the Rootes name at the bottom of advertisements, as in all of the company's literature, from September 1965. Pentastars were also attached to all of the company's cars.

In March 1967, Chrysler gained complete control of the Rootes Group and Sir Reginald Rootes, now 70, also retired, although members of the family remained on the board. The pentastar was made the centrepiece of some advertisements, as in a double-page spread of October 1967: "This is the star of something big. This is the pentastar. The sign of Rootes new deal. You'll see it on every Rootes car. It means new deal cars, new deal style, new deal everything. Follow the star to Rootes big new deal. Stand 121 at the Motor Show." On the facing page, various Rootes cars were photographed in dramatic poses with their pentastars seen close-up. Nevertheless, Chrysler under-estimated the time taken to build up brand identity. "The pentastar campaign was well planned and orchestrated throughout all the Chrysler companies in Europe and did make a lot of sense. The Chrysler name didn't mean much in Europe at that time and there were very few Chrysler cars or Dodge trucks being sold there…. It was, however, difficult for Chrysler executives to accept that a company and cars which were so well known in America and Canada should still mean so little in Europe, compared with names like Humber, Hillman, Sunbeam, Singer, Simca, Commer, Karrier and, of course, Rootes."[33] As John Bullock, Rootes' public relations chief in the 1950s, recalled, General Motors had retained the established Vauxhall name "and even Ford took some time to become established in Europe."[34] Meanwhile the Minx model name was dropped for the basic "Arrow" saloon in 1970, while the Hillman marque name continued until 1977, when the Hunter was rebadged as a Chrysler.[35] The Avenger of 1969 (sold in the United States as the Plymouth Cricket) was a good car embodying many of the virtues of the rival Ford Escort and Vauxhall Viva, but the last car of exclusively Rootes conception—an Imp—left the production line in the summer of 1976. In 1978 Chrysler, after heavy losses, sold its European car-making facilities to Peugeot.

4

Morris

"People feel strong about Morris"

By the 1960s the Morris name was known, above all, for the Minor. The millionth Morris Minor was built on December 22, 1960, and production had been arranged so that this car would be the last of 350 copies of a special "Minor 1,000,000" edition, painted lilac and trimmed in white leather. If the colour looked revolting to most British motorists, it was nevertheless distinctive and—importantly—light enough to photograph well for publicity photographs in newspapers and magazines. A few of the special cars were exported, mainly to North America, but the 318 which remained in Britain were dispatched to dealers for a New Year publicity campaign. As Morris Minor historian Ray Newell recalled in 1986, "Much was made of this great British 'first' in the national and motoring press. Aided by a cleverly produced booklet issued by the Central Publicity Department of the Nuffield Organization entitled *A Million Morris Minors*, the journalists were able to extol the virtues of the cars and put into historical perspective the exact nature of the achievement…. [I]n a shrewd move to ensure protracted coverage, BMC donated the millionth car to the National Union of Journalists for use in its charitable fundraising activities. Alec Issigonis…represented the company at the presentation…staged early in January 1961."[1] Advertisements headed "One in a Million…Britain's most successful car…" showed the regular Minor speeding along and invited readers to "discover exactly why the 'Minor' is Britain's most successful car—a brilliant 'classic' of modern motoring." 1961's celebrations represented a high point for the Minor, for although its engine was enlarged to 1098cc in 1962, at last giving the car an adequate top speed of 75 mph and acceleration of 0–60 in just under 25 seconds, it was rarely advertised or promoted after 1965. Anyone who wanted a

Minor knew where it could be bought, and those who did not want one would not be persuaded by advertising; its good and bad points were too well known. This was particularly true of the Traveller, which throughout its lifetime was rarely advertised as an individual model, if at all. After the first million, a further 293,331 Minors were made before production ended in 1971.[2]

The Minor had been in production since 1948, and, as in 1962–63 with the 1100, BMC used its engineers and designers in publicity which had strong patriotic overtones, and which contributed to the Minor's being one of the few cars actively liked by the public at large as well as by the ten per cent of the population who were motorists. Affection for the Minor, moreover, was not confined to the British, as 48 percent of all Minors built to the end of 1960 had been exported.[3] Nevertheless, few predicted in 1961 that the model would continue for another decade, with the last saloon being made in November 1970, the last convertible in June 1969, the last Traveller—a two-door "woodie" inspired by the American station wagons of the early 1950s—in April 1971 and the last light commercial derivative in February 1972.

The Minor's creator, Alec Issigonis, always acknowledged the car's style to be the product of what he called his "American phase." He was particularly proud of the way in which the front wings blended into the doors in a style which combined styling motifs from the 1942 Packard Clipper and 1942 Oldsmobile. Issigonis openly admired the Packard and its influence was most directly apparent in a prototype for the Wolseley 6/80 (1948–54) which Wolseley's chief stylist, Charles van Eugen, adapted from a proposed six-cylinder, 2215cc Morris called the Six (series MS).[4] The Six was one

Autocar, July 31, 1964

Case proven!

1,250,000 OWNERS SAY IT'S
BRITAIN'S BEST
MORRIS
MINOR 1000
From £515·6·3 Tax Paid · 12 Months' Warranty & backed by BMC Service
MORRIS MOTORS LIMITED, (SALES DIVISION), LONGBRIDGE, BIRMINGHAM, OVERSEAS BUSINESS NUFFIELD EXPORTS LIMITED, OXFORD AND AT 41-46 PICCADILLY, LONDON

SERIES 1000 MORRIS QUALITY ON EVERY CAR

BMC

Morris Minor 1000. By 1964, the Minor's case *was* proven: the millionth had been made in 1961. In its later years, the Minor established a middle-class niche, which perhaps explains this rather esoteric theme. The car was not as heavily advertised in the 1960s as it had been ten years earlier, and was largely left to sell itself at the end of the decade. This four-door is shown outside the Royal Courts of Justice on the Strand; more than 30 years later a similar car, rather decrepit, was often to be found parked a few yards away, in Chancery Lane.

of two medium-sized Morrises, developed from the Minor's overall layout and style, which were introduced with the Minor at the Earls Court Motor Show in London in October 1948. The shorter of the two, with a 1476cc sidevalve "four," was called the Oxford (series MO). These additional models shared bodywork behind the windscreen with each other, although not with the Minor, which was much smaller than either. The Six continued until March 1953 and, after an interval, was replaced in July 1955 by the Isis, which was a long-fronted, six-cylinder version of the Oxford Series II which took over from the Oxford MO in 1954. The Oxford Series II was updated in 1956 to become the Series III[5]

Country Fair, January 1960

Together...

and enjoying life in a

"QUALITY FIRST"

MORRIS

MORRIS OXFORD. Prices from £575 (plus £240.14.2 P.T.)
MORRIS MINOR 1000. Prices from £416 (plus £174.9.2 P.T.)
MORRIS MINI-MINOR. Prices from £350 (plus £146.19.2 P.T.)

MORRIS MOTORS LTD., COWLEY, OXFORD.
Overseas Business: NUFFIELD EXPORTS LTD., OXFORD *and at 41-46 Piccadilly, London, W.1*

When the car starts, baby won't wake! The Oxford's engine speaks in a whisper. Resilient seating cradles you in comfort. Wonderful suspension smooths out the road.

A beautifully behaved car, this handsome Oxford—with the sort of acceleration and performance you'll boast about one day to that youngster in the carri-cot!

Long, low lines / gay colours and duotones / full family comfort / brilliant 1500cc. OHV engine / over 70 m.p.h. and up to 35 m.p.g. / panoramic vision / child-proof locks / and, in everything, Morris Quality First. Twelve Months' Warranty, and backed by B.M.C. Service—the most comprehensive in Europe

9/211

4

Morris Oxford Series V. The rear of the average post-war British car presented a problem for advertisers. It might be sturdy, capacious or tasteful, but it was rarely interesting. This was especially true of the 1954 Oxford Series II, and, although that car had been squared up with embryonic fins and some quirky, delicate detailing as the Series III from 1956, only when real fins arrived with Pinin Farina styling in March 1959 could an Oxford rump be displayed proudly. The car became known by its admirers as the "cathedral tail-light" model, for obvious reasons. Children featured prominently in BMC advertising at this time—less often in illustrations from Ford, Vauxhall and Rootes—and, as a marque theme which was carried over to catalogues, togetherness included couples in Minors as well as families in Oxfords. The theme has been revived in advertising for modern people carriers.

The Hammonds
buy an Estate car—

Hurry, hurry—so the Head of the House of Hammond doesn't miss the 8.16 to town. Stop, start—stop, start—so his Good Lady can do her shopping quickly and comfortably. Their sumptuous new estate car has been a member of the Hammond family only a fortnight, but already they can't imagine how they ever managed without it. And where did they find the money to pay for it? They came to us at UDT. Now they pay for their new acquisition little by little, month by month—and make very good use of it in the meantime.

and make it work hard for its keep

UDT helps people to help themselves

UNITED DOMINIONS TRUST LIMITED · UNITED DOMINIONS HOUSE · EASTCHEAP · LONDON EC3   ASSETS EXCEED £174,000,000

Morris Oxford Series V Traveller (UDT). William Morris initiated his company's association with UDT in 1924, so that would-be motorists would not be denied the pleasures of motoring for want of the last few pounds of a Cowley's purchase price. By 1960, more car buyers than ever were buying on credit as new car ownership, no longer confined to the upper-middle classes, spread rapidly. People with modest means who had previously survived with elderly pre-war wrecks, newly forced off the road by the Ministry of Transport's roadworthiness test, at last bought post-war second-hand, and then new vehicles. This is a very early "Farina" Traveller, based on the Series V Oxford saloon and, like its Series VI successor, fitted with Cambridge rather than Oxford tail-lights. The split tailgate looks more convenient here than it was, as the heavy bottom half had to be unlatched to close the window, which it then clamped shut. The car sold steadily in updated Series VI form for much of the decade.

and was supplemented by an all-steel (Series IV) station wagon in 1957. In 1959 the Series III was replaced by the Oxford Series V saloon, a derivative of Pinin Farina's Austin A55 Mk II Cambridge, while in April 1960 the Series IV made way for a Traveller station wagon version of the new Series V, with which Series designations for saloon and Traveller converged once again. The Series Vs were updated to become the Series VI saloon and Traveller in October 1961 and these models survived until April 1971 and February 1969 respectively. Neither was directly replaced.

Thus what began in 1948 as a coherent three-car model range had diverged by mid-1959 into two ranges—the Minor and the Oxfords—that were visually as well as physically distinct, with only the Minor retaining its 1948 style, mildly updated. During 1959–66, the Morris line further diversified into established rear-wheel-drive models (the Minor and

Oxfords) and Morris versions of BMC's new front-wheel-drive models (the Mini, 1100 and 1800). This made the maintenance of a strong marque identity difficult, and although Morris's "Quality First" slogan survived long enough, in a low-key form, to appear in small print in early brochures for the 1100 and as a "Morris Quality" stamp on some subsequent advertisements in 1963 and 1964, newcomers from the Mini onwards were advertised mainly by emphasizing their technical features. Brand identity was retained by prominent use of the Morris name and—especially in the first and last years of the decade—by a distinctively Morris look to the marque's campaigns. The down-to-earth "People feel strong about Morris" series of 1968 was distinctive and very different from Austin's advertising for essentially the same cars.

By 1960 the Minor, famed in the 1950s for the road-

Country Fair, September 1959

Country Fair, April 1960

Morris Mini-Minor. Contrasting approaches for the Morris-badged version of BMC's new wonder-car. At a time when other BMC marques had adopted photography and simple layouts, it was surprising to find the forward-looking Mini initially promoted with the kind of multiple typefaces and elongated illustration that characterized the mid-1950s—particularly as that illustration denied the reader (to whom the car, being new, was not yet familiar) an answer to his most obvious question, "How viable is it really as a four-seater?" The answer was given in the later piece, which integrated the Mini-Minor into Morris's marque-wide "Together..." campaign which had been running since 1958. To create English-language export advertising, the makers changed "Morris Mini-Minor" to "Morris 850," omitted the price, substituted an export address, removed the tax disc and relocated the steering wheel—for the first advertisement by repainting it and in the second by reversing the photograph.

ability given by its rack and pinion steering and torsion-bar front suspension, was becoming outdated. Its handling was still excellent in the sense that the car was easy to control and light to operate, but its ride was hard and its roadholding no longer outstanding. "Frankly, Nuffield's one-time world beater is starting to fray at the seams," said *Small Car* in 1963, "It must delight Alec [Issigonis] to reflect that because his brainchild was so darned good the average enthusiast will still defend it hotly as having wonderful roadholding and some of the finest steering in the game.... It can still show a lot of rivals where to get off when it comes to holding a line through main road corners...but in ultimate stickability the little car has many rivals and not a few superiors. We even know one guy who can guarantee to spin his at a certain corner every time he gets drunk, *and* pull up within a specified distance of the wall...."[6]

Yet until the Ford Anglia 105E and Triumph Herald arrived in 1959, the Minor range, costing from £590 9s 2d to £696 14s 2d in April 1959, was still directly competitive with external rivals from Ford (Anglia 100E) and Standard-Triumph (Eight and Ten) and with the Austin A35, whose engine it shared. It was also well on the way to becoming a unique institution. "Now it's a big car.... Now it's not!" said a February 1958 advertisement showing the car speeding along in one picture and refuelling in another. "Here, without question, is world supremacy in small car performance. With an amazing economy of fuel and upkeep, the 'Minor 1000' travels four in style and comfort, daylong, as easily as you please...the world's biggest small car buy and one of the all-time 'greats' in motoring."

In 1954, *McCalls* magazine coined the phrase "Togetherness" to describe an ideal of family and domestic life which complemented the injunctions of Dr. Benjamin Spock, whose *Baby and Child Care*, published in America in 1947, reached Britain in 1955. In 1958, Morris adopted the "Togetherness" theme for a marque-wide "Together you'll choose a Morris" campaign. It worked well with the Minor, stilted dialogue notwithstanding. One piece showed a married couple examining a brochure: "I say, that's getaway — 0–60 in 28 secs!," said the husband. "My gracious, how spacious — room for all of us!," replied his wife. "In the hands of a good driver the Morris 1000 can hold its own with cars of far bigger engine capacity. Its economy is almost a legend and its roominess is a boon to wriggling youngsters and expanding elders alike!" added *The Autocar*, in a quote from a 1956 road test at the bottom of the page. In April 1959 the smiling faces of the archetypal nuclear family of the period were shown around copy headlined "The gilt-edged security of family motoring" while another advertisement declared the car "almost as good as money in the bank!" Children were banished from the next in the series, which showed a painting of a young couple embracing with happiness at their decision, while photography arrived in 1960 with the modified slogan, "Together and enjoying life in a 'Quality

First' Morris." Affluence was implied in the picture, in which the people, younger than those of previous years, did not yet have children: "When 'Minor' owners meet there's a mutual admiration society in session — with the Minor 1000 as the star!... Why not join in? The world's happiest motorists are carried unanimously...in the Minor 1000."

Slightly older couples appeared with the £815 14s 2d Oxford Series V in 1959,[7] he with a look of shrewd satisfaction, she gazing up at him admiringly above the headline, "Who says dreams never come true!" The car was seen in side view with small drawings of the interior and boot, and with copy consisting of a list of starred features such as "Fashion-plate colours and duotones," "Big-muscled performance...with economy" and "holiday-size luggage trunk." This "trunk"—which in real life Britons always called a boot — became a feature of Oxford advertising. It allowed the car to be photographed from behind to display its fins without a copywriter's actually having to say "Look — fins!" and risk ridicule. "Trunks like this don't grow on trees!" began a December 1959 advertisement, showing a car in cream with a blue roof, photographed so that it appeared slightly pink. Father loaded the Christmas tree as mother and daughter, laden with presents, looked on. The following year Morris declared, "Christmas holidays are fun together in a Morris Oxford" as Dad — and the car — received the full force of expertly aimed snowballs. BMC, Ford and Standard-Triumph all produced highly attractive Christmas advertisements during 1958–64, and the theme had been a tradition in Morris advertising since the mid-1950s, when an Oxford Series II had been revealed within a garage marked, "Not to be opened until Christmas day — Dad." Such advertising promoted individual models and the values of the marque as a whole —family values, in Morris's case. In November 1961, a white Mini-Minor stood in snow against an idealized winter skyline of deep blue with white branches in the foreground. "Open on Christmas day" read a sign on a fence-post, and behind it two children clambered into the new car.

In 1959's announcement advertising the Mini-Minor was promoted as "Wizardry on wheels!," and, compared with its contemporaries, it was astonishingly advanced for such a cheap car. 70 mph and up to 50 mpg were claimed, although 38–40mpg was a more realistic expectation in normal use. "Revolutionary" features included "'power-pack' engine unit contain[ing] steering, gearbox and differential!" and "4-wheel independent suspension mak[ing] all roads seem smooth!" In the shorter version of the advertisement used for small magazines, front-wheel drive was, curiously, not mentioned, although the alert reader could deduce it from the car's other features and from a small plan of the car showing the engine and people inside. Copywriters might have thought that front-wheel drive lacked novelty on its own account while also carrying associations of unreliability and difficult steering. Some traditional Morris buyers did at first think it "newfangled," and the Mini-Minor's sales (and those of the equivalent Austin Se7en) took time to gather pace, but many of the Mini's other features were so new that traditionalists had not heard of them and, therefore, had no relevant prior opinions.

In Australia, where the Mini was released in 1961 only as a Morris, the word "Mini" was thought to suggest "tiny" in an unflattering way and carry connotations of cheapness, so the car was marketed there as the Morris 850. Advertising manager Ian Milbank devised ingenious announcement advertising, published on March 23, 1961, which consisted of an almost blank page containing a very small births notice in the middle. Headlines highlighted the transverse layout and emphasized the car's novelty: "Which way is an engine? Incredible new Morris 850!" The car's cheerful and "cute" personality was recognized in Australia before BMC in England realized how much these characteristics appealed to domestic motorists, too. British Mini advertising made the most of them in the 1970s.[8]

As a package, the Mini[9] was unique; of "proper" four-wheeled cars, only the cruder, rear-engined Fiat 500 (1957–75) was smaller, and the Mini offered much greater space for passengers and luggage within only slightly greater overall dimensions. Taken individually, surprisingly few of the Mini's features were absolutely novel. The engine was an 848cc version of the "A" Series fitted to the Austin A35; front-wheel drive had been seen on numerous cars in the 1930s and most famously on the Citroën Light Fifteen (as the *Traction Avant* was known in Slough-assembled form to British motorists); independent suspensions (albeit all of them very different from the Mini's, some dangerously crude, and most *via* swing axles at the rear) were a staple of pre-war German and Czechoslovakian thinking; and even the gearbox under the engine had been anticipated in a little-known design of 1950 whose originator had sent details to many manufacturers and corresponded with Alec Issigonis in 1952 while the latter was at Alvis.[10] The rubber cone suspension was a different matter: Issigonis devised it co-operation with the inventor and rubber suspension specialist Alex Moulton, whom he had first met in 1949. The Mini was expected to have the kind of Hydrolastic suspension that arrived with the 1100 in 1962, but although the idea had been considered as early as 1949[11] and Moulton had begun work on it in 1954 while Issigonis was at Alvis, the system was not ready for the Mini's launch and was only fitted to the Mini from September 1964. It survived the introduction of the Austin Mini Mk II and Morris Mini Mk II in October 1967, but British Leyland reverted to the original rubber cone suspension to save costs when the Mini Mk III range arrived in 1969. As fitted to the Mini, Hydrolastic was not greatly superior to the original rubber cones. A great advantage of both systems was that neither intruded very much into the passenger compartment.[12]

When the Morris 1100 — a compact design at a little over twelve feet long and five feet wide — was introduced in August 1962, it was sold above all on its suspension. "The big breakthrough in suspension — Completely new Morris 1100 with Hydrolastic float on fluid suspension" announced the front cover of the catalogue. Inside, a woman was shown swimming in the sea and the secrets of "the car you always hoped would happen" were revealed in paintings which showed various parts of the suspension in different colours: subframes in green, fluid displacers in red, moving parts in indigo and interconnecting lines in pale blue. "Briefly," said the caption, "Hydrolastic suspension employs intercoupled [displacer] units which automatically control fluid displacement [between the wheels on each side of the car], preserving the balance and giving a sensationally level, controlled ride. Anti-rust and anti-freeze, the fluid [essentially a mixture of water and alcohol] is sealed into the system for the life of the car."

The principle was simple. If, say, a front wheel hit a bump, it would move upwards, forcing fluid out of its own displacer, along a pipe running down the centre of the car and into the displacer at the rear wheel, pushing that wheel downwards. The rear of the car would then rise as the front wheel rode over the bump, so that the whole car remained more or less level. If both wheels on one side hit bumps together and each displacer tried to force fluid into the other, rubber diaphragms in the displacers would be momentarily deformed by the fluid, allowing both wheels to move up into the body. When the wheels were competing to displace fluid in this way, the suspension at each wheel would be stiffer than usual. During cornering, the wheels on one side of the car were both pushed into the body, and the stiffness caused by the resistance of the diaphragms to deformation reduced roll. Thus the suspension could be designed to be usually quite soft without making the car unstable on bends. The 1100's low build and comparatively wide tracks increased its composure. The suspension units were made by Dunlop and proved reliable, and if they leaked in old age or the diaphragms sagged, the system could be pumped up by a dealer. Burst diaphragms were rare. The ride was not Citroën-smooth — as one journalist put it, "If you run over a brick, it feels as though you have run over a brick"[13] — but it eliminated much of the bucking and lurching to which conventional small cars were prone on rough roads, and it was notably smooth in normal use.

Cinema advertisements depicted the 1100 ("No metal springs, no shock absorbers, no maintenance") running over grassland and cornering at speed while longer launch films called "Austin Breakthrough" and "Morris Breakthrough" showed Austin and Morris 1100s in the hands of journalists, car enthusiasts and well-known entertainers. The films included interviews with Alec Issigonis and Alex Moulton.[14] Once the Austin 1100 had joined the Morris in 1963, BMC advertisements could feature both cars, and for the 1963 Motor Show a five-page magazine advertisement for BMC's front-wheel-drive models gave the 1100 pride of place. Unlike the first advertisements for the Mini-Minor, it made a feature of the drive arrangement: "BMC have the pull — in unsurpassed road holding, in stability on corners, in control on wet and icy roads, in handling ease and safety — with front-wheel power." The first pages showed an Austin 1100 and a Morris Mini-Minor parked in the sunshine, with small colour photographs alongside of the Mini Countryman, Mini Cooper, Wolseley Hornet, Riley Elf and the M.G. version of the 1100. The middle spread showed a red Morris 1100 in front view, speeding through the countryside, trees on either side passing in a dramatic blur. In the next spread a bare engine and front suspension assembly was seen at ground level; and if the reader looked under the engine he could just see an Austin 1100 in the distance. Shorter versions of the advertisement appeared during 1964. It was all a long way from the static "Togetherness" of 1958–60. Marque advertising specifically for Morris continued to appear occasionally: when the Mini Mk II and 1100 Mk II were introduced at the end of 1967, a dozen photographs of details of red cars were collected together against a black background with the slogan, "Look at all the news from Morris." The effect was unpretentious, yet striking.

The last new Morris of the 1960s, a version of the 1964 1800, arrived in March 1966 and differed from the Austin only in its artificial wood-grain facia, its grille and badging, and in its tail-lights, which wrapped round to the sides of the car.[15] The early 1100, despite its robust and effective suspension, had suffered high warranty costs (mainly owing to engine failures caused by under-specified gudgeon pins which shattered) and the 1800, too, had proved intermittently troublesome. But by 1966 the breed had improved slightly, with lighter steering and reduced oil consumption. In March, the last of the 1800 Mk 1s were promoted in a new Morris campaign which reflected a general trend among family car makers towards informal, down-to-earth appeals in which the advertiser was as much "one of the people" as the motorist. "My 1800 medium-sized? Come inside and say that!" said a suited businessman with a look of determination that was slightly undermined by the irrepressibly wide grin of the car's grille. "Don't size up a Morris 1800 the wrong way, from the outside. Who needs a car big outside? Inside's where you want size. And where you get it in an 1800. From £883. 0s. 8d., you'll find more space in a Morris 1800 than in many a limousine. Honestly. That's one of the reasons people feel so strong about Morris...." In May 1968 the car really matured with the introduction of the Mk II, and the existing slogan was used for the new car in September 1968: "I admit it. This car's even better than my 1800," said an amiable-looking man in slacks and a jumper. The copywriter was optimistic: "His car is a Morris 1800 Mk 1. This car is a Morris 1800 Mk II. Now a Morris man doesn't accept changes easily. He's too conscious he might lose a good thing. But the new Mk II re-

ally is an even better car...." It was, too—but it needed to be.

With the Oxford, the copywriter had a difficult task, as by May 1968 the Series VI had been in production, unchanged except in the smallest details, for nearly seven years. He tried hard. "When I changed my Oxford, I went one better. Another Oxford" said Family Man, accompanied by a family that looked distinctly bored. "When a man changes cars, he wants a change for the better. The Oxford owner buys the same car again. That's a lot more imaginative than it seems. He knows the new Oxford Series VI is powerfully different, better styled—but as economical as before and strong as ever." He didn't sound very "strong about Morris," and the car was only better styled by comparison with a 1959–61 Series V. The younger couple shown in July 1968 with an 1100 Mk II sounded more convinced. With its new, wide grille, this car did look like a new model: "'If Morris ever better my old 1100,' I said, 'I'll buy it!'"...Sold to the man in the blue sweater. A new Morris 1100 Mk II. Even better than the Mk I that he's raved about for the last three years. What's changed in the Mk II? The radiator grille, the roadwheels, the seats, the dashboard finish, the door trim, the rear lights.... What's unchanged? The things that no Morris 1100 owner would want changed. Frontwheel drive that holds the car to the road like a limpet. Hydrolastic suspension that levels out the roughest roads. And transverse engine to give more stretch-out room inside than anything in its class...." Ah—specifics! The copywriter was much happier with genuine acclaim and identifiable features than with vague assurances. His confidence in this best-selling car was palpable, and the grin of the driver was a good deal more confident, too.

By now the Morris name at the bottom of advertisements had become "British Leyland Morris" and the "People feel strong about Morris" campaign was abandoned in 1969. The 1800 Mk II nevertheless continued to be promoted on its spaciousness, an area in which it had no rival. "The fast lane minibus" was an inspired headline. The Morris 1300, now in its third year, offered "More power per pound" in September 1969, and was seen overtaking a Cortina on the road as (for the time being) in the sales charts. "We'll convince you about the Morris 1300 in 11.7 seconds" (to 50mph) was down-to-earth yet without 1968's aggression; and "Give yourself a boost. Power-drive the Morris 1300," above a man dressed head-to-toe in black and wearing gloves and dark glasses, lent a fashionable zaniness.

The final new Morris, a car with no Austin equivalent (though an MG was contemplated) arrived in 1971 with the Morris Marina. Styled by the creator of the Ford Cortina Mk II, Roy Haynes, the Marina was intended to be profitable above all else. It was never an enthusiast's car, however: "That's not a car. Anyone could make that," said Issigonis,[16] who was dismayed to find it fitted with a scarcely-modified version of his front suspension for the 1948 Minor. More than a million of the Marina and its final incarnation, the Ital of 1981–84, were made, but this success was not comparable with those of the Minor or 1100, as the new car market had expanded greatly by 1980. The Marina did not have an auspicious start. As director of quality control, Eric Lord, told historian Barney Sharratt, "I was at a pre-launch presentation of the Marina when up came an image of the car on the moors somewhere with sheep grazing in the background. That was fine but the caption read, 'Beauty with brains behind it.' I said to a fellow director, 'They're pulling our legs aren't they?' They had printed thousands of brochures with that on so I said, 'You'll have to bale those and cut out that sheep or we'll be the laughing stock of the industry.' They had to get Nuffield Press to work day and night to reprint all those catalogues."[17] The true spirit of British Leyland had arrived.

5

Reliant

"Make your family self-reliant"

"In general," said *Small Car* of the Reliant Regal 3/25 in 1964, "it's the kind of thing you would expect if you left a Ford Anglia in a field overnight with a British Railways goods trolley from Liverpool Street Station."[1] Yet the much-ridiculed Reliant three-wheeler had been produced in one form or another since 1935, when Tom Williams founded the Reliant company. Williams had worked for the bicycle designers, Raleigh, for whom he had designed the Safety Seven three-wheeler of 1933–36, and his own company's first product was a three-wheeled van. The Reliant name carried the right connotations for such a vehicle while also allowing Williams to use parts from Raleigh in which an "R" was already prominently cast. In 1937 Reliant began to use bought-in 747cc Austin Seven engines and gearboxes and in 1938, with the Seven about to go out of production, Williams bought the manufacturing rights to the engine and developed his own version of it. In 1953, Reliant began production of its first post-war three-wheeler, the Regal Mk I, in Tamworth, Staffordshire. With its Austin-based engine and an open two-seater body made from aluminium panels on an ash frame and mounted to a steel chassis, the Regal looked modern for its time and was far from crude. A hard top became optional in 1955 and remained until the advent of the fixed-roof Regal Mk V in 1959. In 1956, with the Mk III, the little car gained an appealingly bulbous fibreglass body, and the Regal continued through Mk IV (1958–59), Mk V (1959–60, with a boot at the rear) and Mk VI forms until it was replaced in 1962 by the restyled Regal 3/25, which which was fitted with a new, all-alloy, die cast 598cc engine of Reliant's own design. With the Regal 3/30 of 1967, the new engine's capacity grew to 701cc.[2]

The Reliant predated, and outlasted, all other British three-wheelers.[3] The rival Bond Minicar of 1949–66 always had a character more like that of a conventional microcar, squared up bodies of later types notwithstanding, and Bond itself was bought by Reliant in 1969, who soon discontinued the marque except for the bright orange, wedge-shaped, Reliant-based Bond Bug of 1970–75 which was designed by Tom Karen of Ogle Design. The beautifully built, rear-engined, AC Petite of 1953–58 was unusually comfortable by three-wheeler standards, and appealed both to ex-motorcyclists and to a genteel market that could in theory afford to buy a Ford Popular but which found the Ford's image and austerity repellent. For some buyers the AC was not intended even as a second car in the ordinary sense, for in 1956 it was targeted in *The Field* towards country landowners and estate managers: "AC Mk II Petite — gets you around the estate in all weathers." Only about 4000 Petites were sold, however, and it was never a serious rival to the Regal, although it was potentially very useful for people who had been disabled in wartime as it could be adapted to hand control. AC's subsequent three-wheelers were specialized invalid carriages. The Reliant grew steadily more popular over the years: 20,359 were made between 1953 and 1962, including 8478 of the 1960–1962 Mk VI, and 105,824 of the Regal 3/25 and 3/30 were produced between 1962 and 1973, when the Regal was replaced by the surprisingly elegant Robin.[4] Like Bond, Reliant also produced sports coupes. After a slow start with the original Sabre and Sabre Six of 1961–64 and Scimitar coupes of 1964–70, Reliant achieved much greater success with the Scimitar GTE of 1968–86 than Bond managed with various Equipes during 1963–70.

The arrival of the Mini in 1959 seemed to affect the sales of Reliant three-wheelers hardly at all, not least because the

Reliant appealed to an entirely different market and was perceived to be more easily serviced at home. Owners were loyal. Like its forebears, the 24.2 bhp Regal 3/25 of 1962 was to some extent aimed at value-conscious existing motorists seeking an inexpensive second car, but for the most part the 3/25 was intended for thrifty and conservative former motorcyclists who sought shelter for themselves and their young families. Although it cost as much as a cheap conventional car — £487 for a 3/25 Super in November 1965, for instance, compared with the Fiat 500D's £410 — it was not much more expensive than the smallest four-wheelers. As Reliant's managing director for 24 years, Ray Wiggin, recalls: "The typical three-wheeler buyer was a budget-minded, sensible chap who probably worked as a postman, a bus driver or similar; maybe had a couple of kids. It's true he could have bought a four-wheeled car for less money, but he knew he'd get 50mpg from the Reliant and lower overall running costs."[5] With its alloy engine, the 3/25 weighed less than 896 lb. (eight hundredweight) and so could be driven on a motorcycle licence; its annual road tax was that of a motorcycle, too. Those ex-motorcyclists who never got around to taking their driving tests became a captive market, particularly as they got older. True, some servicing operations required dexterity. *Car* found the engine "hidden away in a manner than would make an Army field-camouflage expert envious. There's an inviting flap in the top — but if you unlock it and open it you find only bits of the chassis, part of the front suspension, and the extreme front end of the engine. The rest of it has to be approached from inside the car by ripping up the carpets and removing three panels held down by four screws. These allow you to look at the engine but for most practical purposes prevent you from actually doing anything to it. You even have to remove one of the panels to check the oil level!" But old Reliant hands were familiar with the layout and newcomers, once acclimatized, did not find it daunting. Useful folk knowledge quickly built up and was readily shared; some 1960–62 advertisements even included the name and address of an owners' club.

This folk knowledge extended to the car's handling, which was surprisingly stable provided that the driver was not too large and did nothing in a hurry. In 1965, *Car* suspected that the 3/25's braking power was deliberately kept down in order to minimize incipient instability. In 1964 the same magazine (as *Small Car*) had found the brakes "frankly poor. You have to press very hard indeed for real retardation, especially at low speeds, and a heavy load makes stopping something of a problem. We hadn't the courage to try for fade, during our Regency."[6] Cornered too hard, or sharply, the 3/25 would lift its inside rear wheel, particularly in left-hand bends; in such cases the maximum possible cornering speed depended upon the weight of the driver and how he moved in his seat. With a similarly heavy passenger, the car would handle more consistently if not necessarily better, and would take longer to stop. Yet the Reliant's insurance record

was good: ex-motorcyclists retained their keen road observation and sense of balance, and could hardly become tearaways in a car that accelerated from 0–50 in 43.2 seconds. The 3/25's top speed was only 63 mph — two miles per hour faster than the earlier Regal Mk VI.[7]

For Reliant die-hards who found three wheels too alarming in the motorway age, Reliant introduced the four-wheeled Rebel in 1964. Yet although the Rebel shared the Regal's engine and essential chassis layout, doors and general demeanour, its overall economy, at around 40mpg, was not outstanding for such a slow car; it was too expensive at nearly £533 19s in 1966 without a heater; and it looked austere, suggesting an escaped prototype from a major manufacturer.[8] Rebel by name, it was the opposite by nature: in abandoning the carefree subversion of three wheels, it conformed too much to appeal to iconoclasts and reminded conventional motorists only of the kind of mainstream small car that it was not. Although produced until early 1973, it never caught on.[9]

Reliant advertising, like the car, was gimmick-free and down-to-earth. Copy concentrated on practical features and was accompanied by realistic photographs which never exaggerated the Regal's proportions. The car appealed to the kind of motorist who, when man landed on the moon, would have wondered if the astronauts had remembered to cancel the milk before going away. The Regal's main advantages over its four-wheeled competition were fuel economy — driven gently, it would give 50mpg to a conventional small car's 40 — and its low annual taxation. But it also competed with other three-wheelers, as in 1958: "With a top speed of 65 mph the Regal cruises happily at 50 mph and can travel for 50 MILES on ONE GALLON of petrol with its 4-cylinder 750-c.c. engine. With normal car transmission and synchromesh gearbox, the Regal Mk. III is the most up-to-date 3-wheeler in the country." "Most up-to-date" did not, of course, mean "most recently introduced" but rather, "most car-like," with the implication than to be car-like was to be modern. If this was not always technically true, it had a psychological authenticity: the Reliant owner went up in the world when he bought a car rather than another motorcycle. And Reliant had a point: although the motorcycle engines and transmissions commonplace in other three-wheelers were in many cases more ingenious than the Reliant's drivetrain, they were often less durable than car engines and could wear out quickly even when they did not break down.

Reliant's advertisement made the most of the optional hardtop, too, showing the passenger compartment in plan view with the top off and the whole car in a front three-quarter view with it on. In 1958 the Regal was "the small car that has everything!"; in 1959 it was "Britain's Finest 3 Wheeler" — a slogan that would continue well into the 1960s. Reliant advertisements were small and inexpensive to publish, but were placed in a wide variety of magazines and newspapers, and each contained the vital selling-points and

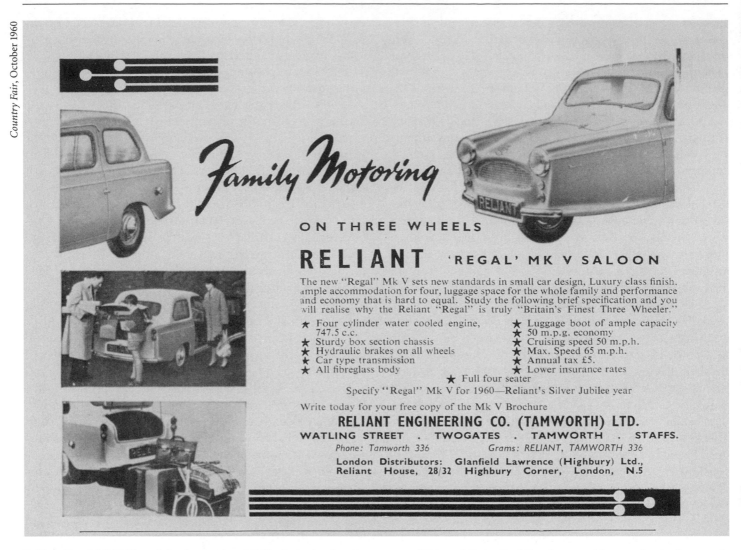

Reliant Regal Mk V. The minimal motorist of 1960 who insisted on a new car could have a Mini, a Ford Popular — or this, a modernized, squared-up version of a model first produced in 1952. The Reliant's main appeal, as a 1962 test of the final (Mk VI) incarnation put it, was "to the ex-scooterist who now has a young family to consider." The copy here is suitably functional, and two pictures are ingeniously made by cutting one in half and moving the pieces to opposite sides of the page. Somehow this summed up the spirit of the car, and in the motorway age its appeal remained specialized, demand being satisfied by steady production of a few thousand a year.

features which remained largely the same from year to year. In 1960–62, copy was accompanied by multiple photographs of the car picking up children from school or being loaded with luggage for a holiday. There was nothing glamorous about the Reliant — other bubble-cars, while they lasted, appealed more to middle-class youngsters seeking novelty — but the Reliant was the most sensible and durable of the breed.

The Reliant's second target market — that of affluent families seeking a second car — was smaller and, to some extent, notional: the idea was not that many affluent motorists would actually buy Reliants, but to make the poverty-motorist believe that his car did not instantly and unambiguously identify him as such. "Make your family self-reliant" said 1957 copy for the Regal Mk III. "Who takes your children to school? Who carries home that shopping? Your wife, no doubt, but not in your car. Give her a second

thought — buy a second car that will do 50 miles per gallon, cruise at 50 mph and yet costs only £5 per year in Tax. Very safe to drive and easy for parking. This is real motoring economy. This is the Reliant Regal Mk III." Behind the Reliant was a faintly drawn large saloon in the traditional style of a few years previously. It looked like a cross between an Armstrong Siddeley and a Wolseley, and in fact almost exactly like an early post-war Jensen Straight-Eight, although that car was so obscure that the resemblance must have been coincidental. It is possible that a subtle point was intended: that the man who would buy a Reliant as a second car would never have been able to afford a prestige model except second-hand, but this is doubtful. To use a new and identifiable luxury car would probably have provoked the wrath of its manufacturer and would have made the Regal look faintly ridiculous. Yet there was no direct correlation between wealth, social status and car choice: aristocrats and intellectuals in particular bought and drove all kind of cars, many of them ancient, obscure or eccentric. Their status was assured — or irrecoverably abandoned — regardless of what car they drove. Fortunately for advertisers, these motorists were, in the nature of things, a small minority.

"The Three Wheeler with the most costs least to run" boasted Reliant in 1963 of the new Regal 3/25, which was shown in three views, each accompanied by starred features such as "wide opening doors," "winding windows" (unlike those of the Regal Mk VI) "spacious boot" and "combined sidelight and flasher." By 1964 the bubble-car craze was declining, and Reliant was understandably bullish: "It all adds up! …Production of the 3/25 is breaking all records — proof that this wonderful little motor car lives up to its good looks in performance and economy. And you only need a Motor Cycle Licence to be able to drive the 3/25. Increased sales — The 3/25 combines comfort with running economy — it's Britain's finest 3-wheeler at a price you can afford. No wonder sales are rising every day and the 3/25 is the *only* 3-wheeler to have increased its sales. Resale value — The resale value of the Reliant Regal 3/25 is higher than that of any comparable small car — it's a safe, sound investment for anyone!" As in earlier Reliant advertising, however, the price was not yet given.

In 1965, the Regal 3/25's price did appear at the bottom of advertisements, and the company's advertising expenditure increased with its sales. Reliant adopted something of the proud iconoclasm in Doyle Dane Bernbach's copy for Volkswagen in the United States, and implicitly mocked the technical pretensions and intermittent unreliability of BMC's small cars: "You'll get sick and tired of your Reliant…. The tough all-aluminium engine has a tiresome habit of going on and on and on…. You cannot boast to neighbours about the revolutionary construction…. The glass-fibre body will show no interesting signs of rust…. You will never enjoy the status of a big-spending

Practical Motorist, May 1965

You'll get sick and tired of your Reliant Regal 3/25. The tough all-aluminium engine has a tiresome habit of going **on and on and on.** *(We expect a life of 100,000 miles before the cylinder liners need to be replaced).* You cannot boast to neighbours about the revolutionary construction. *(We mount our bodies on* **ridiculously old-fashioned** *steel chassis, in the belief that some timid souls like this kind of protection).* The glass-fibre bodywork will show **no interesting signs** of rust. *(It will last for thousands of years, and we haven't yet found a satisfactory way of destroying the stuff).* You will **never enjoy** the status of a big-spending motorist. *(The Regal 3/25 returns 65 miles to the gallon and some* **miserable folk** *do their motoring on as little as twopence a mile).* **Not wildly exciting,** is it? But if you are the sort of wretched fellow who is interested in complete economy, reliability and durability, arrange for a test run at any of 400 Reliant dealers.

Regal 3/25
Britain's top-selling three-wheeler
Four seats, 600 c.c. engine,
from £472 *(inc. p.t.)* 5-cwt. van £374

Write for brochure to:
The Reliant Motor Company Limited (P),
Tamworth, Staffordshire

Reliant Regal 3/25. Few three-wheelers survived the post-Suez boom, but the Reliant was more civilized and useable than most of the others, which appeared to be only on nodding acquaintance with modern car design. The Regal 3/25, which arrived in 1962, was not much cheaper to buy than a utility four-wheeler, but it was cheaper to run and benefited from tax concessions. The facelifted 3/30, made famous as Del-Boy's van in *Only Fools and Horses*, succeeded the 3/25 in 1967. The proud boast here that there was no known way of destroying fibreglass would not be made amid the eco-panic of later years.

motorist…. Not wildly exciting, is it? But if you are the sort of wretched fellow who is interested in complete economy, reliability and durability, arrange for a test run at any of 400 Reliant dealers." With others in the same series published during 1965–66, the advertisement was a minor classic. For the rest of the decade, the status of the little car within its market was assured.

6

Singer

"Motoring's most elegant experience"

When the Rootes Group concluded its takeover of Singer Motors Ltd. in January 1956, it acquired a moribund company and a Birmingham factory that was far from ideal for making cars. Originally "built by BSA during the First World War for small arms manufacture, [it] had what must have been the only vertical assembly line in the motor industry.... Production started on the fourth floor, body trim and paint were on the fifth and final assembly on the sixth. Cars sometimes had to be swung out of the building, turned round manually and then brought in again on the next floor for the assembly to continue. Little wonder that the rate of production was never much more than a steady trickle...."[1] At the time of the takeover, production had declined from 150 per week in early 1952 to approximately 30 cars a week.[2] On the other hand, the factory would be ideal as a spare parts depot for the Group, and Singer had many dealers in strategic locations who could sell a wide range of Rootes cars in the future. Although Rootes' operating motivation throughout was commercial, the takeover nevertheless had a usefully genuine sentimental side: when seeking to persuade Singer's shareholders to accept the Group's offer in 1955, Billy Rootes made the most of his attachment to the firm from his time as an apprentice during 1909–13. Finding his lathe from those days still in use, he placed it in the Rootes museum.[3]

The Group also inherited a history of quality and innovation that went back to 1905, together with a sporting reputation founded, *inter alia*, on records broken at Brooklands in 1911 and on racing successes with 9hp and 1½ litre cars in 1934–35. In the 1930s, however, sustained profitability had proved elusive; an 11hp "Airstream" saloon, streamlined in the manner of the Chrysler Airflow, achieved more publicity than sales, and features such as 1934's twin-trailing-arm independent front suspension, and a fluid flywheel with additional free-wheel to allow clutchless gearchanges, became comparatively less attractive as other manufacturers caught up. In 1929 Singer was Britain's third largest car producer behind Morris and Austin; by 1939 it had been overtaken by Ford, Hillman, Standard and Vauxhall.

In ordinary circumstances Singer would have been unlikely to survive independently for long, but the Second World War reprieved the company and profits from arms manufacture funded the development of the 1947 SM1500,[4] a full-width, six-seater saloon with independent front suspension built to a Packard design under licence and with a body styled by Singer's chief engineer since 1937, Leo Shorter. Inspired by Howard Darrin's design for the 1947 Frazer and Kaiser announced in May 1946, but lacking Darrin's flair, Shorter produced one of the ugliest saloons of its

Opposite: **Rootes Group range, 1960.** Prestige advertising can be tricky. On the face of it there is surfeit of wonders to promote, but, if the appeal of each individual marque is usually quite distinct, the themes one can use for a group's cars *en masse* are limited, and can tend to the banal and generic. Moreover, to show every car can be unwise, as multiple pictures look cluttered while photos of the whole family, as later from BMC, can suggest the slightly mad collection of a man who must have one of everything. Reliability, value for money and good dealer coverage were favourite subjects, and Rootes capitalize here on their main advantage over Ford, Vauxhall and BMC: build quality, in an echo of Buick's pre-war slogan, "When better automobiles are built, Buick will build them." The "elegant yet functional styling" includes three types of fins—blades for the Rapier (naturally), swept-back wings (Alpine) and delicately wrapped-over wing extensions above oval tail-lights for the Minx Series IIIA, which gave it, seen from behind, a slightly severe, querulous look in some colours.

The Illustrated London News, June 25, 1960 (With thanks to Paul Martin)

you get a
TOUCH OF GENIUS
in everything made by ROOTES

HUMBER SUPER SNIPE SALOON

SUNBEAM ALPINE

SUNBEAM RAPIER SPORTS SALOON

Every one of the wide range of cars made by Rootes has that extra something—that 'touch of genius'...showing itself not only in the elegant yet functional styling but also in performance, safety, luxury and economy. When you sit in any Rootes car—Limousine, Saloon, Convertible, Estate Car or Sports model—you are immediately impressed by a gratifying sense of well-being; just as though it had been made specially with *you* in mind.

HILLMAN MINX CONVERTIBLE

SINGER ESTATE CAR

HUMBER—the ultimate expression of ROOTES genius for making better automobiles. Here elegance, luxury and power are brilliantly combined to offer you the finest value at the price today.

HILLMAN—the family car with the quality finish and performance...unbeatable at its price, the result of continuous development over 28 years.

SUNBEAM—the car that gives a new meaning to sports driving. The Rapier...luxury with performance that has won fame in Europe's toughest rallies. The Alpine, sweepingly elegant—up to 100 m.p.h. —and at an astonishingly low price.

SINGER—the car for the connoisseur. Beautifully appointed, supremely comfortable, and high performance with economy. Another example of ROOTES value and that extra 'touch of genius'.

ROOTES MOTORS LIMITED

LONDON SHOWROOMS & EXPORT DIVISION: ROOTES LIMITED
DEVONSHIRE HOUSE · PICCADILLY · LONDON W.1

A better buy because they're better built!

period but also one of the best-built and durable. Pictures of a prototype appeared in the press in 1947 and the car was unveiled at the Earls Court Motor Show in October 1948. A 1952 advertisement promised: "Never believe the man who tells you 'Nobody's making cars that'll last these days.' Here in disproof is a car that from grille to luggage boot is built to last as the best of the old ones lasted. A car that is not built down to a price but up to a name: Singer — a lasting name in motoring."

In some cases, however, the SM1500 owner of the mid-1950s longed not for an excuse to keep the car, but for a reason to dispose of it. The full-width styling with extended boot which Shorter had pioneered in Britain was commonplace by 1952, and the 1497cc (initially 1506cc) SM1500 was over-priced and under-styled for anything other than the sellers' market which it had outlasted. Although the car was reliable, sturdy, spacious and stable, its steering, brakes and clutch were too heavy for many women to manage easily at speed or in confined spaces, and the steering-column gearchange, never one of the best, could be recalcitrant entering second and reverse; many an exasperated driver rammed his knuckles into the mock-wood-painted metal dashboard in the attempt. Singer continued to innovate in small ways, yet unsuccessfully: the SM1500 was updated with a traditional grille to become the Hunter in 1954, but early bonnet and side valances of fibreglass were of such poor quality that subsites had to be designed in steel. A Hunter 75 with a twin-overhead-camshaft 75 bhp engine, launched in October 1955 and advertised in the press, was stillborn. A fibreglass saloon and semi-full-width roadster, both called SMX, were planned in 1953, and the roadster was displayed at that year's Motor Show and developed through 1954 and early 1955, but both projects were cancelled after four of the open cars and perhaps two saloons had been built. Regular SM1500 production was augmented until 1955 by the open four-seater Roadster, a revival of a 1939 design which appealed to Singer stalwarts but which could not compete with genuine sports cars from BMC and Standard-Triumph.[5]

The London Press Exchange's advertising for the early SM1500 was old-fashioned, and the agency's line drawings, portentous copy and fussy borders were at odds with the car's uncompromisingly modern design. Catalogues, however, were more lavish. One in particular included separate sheets, each with a colour painting of the car or its individual features on one side and specifications printed on the other. Artwork by Harold Connolly[6] showed a green SM1500 in front of a multi-storied art deco building, and features such as a locking fuel filler door and capacious boot with

concealed hinges on the lid were proudly highlighted. With the arrival of the Hunter in September 1954, Singer gained a new agency in S.D. Toon & Heath Ltd., who made the most of the model's bold new grille and horse's head mascot. A car sped through the night against an indigo sky: "Mighty Hunters— in Greek mythology, Orion was a mighty hunter; in the constellations he remains immortalized amongst the stars…. The bright star of the motor world today is the Hunter. There is no car made better." There probably *was* no medium-sized family car made better, and although Singer's new owners had no reason to keep the Hunter in production (the last was made in the summer of 1956), the Singer marque name was a different matter. On January 18, 1956 Rootes reduced the price of the Hunter from £1033 4s to £864 17s and that of the Hunter S from £919 7s to £796 7s, renaming the models "De-luxe" and "Special" at the same time. This cleared stocks of complete cars but left a great many engines. There was only one place for them.

Announced on September 25, 1956, the "Elegant new Ginger Gazelle — Admired for elegance…. Applauded for performance" was very obviously a modified Hillman Minx, but a new bonnet and grille and wood trim inside combined with the Hunter engine (with a raised compression ratio) to produce what *The Motor* called "A sturdy new 'Upper middle class' car of popular size."[7] Initially noisy (as the SM1500 had been), the Gazelle was soon quietened with additional sound deadening. At five feet wide and less than fourteen feet long, the Gazelle Mk I was comparatively small, and at £898 7s it was a natural rival for the Riley One-Point-Five introduced at £863 17s in November 1957 and for the similar Wolseley 1500, a spring 1957 débutante costing £796. In spirit the Gazelle lay between the two BMC cars but had a dash of additional glamour, and a Gazelle Convertible was available at £998 17s. A Hillman Minx de luxe, meanwhile, cost £748 7s and a Sunbeam Rapier £1043 17s, which was £30 more than a Ford Zodiac.

At nearly 21 cwt, the Gazelle was heavier than its name suggested and, consequently, was not fast: 0–60 mph in 25.2 seconds and a top speed of just over 75 mph were unremarkable and fuel consumption, at 25mpg, was high. The equivalent 1956 Minx, with a 1390cc overhead-valve engine, boasted 47.5 bhp and managed 0–60 in 27.7 seconds, a top speed of 77 mph and a typical fuel consumption of 37mpg.[8] S.D. Toon & Heath's copy wisely emphasized the Gazelle's features in a style more restrained — and vague — than that used by Basil Butler Co. for the Minx. Selling points included "graceful advanced styling," "exceptional visibility, steadiness, safety" and "complete luxury, with deep com-

---

Opposite: **Singer Gazelle Mk IIIC.** Reinforcing marque identity with the only obvious difference from more mundane models, the theme of this piece was not original, as Austin (inset) had used it for both press and cinema advertising in 1955–56. Singer's boy looks more natural, however, and is allowed a realistic pose. The copy, meanwhile, simply lists the features that distinguish it from the Minx: "efficient sound-proofing" and a "fitted heater" were not universal in small cars at the time. The copy does not emphasize the wood trim inside, mentioning it only in passing, although it admittedly looked like an afterthought on this model. Later Gazelles had proper, full-width wooden dashboards, and looked better for them.

THE FIELD, March 22 1962

IF YOU THINK HE'S PROUD
YOU SHOULD SEE HIS DAD!

THE FIELD, May 10 1956

"She's a real beauty
– my new Austin"

Young James has never once regretted advising his father to buy the new Austin Westminster. She holds the road well, corners firmly, gets away supply at the lights. The steering is steady as a rock at high speeds. The windscreen is good and large. There is room and to spare in the boot. What's more, as James never tires of pointing out, the Westminster has four gears, six cylinders, good lines and ample elbow room, kneeroom and headroom for five people. James, in fact, is proud as punch of his new Austin Westminster. So is his father (at £901.7s. he feels he has got his full moneysworth). So are the rest of the family.

AUSTIN A.90 SIX WESTMINSTER

Buy AUSTIN and be proud of it

THE AUSTIN MOTOR COMPANY LIMITED, LONGBRIDGE, BIRMINGHAM

The Singer Gazelle is a car any man can take pride in

Beautifully finished inside and out, the Singer Gazelle offers all these features at no extra cost: fitted heater, efficient sound-proofing, windscreen washers, bumper overriders, comprehensive range of instruments, really luxurious seats, polished woodwork, lockable glove-box, precise sports-car gearbox, sun visors, choice of seven colour schemes. And, of course, the new, bigger 1.6 litre Rootes engine that gives faster cruising on less fuel.

OPTIONAL EXTRAS: OVERDRIVE · FULLY-AUTOMATIC TRANSMISSION

SALOON: £575 plus purchase tax ESTATE CAR: £655 plus purchase tax CONVERTIBLE: £665 plus purchase tax Also the SINGER VOGUE: £655 plus purchase tax

SINGER GAZELLE

By appointment to
Her Majesty the Queen
Motor Vehicle Manufacturers
Rootes Motors Limited

ROOTES MOTORS LTD

SINGER MOTORS LIMITED, COVENTRY. LONDON SHOWROOMS AND EXPORT DIVISION, ROOTES LTD., DEVONSHIRE HOUSE, PICCADILLY, LONDON, W.1

fortable seating and de-luxe fittings." Advertising continued in a similar vein until October 1957, when the Gazelle Mk II was announced. Still with the original Singer engine, it was promoted in a much more recognizably Rootes style: "Now! Brilliant NEW Singer Gazelle estate car — today's top value for dual purpose luxury motoring. Plus elegant new styling and added luxury to the saloon and convertible." Two small side grilles had been added to the front panel, replacing the collection of slightly crude-looking chrome trim pieces of the Mk I, and the car gained a side flash in a light colour which ran along the length of the car and swept round the rear wheelarch to cover almost the full depth of the body-side behind the rear wheel.

In February 1958 the 1390cc engine used in the Hillman Minx and Sunbeam Rapier was enlarged to 1494cc for the Rapier, and in this form it was fitted to the Gazelle in the place of the old overhead-camshaft Singer engine, which disappeared for good. The resulting Gazelle Mk IIA looked identical to its predecessor and continued until September 1958, when the Minx also acquired the 1494cc engine to become the Series III and the Gazelle was updated again to become the Mk III. Its side flash now reached almost to tail of the car before widening downwards. Still "motoring's most elegant experience," the Mk III was attractively advertised in maroon with a cream flash, accompanied by a convertible in red and white and an estate car in blue and white.

During 1959–62, advertising for the Singer Gazelle was curiously random, but occasionally inspired. A spring 1962 advertisement by Singer's new agency from the middle of 1961, Erwin Wasey Ruthrauff & Ryan Ltd., was arguably the best. A small boy polished the car's grille with intense concentration: "If you think he's proud, you should see his Dad! The Singer Gazelle is a car any man can take pride in." Although not unique — Austin had based a whole campaign around proud offspring in the late 1950s — it was still unusual, and an appealing way to target the car towards thirty-somethings (as they had yet to be called) with young families.

In the meantime Singer essayed several themes. "Foot loose and fancy free" began a September 1959 piece for the updated Mk IIIA with small, wrapped over tail fins.[9] Greatly elongated, the car was shown below a crescent of shoes: "Smooth, effortless [Smiths] 'Easidrive' fully automatic transmission now available as optional equipment at extra cost [£125]. 'Easidrive' puts you miles ahead in performance and leaves you foot loose and fancy free to enjoy these many exciting new Gazelle features:- More power and acceleration with twin carburettors. Improved forward vision through the wider and deeper windscreen. Distinctive new

body line. Normal transmission is now operated by a sports style centre gear shift (If you prefer the column change, it's available at no extra cost.)" Other options included overdrive on third and top gears and those perennial Rootes options, whitewall tyres. (Rootes' 1957 accessories included detachable whitewall tyre rings.) The automatic transmission was a novelty on such a small car, and a great improvement on the 1958 Minx's optional Lockheed Manumatic clutchless gear-change, also used by BMC, in which the clutch was triggered by pressure on the gear lever and the engine was automatically speeded up just before a lower gear was engaged. Examples were known to be reliable but the public had not trusted it, and manoeuvring a car in which the mechanism, or the car's carburettor, was out of adjustment could be dangerous for anything nearby. Manumatic's only real benefit was for drivers disabled in the left leg or foot who could not afford a larger car with automatic transmission. In May 1960, Singer and Rootes advertising merged for a Gazelle advertisement in the style of the Group's prestige "You get a touch of genius in everything made by Rootes" campaign. Usually five cars were shown from the Hillman, Humber, Sunbeam and Singer ranges; in the Singer advertisement the Gazelle saloon, convertible and estate car accompanied copy adapted from regular Gazelle advertising. The range was proving to be a great success.

In September 1960 the Gazelle was photographed alongside one of Britain's great post-war triumphs — the recently completed fully steerable radio telescope at Jodrell Bank in Cheshire which had been devised by Professor (later, Sir) Bernard Lovell at Manchester University and the consulting engineer, Charles Husband. This magnificent structure had generated a good deal of controversy — principally over its cost — but had finally gained public acceptance when it had tracked the carrier rocket of the Russian space craft, *Sputnik I*, a few minutes after midnight on October 16, 1957. Almost a year later, on October 11, 1958, the telescope followed America's first moon rocket, *Pioneer I*, from ten minutes after its launch at Cape Canaveral, Florida until it eventually fell back to earth. Although the rocket failed to reach the moon, the launch was in wider terms a great scientific success. On March 11, 1960, the telescope successfully transmitted a signal releasing the American deep space probe, *Pioneer V*, from its carrier rocket. A few days later, Professor Lovell received a telephone call from Lord Nuffield, now 82 years old, whose Foundation had contributed to the project in its early days. Nuffield asked how much was still owed. Lovell told him: £50,000, "a constant source of anxiety and damaging to our progress," as he later remembered it. "Is that all? I want to pay it off," said Lord Nuffield, and the Jo-

Opposite: **Singer Vogue Mk I Estate Car.** Singer revived an old Humber name in 1961 for this luxury edition of the Hillman Super Minx. Like the Gazelle, it was distinguished from its humbler brethren by a special grille and "triple dot" (rather than oval) tail-lights. Unusually, this car was openly billed as an adapted saloon, in contrast to many rivals which were disingenuously claimed to have been specially designed from the ground up. The elongator, however, is still at work.

THE FIELD. *May 24. 1962*

NEW
SINGER VOGUE
ESTATE CAR

It's loaded with luxury features!

Take the luxurious Singer Vogue saloon. Extend the body. Put in fold-flat rear seats. Include a loading platform. Finish off with a tailgate that extends the loading platform to 79 inches. And there you have the new Vogue Estate Car — the latest way to take five adults (or 700 lb. of luggage) for a really comfortable ride. Here are all the features you expect in a quality car — including a complete heating and ventilation system, excellent suspension and sound-proofing, and twin headlights for night-driving safety.

POWERED BY LIVELY, FULLY-PROVED 1·6 LITRE ENGINE

OPTIONAL EXTRAS: OVERDRIVE ON 3RD AND 4TH GEARS, OR FULLY-AUTOMATIC TRANSMISSION, WHITEWALL TYRES

£705 plus P.T. £265-7-9

ALSO THE SINGER VOGUE LUXURY SALOON

£556 plus P.T.
£246·12·9

By appointment to
Her Majesty the Queen
Motor Vehicle Manufacturers
Rootes Motors Limited

ROOTES MOTORS LTD

SINGER MOTORS LIMITED, COVENTRY. LONDON SHOWROOMS AND EXPORT
DIVISION, ROOTES LTD., DEVONSHIRE HOUSE, PICCADILLY, LONDON, W.1

1042

drell Bank Experimental Station became the Nuffield Radio Astronomy Laboratories, Jodrell Bank.[10] "Anticipating the trend of tomorrow—in the Singer Gazelle there's a harmony of design, luxury and performance that's caught the imagination of far-seeing motorists—everywhere...." said the copy beneath the picture of the Gazelle in front of the telescope. But did Singer's agency know that its chosen backdrop had been paid for, in significant part, by earlier sales of Morris cars?

In July 1961 Rootes introduced the Singer Vogue[11] three months before its mainstream sister, the Hillman Super Minx. "Now—double value with the Singer Franchise!" announced a double spread in *Motor Trader*, showing advertisements for the Vogue and Gazelle side by side. "It's news! It's right in fashion," said the headline of parallel, conventional, magazine advertisement, the last four words written in lipstick by a feminine hand that appeared from the side of the page. "The brilliant new Singer Vogue. Imposing yet not too large for parking, elegant, luxurious...and of modest price. A car to turn all heads with admiration." Features abounded: "The fashionable new Singer Vogue has everything—twin headlamps, smart, sleek frontal appearance and inside...built-in heater and ventilation system, elegant walnut all-in-line instrument panel, dished steering wheel, rear compartment seats three—positioned well forward of the rear wheels." The last of these, a much-heralded feature of full-width bodies in the early 1950s, was rarely mentioned by 1961, and "maximum visibility, fully opening doors, separately stored spare wheel..." were details usually listed in a catalogue.

As with the Gazelle, early advertising for the Vogue concentrated upon tangible features that justified its price, defensively given as "£655 plus purchase tax. See your dealer today." In fact the car cost £956, which was less than the larger Wolseley 16/60 (£993), identical to a Vauxhall Velox (PB) and a substantial £102 more than the Super Minx. The Vogue attracted good reviews. Writing in *The Field*, S.C.H. Davis found the Vogue's styling "much to be admired," while the immediate impressions of J. Eason Gibson in *Country Life* were of "the speed with which the engine warmed up to its work and the silence and smoothness of the car as a whole." It was only approximately two inches longer and an inch wider than the Gazelle, but it looked and felt like a larger car and, at 2455 lb. against the Gazelle Mk IIIC's 2336 lb., was substantially heavier. The models shared a 1592cc engine. A Vogue estate car, "loaded with luxury features," was introduced in May 1962, and was built by Carbodies of Coventry in space formerly occupied by the convertible versions of the Ford Consul, Zephyr and Zodiac Mk II, which

had been discontinued earlier in the year. The Vogue, however, "was never a money-spinner; its main advantage to Carbodies was to keep a number of skilled men employed in the factory, and not to lose them elsewhere. Painting the [Super Minx and Vogue estate] bodies caused problems. Rootes specified the option of two-tone paint, and the masking of the first colour was time-consuming. Moreover when metallic paint was introduced on the model [a pale green was particularly popular] difficulties were encountered in getting a good, even finish on each car: on one panel the paint would be even and shiny, whilst on another it would be patchy and dull and would have to be flatted and resprayed."[12] The Vogue estate car would outlast the equivalent saloon, continuing until April 1967, when it was replaced by an "Arrow" Vogue estate car.

Towards the end of 1964, the Vogue was updated alongside the Super Minx with a squared-up, six-light roofline to create the Vogue III and Super Minx Mk III. Among Rootes saloons, only the Humber Sceptre retained a wraparound rear window. In December 1964 an olive green Vogue was photographed in sharp focus with a fashion model in soft-focus some distance behind, so that only the most determinedly humorous reader would identify the woman rather than the car as the "exciting New Model" announced in the headline. Another model was shown in an almost identical February 1965 advertisement in black and white, which used a realistic, only slightly elongated painting of the car rather than a photograph. The theme echoed Vauxhall's spring 1962 campaign for the Cresta PA. By 1965 the car was beginning to look old-fashioned and was more family car than status symbol. "Ask any Vogue owner what's the best feature of the Vogue" said a March headline. A picture of a glamorous woman was captioned "Luxury"; a man in his sixties applauded "Value" while a smooth-looking thirty-something in a dinner jacket applauded "Styling." "The new Singer Vogue is so full of features that there's something for every motorist to fall in love with" added the copy, as if Rootes were not quite sure where the best market for the car now lay. "The Vogue is for luxury," declared a July advertisement showing a pale lilac car outside the entrance of a country house. Suitcases rather than boxes in the doorway suggested an upmarket hotel rather than a new house for the owners, and the small television set which Vogue Man was taking out of the boot implied—on the most generous interpretation—affluent technophilia. It did make one wonder what was in the couple's suitcases.

In 1964, a third car joined the Singer range. "While the Imp was suffering its early problems, the Singer people kept a respectful distance, but now [sales manager from January

---

Opposite: **Singer Chamois Mk II.** Rootes were not willing to be left out of the luxury sub-compact market and so produced a specially trimmed Imp for the Singer range. The market for the car was closely delineated, and the copywriter used a trick that would become common in later years: he sympathized with the reader's imagined dilemma and then produced a solution. It worked, provided that the target market was attracted to the image of the car. Otherwise, if they could afford a Chamois, they might also be able to afford something bigger.

The Field, April 7, 1966

How to afford a luxury car *and* a home!

Singer Chamois Mk. II—with all the excitement of lively performance, too!

The Singer Chamois Mk. II costs less than £600—and that includes luxury at a level that's surprisingly high in such a modestly priced car, plus performance that's both exciting and economical. See the luxurious Chamois at your Singer dealer.

Seating Comfort-contoured for easy-riding enjoyment of every mile of motoring.

Insulation Body and engine compartment sound-insulated for quietness. Protective underbody coating standard.

Economy Lightweight, rear engine gives 40-45 miles to the gallon. 5,000 mile servicing intervals.

Safety Big, fade-free brakes, all-round independent suspension for sure road holding. Light, precise steering, padded facia surround.

Estate-car versatility Lift-up rear window and fold-down rear seat for easy loading of luggage.

Recommended price **£590.0.5** inc £103.0.5 p.t.

Singer Chamois MK II

ROOTES MOTORS LIMITED
LONDON SHOWROOMS AND OVERSEAS DIVISION
DEVONSHIRE HOUSE PICCADILLY LONDON W.1.

The Field, October 19, 1967

FOR SALE BY PRIVATE TREATY

OUTSTANDING BRITISH ESTATE

The Singer Vogue Estate, a spacious and dignified lounge on wheels in beautiful, undersealed surroundings.

Sumptuous easy chairs, specially figure-contoured and covered in fabulous Amblair keep-cool material. Fully-reclining front seats. Ample space provided for the longest of long legs. Fresh-air heating and ventilating system. Soft fitted carpets throughout.

Huge, 62-cubic-foot storage area, suitable for transporting all manner of sporting and camping equipment, boxes, suitcases, prams and kitchen sinks.

Other special features are:– oil-pressure gauge, water-temperature gauge, ammeter, twin-tone horns, child-proof rear-door catches, twin reverse lights; wood veneer facia, door cappings and centre console. Seat belts extra.

THE ENTIRE ESTATE powered by a superlative **1725** cc engine with facilities for attaining 60 miles per hour in less than 15 seconds and a maximum of 90 miles per hour.

INSPECTION by arrangement with any Singer agent. Keys on request. Offers in the region of **£1019.9s.5d.** will be seriously considered.

PART OF THE NEW DEAL FROM ROOTES   SINGER  **ROOTES**

1956 and now joint head of the Singer division of Rootes] Bill Boss agreed that the time was right to introduce a Singer version. The new car would have to compete directly with the successful Riley Elf and Wolseley Hornet…as well as the Ford Anglia Super and the Triumph Herald 12/50," recall Imp historians David and Peter Henshaw.[13] Introduced in October 1964, the Chamois was a badge-engineered Imp that *Small Car* found better than its recipe promised: "[For his extra £73 over the Imp, the customer] gets better sound insulation…. Second, he gets better front seats. Third comes a wooden dashboard with an oil pressure gauge and a padded top. Fourth, a heater fan and a big Chamois badge on the dash. Fifth, wider-rim wheels and braced-tread [Dunlop] SP41s all round. Sixth, a chrome-and-colour strip down each flank. And, last of all, he gets a Singer badge on bootlid and engine compartment and a fake radiator grille on the front end…. All right, some of the bits weren't necessary; but salesmen, alas, still demand *something* to sell to the mass mimser market. And Rootes has been much more restrained than BMC with the finny Minis [Elf and Hornet] (and produced a far better car, we reckon, in the bargain)."[14] The Chamois name caused confusion, however, with "the controversy (over whether to call it the Shammy or the Shamwa) wax[ing] so furious that our local garageman insists on calling it the Singer Washleather."[15]

Advertising for the little car, which would discontinued in 1970 when the Singer name itself disappeared, was staid and, as with the Gazelle and Vogue, preoccupied with individual features. "The new luxury saloon in the light car class" was photographed beside a river, and the headline could have come from any mainstream marque during the previous thirty years. The list of features began engagingly with a small picture of the original, four-legged, chamois. "Luxury where it matters, economy where it counts" in March 1965 was modest, as was the car's price of £581 11s 3d. In April 1966, Singer got to the nub of the matter with with the Mk II, shown in a tasteful maroon, which had been introduced in the previous year: "How to afford a luxury car *and* a home!" The house was not a modern apartment, a vast-chimnied 1950s bungalow or an art-deco showpiece, but a country cottage with small windows and an agreeably disordered garden. It was the middle-class English dream.

The theme continued with an aspirational edge later in the year, with an entirely new Vogue based on the Hillman Hunter, or "Arrow" saloon.[16] There was a Gazelle, too, scarcely distinguishable from the Vogue and fitted, unless automatic, with an engine co-incidentally of the same 1496cc capacity as that of the original Gazelle Mk 1. Automatic

Gazelles had 1725cc and both had iron cylinder heads; only the Vogue (and, from October 1967, the Vogue Estate Car), also of 1725cc, had an aluminium head. The Gazelle cost £769 19s and the Vogue cost £911 6s 1d. For two such similar cars the price difference was surprising; in the less refined market inhabited by Ford and Vauxhall, only £106 lay between the austere three-speed Victor 1600 at £819 and a much better-trimmed four-speed Victor 2000 at £925. (The most luxurious "Arrow" of all, the Humber Sceptre Mk III introduced in 1967, cost £1138.) Frances Howell of *Homes and Gardens* summed up the Gazelle as "a comfortable, elegant, slightly pretentious car essentially for people who like to travel unadventurously" and found the acceleration "unimpressive."[17] At the end of 1967, "Step up in the world in a Singer and settle back in luxury," in an advertisement for the Singer marque as much as for the Vogue in particular, consolidated an old theme, and a small painting of a white Chamois complemented the green Vogue with white stripe tyres which took centre stage. The copy also described the Chamois Mk II and the Chamois Sport, and the advertisement appeared in several slightly different forms until the middle of 1967. A Chamois Coupe, similar to the Hillman Californian and Sunbeam Stiletto, would arrive later in the year. In October, the estate car was "Outstanding British Estate…a spacious and dignified lounge on wheels in beautiful, undersealed surroundings" in an advertisement which parodied estate agents' publicity, and the theme fitted the slogan at the bottom of the page, "Part of the new deal from Rootes."

Chrysler seemed unsure how to promote the Singer marque in its last year. In October 1968 a bronze Vogue saloon was shown at twilight. Its driver, a middle-aged man with an Inspector Clouseau moustache, looked over his shoulder through the open rear door of the car. The car was "The '69 Swinger Vogue." Not that the driver and his wife were young enough to swing or yet quite old enough for the reader to be sure that Singer were joking. Working within Chrysler's "myth exploders" theme of the year, the copywriter did his best. "Myth: Singers are for people who are growing old gracefully. The 1725cc Singer Vogue has the kind of luxury which most people think went out with running boards. But that doesn't mean you had to be born in the gay twenties to want one…or to afford one. The Vogue is for people who are totally unconvinced that plastic is a satisfactory substitute for wood veneer…." But most people seeking such things in a mid-market car *had*, of course, been born in the "gay twenties." The photograph, one of several moody night-time shots from Rootes/Chrysler marques in

Opposite: **Singer Vogue Estate Car.** Semantic juggling from Rootes in 1967. The new Vogue, lighter and easier-handling than the old car, was a deluxe edition of the "Arrow" series (saloon-only) Gazelle, itself an upmarket Hillman Hunter, which revived a Singer name redundant since 1956. The Minx, meanwhile, was a utility Hunter. This kind of incestuous musical motors did nothing for marque loyalty, and by the end of April 1970 the Singer name was no more, although a few final Vogues were badged as Sunbeams. The "country estate" theme was a favourite with advertisers of station wagons for several years; this was one of the wittier, and comparatively unforced, examples. Others came from Triumph, Opel and that other Chrysler acquisition, Simca.

the late 1960s, was potentially evocative but reproduced variably; occasionally it disappeared into a dark blur. By this time the Vogue and Gazelle cost £1047 and £937 respectively, and both were discontinued when the Singer marque name was laid to rest in 1970. A few remaining cars were badged as Sunbeam Vogues. As Singer historian Kevin Atkinson recalls, "on March 2nd 1970, Rootes finally announced that from April 1st the Singer name would be dropped…. Of the six models produced, three were to go: the Chamois, Chamois Coupe and Gazelle," whilst the Singer Chamois Sport, Singer Vogue saloon and Singer Vogue estate car would become the Sunbeam Sport, Sunbeam Vogue saloon and Sunbeam Vogue estate car.[18] Singer sales were respectable and the Gazelle Mk I-VI, in particular, had been a notable success within its market,[19] but Singers were now so similar to the Hillmans on which they were based that the marque had little remaining *raison d'être*. And Chrysler, above all, wanted its own marque name, unencumbered by old loyalties and affections, to be the one that sold cars in Britain.

7

Standard

"There's a real V.I.P. car"

On July 26, 1956, President Gamal Abdel Nasser of Egypt seized and nationalized the 101-mile Suez Canal which crosses the desert between the Red Sea and the Mediterranean Ocean. He had been prompted by British and American withdrawal of an earlier offer to finance the construction of the Aswan High Dam as part of a continuing development plan; and that withdrawal had in turn been triggered by an arms deal which Nasser had made with communist Czechoslovakia. The British and French stockholders who owned the Suez Canal Company were furious with Nasser, but subsequent military action by Britain and France against Egypt lacked American support, was always controversial with the British public, and failed. Its failure marked a decisive step, psychologically as well as politically, in the retreat by Britain from its former imperial rôle.

The crisis had almost immediate practical consequences in Britain. Fuel rationing was introduced in November 1956 and went on for five months, motorists being issued with coupons according to the size of their cars' engines. The ration varied from six to over ten gallons a month: enough for two hundred miles. Launches and independent road tests of new cars were disrupted. Fortunately the affair was short-lived and the Canal was re-opened in April 1957, but the crisis reminded British motorists of how easily conflict abroad could endanger fuel supplies and created a new interest in economical motoring. Between 1957 and 1962 many different bubble cars, mostly of German and Italian origin, either imported or built in Britain under licence, became common on British roads. For larger cars fuel-saving overdrives, sometimes operating on several gears, also became widespread. The first cars to be made available with the popular Laycock de Normanville overdrive, revealed late in 1949,

were the Standard Vanguard Phase I and the mechanically related Triumph Renown.[1]

Among those stationed in Egypt until the Suez conflict erupted was Captain Raymond Flower, who with designer Gordon Bedson intended to build a range of cars with the Cairo Motor Company, including a microcar and a sports car called the Phoenix. When Flower returned to Britain, he approached Standard-Triumph in Coventry with a view to buying Standard Eight engines and other drivetrain components for an economy car that could be sold to contacts that he had maintained in Egypt. Alick Dick, Standard-Triumph's managing director since 1954, asked the company's general manager, Martin Tustin and its chief engineer, Harry Webster, to meet Flower in Coventry. But although the project was discussed, Flower eventually joined forces with Henry Meadows (Vehicles) Ltd. of Wolverhampton to produce a tiny, four-wheeled car designed by Bedson. With his two brothers, Neville and Derek, Flower promoted the resulting Meadows Frisky with some success during 1957 and 1958. As eventually produced, the car was fitted with a small two-cylinder Villiers (or, occasionally, Excelsior) engine rather than anything made by Standard-Triumph, and was advertised at least until July 1960. Frisky production continued until 1964.

The original prototype had looked ungainly, however, and Flower had commissioned Vignale in Turin to design the bodywork. The result attracted attention at the Geneva Show in the spring of 1957, and achieved publicity in the general press as well as in the motoring papers.[2] Moreover, in parallel with the Frisky, Flower was reconsidering his sports car. As Harry Webster recalled, "One day…a fellow named [Raymond] Flower came to see me…. He asked me, rather indirectly, if we could supply him with a TR chassis, to make an individual sportscar. I asked him what it was going to look like, and he said he didn't know! I asked him how he could make a car without knowing what it looked like, and he said he could get a body built in two or three months! I thought he was joking...." Flower refused to reveal who would design or build the prototype, but a sceptical Webster decided that if Flower really did manage to produce a prototype within three months, Standard-Triumph would pay for it. About ten days later, Flower reappeared with "half a dozen or so styling sketches, we chose one and supplied a chassis and three months later to the day this beautiful [open sports car with two-tone paint and fins, later known as the TR3 Dream Car] appeared! It took me a lot of digging and prying to find out how he'd done it."[3] The name on the side of the car's delivery truck revealed that the car came from Italy, and in due course Webster discovered that it had been built by Vignale.

By this time Standard-Triumph's styling department was in difficulties, and Webster went to visit Vignale where he met the sports car's 36-year-old designer, Giovanni Michelotti. Within a very short time Michelotti was retained as a freelance stylist, and his first project for Standard-Triumph was to update the styling of the Standard Vanguard Phase III which had been introduced in October 1955. The result was the Standard Vignale Vanguard, introduced in October 1958 at £1043 17s. "Shortly after this [Michelotti] decided to leave Vignale and become his own man, so we dropped Vignale and went with Michelotti. He and I became like brothers...."[4] Michelotti would design many cars for Standard-Triumph during the 1960s, including the Herald (1959), TR4 (1961), Spitfire (1962), 2000 (1963), 1300 (1965) and several derivatives of them.

Michelotti's retainer represented a considerable break from Standard-Triumph's past. Between 1945 and 1957, many of Standard-Triumph's cars were designed in-house by, or under, the company's chief stylist, Walter Belgrove, who before the Second World War had been chief draughtsman at Triumph, which was then an independent Coventry company unconnected with Standard. Triumph had made bicycles since 1887 and motorcycles since 1902, and the first Triumph car had been built in 1923, but by the time war was declared in September 1939 the company was in receivership and production of the middle-class Triumph cars had declined to a trickle. The Triumph motorcycle business had been sold off in 1936 and during the Second World War much of the car factory was reduced to rubble by the *Luftwaffe*. The Standard Motor Company, meanwhile, had been formed in March 1903 and by 1945 was one of Britain's "Big Six" car producers (with Morris, Austin, Ford, Rootes and Vauxhall). Standard's managing director, John Black, had joined Standard from Hillman, where he had been joint managing director with Spencer Wilks (who moved to Rover) before the Rootes brothers took over in 1929. Black

became Standard's general manager in 1930 and its managing director in 1933.

From 1931 until 1948, Standard not only made its own cars, but also supplied engines to S.S. [originally Standard Swallow] Cars Ltd., makers of the Jaguar sports cars and saloons; "Jaguar" understandably replaced S.S. as the name of the company and of the marque in 1945. In November 1944, Standard bought Triumph and sold the damaged factory while retaining the all-important Triumph name — which could be used on a sports car line with which to compete with future Jaguars. In the meantime it appeared on large, upmarket (1946–54 Triumph 1800 and 2000, later Renown) saloons and limousines, on a well-trimmed small car (the 1949–53 Triumph Mayflower), and on the 1946–49 Roadster, a curious amalgam of pre-war styles schemed in outline by senior draughtsman Frank Callaby and designed in detail by Callaby at the front and by fellow senior draughtsman Arthur Ballard at the rear. Black insisted that Ballard's end incorporate a "dickey," or rumble, seat — Britain's last — in the style of the pre-war Triumph Dolomites.[5] The result was always controversial, as the self-consciously glamorous front would have been much better suited to a car eighteen inches longer in the doors and with a more sweeping tail.

The original Standard Vanguard, announced in mid-1947 and first produced in 1948, was the first post-war design sold under the Standard name. Designed for world markets, it proved popular in Canada and to a lesser extent in Australia, where it was assembled; and Fergus Motors of New York imported a few into the United States, although the car could offer little that a domestic Ford or Chevrolet did not. At thirteen feet eight inches long, the Vanguard was much shorter that the local product, but quite wide (at five feet nine inches) for its length. Estate car, van and pick-up versions followed. Vanguards, including a convertible, were also built by Imperia in Belgium. The car's 2088cc, 68 bhp, four-cylinder engine was designed also to be fitted to the Ferguson tractor which Standard had manufactured from July 1946, and which was at first powered by a Continental engine imported from America. The new Standard engine was fitted to the Roadster from October 1948 and to the large Triumph saloons from February 1949; a higher-powered version was used in the 1953 Triumph TR2.

The new model took its name from the ninth H.M.S. *Vanguard*, Britain's last battleship, which had been launched in 1944 and would be broken up in 1960. John Black had served with the Royal Naval Volunteer Reserve (RNVR) during the First World War and was eventually demobilized as a Captain from the Royal Tank Corps in France; in peacetime he still preferred to be known as Captain Black and was a keen yachtsman. Standard-Triumph's penchant for model names with naval connections would outlast Black's chairmanship of the company, which ended in January 1954. But in 1947 the choice of name was good for public relations and suited the export-orientated spirit — and styling — of the car.

In overseeing its design, Black knew what he thought would sell, and in 1945 he sent Walter Belgrove to seek inspiration from a 1942 Plymouth he knew to be parked outside the American Embassy in Berkeley Square in London. For the new car, Black demanded a 92-inch wheelbase and a body with filled-in sides that would be high enough for him to enter with his hat on. He was unhappy with Belgrove's proposal, however, and sought a second opinion from the American freelance stylist George Walker, who would shortly afterwards take over Ford's styling studio in Dearborn. "Gee, it's as high as a haystack," said Walker, to the fury of Belgrove, on whom Black had, after all, imposed a highly restrictive brief.[6] With junior colleagues Vic Hammond, Leonard Warner and Leslie Ireland, Belgrove developed the design and Black reluctantly granted an extra two inches in the wheelbase. The finished six-seater fastback was still short and high, a little too large for most home-market motorists yet a little too small for export buyers used to American cars, but despite teething troubles with suspensions and dust sealing it was assembled in several export markets as well as in Britain and was moderately successful.[7] In 1952 it was updated by Arthur Ballard with longer doors and an extended, separate boot to produce the Phase II, and a version with a diesel engine appeared in 1954.[8]

Yet although the Vanguard was modern, it was not really good-looking. "One only has to note the number of Vanguards on the road to know that the earlier models were successful," remarked S.C.H. Davis when testing a Phase III in January 1956, "Yet I never thought them attractive to look at, a certain sturdiness, a lack of those fine lines for which the Italians, as example, are noted, suggesting utility in the true sense of the word rather than speed. Yet they had the speed [78.8 mph according to *The Motor* in May 1952], and appearance could not have weighed against them in the final choice. But the car is beyond doubt very much better now...."[9] Belgrove had produced a Phase III proposal which, with hindsight, preserved the original Vanguard's sleekness while improving its proportions. But John Black had other ideas. In 1953, unbeknown to Belgrove, he had met the American industrial designer, Carl Otto, and commissioned from him a proposal for the next Vanguard. Otto then asked Tucker Madawick to work with him on the project.

Madawick had begun his career in 1935 as one of the initial intake at the Pratt Institute, New York — the first school in the United States to offer a course in industrial design.[10] In 1939 he joined Ford in Dearborn as an apprentice designer and produced the full-sized pastel renderings of Lincoln, Mercury and Ford cars for the 1939 World's Fair. After the Second World War he worked for J. Gordon Lippincott in Manhatten on, among other things, Preston Tucker's rear-engined car. In 1947 Madawick began working in Raymond Loewy's studio at Studebaker in South Bend, Indiana, where he met Carl Otto, who had worked for Loewy since 1935. Otto and Madawick were sent to Lon-

don where they re-opened Loewy's office at 32, Upper Grosvenor Street and where, under Otto's guidance, Madawick "was given responsibility for Loewy's account with Austin and a brief for the design of the A40 Somerset"[11] — the car that would replace the A40 Devon of 1947–52. Otto and Madawick divided their time between the Grosvenor Street office and Austin in Longbridge. Not that Austin's eventual designs contained much of their work: "We couldn't get [Austin's stylist, Dick Burzi] into the city. We thought if we could get him to London we could buy him lunch and see if we could get to the inside of things. But he was a man of excuses. We were not that compatible with Austin.... Although the Somerset was a combination of us and Burzi, basically Austin went in-house rather than use much of our stuff. On the phone to Loewy, [Leonard Lord, Austin's chairman] said he had only brought us in to make sure they could compete with American designs and that broke Raymond Loewy's heart. It was quite a bald statement but at least the man was honest."[12] Early in 1950, Madawick returned to the United States and subsequently rejoined the Studebaker programme, and Loewy's London office closed in 1951. But in 1952 Carl Otto set up his own consultancy on New York's Fifth Avenue and shortly afterwards invited Madawick to join him.

Madawick produced a quarter-scale Vanguard proposal in the consultancy's New York studio,[13] and its arrival in Coventry surprised the Standard stylists, as Vic Hammond remembered: "All of a sudden this...great box arrived from America addressed to Walter Belgrove.... Inside was a clay model proposal...which Tucker Madawick had produced in...New York. It was a typical American car with a Loewy Studebaker-type front and those French bezels like on the Consul. It was a case of 'What the bloody hell is this?'"[14] The model looked rather like a 1952 Lincoln or Mercury with a squared-up roofline quite similar to that of the later *Heckflosse* or "fintail" Mercedes-Benz. Black asked Belgrove to modify the model, and Belgrove worked with Otto to create the final car.

The eventual production design was neater and more cohesive than Tucker Madawick's original proposal but nevertheless contained elements attributable to individual earlier American cars. The grille — an almost rectangular opening with a ribbed bar across the middle — was reminiscent of the 1953–54 Plymouth; the indicators built into the ends of the bar looked like those of the 1949 Ford; indentations in the body sides recalled the 1953 Studebakers; the large, circular tail-lights echoed those of the 1952–54 Ford; and the wraparound rear window was generic-American but probably closer to Ford's than to any other. Inside the car, the instrument binnacle once again reflected American Ford practice, as did the way in which the tops of the front door trims blended into the dashboard, for which the most obvious parallel lay in the 1954–57 Simca (originally Ford-France) Vedette.[15] Fortunately, all of these cars were virtually unknown in England at the time.[16] The Vanguard Phase III was launched at the Earls Court Motor Show in October 1955 at £849 14s 2d. Unfortunately, however, Belgrove did not get on with Standard's chief engineer since 1931, Ted Grinham, who after Black's departure in 1954 had become the company's deputy managing director. At the October launch, Grinham criticized the Phase III's design to anyone who would listen with the result that Belgrove confronted him on the stand, and, after a full-scale row with Grinham, left Standard-Triumph for good. Grinham retired at the end of 1956.

The Vanguard range was developed to include a new estate car and Sportsman saloon from September 1956 and, from October 1957, an Ensign saloon with a sleeved-down 1670cc engine and simpler exterior and interior trim. It cost £899 17s compared with the Vanguard's £1013 17s. The Sportsman was a high-performance (90 bhp) luxury saloon with a faux-traditional grille which was originally intended to be sold as a Triumph Renown. At £1231 7s, it cost much more than six-cylinder rivals from Austin, Morris, Ford and Vauxhall, and was an unequivocal flop.[17] Flower's visit came just in time.

Advertising for the Phase III was heaviest during the pre-Vignale years of 1955–58. Some early advertisements showed a left-hand-drive (though British-registered) car in two-tone light and dark greyish-pink while modest paintings of the car in a single dark colour accompanied monochrome advertisements. The Vanguard was incorporated into 1955's "IT" campaign which which was most effective with the small Eight (1953–59) and Ten (1954–61), allowing headlines such as Here "IT" is!," "The pleasure of IT!," "They're proud of IT!," "IT's ours for good!" and, in the Vanguard's case, "IT makes history!" The rest of the copy was less exciting: "Those Internationally Tested qualities found in all Standard cars are now presented to you in a NEW Standard model — a car for this day and age, superb in its comfort and up-to-the-minute refinements.... Fitted with the famous 2-litre engine that has already proved its reliability in hundreds of thousands of Standard-made vehicles since the war, the new Vanguard III brings you such features as automatic entry lights to all doors; front doors that can be locked internally or externally as desired...simplified, finger-light controls...two tail and stop lamps and reversing light placed so that all are easily seen by following vehicles...." An unexpected feature was saved for the end: the Phase III's "electrically operated screen washer" was unusual in 1955, when for many manufacturers a screen washer of any kind was in theory still an extra. Most were operated by

manual plungers until well into the 1970s. For a mass-produced, four-cylinder family car, the Vanguard was very well equipped.

In 1957 "IT" was replaced by the headline, "Time goes further with a Standard" above photographs of small cars and Vanguards in homely and rural settings. In the spring of 1958 a hatted and sober-looking man and his wife admired "That *extra* look!," "That *extra* satisfaction!" and "Those *extra* qualities!" in the Ensign, although the emphasis was on space and durability rather than gadgets. Much was made of the Ensign's "...really exciting performance — 79m.p.h. (Autocar Road Test) from its 14 horsepower (1670c.c.) wet liner engine of unequalled durability." The reference to old-fashioned horsepower was eccentric by 1958, but, as Graham Robson recalls, "Way back in 1955...the [sales] department had started asking the board to approve a new (RAC rating) 12hp/14hp car, 'as in our view this car is in the greatest demand.' Although RAC ratings had been officially obsolete since the late 1940s, many long-established managers were still wedded to the old language.... At that time [managing director] Alick Dick and [his deputy] Ted Grinham's first response had been to develop the...Vanguard III-based Ensign."[18] As an austerity edition of what, at fourteen feet four inches long, was to British motorists a large car, this first Ensign was not successful.

Nevertheless, in 1958 Giovanni Michelotti, who would become famous for the speed at which he worked, "made a most surprising alteration alteration to the whole character of the car by what amounts to a few masterly changes."[19] As an essentially American production, the Phase III was not the easiest of cars to update, but a simplified grille, deeper front and rear screens, more modest tail-lights, new wheel trims and a three-layer colour treatment gave the Vignale Vanguard a much lighter, more European air than that of the 1955 original. For traditionalists, an all-black paint scheme was available to special order. Amusingly, the makeover included a "crossed flag" badge on each rear wing, the left and right flags symbolizing not sporting success, but the maritime codes for "V" (a red cross on a white background, for Vignale) and "S" (a blue rectangle on a white background, for Standard) respectively. Naval men instantly recognized them as standing for "I require assistance" and "My engines are going astern," which described the likely state of Vanguard sales without Michelotti's intervention quite well; but the car, while popular with the armed services generally, was most widely used by the Royal Air Force.[20] The flags later appeared on coupe and convertible versions of Michelotti's

Opposite: **Standard Atlas.** The epic-journey theme, rare in post-war advertising (see "Sahara tested," bottom right), didn't help this, the runt in the litter of forward-control vans produced by the major car makers in the late 1950s. The Atlas was slow (with the 948cc engine of the Standard Ten and early Triumph Herald), ill-handling (hitting a bump while braking with nothing in the back could lift the tail off the ground) and crude inside. The driver sat on a tiny seat and grappled with a bent-rod gear lever, two feet long, which emerged from the gearbox at the rear of the cab and was cranked forward over the engine cover beside the driver. This catalogue-in-miniature showed what could be done with one basic design, but others did it too, and sales remained slow even after a 1670cc Standard Ensign engine was adopted later in the year.

The Field, June 2, 1960

ATLAS — allways the best

Whether it's bread, milk, people, or frozen fish, whatever the load Atlas is *allways* the answer. Atlas has everything: easier maintenance, taxi-turning, greatest load space, low loading level, high headroom, sliding or hinged cab doors. Wherever you look, there's an Atlas doing better, faster, more economical work. For instance . . .

The Atlas Kenex Caravan

. . . has more body height and width than any comparable competitor outside the Atlas range, giving generous cupboard space and comfortable dining and sleeping for four people. Unmatched reliability, manoeuvrability and economy.

The Atlas Lomas Ambulance

. . . has sound insulated engine, maximum interior room, low loading level, wide rear door with single action closing. It carries one stretcher case, three to four sitting patients plus attendant — or two stretcher cases and attendant. Interior equipment can be varied, of course, to suit individual requirements.

The Atlas Barham Bros. Milk Float

. . . has remarkable running economy under start-stop conditions, a strong, hygienic alloy floor with storage compartment beneath, strong body pressings eliminating the need for additional side posts and driver access from either cab door. Atlas Milk Floats are the most manoeuvrable on the roads today.

The Atlas Botwoods Insulated Van

. . . has a wide side loading door and low loading level for easy, speedy kerbside delivery. It has flat-topped wheel arches and a greater capacity than any other van in its class, enabling an insulated compartment of 80 cubic feet to be fitted.

The Atlas Kenebrake

. . . has more head clearance than any other vehicle in its class, an incredibly tight turning circle and plenty of room to carry up to 12 passengers, including the driver, in real comfort. Wide rear and side doors.

The Atlas Pickup

. . . has all the virtues of the Atlas Van with a steel tailboard which can be locked horizontally or dropped right down, extra large rear cab window, and reinforced all-steel chassis and body.

STANDARD ATLAS 10/12 cwt

Van £475 Pickup £465

SAHARA TESTED

In October 1958, a production model Atlas covered the 10,000 miles from Cape Town to Tangier via the Sahara desert.

. . . and STANPART *service wherever you go!*

WITH A TWELVE MONTH GUARANTEE, OF COURSE

STANDARD TRIUMPH

STANDARD-TRIUMPH GROUP COVENTRY. LONDON SHOWROOMS: BERKELEY SQUARE

next design for the Standard-Triumph, the Triumph Herald, and on Vignale's own TR3A-chassised Triumph Italia of 1959–62.

In November 1958, a two-tone coffee and pale lilac Vignale Vanguard was painted outside Westgate in Warwick in the second of a series of Christmas advertisements; the first, in November 1957, had shown a dark pink Ensign in the snow outside a large country house. In the summer of 1960, the Vanguard was painted in a ground-level view without background: "The classic marriage — Italian artistry and British craftsmanship are brilliantly combined in the sleek, new Vignale Vanguard. The result — breathtaking beauty of line and outstanding performance, [0–60 in 21 seconds and 83mph] with the reliability of Standard engineering." A small picture of the Ensign, "For budget motoring" was included in a May 1960 version of the advertisement but had disappeared by July; the model would reappear with a 2138cc engine as a De luxe in May 1962 which (at £744 17s 11d in January 1963 when a Ford Zephyr 4 cost £772 13s 9d) offered better value than the original and thereby found a small niche.[21] But the regular Vanguard of 1955–63, even in updated form, never became really popular, not least because it was heavy to drive and cumbersome, particularly in its steering and brakes.

There might have been another factor, too. "For their time," remembered Ralph Thoresby of *Motor* in 1967, the Vanguard Phase III and Ensign "were surely quite magnificent cars — comfortable, beautifully made for the money, utterly reliable, rugged, powerful and above all, likeable. Yet they never sold well and their second-hand values were often chronically low. The only reason I could ever find for that state of affairs was that perhaps the styling was neither 'flashy' nor 'quality' but fell uneasily half-way between."[22] Exactly so. A July 1960 advertisement showed three uniformed men — perhaps doormen, perhaps service personnel — in a line. "There's a real V.I.P. car" said one to the others. At the foot of the page a black Vanguard estate car was seen with a chauffeur at the wheel and, incongruously, with whitewall tyres, which no VIP would have specified. The taint of officialdom was authentic, and for private motorists in the 1960s prestige that was official and public was not nearly as desirable as that which was social and private. No-one was ever inspired to success and acclaim by the prospect that one day they might be able to buy a Standard Vanguard. Later surveys by Standard-Triumph showed that the Vanguard's successor, the highly successful Triumph

2000, reached "exactly the clientele the Vanguard Six had always missed — doctors, architects, solicitors, young businessmen and accountants among them."[23]

By 1960 the four-cylinder Vanguard was not selling well; the Triumph Herald, introduced in April 1959, was blighted by quality control problems; and Standard-Triumph's difficulties were compounded by a credit squeeze imposed by the government in April 1960 which had reduced sales of all new cars. In April 1961 the company was taken over by the commercial vehicle manufacturers Leyland Motors, who appointed their own new chairman, Henry Spurrier, in May and a new managing director, Stanley Markland (previously Leyland's joint general manager and works director) in September. Planning for the Vanguard's replacement had begun in 1957. After two false starts — a modish four-door hardtop cancelled in September 1960, and a Standard-engined 1961 Rambler American briefly considered at the suggestion of American Motors' president, George Romney — work began on the Vanguard's successor in the spring of 1961. It was to be styled by Michelotti and from the outset was intended to be badged as a Triumph.[24] Happily, the original plans had included a two-litre, six-cylinder, 1998cc engine, which from October 1960 was fitted in the Vanguard to create the Vanguard Luxury Six. Introduced as a companion model to the four-cylinder car at £1051, the Six soon supplanted the original Vignale, of which the last were sold at the end of 1961 and early in 1962. The Vanguard had never been smooth, and the new engine made it much more pleasant to drive.

Advertising for the Luxury Six was homely, a little bizarre, and in the summer of 1961 harked back to the middle-class styles of the 1930s: "Vanguard Six leads the £1,000 class with the newest 6-cylinder engine in Britain" announced the copy. The new car, looking identical to the established four-cylinder model, was seen on a raft or makeshift wooden landing platform, crossing a river surrounded by farmland. A small church and a few outbuildings stood in the background. "The new Vanguard Luxury Six is a challenging entry in the 6-cylinder market. These are the facts to reckon with. The driving is a delightful combination of the handling of a light car with the effortlessness of 'big engine' motoring. Try it for yourself. The individuality is built-in. So is every luxury refinement you could ask for. The power is 85 gross BHP, spurred by the semi-down-draught 'inclined' twin Solex carbs...." And so, soporifically, on. And the raft? All was revealed in small print at the end:

Opposite: **Standard Vignale Vanguard.** For the Christmas numbers and annuals of popular magazines many advertisers abandoned features and performance figures for lavish illustration and brief, often humorous, copy. In 1961 Morris placed a Mini-Minor behind a wooden sign that said, "Open on Christmas Day," while Ford's "On the first day of Christmas my true love gave to me...one new Capri" (1962) was guaranteed to raise a smile whatever one thought of the car. Standard, however, were still stuck with a 1955 shape contrived by consultant Carl Otto, Tucker Madawick and in-house designer Walter Belgrove in an American style now superseded. Although updated in October 1958 by Giovanni Michelotti of Vignale, the effect of whose improvements was out of all proportion to the actual changes made, the design had to last until 1963 when the final, six-cylinder version was succeeded by the Triumph 2000. This Warwick scene therefore plays down the Vanguard itself while emphasizing the heritage of the Standard-Triumph marque; the cars were built approximately eight miles away, in Coventry.

A Standard Vignale Vanguard at Westgate, Warwick

The Standard Motor Company wish all owners and prospective

owners of their cars a very happy Christmas

and a prosperous New Year.

The Standard Motor Company Limited, Coventry, England

Triumph Motor Company (1945) Limited (A wholly owned subsidiary)

"The ferryman's a woman. Grove Ferry, on the Great Stour in Kent, is one of Britain's last hand-drawn ferries, a young and feminine hand, too. It has been a ford since the XIth century. Charges are modest: beasts, 1/2d; persons, 1d; horses, 1d a leg. With 85 brake horsepower, the Vanguard Luxury Six saloon was only charged 1/- [one shilling]. Waiting its turn behind is the Vanguard Luxury Six estate car." For most people, a ford was a Ford, particularly in a car advertisement, and a new Zodiac (Standard-Triumph having thoughtfully brought it to mind) was £39 cheaper. And should a new model have been shown on an ancient ferry? Not if most of it was designed in 1953 it shouldn't. Production of the six-cylinder Vanguard and four-cylinder Ensign De luxe trickled on until May 1963, when the Standard marque was laid to rest. The cuckoo that was the post-war Triumph had finally outgrown its adoptive parent, and a whole range of innovative Triumph sports and luxury cars would attract motorists during the rest of the decade and beyond.

8

Vauxhall

"Everyone drives better in a Vauxhall"

When David Jones, Vauxhall's director of styling from 1934–71, died in March 2000, his obituarist, Jeremy Dixon, recalled, "During and immediately after [the First World War] he came under the spell of [the philosopher and mystic, George I.] Gurdjieff, his movement and John Bennett…he attended the 'Movement' at Bennett's house…most weekends, with trips to Paris to visit Gurdjieff…. He became briefly a spokesman for the 'Movement.'"[1] Jones had studied illustration and sculpture at the Royal College of Art in the late 1920s, where he was influenced by the sculptor Henry Moore, and was briefly apprenticed to another sculptor, Barry Hart, before joining Vauxhall in 1932, initially "just to raise enough money for a holiday in France."[2] But he also served an apprenticeship with Harley Earl in Detroit in 1937 and, according to Dixon, "[t]he decade of the 1950s was Jones's most creative period at Vauxhall. In retrospect, there is a clear connection between the streamlined forms of motor car styling and the work of sculptors such as Moore and [Barbara] Hepworth. This might be seen as his particular English contribution to what was essentially an American initiative."[3]

Jones's background, which combined an openness to Detroit's design methods with an involvement in branches of European art not normally connected with automobiles, would have surprised many car buyers in the 1950s. Vauxhall's streamlining was symbolic rather than empirical,[4] and in the late 1950s many conservative middle-class British motorists shunned Vauxhalls as being designed without regard for the "good taste" which they associated with experience of the fine arts.[5] Yet while the influence of American designs on Jones was strong, his conformity to them was co-operative (or, to a cynical mind, pre-emptive) as much as reactive. In 1980 Maurice Platt, Vauxhall's chief engineer from 1953 to 1963, recalled, "As in the case of other divisional executives, David's 'line' responsibility was to Vauxhall's management. His activities were never *directed* [italics original] from Detroit but he was strongly influenced by the styling fashions which were being developed in Harley Earl's studios."[6] Similarly, in 1967 Platt's successor, John Alden, said of the new Vauxhall Victor FD: "The whole of that new engine and car was developed at Luton, with Davy Jones styling it from the raw clay…."[7]

Vauxhall's early days were very different. The company began making cars in London in 1903 and moved to Luton in Bedfordshire in 1905, becoming a respected producer of specialist luxury models— most famously the 30/98 of 1913–26— before being taken over in 1925 by General Motors, who wished to expand their operations to Europe and had considered taking over Austin or Citroën. In the company's later phrase, the "first major fruit" of the association was the six-cylinder, middle-class (£280 —£295) Cadet of 1930, which in 1931 was fitted with Britain's first synchromesh gearbox.[8] Ease of handling, value for money and smoothness became dominant themes in Vauxhall advertising, and would remain so throughout the 1950s and early 1960s.

After the Second World War, the 10hp of 1937–40 was revived until September 1947, while its 12hp and 14hp companions continued until the late summer of 1948, when they were succeeded by four-cylinder Wyvern and six-cylinder Velox saloons. These new (L-type) cars shared a body adapted from that of the 1937 "Ten," its central section still visibly pre-war, while the front and rear were new. In August 1951, new, full-width Wyvern and Velox (E-type) models arrived, visibly products of General Motors, albeit with styling which "savour[ed] more of the late '40s than the early 50s" according to *The Motor*.[9] At first the new cars took the old Wyvern (1442cc, side valve) and Velox (2275cc, overhead valve) long-stroke engines, but in April 1952 they were fitted with new, short-stroke, overhead valve engines, respectively of 1507cc and 2262cc. A luxury Cresta version of the Velox joined the range in October 1954 for the 1955 model year to compete with the equivalent Zephyr Zodiac introduced by Ford in October 1953. This three-model range continued, with improvements for the 1956 and 1957 model years, until the Wyvern was dropped early in 1957 to make way for the first Victor. The Velox and Cresta were replaced by the new (PA) Velox and Cresta saloons in October 1957. It was with these 1957 designs that Vauxhall entered the 1960s.

The new (F-type) Victor was unveiled on February 7, 1957.[10] *The Times*, sounding a little like a benign Martian describing events on a distant Earth, reported that "[t]he introduction of a new Vauxhall car, which has been widely discussed in motoring circles for some time, was confirmed yesterday when an audience of 2,400 Vauxhall home and overseas dealers and members of the Press were given a private view of the car in a spectacular show produced by Mr. Ralph Reader at the Gaumont State Theatre, Kilburn [in west London].... In the competitive state of the car market, price is one of the key sales features, and after the expectation of the audience had been suitably titillated, the prices of the new Vauxhall model were announced...."[11] The standard model cost £728 10s and the Super, with extra equipment inside and additional chrome and stainless trim outside, cost £758 17s.[12] Similar announcement parties were arranged for local dealers where, as the Victor revolved slowly on its turntable, a gramophone record announced the new car and highlighted the advantages of Victor ownership.[13]

With its panoramic windscreen, tail fins and elaborate decoration in chrome and stainless steel, the new design immediately attracted controversy. It had been devised by the application of a stylistic doctrine conceived by Harley Earl to sell American cars to Americans, and, of two styling clays completed under David Jones, General Motors president Harlow H. Curtice unhesitatingly chose the more extreme when he visited Luton in 1954. This clay was further developed by Earl's staff in Detroit during repairs after it was sent to Fisher Body, where the prototype Victors were built.[14]

Platt had misgivings about the practicability of a panoramic windscreen in a monocoque body. "Asked for my opinion upon the engineering implications, I recall voicing three objections...extra cost, extra weight and the 'kinky' front pillars of which no-one had any experience in an integral body structure.... [But] Curtice felt certain that the commercial advantages outweighed all counter-arguments and no one felt sufficiently reckless to suggest that the panoramic windscreen was a costly gimmick of uncertain acceptability outside the United States."[15] To car buyers un-

familiar with it, Detroit's idiom could seem needlessly bizarre, like a fragment of a private design conversation accidentally broadcast to startled passers-by. As Platt and his team were ruefully aware, the Victor was a panoramic pioneer. GM's American sedans and hardtops relied on separate chassis frames while the equivalent monocoque Opel Olympia Rekord, with a slightly neater panoramic windscreen and styling of the same school as the Victor but with cleaner lines and details, would be announced later in 1957 as a 1958 model.[16]

Early Victor advertising emphasized the imagined utility of individual features as much as overall style: "First car in the country with the panoramic windscreen, the Victor's road vision is such that the tips of all four wings can be seen at a glance by the driver.... First with the new concealed exhaust system.... First for appearance, with the lines of a new generation of low, swift cars—in a range of eight beautiful colours." The "new concealed exhaust system" was a tailpipe that discharged through the end of the right-hand rear bumper on the Victor Super—an American feature that prevented grounding on inclined driveways (although this was not a particular problem in Britain) but which made the bumper rust quickly. A painting of a Gipsy Red Victor Super, elongated but with accurate detail, was shown surrounded by gold "Vs" against a yellow background beneath the headline "Salute the Victor." For motorists who disliked the new style, this was an irresistible invitation to rude rejoinder.

On February 28, 1958 a station wagon version, fitted with heavy-duty tyres, rear axle and rear springs, and equipped to Super specification, was introduced as a single model and advertised in March as "New—The Victor estate car...finest of them all. Low [*sic*] and behold the fresh new look of the future...an eye-catching, dual purpose estate car, with crisp, low lines...." With a "counterbalanced tail door" rather than a split tailgate, the Victor was the most modern medium-sized estate car of its time. In the trade press, Vauxhall drew dealers' attention to the advertisement: "On March 8th over 12 million people saw this Victor estate car advertisement in the 1/2 page advertisement in the *Daily Express* and they're coming to you to buy. Don't miss this splendid opportunity to sell the Victor estate car...finest of them all...."[17]

The estate car cost £931 7s and was available in four two-tone colour schemes as well as in five single colours, and was announced alongside Newtondrive two-pedal control, which used a centrifugal clutch that disengaged whenever the engine speed fell below 900 rpm (unless the choke was out, when the speed was higher), and was otherwise disengaged by an electric switch in the gear lever knob. Like the Manumatic used in BMC cars, it required the mechanism and the car to be in optimum condition and was not popular, but it cost a modest £25 10s. The driver had to remember not to touch the gear lever except when changing gear, and, if the clutch lining were to last, not to start or pull hard from low speed in top gear.

Road testers were divided about the Victor. Most liked its handling and light controls; not all liked its styling. J. Eason Gibson, testing a 1958 estate model for *Country Life*, found its appearance "most disturbing." *The Motor*, studiedly polite, said that the saloon was "not likely to be outmoded for many years to come." S.C.H. Davis, testing a saloon for *The Field*, was more generous. The stylists, he said, had "done their work well, so one can allow them an occasional curve which is curious and non-functional." In a test of the estate car in 1958, he began, "The Vauxhall Victor has been a favourite of mine since its first rather sensational appearance…." Yet in 1959, he recalled, "[The original Victor's] styling caused considerable argument and some dispute. But [sic] from the very first I liked it for the way it handled, its cornering, and, in particular, for its comfort…." Nevertheless, he found its replacement, the Victor FB of 1961, "brisk, likeable and much more pleasant to look at than any of its predecessors."[18]

In 1957 the *coup de grâce* was administered by *The Autocar*, who left behind for ever the diffident style lampooned by *Punch* in 1954: "The variety of exterior curves and mouldings, coupled with the very wide application of chromium plate, give a flamboyant effect to the exterior which may appeal in export markets more than to the more conservatively-minded British motorist…. A rather disappointing feature of the car is the poor standard of coachwork construction. Both wing lines…can be seen to have ripples…. It is fair to suggest that the ready performance of this new model may well bring it success in the large market to which the specification appeals. But it would appear that further development work is required before the Victor may be recommended without reservation."[19] Vauxhall subsequently cancelled its advertising in the magazine for several months.

Most of the car's problems were caused by a lack of development. The first Victor prototype had run in Detroit in October 1955, and Harlow Curtice decided shortly afterwards that the new car would be announced in April 1957; early in 1956 the launch date was brought forward again to February 1, 1957, allowing the car to be shown at the Geneva Motor Show in March of that year.[20] This new timetable resulted in skimped development, poor build quality and a consequent rust-proneness in early Victors that undermined Vauxhall's long-term sales to a much greater extent than the early announcement increased them in the short term. The vice managing director of a Dutch GM dealership recalled, "I can tell you that Vauxhall built fine and reliable cars until 1957. But after 1957, the start of Victor production, we had daily to [deal] with technical problems around bodywork, engines, transmission, steering, paintwork and so on. Also the Viva (since 1964), the Velox, Cresta, and Viscount were of bad quality, so bad that we never got a fine, reliable GM product anymore. The sales results were so bad that around 1970, I had to reduce the number of employees from 95 to 16…."[21]

Vauxhall's greatest difficulty with the early Victor was with inconsistent clearances round the doors, which caused the seals both to leak and to pinch, a problem exacerbated by the complexities involved in designing and producing the car's reverse-raked windscreen pillars. And, as Maurice Platt remarked, "the publicity given to the announcement of a brand-new model results in an immediate and pressing demand for deliveries from dealers and customers."[22]

The Victor was widely advertised, first separately as a new model, and later in range advertisements alongside the Cresta, too. Illustrations from advertisements sometimes also appeared in catalogues; for example, the Gipsy Red Super in announcement advertising reappeared in the 1958 brochure with that year's hooded headlamp rims skilfully added. By September 1957 the Victor was being trumpeted as: "The success of the year…. The Victor recaptures the thrill you had with the very first car you owned…." Overseas readers of British magazines were encouraged to "see Britain in your own new Vauxhall, delivered the day you arrive…. You can choose left-hand or right-hand drive. There are many different colour combinations, upholstery alternatives of Nylon, Rayon, leather or Vynide." Motoring journalist Mike McCarthy remembered in 1991, "[W]hen I was a kid in Africa, my sister got married. She and her new husband came over to England for their honeymoon, and bought themselves a wedding present. It was a brand-new Victor, finished in a gaudy metallic lime green…with a 'tropical' kit which included a then-fashionable sun visor…over the windscreen. The first time they took it over 60mph, this visor blew off…. My other sister and her husband stuck to German machinery. First there was an Opel Olympia. My brother-in-law liked it so much he named his pet monkey Opel…."[23]

"Nothing rivals the 1958 Vauxhalls for value!" declared January 1958 advertising, which used a touched-up monochrome front-three-quarter photograph of the car from which the tail was curiously cropped just behind the rear doors, as if the original picture had been too large for the page. It was neatly reinstated — albeit in exaggerated length — in February's version of the advertisement. Practical features were described under cross-headings such as "Advanced styling," "Smoother ride," and "Greater safety." Some Victor advertisements were aimed specifically at female motorists. Readers of *Vogue* in the early summer of 1958 would "arrive in wonderful style…. All heads turn as you arrive…in your new Vauxhall Victor. For here is the most handsome, eye-catching of lower-priced cars…." The copy in this series was feminized with words and phrases such as "simplicity itself," "magical" and "exciting," and the appeal was personalized: the buyer would be "admired wherever you go…" and would "take pleasure in choosing from a range of modern colours the one that expresses your own personality" (although that metallic lime green was for export-market personalities only). In November 1958 the estate car, a "space-conscious four-seater," was included in a *Vogue* feature by Nancy Mitchell on fashionable clothes and cars.

In October 1958 the slogan, "Everyone drives better in a Vauxhall" appeared prominently at the foot of a two-page advertisement which trumpeted the Victor as "Britain's No. 1 export car, first choice of 125,000 motorists at home and abroad.... You've only got to be at the wheel of a Victor for five minutes to know what superlative value you're getting for your money.... And all over the country, Vauxhall Square Deal Service when you want it...." Many buyers did want it, but as a design the Victor was not inherently unreliable and it was, as *The Autocar* had predicted, an export success. Victor exports between February 1957 and February 1959 (when the Series 2 was announced) outnumbered those of any other single British model. In the United States, Pontiac dealers sold 17,365 Victors during 1958, and over 20,000 in 1959, with sales only falling in 1960 (to 10,958) when the market for imported small sedans contracted and stories about rust, unreliability and erratic service began to spread.[24] A large car hire firm in America bought 100 Victors for its self-drive fleet,[25] and over 11,000 were sent to Canada in 1958. Vauxhall's 1959 Motor Show publicity "newspaper," *Vauxhall News*, highlighted exports to Hawaii, Iran, Mexico, New Zealand, Mexico, Sweden, Switzerland and Venezuela, while other Victors went to the Benelux Countries and to the British Commonwealth. Many Victors were exported in "completely knocked down" (ckd) kit form for assembly at local General Motors plants. In January 1960, Envoy (sedan) and Sherwood (wagon) versions of the Victor Series 2 were announced exclusively for the Canadian market. Described on the cover of the catalogue as a "new British car designed and built especially for Canadians," the Envoy was sold by Chevrolet/Oldsmobile dealers, and it was replaced by an equivalent version of the 1961–64 Victor FB. Built in three sedan forms—Standard, Special and Custom—the Envoy differed from the Victor mainly in styling and interior trim details, the most obvious changes being to the grille and side-lights, tail-lights and body side decoration.[26]

By February 1959, 145,000 Victors had been built and an updated, Series 2, Victor was introduced with cleaner styling than that of the Series 1. The bonnet, roof and door pressings were more simply styled and there were plainer bumpers, lights and grille, with less chrome decoration inside the car. "This test confirms that much development work and attention to detail have gone into the Victor since

its introduction..." pronounced *The Autocar*, with a headmasterly satisfaction.[27] A De Luxe saloon, with leather seats and standard two-tone paint, was included in the range, and advertisements continued to use paintings which lengthened and widened the car to (roughly) the size of a Chevrolet Corvair, although a photograph of the De Luxe accompanied an intriguing late-1959 advertisement which reproduced large sections of a flattering road test by racing driver Roy Salvadori in *Sporting Motorist*, a new magazine produced by the owners of the famous *Autocourse* annuals. At the end of 1959, the new Victor was shown above a much smaller picture of an updated Cresta under the headline "Marvellous new cars...these 1960 Vauxhalls!" The copy quoted Salvadori's test and aimed the car upmarket: "A pride-and-joy car, the 1960 Victor...long-looking and low, clean-looking and modern; the sort of car the discerning motorist falls for the moment he takes it on the road." A similar advertisement, with the same headline and Cresta-specific copy, transposed the pictures, showing the Victor rather than the Cresta in a small scale at the foot of the page.

In the spring of 1960, W.S. Crawford Ltd. devised a short series of advertisements for the Victor under the headline, "You may not know the driver...but you recognise the car," which used distinctive drawings in pen and ink and implicitly acknowledged that the car had been controversial. The Victor was targeted towards those who *did* like it. A distinguished-looking passer-by watched the car approach: "You recognise the fine, graceful lines.... You've seen them time and again, and you've admired them. You've come to know that *these* are the lines of particular cars: distinctive cars...*Vauxhalls*.... For the handsome appearance of these Vauxhalls is, in truth, a reflection of the advanced engineering design. That long, low, modern look...means low centre of gravity and better roadholding. And large panoramic windows mean really wonderful all-round vision.... The *looks* are obvious. The good *sense* you can appreciate only by getting behind the wheel and having a trial run yourself...." 1959–60 advertising for the estate car was more conventional. The early opening copy line, "Always acknowledged as a very good looker," gave way to a "city saloon...country wagon" theme (though the use of "wagon" without "station" was unusual in Britain), and the owner was shown on one side of the car in a city suit and on the other (optimistically) in country tweeds. Most later advertisements showed the estate car with the tailgate open under lighthearted headlines such as "Space travel," "Wide open space," and "Goodness spacious."

In August 1960 the F-type Victor was restyled for the last time with a new five-bar grille, deeper rear window, a

Opposite: **Vauxhall Victor F-type Series 2.** If you're different and can't hide, stand out with confidence. Packard and Edsel made a virtue of controversial looks in their 1958 advertising, and Vauxhall tried the same trick in 1960. The copy, too, is American in style: remove anglicisms like "petrol" and change the marque name, and it could almost have been written for the 1953 Chevrolet. The type of illustration and layout, with its homage to the 1920s and use of black and white without shades of grey, was unique to this Victor campaign, and stood out in a year when advertising for rival medium-sized saloons—and even parallel advertisements for the Victor Estate Car—used photographs.

You may not know the driver

...but you recognise the car

A Vauxhall, of course. And very nice, too. You see so many, so often, yet you *notice* each one. No doubt about it, they do look good.

But there's much more to a Vauxhall than graceful line and gloss of finish. There's something very special about the whole engineering design. A power-packed engine that really makes the most of your petrol; a low centre of gravity for roadholding and safety; panoramic windows that ensure all-round vision and easy parking. These are only a few of the obvious Vauxhall advantages.

Why not visit your Vauxhall dealer, get behind the wheel, and go for a trial run? You've *seen* there's nothing quite like a Vauxhall. Now you'll *feel* it too. No strain, no effort, just the sheer enjoyment of effortless driving.

VICTOR £505 + £211.10.10 PT (£716.10.10)
VICTOR SUPER £530 + £221.19.2 PT (£751.19.2)
VICTOR DE LUXE £565 + £236.10.10 PT (£801.10.10)
VICTOR ESTATE CAR £605 + £253.4.2 PT (£858.4.2)
VELOX 6-cylinder £655 + £274.0.10 PT (£929.0.10)
CRESTA 6-cylinder £715 + £299.0.10 PT (£1,014.0.10)
Vauxhall Motors Limited · Luton · Bedfordshire

EVERYONE DRIVES BETTER IN A

VAUXHALL

modified boot lid, a new dashboard and other trim modifications inside and out. October 1960's "Drive into the motorway age!" was topical, the M1 motorway having been opened in November 1959, and highlighted features included "new big-end bearings for the famous Victor engine," a useful precaution as many motorists cruised at much higher speeds than before; there would be no motorway speed limit until April 1965. "Everyone drives better…" a slogan that first appeared in 1958, continued until 1961, when a slightly desperate-sounding series of monochrome advertisements, headlined "Own a wonderful world! Own a Vauxhall," showed paintings of the Victor against line-drawn holiday backgrounds and described selling-points such as "space for everything" and "family-budget prices." The hectic copy continued in more conventional advertising for the last of the estate cars, too: "It not only takes, but gives. Gives comfort, with its fabulous load-loving suspension…. Gives fun, with its vigorous fuel-eking engine…."

American advertising for the Victor Series 2 used both paintings and photographs and showed the car with left-hand drive in British settings while emphasizing its American features. "Britain's Vauxhall — this is the fine small car from England sold and serviced by Pontiac dealers throughout America" was a typical, sensible headline, as was "Pamper your pride as well as your purse — go Vauxhalling" — even if fewer Americans than in 1958 were willing to take the risk. Victor advertising in mainland Europe could be imaginative, too. A Swiss 1961 piece, appropriately from agent Victor N. Cohen, showed the upper half of the car in profile, cropped just below the side fluting and driven by an attractive model, against a pure white background. Above the car was an apple, as big as the car's roof, with an arrow through its centre. This juxtaposition of cars with simple objects related to them emotionally, but not spacially or logically, had yet to feature in home market British car advertising.[28] The model was finally discontinued in July 1961, after 390,745 cars had been built. It had been a qualified success, promoted by advertising that was occasionally, as in the spring of 1960, unique and distinctive. Four more Victor series would follow, the last of which, the FE, would continue in India, as the Hindustan Contessa, into the 21st century.

The Velox and similar, more luxurious, Cresta, which replaced the E-series "sixes" in October 1957, were never as controversial as the Victor, and potential difficulties with windscreen pillars and door seals were prevented before production began. Harlow Curtice, recalled Maurice Platt, was impressed when he visited Vauxhall in the middle of October 1955: "David Jones had staged his styling exhibits with customary skill, the centrepiece being a beautifully executed,

full-scale representation of his concept of Model PA…. Daringly flamboyant, but free from the fussy quirks which marred the Victor, it was in my opinion the *tour de force* of all the new models for which David was responsible during his long career at Vauxhall. The panoramic windscreen looked much more attractive in the setting of a car that was six inches wider and two inches lower than the Victor…. Later on, when we experienced production difficulties with both our new models, the PA…was never so harshly criticized as the Victor; good-looking motor cars, like handsome people, are forgiven many shortcomings."[29]

But the PA was almost as rust-prone as the Victor, and for many of the same reasons, which included inconsistent paint finishing and the absence of full wheel arches inside the rear wings, which resulted in mud being thrown up into the wings and panelwork beneath the three-piece rear window (a feature shared with many of GM's 1957 cars in America). The windscreen added significantly to the torsional strength of the body, and could shatter if the car had corroded and was jacked up carelessly in the wrong place.[30] E.J. Attree, who worked in Vauxhall's engineering department in the late 1950s, recalls, "Vauxhall went down in a welter of rusted body shells, starting with the E-type…and following on with the appalling 1957 F-type, the Victor; the débâcle was completed by the nearly-as-awful 1958 PA…. The frantic rusting was aided and abetted…by much dreadful design work, courtesy of GM in the States in the case of the F-type, leading to many both normal and bizarre field complaints…the body shells of the F and PA broke up beyond economical repair after 500 miles in East Africa and similar rough but dry territories. The datum at the time was the Peugeot 203 and 403, which would last 5000 miles before repair, and their reputation for durability carried on into the 404."[31] But the Peugeot was known as one of the most robust cars of its period, and Stuart Bladon, who used one of the first Friary estate car conversions of the PA in Yugoslavia in 1959, found that, apart from trouble with wheels and tyres, "everything else stood up to the bad roads very well indeed."[32]

The Velox and Cresta were easier to advertise than the Victor, and they represented good value at £983 17s and £1073 17s respectively. The potential market for large, six-cylinder models was smaller than that for the four-cylinder Victor[33], but Vauxhall had fewer rivals in the six-cylinder field and the sixes competed mainly against Ford's Zephyr (£916 7s) and Zodiac (£1013 17s). The Vauxhalls were widely exported but, unlike the Fords, did not officially enter the United States although occasional examples trickled in. The Velox and Cresta immediately became known for their bright colours — single tones on the Velox, two-tone schemes

Opposite: **Vauxhall Victor Super F-type Series 2.** "Completely proof against dust, draughts, water"… That was more than could be said for early F-types, even before they started rusting, which they did rapidly. Series 2s like this 1961 car (distinguished from the 1959–60 model by the five-bar grille and deep rear window) lasted better — say six years rather than four or five — though the vicious winter of 1962–63 sent many to an early grave. The curious mixture of 1930s-style worthiness and camp prose in this piece was unusual by the early 1960s; like the car, such things were no longer fashionable, and would make way for more confident advertising when the new FB Victors came along later in the year.

THE FIELD. *February 16 1961*

Own a wonderful world!
Own a Vauxhall

Own a 1961 Vauxhall Victor and possess the wide world around you, the big outdoors, sea and country and sky. Own a Victor and command a host of luxurious, wantable features :

'Motorway age' engine

High cruising speeds. High average speeds. Vivid performance with outstanding economy and long life.

Space for everything
and everybody

Ample room for 4 adults and 2 children, plus 19 cubic feet of luggage in the big, flat-floor boot.

All-round vision

Panoramic windscreen, low glass-line. Vast rear window that goes high into the roof. Better vision, greater safety.

Vauxhall extra quality

Splendid finish outside. Splendid finish inside. Elegant facia. Vauxhall chrome-on-nickel-on-copper plating. Underbody sealing. Underwing sealing. Completely proof against dust, draughts, water.

All-synchro magic

Synchromesh on all gears including bottom. Touch-perfect steering. Road-perfect brakes. Better to drive. Safer to drive.

Family-budget prices

Victor prices from £723.12.6 inc. PT.
Victor Super, above, £535 + £224.0.10 PT (£759.0.10).
Velox and Cresta prices from £929.0.10 inc. PT. Go to your nearest Vauxhall dealer and have a free trial run!

Vauxhall Motors Limited, Luton, Beds.

EVERYONE DRIVES BETTER IN A VAUXHALL

More than a thousand Vauxhall dealers offer top quality service with factory-trained mechanics and charges based on standard times.

on the Cresta—which were regularly updated. Most famous of all were the pinks, such as the light Mountain Rose (1957) and darker Royal Glow (1958), which were daring even in a period (1955–59) when colour schemes were generally becoming less conservative. Rootes had led the way in 1953 with the Hillman Californian and in 1955 with its almost-successor, the Sunbeam Rapier. But the greyish-lilac offered with deep maroon in the first monocoque Humber Hawk of 1957 (and in its leather interior) was not *quite* pink. Goodyear, meanwhile, used a pink Cresta to advertise its new "3.T Nylon Tyres" in upmarket magazines in May 1959, and a similar advertisement five months later showed an updated Cresta in two-tone lilac and mauve. Vauxhall's publicity photographs depicted the Cresta with imaginary owners posed in ball gowns and dinner jackets against a pure white background in a style pioneered in the early 1950s by Boulevard Photographic in the United States.[34] Catalogues (of which at least one featured a pink Cresta on the cover) showed both photographs and paintings of the cars. As with many marques, paintings remained popular in catalogues after they had become rare in press advertising, and some catalogues for the last of the PAs featured highly attractive artwork.

Most advertising for the PA was in black and white, and early pieces were modest. "Vauxhall leads again…" began a monochrome October 1957 advertisement for the Vauxhall range, "The Victor—the most successful car for years…and now, the entirely new Vauxhall Sixes…. Now the new Velox and Cresta sweep powerfully into the lead of 6-cylinder, 6-seater design. Handsome in looks, with one clean, unbroken line from headlight to tail…. See them at the Motor Show. Take them on the road…. The new Velox and Cresta will be [in your local Vauxhall dealer's showroom] soon. Watch out for local announcements." Paintings of the Cresta lengthened it only slightly. The following October, a list of starred features was headlined "It all adds up to a Vauxhall!" in a similar-looking advertisement, which underneath pictures of the two cars continued, "At the show or on the road, look out for the new good looks of the Vauxhalls, in their distinctive 1959 colours. Notice how perfectly those clean, *modern lines express the car of today*" (italics original). Although the advertisement looked similar to that of the previous year, the Cresta was identifiably a 1959 model, its front quarter-light pillar moved back a little from the original, 1957, position.

A September 1958 advertisement for the Velox and Cresta highlighted the available colour schemes by illustrating an Imperial Ivory and Royal Glow Cresta with two models who looked at colour samples spread around them. This theme was unique in British car advertising and the piece appeared in several magazines without a specifically female readership. Later advertisements photographed the Cresta in upmarket settings, and included in one night-time photograph the kind of country house also used by Daimler (1956) and Austin (1958). The copy was in modern typefaces with plenty of white space between the lines: "People going places…. On occasions like this, when everything about you must be in the superlative, you'll be glad you chose a Cresta. Here is a fine car that perfectly expresses your good taste [*sic*]; a car combining new beauty of line with the most advanced engineering features…. Go Vauxhall." In February 1959 the car was shown outside that other staple of aspirational advertising, the theatre, with a modified opening copy line, "Whenever you find yourself at the centre of the scene…" and—in an appeal to middle-class allegiences rather than through pessimism or oversight—an Automobile Association, or AA (information and breakdown service) badge attached to the grille. "Only a trial run in the new Cresta (or Velox) can fully demonstrate to you its many advantages over other 6-cylinder cars," concluded the copy. Five months later, "Go ahead people" were shown beside a boating lake, anticipating the way in which fun would rival static status in middle-market advertising during the 1960s.

In August 1959 the sixes were improved with stiffer body shells, one-piece rear windows, deeper grilles slightly like those of the 1955–56 Packard, narrower side trims and new colours which included two-tone layouts in three layers. In August 1960 the engine was enlarged to 2651cc, increasing its power from 83 bhp to 95 bhp (gross) at a slight cost in smoothness. Updated exterior trim gave the Cresta in particular a more sober and substantial appearance.[35] Yet the design was rapidly becoming outdated, and during 1960–1962 advertising increasingly concentrated on features such as the larger engine and Hydra-matic transmission, which was optional from October 1960.

An estate car, produced by Friary Motors Ltd. in Basingstoke, Hampshire was announced in May 1959. During the 1950s, Friary Motors Ltd. was a car dealership owned by the former owner of Aston Martin until 1947, Gordon Sutherland, who in 1950 had bought E.D. Abbott Ltd. of Farnham, Surrey. In 1958, Abbott's chief designer, Peter Woodgate, designed an estate car conversion for the PA. But Sutherland decided not to build the car under the Abbott name, which was already associated with the firm's existing, rival, Farnham conversions of the Ford Consul, Zephyr and Zodiac. So Friary Motors Ltd. bought a factory at Hatch,

Opposite: **Vauxhall Velox Hydra-matic (PA).** Copywriting in transition. The layout is pure Detroit, circa 1955, but the photograph and continental setting are what one would expect from an English advertisement in 1961. This piece appeared in the sepia-tinted holiday supplement of a women's magazine but, colouring apart, it is mild by comparison with many. Ford had offered an automatic on the rival Zephyr and Zodiac as long ago as October 1956 and made much of it in a 1958–59 campaign featuring *haute couture* creations of the fashion designer, John Cavanagh. "Ford sets the fashion" became "Ford automatically sets the fashion," as being first with the feature allowed Ford to be first with the best slogan, too.

Happier holidays
with
fabulous *Hydra-matic*

Holidaying at home — touring abroad — Hydra-matic brings a wonderful new simplicity and relaxation to driving. Hydra-matic is the new automatic transmission, optional on the Vauxhall Velox and Cresta. There is no clutch to engage or disengage. Gear changing is done for you – so beautifully smoothly you'll never notice it happening. Effort and driving strain are reduced. Safety is increased.

In heavy traffic and hill-climbing the necessity for repeated gear-changing and clutch-work is gone! Motoring becomes fascinatingly simple. And yet – Hydra-matic still lets you demonstrate all your driving skill when you want to. Ask your nearest Vauxhall dealer all about it. Better still, arrange to have an early trial run and feel the wonderful difference yourself. Driving is a holiday with Hydra-matic !

HYDRA-MATIC VELOX £775 plus £324.0.10. P.T. £1,099.0.10.
HYDRA-MATIC CRESTA £835 plus £349.0.10 P.T. £1,184.0.10.
ALL SYNCHRO-MESH MODELS :
VELOX £655 plus £274.0.10. P.T. £929.0.10 ● CRESTA £715 plus £299.0.10. P.T. £1,014.0.10.
VAUXHALL-FRIARY ESTATE CARS from £1,222.5.10 inc. P.T.
All-synchro plus overdrive £63.15.0. extra inc. P.T.
All powered by the new 2.6 litre six-cylinder Vauxhall engine.

EVERYONE DRIVES BETTER IN A VAUXHALL

Vauxhall Motors Limited, Luton, Bedfordshire

The Field, April 5, 1962 (Inset author photograph: sole surviving 1957 Velox Dormobile seen by chance in Ongar, Essex, in 1985)

VERY DISTINGUISHED ESTATE CAR

There's an air of quiet distinction about the Vauxhall Friary Estate Car. Elegant in town, powerful on the open road, rugged in the country, it makes a virtue of versatility. The thoroughbred lines you can see for yourself; what may surprise you is the immense carrying space – 6′ 5″ long, more than in any comparable estate car. All that space, and all the power of Vauxhall's 2.6 litre engine – yet the Friary Velox and Cresta are as easy to handle as only a Vauxhall can be. Very distinguished estate cars.

Friary Velox £1,258.6.5 inc. PT. Friary Cresta £1,348.0.2 inc. PT.
Laycock Overdrive £65.12.6 extra inc. PT. Hydra–matic transmission £175 extra inc PT.

Vauxhall Friary | Velox and Cresta

Vauxhall Motors Ltd., Luton, Beds.   Hydra-matic is a registered trade mark

near Basingstoke, in which to build the PA, which would be marketed under the Friary name. At the Motor Show in October, the public were enthusiastic, but on the day following the end of the show a serious fire destroyed the Friary factory together with many cars. Only in the spring of 1960 did the conversion become readily available again. It was advertised separately from the standard PAs, as in May 1960: "'Skittles anyone…?' asks the man who's just bought himself a Vauxhall-Friary estate car. He's boasting, of course, about its incredibly long floor when the back seat is folded…. Production of the Vauxhall-Friary has been substantially increased so you can probably have one in time for your summer holiday if you see your Vauxhall dealer now."[36] Costing £1222 as a Velox and £1309 as a Cresta, this car was not entirely an innovation for Vauxhall, as the Grosvenor Carriage Co. Ltd. of Kilburn, west London and Martin Walter Ltd. of Folkstone, Kent had both offered estate car conversions of the Velox E-type from October 1956. But "neither [model was] ever properly developed, and it was left to Friary Motors three years later to show that they had missed a market opportunity."[37] Martin Walter would return with attractive estate car conversions of subsequent Crestas (PB and PC).

The 1960–62 Velox and Cresta were advertised both individually and together. A May 1960 advertisement for the Velox made a feature of the car's name; "V.e.l.o.x — pronounced sensation! Some people say Vell-ox. Some people say Vee-lox. But all Velox owners say *sensational*…." The copy accompanied a stylized painting of the car, which was a novelty by 1960 and even more so by March 1961 when a similar illustration, again of a Velox, was used to promote the Velox and Cresta within the "wonderful world" theme also used for the Victor. Both advertisements employed a marque-wide "look" common to Victor advertising. Hydramatic was promoted vigorously in pieces without equivalent in publicity for the Victor, which was available only with manual gears. In February 1961 a very sober-looking Hydramatic Velox was shown in the Alps; other advertisements depicted a 1961 Cresta trickling through London: "Traffic…traffic…traffic…stop…amber…go…zebra…. The only driver who's completely happy here is the one in the Hydra-matic Vauxhall." At the end of the year, 1962 models were offered with optional disc brakes at a modest £21 17s 6d over the car's basic price of £1043. This time the car was shown outside a more modern, continental house in the daytime.

By 1962, the PA was looking old-fashioned. Like many other advertisers in a similar position, Vauxhall promoted the car as distinguished, the Cresta offering "very distinguished motoring" while the Friary was a "very distinguished estate car." In July 1962, in one of the last advertisements for the PA, a photograph of a Velox rolling through a bend accompanied quotations ("As virile as they come") from a road test for the *Sunday Pictorial* by racing driver Jack Brabham, and styling was not mentioned at all. The most distinctive late advertisements for the car were a short series from March, April and May 1962, aimed at female readers, whose style echoed much car advertising in mainland Europe. The faces of three very different models accompanied copy that reflected their expressions. "Privileged pair!— Together you sing through the countryside, laughing at the miles. You go elegantly to town, admired and sometimes envied. You arrive relaxed and *very* sure of yourselves. You and your new Cresta. You look so well together," promised one piece, while another model, who looked more than capable of cutting up traffic if in the mood, was captioned "Witch!— You skim the countryside, melting the miles. You charm your way through town. You arrive serene. Is it your magic — or is it your new Cresta with Hydra-matic to do all the gear-changing for you?"

In the early 1960s, with new Victor and six-cylinder ranges, Vauxhall styling changed completely. Fins and chrome, which had never been taken up as enthusiastically by other British manufacturers as by Vauxhall, were in decline in the United States and were becoming outmoded in Britain almost as quickly. Old advertising styles were abandoned too, and although there was no cohesive look to Vauxhall advertising between 1962 and 1966 — that would have to wait until the "Vauxhall Breed's got style" campaign of 1967 — there was a consistent realism. With few exceptions, Vauxhall advertising during these years used photographs of cars seen in daytime settings with owners who, if socially optimized, were essentially plausible.

In September 1961 Vauxhall announced the new Victor FB range under the slogan, "the clean line of good design." This induced in Britain's motorists the kind of smile that greets the late convert. For Vauxhall had converted, and the slogan was used in headlines and copy throughout the model's life. Commentators, too, praised the new design. So great was the change in Vauxhall's design philosophy that the company considered dropping the "Victor" name, "to emphasize the extent of the changes which had been made."[38] It was the general manager of General Motors Overseas Operating Division (GMOO), Pete Hogland, who recommended that it should continue. The decision to produce the car was made in 1959, when it was approved by GM's new president, John Gordon. According to

Vauxhall Cresta Friary Estate Car (PA). A subdued advertisement for a car that only had a few months to run by April 1962. "There's an air of quiet distinction" was pure wishful thinking, as no amount of Wolseleyish prose and modesty in illustration could disguise the car's exuberant styling. The new model that succeeded it later in the year was much more conventional, although it is the PA which is the more sought after by collectors today. Curiously, Martin Walter's 1957 "Dormobile" conversion of the earlier Velox E-type (inset), though intended as a specialized vehicle for camping during long tours abroad, had looked much more integrated as an estate car.

The BIG Vauxhalls for '62!

Choose from 2 models... 3 transmissions... 15 colours!

With the new 6-cylinder models for 1962, Vauxhall gives you the *choicest* big-car motoring. More comfortable, more exhilarating, safer than ever before, these beautiful cars are now offered with a very wide choice of alternative equipment.

TWO MODELS – Cresta and Velox! Both luxury cars in every detail except price. Optional for 1962 are power-assisted brakes (disc type on front wheels) and individual front seats.

THREE TRANSMISSIONS –

HYDRA-MATIC, the simplest, smoothest and safest automatic transmission ever devised.

OVERDRIVE, which gives you the benefit of two extra gears.

ALL-SYNCHRO (fitted as standard), the easiest non-automatic gear changing—women drivers particularly like "synchro" in first gear.

Have a look at some of the other fine quality features shown here. Then check them for yourself at the nearest Vauxhall showroom. A trial run will prove everything in the pleasantest possible way.

Power '62
'Motorway age' 2.6 litre, 6-cylinder engine. High average speeds. Jubilant performance. Welcome economy. Long, long life.

Safety '62
New zone-toughened safety glass windscreen. New wide-sweep wipers. For high speed drivers, disc front brakes with power assistance (optional extras).

Comfort '62
Ample room for six adults, loads of luggage. Choice of a full-width front seat, or individual front seats. Many detail refinements and extra quality features.

Hydra-matic '62
Simplest, smoothest safest automatic transmission. Takes the tension out of traffic driving. Velox and Cresta are the only British cars below £3,000 to offer it.

Colour '62
Fifteen colours—plus, for Cresta, nine two-tone combinations – to which Vauxhall's new long-life, high-lustre paint imparts an impeccable finish.

Prices '62
Velox £655
plus £301.8.11 P.T. £956.8.11
Cresta £715
plus £328.18.11 P.T. £1,043.18.11
Vauxhall-Friary Estate Cars
from £1,258.6.5. inc. P.T.
LAYCOCK DE NORMANVILLE OVERDRIVE
£65.12.6 extra inc. P.T.
HYDRA-MATIC TRANSMISSION
£175 *extra inc.* P.T.

Vauxhall Velox & Cresta

Vauxhall Motors Limited Luton Beds

Maurice Platt, "we were able to show Gordon a full-scale styling representation…. David Jones…had demonstrated the versatility of his talent by creating a simple, restrained, yet attractively styled saloon, only fractionally larger than the existing Victor. The panoramic windscreen had been discarded and the body presented few design or manufacturing problems. Although we had been in touch with Chevrolet during the evolution of the Corvair and had also studied the design of various rear-engine and front-drive cars, prudence prompted the retention of a conventional front-engine rear-drive configuration for our new Victor which must, above all, be free from teething troubles. However, there were a number of worthwhile modifications to the engine and front suspension plus [the option of] a new, four-speed 'all-synchro' gearbox. The new Victor was approved, with very few reservations…."[39]

Early advertising for this Victor showed a touched-up photograph of a Victor De Luxe in two-tone pink, the shades less striking than those of the original Cresta. "The new Vauxhall Victor is a car of outstanding quality and grace. Every contour bears the hall-mark of good design. Every detail has been planned with scrupulous care to match the clean good looks…" promised an announcement advertisement in September 1961. A more down-to-earth parallel piece highlighted, among bullet-pointed features, "meticulous anti-rust treatment including under-sealing of body and wings. Superb paint-finish in Vauxhall's new formula synthetic-cellulose enamel." In June 1962 a painting of the car was shown below the headline, "Good design speaks for itself and for you," while in January 1963 — in the middle of one of the hardest winters of the century — the car was shown driving down a slushy country lane with the headline, "Nice day for a Victor" — at a time when such conditions were driving many of its 1957–58 predecessors to early disintegration. "The Victor ignores the weather; snubs it; triumphs over it…. The clean line of the body 'takes' paint admirably; *under* the body, mud and poisure traps have been virtually eliminated," said the copy, "Your Vauxhall dealer…[will] be glad to arrange a trial drive for you in the impervious Victor. Any time. Whatever the weather." In April 1963 the Victor was "…just like one of the family. Which one?" in an advertisement in which the car was shown with "Mum"…"Dad"…"son" and "daughter," echoing their characteristics ("tireless…dependable…tough… stylish"). The theme had been popular with advertisers of British cars in the 1930s. A June 1963 piece began, "The clean line of good design is doing fine" — which it was. Maintenance, meanwhile, was usefully reduced: where earlier Vauxhalls had numerous grease nipples needing frequent atten-

tion, the new Victor had only four, which by 1963 were claimed to need greasing only every 30,000 miles. "Hello stranger!" said one headline, showing a grease gun and a Victor on a garage hoist.

In July 1963, the Victor was updated with a new aluminium grille, a revised rear number plate arrangement and a 1594cc engine.[40] "Let's take *my* car!," said the owner in a March 1964 advertisement, "That's what *you'll* be saying for a long time to come, if you buy a Vauxhall Victor…. Magic Mirror acrylic lacquer keeps its showroom shine without polishing." J. Eason Gibson, trying out a De Luxe estate car in 1964, admired its "expensive shade of maroon" and the "pleasant change" from earlier "pastel shades" represented by the new colours: "Since it was first introduced…the Vauxhall Victor estate car has made many friends, because of its roominess for both passengers and luggage and its gentlemanly appearance."[41] Canadians continued to receive Envoy sedans and Sherwood wagons, neatly trimmed with the grille, side flashes and tail-lights of the VX 4/90 at the top of the British Victor range. Colours included a striking mid-blue with pale blue side flash. The new Victor was available on an "order basis only" in the United States during the 1962 model year.

The estate car, available initially as a single model trimmed to Super specification and from late 1962 as a De Luxe as well, was a success, the styling of the rear perfectly matching that of the saloon. The tailgate incorporated a curved window, more expensive to produce than a flat pane, which wrapped into the roof and improved headroom during loading, reducing the height to which the tailgate had to rise, and so making it easier to close. *Small Car* considered that "appearance-wise the Victor pleases most of the people most of the time. Turn your mind back to its Mark 1 [*sic*] saloon predecessor (which won more than one prize for the ugliest postwar car) and you must give Vauxhall full marks for owing up when they've made a mistake and putting it right in a high, wide and handsome way."[42] Early advertising for the estate car followed the general theme and appearance of that for the saloons, but the De Luxe, costing £804 2s 1d compared with the £737 12s 11d for the 1961 original, was aimed upmarket and shown with sportsmen and horses. Estate car design would become a Vauxhall forte, especially with the Viva (HB) of 1967.

The Vauxhall VX 4/90 crowned the Victor range. Costing £984 3s 1d, it had appeared at the 1961 Motor Show but was first produced early in 1962. With a twin-carburettor, aluminium-head engine[43], it was much faster than the ordinary Victor and with special trim and equipment it was also more luxurious — except, perhaps, in its seats, as those of the

Opposite: **Vauxhall Cresta (PA).** By the end of 1961, the 1957-style six-cylinder Vauxhalls were in their last year. Motorists had long since decided whether or not they liked the PA's style (a Cresta is shown here), and where 1958's "three-window" model had appeared outside a traditional country house at night with its owners in evening dress, this house is smaller and simpler, with an owner who is young and smiling rather than dutifully aspirational. Happily for the copywriter, the car was still modern in its features, which are described in a mid-Atlantic style with a sideways glance at the rival Ford Zephyr and Zodiac, which did not yet have the Vauxhall's useful all-synchromesh gears. The "motorway age" engine gave a 0–60 time, in a manual car, of about 16-17 seconds and a top speed of 90-95 mph.

YES!
THE NEW VAUXHALL VICTOR

The car that says **YES!**
to everything you ask of it

Good looks. Good design. Performance with safety. Quality with outstanding value. If you're talking about the new Victor, the answer is YES all along the line. Because here is a car that is every bit as good to look at as it is to drive. A car with beautifully clean contours, superb finish and immaculate attention to detail. A car to drive and *enjoy*. Your Vauxhall dealer will be delighted to provide proof that the new Victor says YES to everything *you* want in a car.

3-speed or 4-speed ALL-synchro gears
(3-speed column change, or optional 4-speed floor-mounted lever)

More comfort, more space for 4 or 5 adults
(extra legroom front *and* rear. 21½ cu. ft. luggage space)

Maintenance costs cut by two-thirds
(only 4 nipples which require lubricating only every 12,000 miles)

Superb, long-lasting paint finish
(in new formula synthetic-cellulose enamel. 14 attractive colours)

Victor Saloon £510 + £234.19.9. P.T. (£744.19.9)
Victor Super £535 + £246.8.11. P.T. (£781.8.11)
Victor De Luxe £580 + £267.1.5. P.T. (£847.1.5)
(including leather upholstery and heater)
Victor Estate Car £590 + £271.13.1. P.T. (£861.13.1)

See and try the new Victor
at your local Vauxhall dealer's.
Or write for catalogue to
Vauxhall Motors Ltd., Luton, Beds.

THE FIELD, with which is incorporated *Land and Water* and *The County Gentleman*, is published every Thursday, price 2s. 0d., by THE HARMSWORTH PRESS LTD., 8, Stratton Street, London, W.1, Thursday, October 26, 1961. Printed by GALE & POLDEN LTD., 28, Craven Street, London, W.C.2, and Aldershot, Hampshire. PRINTED IN GREAT BRITAIN, and registered as a newspaper for transmission in the United Kingdom and to Canada by magazine post. Entered as second class matter at the Post Office, New York, N.Y. March 1897.

Vauxhall Victor (FB). Good looks? Immaculate attention to detail? In a Vauxhall Victor? Well, yes actually, at least by family car standards, and even yes to reasonable rust resistance. Stylist David Jones managed to incorporate American touches such as the body side creases (pure 1961 Chevrolet) and tail-light pods (originally 1949 Ford but also found on GM's German Victor equivalent, the Opel Rekord P2 of 1960–63) without producing an American-style car. Only the door handle design was curious, with a button that moved sideways into the handle rather than into the door; it was slightly awkward, but did allow the dextrous, hands full, to open the door with an elbow. Most colours were more conventional than the two-tone pink shown in catalogues and early advertising, and the FB was probably the best-liked Victor series. Quite a few survive.

go on then – DRIVE

the VX4/90 understands

This is a car that *responds* to driving. Vauxhall build it for the motorist who needs 4/5 seats and a big boot, exceptional maintenance economy – yet who wants a car for *driving* as well as mere transport.

The VX4/90 gives you vivid motoring with the velvet touch. It accelerates nimbly to almost 90 mph (0-50 mph in 11.9 seconds); its steering and suspension are taut and true; the floor-mounted lever operates four sweetly-matched gears, *all* synchro. That's vivid motoring! And the velvet touch is everywhere in the car: in the extra safety of power-assisted disc front brakes; in the rich upholstery, the heater, the other de luxe appointments.

Go on then, *drive* a VX4/90. Your Vauxhall dealer will be pleased to arrange a trial.

More than a thousand Vauxhall dealers offer top quality service with factory-trained mechanics and charges based on standard times.

305

VAUXHALL
VX4/90

1.5 litre 4-cylinder engine. 81 bhp at 5,200 rpm. Aluminium cylinder head. Twin carburettors. Special inlet manifold. 4-speed all-synchro gearbox, short floor-mounted lever. Power-assisted brakes, discs at front. Specially tuned suspension for fast, tough driving. Lubrication every 30,000 miles.

£814.19.7 *inc. £140.19.7 tax*

Vauxhall Motors Limited · Luton · Beds

Vauxhall VX 4/90 (FB). An action shot, of a kind unusual in Vauxhall advertising before the middle of the decade, shows the car with which Vauxhall beat Ford into the mass-produced GT saloon market in 1962. It was distinguished from the regular Victor by a different grille, side flashes (revived from the 1957 E-type Cresta and subsequently copied by other marques), inverted T-shaped tail-lights and special wheel trims and colours. Less obviously, the engine and interior were upgraded too, as the copy reveals.

Victor De Luxe, in leather, were exceptionally comfortable. Part sporting, part sybaritic, the VX 4/90 fitted no established niche. It was a pioneer in an expanding but specialized market which still associated performance in a compact car with expensive continental models. The VX 4/90's most obvious distinguishing feature was a side flash, similar to that of the 1957 Cresta E-type.[44] Early 1962 advertising emphasized the VX 4/90's sporting character by showing the car speeding along a main road and emphasized its features. In June 1962 the headline, "Vivid motoring" was superimposed on "Velvet touch" in a fainter grey, with a picture of the car at speed accompanying a list of features. Showing the car with other Victors in September 1962, the copywriter said, "The VX 4/90 has made motorists think again about 'performance' cars. It has shown that real liveliness and real luxury *can* go together in a roomy four-door saloon...." In February 1963 the theme was consolidated: "Go on then — DRIVE — the VX4/90 understands." Sporting drivers compared the VX 4/90 with the Cortina GT introduced in April 1963. The Vauxhall was more luxurious than the Ford, less sporting, but more refined.[45]

The mid-1960s were years of consolidation. New Velox and Cresta (PB) saloons, announced in the first week of October, 1962, adopted much of the restrained demeanour of the Victor, along with the "clean line of good design" as a theme in elegantly photographed brochures. Some commentators found the new sixes a little *too* utilitarian, partly for their innate sobriety, and partly because the doors were so obviously shared with the Victor, following a practice famously adopted by BMC with Austins.[46] Moreover, Vauxhall offered no equivalent to Ford's £846 12s 9d Zephyr 4, with its four-cylinder engine in a six-seater body. The Velox, at £936 0s 3d, was comparable with the Zephyr 6 at £929 2s 9d while the Cresta, at £1046 0s 3d, paced Ford's Zodiac at £1180 15s 3d. Yet, as with earlier models, the characters of the Fords and Vauxhalls were different, the Velox and Cresta, with their three-speed gearboxes (augmented by optional overdrive and Hydra-matic), more closely mirroring American compacts. The Cresta, although never as magisterial as a large Humber or Austin, was luxurious by British standards with a specification that included elaborately patterned door trims (something of a Vauxhall speciality) and walnut dashboard trim. Nevertheless, only a modest 87,047 PBs were sold in three years.

At the Motor Show in October 1963, the specialist independent coachbuilder Harold Radford announced a low-production, super-luxury Cresta Executive at £1524 6s 11d. With twin headlamps, spotlights, bumper overriders, special wheel covers, a ribbed finishing strip on the tail and beautifully painted, Radford's Cresta Executive looked quietly distinctive in a way that earlier Vauxhalls never could. The interior, with sliding division, picnic tables, transistor radio, adjustable reclining seats and reading lights, was hand-trimmed in leather, and the boot was carpeted.[47] At the same time, Martin Walter introduced estate car conversions of the Velox at £1202 17s 1d and of the Cresta at £1305 11s 3d, with heavy-duty springs and tyres and "67 cubic feet for cargo inside the handsomest body of them all!." In October 1964 the sixes gained a 115 bhp (net) 3.3 litre engine developed from an earlier Chevrolet design which, coupled to a four-speed gearbox (the three-speed remaining optional) consolidated the cars' effortless character. In April 1965 Powerglide replaced Hydra-matic as the optional automatic transmission, an apparently retrograde step even with an engine giving 175 lb. ft. of torque (net) at 2200 rpm. Hydra-matic had received its own advertisement in February 1963, at least in motoring publications: "Hydra-matic is a registered trade mark. Why? Four car makers in Britain can offer Hydra-matic.... One is Vauxhall. The other three don't concern you unless you have more than £2,500 to spend.... It is a highly advanced piece of engineering, and naturally other makers would like to copy it. That's why the design is protected by patents...."

Headlines for the range were conventional. "This is the rugged, practical, robust, *sensible* new Velox" reassured readers of the convert's earnest intent; and "The looks will win your heart at once — later you'll discover its dependability!" could have been written for an Austin. 1963's "It is, quite simply, a great motor car," within copy rather than as a headline, sounded enthusiastic rather than grandiose. "Test drive the magnificent Vauxhall Cresta. Learn what it means to have 113 brake horsepower right where you need it!" appealed to motorists new to large-engined cars in 1964, while "New for '65: the 3.3-litre Vauxhalls — The most powerful and luxurious cars in the £1,000 class" struck a suitably mid-Atlantic note. Snob-appeal arrived in the same year: "For successful men who prefer to drive their own cars..." and "Most powerful car in the £1,000 bracket — the car you like to drive yourself" were headlines in an established tradition of aspiration. Illustrations were occasionally dynamic: a 1963 Velox was photographed from the front, speeding under a motorway bridge ("the new Velox takes it easy at 85 m.p.h."), although it did not look its best from this angle, with the edges of the front wings curving down in something like a frown. But at night, with London's Big Ben or a palatial column nearby and with side-lights glowing, it was almost the "glamorous saloon" claimed.

In October 1964, the 1961-style Victors were replaced by

Opposite: **Vauxhall Velox (PB).** "Sensible...good design and excellent proportion...simple lines...remarkable harmony...." A new era had begun in Vauxhall styling and advertising, which from 1962 to 1966 concentrated on practical features rather than gimmicks. The theme of this picture, however, was inherited from the moody shots that sometimes promoted the PA in the middle of its run; and note the hint of a classical façade, that most ancient of snob motifs.

This is the rugged, practical, robust,
sensible new Velox

What, this glamorous saloon? Yes indeed. At heart the Velox is powerful, purposeful, eager for work and reliable as daybreak. Its elegance comes from good design and excellent proportion—so it looks as splendid on motorways as gliding through town.

The new Velox looks what it is: a great motor car. These simple lines enclose a car in which every part matches the rest perfectly.

There is a remarkable harmony between the big six-cylinder engine, the all-synchro gearbox and the power-disc brakes; between the supremely good driving position, the elegant fittings and the comfortable ride for six people. Add it all up, you get a great—and beautiful—car.

Add it all up for yourself. Arrange a trial drive with your Vauxhall dealer. (He is one of over 1,000 Vauxhall dealers who offer top quality service with factory-trained mechanics and charges based on standard times.)

VAUXHALL
VELOX

£840.7.1 (£695 + £145.7.1 p.t.)

Ample room for six BIG adults. Power-assisted brakes (disc at front). Lightly stressed 2.6 litre engine. All-synchromesh gearbox with optional overdrive, or Hydra-matic* automatic transmission. Lubrication every 30,000 miles. The more luxurious CRESTA costs £943.1.3 (£780 + £163.1.3 p.t.)

Vauxhall Motors Limited · Luton · Beds.

*Hydra-matic is a registered trade mark.

the Victor 101 (FC), a car "produced as ample, inexpensive family transport," with "sporting pretensions [having] little importance in Vauxhall's current ideology which stresses spaciousness, comfort, ease of control and style."[48] Yet it was never as well liked as its predecessor, and no-one seemed sure why it had acquired a new name: its wheelbase was 100 inches, its power 68 bhp. Somehow, too, it lacked the earlier model's character and "rightness." Announcement advertising used glittery paintings against blurred, light-infused backgrounds in an American style. Copywriters made much of "curved door and curved window [or "space-curved"] design," which allowed the body sides to taper inwards towards the roof without the doors having to be styled with a three- or four-inch "shoulder" below the waistline to give the thickness that would accommodate the retracted windows. Curved side glass (also fitted, with a shallower curve, to the 1963 Viva) was not a Vauxhall innovation — it was a feature of Chrysler Corporation's 1957 Imperial, among others — but the Victor's glass was more curved than most and its doors thinner than many. The saloon, available as a standard model, Super or De Luxe as before, was targeted towards the family man, while the estate car was heavily promoted in upmarket rural magazines with the usual entourage of horses and dogs. "It's yours. You can hardly believe it. So you keep on looking. Just to prove it," in October 1965, could be misinterpreted, and the passing horse looked bemused, as well he might. "Space Setter" in May 1966 suggested "pacesetter" — a failsafe in any car advertisement — and was clever: an alert reader would see the red setter dogs in the back. But could November 1966's caption, "Gold Medal Winner Earls Court Motor Show Awarded by the Institute of British Carriage and Automobile Manufacturers for Section 19 Estate Cars" justify the headline, "How to improve on a winner"?

In truth, Vauxhall's copywriters had a difficult task. In the late 1950s they had sought to make flamboyant designs acceptable while knowing that motorists who read advertisements had opinions of their own. In the 1960s the company could offer no distinctive theme like BMC's engineering or Ford's value for money and rally-inspired sportiness. Vauxhall had withdrawn completely from an already minimal involvement in motor sport when the VX 4/90 of Canadian driver Sam Nordell fell into a deep ravine during practice for the 1964 Monte Carlo Rally, killing Nordell. The need to persuade the reader with details of engine specifications, colour schemes and trim and transmission options inspired in the copywriters of W.S. Crawford Ltd. some of the longest

copy of its period. The more the reader knew, the more likely he was to buy. This philosophy was taken to its limit in a January 1965 advertisement for the VX4/90 which adopted the form of a magazine article. The headline, "A new VX4/90 — Sleek, roomy, civilized," was surmounted by a sub-heading, "Good news for family men who miss the breezy days of sports car motoring!" By using "A new..." rather than "The new...," the copywriter suggested distance and rational objectivity. Two short paragaphs in a fairly large typeface opened the copy, while the remaining 250 words appeared in smaller type under subheadings such as "Smoother performance," "Controls" and "A driver's car." The style was discursive, and the car itself was shown simply and neutrally, parked in sunshine under a willow tree with no owner or admirers in sight.

With the Viva of 1963, Vauxhall had two advantages: the Ford Anglia was four years old and looking out of date, and technically audacious rivals from BMC and Rootes were racking up warranty claims by the thousand. The same had been true at first of the ingenious if essentially conventional Triumph Herald. Criticized by some as being the embodiment of "biscuit tin" design, the Viva was nevertheless liked by many who did not usually like Vauxhalls. It combined simple engineering with lightness of control and a uniquely large boot in its class. Despite slightly peculiar, skittish handling bestowed by a transverse-leaf front suspension that was better in theory than in practice, the felicitously named Viva was a great success. With 1057cc, "It was the first of the light, cheap, family saloons with as much room as more expensive cars. The notable point about the Viva was that it was designed to be easy to manufacture. Like the Opel Kadett, based on identical principles, it was a dull car without any engineering innovations; but it was remarkably cheap to manufacture and could be sold at a competitive price [£527 7s 11d].... With the help of the Viva, Vauxhall sales expanded to 13 per cent of the British market, the highest ever achieved."[49] From May 1965, extra luxury with a side flash, revised tail-lights and new grille became available in an "SL" model, while from October extra performance could be had in a "90" — or with the SL package, in an SL90.

Early advertisements showed the Viva speeding along dusty tracks while press photographs and other publicity demonstrated its turning circle by making circles in the sand — a theme which challenged the Triumph Herald on its home ground and in its setting anticipated the Vauxhall campaigns of 1967–68. In the summer of 1966, Vauxhall

Opposite: **Vauxhall Victor 101 (FC).** Anything but Room 101 on wheels for the advancing suburbanite at last able to afford a new family car. An advertisement like this would not appeal to the reader who did not want to live, with minimal privacy, on an ultra-neat new housing estate, and the tone of the copy was faintly patronizing, as if written in the belief that people who did want to live there were practical and down-to-earth but not very bright. Every significant feature is carefully described in short paragraphs printed in clear typefaces. The car, like the location, was conventional, having evolved gently from the earlier FB. Curved side windows were also found on the German Ford Taunus 17M of 1960, the Opel Kapitän of 1964, the 1960 Lancia Flavia, the British Ford Zephyr and Zodiac Mk III (1962) and BMC's 1100 (also 1962), and so, although fitted to the Viva, were not a first for Vauxhall in Europe.

THE FIELD, *August 19 1965*

Owning a Victor 101 is like driving home a brand new car every day

There's nothing to touch the marvellous feeling when you take possession of a brand new car. When the car's a Victor 101, you get this same, proud feeling every time you drive it.

Feature for feature, point for point, the Victor 101 gives you more real car for your money than any of its competitors on the road.

Step inside. You'll see immediately that the Victor 101 is a *big* car. The sides of its elegant, wind-tunnel-tested body are specially curved to give you four valuable extra inches. Ample room for three abreast seating. And the enlarged boot measures 23 cubic feet.

Start the engine. Feel the extra power of the world-tried Victor engine. Cruise comfortably between 70-80 m.p.h. Halt comfortably too, thanks to the powerful brakes. Big drum brakes on all wheels with duo-servo at the rear. Power-assisted brakes, with discs at front, an optional extra.

Enjoy the luxury of the Victor 101 De Luxe. Sink your feet into the cut-pile carpeting, sit back in comfort in the individual front seats of soft Ambla, or optional leather if you prefer. Enjoy the steady flow of warmth from a new heater that heats the back of the car as efficiently as the front.

'New car' looks. This year, next year, year after year. The Victor 101 is protected outside by Magic Mirror acrylic lacquer, that keeps its showroom shine for years without polishing. Factory-applied underbody seal protects the car from mud, slush and grit.

If you would like to try this exciting car for yourself, contact your Vauxhall dealer. He'll bring a brand new Victor 101 right to your door.

Victor 101 Saloon   £690.6.3.
Victor 101 Super   £718.2.1.
Victor 101 De Luxe £774.17.11.
NOW WITH POWERGLIDE
world's smoothest automatic transmission.
Extra cost £96.13.4 on all Victors.
Prices include purchase tax and are ex-works

VAUXHALL
VICTOR 101

NOW!
VAUXHALL
VIVA

The 1 litre car with the millionaire ride

£527 inc p.t.

Compare the Viva with any car in its class. World-wide tests have proved its superiority in all these points: speed, handling, steering, roominess, suspension, and all-round finish. But drive one, find out for yourself!

Real comfort for four
S-T-R-E-T-C-H-I-N-G space for four big people. In all, more interior room *than in any comparable car.* Wide doors for easy access. Real 'millionaire' comfort in the specially sprung and padded seats.

Big car performance
Undoubtedly fastest in its class. Top speed 80 plus. Over 70 in third. Beats comparable cars in all speed ranges. Four-speed all-synchromesh gearbox. High performance engine. Optional disc brakes.

Roll Control Suspension
Viva's suspension will amaze you. You get 'millionaire' smoothness even on very rough surfaces. Sports car cornering with none of the pitch-and-toss some light cars have. Unique 'roll control'.

Best Steering and Handling
Carefully designed front-engine layout gives perfect handling and very easy access for service. Viva's steering effort is *lightest in its class.* Turning circle 29 ft., ideal for tight parking.

Carefully Designed Controls
All controls easy to reach. Headlamp dipper, flasher, horn and direction indicators controlled by one lever on steering column. Short gear-lever and handbrake fall perfectly to hand. Maximum all-round vision.

Enormous Boot
Viva first again on luggage room. Space for 10½ cu. ft. of hard suitcases. Lots more for soft baggage. The Viva's finish is meticulous. 5 gallons of paint protect the exterior. Complete underbody seal is standard.

VAUXHALL
VIVA

Vauxhall Viva, 4 cylinders, 1057 cc.
Saloon £527.7.11 (£436 + £91.7.11 p.t.)
De Luxe Saloon with heater,
Screenclean, etc., £566.1.3.
(£468 + £98.1.3 p.t.)
See the Viva at your Vauxhall dealer's now!

DESIGNED FOR OUT AND OUT RELIABILITY

Vauxhall Viva (HA). The miniature diagrams recalled earlier Victor advertisements—not to mention pre-war American advertising—but they were more technically orientated than 1961's, and the theme of this piece, which marked Vauxhall's re-entry into a market that it had deserted since the war, was resolutely functional. There is more than a hint of knocking copy in the reference to the "carefully designed front-engine layout" which implicitly contrasts the Viva with various imported continental models and, of course, the Hillman Imp. "A little better than average if not quite in the millionaire class" was the verdict of *Small Car* on the suspension in 1964, demonstrating that memorability can be a two-edged sword. Survivors occasionally turn up in scrapyards even today, in surprisingly good condition underneath.

If you want a car that's more spacious, powerful, handsome and luxurious—this one has it all. New Cresta. By Vauxhall.

Is this the car you've been waiting for? A car that's big and beautiful and seats six in easy comfort? A car that glides along motorways with scarcely more than a discreet purr? A car that out-accelerates practically every other saloon on the road?

You've been waiting for the new Cresta. By Vauxhall.

It's big. Long. Spacious. Four extra inches of shoulder room, but no wider than the previous Cresta. 30 cubic feet of boot!

The new Cresta is all luxury motor car. Sleek. Stylish. Roomy. Fast. Turn on the power. Six cylinders with 140 b.h.p. eager to serve you.

There's a choice of 3-speed column-change with or without overdrive, or 4-speed all synchro with floor-mounted lever. If you want to let the car do all the work, have your Cresta with Powerglide, world's smoothest automatic transmission. And power steering too, if you wish.

There are two models to choose from.

The Cresta with single headlamps. The Cresta de Luxe with twin headlamps and special luxury features. Both have what you're looking for in luxury motoring.

Cresta   £956 . 2 .11
Cresta de Luxe   £1058 .17.1
Prices include P.T. and are ex-works.

See your Vauxhall dealer and book a trial run.

VAUXHALL. BRED FOR SUCCESS. — BETTER THAN EVER FOR '66.

1250

Vauxhall Cresta (PC). American-style advertising for the last and biggest Vauxhall to bear the Cresta name. Vauxhall employed that old Ford trick of moving existing models upmarket while bringing in new, smaller cars at the bottom of the range. The twin headlamps of this de luxe model make the car look more than ever like a Chevrolet, and Powerglide had first been offered on that marque's cars in 1950. Early advertising for the model seemed quite ad hoc, flitting from theme to theme and layout to layout, with only minimal continuity or resemblance to copy for other models, but in 1967 the Cresta joined other models in a marque-wide "The Vauxhall breed's got style" campaign from agents Masius, Wynne-Williams, who targeted the growing number of company car drivers, and emphasized the marque's main selling-point over Ford.

The quiet world of Powered Luxury

Viscount by Vauxhall is the Powered Luxury car.
It is this powered luxury that makes the Viscount one of the quietest and smoothest motor cars on the road today and also one of the safest.
Power—instant power—from a silk-smooth 3.3 litre six. Power brakes and power steering to ease your driving and give you extra assurance and precision.
Plus Powerglide—smoothest fully automatic transmission.

And power-operated windows too—a feature normally associated with cars costing four times as much.
Yet the multi-power Viscount, complete with a galaxy of luxury appointments—like reclining seats and best hide upholstery—costs only £1,483 inc. P.T. (£1,397 with manual 4-speed change). Delivery charges extra.
Contact your Vauxhall dealer and ask him to arrange for you to test-drive the new Viscount.

Never before such powered luxury in a £1,500 car

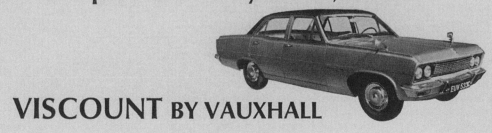

VISCOUNT BY VAUXHALL

teamed up with *Punch* magazine in a suitably whimsical series that emphasized boot space ("You can get 2,568 copies of Punch in a Viva boot...") and promoted the magazine alongside the car ("It's nice to have the good things in life. *Punch* weekly, Viva every day"). The audience was middle class, much of it seeking a second car for shopping: "Gears as sweet as a waltz by Strauss" joined Jensen's reference to Bach in appealing to music enthusiasts. "The engine is a cheerful revver, the synchro on all four carefully chosen ratios actually works (*and* goes in from rest every time)..." enthused *Small Car*.[50]

With the advent of a new Cresta (PC) and Cresta de Luxe in October 1965 and a super-luxury Viscount in June 1966, Vauxhalls acquired a corporate, "coke-bottle" style which was consolidated with a new Viva (HB) in September 1966 and with a new Victor (FD) in October 1967. The style had been prefigured in a slight kick-up in the waistline of the 1961 Lincoln Continental, and in the late 1960s it was enthusiastically adopted by GM in America for cars such as the 1965 Oldsmobile and the full-size 1967 Chevrolet. Not that British motorists often saw either car: new American designs became known to most through films, *Observer* books and toys.

Late in 1966, Vauxhall gained a new advertising agency, Masius, Wynne-Williams, who, for the first time since the Vauxhall line had diverged into separate models in 1957, brought the marque's advertising within a single campaign, "The Vauxhall Breed's got style." It was a quirky slogan, very much of its period, and although it spawned some eccentric copy it was distinctive and youthful. The Cresta had initially been advertised by W.S. Crawford Ltd. with a mid-Atlantic slogan ("Bred for success—better than ever for '66") and an emphasis on acceleration ("There are times when a man must put his foot down") and styling ("Cresta by Vauxhall is a way of life—a big, beautiful way of life"). The advertisements of 1965–66 which showed this barrel-sided cruiser, with its enormous rear overhang, speeding down the motorway on 5.90 × 14" tyres, must have frightened many a sporting motorist. Sales were modest, at 60,937 in nearly seven years, compared with nearly 663,000 of the new Viva in just under four years.[51] According to one contemporary account, "The top-of-the-line Cresta [PC] was a serious mistake and was manufactured only in special batches.... The failure of the Cresta was openly blamed upon styling dictated from Detroit against the views of Luton...."[52] But this Cresta was larger and more specialized than its forebears, and it competed effectively against the Ford Zephyr V6 and Zodiac Mk IV of 1966–72.

The Victor FD, despite the advantages of a new (if leak-prone and, with a single Zenith carburettor, rather strangled) overhead-camshaft engine and rear suspension by coil springs, parallel trailing links and Panhard rod, sold less well than its makers expected.[53] It was, however, squeezed from below by the Ford Cortina 1600 and from above by the Rover and Triumph 2000s. The Victor 1600 in particular, with an austere painted dashboard and bench seats, drum brakes that quickly went out of adjustment and a generally utilitarian tin-and-plastic air, was too visibly a fleet car—a stigma which unavoidably attached itself to the better-trimmed Victor 2000. Fitted with the 2000's disc brakes and two-litre engine as options, and with the four-speed gearbox more usual in that car, the 1600 offered fine value for money at £859 19s 8d. Yet many family motorists preferred a car that was smaller and easier to park, and which did not so obviously bring the office home.

The new Viva was much more successful, and the adoption of American, computer-assisted production methods enabled it to be offered in a great variety of models based around two-door, four-door and estate car bodies. It offered genuine competition to some versions of the Ford Cortina even though it was not directly comparable with that car. Versions with the Victor 1600's overhead-camshaft 1599cc engine supplemented the original overhead-valve 1159cc models from June 1968; four-door saloons arrived in October of that year; and specialized variants included a "Brabham" conversion of the two-door 1159cc Viva 90 and SL90 during 1967–68: "What happens when a 3-times-world-champ racing driver breathes on Britain's most exciting 1-litre saloon? Brabham Viva!" A 1975cc GT arrived in March 1968, for its first 16 months with a matt-black bonnet and pretend-sporting wheel trims that imitated bare steel wheels, and subsequently with more conventional Rostyle sports wheels and paint. Capable of 104 mph and 0–60 in 11.6 seconds, it was fast if a little rough-and-ready, and was particularly popular in Canada. A few SL90 convertibles by Crayford of Kent were sold by Wallace Arnold of Leeds. In 1967 and 1968 the Viva was Britain's third-best-selling car (behind the Cortina and BMC 1100/1300) before being overtaken by the Ford Escort in 1969 and additionally by the Mini in 1970.[54] The Vauxhall Epic, a Viva HB for the Canadian market, mimicked larger cars with its four headlamps, special grille, and side trim strips between the wheel arches.

Masius, Wynne-Williams sought to inject dynamism and personality into Vauxhall advertising. This was an uphill task with the last of the homely Victor FCs, although it was attempted valiantly with headlines such as "You can

Vauxhall Viscount (PC). In Britain, as in America, competition between Ford and General Motors continued not only between ranges, but model-for-model. In January 1965, Ford introduced a super-luxury Executive version of its Mk III Zodiac, the Viscount arrived in June 1966, and Ford's Mk IV Executive followed in October. (Hooper Mk III Zodiacs and Radford Crestas of a few years earlier, being finished by outside coachbuilders and produced only in tiny numbers, had passed largely unnoticed.) In theory the Ford was more advanced than this Vauxhall, but the Mk IV's rear suspension produced odd effects and Vauxhall arguably won the battle of the features—though not the longer-term contest—with this car's power windows and vinyl roof. The Viscount continued alongside the Cresta until both were discontinued in 1972.

Look Dad. Fourdoor.

New family-tuned Viva.

Look Dad! Success-story Viva now comes fourdoor too.
For fourdoor freedom. And getting-in-and-out-ease.
1159cc economy or 1600cc power. Deep body-contoured seats.
Fitted front seatbelts. And a 16 cu.ft boot.
Viva fourdoor or twodoor. Now with a safety package
including energy absorbing steering column.
Twodoor from £658. Fourdoor from £759.
Purchase tax paid.

The Vauxhall Breed's got style.

Vauxhall Viva (HB). Look Dad. A lively Vauxhall advertisement! In 1966 the original Viva gave way to a slightly larger and more upmarket car that competed head-on with Ford's new Escort from 1968, and which was much better-looking than the Ford. The treatment of the wheel arches and lower body sides, which made the car look longer than its 13' 5" and improved greatly on the high-sided austerity of the 1965 Opel Kadett, followed the 1963–65 Buick Riviera and contributed to what, in two-door form, was arguably one of General Motors' best post-war designs. Although by 1968 the deserted beach was nearing the end of its usefulness as an advertising motif, having become a cliché, the dynamic theme transferred well to television advertising — in which Vauxhall (mainly with the Viva and Victor) were second only to Rootes/Chrysler (mainly with the Imp) during 1966–70, at a time when the medium was used quite sparingly by car makers and importers. This photograph, unusually for the late 1960s, has been heavily and obviously retouched. The "safety package" is a sign of the times.

The Scots Magazine, March 1969

Overhead cam power rockets Victor 1600 along. Underbody seal protects that body beautiful.

And you feel trailblazer.

Here's Victor value:
1599cc overhead camshaft engine with crossflow head for freer flow. With fully-machined chambers for cleaner combustion. Coil suspension and widetrack stability. A Vauxhall safety package including the energy-absorbing steering column. Full-width, or optional individual, front seats. Saloons (including underbody seal, fitted front seat belts and purchase tax) start at £897. Racy, spacy estates from £995. So find yourself a trail. Start blazing.

The Vauxhall Breed's got style.

Vauxhall Victor 1600 (FD). Underbody seal didn't protect that body beautiful, as the early FD was almost as rust-prone as the F-type. The fit of the body panels was variable, too, as advertising photos sometimes revealed with embarrassing clarity. And in life, as in copy, 1969 Vauxhalls spent a lot of time off the road — on average, six days in their first year for non-routine repairs, according to a 1971 report from *Motoring Which?* who declared Vauxhall's reliability record the worst of any make tested. Yet for all that, the FD was quite a good family car of its period, reliable once production faults had been corrected, and, to most eyes, good-looking.

The Geographical Magazine, April 1970

**Vauxhall
use six kinds of
make-up to
keep the body
beautiful.**

If you start off with a beautiful figure, what more could you want than a lovely complexion as well? Some people have all the luck. We call them Vauxhall owners. They get it both ways. A superb body that's been given the most elaborate beauty treatment in the world.

First the foundation cream. Phosphate in our language. The number-one barrier against rust and a perfect base for primer. The phosphate treatment is a seven-stage process in itself.

Then the primer. A deep dip. And then coat after coat after coat.

Now the paint. The real thing. Acrylic lacquer—a Vauxhall first. One, two, three double coats of it. And finally a 'reflow' process in which the paint is heated to melting point, then cooled—leaving a clear, hard surface skin with the brilliant colour imprisoned beneath.

The finish is so glossy, we call it 'Magic Mirror'. So resistant to atmospheric conditions you only need to wash and wipe, to bring up that showroom shine.

Then there's make-up in places you wouldn't think of. Aluminised wax injected inside the body sills. (Another rust inhibitor.) And underbody seal that comes as standard. Because our beautiful bodies deserve all the protection we can give them.

And on hubs and bumpers, triple nickel chrome—built to take the knocks and still come up shining.

These are just some of the ways we make sure a Vauxhall never looks its age. But it's what's underneath that counts. Vauxhall means quality through and through. And remember. You too can have a body like ours.

Victor 2000 SL.
Power at your command. Lavish new instrumentation. Advanced new electrics, including alternator. Opulent new upholstery. New steering column lock. New-get-in-and-get-out room at the back. New luxury all round. £1040.4.2. (Recommended retail price 'ex factory' including p.t., fitted front seat belts and factory applied underbody seal.)

Cosmetic containers by Charles of the Ritz

Vauxhall Victor 2000 SL (FD). Paranoia, or how necessity can create an enjoyable advertisement about an unexciting subject. FD Victor sales never approached 1967's projection of 100,000 a year, and by 1970 corrosion was beginning to set in on early examples. Cue for an imaginative campaign emphasizing durability. Yet although 1970 models were better protected than 1968–69 cars, those angular wings and tucked-under wheelarches still harboured mud — and the processes lovingly described here were not always carried out diligently on the production line. The advertisement showed what could be done with studio photography, which, with the amusingly labelled jars and bottles in the foreground, lends an intimacy impossible with older-style artwork.

pack 5 wrestlers into Victor. Plus all their luggage. And still feel spacecraft," and "Zip up a 1-in-8 hill? In top gear? Victor 101 can. And you feel greyhound." Features were listed in the "Victor style file" below, and, with glorious improbability, a green car was shown against a low sun, speeding across a desert landscape. Similar settings were used with Vauxhalls of all sizes thoughout the campaign, giving the marque's advertising a distinctive, range-wide flavour for the first time in ten years. Early in 1968, the "great '68 symbol — sleek, scorchy new Victor," was shown racing across the sand towards a post on which rested a new Victor engine, proudly displaying its exposed timing belt, of a kind used on the Pontiac Tempest, made for the Victor by Uniroyal in Edinburgh, and on which the basic research had been carried out over several years at the GM Technical Center in Michigan. It was a first for Britain and subsequently became commonplace in Europe.

The new agency's headlines, expressing the period's scatty iconoclasm with surreally military briskness, were easy to parody but quite difficult, once read, to forget. "Victor's 54in. widetrack coil suspension grips. But tight. It's the 4-wheel limpet," "Victor sports an overhead camshaft. 104 horses from a 2 litre engine. Get Victor power. Go horizon hunting" and "Victor 3300 estate. Big jetsmooth six. Turn 140 horses loose. And spread yourself into the space age" were typical. Copy sometimes quoted favourable road tests from national newspapers and motoring magazines, and photographs were frequently touched-up — sometimes very obviously — although variable panel fit was quite difficult to disguise.

In 1968 copywriters made the most of the Vivas' variety with a standard copy line, "One of the ten called Viva," whichever version was featured, while the Cresta was "The gentle giant from Vauxhall" and the Viscount, with "The swish of pushbutton windows" was "the breed's biggest and costliest." Some advertisements in motoring magazines used long copy with diagrams of features to show, for instance, "why...people say [Viva's] Britain's sportiest 1-litre saloon."

Sometimes copy was genuinely inspired—"The Lazy Fireball" captured the spirit of the six-cylinder, Victor-based Ventora perfectly. Occasionally a copywriter seemed to inhale the spirit of the times a little too freely, as in 1967: "Drive Viscount—feel house of lords. Drive Cresta—feel thunderpower—Drive Viva—feel dollyrocket." *Dollyrocket*? 1957's F-types, with their "luxurious, washable upholstery," must have turned in their rusty graves.

◆

PART TWO

Luxury and Sporting Marques

Aspiration and Escape

◆

It is perfectly usual among educated people to recognize the attractions of a simple life unencumbered by multiplying wants, and it is equally usual for wants in these circles to multiply continually with results which are often…less unpleasant than they are made out to be. So it becomes increasingly difficult to reach the ideal of simplicity but even more difficult to abandon it — as an ideal. New and opprobrious names are invented for the process of multiplying wants and acquiring the means of satisfying them — such as 'Keeping up with the Joneses.' Advertisers are more and more bitterly assailed in words as they become more effective in forwarding this process.

— Walter Taplin, *Advertising: A New Approach* (rev. ed.), 1963

9

The "Bond Bombshell" and Other Specialists

If most car advertisements in the 1960s were for family cars, a significant number nevertheless appeared for luxury and sports models. The semi-specialized marques of the big producers— M.G., Riley, Wolseley and Vanden Plas from BMC (later British Leyland); Humber and Sunbeam from Rootes (later Chrysler); and Triumph from Standard-Triumph (as the company continued to be called even after the Standard marque was discontinued)— all advertised their saloons and saloon-based coupes extensively. By contrast, the pure sports cars, being mostly for export and easy to sell anywhere, did not need to be widely advertised in general magazines and newspapers and, with their distinct individual characters, were usually well known already to potential buyers. The small sports specialists, on the other hand, simply could not afford heavy promotion. Most of their advertising appeared in magazines for enthusiasts.

The "luxury" and "family" catagories, of course, overlapped. Any four-seater could, after all, transport a family; many cars within the main producers' luxury marques were variants of Austins, Morrises and Hillmans; and some family cars were much larger and more expensive than some luxury models: in the spring of 1962, for example, a Ford Zodiac Mk III cost £1071 while a Riley Elf cost a mere £654. The "mere" was relative, however: a standard Austin Mini cost £496. Some marques fell into one category or the other by the narrowest of margins: Singers, as luxury Hillmans, were generally seen as well-equipped family cars whereas Rileys were slightly more sporting and luxurious by virtue of their ancestry and the characteristics of the compact One-Point-Five.

The appeal of a particular car was to some extent determined by the image of the marque of which it was a member. There was nothing inherently luxurious or sporting about the Triumph Herald, with or without the wooden dashboard of 1961–71, but "Triumph" did not immediately bring to mind utility and many Herald buyers thought it sportier than a Ford Anglia, although there were good technical grounds for concluding otherwise. The Herald was elevated by association with its sporting derivatives— the Spitfire, GT6 and Vitesse — and, more indirectly, with the modernity of the Triumph 2000 and its younger brother, the Triumph 1300. Fortunately for salesmen, motorists continued to interpret the experience of driving a car according to expectations arising from the apparent values of the marque as a whole. As most people never drove their own cars' immediate rivals, their interpretations were not vulnerable to recalibration by knowledge of alternatives. And almost any new car would feel better than the worn-out example of an older model traded in.

The overlapping characteristics of cars from "family" and "luxury" marques were reflected only partly in overlapping advertising styles, even if one allows for advertisers' need to distinguish related individual models from each other. Yet to some extent, and with exceptions, the more expensive the car, and the fewer the characteristics it had in common with more mundane models, the more distinct was its advertising. Among the thousands of advertisements published over a decade exceptions to any rule can be found, but some trends were all but universal. Luxury models tended to be aimed exclusively towards men, who in the early 1960s were often seen alone in semi-public formal or business contexts rather than at home. If they rarely looked happy with their purchases, this was not because they were dissatisfied — rather, a stern look suggested power and importance. The formality and the sense of being "on duty," socially or professionally, diminished towards the end of the decade. Copy for business cars often used longer words and sentences than would be used to promote family models: Rover adopted a reserved style; advertising from Jaguar and Vanden Plas was almost comically effortful at the beginning of the decade as copywriters wheezed up to social altitudes which they occupied only precariously; Wolseley, by contrast, came to adopt a more natural style than formerly; and Triumph's copywriters, generally speaking, concentrated on equipment and technical features, and appealed to progressive motorists' rational instincts. Humber, meanwhile, presented prestige less solemnly than most.

At the very top of the market — the world of Bentley, Rolls-Royce and Bristol — copywriters' language was measured but usually simple. In general, the prestige marques closest to the family-car mainstream took the greatest trouble to distance themselves from it, and it was in the lower reaches of prestige car advertising that gadgets and features were listed with the greatest care. The debate between motorists who thought that prestige was conferred by individual features and those who sought it in build quality and marque values would intensify in the 1970s. The Mercedes-Benz, for example, was notoriously poorly equipped for its cost, but the equipment that it did have was unlikely to fail or fall off.

It was the top of the price range, too, that most of the hand-built specialist cars were to be found, partly because a hand-built car looked and felt special, partly because low production runs did not allow expensive body tooling (and so required handwork whether it was intrinsically appealing or not), and partly because only if a car were expensive could it justify the labour needed to produce anything but the simplest open bodywork. The more complex a body design, the greater the amount of labour needed — which was one reason why hand-built four-door cars were so rare. The Lagonda Rapide was a pure indulgence by its manufacturer and standard Bentley and Rolls-Royce bodies, though hand-finished, were series-produced in comparatively large numbers by Pressed Steel at Cowley. Family cars, conversely, had to be inexpensive and could only be so if they were made in huge numbers. The exception, cheap in absolute terms if not especially good value, was the austere Reliant Rebel, which rather proved the point, and even that car was possible only because the Regal three-wheeler already existed. The Regal, however, had remained viable as a closed car after the mid-1950s because its body could be made from fibreglass, and this was the material that gave a lifeline to a second category of specialists — the makers of medium-priced sports or sporting cars like the Reliant Scimitar,[1] the Morgan Plus 4 Plus, Lotus cars from the Elite of 1957–63 onwards, the Gilbern and the Bond Equipe. All were produced in small numbers for devotees and none was extensively advertised.

Eminent among specialists was Bristol, whose bodies, hand-crafted in aluminium over steel framing, rested on separate chassis. The company was widely believed not to advertise at all, but although this would become more nearly the case in later years Bristol did advertise in the 1960s, albeit infrequently and modestly, in upmarket magazines such as *Country Life, The Field* and *The Illustrated London News* — usually at the time of the Motor Show in October. Advertisements occasionally appeared at other times, too, as when the 407 was coming to the end of its run in May 1963. The car was shown in side view with a short quotation from *The Motor* and the studiedly laconic copy: "Bristol 407. 5 Litre V8 engine. 122 mph plus; 100 mph cruise; 0–80 mph in 16.2 seconds. Luxurious full four-seater saloon." In October 1964 a Bristol 408 was "one of the world's few cars of obvious distinction..." and offered "High performance with unobtrusive elegance." Long copy was rare and the company avoided hyperbole, as in October 1968: "Bristol 410. Bristol cars have been handbuilt, for over 21 years, to the highest standards of automobile and aircraft construction and inspection. Many of the very first cars are still giving excellent service and we are proud to have many owners who have had all models. Throughout the series the emphasis has been on a massive separate safety chassis, with a luxury coachbuilt body. The latest type 410 provides dignified express travel for four six-foot persons in absolute silence and drawing room comfort with more than adequate head room front and rear. In spite of its sheer luxury the Bristol 410 one of the world's fastest accelerating cars, and probably represents the best compromise in today's motoring conditions, for those who can afford and appreciate the best." A 5130cc Chrysler V8 had taken over from Bristol's own 2216cc two litre "six" in 1961, and the V8 grew to 5211cc with the 409 of 1965 and to 6277cc with the 411 of 1969.[2]

Similarly specialized was the AC 428. Based on the chassis of the legendary AC Cobra which had been produced, mainly for the American market, from 1962–68,[3] and with bodywork styled by Pietro Frua and built by Frua in cooperation with Maggiora of Turin, the AC 428 was announced in October 1965 and series-produced from 1967 onwards. It was available as a convertible or fast-back fixed-head coupe. But it was not as well built as the Bristol: "We pretty well rebuilt the bodies when we got them. Frua did all the bright trim brasswork but we had it chromed over here. We tried to protect the sheet steel but at that period there was no way to be sure of getting into the box sections," recalled Derek Hurlock of AC in 1983.[4] As its engine produced 385 bhp at 4000 rpm and 462 lb. ft. of torque at 2800 rpm, the AC 428 was so powerful that "the kickdown action [of the prototype convertible] was sufficiently violent to be dangerous if one was using it to pass on a wet road, and particularly in view of the fact that £4500 cars are usually bought by rather sporting fuddy-duddies who tend to drop teeth in their laps if anything untoward occurs."[5] A half-page advertisement

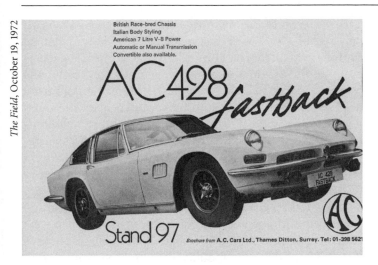

The Field, October 19, 1972

The Field, October 16, 1969

AC 428 Fastback and Bristol 411. Two very different approaches to the super-luxury closed car. Both were produced in very limited quantities, the AC especially so— 29 Fastbacks were made as against 287 of the 411—and, as often with such specialized cars, they were advertised only occasionally. Both were powered by high-quality American V8s— Ford for the AC and Chrysler for the Bristol. The AC, bodied in steel of varying quality by Frua, rusted easily and extensively, but the Bristol, British-built with aluminium panels, was a much more robust and practical car. A great boon was its comparative narrowness, which reduced journey times to a surprising extent in London and on country roads.

showed the fastback in October 1968: "There is only one motor car in the world which combines supreme comfort with the performance of a racing car, and can be driven in top gear at 15 mph…the AC428." In 1970 the car was "the Best of Two Continents. British Chassis and Workmanship. Italian Body Styling. American 7 Litre V-8 Power. Race-bred Chassis. Automatic or Manual Transmission. Convertible also available." By 1969 it was less expensive than the most exotic Italian sports cars, but still cost £5573 when an Aston Martin DB6 was only £4229, a Jensen Interceptor £4460 and a fixed-head Jaguar E-type £2225.[6]

More obviously fuddy-duddy was the Alvis, a 1950s car for 1960s motorists who hoped that time would stop still, if only while they were at the wheel. At the beginning of 1960 a 3-litre two-door sports saloon cost £2827 (slightly less than, say, a Daimler Majestic Major) while a convertible (called a Drophead Coupe) cost £3111 or nearly £300 more than a Mercedes-Benz 190SL convertible. By November 1961 it cost £3202, or fifty percent more than a Jaguar E-type (£2160). It was advertised more extensively than the Bristol, although the half-page advertisements that appeared in up-market magazines hardly constituted media saturation. Even at the end of the marque's run in 1967, Alvis advertising was old-fashioned, and in 1963 the Three Litre Series III (TE 21) with new, vertically stacked headlamps, was shown with horses outside a country house in a rare full-page advertisement in a style otherwise long extinct. "Improved performance and re-styling are the features of the new Alvis Series III Saloon and Drophead Coupe which are being shown for the first time at Earls Court this year. The Graber-styled body has been given a new frontal design, incorporating a twin headlamp system. Steering and front suspension have been modified to give better handling, and engine power has been increased to 130 bhp at 5,000 rpm giving im-

proved top speed and acceleration characteristics" said the copy, stolidly. Understatement could inspire expectation, but it could also kill imagination stone dead. The 1959 car, with 115 bhp, had reached 103.5 mph and 0–60 in 13.9 seconds, which was admittedly faster than its looks suggested.[7]

In one respect Alvis advertising was advanced: 1961's full-page Motor Show advertisement had shown a woman at the wheel, ink-drawn and charcoal-shaded in fashion-supplement style, when in almost all advertising for large cars men still drove. "Talk about Alvis…" said the headline, "and they are talking about the Alvis 3-litre. Drophead coupe or saloon, each has Park Ward coachwork and Graber styling. See both cars at Earls Court on Stand 98." With its heavy controls the Alvis was not a woman's car (but then, neither were ambulances and other heavy vehicles that thousands of women had driven in the war), yet the Alvis was elegant in a self-consciously tasteful way and unusual, for its size (nearly sixteen feet), in having wire wheels— a feature inherited from the low-production, three-litre TC 21/100 Grey Lady of 1953–55. The body design had originally been presented at the 1955 Paris *salon* by Hermann Graber, who built the first sixteen or seventeen cars, while the remainder, in a slightly simplified style, were built from late 1958 onwards by Park Ward in London.[8] Most Alvis advertising in the early 1960s showed simple photographs of cars against conventional backdrops with just the Alvis marque name, and outline details. Descriptive copy was rarely attempted as the reader either wanted — and could afford — an Alvis or he did not (or could not).

The Armstrong Siddeley Star Sapphire, a 3950 lb. luxury saloon with aspirations to Bentley opulence, fell just within the decade, and had a similar performance to the Alvis. It was the last of a line which had begun in 1952 with the Sapphire. Advertising for that car, named after the Sapphire jet, had emphasized the car's aircraft connection with headlines such as "The Gentleman's Carriage...Jet-Bred" and "The Pedigree Car with the Jet-Bred Engine" as well as the more conventional "20 miles to the gallon! Top speed 95 m.p.h. 120 Brake Horse Power." Saab would make a similar connection thirty years later. The Sapphire's sphinx mascot, traditional for the marque, had been updated with small jet engines, by which it was "in no way enhanced," in the view of S.C.H. Davis who, with a motoring memory long enough to include most marques' early days, noticed such things. As with Alvis, Armstrong Siddeley cars were a comparative sideline for their manufacturer. "Member of the Hawker Siddeley Group" said the company proudly at the foot of its advertising until 1959 when Armstrong Siddeley Motors Ltd. merged with Bristol Aero Engines Ltd., whose name then took over at the foot of each advertisement. In the summer of 1960 a double-page advertisement included a small picture of the car amid photographs of aeroplanes powered by Olympus, Proteus and Viper engines.

The 3950 lb., 3990cc Star Sapphire was less ponderous than it looked, and each of the 980 produced between 1958 and 1960 was tested to 100 mph. "A good one should do 110 mph" according to Geoff Harris, former Hawker Siddeley apprentice and long-time owner and devotee of the marque.[9] The Star Sapphire was beautifully upholstered in two-tone leather, superbly built, and lasted just long enough for its advertising to mark the transition from 1958's static portraits ("The managing director's car") and May 1960's painting of a two-tone green car in motion with jets overhead ("In the top flight of Britain's Quality Cars— at £2,498!") to October 1960's dramatically blurred image of a maroon and cream car photographed from above as it sped along the motorway ("Luxurious Power — Quiet Comfort"). The last Star Sapphire saloon was made in July 1960 and the last limousine two months later.

Alone among the old guard, Morgan survived by producing a car unaltered in its essentials (though constantly updated in detail and in its engines) since the 1930s. The first four-wheeled Morgan sports model, with an 1122cc Coventry Climax engine, had entered production in 1936. The present-day, Ford-powered 4/4 remains recognizably its successor and, at £25,000 or so, is similarly inexpensive for a hand-built car. The 1936 4–4 cost £185, or the price of a good 10hp family saloon. In 1963, partly with the American market in mind, Morgan reached towards modernity with the Plus 4 Plus, an unaltered Plus 4 chassis with a fibreglass hardtop body designed by EB Plastics of Tunstall, Stoke on

Trent. The body was well made and attractive by the standards of its kind, even if some details (the heavily domed roof in particular) were curious. But in October 1964 it cost a substantial £1276 7s 1d compared with the £817 3s 9d of a standard Morgan Plus 4 two-seater. A Morgan was always a deliberate rather than default choice, and people who chose it wanted the original, whilst those who wanted a modern-looking sports car wanted one that was modern in all respects. A Triumph TR4 — whose engine powered the Plus 4 Plus—cost £949 2s 1d with a hardtop. The three advertisements published for the Plus 4 Plus (in 1963, 1964 and 1966) portrayed it as a girl's car ("Make friends with a Morgan..."; "definitely a Morgan Girl!") but neither girls nor men were convinced. Only 26 (and two spare body shells) were produced before the body moulds were destroyed in a fire in 1967. Eight of the cars and the prototype were sold in Britain, and the remainder were exported.[10] The experiment would remain a one-off. As with Austin and other British manufacturers in the early post-war years, Americans did not want every British car, but those that they did want they wanted to be traditionally British. An American who wanted a Morgan preferred the original, and if he would not take the original no other kind would persuade him. The same was largely true of the marque's home market, too.

Regular Morgans were a different matter, and they received a celebrity testimonial long before such things were common. "Hands up all those who want a full four-seater Sports Car?" said a July 1966 advertisement, "Well, you can't have this one, it's mine! says Lynda Baron of BBC Television programme BBC3." In October, Lynda stood up on the seat of her car, arms in the air, grinning broadly. "Love Affair," began the copy in very "sixties" swirling capitals, "Lynda Baron — Star of 'B.B.C.3' said 'I'm madly in love. With Morgan. He's a thoroughbred — masculine and very rare and everything I can think of that's marvellous and I've bought him.' ...The 'trend-setting' people like Lynda choose Morgan — why not you?" Happily, the waiting list for regular Morgans remained long.[11]

Only rarely did advertising for sports cars overlap with that for saloons, however useful the "halo effect" of a sporting line might be in selling family cars. The glamour of the Austin-Healey, despite its name, never really transferred to cars like the Cambridge and Princess, and nor was it expected to, although mechanical commonalities helped the sports car owner. In 1960, separate advertisements for the Austin-Healey 3000 and Sprite were published individually and — in identical form — side by side with advertisements

Opposite: **Austin Healey 3000 Mk I.** Advertising for the Austin Healey sports car was integrated into the main Austin campaign by 1960. Colour photography showing cars in motion became common at the turn of the decade, and is used here to striking effect. Traffic scenes, like this one in London's West End, remained rare, however, as they only worked if the product contrasted well with the cars in the background. Here, the photographer is looking down Shaftesbury Avenue from the foot of the statue of Eros at Piccadilly Circus. The 3000 was aimed at the young professional man, and, as similar looking enthusiasts could often be seen driving such cars in London forty years later, this picture looks surprisingly modern.

AUSTIN AHEAD

Austin Healey 3000; 6-cylinder, 2912 ccs engine. Disc braked. THE AUSTIN MOTOR COMPANY LIMITED · LONGBRIDGE · BIRMINGHAM

The day's work is over. Office doors close, theatre doors open. A thousand lights spring to sudden importance. The city pulses with a new excitement. And round the stained old buildings the evening begins. And, of course, if you own an Austin Healey the evening before you is livelier, longer by far. For here is a car that quickly makes nonsense of clogged city traffic. Adroit and nimble, it darts off the mark:

AUSTIN LOOKS YEARS AHEAD

winkles through narrow, winding streets. Alert and safe, it stops in a twinkling trice. And once on the open road the Austin Healey responds to its freedom with lightning ease. It bounds past stragglers, purrs round corners, sends the highway flooding past at 100 mph and more. A powerful car, yet skilful and disciplined too. An Austin car—so obviously years ahead.

By Appointment to
Her Majesty The Queen
Motor Car Manufacturers
The Austin Motor
Company Limited

Backed by
BMC 12-month
warranty
and BMC
service

for Austin saloons. In April a red Sprite was photographed on a playing field, its "pair" on the opposite page a blue Cambridge on a forest path. The Austin virtue of dependability was implicitly added to the other endearments of the Sprite: "One of the pleasures of owning an Austin Healey Sprite is that you don't have to hurry. The wind's on the heath (as someone said) and life is very sweet. You two in the car can take it easy, and let the harriers do the hurrying. The point is, of course, that the Austin Healey Sprite is a speedy little car. And more speed, less haste, less hurry. Where the traffic trundles along on leaden wheels, the Sprite just cuts through. On the open road it overtakes with the easiest snap of acceleration. Sharp corners and steep hills don't disturb its comfortable stride. For the Sprite is an athletic car; a young man's car at a young man's price. It's an Austin — and it is years (or should that be *miles*?) ahead." If the prose did not soar and its tendency toward homily and vague quotation suited family cars better, its unpretentious ordinariness was a virtue, too: the Sprite was a sports car for middle-class people with conventional lives and modest incomes. At £632, it was affordable, and nearly 50,000 were sold between 1958 and 1961.[12]

Copy in motoring magazines could be more spontaneous. "Get into an Austin-Healey Sprite — and see what you get out of it!" was a headline within a regular campaign but it suited the car, as did the copy: "Almost no spot's too tight for an Austin Healey Sprite to wriggle out of. It slips through a chink in the traffic, parks itself neatly in the tiniest kerbsite niche. And a car that loves its freedom, too. On high days and holidays it's alive with eager, impatient power." If the copywriter sounded as if he were describing a pet, his was an approach that the car's "frog-eye" looks invited.

The big Healey was aimed at a very different audience. Where the Sprite was shown in the countryside, a 1960 Austin-Healey 3000, in two-tone black over red, appeared in London: "The day's work is over. Office doors close, theatre doors open. A thousand lights spring to sudden importance. The city pulses with a new excitement. And round the stained old buildings the evening begins. And, of course, if you own an Austin-Healey the evening is livelier, longer by far...." If the rhythm of the copy was familiar, the imagery was very different: "It bounds past stragglers, purrs round corners, sends the highway flooding past at 100 mph and more. A powerful car, yet skilful and disciplined too." It had always been glamorous: in 1956 its similar-looking predecessor had appeared in pale turquoise with a mink-clad model and a cuddly tiger the size of a labrador: "Beautifully fast, the Austin-Healey." Ten years later the 3000 Mk III was photographed in metallic light blue. As a man drove, his girlfriend tried to escape through her window. The copy appeared at an angle at the bottom of the page: "If you're the nervous type go buy something else, the Austin Healey 3000 isn't for you. We don't like to say it, but a lot of people just

aren't right for the 3000. Punch the accelerator at a green light, and feel the power of the big 3 litre engine. When you're moving fast, there isn't time to turn and look at the primroses...."[13]

The appeal of the Lotus Elan (1962–73) was more esoteric and the car itself much more sophisticated. The Lotus Elite of 1957–63, with the world's first fibreglass monocoque body, low-drag styling by Peter Kirwan-Taylor and a 1216cc, 75 bhp Coventry-Climax engine had appealed to enthusiasts world-wide. In an American advertisement the Elite appeared in a church, a blindfolded man in a morning suit beside it, a priest in front. "I do!" said the man. The copywriter explained: "He found it appalling just to go out and buy it! So, it was practically a marriage. Lotus Elite stands on ceremony. It's not just a car to be taken up with lightly. Lotus Elite demands that certain type of man characteristic of nobility. In a word, the union must have 'taste.' Lotus Elite is a $6,000 Grand Touring English sports car of excellence. The blood is racing! The breed is speed! The dowry: four cylinders, disc brakes and independent suspension all the way round...." The Elan, too, was intended for the knowledgeable, and the factory was later horrified by some of the lash-ups produced from Elan kits that it was called upon to put right. "This is the Lotus Elan," said a 1963 advertisement, "Not for fools or primitives but good minds unwinding — the Lotus Elan — racing Lotus, engineered into the lithe lines of the most luxurious sporting vehicle ever. 0–60 m.p.h. in 7 seconds from 1600cc — a unique frame design and Chapman designed suspension. From £1,095." The car was photographed simply, top up, its driver about to turn onto a deserted main road. Most advertising for the car was placed in magazines for enthusiasts rather than in the general media, as in June 1964, when a testimonial appeared in *Small Car*: "'I drive my Lotus Elan for pleasure — not because I have to' says World Champion Jim Clark," who sat in a kilt on the front corner of a red Elan with a silver roof parked outside a house in the countryside.

As the Elan's reputation grew, so did its potential market: "Winner takes all" said a 1965 advertisement, a girl standing up in the car, "Take the girl, take the opposition, take the liberty of time out in the Lotus Elan S.2. It's a winner — designed from World Championship winning experience.... A car engineered in the best male traditions: full of ideas and technical talking points.... The most accomplished car on the road today." Occasionally the "talking points" theme misfired: in 1964 the car was "a moveable feast of technical talking points designed around your need for conversational comfort and perfect taste" — which suggested social insecurity rather than informed enthusiasm. But the Elan was arguably the most modern sports car of its time, a kit-car only in the literal sense that it was available as such, in need of careful maintenance certainly (and therefore not as reliable as more mainstream sports cars in ordinary use) but well-equipped, light (1500 lb. or so) and, above all, with

The Field, August 27, 1964

superb handling.[14] The larger, fixed-hardtop Elan + 2 of 1967–74 was aimed at a more socially self-conscious clientele, as in 1969, when a white car appeared outside a plush modern hotel at night: "Elegance breeds elegance. Doors open wide to the fortunate few whose success has permitted them the luxury of a Lotus. Its engineering integrity and traditionally superb Lotus styling make it an outward indication of your discerning taste. For details and brochures telephone 01–240 1902. 'You have obviously arrived in a Lotus.'" This was aspirational copywriting by numbers, and the car never encroached seriously on the mainstream coupe market. As a car, however, it spoke for itself and therefore — paradoxically — said comparatively little about its owner.[15]

The Elan did wonders for the reputaton of fibeglass cars in general, which had suffered in the 1950s when the material was new and associated with crudely finished two-seater bodies intended for the chassis of secondhand upright Fords. The motorist of 1969 who found the Elan + 2 too delicate, expensive or overtly sporting had an unconventional alternative in "The Go-ahead Gilbern," a more conventional-looking, fibreglass-bodied sports saloon which buyers usually bought in kit form to avoid purchase tax. "Cruise into the seventies (80s, 90s, 115mph Plus!) with the exclusive Gilbern Invader. The Invader puts most other cars on the road in their place…in your driving mirror" said one advertisement. "More power to your elbow room" said the headline of another. "A full four-seater with the thrust of a formula 2. That's the Gilbern Invader — the individual…" added the copy, before listing features such as "3 litre [Ford] V-6 power unit developing over 140 b.h.p. 0–60 in under 10 seconds…. Phone for a test drive. Arranged anywhere at short notice." It was a kind offer from a company based in Glamorgan, Wales, though whether a man who could not find his way to Wales should have been allowed to assemble a 115 mph car was another question. Small manufacturers worked hard for their sales.[16]

The Bond Equipe, by contrast, was sold complete and, in due course, by Standard-Triumph's sales organization. Announced by the three-wheeler manufacturers in mid-1963, it combined the mechanical reliability (more or less) of a mass-produced steel car with the specialist appeal allowed by fibreglass. The Equipe was based on the Triumph Herald, whose doors it combined with a fastback tail and a semi-streamlined bonnet. Early advertising was optimistic: "Now — a thoroughbred G.T for the connoisseur. Until now, the gulf separating Gran Turismo from family saloon was thought to be unbridgeable. Here now is the car that has

Right: **Lotus Elan S1.** A modest piece for a sports car that would become famous, not least in *The Avengers.* The Elan is quite openly depicted as an extension of its owner's self-image, and the flattery is less than subtle, although "need for conversational comfort" imputes an insecurity to the purchaser that he might not relish. But the slight gaucheness of the sales pitch cannot obscure the impressive performance figures.

Naturally, your discrimination brings you the best. In the Lotus Elan you have selected the proper symbol for your understanding of performance, for your interpretation of elegance. It takes you from 0–60 mph in 7 secs, 0–80 in 13.8 secs and to a cool, assertive maximum of 115 mph. A car with many exclusive features; a movable feast of technical talking points designed around your need for conversational comfort and perfect taste. Power of World Champions, Lotus Elan.

Basic price £1,148 inc. heater and close ratio gearbox, plus purchase tax £239.14.7. Hard top an optional extra at £68.

For the name and address of your nearest distributor contact
LOTUS CARS LIMITED · DELAMARE ROAD · CHESHUNT · HERTS

done the impossible — a car that has the lines, excitement and comfort of a G.T., the economy of a family saloon and is backed by a world-wide spares service through Standard Triumph Agents. If you find ordinary cars commonplace, the Bond Equipe is the car for you." It cost £822 4s 7d. Road testers were less ecstatic, and complained of leaks, vicious body shake, the lack of a boot lid, side windows that bowed out at speed, a light switch dangerously above the ash tray, and noisy suspension with the usual Herald vice of sudden oversteer. But the interior was praised for its special bucket seats and good general finish, and the Bond's performance — from a Triumph Spitfire engine — was broadly comparable with that of the Herald Coupe which had been discontinued in October 1964.

The Bond Equipe GT 4S of 1964–70, with a reshaped tail and four headlamps, was better-looking and faster, if a little slower in its acceleration. "Different! that's the Equipe G.T." said 1964's half-page advertisement for the first version, with the word "different!" curving wackily round from the picture of the car in side view to the block of copy below, which listed its features in bullet points. Another version of the advertisement showed the car in a rear three-quarter view, accelerating up the page, with copy angled downwards from left to right to match. In 1969 the GT 4S was "The 1300cc shopping basket. The Bond Equipe GT 4S is a two-timing type of car. Two ways. For a start, girls go for the Bond in a big way. They go for the looks, the easy handling and easy parking…. Don't get us wrong, though, it's a man's car too. Because it's exclusive. Because there aren't many around. Because it's got a sporty Mark III Spitfire engine, all-round independent suspension-type roadholding…."

Finally, in 1968 came "The Bond Bombshell," a restyled Equipe 2 Litre GT with, at the front, something of the look of the Jensen Interceptor. Enhanced by a leather-jacketed girl leaning on the bonnet with a "So what are you going to do about it?" expression, the 2 Litre GT was a "fleet, four-seater fastback with a smooth 95 b.h.p. 2-litre Standard Triumph engine beneath its bonnet. A car that can soar to 70 m.p.h. in seconds and reach 100 in top." Perhaps accidentally, the number of seconds was not stated, which did little for the advertisement's credibility, but *Autocar* managed a respectable 14 seconds, which compared well with the 16–17 seconds needed by a Vitesse with a similar engine. If the Bond was unremarkable,[16] the headline was characteristic of its period, and continued a theme suggested more subtly by Aston Martin in 1963.[17]

10

Aston Martin and Lagonda

"Body beautiful (with a nature to match)"

In 1961 *The Autocar* began its test of an Aston Martin DB4, "With a top speed of over 140 m.p.h. and a price in Britain of over £4,000, the Aston Martin DB4 truly can be said to live up to its makers' claim '...the ultimate symbol of success.'" In 1965, the magazine tested a DB5: "Like the fourth dimension, subjects and experiences beyond our personal comprehension are virtually impossible to visualize with any degree of reality.... To be told 100 m.p.h. (with certain qualifications) is a safe speed would cause a large majority of everday motorists to throw up their hands in horror and launch forth on a counter-attack on the dangers of high-speed driving. Yet they could be silenced simply and forever by a short trip over ordinary trunk roads in an Aston Martin DB5." The test concluded: "It is a car requiring skill and muscle — a man's car — which challenges and satisfies and always excites."[1]

In the 1960s road testers of Aston Martins found themselves caught between rapture on the one hand and, on the other, the quest for the objectivity which required them to note wind noise, exhaust resonance, feeble handbrakes, reverse gears that needed two hands to engage, and other details in which the average family car was superior. Occasionally testers seemed to be surprised by good detail: "Electrically operated windows are fitted, designed by Aston Martin, which are quite the best of their type we have yet experienced. They are virtually silent, extremely quick, and can be held back against the motor as a safeguard against fingers getting trapped," said *The Autocar* in its test of the DB5. But the personality of the car dominated: "From the moment the car moves one has the sensation of great power straining at the leash under control," said S.C.H. Davis in 1964, "If ever a car had animal characteristics this one has.

One cannot think of it as feminine.... Of course, this is not a car for the inexperienced.... Originally Lionel Martin could not suffer driving foolishness gladly. Once he wired an owner, who had had trouble with the gears, that 'Gears should be changed with the finger and thumb of one hand' — and lost a customer. But the idea behind the first Aston Martin has achieved its target in these days."[2] Customers with more money than driving skill who bought Aston Martins had an incentive to improve: "[B]eing, as it were, permanently in the public eye like all exceptional cars, it encourages one to drive it courteously and well in towns and in crowded traffic conditions, for one knows that, as soon as the open road is reached, one can accelerate clear and pass the lot!" said *The Autocar* about the DB4. And Aston Martin had an incentive to improve, too. As introduced in October 1958, the DB4 was under-developed: "It soon became apparent that the DB4 had been launched prematurely, in response to pressure from [David Brown] and the dealers. Lack of pre-production development really began to tell early in 1960, when unusually warm weather brought a spate of bearing failures on cars run at sustained high speeds in France and Italy. The problem was so serious that Tadek Marek, Aston's engine designer, was sent to Paris to investigate...."[3] The problem proved to be the lack of an oil cooler.

The circumstances suited the car; the breakdowns did not happen on the A3 — or even the Preston By-Pass or M1. The Aston Martin was an international car *par excellence*. When it broke down in did so — at least sometimes — in glamorous locations. It was also a car that needed little advertising and, by and large, received little. The DB4 of 1958–63, one of the most beautiful cars in the world with styling by Touring of Milan and a *Superleggera* body con-

The Field, June 21, 1962

...to serve with distinction

Bringing new lustre to a renowned name, the new Lagonda Rapide has attracted the highest praise from world motoring commentary. The guiding concept in the development of the Lagonda was, in the words of Mr. David Brown, "...to create something which should from the very outset invade the future audaciously, and set such an advanced standard of mechanical perfection, beauty of form, and all-round performance, that no other car would compare with it". The new Lagonda Rapide is a car of outstanding beauty and distinction, capable of speeds in excess of 125 m.p.h. and with a specification so complete that no additional equipment is required. The new 4-litre Lagonda Rapide takes its logical place as a leader among the really high performance cars of the world.

ASTON MARTIN LAGONDA LIMITED
LONDON SHOWROOMS: 96 97 PICCADILLY, W.1
LONDON DISTRIBUTORS:
BROOKLANDS OF BOND STREET LTD. W.1

THE DAVID BROWN
LAGONDA RAPIDE
THE FINEST OF FAST CARS

Lagonda Rapide. Edsel meets Maserati in 1962. The copy sounds home-grown and in parts frankly odd, with a headline reminiscent of a corny film trailer and some tortuous prose of the find-a-portentous-word-and-jam-it-in-anyhow school. The car was based on the contemporary Aston Martin; 55 were sold between 1961 and 1964. It is little known today, although a few have survived in the hands of collectors who appreciate the fine workmanship and nearly 240 bhp.

structed from magnesium-aluminium panels shaped over a framework of small-diameter tubes, was always in demand. Production was held down by the development and production demands of David Brown's pet project of the turn of the decade, the £5251 4s 6d Lagonda Rapide. Aston Martin's general manager of the time, John Wyer, estimated that "each Rapide was built at the expense of three Aston Martins, with no commensurate return in profitability or reputation."[4] There was no doubt that more Aston Martins could have been sold, even at the 1961 price of £4085 (or £4668 for a DB4 GT). In a November 1960 advertisement, "The breathtaking Aston Martin DB4," shown in front view at ground level, sped along a country road towards the camera in the kind of photograph that would become popular with much less exclusive marques within a few years. In May 1962 the DB4 was seen in a field in summer (a setting that Reliant would use for its Scimitar GT in 1966), the "Choice of the

perfectionist. With its unique heritage of international racing triumphs, the DB4 Aston Martin is the embodiment of all that is most desirable in automobile engineering. No other car in the world so successfully equates fantastic performance with the very highest standards of safety and luxury. The Astonishing Aston Martin." Another 1962 advertisement in the same series, with the same headline and slogan, showed the car in a simple photograph against a black background with white-on-black copy. It was tasteful, inexpensive to produce and, to modern eyes, even mundane. But in 1962, white-on-black copy with a photograph against a black background did not yet constitute the default style for sports car advertising that it would later become.

During 1963–68, Aston Martin advertising remained infrequent but became more lavish.[5] In 1963 the company used the same headline and similar copy in the first half of the year for the DB4 Vantage as for new DB5 in October. The

Opposite: **Aston Martin DB4 Vantage.** No need to flaunt it if you've really got it. An unassuming yet clever piece for one of Britain's most prestigious marques, combining sensuality with a cosmopolitan feel. Anyone with £3750 to spend when a Cortina cost £640 was likely to be something of an individualist, so the reader is allowed to create his own background for the car. The citation of a European journal is unusual for the period, but it suited this car as buyers of specialized machines often read the international motoring journals and reviews.

ASTON MARTIN DB4 VANTAGE

BODY BEAUTIFUL

(with a nature to match)

The pleasure to be had from owning an Aston Martin is something that must be experienced to be believed. ■ The delight in those well bred lines, in the sheer luxury of superb English coach hide upholstery is understandable : they are things that everyone can see and admire

The *particular* pleasure is your own. ■ This car has a nature like an angel. So responsive you can accelerate from zero to 100 mph and back in under 25 seconds. So docile and forgiving, your control and mastery of every situation is supreme. No other car offers such performance

('Revue Automobile', August 2nd, '62, report it as the fastest four-seater car they have ever tested) together with such amazing flexibility. ■ The price £3,746.7.11 incl. P.T. Colour to your choice and leather suitcases made to match the upholstery of your car, if you wish.

ASTON MARTIN

ASTON MARTIN LAGONDA LIMITED, A SUBSIDIARY OF THE DAVID BROWN CORPORATION LIMITED, FELTHAM, MIDDLESEX. FELTHAM 3641. CABLES ASTOMARTIA FELTHAM. LONDON SHOWROOMS 96/97 PICCADILLY, W.I.
CONCESSIONAIRES FOR THE HOME COUNTIES : BROOKLANDS OF BOND STREET LTD. 103 NEW BOND STREET, W.I.

ASTON MARTIN

CRAFTSMAN BUILT MOTOR CARS FROM £4,600/ASTON MARTIN LAGONDA LIMITED, NEWPORT PAGNELL, BUCKS.

Vantage was photographed against a plain white background while the later DB5 was seen on gravel with a lawn and trees in the background. Under the headline, "Body beautiful (with a nature to match)," the copywriter described the DB5: "The pleasure to be had from owning an Aston Martin is something that must be experienced to be believed. The delight in those well bred lines, in the sheer luxury of superb English coach hide upholstery is understandable: they are things that everyone can see and admire. The *particular* pleasure is your own. The new 4 litre Aston Martin DB5 has a nature like an angel. So responsive you can accelerate from zero to 100 mph and back in under 23 seconds.... No other car offers such amazing flexibility with such a splendid performance. Astons took 1st and 3rd at the 1963 Monza *and* broke the lap record. Also 1st and 2nd at the Coupé de Paris. Colour to your choice and leather suitcases made to match the upholstery of your car, if you wish." A 1965 colour advertisement was less original but, by virtue of its colour, more arresting. A silver DB5 was parked outside a country house in a style of illustration revived from the late 1930s and 1940s; the copy was written in a semi-italic, invitation-card typeface: "For you, a possession that reflects immaculate taste and rare discrimination. Of nearly two million British cars produced annually, Aston Martin account for just three a day.[6] Each painstakingly hand-built by master craftsmen...true devotees of the marque. The DB5 is the fastest regular 4-seater G.T. car in the world. Top speed exceeds 150 m.p.h. Stops from 100 m.p.h. in 6 seconds. Murmurs through traffic and arouses interest everywhere. Experience the ultimate in high-performance motoring—DB5 Aston Martin." Copy in a much smaller typeface then listed specifications (282 bhp was claimed for the standard engine, and 325 bhp for the Vantage) and described the car's features, while dealers were listed in a narrow panel on the opposite page.

One of the most appealing Aston Martin advertisements of the decade was placed by the dealers, H.R. Owen, in July 1967. The scene was a forest path, and in the background, out of focus, was a maroon DB6. In sharp focus in the foreground, to the left of the car, a heart with an arrow through it was scratched on a tree trunk; the lovers were "H.R.O" and "D.B.6." The copy explained all: "...so now you all know! Well it was bound to get out sooner or later. The fact is that the amazing affair between H.R. Owen and Aston Martin has become pretty hot news. The combination of the world's greatest grand tourer and Britain's most exciting retailers just had to be a winner. It's less than two

years since H.R. Owen were made the Aston Martin distributors for London and now they outsell everyone else in the world. They do this because they have a specialist team of Aston lovers to give their customers the service to match the car. H.R. Owen are proud to be linked to the name of Aston Martin." Dealer advertisements were rarely exciting and, advertising being expensive, their wit tended to be fairly home-grown and leaden-footed; but H.R. Owen's was easily one of the best dealer advertisements of the decade, and comparable in its originality and presentation with mainstream car campaigns.[7]

In 1968 Aston Martin produced two double-page advertisements, each with a colour photograph of a car and introductory copy on one page, and the longest copy of the decade, in the form of an article, on the other. The first advertisement, for the DB6, appeared in the spring. At the bottom of the introductory copy, in a typeface half-way in size between those of the text and the headline, was written "Part 1." A silver car was photographed in front three-quarter view against a black background. It stood on a Union Jack. "When 'only the best is good enough'—At Newport Pagnell, where Aston Martin cars are manufactured, there is a deep-seated resistance to the sacrifice of any quality standard. So, in the best traditions of British craftsmanship, only the best is good enough. This first in a series of special features about the Aston Martin shows how that insistence on quality derived from the make's long, proud history [since 1921] is reflected in the current models, the DBS, the DB6 and Volante convertible." The article on the facing page described the philosophy behind the cars, racing successes and—under the sub-heading, "1/16 of an ounce" (the maximum variation in weight allowed between an engine's pistons)—the way in which each car was constructed and tested. The length of the article varied a little according to the page sizes of the magazines in which it appeared. In the summer, "Part 2," with a dark blue DBS seen close-up on a country road, was headlined, "'Above all, make it an Aston'"—apparently David Brown's brief in October 1966 to the design team shown gathered around a quarter-scale model of the car on the facing page.[8] The DBS was a car in a very different style from the Touring DBs. "I was influenced by GM when I was doing the DBS, so I suppose you can see a bit of Camaro in the rear wing shape" recalled the car's designer, William Towns, in 1986.[9]

In 1968 the DB6 and the DBS appeared in black and white advertisements with "Aston Martin" in large letters at the top and, with either car, the same copy at the bottom:

Opposite: **Aston Martin DBS.** Most car advertisements contain a headline, descriptive copy, and a picture with a car in it. But not all. In America Duesenberg notoriously showed owners in vast houses above the single line, "He [or she] drives a Duesenberg," with no car in sight. In the 1950s, Rolls-Royce photographed majestic grilles close-up beside the famous slogan, "The best car in the world," while for a few years in the 1930s several British advertisers had written memorable copy while showing neither car nor owner. Distinctiveness was necessary for a specialist producer with a small advertising budget, and this piece, one of a pair from Holmwood Advertising in 1969, shows a car in need of advertisement, as it was then less well known than the still-current DB6. It would shortly be joined by the almost identical-looking DBS V8, the characteristic Aston Martin of the 1970s.

"Aston Martin — elegantly virile — a potent blend of exhilarating performance and seductive comfort. Its precision four-litre unit set in a race-bred chassis to give swift, secure travel. Here's the best in British craftsmanship. Here are the highest standards of comfort and finish. Here are cars for the discriminating motorist. DB6, Volante, DBS — cars for all seasons from £4,500." It was all a little generic — and "unit" jarred — but in 1969 a more distinctive style emerged in which the DBS was photographed in rural settings without any copy at all, the picture in each case framed by a narrow white border on a black page with "Aston Martin" in large letters below. The series was as distinctive, in its way, as 1963's advertising had been for the DB4 Vantage and DB5.

11

Bentley

"Take a Bentley into partnership"

By the 1960s, with the exception of a few coachbuilt cars, the Bentley was a beautifully badge-engineered Rolls-Royce — Rolls-Royce having taken over Bentley in 1931. In the early post-war years, however, there were Rolls-Royces without equivalent Bentleys. The Silver Wraiths of 1946–59 and Phantom IV of 1950–56 had no Bentley sisters, whilst only in 1949 was the Bentley Mk VI, which had been introduced in 1946, followed by an equivalent Rolls-Royce Silver Dawn; and that car was reserved for export. Few people wished to drive a car as ostentatious as a Rolls-Royce through the rubble of 1945, and the Bentley, which suggested enthusiasm as well as mere wealth, was less aggressively prosperous. In 1952, however, the Mk VI became the R Type with an elegant extended boot devised by Rolls-Royce's chief styling engineer from 1951, John Blatchley, and the Silver Dawn was similarly updated and made available on the home market. Special bodies were a different matter; there was never, for example, a Silver Dawn Continental, and the Bentley Continental was rarely advertised, although in 1955 new two-door and convertible models by Park Ward merited a modest half-page, with short copy below a simple photograph of the convertible, or drophead coupe: "Bentley announce Two Continental Models — The elegant Drophead Coupe and the new Sports Saloon by Park Ward provide exhilarating motoring for four passengers at speeds up to 120 m.p.h. These new models, which are available with the automatic gearbox, are the only additions to the existing range of Rolls-Royce and Bentley cars which continue in their present form and were exhibited at the Earls Court Motor Show." And that was it. The price — not given in the advertisement — was £6765 14s 2d for either car.

The mainstream Bentley R Type and Silver Dawn were succeeded in April 1955 by the Rolls-Royce Silver Cloud and equivalent Bentley S1,[1] which were (and are) widely considered to be John Blatchley's finest work. In 1959 both models, as the Silver Cloud II and Bentley S2, acquired an all-alloy, 178bhp (net), 6230cc V8 engine,[2] and in October 1962 Blatchley's styling was updated with twin headlamps and a slightly lowered bonnet line to create the Silver Cloud III and Bentley S3. In 1965 these cars made way for a new Rolls-Royce Silver Shadow and a parallel Bentley T1. Of the 1955–59 cars, more Bentleys were built than Rolls-Royces, although the proportions were reversed for the V8 models.[3] Between 1965 and 1980, when they were replaced by the Rolls-Royce Silver Spur and Silver Spirit, and by the Bentley Mulsanne, more than ten Silver Shadows would be built to every Bentley T1.

In the 1960s, therefore, Rolls-Royce was very much the senior marque, and this was reflected in Bentley advertising — or, rather, in the lack of it. Bentley advertisements appeared regularly during the early 1950s; when the 'S' Series was new in 1955; occasionally during 1957–59; and in 1960. But only a few different advertisements were published and Bentley's advertising expenditure, as distinct from that for Rolls-Royce and for Rolls-Royce and Bentley together, was otherwise minimal. By the late 1960s it was virtually nil.[4] In the 1950s some of the most attractive advertising for Bentley and Rolls-Royce cars was produced by Hooper for low-production coachbuilt models such as the four-door Bentley 'S' Series saloon in red and silver seen in *Country Life* in October 1955, or the more conservatively styled Rolls-Royce Silver Wraith Touring Limousine, in two-tone green, shown in *The Field* at the same time. "This car will be shown at the Motor Show, Earls Court stand 106, Oct 19 to Oct 29," said the captions in both cases. The advertisements were for the coachbuilder as much as for the individual cars, whose bodies were typical examples of Hooper's work.

In the early 1950s, however, Bentley established what would be a long-term niche with advertising that was highly attractive and that combined unusual illustrations with the minimum of copy. "Take a Bentley into partnership" made an explicit appeal to the successful businessman rather than to the aristocrat, and R Types were seen alongside factories, building sites and refineries rather than with country mansions or at cocktail parties. Everywhere the Bentley went, something was being built, as Britain was reconstructed after wartime bombing. The theme appealed to the potential buyer's constructive spirit and soothed his conscience in a war-ravaged country, suggesting that he was a force for the national good rather than a mere opportunist. Such an accusation was easily made when a Bentley cost £4392 15s 10d, by the end of 1954, compared with the £529 10s 10d needed for a Morris Minor. If the image was a soothing fiction, at least in part, it was nevertheless compelling. Bentley's artwork, usually in black and white and often impressionistic, blended strong lines and a confident use of dark tones for brickwork in the foreground with light, almost ethereal suggestions of skeletal buildings in the distance. The theme also reflected marketing reality: a Bentley represented "new money" as a Daimler, Armstrong Siddeley, Lea-Francis or Riley did not, and even the unostentatious Mk VI, shorter and less deliberately elegant than the long-tailed R-type, was very much a car for the industrialist. When "old money" could in theory afford to buy a Bentley, it usually kept its head down. In 1950, or even 1955, one needed to be comparatively detached from the population in order to feel comfortable driving through it in a new Bentley every day. The industrialist's loyalties lay in the world of business rather than with his neighbours at home.

The industrial theme continued in early advertising for the 'S' Series, described in 1956 simply as "[a] new motor car representing a logical advance in the design of chassis and coachwork." Later in the year, the car was photographed rather than painted, and admired in a City setting by a prospective, rather than actual, owner. The picture was accompanied only by the Bentley badge and slogan. During 1957–58 the S1 was photographed in the countryside. Copy was laconic: "Power assisted steering is now offered on the Bentley 'S' Series as an optional extra." Nothing more, after all, needed to be said about a model, now well-received and established, costing £5543 17s. (The equivalent Rolls-Royce was a notional £50 more expensive at £5693 17s). In a second, similar advertisement the Bentley was photographed

from the side at ground level, against a backdrop of flat farmland. The copy, apart from the slogan at the bottom, simply quoted *The Autocar*: "The latest Bentley model offers a degree of safety, comfort and performance that is beyond the experience and perhaps even the imagination of the majority of the world's motorists." In March 1958 an S1 whooshed through a London park as City men walked by: "The Bentley 'S' series saloon combines silence and luxury with safety and speed"—although this time the words came from the copywriter. The slogan, "Take a Bentley into partnership," meanwhile, had disappeared; for the world of the late 1950s it risked making too specific an appeal and it worked better with artwork than with the photographs now commonplace—and expected—in modern car advertisements. Possibly, too, the delicacy and elegance of the new model's styling told against the industrial theme: beside it buildings—and, by extension, perhaps the world of business—looked less appealing.

Long copy arrived with the V8 in October 1959. The front of the car was photographed as it sped along. Both car and background were blurred, but the Bentley was identifiable by its radiator shell, lights and bumper. The copywiter adopted a formal style already familiar in Jaguar advertising: "The Eight Cylinder Bentley.... An eight cylinder aluminium engine of vee design now becomes the standard unit for the Bentley S2 and Bentley Continental. Delivering greater torque over the entire speed range, it replaces the six cylinder engine which has reached the peak of its development within the prescribed standards of silence and smoothness. These latest Bentleys follow the great tradition of the marque in combining a fine road performance with safety and comfort of the highest order.... Other features available on these cars include fully automatic transmission, power-assisted steering, electrically operated ride control, redesigned and more flexible air conditioning, electric rear window demisters and press button window lifts."

It was measured, it was rational, it was conscientious and it was complete: but somehow the magic of the car dissipated under the dead weight of "unit" and the almost painful honesty of "more flexible air conditioning"—even if the original system, imported complete from Chrysler, had sometimes been criticized as needing frequent re-adjustment at the wheel.[5] It was even lambasted by Rolls-Royce's advertiser in America, David Ogilvy. As Ogilvy recalled, "[T]he manager of the American company went down and got these new air-conditioned Rolls-Royces off the boat. The first one he drove round Central Park. He didn't go halfway round Central Park before the windows fogged up. He couldn't see out.... I wrote this dreadful letter resigning.

Opposite: **Bentley S2.** Wonderfully simple in conception and aimed at aspiring buyers rather than existing Bentley owners, this advertisement implies that the driver himself has power but does not need to say so. Envy of the owner is transmuted into the pursuit of perfection, and so the onlooker is flattered by his own ambition. He probably won't mind the tyre howl and body roll, which is visible even here.

"I'll get a Bentley"

This is automobile engineering at its best. This is power. Power that flows from the eight-cylinder engine and effortlessly answers every demand. This too is the power to stop safely and surely . . . without fail, without fade. This is a complete partnership between owner and car.

Even then I thought it was dreadful. Now I think it was unpardonably offensive. But do you know, they didn't take offence at all. The head of Rolls-Royce, who was an engineer, wrote back and said I don't blame you at all. I think you have a point."[6]

Perhaps the most attractive advertisement for the Bentley 'S' Series appeared at the turn of the decade, in November 1960 and subtly incorporated the old theme within a much wider appeal. A fifty-something motorist, seen from the passenger seat of his own car, looked out of his window as he passed a junction, almost certainly in London, from which a Bentley was emerging. "I'll get a Bentley…. This is automobile engineering at its best. This is power. Power that flows from the eight-cylinder engine and effortlessly answers every demand. This too is the power to stop safely and surely…without fail, without fade. This is a complete partnership between owner and car."[7] Testing a Bentley S3 in 1963, S.C.H. Davis made the point in a different way: "Every control, however small, handles as though produced after much earnest experiment to attain perfection…. This is motoring as motoring should be."[8]

12

Daimler

"Prestige motoring in the modern manner"

"When the Beatles were awarded their M.B.E.s, one of my ship's chefs returned his M.B.E. that he had so gallantly won during the war for courageous action. I applauded his decision…. It was the Beatles and their imitators, and the unkempt, immoral generation who emerged under the intoxication of their music, that brought England and its elegant age to an end. My world, which we had restored after the last World War to the status it had once enjoyed, suddenly disintegrated…. Where has our world of elegance gone? What has happened to our virtues?"[1]

If this was the timeless lament of former socialites down the ages, it was also personal, as the social world of the speaker in 1969, Lady (Norah) Docker, wife of Daimler's chairman from December 1941, Sir Bernard Docker, had long since disintegrated. In May 1956 Sir Bernard was forced out of his chairmanships of both Daimler and its parent, the Birmingham Small Arms (BSA) group, having held the latter since 1940. The Dockers' extravagant and, diplomatically speaking, accident-prone, lifestyle — in which Lady Docker took the lead — was too much for the boards of Daimler and BSA and many other organizations with which Sir Bernard Docker had been connected. The couple's most visible indulgences were five Hooper-bodied "Docker Daimlers" displayed at the Motor Shows of 1951–55. Ostensibly built to generate publicity for the company's production cars, they cost far more to build and promote than the company could ever have recouped through consequent sales of production models, and they attracted mixed reviews. While their craftsmanship was admired, and brought welcome publicity to Hooper, many thought them vulgar. For the latter reason, they might have lost Daimler as many sales to its natural clientele as they gained, while motorists drawn to such

flashy and fabulous creations often preferred more ostentatious makes for their own use. The three or four of the five "Docker" cars that remained with the company in 1956 were stripped of most of their special equipment, resprayed, and sold off.[2] The last Hooper-bodied show car, possibly intended at first as a sixth Docker Daimler, was a two-door Daimler Continental displayed at the 1956 Motor Show in a striking but not outlandish colour scheme of beige over light green.[3]

Nevertheless, there were models in Daimler's attractive but diffuse and minimally profitable production car range of the mid-1950s that reflected Lady Docker's spirit and influence. The first was the 1953–58 Daimler Conquest, a 2433cc, six-cylinder "small" Daimler developed from the four-cylinder Lanchester Leda and Fourteen of 1950–53. Medium-sized and medium-priced, the Conquest brought Daimler motoring to a market for which the 3½ litre or 4½ litre Regency Mk II of 1954–55 (£2324 or £2778) was much too grand and specialized. Lady Docker recalled, "I was ashamed, when I married Bernard [in 1949] to discover that, both at home and abroad, the superb Daimler car was in danger of becoming a relic…. I induced [him] to re-examine the firm's marketing policies. I told him: 'The only people who know about the Daimler are the Royal family! I know you couldn't find better customers, Bernard, but Daimler can't survive on status alone. It's got to sell to the masses…. Why can't you manufacture a smaller Daimler, suitable for the family?'"[4] By Daimler standards the subsequent Conquest was certainly series-produced, although at £1511 (or £1066 before purchase tax), it was not for "the masses" in any but the most elevated, or snobbish, sense.

In October 1955 the Regency Mk II was replaced by the

similar-looking, 3½ litre One-O-Four (1955–59) which cost £2829 as a standard saloon and £3159 as a Lady's Model with "a new burr walnut instrument panel with special drawer and patent touring map; attractive new instruments [in a highly styled, polished metal surround at the centre of the dash, with specially labelled switches]; power operated windows; elegant vanity case; four aeroweight suitcases; picnic case and ice-box; telescopic umbrella; shooting-stick; sheepskin rug and travelling rug" according to announcement advertising. The features reflected the equipment of Hooper's "Docker Daimlers" and in the spring of 1956 the price of the Lady's Model was reduced to £3076 to enable "the special Lady's items to be purchased as optional extras item by item to choice." But no car company could survive on such products: only 400 of the Regency Mk II and 561 of the One-O-Four were built.[5] In the short term, Daimler was protected by its parent company, BSA, who had taken over the company in 1910 and who had bought Hooper in 1940, and until the early 1950s the company's famous fluid flywheel transmission, fitted to all Daimlers from 1931 to 1956, had been a genuine boon.[6] But by the mid-1950s Rolls-Royces and Jaguars were available with automatic transmission, the Rover 75 had acquired synchromesh on second gear in September 1953, and automatic gears arrived on six-cylinder BMC saloons, the Humber Super Snipe and the Ford Zodiac during 1956. A Borg-Warner automatic became optional on Daimlers in 1957 and was standard equipment on the Majestic saloon of 1958. In May 1960, Daimler was taken over by Jaguar.

Jaguar inherited two Daimler models and two Daimler engines with potential. The first car was the fibreglass-bodied SP250 sports car introduced in April 1959 with a new 2548cc, 140 bhp, Cadillac-influenced V8 engine designed by Edward Turner, head of BSA's Automotive Division and formerly of two motorcycle makers, Ariel and Triumph. At £1395 the SP250 cost more than an M.G. or Triumph TR3A (whose chassis layout it largely shared), but less than the earlier Conquest Roadster (£1673), which had been sporting but not a traditional sports car in the English sense. As often with charismatic sports cars, the SP250's advertising was unremarkable: "Announcing the new Daimler sports car — 2½ litre V-8 type SP250. Designed to give the enthusiast a truly practical Sports Car, the Daimler SP250 is an entirely new conception which for performance, servicing ease and reliability is unrivalled." 1960's copy was livelier, but still unoriginal: "The sensational V8 S.P.250. Sensational! That's how the world's press has described the Daimler SP250...a new speed sensation by Daimler — V8 engine for velvet

power, disc-brake safety at *every* wheel." Daimler claimed a 0–100–0 time of 30 seconds. *The Autocar* managed 0–100 in 26.3 seconds and a maximum speed of 121 mph,[7] and the car could accelerate to 60 mph in 8.9 seconds. The SP250's styling was controversial — it attracted more jokes about marine scavengers even than the Ford Anglia — and early versions suffered ferocious body shake, but the chassis was improved and the engine was widely considered one of the best in the world. The car sold much less well than had been hoped, however: although it continued until late 1964, only 2645 were made, of which probably fewer than 1000 were imported into the United States, where after the Jaguar takeover of 1960 they were sold, often reluctantly, by Jaguar dealers.[8] A more conventionally styled successor called the SP242 was developed under Sir William Lyons' guidance during 1962–63. It looked a little like a cross between an MGB (from the front) and a Park Ward-bodied Bentley Continental S2 (from the rear), but it was old-fashioned in all but its engine and styling by 1963 and did not enter production.[9] The engine would survive in the Daimler 2½ litre V8 (later, V8–250) of 1962–69.

In 1958 the One-O-Four was selling slowly and its semi-full-width body, with prominent wing lines running across the rear doors like those of a 1953 Buick, looked old-fashioned. In June 1954 BSA had bought the coachbuilders Carbodies, who made low-production, especially convertible, bodies for Austin, Ford, Daimler and others, and Daimler asked Carbodies to develop new rear doors and wings for the One-O-Four body at minimum cost.[10] The new car, called the Majestic, looked slab-sided at the rear and therefore rather heavy and official, but it was undoubtedly more modern than its predecessor. Announced in July 1958 with an improved, 3974cc engine, disc brakes and standard automatic transmission, the Majestic cost £2495 compared with £2395 for the One-O-Four, which stayed in production until 1959. "There's nothing to touch the Daimler Majestic for luxury, performance and price" said an early 1959 advertisement, which claimed "over 100 miles-an-hour — a top speed which is achieved quietly and entirely without fuss" — something beyond the optimistically named One-O-Four. The new model handled well and attracted good reviews, which were quoted at length in an April 1959 advertisement, and during the spring and summer of 1960 the Majestic was painted against impressionistic renderings of fashionable, rather than traditionally upmarket, venues. In one advertisement a silver and maroon car appeared outside a luxury bungalow with what looked like a circular swimming pool until one noticed a very small duck. "Effortless and thrilling

Opposite: **Daimler SP250 (Capstan cigarettes).** Advertisers of many non-automotive products used cars as backdrops in the 1960s to suggest style and modernity. This interior belongs to the individualistic, fibreglass-bodied sports car which used Daimler's small V8, later found in the Jaguar-based 2½ Litre V8 saloon. The spring-spoke steering wheel with central indicator switch was old-fashioned when this piece appeared in 1962. Smoking was popular at the time and compulsory health warnings lay in the future, although the SP250's heavy steering required its driver to be sound in wind and forearm. British press advertising for cigarettes ended on February 13, 2003. Television advertising for cigarettes (though not for cigars or pipe tobacco) had ceased at the end of July 1965.

The Field, July 12, 1962

THE FIELD, July 12 1962
WATER
AMPS
never
go
without
a
CAPSTAN
C.C.87
To match the smoothness of a well-tuned engine...the smoothness of a perfectly made cigarette. A Capstan naturally. With every strand of the fine Virginia tobacco *vacuum-cleaned* for extra coolness. Give Capstan a trial run today. You'll be impressed with their performance.
W. D. & H. O. WILLS—A WORLD-FAMOUS NAME FOR FINE VIRGINIA TOBACCOS FOR NEARLY 200 YEARS
20
CAPSTAN
MEDIUM
CAPSTAN

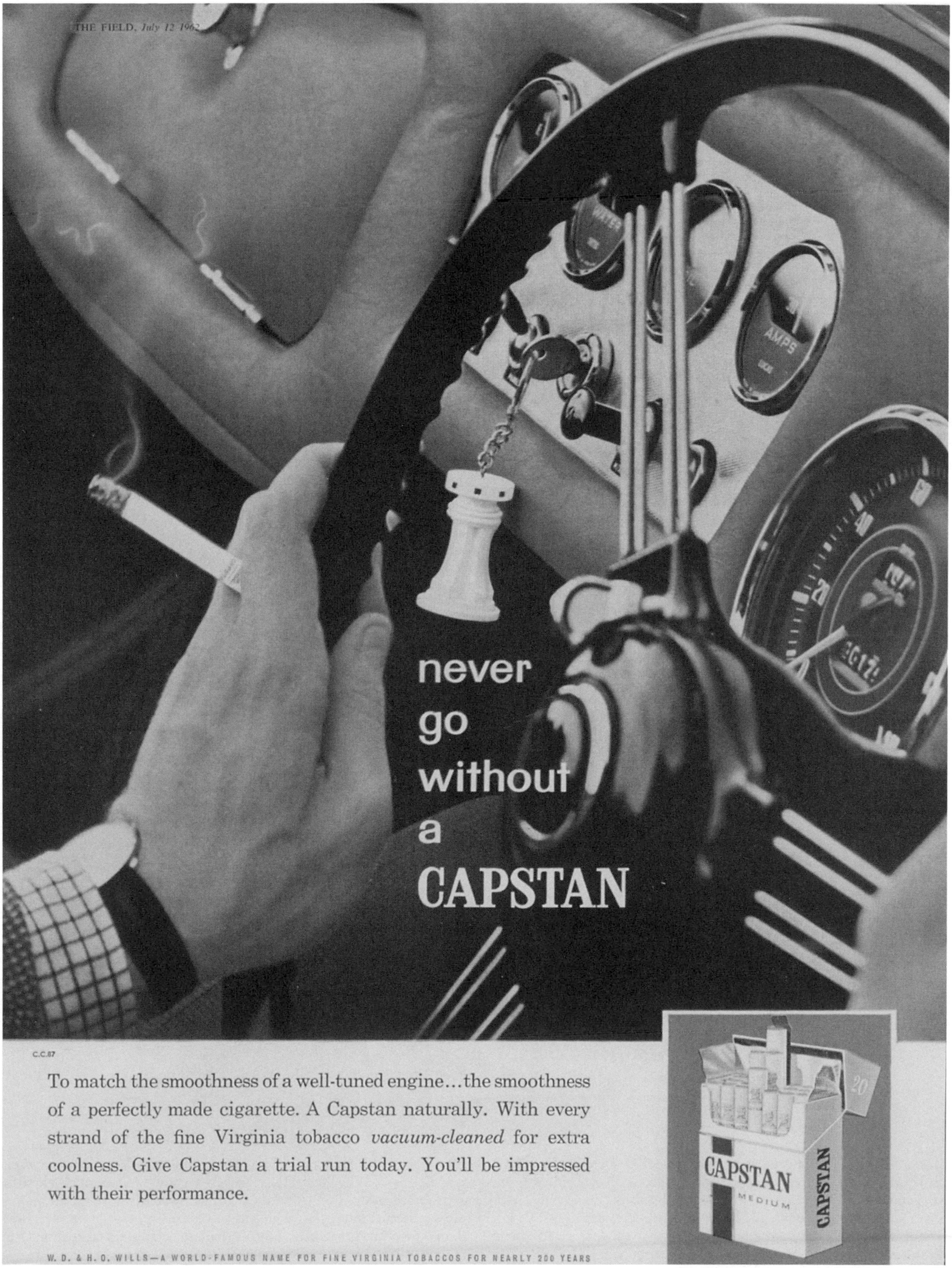

The Illustrated London News, July 21, 1960 (With thanks to Paul Martin)

high performance
high quality—this
is **MAJESTIC**
motoring!

Effortless and thrilling acceleration to over the three figure mark
— superb handling — fade-free response from all-wheel disc
braking — the style and luxury expected from Daimler — and you
have Majestic motoring. With automatic transmission and full
six seater comfort, the "Majestic" sets an unrivalled standard
of value at the realistic price of £2,495 (incl. P.T.).

relax in a

DAIMLER MAJESTIC

with disc-brake safety at EVERY wheel

THE DAIMLER COMPANY LIMITED · G.P.O. BOX 29 COVENTRY

London Distributors and Showrooms: STRATSTONE LTD. 40 BERKELEY STREET, W.1.

BY APPOINTMENT
TO HER MAJESTY THE QUEEN
MOTOR CAR MANUFACTURERS
THE DAIMLER CO. LTD.

Daimler Majestic. Sir Bernard and Lady Docker left Daimler after a tempestuous boardroom battle in 1956, and in 1960 the company merged with Jaguar. Yet this advertisement appears tranquil and old-fashioned — at first glance. The illustration, however, shows a modern block rather than a classical façade, there are no pretend-aristocrats in sight, and the copy concentrates on the merits of the car as machinery rather than on any supposed social cachet. £2500 may have been a "realistic" price, but it was a lot of money in 1960, and so the car's potential market, however appreciative, remained small. Surprisingly, Daimler's campaign had an American precedent: Lincoln had associated its clean-lined new sedans and hardtops with modern architecture in 1952.

THE NEW 4·2 LITRE
Daimler SOVEREIGN

Daimler enthusiasts everywhere will welcome this elegant and powerful new model which combines the very latest developments in modern high performance engineering and built-in safety with all the true characteristics that have made Daimler prestige motoring world famous. The new Sovereign is a car, which despite its compact dimensions, provides a spacious and luxurious 5 seater interior equipped with every refinement for the comfort of driver and passengers alike. Powered by a new 6 cylinder, twin o.h.c. 4.2 litre engine giving a flow of smooth effortless power at all speeds with remarkable acceleration and flexibility, it is equipped with either the latest Borg Warner Model 8 automatic transmission with dual drive range or new all-synchromesh gearbox with overdrive. 'Varamatic' power steering is standard. Independent suspension all-round, four wheel disc brakes with dual hydraulic systems, selective interior car temperature control,

and a high efficiency cooling system are among its many outstanding features. Electrical equipment includes an alternator and pre-engaged starter, four-headlamp system, heated backlight fitted as standard, and transistorised clock mounted in padded safety screen rail. High quality leather hide upholstery, reclining front seats, centre folding arm rests front and rear, a fully lined 19 cubic feet luggage boot and twin fuel tanks with a total of 14 gallons capacity. With its most impressive appearance and the completeness of its specification, this fine new Daimler marks still another step forward for prestige motoring in the modern manner.

Stand 120 Earls Court
LONDON SHOWROOMS: 40 BERKELEY STREET W.1

THE DAIMLER RANGE FOR 1967 ALSO INCLUDES THE 2½ LITRE V8 SALOON, THE 4½ LITRE V8 MAJESTIC MAJOR SALOON AND THE EIGHT-SEATER LIMOUSINE

Daimler 4.2 Litre Sovereign. Rationalization continues. Unlike the V8, this car had a Jaguar engine, and the style of the copy reflects earlier Jaguar rather than Daimler advertising. It is convoluted and pretentious by modern standards, though the emphasis is on the car as technical object rather than on any abstract idea of class. This was wise, as Jaguar had not yet completely recovered from its spiv/self-made plutocrat image of the 1940s. The continuity in illustration and layout from one decade to the next was unusual, particularly given the revolution in advertising styles elsewhere.

Formula for
prestige plus performance

THE MARQUE	DAIMLER
THE ENGINE	140 b.h.p. Daimler 2½ Litre V8
THE DRIVE	Automatic Transmission with Full Driver Control
BRAKING	Disc Brakes on all four wheels

In every detail of its outstanding performance the new Daimler 2½ litre V8 saloon matches the high standard of luxury and refinement traditionally expected of this famous marque. Whether at high speed on the motorway or leisurely manoeuvring in town traffic—the turbine-like smoothness of its engine is truly remarkable. The fully automatic transmission gives full engine braking in *all* ratios and, moreover, provides for driver control with all its advantages. With disc brakes on all four wheels, and with power steering as an optional extra, this lavishly equipped 5 seater saloon truly provides prestige motoring in the modern manner.

LONDON SHOWROOMS: 40 BERKELEY STREET, W.1

Daimler
2½ LITRE V8 SALOON

acceleration to over the 3 figure mark — superb handling…the style and luxury expected from Daimler — and you have Majestic motoring…. [R]elax in a Daimler Majestic with disc-brake safety at every wheel," said typical copy.[11]

The Majestic really came into its own in 1959, when it acquired the second of Edward Turner's V8 engines, similar to the 2½ litre of the SP250 but much larger at 4561cc. It also acquired a boot neatly extended beyond the rear wing line, and was called the Majestic Major. Production began in 1960. The name might have been a little comical — any advertising line such as "Come and see the Majestic Major!" would, after all, have suggested a music hall act rather than a car — but there was nothing comedic about its performance. It was much, much faster than its appearance suggested — so much so that, had its engine been put in large Jaguars after 1960 (a version of the Jaguar Mk X was seriously considered), or had the car not been so heavy at over 4200 lb., or looked so old-fashioned, it might have undermined Jaguar's reputation for unbeatable performance. The Majestic Major was produced until 1968 (and as a limousine, too, from 1961) but it was, perhaps, suspiciously under-advertised in the early 1960s and from 1962 it usually appeared alongside the 2½ litre V8, with brief copy that mentioned its "4½ litre engine," "Automatic transmission and "20 cubic ft. capacity luggage boot" and occasionally its top speed (120 mph), but kept quieter about its power (220 bhp) and acceleration (0–60 and 0–100 mph in 10.3 and 30.9 seconds) than the reticence expected in luxury car advertising strictly required.[12]

During 1962–66, Daimler did not advertise extensively, and those advertisements that did appear concentrated more than most on the whole marque range rather than on individual models. Like Jaguar, Daimler continued with paintings until 1967, and although Jaguar's agency, Nelson Advertising Service, took over Daimler advertising from the London Press Exchange Ltd. at the beginning of 1961, the two marques continued to be promoted in separate campaigns. The marques' distinct, if related, styles of advertising continued until 1966–68, when they began to resemble each other more closely, although similar advertisements did not always appear at the same time. An October 1966 advertisement for the "new Daimler 4.2 litre Daimler Sovereign," for example, looked as similar to a piece for the Jaguar 420 as did the cars themselves — but the Jaguar advertisement was published in 1968.

The great advantage of the Daimler Sovereign over the Jaguar 420 was its marque image. According to *Car*, "In this class, the Jaguar has always had to contend with a slight aura of bookmakerish vulgarity which despite being no fault of the car's must have cost the firm a sale or two. Their upper-echelon salesmen must have been quite relieved to lay hands on the regal name and reputation of Daimler; certainly they lost no time in Daimlerising two of their models to apparently good effect. (Imagine, apart from all else, the effect of the name Daimler as distinct from Jaguar on the attitude of some [magistrates'] benches which remain in blissful ignorance of the meaning of badge engineering.) The Daimler Sovereign, then, is to all intents and purposes a Jaguar 420 with marginally different trim, a new radiator grille, and a cheeky £134 slapped on the price tag."[13] The later Daimler Sovereign of 1969 onwards, based on the 1968 Jaguar XJ6, would provide much the same kind of alternative car, and the Daimler name would be used on the most luxurious of Jaguar saloons in the 1970s. As so often at the end of an up-market, badge-engineered car's production run, the final advertisements for the Sovereign showed its grille, close-up: "Nobody has ever been sold a Daimler Sovereign. The Daimler Sovereign sells itself. When you go and look at one you will see why." The copywriter then listed features and details of its specification before adding, "There is something else, too: only a Daimler has the distinguished Daimler radiator."

If the Majestic Major was the last pure Daimler, the 2½ Litre V8 was the last individual car of the marque. In its body and trim it was a Jaguar Mk 2 in all but small details, yet with the engine of the SP250 and standard automatic transmission it was not simply a late invention by Jaguar. The V8 engine had been fitted in a Conquest development car in the late 1950s, and a V8 saloon, based around a much-modified Vauxhall Cresta body shell, had also been considered.[14] In 1964, S.C.H. Davis assured readers of *The Field*: "This car has a marked character, entirely different from that of the equivalent machine in the Jaguar range. This is *not* a Jaguar with Daimler radiator grille and name plate. It can stand on its own."[15] It was a faster car than the Jaguar 2.4 litre Mk 2 but slower than the 3.4 litre. It was announced in October 1962: "Presenting the new 2½ Litre V8 saloon by Daimler — In the Daimler 2½ Litre V8 saloon, Daimler tradition is continued in the modern manner with all the attributes of high quality and fine workmanship associated with this famous marque faithfully guarded…. Lavishly equipped with every conceivable appointment and refinement devised for the comfort of driver and passengers…here is the kind of Daimler which so many Daimler enthusiasts have long demanded and which truly provides prestige motoring in the modern manner." The last phrase was used in later advertising for the car, and during 1964–67 was used as a slogan for the marque as a whole.

Early advertisements for the 2½ Litre V8 did not mention its price, which was comparatively high: in October

Opposite: **Daimler 2½ Litre V8.** At first sight this advertisement looks almost as old-fashioned as that for the 1960 Majestic, but the copy is recognizably of the sixties, as are the car's features. It may have looked like a Jaguar, but the special (and notably efficient) engine and a modified interior gave the V8 a distinct character which was highlighted in advertising. Both Jaguar and Daimler used paintings with their copy for most of the decade, bucking the general trend. This piece is aimed at successful businessmen and is livelier than the copy that promoted Conquest saloons and coupés ten years earlier.

1964, for example, the car cost £1598 19s 7d compared with the £1556 17s 11d asked for a 3.8 litre Jaguar Mk 2. Yet the small Daimler reached parts of the prestige car market from which Jaguar, by virtue of its image, was excluded, and an estimated 17,620 were sold between 1962 and 1969,[16] making it a highly successful model. In 1962 the Jaguar Mk 2 became the Jaguar 240 and 340, and the Daimler was updated at the same time to become the V8–250, for which, as for the Jaguars, the heavy ribbed chrome bumpers, of a pattern first seen on the Jaguar Mk VII of 1950, were replaced by slim bumpers in a more modern style. By 1968 the car was old-fashioned but still distinctive: "Step up your motoring enjoyment…with real V8 performance" said an April 1968 headline, with copy that emphasized the engine's flexibility and the luxury within the car: "The cost of the V8–250, which can be as low as £1,738.11.8 (inc. p.t.) is no measure of its outstanding quality — but the pride and enjoyment you will get from owing it is perhaps immeasurable. Ask your dealer to arrange a trial run soon — we are confident that you, like many other discerning motorists, will find it a most convincing experience." Many did, and kept their cars for a long time.

13

Humber

"Luxury with a capital H"

In September 1967, the Rootes Group published its last advertisement showing the Humber Super Snipe. "Goodbye old true and faithful servant. You were magnificent. Posh. Plush. Pricey. No doubt you will carry on carrying your many appreciative admirers for years to come. Though you are a long, long way from being put out to pasture, you're going to have to move over the the young new HUMBER. It's all part of the new deal from ROOTES. Please observe one moment of silence before turning the page." A black Super Snipe was seen in profile, driving off the end of the page, grief-stricken chauffeur at the wheel. When the reader turned over he discovered: "The Astonishing new Humber Sceptre. We'd like to launch it with a 22-gun salute. 1. Bang! Distinctive new styling. 2. Bang! Beautiful black leathercloth roof covering. 3. Bang! Gold coachline on body beautiful." Eighteen bangs later the copywriter reached "Bang! Illuminated lockable glove box with vanity mirror" and concluded with "that final ineffable thing: Humber quality all for £1,138! And lots and lots of other things like coat hooks and hand rails, lockable petrol cap, warning light if you're running low on fuel, safety-ledge wheels…. Gentlemen, be seated." Any reader still able to look at a Sceptre Mk III without wondering if it was going to backfire had until 1976 to buy one. It would be the last Humber.[1]

The large Humbers were old fashioned by 1967. Although favoured by government ministers, by the police as patrol cars and even by Britain's Prime Minister of 1964–70 and 1970–76, Harold Wilson, they had become cars which everyone respected but which few people actually bought. By the end of 1966 Rootes had decided their fate, and Chrysler's acquisition of a controlling interest in the Group in March 1967 ensured that nothing similar would be built in future.

In the short term, the demand for big cars would be met by imported Valiants while the next big Humber, styled in Coventry, would be built both in Britain and at Poissy by Simca, which Chrysler had controlled since 1963. In the event, as Graham Robson recalls, "…at the beginning of 1970, the British end of the project was cancelled. Tooling already being installed at Humber Road for production of [the British V6 engine for the Humber-badged version] was ripped out. The Simca-engined car was launched later in 1970 as the Chrysler 180; cynically advertised in France as 'An American, from Paris', it was *not* a success."[2] Nor, in Britain, were the Valiants, even if the Valiant Charger, advertised in bright orange in 1973 as "the grown-up sports car," had curiosity value for its muscular hardtop design and 230 bhp, 5.2 litre V8 engine.

Yet the big Humbers had been regularly updated, and the most radical change of all was contemplated shortly before Chrysler took full control of Rootes. In 1964, while the Sunbeam Tiger was being developed, "a [four-light, Series IV] Super Snipe was fitted with a 318 cu. in. Ford V8 breathing through a four-barrel Holley carburettor. This silver Humber certainly 'moved' in a most un-Humber way!…the development section told [Rootes test driver Michael Heath] not to exceed 6000 rpm. So off he went and on reaching the M1 [motorway, then without speed restriction] decided to 'see what she would do' up to this limit. He got the car to just under this limit but the noise of the engine was deafening and the car was moving across all three lanes! On returning to the Stoke plant he told one of the engineers of his experience. It wasn't surprising, he was told, as at that engine speed the car would have been travelling at around 145 mph!"[3] The project was continued with Chrysler engines and in January 1966 the company's technical library "issued detailed instructions for the preparation of publicity material."[4] Production was intended to begin by July 1966.[5] Yet the V8 was eventually dropped during Chrysler's reorganization of the Group and production of the Hawk, Super Snipe and Imperial continued until the summer of 1967.

In its advertising from 1957 to the spring of 1964, Humber[6] made the most from the least, adapting, modifying and re-arranging copy and illustrations as the cars were improved in detail.[7] The resulting advertisements were colourful and distinctive and, perhaps surprisingly, not usually pretentious. The marque's occasional flights of social fancy were so innocently overstated that they inspired a smile rather than insecurity or resentment. The saloons and estate cars were often advertised alternately, and regular improvements to both models justified fresh announcements. Subsequent road tests by motoring journals generated extra publicity, as did several film placements and a class victory by Raymond Baxter in the 1961 RAC Rally. In the middle of 1959, photographs began to appear in Super Snipe advertising, and although paintings reappeared between late 1962 and the summer of 1963 (albeit in a less impressionistic style than previously) they disappeared for good in 1965. The abandonment of paintings marked the end of a long tradition. Until the early 1960s Rootes advertisements and catalogues sometimes included artwork by the famous aviation artist, Frank Wootton, who under commission by Astral Studio produced striking portraits of Sunbeam-Talbot, Sunbeam and Humber cars in particular. As a freelance artist after the Second World War he had also worked for Alvis, Bentley, Jaguar, Land-Rover, Rolls-Royce and Rover.[8]

Announcement advertising for the new Hawk, which cost £1261 7s as a saloon and £1381 7s as a Touring Limousine with wind-down glass division, was typical of the Rootes Group and of its period. An elongated car, in a three-layer colour scheme of maroon over beige over maroon, was set against a background of deep marine blue that looked like waves of a gently rolling sea photographed at dawn. Small stars twinkled in the background: "See the new Humber Hawk — More power — More Room — More M.P.G. — and Greater Safety!" The overall look was like that of much American car advertising of a few years earlier, toned down for British middle-class sensibilities. Surprisingly, the car's colours were less radical than some actually offered: in real life the beige was more like lilac and the maroon more akin to dark chocolate with a reddish tinge. The lilac was carried through to the leather interior, and complemented a dashboard in wood-effect painted metal that was given away only by the feel of the glovebox lid and by the shape of a recessed centre panel containing a clock and controls for the lights and ventilation. Veneer could not have been applied to such a panel without splitting.[9] Real wood appeared towards the end of 1958, when advertising for the new Super Snipe invited the reader also to see the Hawk, "now with a greatly

enriched interior." The phrase was a Rootes favourite and had been used in 1954, when the earlier (1952–57) Super Snipe, its styling essentially that of the 1948 Hawk Mk III, had gained a wooden dashboard and door cappings and other improvements. With typical Rootes economy, the new Hawk adopted a 2267cc overhead-valve engine first seen in the 1948 Sunbeam-Talbot 90 and fitted to the Hawk Mk VI from 1954. 1957's copy modestly described it as a "greatly improved power unit"; its origins lay in the 1669cc Humber Twelve of 1933.

At 3080 lb. the new Hawk was a solid car, and at just under fifteen feet five inches long and nearly five feet ten inches wide it had the largest monocoque body then built in Britain.[10] It looked quite unlike the separate-chassied Hawks Mk III–VIA of 1948–57, even though both basic types were styled under the influence of Raymond Loewy Associates. In 1948, when Loewy's company had an office in London, that influence was most apparent in the Minx Phase III, whose general contours were shared by the Humber. But where the 1948 production cars had an obvious stylistic prototype in the 1947 Studebaker, the production 1957 Hawk appeared to have been inspired by no particular American model and looked, if anything, like a 1955 Chevrolet. A generally squared-up rather than streamlined appearance; a slight kick-up in the rear doors; front and rear screens that wrapped round only far enough to take the pillars to, rather than beyond, the almost vertical; two-tone paint separated from the outset by stainless trim along the sides of the car; an upright and essentially rectangular grille; peaked headlamps; and a certain severity of outline underneath the two-tone paint all suggested General Motors rather than Studebaker. According to William Towns, then a young trainee stylist with Rootes, this was no accident: "William Rootes brought back a Chevy brochure and decided the next... Hawk and Snipe had to look like this: the tail treatments are identical to the...Chevy if you look at the cars today. Later, a Dodge tail fin was applied — unsuccessfully, thank God — to a Minx. Too awful."[11] True the Hawk retained a family resemblance to the 1956 Minx, styled alongside it, and the Minx did look like a 1953 Studebaker. Yet without the Minx to link them, the Studebaker and the new Humber did not seem to be related, and the resemblance was directly apparent only in early clays.[12] As the new car was developed, it faded away. The Hawk and Super Snipe estate cars, introduced in October 1957 and October 1958 respectively, featured rear side windows with curved ends like those of 1955 Chevrolet and Pontiac station wagons. The estate cars were assembled at the Singer factory in Birmingham until Carbodies took over their assembly during 1961, when Rootes needed all available space in order to build the Hillman Super Minx and Singer Vogue in parallel with, rather than as replacements for, the regular Minx and Gazelle.[13]

In October 1957 the original advertisement for the Hawk was altered economically from "See the New Humber

Hawk" to "Drive the impressive Humber Hawk," and shortly afterwards the new Hawk Estate Car took centre stage, and was advertised not only on the Hawk staples of power, comfort and safety, but also on its "BIG load and passenger space." The new copy appeared either with a russet and cream car or — more usually — with a two-tone green one, which suited the rural backdrops chosen. Later versions of the advertisement used the same illustration against a new background and with extra passengers inside. The headline, "Humber Luxury, Performance, Styling PLUS Estate Car Versatility," was typical of Rootes in being both aspirational and practical. When the Hawk gained a wooden dashboard, the saloon was painted in a style more impressionistic than the original, although the car's colours of russett and cream were similar to 1957's scheme. "The incomparable Humber Hawk" now had "a greatly enriched interior, combining luxurious comfort, elegance and a smooth yet powerful performance with the highest standards of road holding and reliability."

When the Super Snipe arrived on October 1, 1958, Humber's emphasis switched to that car. With a smooth and durable 2651cc, six-cylinder, 112 bhp engine designed for Humber by Armstrong Siddeley along the lines of its existing 3.4 litre Sapphire "six," the Super Snipe was offered as a Touring Limousine at £1643 17s or as an estate car at £1751 7s. At £1493 17s, the Super Snipe saloon cost just £232 10s more than the Hawk and, like the Hawk, could be ordered with overdrive or automatic transmission. The standard column-change gearbox had three speeds to the Hawk's four and synchromesh on bottom, which the Hawk lacked. The interior included walnut picnic tables and a separate radio volume control for the rear passengers, and power-assisted steering was optional. "This new car represents the Humber attack on the difficult and variable luxury market," announced *Motor Trader*. "Technically it is chiefly noticeable for its new engine…. The whole tone of the car is consonant with its market."[14] With its elaborate grille and three-layer paint schemes divided as on the Hawk, the highly styled Super Snipe was the most luxurious British car designed in a mid-Atlantic rather than traditionally English idiom. S.C.H. Davis found it "a pleasant shock" to find how little the car cost, given its power and equipment, and he was amused by the "Snipe" emblems on the bonnet and boot: "There is no knowing what a stylist will do with such things as badges if left to himself, the result in this case being intriguing. When I last tried to abolish snipe by gunfire those agile, fast little birds were not noticeably provided with necks like storks. Their image, as provided on the bonnet of the Humber, is mainly neck, while the version on the tail resembles nothing so much as a demented duck."[15] The bird had long given its name to Humber: the first Snipe had appeared in 1930 (as did the first Imperial) and a 4.1-litre Super Snipe, more powerful than the plain 3.2-litre Snipe of the time, had arrived in 1938; the first Hawk had been a Hillman of 1935–37.

In October 1958 the Super Snipe Series I, "the most luxurious and beautiful Humber ever made," was shown in two-tone black and silver outside a palatial country mansion, its owners in evening dress. It was a style of advertising popular in the United States with Cadillac (and with Packard, Duesenberg and others before the Second World War) but rarely seen in post-war Britain. The Super Snipe was "[t]he aristocrat of cars…. A beautiful car of undoubted quality, luxury and exceptional comfort. A car whose very silence whispers its supremacy…." Less high-flown copy was substituted in an otherwise identical advertisement for *Vogue* magazine a month later: "New 2½ litre six-cylinder engine giving remarkable flexibility of performance. Deep seat luxury for six, exceptional riding comfort and the reassurance of utter safety at all times." In June 1959, Humber's copy retreated from tangible features but became less formal: "Here is a car with a distinctive personality of its own expressed through a superb elegance of line, luxurious comfort and a brilliant performance." Colours and settings became more down-to-earth, too: a sober two-tone grey car without whitewalls appeared on a forest path at dusk and in a former stable used as a garage. The same copy was used for both advertisements and — unusually — for early advertising for a updated Super Snipe Series II, which arrived in October 1959.[16]

Seen side by side, Rootes' 1959–60 advertisements for the Super Snipe Series I and II reveal how ingeniously the Group minimized costs, and how last-minute changes to cars' specifications, useful in themselves for publicity, could play havoc with the lead times needed by photographers and advertising agencies. In November 1959 a new Series II with whitewall tyres was shown in two-tone green with the side flash which distinguished it from the Series I taking the darker colour. But the country house behind the car was in a suspiciously similar style to the stable which had sheltered the Series I, and the new car had the same registration number and red interior as its predecessor. The new picture included the Series II's roof-mounted rear-view mirror and subtly updated grille (with five rather than six horizontal bars) but retained the earlier car's bonnet badge. The picture had, needless to say, been confected from an old photograph before the badging of the Series II could be finalized. By February 1960 the correct bonnet script had appeared and new copy refered to the "New 3-litre Super Snipe" and to the "Self-adjusting front disc brakes" specific to the Series II. Yet the updated copy had already appeared in a December 1959 advertisement that had used an unrelated picture of a Series II which was up-to-date in every detail, including the bonnet script.[17] This picture, however, was a painting rather than a photograph — as was the illustration in an October 1959 advertisement for the estate car, which had appeared within weeks of the Series II's announcement with up-to-date body coachwork details and estate-specific copy mentioning the Series II's new engine and brakes.

When specifications changed quickly it was often easier and cheaper to touch in an old photograph or even commission new artwork at short notice than to arrange for new colour photographs to be taken. This was one reason why colour photography took such a comparatively long time to catch on. Fortunately Humber sales did not depend on it: "There was no difficulty in selling Humbers in those days. They were lovely cars, very well finished and trimmed, and they were also very good value," recalls David Allen, who worked in Rootes' sales and marketing organizations at the time.[18]

With the 2965cc Series II, Humber entered model-for-model competition in the three-litre class with a car £56 more expensive than the manual Vanden Plas Princess 3-litre introduced at the same time, and £159 more expensive as an automatic. But when the Super Snipe was updated again in October 1960 to become the Series III,[19] it became cheaper than the Princess at £1532 to the BMC car's £1626 or, for the automatic, £1688 to BMC's £1699. The Series III featured a new, full-width grille and was the first British car to have four conventional headlamps as standard equipment. Curiously, little was made of this innovation in advertising, possibly because the headlamps and their advantages were so obvious; the unique feature emphasized in copy for the estate car was that it was the "only British Estate Car in its class with easy-loading tail gates giving an extension for lengthy articles" — in other words, the lower half of the split tailgate was supported sturdily enough to carry weight. As ever, the estate was shown in the countryside while in October 1960 the saloon sped through the gates of a sun-denched mansion, diplomatic "CD" plate discreetly attached beneath the front bumper. A spring 1961 advertisement showed a crimson-tinted black and white photograph of the car under the headline, "Masterpiece," with copy to suit, which listed the car's features and emphasized its value for money. With the Series III, the earlier car's side flash was replaced by a simple stainless steel trim strip, the gaudy colour schemes of 1958–60 disappeared, and the colour photographs used in subsequent "masterpiece" advertisements during the summer showed a car in distinctive but restrained duck-egg blue with a very dark blue roof. In November 1961 the colour scheme was reversed for a dignified-looking car seen in London. With Big Ben and the Houses of Parliament in the far distance, the car was admired by a city gent holding — surreally — a telescope: "If your horizons have widened…have a Humber complete the picture. Every picture tells a story — every Humber tells the right one. This one could be called 'the partnership of assurance'…." Well, it could be — but only by a copywriter, and the aspirational copy which followed was rather lamely generic. Yet the

change of tone and sober colours consolidated the car's appeal to the more conservative part of its natural market. In June the car was shown on a deserted beach above the same copy, its owner now in a beach robe, still clutching the telescope.

For the Super Snipe Series IV of October 1962, distinguished from the Series III mainly by a rear window that wrapped round less sharply at its bottom corners, copy was divided into a general introduction ("A policy of continuous, logical development has brought the Humber Super Snipe to its present eminence…. Here is an elegant and distinguished car…. A car you will be proud to own") and a list of starred features such as "Improved suspension and steering" and "built-in ventilation, with four swivelling ventilating windows." The car appeared in single-tone, sober colours with narrow whitewall tyres and without background, in artwork that looked almost like photography. A separate box gave the Series IV's price of £1541 0s 3d with that of the Hawk (£1204 2s 9d). In a new campaign at the end of 1962 the Series IV promised "Luxury with a capital H." A smiling doorman held an umbrella in one hand and mock-saluted the car's owners with the other in a studio pose similar to those used by Ford two years earlier. At the end of 1965 Humber's new agency, Erwin Wasey Ltd., returned briefly to its predecessor's theme of 1958: "Carriages at midnight…. The Humber Super Snipe glides effortlessly and naturally into the most gracious way of life. Stately in its comfort, it offers you the luxury of English hide upholstery and styling at a truly aristocratic level." This time the car was finished in a distinctive but unflamboyant metallic dark purple and the country house was discreetly aristocratic, like those used by Austin and Vauxhall in 1958 for the A105 Vanden Plas and Cresta, and admirers wore evening dresses rather than formal gowns. The Super Snipe, now a Series V, displayed a new, six-light roof design also seen on the equivalent Hawk Series IV and Imperial introduced with it in October 1964.

The Imperial, with "coachwork by Thrupp and Maberly"[20] in saloon or limousine forms and with standard automatic transmission, was announced as "a new conception of executive luxury" at £1795 18s 9d, and in 1966 it was promoted as a business asset. A tycoon sat in the back, his cigar, dictaphone and papers illuminated by a reading lamp in the roof of the car: "Every top man has his team…and the star of this team is the Humber Imperial, which provides him with a degree of luxury unprecedented in this price range…." The copy went on to list the Imperial's special features such as a leathercloth roof, "deep nylon rug" and adjustable rear dampers. Another press advertisement, selected

---

Opposite: **Humber Super Snipe Series III.** By 1962 the Super Snipe had lost the brash details of earlier versions, and the neat twin headlamps, grille corners and wrap-around indicators recalled the 1958 Edsel. The picture is unusual for using the kind of backdrop for a photograph that was more popular in earlier advertisements which used paintings. The copy has an American feel, and its theme was echoed in 1963 Buick advertising, which targeted an equivalent market. This piece is clumsy, however, with too many clichés, and the worst of them, "every picture tells a story," was the kind of platitude that fitted badly with the dynamism and "assurance" promised by the makers.

THE FIELD. *November 23 1961*

If your horizons have widened…
have a **HUMBER** complete the picture

Every picture tells a story—every Humber tells the right one. This one could be called "the partnership of assurance"—a man and his Humber. He can rely on it. On the way it performs (brilliantly), on the way it looks (every inch a thoroughbred), in the way it accommodates (generously, luxuriously). Able to deal with any conditions that climate, roads and traffic can devise. And safe. Very safe. Very strong. Imposingly elegant in any company. And it is for these very important reasons that at a certain moment in your life (perhaps now?) a Humber will fit your aspirations like a glove. The 3-litre, six-cylinder Super Snipe Saloon has front disc and large rear brakes, dual headlamps and outstanding suspension. Fully-automatic transmission, power-assisted steering, individual front seats and overdrive (on normal transmission models) available as extras.
THE HIGHLY SUCCESSFUL HUMBER RANGE CONTINUES UNCHANGED AND WILL BE CURRENT IN 1962

> SUPER SNIPE SALOON
> Unrivalled by any other car
> approaching its price
> # £1532.9.9
> (£1050 PLUS P.T. £482.9.9)
>
> HUMBER HAWK SALOON
> Remarkable value at
> £1277.5.7
> (£875 PLUS P.T. £402.5.7)

ROOTES MOTORS LIMITED

HUMBER LIMITED · DIVISION OF ROOTES MOTORS LIMITED · LONDON SHOWROOMS AND EXPORT DIVISION: ROOTES LIMITED · DEVONSHIRE HOUSE · PICCADILLY · LONDON · W.1

the HUMBER with a dual personality

HUMBER SUPER SNIPE ESTATE CAR

An estate car with a difference. A superb, commanding aristocrat with all the good looks of a saloon—yet it quickly converts into the most spacious load carrier. The luxurious interior provides ample room for six people and their luggage or, with the rear seat folded flat, load space for 840 lbs of bulky goods and full seating for three. The back-light is hinged and the tail-gate opens out to accommodate lengthy loads. The 3-litre, six-cylinder engine gives a supremely effortless performance. Front disc brakes ensure fade-free braking safety. Improved steering and suspension mean precise control with a smooth balanced ride in all conditions. All-steel unitary construction gives tremendous strength.

HUMBER HAWK ESTATE CAR

The Humber Hawk Estate Car is superbly roomy and comfortable. Combining craftsmanship and luxury with a rugged and remarkably economical four cylinder engine, it offers value that is quite outstanding.

£1,295 plus P.T. £270.7.1   **£1,095** plus P.T. £228.13.9
Overdrive or fully-automatic transmission, power-assisted steering and whitewall tyres extra.   *Overdrive and whitewall tyres extra.*

ROOTES MOTORS LTD

Humber Limited
Division of Rootes Motors Limited
London Showrooms & Export Division
Rootes Ltd. Devonshire House
Piccadilly London W1

Humber Super Snipe Series IV Estate Car. Old-fashioned copy and illustration for an old-fashioned station wagon, complete with split tail-gate, wraparound windscreen and 1958 American styling. Amusingly, the rear reflector on the driver's side doubled as the fuel filler cap. The "dual personality" theme was used by Hillman in 1955 for their Husky utility wagon. The Super Snipe was not directly replaced when it went out of production in 1967, and this version was much missed by mayors, antique dealers and field sports enthusiasts. A few survive.

ROOTES MOTORS LTD

BY APPOINTMENT TO
HER MAJESTY THE QUEEN
MOTOR VEHICLE
MANUFACTURERS
ROOTES MOTORS LTD

Present the new Humber Imperial

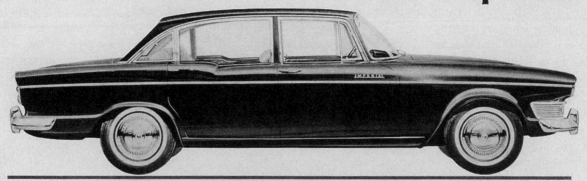

A new conception of executive luxury

From a long tradition of distinguished cars the new Humber Imperial approaches the ultimate in comfort and luxury at a very modest price. The sleek hand-built coachwork with distinctive black leather finish to roof, is richly styled in West of England Cloth upholstery, deep pile carpets and polished walnut veneer. Electrically adjustable rear shock absorbers ensure a comfortable ride over all terrain, and fully-automatic transmission and power-assisted steering are fitted. Every passenger comfort is catered for, including fully-reclining front seats, front and rear heaters, also push-button radio, adjustable reading lights, three cigar lighters and folding tables. The Humber Imperial is available as a limousine with division or as a high performance saloon.

Coachwork by Thrupp and Maberly

Smooth, silent 6-cylinder 3-litre engine with vivid acceleration; Front disc brakes; Borg-Warner fully-automatic transmission; 'Hydrosteer' power-assisted steering; 'Selectaride' electrically adjustable rear shock absorbers.

Saloon **£1,795.18.9** (inc. £310.18.9 p. tax)
Limousine **£1,916.15.5** (inc. £331.15.5 p. tax)

NEW HUMBER SUPER SNIPE Beautifully styled and featuring even more luxurious seating ; elegant new 'low-line' look ; more power ; improved suspension, quieter running. Price : £1,511.19.7 (inc. £261.19.7 p.t.) Limousine and Estate Car versions also available.

NEW HUMBER HAWK The biggest family car at a 'family car' price . . . now extensively re-styled. Sleek new lines ; new all-synchromesh gearbox, new light steering, improved suspension. Price : £1,095.2.1 (inc. £190.2.1 p.t.) Limousine and Estate Car versions also available.

HUMBER IMPERIAL · SUPER SNIPE · HAWK

LONDON SHOWROOMS AND EXPORT DIVISION ROOTES LTD DEVONSHIRE HOUSE PICCADILLY LONDON W1

Humber Imperial. A name redundant since 1954 was revived for this super-luxury Super Snipe derivative. Ironically in a year when Chrysler took a large shareholding in Rootes, this version marked a move away from the American-style wraparound front and rear screens of the type's earlier years, although Imperial was a Chrysler moniker too, dating back to the 1920s. The use of the word "executive" indicates the period, as does "conception of," which in later years would almost certainly have been "concept in," although the former might sound more measured and weighty.

as one of the best of the year by the advertising annual *Modern Publicity*, showed the Imperial's owners close-up through its side windows, their driver in front at the wheel: "Only a private chauffeur can add to the luxury of a Humber." As a super-luxury edition of an established big saloon, the Imperial anticipated the Ford Zodiac Executive (1965) and Vauxhall Viscount (1966). Yet by 1967 the basic design was obsolescent and, as with Singer Hunters in 1956, stocks were cleared by reducing prices. "Now's the time to buy a Humber — prices down by as much as £175. No change in specification or quality" announced Chrysler, its pentaster nestling between "Humber" and "Rootes" at the foot of the page. Soon they were all gone.

The best-selling and most modern Humber of the mid-1960s, quite different from the big cars in its feel and potential market, was almost not a Humber at all. *Small Car* began its test robustly: "We…introduced the malicious phrase badge-engineering to British enthusiasts' vocabularies for just one reason. We maintain that by calling a spade an earth-moving instrument the average UK volume manufacturer is deluding himself just as much as the public.…" Yet the magazine acknowledged that sometimes "badge-engineered cars do in fact often have virtues their parent models lack.… In fact we believe there is a definite place for most badge-engineered cars—as cars.… [Their manufacturers'] mistake…lies in retaining the badges and not in building the cars." Almost in spite of itself, it found the Humber Sceptre "a bright newcomer…remarkable…rugged as a Volvo, quiet as a Rover, [it] made an uncommonly deep impression on us as a fine offering."[21]

Based on the Super Minx, the Sceptre had originally been planned as a new Sunbeam Rapier Series IV, and pre-production prototypes carried Rapier badges.[22] As Rootes development engineer Don Tarbun recalled in 1987, "Both the [Sunbeam] Venezia and the Humber Sceptre were thought of as possible replacements for the Rapier, but they were grossly overweight and never performed well. In the case of the Sceptre, we called it a Humber and it sold, whereas the Venezia was never productionised."[23] As introduced in January 1963, the Sceptre was only slightly heavier than the eventual Rapier Series IV.[24] The Sceptre's twin headlamps resembled those of the Singer Vogue but its grille was unmistakeably that of the Rapier. The centre of the steering wheel bore a large "S," which could have stood for "Sceptre" had not the game been given away by the sword, like that in badges of earlier Rapiers, which ran through the letter.[25] At £997 8s 9d the Sceptre was expensive compared with the £768 17s 1d Super Minx but it was a substantially different car, with an 80 bhp, aluminium-head (and, for its first few months, twin-carburettor) version of the 1592cc engine fitted in the Rapier since 1961, giving 0–60 in 18.2 seconds and a top speed of 85 mph. The understeer of the Super Minx was largely abolished by a stout anti-roll bar.

In its body and interior styling, the Sceptre showed both Chrysler and Chevrolet influences. Its double-curved windscreen, much larger than that of the Super Minx and Vogue, echoed Chrysler Corporation's contemporary (1957–63) Imperial, and Chevrolet's 1958 style dominated the Sceptre's lowered roofline, wraparound rear window and tail. The Sceptre's fins were shared with the Super Minx and Vogue and its tail-lights with the Hillman, but the resemblance was closest with the stainless trim chosen for the Humber. The Humber's greatest selling-point, however, was its interior, the first in a British saloon to be really fully equipped but to spurn wood and leather. The dashboard, with two hooded dials ahead of the driver and four auxiliary instruments alongside them above the minor controls, was covered only with black vinyl. Beneath the minor controls was a small console containing the gear lever. By contrast, the car's high-quality woollen carpets, bucket seats and door trims were in a colour matching the bodywork — they were mid-green, for example, in a car with a dark green body and pale green roof and rear deck. "It gives you a wonderfully pampered feel to sit among so many separate instruments and switches, and everything operates with satisfying precision…" purred *Small Car*. S.C.H. Davis of *The Field* appreciated "that the car has a fine set of instruments of true engineering type, not fancy ones," and quoted a friend who had been reminded of aviation cockpit drill. "One certainly gets the impression of tasteful comfort quickly" said Bill Hartley of *The Illustrated London News*. J. Eason Gibson of *Country Life* found the fittings impressive and the layout "good," feeling only that "a slight over-exuberance had been allowed" in the design of the fascia. No wonder: the passenger's grab handle, across a recess in the top of the dashboard, was exactly like that of the 1958–60 Chevrolet Corvette; the perforated chrome spokes within the horn ring followed the pattern, if not the shape, of those in some 1958–60 Chevrolets; and the circular gauges and their hoods, though not their arrangement, recalled the full-size Chevrolet of 1959–60.[26] No British manufacturer had ever produced anything similar before. Perhaps fortunately, the Sceptre was not sold in the United States.[27]

It was no surprise that a car as hastily rebranded as the Sceptre should be advertised at first with paintings rather than the photographs adopted later, and from the outset the model was promoted on its equipment: "Rootes present the superbly equipped Humber Sceptre. Humber luxury in a new sports saloon! Never before has there been a car so superbly equipped with such a performance…at so modest a price!" Ten selected features such as "New self-cancelling overdrive on top and third gears fitted as standard" and "Generous space in the carpeted boot" were listed, and they included that 1963 selling point, "No greasing points." In 1960 it was not uncommon for a car to need grease at fifteen or twenty points every 1000 miles. Owners, not surprisingly, sometimes ignored the nipples which their particular grease guns could not reach, and there was no guarantee that a garage, finding a nipple blocked, would replace it rather than simply squirt and hope. By the summer of 1965 the Sceptre was selling steadily[28] and its interior — by now with a restyled steering wheel hub — was promoted as "The inside story of out and out luxury" and given as much prominence as the exterior design. A mid-1966 advertisement for the 1725cc Sceptre Mk II ("For the man who wants to do more than just sit there and steer") pioneered the use of multiple close-up photographs arranged in rows to highlight individual instruments, switches and other details, and showed the whole car only in a small picture at the foot of the page. The idea would be taken up by other advertisers of super-equipped family cars later in the decade and during the 1970s.

In 1967 all of the old Rootes cars, their origins lying in the mid-1950s, were discontinued, and by 1968 the company sold only "Arrow" saloons and estates; the related, fastback, Sunbeam Rapier; and the Imps. The Humber Sceptre Mk III, a much less extensive deviation from the Hillman Hunter than the Mk 1 had been from the Super Minx, had settled down by mid-1968 and "in Prussian Blue photographed by John D. Green" was shown in a moody, rainy, night-time street scene: "What's the new deal to men already flushed with success? The New Humber Sceptre. £1,259. Rootes' new deal is your new deal."[29] The original car had been successful within its market and an excellent image-booster for an ageing saloon range, but it had not been especially profitable. David Allen, a member of Rootes product planning department from 1966, recalls, "The original Sceptre…was one of the first medium-sized luxury sports saloons, along with the Rover and Triumph 2000s. Our problem was that we didn't have a two-litre engine, so [we] lost out on image as well as performance. I think the Arrow-series Sceptre was just about acceptable, but it no longer had any exclusivity, apart from its traditional Humber interior. Like [British Leyland] the company was trying to keep too many balls in the air at once."[30] Nevertheless, the new Sceptre sold only slightly less well than its predecessor, and kept the Humber name clinically alive — if not gambolling round the automotive garden — for almost another ten years.[31]

14

Jaguar

"Grace…Space…Pace"

The ideal for a car manufacturer is to need no advertising at all. The product is announced, it is well reviewed, its reputation spreads rapidly by word of mouth to the whole population; it is bought by everyone who hears about it and who can afford it; as many are sold—instantly—as can be made; each one is as profitable as any product of its kind can be; and all other manufacturers see the car, exclaim—"It is marvellous; we can never compete!" and collectively give up car manufacture for market gardening. In the 1950s and 1960s, with some models and in some years, Jaguar came as close as any British luxury car manufacturer to this ideal. The cars offered wonderful value for money. The question unavoidably on the mind of someone with, say, the £1579 that bought a 3.4 Litre Mk 2 at the beginning of 1960, or the £1884 that secured a big Mk IX,[1] was— why *not* buy a Jaguar? And the reason was often purely social: the man who chose a Daimler Majestic (£2495), Rover 100 (£1538) or Mercedes-Benz 220 (£2249) did not wish to be thought a Jaguar type of man. Yet in truth Jaguar drivers were diverse: for every "spiv" there was an enthusiast who polished his cam-covers lovingly, and the marque was perennially popular with businessmen and in the "gin belt" of the home counties around London which, despite its apparent homogeneity to outsiders, incorporated a wide variety of incomes, world-views and occupations.

If some other cars—the Daimler, Rover and Mercedes-Benz among them—had more deep-down quality, Jaguar had some of the best engines in the world and combined them with speed, robustness, good handling and, by 1960, four-wheel disc brakes. Admittedly the earlier, drum-braked 3.4 litre (retrospectively called the Mk 1), weighing 3250 lb., with 190 net bhp and capable of 0–60 in 11.2 seconds (and 120 mph flat-out), had been a frightening car if driven to its potential. "Regrettably, the brakes of the model submitted for test fell considerably below desirable standards of performance" thought *The Autocar* in 1957, and, with a rear track slightly narrower even than that of the Morris Minor, the Mk 1 could swing out its tail unpredictably, especially in the wet.[2] Motorists changing from less powerful cars sometimes became over-excited, with predictable results. But the Mk 1 acquired disc brakes later in 1957 and the Mk 2, introduced in 1959, was a much better car. And Jaguars had quality of their own, too: "I insisted on keeping the best features of coachbuilding after we went for the pressed-steel bodies," recalled Sir William Lyons,[3] "We kept plenty of wood in the doors, for example, so there would be a nice, solid 'clunk' when you used them."[4] Lyons kept his factory's costs—and his suppliers' prices—as low as possible and, like Fords in the family car market, Jaguars were designed with features and trim that would give the maximum pleasure to owners for the minimum expense in production. In this respect the cars sold themselves, rather than waiting to be discovered. A Jaguar was never modest.

Opposite: **Jaguar Mark X.** This advertisement suited its subject. In real life the car looked like a humorous parody of its kind, and its proportions are exaggerated here only a little. The front doors, which extended nearly a foot beyond the windscreen pillar, were very heavy and, owing to the curvature of the body sides, inclined to close under their own weight, and so were spring-assisted. Yet in spite of its size the Mark X performed, handled and rode well. The copy, pompous and overblown in Jaguar's best tradition, includes many of the mannerisms of style, vocabulary and sham-antique phrasing that characterized the business-speak of popular film caricature. The result was a delightful pastiche that is a collectors' item for Jaguar owners today.

new grace .. new space .. new pace

a completely new JAGUAR .. *a successor*

to the Mark IX, now joins the famous Mark 2 and 'E' Type models

The Jaguar Mark X, although an entirely new car in construction, design and appearance, stems from a long and illustrious line of outstanding models which have been identified during the past decade by the symbols Mark VII, Mark VIII and Mark IX. All have been highly successful in their own right and have formed important links in a chain of development culminating in the creation of the finest car yet to be produced in the Jaguar big saloon tradition—the Jaguar Mark X.

This elegant model is of monocoque construction and is powered by the world-famous Jaguar XK 'S' Type 3.8 litre twin overhead camshaft engine with three carburettors. This highly versatile engine by reason of its flexibility, smoothness and silence is ideally suited for use in such a car as the Mark X where every emphasis has been placed upon refinement of performance. Producing 265 horsepower, the engine, save for minor details, is identical with that fitted to the recently introduced 'E' Type Grand Touring Models, and it endows the Mark X with a degree of performance superior even to the Mark IX which it now supplants. Independent suspension front and rear and disc brakes on all four wheels enable full advantage to be taken of this performance with safety and comfort, whilst the luxurious furnishings and appointments include such refinements as reclining seats, folding tables and high efficiency dual-control heating installation.

With new grace in its smooth flowing lines, with new space in its roomier interior and with new pace in its magnificent road performance, the Jaguar Mark X provides a special kind of motoring which no other car in the world can offer.

The Mark Ten

London Showrooms: 88 Piccadilly, W.1 ON STAND 121 EARLS COURT

Nor was Jaguar advertising, though the introduction of the 2.4 litre (Mk 1) was perhaps too much for a sensitive copywriter in 1955: "To the already famous range of Jaguars exemplified by the Mark VII and XK140 models, comes the 2.4 litre Jaguar saloon, a brilliant newcomer in which will be found the embodiment of all the highly specialised technical knowledge and engineering achievement that have gained for the name of Jaguar the highest international repute…. To those motorists whose desire for a car of compact dimensions is a matter of personal preference the opportunity is at last presented, not only for satisfying that desire, but for gratifying a natural wish to own a car, the mere possession of which indicates insistence on owning nothing but the best…a Jaguar." In 1961, he—or a faithful pupil—had another go with the Mk X: "The Jaguar Mark X, although an entirely new car in construction, design and appearance, stems from a long and illustrious line of outstanding models which have been identified during the past decade by the symbols Mark VII, Mark VIII and Mark IX. All have been highly successful in their own right and have formed important links in a chain of development culminating in the creation of the finest car yet to be produced in the Jaguar big saloon tradition." The words "big saloon" did not really go with "tradition"; the reader could feel the copywriter really wanting to say, "Look at this big fast car!" yet feeling compelled against his instinct, and perhaps against his better judgment, to sound like a minor local worthy after a very long lunch. The Mk 10, as it was soon called, was designed with the American market in mind (where it arrived in February 1962), but it was not fast by American standards while being too big for most British buyers. It did, however, incorporate many features (especially independent rear suspension) of the future XJ6, and its floorpan and much of its drivetrain found a home in the Daimler DS420 limousine of 1968–92. The Mk 10 was rarely advertised nationally after 1961.[5]

These announcements were not typical of all Jaguar advertising, even in 1955–62. Early (1957) copy for the Mk VIII was much more straightforward ("Here to join the world-famous Mk VII, XK and 2.4 litre models, is the Mark Eight—one of the most luxurious models ever offered as a series production car…") and announcement copy for the S-type,[6] while reverting a little to portentous type, was short at about 100 words to 1955's 400. Individual features were described separately in bullet points. Like many manufacturers, Jaguar advertised most heavily in October, particularly when a new model was announced at the same time, as was often arranged. In the "fallow years" of 1960 and 1962, Jaguar's October/average month expenditure ratios were 3.6:1 and

4.7:1 respectively, compared with 7.8:1 in 1958 (with the Mk VIII's introduction), 11-5:1 in 1959 (with the introduction of the Mk 2) and 9.9:1 in 1964, when there were no completely new models to announce but many improvements. 1961 was an unusual year with a launch campaign for the E-type in March (estimated at about £32,000) and another for the Mk X in October (estimated at £50,000 or so). The average monthly expenditure during the rest of the year was about £7000.[7] When there were no new models to announce, advertising was, of course, needed to maintain interest in the existing saloon range. Jaguar's sports cars, however, hardly needed to be advertised in the ordinary way at all, as most were exported, motoring journals provided a great deal of publicity, and the E-type was its own publicist. In Britain it appeared most famously in an advertisement for Super National fuel rather than in advertising for itself.[8]

In the early 1960s, Jaguar's range advertising developed into a continuing campaign not just for individual models, but for the distilled values of the marque itself. In the late 1950s, Motor Show publicity had shown five different models and described them individually, but in August 1959 a Mk IX and a 3.4 Litre (Mk 1) were shown with a slogan, "Jaguar—a special kind of motoring which no other car in the world can offer," that would appear—sometimes prominently, sometimes within copy for an individual model—until 1968. In November 1959 it appeared with a red Mk 2, photographed outside a grand-looking if not quite aristocratic country house, accompanied by the Jaguar name and "Grace…Space…Pace" with the caption, in very small print beneath the picture, "The 3.4 litre Mark 2 Jaguar." Advertising of 1960–62 for the Mk 2 retained this layout and treatment while reverting, against the general trend of the time, to paintings, which suited the lines of contemporary Jaguars well. Mk 2s in different colours appeared on a country road, on the M1, and accelerating through Marble Arch ahead of taxis and slower cars. The paintings, too, would last until 1968.

Within Jaguar's marque-wide campaign of 1959–66, three particular series stand out. A March 1960 advertisement displayed the trophy from Jaguar's 1951 Le Mans victory with the tiny caption, "One of the Trophies won by Jaguar in their Le Mans victories of 1951, 1953, 1955, 1956, 1957." Above the sculpture was the simple copy: "Sculpted grace…and a special kind of motoring which no other car in the world can offer." At at the top of the page was a very small picture of the Mk 2 in front view. In October the sculpture was replaced by a Jaguar "leaping cat" mascot, and in November the mascot was seen, close-up, on the bonnet of a Mk 2: "You enjoy a very special kind of motoring—when

---

Opposite: **Jaguar Mark 2.** In its early years, Jaguar had been dogged by a reputation for spivvery, but during the 1960s the marque came to be more widely appreciated. This advertisement typifies a new, lighter style of copy that eventually prevailed. The continued use of paintings rather than photographs gave the required impression of old-fashioned substance, and the overall effect, given the nature of the car, is unpretentious. The Mark 2 achieved lasting popularity.

The 3·4 Litre Mark 2 Jaguar

JAGUAR

GRACE . . SPACE . . PACE

*—a special kind
of motoring which no other
car in the world
can offer*

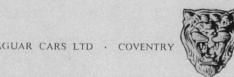

JAGUAR CARS LTD · COVENTRY   *London Showrooms* 88 PICCADILLY, W.1.

THE FIELD, *March 22 1962*

grace...

space..

pace

Three basic models constitute the Jaguar range;
the Mark 2, the Mark 10 and the "E" Type.
Each is endowed with its own individuality, each is
outstanding in its performance and, together,
they satisfy every requirement of those motorists
who, however diverse their needs, have a common
aspiration—to enjoy a special kind of motoring
which no other car in the world can offer.

JAGUAR

LONDON SHOWROOMS 88 PICCADILLY W.I.

550

Jaguar range, 1962. One of a famous series that revived and slightly adapted a pre-war M.G. slogan, this advertisement is that rare thing — a timeless piece which is greater than the sum of its deceptively simple parts. The style of the copy, so unappealing when used to describe the mechanical features of an individual model at length, finds its true rôle in defining the values of a marque. Add a subtle, artful use of layout, carefully chosen typefaces and plenty of white space to draw the reader's eye to the superbly drawn illustrations, and the result is a masterpiece of elegance and restraint.

Getaway people

get Super National

Pale sunrise and purple evening...getaway hours! Sleek, beckoning roads and away-from-it places...getaway playgrounds! Put your right foot down! Relish the power of Super National. Getaway people get Super National.

GETAWAY PEOPLE **GET SUPER NATIONAL**

SUPER NATIONAL

SUPER

National

Jaguar E-type Series I (Super National fuel). A famous advertisement, this piece captures the sense of euphoria that many advertisers attempted with varying degrees of success. The E-type was among the most glamorous cars of its period — and was also a favourite getaway car. This is an early roadster, unusual in Britain for being fitted with whitewall tyres and chrome wire wheels. An early-fifties Standard Vanguard trundles past the petrol station as the Jaguar fills up.

you own a Jaguar." In the spring and early summer of 1962, Jaguar's artist drew the noses of the Mk 2 ("grace…"), Mk 10 ("space…") and E-type ("pace…") in charcoal, and the trio was accompanied by brief copy whose theme — the values of the marque as a whole, rather than the mechanical details of individual models — perfectly matched the copywriter's self-consciously elevated style. A colour version of the advertisement, with the cars painted in black, dark green and red respectively, looked slightly crowded by comparison but was still distinctive. Finally, during 1965–66, the "leaping cat" was painted on a bonnet, in profile, against a glorious sunset, each version of the advertisement quoting one or more eulogies from recent road tests by *Motor*, *Autocar*, or national newspapers. "Superlatives about Jaguars are inclined to be repetitive" said one; "Always a leap ahead" said another headline, unimprovably, with three quotations below.

In 1967 the magic faded a little from Jaguar's advertising, and in May 1967 stolid copy threatened to return with the 420 (1966–68), in effect an S-type with a 4.2 litre engine, improved steering and brakes and a squared-up front in the idiom of the Mk 10. [9] "The difference between what your money can buy in terms of ordinary motoring and the superlative qualities offered by a Jaguar is still more marked with the introduction of this latest model…," said the copywriter. The headline, "The 420 Jaguar sets the highest standard yet achieved in motoring values" was uninspired, too, although equivalent headlines for the S-type in April ("Can you afford *not* to own a Jaguar?") and for the 2.4 Mk 2 in May ("The joy of Jaguar motoring begins at £1,341") were snappier. In all three pieces the cars were shown in plain monochrome photographs without backgrounds. In July 1968 a 420 sped through the same Marble Arch — in front of the same taxi — as the Mk 2 in July 1961: seven years was probably a record for the re-use of artwork in a car advertisement. Not that the car itself was lacklustre: "A saloon that for a combination of speed, comfort and safety is as good as any in the world…regardless of cost" (£2077 3s 11d) said the headline, quoting *Motor*. In America the front of the 420 was dramatically photographed in the rain at ground level: "This is the new Jaguar 420 Sports Sedan. If you love our XK-E, this is the only sports sedan you could be happy with."

A real change in Jaguar's advertising came in October 1968, with the XJ6, a model that would stay in production in updated form until 1986, and would also be produced as a V-12 from 1972 until 1991. It is almost impossible to overstate the impact made by the XJ6 when it was launched: "If

Jaguar were to double the price of the XJ6 and bill it as the best car in the world, we would be right there behind them," said *Autocar* in June 1969. "With two new [4.2 litre and 2.8 litre] engines up their sleeves, Jaguar are in the most enviable sales position of any manufacturer. As more and more XJ6s get delivered, the standards by which other cars are judged will inevitably go up. We of *Autocar* see it as a new yardstick, a tremendous advance guaranteed to put it ahead for several years at least." There was one *caveat*, however: "With stricter quality control…and more expensive fittings it would wipe up the quality car market."[10] A lack of quality control would become a serious problem in the 1970s. But in 1968–69 such difficulties were, for the most part, in the future. For *Road & Track*, Cyril Posthumus considered the XJ6 "without question…one of Britain's out-standing cars of today," and described how Jaguar's suspension engineers had achieved remarkable handling, ride and refinement by designing the car around Dunlop E70 radial types of very low profile. "Is it not significant that the waiting time for an XJ6 in England is now over 12 months, that black market examples regularly command an extra $1000–1200, and that recently a group of would-be Swiss buyers flew specially to London to protest at British Leyland HQ that their market for the car was being discriminated against? It is surely a car worth waiting for."[11] When the model was announced to the press and motor trade at the Royal Lancaster Hotel on September 26, 1968, ten cars were on display. "Little did they know that they were looking at one fifth of all XJ6s then ready for sale" recalled Jaguar historian Andrew Whyte in 1986.[12]

With October 1968's launch advertisement for the XJ6, the old re-hashed illustrations and soporific copy disappeared for ever. "Creating an exciting new world of luxury motoring. The new Jaguar XJ6," it began. "Four years ago, Jaguar gave their designers a brief: 'Design a saloon car that sets new standards of comfort and luxury, road-holding and ride, steering and braking, performance and safety — all in one car — with a level of outstanding value that Jaguar have traditionally made their own.'" The copy, accompanied by four views of the car, described features and invited the reader to try the car for himself. It was one of the most convincing advertisements of its kind. In June 1969, copywriters made the most of the demand for the car: "Don't blame him. Blame Jaguar" said a headline below a picture of a customer berating a salesman for being unable to sell him a car: "You will have to wait a while for your new Jaguar XJ6. In fact, quite a while. If you order one now, it'll be several months before you take delivery." Under the sub-heading,

Opposite: **Jaguar marque, 1966.** Jaguar's marque identity — what would now be called branding — reached its zenith just before the company merged with BMC to form British Motor Holdings in July 1966. BMH would merge with Leyland to form British Leyland in January 1968. This piece, with its unimprovable headline, is one of a series quoting independent testers, who provided plenty of flattering assessments from which to choose. Jaguar's mascot was ideal for this kind of advertising: it was horizontal, suggesting speed; it represented a powerful and attractive animal with lasting appeal rather than a mechanical or artistic abstraction; it was socially and culturally quite non-specific; and, best of all, it appeared on the car as it appeared here, in chrome, glinting against the sunset.

Always a leap ahead

"A long test mileage in this car (The Jaguar 'S' model) moved us to superlatives and at just over £1,800 for the 3.8 litre manual version there is no other car which can match the near perfect blend of effortless high performance and comfort and sell at that price." MOTOR

"The Jaguar Mark Two 3.4 saloon, which has assumed a unique place in our social living . . . is probably the most remarkable car of our generation." SUNDAY EXPRESS

"From practically every point of view a car which calls for superlatives in its assessment . . . the luxury of the Mark Ten's 100 m.p.h. cruising on a motorway approaches the refinement and isolation from one's surroundings that goes with modern air travel." AUTOCAR

JAGUAR

Grace . . . Space . . . Pace

LONDON SHOWROOMS: 88 PICCADILLY W.1

The Field, October 17, 1968

Creating an exciting new world of luxury motoring
The new Jaguar XJ6

FOUR years ago, Jaguar gave their designers a brief: "Design a saloon car that sets new standards of comfort and luxury, road-holding and ride, steering and braking, performance and safety—all in one car—with a level of outstanding value that Jaguar have traditionally made their own."

Now, Jaguar announce the 2.8 and 4.2 litre XJ6 models.

Come and see how completely the XJ6 fulfils its brief. Look down at the long, low roof. The steel body was rustproofed, painted 7 times, baked 3 times: now a pool of colour holds your reflection. Step inside. Beneath your feet, deep pile carpet. Beneath that, thick felt. Road noise, already minimised by fine engineering, will be lost in its soft meshes. Your seat holds you in a sustaining but never restricting embrace. Adjust the seat. Adjust the fully reclining backrest. Adjust the steering column. Adjust the temperature control of the new ventilation system. Comfort is total. Pause to admire the view. Visibility all round is virtually unrestricted. Switch on—and watch the rev. counter! It's the surest way to know that the engine is running. With the body insulated from front to rear, and double silencers on both exhausts, you can hardly expect to *hear* it. And with the engine doubly-insulated—its front rubber mountings rest on a separate suspension beam itself rubber mounted to the body—you'll have a job to *feel* it.

Two pedals or three? The XJ6 offers a choice: 4-speed synchromesh gearbox (with overdrive if you wish) or full automatic transmission. Disc brakes on all four wheels are servo-assisted.

As you move forward, feel how responsive and light the steering is. There's a hazard on the road. You brake hard and discover one of the most reassuring things about the XJ6. The stop is rapid, yet the nose dips only slightly. This is 'anti-dive geometry' at work to give extreme stability. This Jaguar *lopes*: it does not bound.

Unleash the XJ6 along a familiar road. The hills seem smaller. The bends less sharp. The road smoother—shorter. The XJ6 has cut it down to size. There are several reasons for this. The power of a twin-overhead-camshaft, six cylinder engine, race-bred for reliability as well as performance. The road-holding of wheels set wide apart and independently suspended. And the tyres, specially made by Dunlop to meet Jaguar's demand for an unprecedented reserve of cornering power, are wider than anything you will see off a race track. The precision of rack-and-pinion steering straightens the road. The fully independent suspension smooths it. Road-holding, braking, acceleration, steering, tyres, and fatigue-banishing comfort all add up to a new standard of safety.

One question remains. What happens if the XJ6 is involved in an accident? It has to be faced, and Jaguar have faced it. In the interior: recessed knobs, handles and switches, soft sunvisors, padded dash surround, burst-proof doorlocks, collapsible steering column. In the layout: fuel tanks are in separate compartments. And if the engine were forced back it would be deflected away from the passenger compartment not into it. The front and rear sections are strong indeed, but they cannot match the passenger compartment. In a collision, the ends will absorb impact as they crumple, before the centre section is affected.

But mere words cannot do full justice to the work of four years. Only a detailed inspection can. So see and try the XJ6 soon. You will be glad that you did.

NEW JAGUAR XJ6

The Jaguar range also includes the 240 Saloon the 420 'G' Saloon and the 'E' Type G.T. models
London Showrooms, 88 Piccadilly, W.1.

"There are always fewer Jaguars than people who want one," the copywriter attributed the delay to the company's "comprehensive system for checking" everything from steel quality to the walnut inside. "Another Jaguar fault is patriotism. They are exporting 50 percent of XJ6s. Fine for the Chancellor — if not for you. Plan ahead — and Jaguar will get your car to you as soon as humanly possible." In July, a happy new owner was shown with his car: "I'd forgive Jaguar anything — This is Mr. John Viall of Kensington. He waited impatiently for months before his Jaguar XJ6 was delivered." He was, of course, delighted. "After such a long wait I was getting bad-tempered about it. But now, after driving the XJ6 for four weeks, I'd forgive Jaguar anything…. It's a fantastic car…." The campaign was an unusual adaptation of the "we know where you're coming from" approach to copywriting which had been gaining ground throughout the industry, and particularly with British Leyland, since 1967.

Jaguar's new advertising style extended to October's range advertising, too. In the mid-1960s, all Jaguar saloons (Mk 2, S-type, 420, 420G) had looked similar, not least because the S-type and 420 were extensive adaptations of the Mk 2. But this was not the case by October 1969: "Jaguar proudly present their non-range range. Other motor manufacturers, at this time of the year, present to the public their range. And by that they mean a basic design in different sizes. Jaguar have no range in that sense. They have three entirely different models, in three entirely different classes — and each unassailably the head of its class." The copy gave brief details of the models and starting prices — £2293 for an E-type, £1999 for an XJ6, £2670 for a 420G — in what was a very simple, effective, advertisement for new circumstances.

By 1969, Nelson Advertising Service had been Jaguar's advertising agency for thirty-five years, but at the end of the year the account was relinquished to Benton & Bowles. The 1970s brought difficulties for Jaguar, but they also brought some fine advertising. In 1972 a middle-aged man lay in bed, looking into the far distance with a wistful smile, the XJ6 catalogue in front of him on top of his newspaper. "For pity's sake, John, buy the wretched thing" said his wife. "One drive is worth a million words" said Jaguar's slogan. In 1974 two Jaguar drivers passed each other on a country lane and shook hands. "Double first in economics" said the headline. By 1976 the scene would have reminded readers of the joke that a Jaguar owner needed to keep a second car for when the first broke down, but it was a safe enough advertisement two years earlier. Arguably the best advertisement for the XJ6 appeared in those economically turbulent days of 1976. Even if not every example lived up to the copywriter's promise — the wisecracks were understandable and easily made — the copy, as copy, was magnificent. A fashionably mid-green car, seen from behind, drove gently along a mountain road in the morning mist: "It will reassure you when you need it. It will help restore your confidence should it ever desert you. It will soothe and solace you after a hectic day. It will insulate you from the noise and chaos of the outside world. It will rebuild your morale; your ambitions. But most of all, it will remind you that your life has not been totally without success."

Opposite: **Jaguar XJ6 Series I.** Ecstatic reviews greeted this car on its announcement, and many considered the XJ6's ride and refinement unsurpassed. This advertisement makes much use of detailed description, but the lifeless verbosity of some earlier pieces has disappeared, to be replaced with an effective article. It is a sign of the times that a paragraph is devoted to safety features which go far beyond the padded dash tops and lap belts of earlier years. The British Leyland symbol would remain for some time, sadly.

15

Jensen

"Pianissimo Power"

In 1963 *The Motor* found the Jensen C-V8, which had been launched in October 1962, "one of the fastest cars we have ever road tested and certainly the fastest full four-seater."[1] With a steel-tube chassis and fibreglass bodywork, the C-V8 weighed only 3360 pounds or so, and with a 5916cc Chrysler V8 engine it accelerated from 0–60 mph in 7.7 seconds and had a top speed of 136 mph. A 6276cc C-V8 Mk 2, tested by *Autocar* in April 1965, managed 129 mph, 0–60 in 6.7 seconds, 0–120 mph in 30 seconds and the standing-start quarter-mile in 14.6 seconds.[2] Unsurprisingly, it was equipped with four-wheel Dunlop disc brakes, as the earlier Jensen 541 had been from October 1956. The C-V8 was also a refined car: "[T]he lack of obtrusive wind noise is exceptional when [the front quarter-vents] are closed. The Jensen holds 110 mph with complete ease and in deceptively restful silence; even at 120 mph voices have to be raised only a little for easy conversation," found *Autocar*. Without power steering, however, it was not effortless to drive, even if most examples were automatic. "Rather heavy controls make the Jensen very much a 'man's car'," said *Autocar*. Testing a new Jensen FF in 1966, L.J.K. Setright of *Car* agreed: "[T]he C-V8 was a car that was splendid and dependable, fast and controllable so long as one never drove beyond about six-tenths. But once let your enthusiasm get the better of you...all sorts of untoward things are likely to happen. The C-V8 was the sort of car that required a certain amount of brutish and insensate heaving at the wheel, the sort of car that is called a 'man's car' by those who sell it and presumably also by those who buy it, though what those who do not buy it call it may be somewhat different."[3] *Autocar* had called it "a superb concept carefully disguised as the ugliest car in the world."[4]

The curious thing about the Jensen C-V8 was that it appeared to have been deliberately designed to be controversial. Its four headlamps, stacked in slanting, oval recesses, drew the eye away from the rest of the car which was characterful but much less extreme.[5] In fact the C-V8 was not produced in the style intended by its designer, Jensen's body design and development engineer, Eric Neale: "[T]o try and maintain good airflow...I placed the lamps in position following the contours of the body; the smaller lamps inboard of the larger ones and mounted lower and further forward.... I was always dismayed that...one very important fact was never published, i.e. [that] the headlamp clusters were designed to have a pear-shaped perspex cover held in the peripheral chrome mouldings.... However, at the last minute Richard Jensen said no, he was scared of their affecting the light emission. If I had known earlier that we were not to use the perspex covers I would have designed the headlamp layout differently, and of course there would have been no need for the peripheral chrome-plated mouldings; I would have designed separate bezels for each lamp."[6] On the C-V8 Mk III of 1965–66, all four headlamps were the same size and the bezels were removed, giving the car a less aggressive and more finished look, and Melamine mock wood in the dashboard was replaced by walnut veneer. Not that everyone disliked the original design: it suited the overall character of the C-V8 and was distinctive at a time when the prevailing fashion was for slimness and delicacy. Eric Neale's next and last designs for Jensen, the P66 Interceptor coupe and convertible of 1966, though they never reached production, would follow this trend.[7] In the meantime television appearances helped the C-V8: Tony Good of Good Relations had been Jensen's public relations consultant since

1964 and became a Jensen director in 1968. "[We] tried to get the car into non-motoring magazines, to make it a car to aspire to. We talked to TV producers, and said we'd lend them a car. The breakthrough came when we got one into *The Saint*, and that led to the C-V8 being used in [the ATV adventure series with Steve Forrest as] *The Baron*. It was an ugly car but we did establish a certain cachet."[8]

The C-V8's body, well-made, well equipped and full of thoughtful details such as front seat backs in which inflated rubber bags could be inserted from behind and moved so as to provide just the right lumbar support for individual users, had been developed from the earlier 541 first seen in 1953.[9] The only unusual styling features of that car were streamlined fairings above the wheelarches similar to those seen on some coachbuilt Italian bodies a few years earlier and on the Mercedes-Benz 300SL, and an ingenious radiator opening which contained a flap, pivoted horizontally at its widest point, which covered the entire opening when the engine was cold and which opened progressively to admit air as the engine warmed up. A rather odder-looking convertible was proposed by the coachbuilders E.D. Abbott of Farnham but not taken up,[10] and the Jensen 541S of 1960–63 was fitted with a conventional grille.

Earlier Jensens had been very different, though the firm was not new to American V8s. The first Jensen production model, the immaculately coachbuilt S type of 1934, was powered by a modified Ford V8 engine. The firm also produced light commercial vehicles, principally the light and versatile JNSN from 1939 and the Jen-Tug from 1946. During 1946–52 Jensen built a handful of PW saloons, initially with Meadows straight-eight engines, then with pre-war Nash straight-eights when the Meadows engine proved unsatisfactory, and subsequently with the six-cylinder, 3993 cc, 130 bhp engine of the Austin Sheerline. There was also a four-door PW convertible. In 1949 the PW was joined by a similarly Austin-engined convertible and sports saloon—for which the name "Interceptor" was suggested by Lord Strathcarron—and a smaller car in a similar style was designed and built for Austin and appeared in 1950 as the Austin A40 Sports. Jensen subsequently built the bodies of the Austin-Healey 100 and its derivatives until the Austin-Healey 3000 Mk III, as it eventually became, ceased production in 1967. From 1960–63 Jensen also finished and painted bodies made by Pressed Steel for Volvo's P1800 sports coupe, and in 1964 the company helped to develop the Sunbeam Tiger which it built until 1967.[11] The C-V8 of 1962–66 therefore represented quite a small part of Jensen's work at the time, and the car was too specialized to be very profitable.[12] The Austin-Healey 3000 provided most of Jensen's income.

In its first and last years, the C-V8 was promoted only lightly, but advertising published in 1964 and 1965 was surprisingly attractive for a period when specialized sporting cars were often promoted erratically and sometimes hardly at all. According to Tony Good, "Our biggest problem was Jensen had no advertising budget. The best we could do was get Chrysler to fund ads because Jensen used its engines. Jensen needed a really sexy product."[13] Two advertisements for the C-V8 appeared in upmarket magazines in the middle of 1964. The first was, in effect, a catalogue in miniature that mixed monochrome and colour pictures. The page was divided horizontally at a point two thirds down its length, and the upper two thirds were then split vertically. On the left-hand side the interior of a left-hand-drive C-V8, photographed through the passenger's door, appeared in red with tan carpets; on the right, a monochrome photograph of the front of the car was placed below copy which emphasized the car's special features and tangible characteristics: "If the going is rough in a Jensen C-V8, switch the road off. The Jensen C-V8 is always smooth. It has an incredible ride-control you can adjust to different road conditions.... The smooth fibreglass body and the effortless ease of the automatic transmission hush wind and engine noise to the level of a whisper. The C-V8 is engineered with the fine care that makes the term 'craftsman-built' a cliché. (Ask a Jensen workman to show you the best tooling equipment in the factory and he will probably show you a plain, simple gauge and his bare hands.) You may never drive the Jensen C-V8 at 135 mph...but it is agreeable just to know you can lick anything in sight.... It is the only car of its kind." Along the bottom of the page was a colour picture of the dashboard, one of the car's best features.

In the second advertisement the C-V8 rested in a forest under the slogan, "Pianissimo power," with copy to match: "You could cruise at over 100mph and not miss a bar of a Bach recital on the radio. The Jensen C-V8 is probably the quietest fast car on the road. It is a superbly comfortable four-seat saloon with an enormous boot; a Grand Tourer in the grand manner. The interior is opulent; the lean sculptured lines enhance a performance that sweeps you to a hundred in under 20 seconds, and on to more than 130 mph...." The car looked its best in this setting and in the subtle metallic grey chosen, to which the forest light lent an rich amber glow. In July 1965, by contrast, a monochrome half-page advertisement showed the Mk III outside an office block at night: "The Chairman's working late tonight. It's been a long day. But soon he'll be able to relax in the quiet warmth of his Jensen C-V8. Turn the ignition key and feel the hush pulse of the 6 litre V8 take over. The Jensen C-V8 is geared to meet the demands of modern business. Content at times to glide leisurely through city streets, at others to take the fast lane effortlessly at speeds in excess of 120 mph. The C-V8 is a car for the top man. Calm. But very powerful. Very safe." The Chairman would have to hurry, however, as in November 1965 a national speed limit of 70 mph was introduced for the first time; the advertisement was one of the last of its kind.

Unlike the C-V8, the Interceptor and FF were designed from the outset to appeal to their potential market — to be,

PIANISSIMO POWER

You could cruise at over 100 mph and not miss a bar of a Bach recital on the radio. The Jensen C-V8 is probably the *quietest* fast car on the road. It is a superbly comfortable four-seat saloon with an enormous boot: a Grand Tourer in the grand manner. The interior is opulent; the lean sculptured lines enhance a performance that sweeps you to a hundred in under 20 seconds, and on to more than 130 mph. Automatic transmission, or for those who prefer manual control, a 4-speed gear box. Powerful servo-assisted disc brakes all round. Adjustable ride-control.

JENSEN C-V8

FOR DETAILS ■ CHARLES FOLLETT LTD., 18 BERKELEY STREET, LONDON, W.1. MAYFAIR 4300 ■ ROSSLEIGH LTD., 183 BOTHWELL STREET, GLASGOW, C.2. CITY 3041 ■ NEWBURY MOTORS LTD., MANOR LANE, HALESOWEN, HALESOWEN 1641 ■ NORTHWOOD MOTORS (HULL) LTD., GEORGE STREET, HULL, HULL 25630 ■ FRANCIS MOTORS, HUMBERSTONE ROAD, LEICESTER, LEICESTER 66304 ■ GUY SALMON (TEDDINGTON) LTD., HIGH STREET, TEDDINGTON, TEDDINGTON 5377 ■ CULLEN'S (LANGFORD) LTD., LANGFORD (A38), NR. BRISTOL, CHURCHILL 541. LONDON SERVICE DEPOT: LYTTELTON GARAGE, LYTTELTON ROAD, LONDON N.2. MEADWAY 5161/4. EXPORT ENQUIRIES TO:- JENSEN MOTORS LIMITED, WEST BROMWICH, STAFFS. WEST BROMWICH 2041.

Jensen C-V8 Mk II. Perhaps the best of the "deserted wood" advertisements of the early 1960s, and remarkable from a producer as small as Jensen, whose main work at the time lay in assembling sports cars for BMC (Austin-Healey 3000), Rootes (Sunbeam Tiger) and Volvo (P1800, until 1963). This inspired piece promoted a controversially styled car with a Chrysler engine, Torqueflite self-changing gears and a robust fibreglass body. The copy is surprisingly modern in its style, although forty years later the reference to Bach might be deemed dangerously élitist(!) 499 C-V8s were built between 1962 and 1966; this is a 1964 Mk II with Selectaride adjustable rear dampers and a 330 bhp engine.

PRESENTING THE INCOMPARABLE
JENSEN INTERCEPTOR & FF

The sleek new look for Jensen, 1967. The distinctive Interceptor combines inspired Italian styling with Jensen's own advanced British engineering. This is a true luxury car, combining armchair comfort for four with high-performance motoring at its liveliest.

A power-packed heart to quicken your own
The heart of the Jensen Interceptor is the big, silent, performance-proved Chrysler V8 engine – over six litres of inexhaustible drive for exhilarating acceleration. Yet the Interceptor remains cool and calm in town and on the open road at speeds over 130 mph !

Here are some more reasons why the Interceptor deserves closer study
Exciting Italian styling ☐ Highly advanced Torqueflight automatic transmission (with full over-riding control) for silken gear changes and lightning acceleration ☐ Selectaride driver-controlled adjustable shock absorbers for perfect riding ☐ High-efficiency rack and pinion steering – power assisted, if specified ☐ Fully reclinable front seats ☐ Thermostatically controlled heating and ventilation system ☐ Independent swivelling ventilation outlets for front and rear ☐ Independent demister fans for rear window ☐ Electrically-operated windows ☐ Comprehensive instrumentation on an aircraft-style central console ☐ Safety belts fitted as standard ☐ Safety warning lights on trailing edges of doors ☐ Self-adjusting disc brakes on all four wheels ☐ First-aid kit ☐ Dished wood-rim steering wheel ☐ Transistorised radio with twin rear speakers ☐ Deep-pile Wilton carpeting throughout.

Ring Tate Gallery 3195 and name your day!
Test drive the Jensen Interceptor or Jensen FF. Ring TATe Gallery 3195 today and make a date – or contact Jensen Motors Ltd. for full details and the name of your nearest Distributor or Dealer.

The Jensen FF : 4-wheel drive for supreme safety
Far in advance of any other car on the road, the brilliantly styled, luxuriously appointed Jensen FF incorporates the world-famous Ferguson Formula 4-wheel drive and Dunlop Maxaret skid-resisting braking system. The Jensen FF defies comparison. With all four wheels gripping and driving, it is almost impossible to skid or spin even on the iciest surfaces.

INTERCEPTOR
Basic £3,043. Incl. P.T. £3,742.11.2

FF
Basic £4,343. Incl. P.T. £5,339.19.9.

JENSEN MOTORS LTD., WEST BROMWICH, STAFFS. TEL: WEST BROMWICH 2041

768

Jensen Interceptor and FF. A new advertising style for a new car in 1966. This was one of the most technically interesting, as well as exclusive, cars of the decade, with Italian styling in marked contrast to the eccentricities of the C-V8. The emphasis of the copy—more or less a simple list of features—was on the face of it a recipe for dullness, but for the enthusiast it was anything but dull, particularly as the specification of the four-wheel-drive FF was decades ahead of its time.

in Tony Good's phrase, a "really sexy product." The market responded in kind: 6407 Jensen Interceptors and 320 of the FF were made during 1966–1973 and 1966–71 respectively.[14] The FF was distinguished from the Interceptor by its longer bonnet with two air outlets rather than one behind each wheelarch and, on the earliest examples, by a roof of brushed stainless steel. The beautiful new design was by Touring of Milan, albeit modified by Vignale who built the bodies of the earliest cars before quality control problems led Jensen to transfer body construction and finishing to its own factory. Announcement copy in October 1966 was conventional: "Presenting the incomparable Jensen Interceptor and FF. The sleek new look for Jensen, 1967. The distinctive Interceptor combines inspired Italian styling with Jensen's own advanced British engineering. This is a true luxury car, combining arm-chair comfort for four with high-performance motoring at its liveliest." The Interceptor cost £3742 11s 2d while the FF was a very expensive car at £5339 19s 9d. It was, however, one of the safest cars in the world with four-wheel drive and Dunlop Maxaret anti-lock braking. The "pulsing" of the brake pedal, slower than that in aircraft brakes of the time or in later car systems, surprised road testers, but in its first few years the FF — and to a lesser extent the Interceptor — attracted rave reviews. All FFs, and most Interceptors, were automatics, and almost all cars had power steering. L.J.K. Setright felt it "reasonable to drive at perhaps seven-tenths...although there is always the feeling that if you were to escalate another tenth it would bite."[15]

In 1968, *Autocar* drew an analogy: "When we first drove the Oldsmobile Toronado we were apprehensive about how a large American car would behave with front-wheel drive. We were surprised at how much earlier the 500 lb. ft. of torque could be applied in a bend and how controllable, and therefore safe, the Toronado was. Steering the Jensen FF into a corner is uncanny, because the car seems to pull itself round with a combination of all the best front-drive and rear-drive characteristics. It is as much in advance of the Toronado as the Toronado is ahead of the rear-drive Americans."[16] "If you've got four wheels, use them," said the headline of Jensen's advertisement on the page following the test, and the advertisement concluded, disarmingly, "Even though it lacks the total assurance of the four-footed FF, the two-wheel drive Interceptor is eminently safe...." But the Interceptor did have its limits, as *Autocar* discovered in 1969: "Up to a very high cornering speed there was predictable understeer, but beyond what we found to be a very critical and sudden limit the back end would break away regardless of the amount of power being applied to the rear wheels.... It is the behaviour in an emergency which worries us, because once adhesion has been lost, recovery takes too long and when correction does take effect it is with a sudden whip which is very hard to catch."[17] Advertising for the 1967 Motor Show looked, at first, like that for the previous year, as the photographs and layout were identical. The copy, however, had changed: "'Car of the year'—*Car Magazine*. The Jensen is probably the most desirable car on the road today. It's body styling is an inspiration. Its engineering is first class. It delivers an outstanding road performance that is totally without temperament.... Jensen Interceptor and FF — supremely safe, utterly reliable."

The year had been a difficult one for Jensen. The Austin-Healey 3000 and Sunbeam Tiger had both ceased production, and although in hindsight one might wonder how long basic designs dating back to 1952 and 1959 could have been expected to sell in practicable numbers, the loss of both contracts within such a short time was a severe blow to the company. Secondly the FF, for all its virtues, sold poorly. As Tony Good recalled, "Buyers liked the idea of safety, but they wouldn't pay a premium for it.[18] In April 1970, the long-time distributor of the Austin-Healey 3000 and of many other British cars in America, Kjell Qvale, acquired a majority shareholding in Jensen, and serious plans began for the car that would become the Jensen-Healey of 1972. Fortunately Jensen retained some highly skilled and dedicated workers: "I'd improved that Jensen so it was a lovely car," remembers Qvale, "We built that Jensen off the most horrible tooling you've ever seen. The panels were barely shaped. We spent 650 hours putting that car together, and the guys who did it were geniuses — they were from the original group of workers, not those hired for the Healey. We could have carried on selling them. But the size of the operation made it impossible to exist just with the big Jensen."[19]

In the longer term, however, luck was not on Jensen's side: the 1973 oil crisis reduced Interceptor sales dramatically and, without an advertising budget, Tony Good "was forced—ingeniously—to promote the Interceptor solely through smooth, middle-aged celebrities who would strike a chord on both sides of the Atlantic."[20] Many were provided with Interceptors when they visited London. Even in 1961 the average Jensen 541 buyer had been in his mid-fifties. The Lotus-engined Jensen-Healey, meanwhile, proved troublesome, and the company ceased trading in May 1976. Interceptor production was revived on a small scale between 1983 and 1992, and the Jensen name itself reappeared when a new model, the S-V8 sports car, with a 4.6 litre Mustang Cobra V8 engine and styling cues from the C-V8 and P66 Interceptor, appeared at the 1998 Motor Show. Twenty S-V8s were made before the company went into administration in July 2002, and in 2003 a final dozen were expected to be built from remaining parts by SV Automotive of Carterton near Witney and to be sold by the Witney classic car specialist, Oselli. The marque was characterful — if demanding of its backers — to the last.[21]

16

MG

"Safety Fast!"

The most famous MG advertisements—those widely quoted from memory twenty or thirty years later—were published in the 1970s. MG notoriously promised "Your mother wouldn't like it," adding mischievously, after the performance statistics, "Fantastic ride."[1] In "You can do it in an MG" (May 1974), a man descended a prison wall on the end of a sheet to his blonde girl-friend below, who sat patiently in the passenger seat of her (or his?) orange MGB roadster. "0–50 in 8.0 seconds. 37.6 mpg at a steady 50 mph. You can still have fun at fifty." Only David Ogilvy's "ticking clock" advertisement for Rolls-Royce in America became as well known on both sides of the Atlantic.

During 1975–76, MG advertising gave way to some extent to that for MG's in-house British Leyland rival, the Triumph TR7 ("It looks like you can't afford it"). But MG bounced back in 1978–79. A short series for the MGB and Midget roadsters carried the headline: "Some day, you'll settle down with a nice, sensible girl, a nice, sensible house and a nice, sensible family saloon. Some day." The copy then varied according to the picture: a red MGB splashed through an incoming summer tide as the sun went down, spray flying over the couple within: "Some day your family will be too big for a sporty 2-seater. And as for the wind whistling through your hair, there's no guarantee you'll have much hair left for it to whistle through. So, if you've always told yourself you're going to have an MG some day, make sure you don't leave it too long. Sports cars aren't the only things that overtake you."

In another advertisement in the series, a dark green Midget sped along a country lane in summer: "Some day, you'll settle down.... Meantime, let your hair down, put your hood down and push your foot down. After all, you've no

commitments to slow you up...feel the sun on your face and the wind whistling past your ears. Play tunes on the gearbox through the country backroads. True, there are only two seats. Who needs a charabanc for what you have in mind? Your MG days don't last forever." A more risqué version showed the Midget in woodland, its owners' clothes—or some of them—draped over the windscreen and door frames. If the execution was newly explicit, the theme was the same as for the Ford Consul Capri more than fifteen years earlier. The point was made slightly differently in 1979 with the MGB GT, shown in black on a black marble floor against a jet-black background, turn signals alight to lend a little colour: "Psychologists say a saloon car is a wife and a sports car is a mistress." Small print elaborated: "Beautiful body. A joy to handle. And rumoured to be rather fast." Feminists growled in outrage; respectable forty-somethings smirked; psychologists wondered what exactly the human equivalent might be of a Vauxhall Victor, and whether anyone would marry it; progressives bought Scimitars or Lancia HPEs. But the MGB GT, an antiquated but comfortingly known quantity, still inspired affection at the end of its life.

It was all a long way from M.G. advertising in the late 1950s and early 1960s, which in mainstream British media was mainly for the M.G. saloons—ZB Magnettes during 1957–58; Magnettes Mk III and IV from February 1959 to 1966 (though rarely afterwards, as sales had declined to a trickle);[2] and occasionally for the MG 1100—"The Most Advanced MG of All Time"—during 1962–65. This "Latest concept of Alec Issigonis...with the elegant line of Pininfarina," as the catalogue called it, had handling to suit its adoptive marque, even if it was essentially, in the words of *The Motor*, "a faster, luxury version of the Morris 1100." Testing the four-door version sold on the home market, S.C.H. Davis noted that the MG was "considerably more expensive than the Morris."[3] But the MG 1100 was an interesting and quite speedy small car (giving 87 mph and 0–60 in 20 seconds) whatever one made of its provenance.

The ZA Magnette, MG's first fully post-war saloon, had a "rightness" about it that its Nuffield companions, the Riley Pathfinder and the Wolseleys 4/44 and 6/90 never matched.[4] "For my kind of motoring — it must be an M.G." said a spirited-looking, spripy-bloused woman in July 1956: "'I'm a keen motorist and I pride myself on driving rather well. I chose my M.G. Magnette not only for its lovely lines, but because it is such a delightfully easy car to handle.'" The copywriter continued: "Everything about the M.G. Magnette brings out the best in a driver. Steering is positive and feather-light, braking smooth and sensitive. The comfortable driving position is planned to ensure correct posture…. Controls, too, are ideally placed. The short lever, mounted directly above the gear box, makes gear-shifting smooth and precise." A floor-shift arrived on the equivalent Wolseley, too, when the 4/44 was replaced by the similar-looking 15/50 in mid-1956.

In January 1957 a cloth-capped, tweed-jacketed fortysomething relaxed against his new ZB Magnette with a cigarette and concurred: "For my kind of motoring — it must be an M.G. Whether you're rendevous-ing at the Ritz or rallying with your club, the versatile M.G. Magnette rises magnificently to the occasion…. Lively, flexible and modest in her demands for fuel, the graceful Magnette provides true sports motoring in comfort and luxury." A pipe-smoking driver — subtly downmarket of his cigarette-smoking predecessor and with a more stolid style to suit — agreed in March: "Everybody admires my M.G. Magnette. She has a lovely line, a lively engine and she gives me sports motoring in real luxury!" "The man who regards his car as something more than a comfortable means of transportation will find much to delight him in the celebrated M.G. Magnette. For this is a car of rare character, luxuriously equipped, well-mannered in town traffic and really exciting to drive on the open road," added the copywriter earnestly. Liveliness returned with the ZB Varitone in February 1958: "Drive a Magnette — it brings out the expert in you," and the slogan became a headline later in the year. By 1958 the Magnette was a genuinely well-loved car, and considered one of the best, and best-handling, saloons of its day.[5]

Alas — this was not true of the 1959 Magnette Mk III. Unkind things have been said about the "Farina" Magnette, most of them true, although comparison with the ZA and ZB was bound to leave almost any successor wanting. "Completely new — with a flawless sporting pedigree" announced BMC in February 1959, "The M.G. Magnette Mark III is today's concept of safety fast motoring, the sports saloon with the spacious air and the continental line…. Here is luxurious high performance at a remarkably modest cost."

It was "planned to bring out the expert in you" according to the slogan, soon dropped, at the foot of the page. But the slogan was apposite: the Mk III handled so poorly once its dampers were a little worn that real expertise was needed to control it at speed or on winding roads in poor weather. A 1966 advertisement, showing the improved Mk IV in town at night, reminded Mk III owners why they would not buy the model again: "Rain and night falling. Soft splash of wipers and squelch of tyres. Wrapped in warmth…cocooned in luxury…sports car ride with big car opulence…." For readers without experience of the car this was an urban dreamscape; for anyone who had lost the tail of a Mk III on a wet Hyde Park Corner in December it revived nightmares. Some Magnettes had two inches of free play at the steering wheel even when new. "[I]t is a great pity that on the M.G. the performance of the excellent engine and the driver's enjoyment of the smooth gearbox, with its well-chosen gear ratios, should be limited by the features of the chassis," said J. Eason Gibson of *Country Life*.[6] The car was, however, reliable and attractively finished, with a good gear change, leather seats and a wooden dashboard. It cost £1072 7s, or £1081 2s with two-tone paint. Two-tone green (the darker colour on the roof, fins and boot) particularly suited the model and was popular. For the Mk IV of 1961–68, contrasting colours were divided by stainless trim running along the body sides.

Faced with a model almost identical to its Austin, Morris, Riley and Wolseley companions (and built alongside the last three of them, at Cowley), MG's copywriters had an impossible task. No-one expected the other "Farinas" to handle like sports saloons (even if some old Riley hands still lived in hope) but with MG expectations were high, and the reality was roll-oversteer. "*Do* look now — its pedigree is showing!" declared a copywriter in April 1960 with the subversive abandonment of a man who knows his cause is lost. "Let me drive"—"Let's toss for it" argued a fifty-something couple in August about "the car for the young of all ages." In March 1961 the Mk III was "streets ahead — miles ahead — the car that recaptures the desire to drive." In May, following a reduction in Purchase Tax, it was "a family car and a sporting car in ONE price" (£1012 12s 6d). In October, with wider tracks, anti-roll bars at the front and rear and relief all round, it became the more manageable Magnette Mk IV. "The Prestige of the MG Family Tree" began a new campaign, ingeniously: "Start with a Midget…graduate to an M.G.A.1600…marry into a Magnette…." In copperplate script the new car offered "Family Motoring plus Sporting Performance…. On the road the less time you take overtaking — the greater your safety. M.G. sporting performance gives you that tremendous advantage…." This was a more modest claim than the "luxurious high performance" promised in 1959.[7]

In 1963, pure snobbery arrived. A Mk IV stood in an expensive suburban lane. "Look! They've got an MG" said a

The Field, October 22, 1964

The M.G. Car Co. Ltd., Sales Division, Longbridge, Birmingham
London Showrooms: 40 Conduit Street, W.1
Overseas Business: Nuffield Exports Ltd., Cowley, Oxford & Piccadilly, W.1

THE **BRITISH** MOTOR CORPORATION LTD
12 Months' Warranty and backed by B.M.C. Service—
the most comprehensive in Europe

Breeding counts

JB 3182

Your new Magnette has a pedigree direct from the K3 Magnette built in 1933 by the M.G. Company one of which won the T.T. in the hands of Nuvolari. Your Magnette owes its advanced design to such feats in pre-war days. Like every M.G. it still has much of the excitement of earlier sports cars because M.G.'s are still built by enthusiasts for enthusiasts—from the K3 to your automatic Magnette today.

123 UML

Safety Fast! **MG MAGNETTE** Automatic £974.17.6 (inc. £169.7.6 P.T.)
Manual Gearbox Model £892.14.2 (inc. £155.4.2 P.T.)

816

MG Magnette Mk IV. Exactly! Breeding did count for many buyers of the earlier Z-series Magnette, and this was not even a cross-breed. The grille was the car's most individual feature, and it is therefore displayed here. The copy has been written carefully, implying a more substantial link with the past whilst not actually stating it. The emphasis in this and other advertisements for the car was less on its tangible virtues than on the impression it would make, as this Magnette possessed all the characteristics, endearing and otherwise, of the Morris Oxford that sired it.

speech-bubble from an ivy-smothered upstairs window be-hind a hedge. "Not everyone can afford a Magnette, but those who can, get automatic transmission on a reasonably-priced car..." added the copywriter. In March the car was parked at an airfield, as the same bubble emerged from an aeroplane passing overhead. The same copy emerged underneath, too. In May, a Magnette in Riley-ish coffee and cream, resting on a hill-top, was "an automatic choice" at £973 17s 6d compared with £891 14s 2d for the manual version. But in January 1964 the copywriter was back to his old tricks. A bright red Mk IV appeared in front view with a pre-war model in a smaller picture above: "Breeding counts—the new [sic] M.G. Magnette has a pedigree direct from the K3 Magnette built in 1933 by the M.G. Company a proto-type of which won the T.T. in the hands of Nuvolari...." Whether by accident or design, the post-vintage model shown looked suspiciously like an MG TC, *circa* 1946. In April, with the rest of the advertisement virtually unaltered, it became a K3 Magnette. "What's twice as good as owning an MG?" the company asked a year later. "For a mobile-minded family, there's only one thing better...and that, of course, is two of them"—a Magnette for him, and a little red Midget for her.

The little red Midget[8] was many people's ideal of an MG before the "B" arrived in 1962, and for some time afterwards. The MGA Coupe with fixed hardtop of 1956–59 provided sophistication for a niche market, as in 1958 when an upper-class woman got into her car outside a country cottage: "Lovely—lively—luxurious—the Thoroughbred MGA all-weather Sports Coupe." More specialized, in the same year, was the "Twin-cam MGA with disc brakes—Yes, this is it! A phenomenal new power unit based on the EX 181 in which Stirling Moss achieved 245.6 m.p.h...in August 1957. For three years this twin o.h.c. 1588c.c. engine has been developed, and is now available, together with disc brakes, as optional equipment on new models only. Power output is 108 b.h.p. at 6,700 r.p.m. From 0–90 m.p.h. takes only 24.6 secs. (see 'The Motor')...." In Graham Robson's words, this car was "technically interesting, but not always properly built and adjusted, and...very definitely a com-mercial failure."[9] In the 1960s, MG's production cars would be mechanically conventional.

The sports cars' advertising was conventional in the mid-1960s, too. Styles of illustration and typefaces were shared with advertising for the Magnettes in marque-wide campaigns. "Look! They've got an MG" was heard from an-other upstairs window when a Midget Mk I appeared below

("Not everyone can aspire to a Midget..."). 1964's old-and-new theme worked well for the the MGB and Midget, and during the summer both models were shown with the orig-inal sports M.G., "Old Number One" of 1925. "First of the line" said the copywriter for the MGB, "Patriarch of a noble race — the first sports M.G. ever made — the start of this great line of high-performance cars.... Try the superlative M.G.B. for real 'Safety Fast' motoring." "Superlative MGB," M.G.'s main slogan for the MGB for several years, appeared in beau-tifully illustrated catalogues as well as in advertisements; and the long-standing marque slogan, "Safety Fast," ap-peared in British MG advertising until 1966. The equivalent 1964 piece for the Midget began: "Vintage Year? ...The ma-turing of good wine is a process which cannot be hurried. Likewise with M.G. 40 years of steady development and en-thusiasm have gone into the making of today's Midget. The Mk II Sports Convertible has fully wind-up windows and adjustable quarter lights, lockable doors with exterior han-dles, curved windscreen, new suspension, increased power, new de luxe cockpit plus the vast resources of B.M.C." By October 1964 the MGB — always a sturdy car — had begun to accumulate competition experience. A standard model in cream with wire wheels, fog lights and numerous badges was shown beside a competition version[10]: "Proved on the track — right on the road. Driven by Paddy Hopkirk and An-drew Hedges at Le Mans, the M.G.B., very little modified from the standard production model you can buy, covered 2392 miles in 24 hours at an average of 99.9 miles per hour to win the 'Motor' trophy for the highest placed British Entry...." It was a compelling photograph, and the angled block in which the copy was arranged, very unusual in post-war advertising,[11] lent drama.

If the "squelch" of a Magnette's crossplies on a wet night was enough to make a reader take up cycling, the theme suited the Midget and MGB in 1966: "Tyres gripping...wheels humming...driving urge to master the miles with a come-on-let's-go roar. You in your slung low sweet chariot — heart thumping, pulse quickening little bomb on wheels. Foot down and Zip-Zip-Away! Man, this is what sports car mo-toring is all about! MG Midget Mk II sports convertible. £623.17.1." Alternatively, "When you get a sudden, mad urge to to nowhere in particular...burn up the miles...feel the whip of the wind. Is it love, fate — or a touch of the com-pulsive, highly contagious MGB's?" The MGB was red, al-though in some magazines it came out as dark orange, which suited the flavour of the copy.[12]

A real orange car appeared in 1970 in calmer mood,

Opposite: **MG Sports Sedan.** An American advertisement for the nearest saloon equivalent of the famous MG sports cars. Like many imported subcompacts, it targeted affluent, leisure-focused American families who wanted an interesting second car for about the same price as a hum-drum domestic sedan. American traditionalists were not impressed: "It's got a top on it like a box.... The American people who buy the cars I manufacture don't want things like that" said Henry Ford II to MG 1100 owner and Ford chronicler Booton Herndon in 1969, amid remarks critical of British cars that were omitted from the English edition of Herndon's book. Sales of the Sports Sedan were modest in the US, where the car was succeeded in 1968 by the essentially similar Austin America, but the MG (mainly in four-door form) gained a steady following in Britain. Collectors now restore them.

sports . . .   . . . sedan

Paint a stripe along its top; a number on its side . . . and you're ready to compete.

Pack it full with Mom, kids, pets, lunch and you're on your way to a picnic. That's the joy of owning the new MG Sports Sedan. It's the amazing combination of racing potential and sedan comfort at a price so low ($1898*) that you owe it to yourself to give it a trial run.

Make no mistake about it, this MG is a sports car . . . designed and built in true British sports car tradition . . . packed under its hood, a sports car power plant—the world's number 1 competitive engine . . . . . . an engine that sets crosswise instead of lengthwise. This simple maneuver finds 80% of the car's length devoted to luggage and passengers, 5 passengers. Even long-legged riders will find the back seat as big as a bathtub . . .

. . . while up front, sports car enthusiasts sit snugly in two buckets . . . Dual carburetion . . . 4-speed stick shift . . . Crunchproof synchromesh gear box . . . Speeds in excess of 80 mph, the guts and spirit of a true MG. But Mom likes this MG because it's a tiny marvel in big city traffic. It parks in a pocket, stretches budgets (24 to 30 mpg). It goes shopping, visits Grandma, hurries to the station, hushes to church and sits comfortably at a drive-in movie.

But on the road, when you're all by yourself—it's an MG. Flattens hills, corners like a cat. Sports car disc & drum combination brakes for safer, surer stops. Revolutionary fluid suspension system (no springs, no shock-absorbers) for a creamy smooth ride. Front wheel drive . . . the engine pulls instead of pushes . . . incredible stability (especially on slippery roads).

The MG Sports Sedan—a car that anyone can drive with enjoyment, comfort and confidence. A little giant, bigger on the inside than it appears on the outside.

Put a racing stripe on its top . . .

. . . or a picnic basket in its back. You have at your command an obedient servant, a sporting spirit—an elegant rascal.

And even sports car drivers wave . . .

 MG SPORTS SEDAN $1898.00*

*Suggested retail price East Coast P.O.E. includes: turn signal; windscreen washer; spare wheel; tool kit; ash tray light. (heater, white-walls and racing stripe optional)

FOR OVERSEAS DELIVERY INFORMATION, WRITE: BMC, DEPT. G-1, 734 GRAND AVE., RIDGEFIELD, N. J.

PRODUCT OF THE BRITISH MOTOR CORPORATION, LTD., MAKERS OF MG, AUSTIN HEALEY, SPRITE, MORRIS AND AUSTIN CARS

parked on a forest path: "The sports car for the enthusiast" said the caption, with the owners very obviously not thinking about cars: "The MGB is the car for the man who's been around. Tried them all. But won't take less anymore. He knows what he's after. And he knows he can get it in an MGB. He's after performance. Like 0–50 m.p.h. in a cool 9 seconds…. Sport the real thing. MGB." In July a Midget appeared in a similar setting, top up, the driver somewhere else. Inside, seen through the open window, a girl sat in the passenger seat, a faraway look in her eyes as she absently fingered the raised chrome handbrake: "85 percent of MG Midget owners are men—which means lots of girls will be relaxing in our new, thick contoured rake adjusting seats. A scene we're sure will appeal to both driver and passenger…. The MG Midget will give you dynamic accleration. Magnificent high speed cruising. And economical fuel consumption…. The girl you'll have to get for yourself."

American MG copy adopted a very different style but was equally distinctive, and in the United States advertising for the MG 1100—as the MG Sports Sedan—was imaginative. Novelty helped: "This proud, defiant, staunch British grille can be yours for only eighteen hundred and ninety eight dollars (and the price includes an MG Sports Sedan)" said a 1963 advertisement: "Λ sports car? Name one more sportive: deep-lunged MG engine…marathon endurance…the conformation of a thoroughbred. Altogether, a most spirited little speedster. A family sedan? Rather! You might say, this is a grown-up, married MG." With white stripe tyres and special wheel trims it looked subtly different from the British version. Another advertisement showed a car in two halves—on the left-hand side a racer painted a white strip down the roof, chequered flag on the ground beside him; on the other side, Mother got into the driving seat as Father prepared to hand her a cat basket: "Paint a stripe along its top; a number on its side…and you're ready to compete. Pack it full with Mom, kids, pets, lunch and you're on your way to a picnic." Sporty features included "4-speed stick shift…crunchproof synchromesh gear box…speeds in excess of 80mph…."

In 1965, copy for the Sports Sedan played on the MG's uniqueness, just as Doyle Dane Bernbach had done with the VW since 1959. In October the Sports Sedan and the VW appeared side by side below the headline, "Popularity contest: Who won?" "Who else!" began the copy, "Of the 28,000 auto-wise readers polled by *Car & Driver* magazine, 27.5 percent named VW the 'Best Economy Sedan.' Some 18 percent nominated our MG Sports Sedan. Well of course! The Winner had a 12-year head-start on us. Result: Volkswagen is owned by 1,364,639 U.S. drivers. MG's Sports Sedan has improved the scene for approximately 20,000—thus far. Owner ratio: 68.2 to 1. Preference ratio: about 3 to 2." The copy described the MG's "living room for 5 (5 adults, not elves)"—a strong point for the MG and a weak one for the VW—its "race-proved" twin-carburettor engine, front-

wheel drive that "has Detroit wondering…worrying…working" and "exclusive Hydrolastic Suspension, a cushy mixture of alcohol and water that makes metal springs and shocks old hat…. Congratulations, you lusty, close-fisted 18 percent. As for you, VW, wait 'til next year." Surprisingly — or perhaps not, if to do so would have risked coming too close to direct knocking copy—this advertisement did not mention the MG's great advantages over the rear-engined VW, which were its handling and remarkable roadholding.

But BMC/Hambro Inc. did mention these selling-points in June, in an advertisement devoted to the suspension. Two feet and an adjustable wrench could be seen underneath a parked Sports Sedan: "Please don't drink the suspension system—Not good for you: we had to add dye to the alcohol-and-water mix to avoid paying a liquor tax on every MG Sports Sedan we import. Besides, there are greater kicks to be had from our new Hydrolastic Suspension. Teamed with front-wheel drive, it gives our five-passenger economy sedan the qualities of an expensive sports car…. You corner flat, ride level and hold firm to the road. Most intoxicating, whether you motor for fun or family…. And it's all yours at a price usually referred to as laughably low. Want a drink? See your favourite bartender. Want the sporting life in a family car? See your MG dealer. In either case…cheers."[13]

Despite its comparative fragility and proneness to rust in damp climates, the little MG sedan became well-liked by many enthusiasts. Yet among small European sedans only the Volkswagen remained really successful in the United States. After the lamentable experience of the Renault Dauphine in 1959–61, Americans increasingly came to see the reliable and robust VW, despite its eccentricities, as a one-off European small car that worked. Most of the others—bought, unlike sports cars, by busy families for use with only scheduled maintenance rather than by young men for tinkering with—were "if only" cars: if only the transmission didn't break after 15,000 miles; if only the floor didn't rust out; if only the engine didn't need to warm up for ten miles before it could accelerate onto the freeway; if only Mom hadn't got stranded that day when the children were young, and hungry, when the dealer couldn't get parts because of an industrial dispute in Birmingham, England… But it did, she did, and he couldn't because there was, so the family's next shopping car would have to be a VW or American compact or, from the late 1960s onwards, a small Japanese car. The Sports Sedan was followed by the similar Austin America in 1968, but neither car acquired a wide following.

American advertising for the Midget and MGB[14] in the late 1960s was interesting for its imaginative headlines. At first they were tame. "Introducing the MGB/GT. A quietly sensational touring machine steeped in British luxury yet priced at a modest $3,095" in May 1966 was unaffected and to the point, but by December the copywriters were warming to their task: "The new MGB/GT looks and handles like a $6,000 machine. At $4,000 it would be a real buy. At $3,095 it's practically licensed stealing." In January 1967, MG were direct: "This is the MGB. You turn it on. It turns you on," and in February the copywriter employed a psychological approach that would never have been attempted in England at the time: "The new MGB/GT can help save your marriage. Read why." Because it was roomy *and* comfortable *and* easily driven by a woman *and* responsive to a man's sports driving, *and* kind to the family budget. The themes were standard for "his and hers" copy, but the treatment was unique. If this tactic appealed particularly to a college-educated audience, pretty girls appealed to everyone, as in a July 1969 advertisement which gave voice to one of the great enduring themes in car advertising: "If you want to know the kind of man he is, take a good look at the car he drives." Not that MG's girl would be impressed by mere pocketbook-waving[15]: "The MGB man likes to shift for himself…. He's a no-nonsense guy…. Point for point, the MGB is in a class by itself. But then again, so is the man who drives it." Similarly the GT, in May 1970, was "like the man who drives it. The exception rather than the rule." When so many were lusting after high-horsepower V8s, any import driver had to be a little bit exceptional, and in April 1971 the car became "The thinking man's GT." In July 1970 British Leyland declared: "People don't buy the MGB just because it's different. But because *they* are." It was a circular argument if it was an argument at all, yet in a world of personalized cars, subdivided market sectors and multiplying imports, individuality — and individualism of outlook — conferred status as never before.

17

Riley

"Riley for Magnificent Motoring"

The Rileys of 1946–55 were a hard act to follow. Although Lord Nuffield (formerly William Morris) had taken over Riley (Coventry) Ltd. in September 1938 and resold the company to Morris Motors, the post-war 1½ Litre (RMA and RME) and longer-bonneted but otherwise similar-looking 2½ Litre (RMB and RMF) saloons[1] were Rileys in spirit and mechanical fact as well as in name. They were also inspired in part by the best pre-war continental cars: Riley examined two examples of the Citroën *Traction Avant* in 1937 and stylist Bert Holmes was influenced not only by earlier Rileys, but also by the BMW 327.[2] The post-war saloon body was built from steel panels attached to an ash frame, while the roof was made from expanded metal, padded, and covered with black fabric. The whole was mounted on a sturdy steel chassis with torsion-bar front suspension and steering by rack and pinion. The 1½ Litre stayed in production until 1955, while the 2½ Litre was replaced in 1953 by the Pathfinder. The earlier cars soon became known by enthusiasts for the marque as the "last proper Rileys."

The Pathfinder, which marked the half-way point in Riley's transition from pure independence of design to pure badge-engineering, was first Riley to bear a strong Nuffield (though not, as yet, BMC) identity. It inherited the old 2½ Litre engine but sported a new, full-width, faintly Italian-looking body on a new chassis. Quiet, spacious and fast for its time, the Pathfinder was badly let down by a troublesome, Buick-inspired (but not Buick-reliable) coil-spring rear suspension whose Panhard rod sometimes broke free, and by brakes with a damage-prone servo bolted to the chassis under the rear seat pan. The servo was required by Girling's new twin-trailing-shoe drum brakes, which resisted snatch and fade but required heavy operating pressures. "Regrettably service problems of varying degrees of severity occurred on this model throughout its production life, many of which remained unsolved. In the attempt to continue the unusual features which would appeal to discerning Riley owners, they were not very well developed," recalled the car's designer, Gerald Palmer, who was best known for the acclaimed Jowett Javelin of 1947–53.[3] One Pathfinder was "obtained after the previous owner had commissioned a complete re-fit of the braking system at vast cost. The cause of the problem, as we discovered after purchasing the car for little more than had been spent on the re-fit, was some sixpenn'orth of tubing which perished inside some metalwork in the region of the front cross-member. Once cured, the brakes were fine."[4]

Gerald Palmer had designed the Pathfinder alongside the Wolseley 6/90, but the Pathfinder's successor, the similar-looking, six-cylinder Two-Point-Six of 1957–59, was derived directly from the Wolseley at Abingdon. According to Don Hayter, the future designer of the MGB, who had moved to MG from Aston Martin in 1956: "It was a very friendly, 'get-on-with-it' atmosphere at MG at the time…. They were building the Riley 1.5 and Pathfinder as well as the

Riley One-Point-Five Mk III. Old-fashioned advertising for a sporting compact that gained a good reputation for performance. As a luxury car it was compromised by a small cabin and a peculiar driving position, and the interior trim of early versions was a bizarre, multicoloured confection of various fabrics that was more Standard Sportsman than English traditional. The equivalent Wolseley, advertised separately, was slower, but less so than expected, for the Riley's headlamp peaks reduced its top speed by several miles per hour.

The Field, April 12, 1962

One-Point-Five

BIG CAR LUXURY

SMALL CAR ECONOMY

SPORTS CAR PERFORMANCE

For the motorist who wants to shorten the distance between two points and add to the pleasure of those away-from-it-all weekends, this is it. The *improved* RILEY One-Point-Five. The car that offers you all the luxury of a superbly appointed limousine—plus all the pep, the pace of a thoroughbred sports car. It gives you more miles per gallon, more fun-per-mile. Twin carburetters? But, of course. Fine leather upholstery, too. And deep pile carpets. And all the trimmings for which the RILEY is traditionally famous.

Price £580 plus £267.1.5 P.T. including surcharge.

IT ALL ADDS UP TO EVEN MORE MAGNIFICENT MOTORING

THERE'S 'SOMETHING SPECIAL' ABOUT THESE OTHER RILEYS, TOO

RILEY FOUR-SEVENTY-TWO: *Spacious luxurious family saloon with optional automatic transmission. Price from £745 plus £342.13.11 P.T. including surcharge.*

RILEY 'ELF': *World's newest, most elegant small car — for Magnificent Motoring in Miniature. Price £475 plus £218.18.11 P.T. including surcharge.*

Every Riley carries a Twelve Months' Warranty and is backed by Europe's most comprehensive service—B.M.C.

R.12

RILEY MOTORS LTD, SALES DIVISION, COWLEY, OXFORD · LONDON SHOWROOMS: 8/10 NORTH AUDLEY ST, GROSVENOR SQUARE, W.1.
OVERSEAS DIVISION: NUFFIELD EXPORTS LTD, OXFORD & 41/46 PICCADILLY, W.1.

This is a man who really cares—a
discerning man who enjoys the better things in life;
who takes pride in everything he does. . . . He
drives well; takes pleasure in driving.
So he buys Riley. Currently he's driving the
4/Sixty Eight—more than a car, it's a symbol
of magnificent motoring. Designed for
the Man who Really Cares . . . designed for *you!*

Riley for men who like finer things in life

✳ *Styling*—elegant (Pininfarina) ✳ *Interior*—spacious
(five-seater) and luxurious, with leather upholstery,
walnut veneer facia, deep pile carpets
✳ *Engine*—sports-tuned, twin-carburetter, 1½ litre, developing 68 b.h.p.
✳ *Gearbox*—4 speed, with floor-mounted gear lever
✳ *Roadholding*—superb ✳ *Acceleration*—vivid, 0-50 m.p.h. in 12.9 secs.
✳ *Top Speed*—over 88 m.p.h. . . .
Ask your local Riley Dealer for a trial run now.

Price **£725**
plus £303.4.2. P.T.
Duotone colours extra

FOR MAGNIFICENT MOTORING—THE RILEY **4 SIXTY EIGHT**

Price **£575**
plus £240.14.2. P.T.

R115

The Lively Riley One-Point-Five

For the motorist who wants big-hearted
performance in a compact
four-seater saloon, the lively
Riley One-Point-Five is the
answer. Long stride cruising
in the 80's. Sparkling
acceleration. The luxury
appointments on this fine car
include leather upholstery
and polished walnut veneer finish.

*Every Riley carries a Twelve
Months' Warranty backed by
Europe's most comprehensive
Service—B.M.C.*

RILEY MOTORS LTD., *Sales Division, Cowley, Oxford*
London Showrooms: 8-10 North Audley Street, Grosvenor Square, W.1
Overseas Division: Nuffield Exports Ltd., Oxford and 41-46 Piccadilly, W.1

456

Riley 4/Sixty Eight. Implicitly aimed at the older male motorist, this Riley was one of the more exclusive "Farina" variants (10,940 were made between 1959 and 1961, compared with nearly 150,000 A55 Cambridges during the same period). It was, however, only a "symbol" of magnificent motoring, rather than the real thing, and that, for the Riley purist who retained his old-style RME, was precisely the point.

THE FIELD July 6 1967

We often sell this car to people who haven't got a chauffeur

It's hardly surprising. After all, why waste the Riley 4/Seventy Two on a Chauffeur? It's only human to want to keep it to yourself—the pride, the pleasure of driving a pedigree sports saloon like this, the day-long comfort of the effortless automatic drive, the exhilarating response from the twin carbs., the instruments sparkling in walnut. Give all this to a chauffeur—and what have you got left for yourself? Just room-to-stretch luxury for four (not counting the chauffeur), a lot of real leather—and carpet, carpet everywhere. Loads of comfort. But not so much fun.

So at least take the test-drive yourself. Then you'll know what you have to lose! And remember—the Riley 4/Seventy Two is backed by BMC's expert, nation-wide service.

THE BRITISH MOTOR CORPORATION LIMITED

BMC RILEY
4/SEVENTY TWO

£1020.1s.8d. INCLUDING £191.11s.8d. P.T. (OR £936.10s.0d. INCLUDING £176 P.T. WITH MANUAL GEARBOX).

RILEY MOTORS LTD., SALES DIVISION, LONGBRIDGE, BIRMINGHAM. OVERSEAS DIVISION: BMC EXPORT SALES LTD., BIRMINGHAM AND 41/46 PICCADILLY, LONDON W.1.

Riley 4/Seventy Two. Wishful thinking as the "Farina" saloon, with a larger engine and wider track than the 4/Sixty Eight, enters its twilight years. It wasn't a "pedigree sports saloon," of course, but its wood and leather interior was something no Ford or Vauxhall could boast, even if the huge steering wheel suited tall people best. "The day-long comfort of the effortless automatic drive" indicated the target market, most of whom were not so befuddled that they could not tell a thinly disguised Morris Oxford when they drove one.

She's gay
She's safe
She's unashamedly fast

Pert looks. Trim lines. Compact measurements.
This beautifully appointed little Riley has them all.
And more. *Independent suspension on all four wheels* gives
better road-holding, added comfort. *Front-wheel drive
and sideways mounted engine* permit exceptional space
for four adults and their luggage. Economical 848 c.c.
O.H.V. engine achieves up to 50 m.p.g., over 70 m.p.h.
Price £475 plus £179.2.9 P.T.

FOR MAGNIFICENT MOTORING
IN MINIATURE

She's the  elf

*Every Riley carries
a Twelve Months'
Warranty and is
backed by Europe's
most comprehensive
service—B.M.C.*

There's something special about these other Rileys too!

RILEY FOUR-SEVENTY-TWO

Spacious, luxurious family saloon with
optional automatic transmission. Price from £757
plus £285.1.6 P.T.

RILEY ONE-POINT-FIVE

Compact, richly appointed, really fast. For the
sporting motorist who likes his comforts. Price
£580 plus £218.10.3 P.T.

RILEY MOTORS LTD., SALES DIVISION, COWLEY, OXFORD · LONDON SHOWROOMS: 8/10 NORTH AUDLEY ST. GROSVENOR SQUARE W.1.
OVERSEAS DIVISION: NUFFIELD EXPORTS LTD., OXFORD AND 41/46 PICCADILLY, W.1.

ZA Magnette and there was very much in common with the Wolseley people at Cowley. Those were the days of putting side flashes on and bigger backlights, so they gave me a Wolseley body and said, 'Do us a big backlight.' I did a big wraparound backlight, styled it in and took the drawings over to Cowley; they just modified the body very quickly. I then drew a new front end with a Riley radiator instead of a Wolseley, and that became the big Riley 2.6—I also did a very complicated walnut fascia for it. That same big backlight was taken across to the Magnette [ZB] Varitone, too."[5] The Two-Point-Six was the first entirely badge-engineered Riley and, from its inception in 1957 to the marque's demise in October 1969, Riley would shadow Wolseley, model for model. There would be no Riley without an equivalent Wolseley. The reverse was not the case, however, as neither the Wolseley 6–99 (later, 6/110) nor the Wolseley 18/85 ("landcrab") had Riley shadow models—although a Riley equivalent to the 18/85 was briefly contemplated. In the meantime, the Two-Point-Six was more reliable than the Pathfinder if, inevitably, less characterful. "One of the most advanced cars you can buy today!" claimed Riley's copywriters, emphasizing the "clean-cut elegance" of its "continental lines." "Now Riley Fit Lockheed Brakes. Owners can speed with safety knowing that they have at all times the extra stability and extra power for instantaneous braking…. The safest brakes in the world" crowed a Lockheed advertisement on the front cover of *The Autocar*.[6]

With the introduction of the Riley One-Point-Five at £863 17s in November 1957, the marque gained a new lease of life. True, it was badge-engineered life, as the new model looked almost identical to the cheaper Wolseley 1500 introduced in May, and both cars were based on a proposed replacement for the Morris Minor that did not reach production.[7] But the Riley had a sporting character together with—in the Riley spirit—agile handling and a good power to weight ratio which allowed it a 0–60 time of 17.4 seconds and a top speed of 83.5 mph. The new car was only twelve feet, nine inches long.[8] The One-Point-Five was updated in May 1960 and in October 1961 to create Mk II and Mk III versions respectively, and continued in production with the Wolseley 1500 until April 1965.[9] The name "One-Point-Five" was cumbersome and affected, but it provided continuity with the Two-Point-Six introduced in September and distinguished the new model from the earlier 1½ Litre.

In the early 1950s, Riley advertising had been confident and patrician—and sometimes very colourful, with artwork among the best in the world. Pathfinder advertising, on the other hand, had been more blandly aspirational ("You enjoy motoring as never before…," "The day you drive your Riley

Pathfinder home…," "It's time you tried the brilliant Riley Pathfinder") and illustrations of the car, competently mainstream, suggested something less than the "magificent motoring" promised by the marque's long-standing slogan. The shape of the Pathfinder did not lend itself to artistry: the sleeker the artist made it, the more slab-sided it appeared, yet in the flesh, in a dark colour, with its low roofline and large wheels, it looked quite distinguished. Copywriters seemed to be weighed down by BMC's hopes for it: "At once you will see why it is the car on which so many men have now set their hearts." This was trusting too much to fate. But confidence returned with the new, compact four-seater, as in January 1958: "You'll like the winning ways of the new Riley One-Point-Five…. Here's a new, smaller Riley…that gives a truly breathtaking performance. You'll enjoy its flashing acceleration, its effortless cruising in the 80's. You'll give full marks to its excellent steering and roadholding. You'll drive with confidence and pleasure in a car that gives you power with safety." The two-tone car was painted almost exactly as it appeared in real life—at most an inch was added between the front wheel-arch and the door—and small diagrams showed the front suspension (with torsion bars again, as on the Minor), the dashboard (walnut-veneered) and boot (with a separate spare wheel compartment).

In 1961, *The Autocar* found the One-Point-Five's engine "amazingly smooth and willing, and [it] revved very freely indeed," but like most testers criticized the car's driving position, considering it "agricultural," though not uncomfortable. In 1958 J. Eason Gibson of *Country Life* thought that it would cause fatigue to tall drivers. Everyone noticed a lack of leg room in the rear with the front seats back, and most who sampled early cars wondered about the interior colour scheme. "An amazing variety of different materials of assorted colours [is] used in the internal trimming of the car, which gives an impression of untidiness and cheapness," Gibson admonished. "Much highly polished wood enhances the interior" said S.C.H. Davis tactfully in *The Field* in December 1957, when a small picture of the interior was captioned "The surprisingly spacious interior of the new Riley is finished in tasteful duo-tone shades…." The "surprisingly," of course, indicated its lack of spaciousness; kindly (and realistic) testers arranged their expectations so as to be able to be pleasantly surprised. Later cars were more conventionally trimmed. But Davis liked the car and, testing the Mk II in April 1961, reflected: "When the Riley became one car in the long range manufactured by [BMC], dyed-in-the-wool Riley enthusiasts were not too pleased. However, a large and magnificently equipped factory has very much more chance of producing the right type of car at a com-

Opposite: **Riley Elf Mk I.** Is she really? Another badge-engineering exercise from BMC, the Elf was a good example of the new breed of anti-utilitarian small car. "Pert" is not a word that could have been used in quite the same sense in later years, and the headline would have been unwise even a decade later. Like the similar Wolseley Hornet, the Elf was marketed as a woman's shopping car, although (as was not the case in at least one Wolseley advertisement), it is assumed that the driver has chosen it for herself and has not merely been lumbered with it by her husband.

petitive price — provided that there is a genuine market. The Riley proves the point. There are two models, both with 1,500 c.c. engines. But one is a large and luxurious saloon, a carriage in the accepted sense of the term, and therefore not quite a Riley. But the other, the One-Point-Five, is genuinely a Riley which no tradition-bound Riley owner can scorn…"[10]

The car soon became popular with saloon car racers and motoring enthusiasts, the Wolseley 1500 being staid by comparison, and advertising emphasized its enthusiast appeal: "Everyone acclaims the lively One-Point-Five" said a September 1958 headline as three men raised their hats to it, music-hall style. An April 1959 advertisement began: "If you like the 'feel' of a finely engineered car, the response of a sports-tuned engine, the positive feel of good steering, sureness in cornering — if you value these things, the Riley One-Point-Five is for you." Three years later the car offered "Big car luxury — Small car economy — Sports car performance." In 1963 the Mk III, now photographed rather than painted, was "So luxurious, so lively, so easy to handle." By July 1964 the car was being challenged by a new generation of GT saloons from Ford and Vauxhall, and its handling — never outstanding, though adequate for a car with such relatively soft suspension and high build — was outclassed by that of BMC's new front-wheel-drive cars. The copywriter placed more emphasis on the Riley name: "The Riley world of magnificent motoring — Big car luxury. Small-car handling. Twin-carburettor performance. The kind of acceleration you expect from a high power/weight ratio. The luxury that comes from real leather….A great car. A fine name. A proud symbol of the exclusive, enviable world of the pace-setting Riley owner. £701. 7. 11., including £121. 7. 11. P.T." Overall sales of 39,568 in seven and a half years were certainly respectable, and made the One-Point-Five the best-selling Riley.[11]

Where the tangible was unremarkable, copywriters had to emphasize the intangible, especially with the "not quite a Riley" that was the Riley 4/Sixty Eight. It was quite a convincing Austin Cambridge, however: "The combined steering and cornering characteristics appear to give passengers the impression that they are being driven very fast; this has the effect of setting a limit on the cruising and maximum speeds that can be habitually used," said J. Eason Gibson.[12] "For the man who really cares — The new Riley 4 Sixty Eight. here's a superb new Riley for the man who really cares about motoring! Long, low, elegant, spacious and luxurious…" said BMC in April 1959 beside a line-drawn head-portrait of a square-jawed businessman stroking his chin. The opening slogan lasted for a year, though what the man really cared about was (wisely) never specified. In January 1960 BMC were perhaps a little too honest: "Are you three men in one — part business man, part family man and with a dash of the debonair sportsman? There is just a little coterie of such enthusiasts to whom we think the Riley 4/Sixty Eight

will appeal…" In May the family won, as Father stood by the car waving to a friend in a boat while the children played in the back. Mother, meanwhile, leaned forward at the wheel as if willing the car not to grind to a halt, and looked as if she was about to burst into tears. Sometimes photographs were safer. In June photography did take over with the headline, "You are really someone in a Riley!." A September advertisement began, "Riley for men who like finer things in life." In November the car was seen from above, its boot and bonnet lids removed, being inspected by the owner and other admirers: "Take a good close look at the Riley." More dynamic photography arrived with the 1961 headlines such as: "For you who want high performance with your luxury" (above a speeding car), "For you who recognize true value" (above a ground-level front view), and "For you who like refinements with your speed" (above a photograph of the instruments at 45 mph and 3600 rpm).[13]

When the £1028 4/Sixty Eight was replaced by the £1088 4/Seventy Two in October 1961, early advertising did not mention the new model, but showed just a grille which could have been from either car. This enabled the advertisement to run during October and November and ensured that readers were not discouraged from buying the earlier model, still available in local showrooms. The copy was general and high-flown: "Riley for Magnificent Motoring — To generations of motoring enthusiasts the timeless beauty of the Riley has been a symbol of 'magnificent motoring.' It is no less so today. Whichever of the exciting models claims your interest, the noble name of Riley is a proud reminder — to you and to the world — that here indeed is 'something special'…" The new 4/Seventy Two had more power than the old (with 1622cc and 68bhp rather than 1489cc and 64bhp) and handled better — and it was also available as an automatic: "Three big new reasons why you can enjoy even more magnificent motoring" as model-specific advertising put it early in 1962.[14] By 1963 photography was established in Riley advertising for good. In 1965 the finned saloon, in brown and cream, received the obligatory "deserted beach" treatment: "Just imagine…the thrust of twin carbs, the sporting character enthusiasts demand, the day-long comfort of automatic transmission — all in one luxurious family 5 seater. A Riley? *Of course!*" The wood and leather interior was the car's best point by 1967, when Ford, Rootes and Vauxhall relied increasingly on plastic mouldings and vinyl: "We often sell this car to people who haven't got a chauffeur," announced Riley in July 1967, in one of a short series of colour advertisements which included beautiful close-up colour photographs of 4/Seventy-Two, Riley Elf and Riley Kestrel interiors.

The Elf, introduced in 1961, was trimmed in traditional Riley style and at £694, compared with £526 for a basic Austin or Morris, was the most expensive as well as the most luxurious of BMC's Minis.[15] According to a 1963 headline it was the "Most luxurious small car in the world" — which was true (until the Radford Mini de Ville arrived) if wood and leather trim constituted luxury; less so if luxury meant smooth suspension and room to stretch out. Although the Elf was obviously based on the Mini it was not, at first, advertised on the fact, although any pretended distance was abandoned by 1967, when the car was "The Mini with the most — Meet the new Riley Elf Mk. III. The craftsman-built "mini" with the Riley pedigree. The world's most advanced small car, with the world's most advanced specification." This included "concealed door hinges" and "wind-away front windows" which no regular Mini yet boasted. By now the car had Hydrolastic suspension as well as a "carpet in the boot" and "an impressively full range of instruments sparkling in walnut"—which extended to glove boxes, as it did not in the equivalent Wolseley Hornet. "Travel First Class" invited an October 1967 advertisement showing a young husband giving the keys of a red Elf to his wife in the car. "Buy British Riley" said the slogan on the couple's suitcase. It was "the elegant British super-mini" at a time when the super-mini hatchback, as we know it today, had yet to be invented. A similar advertisement with the same headline and theme appeared for the Riley Kestrel 1300.[16] In February 1969 a white Elf was photographed at ground level, the front of the car just fitting within the page, a bright, lightly clouded sky in the background. With just six months to run, it was the "Mini-most." In May a white 1300 Mk II, photographed in an almost identical pose and setting, was headlined "The 1300 ct. Diamond"—the diamond being the Riley badge, "fair and square on the nose of the Riley 1300 Mark II. A spaciously sporty grand alliance of a car." Perhaps the best of several inspired Riley headlines of 1967–69 appeared in mid-1967 for the Riley Kestrel, as the marque's version of the famously Hydrolastic Morris 1100 was then called[17]: "Luxury Car Runs on Water," it said. If only.

18

Rolls-Royce

"The Best Car in the World"

In the 1960s Rolls-Royce advertising was well known for its longstanding slogan in Britain, "The Best Car in the World," and for an American advertisement for the $13,995 Silver Cloud devised by David Ogilvy in the late 1950s and placed in two newspapers and two magazines at a cost of $25,000. "When I got the Rolls-Royce account," Ogilvy recalled in 1983, "I spent three weeks reading about the car and came across a statement that 'at sixty miles an hour, the loudest noise comes from the electric clock.' This became the headline, and it was followed by 607 words of factual copy."[1]

In later years Ogilvy was scathing about car advertising in general: "Car manufacturers assume that you are not interested in facts. Indeed, their advertising is not aimed at consumers. Its purpose is to win an ovation when it is projected on the screen at hoopla conventions of dealers. Showbiz commercials have that effect. Sober, factual advertising does not. If their engineering was as incompetent as their advertising, their cars would not run ten miles without a breakdown. When I advertised Rolls-Royce, I gave the facts—no hot air, no adjectives. Later, my partner Hank Bernhard used equally factual advertising for Mercedes. In every case sales went up dramatically—on peppercorn budgets."[2]

In one version of Ogilvy's famous advertisement, the Rolls-Royce Silver Cloud was photographed in an affluent, tidy but unflamboyant street, approached by a mother and daughter in riding gear. The headline, which quoted "the Technical Editor of The Motor," was followed by thirteen numbered paragraphs of which the last concluded, before giving the car's price and inviting the reader to contact dealers listed on the opposite page, "People who feel diffident about driving a Rolls-Royce can buy a Bentley." In 1963

Ogilvy remarked, "Judging by the number of people who picked up on the word 'diffident' and bandied it about, I concluded that the advertisement was thoroughly read."[3] It was: the facts may have been "sober" in the sense that they were demonstrable and presented simply, but, like the car as a whole, they were conversation pieces. The advertisement could be grounded in reality because the reality was intrinsically worth talking about.

Ogilvy used the advertisement as an example of the merits of research as the basis of effective advertising. The research had to be into the product itself, to give the copywriter something interesting and persuasive to say about it; and also into how effective different advertising techniques had been in the past, so that approaches known to be unsuccessful were not repeated. It was entirely possible for advertising to *unsell* a product if it repelled people who would otherwise have bought it yet failed to persuade potential new customers. For Ogilvy, an advertisement only worked if it sold what it was advertising. Artistry and creativity, in themselves, were neither here nor there. True, it was never possible to prove empirically, beyond a certain level of generality, which advertisements worked by this definition and which did not. Only by recording the exact causes of every individual's decision to buy or not buy a product for which he had seen an advertisement could the effectiveness of the advertisement be gauged definitively. Even then, one could never know how well any of an infinitely large number of alternative advertisements, never devised, might have worked by comparison. Neither theories of motivation nor an individual's recollections of his own impulses could ever correlate exactly with the mental processes that caused him to buy one car rather than another. But if advertising could never be truly scientific, research could nevertheless help an advertiser to find out what *could* be known. One might not achieve certainty of prediction, but one could do better than competitors who were less well prepared.[4] In Rolls-Royce's case, the competition included not only Mercedes-Benz, Imperial, Cadillac and Lincoln Continental, but also boats, real estate, fine art, and financial investments.

Ogilvy's counsel was one of commercial pragmatism rather than theoretical perfection, and in upmarket advertising the appearance of rationality within an advertisement itself, as well as in its conception, was as important as the reality. It enabled the consumer to feel that he was being rational, too, and that mattered when he was spending $14,000 on a car. With the Silver Cloud, Ogilvy — who had the great advantage of speaking naturally in the language of many of his potential clients — appealed to the consumer's image of himself as a person readily engaged and amused, but nevertheless deliberating and rational, just as openly as Cadillac appealed directly to a desire to be envied or thought successful by strangers. In this context the supposedly rational consumer's attachment to rationality was not itself rational, but rather pre-rational: it was an emotional attachment to a way of proceeding that was not itself founded in that way's own precepts or in dispassionate analysis. And, with a Rolls-Royce, the facts were interesting, and stayed in the mind: "The finished car spends a week in the final test-shop, being fine-tuned. Here it is subjected to 98 separate ordeals. For example, the engineers use a stethoscope to listen for axle-whine.... A picnic table, veneered in French walnut, slides out from under the dash. Two more swing out behind the front seats.... You can get such optional extras as an Espresso coffee-making machine, a dictating machine, a bed, hot and cold water for washing, an electric razor or a telephone." The Rolls-Royce came with toys, and they were fun.

British Rolls-Royce advertising was just as distinctive, particularly in the early 1950s with the Silver Wraith. There was nothing modest (or diffident) about a Rolls-Royce on either side of the Atlantic. In one advertisement the car's radiator was drawn as it would be seen by someone kneeling directly in front of the left-hand wing, looking towards the far headlamp. The classical immensity of the grille filled almost the whole page, its bars like columns standing close together, the Spirit of Ecstacy a giant, exotic bird poised to take off from far above. The freestanding headlamp beside the grille, in the style of twenty years earlier, looked imposing in itself. There was no copy, just "The best car in the world" in small capital letters. In another piece, a photograph was taken from just in front of the windscreen on the left hand side of the car, along an immaculately polished bonnet to the mascot at the end. Neo-Gothic buildings were reflected in the deep paint, and the picture was taken with a long exposure so that passing traffic appeared as ghostly smudges through which railings and parked cars could be seen behind.

Frank Wootton painted illustrations for the announce-

ment of the Silver Cloud in 1955, and in 1957–58 it was promoted with simpler advertising in a style similar to that used (by the same agency, Dorland Advertising Ltd.) for the Bentley S1. In December 1957 the front of the Silver Cloud was photographed from a point to the left of the grille about ten feet above the gound, so that almost the whole of the front of the car could be seen. Earlier in the year the car was shown in a simple, front three-quarter photograph, without background, for the announcement, as with the equivalent Bentley, that "Power-assisted steering is now offered on the Silver Cloud as an optional extra." In 1958 the car appeared outside a modest country house at night without copy except for the famous slogan, its grille illuminated by the headlights of another car. Though appealing in its own right, this advertisement was surprisingly conventional for Rolls-Royce as exactly the same theme was used in 1958 by Austin, Humber and Vauxhall for six-cylinder executive cars in the £1000 — £1500 class. By the end of 1958, a Silver Cloud cost £5693 17s. In January, S.C.H. Davis had tested a long wheelbase model: "Not cheap by one yardstick, it is wonderful value for money by another. True, for that money it should be good. It is worth every penny," he concluded.[5]

In November 1959 a "new engine for the best car in the world" was announced with a photograph of the Spirit of Ecstacy glittering against a pitch-black background with streamlines, like horizontal icicles, trailing behind it. The copy was longer than usual, similar to that for the equivalent Bentley, but crisper: "Aluminium alloy engine. Developed by Rolls-Royce over the past five years, the new engine in the Phantom V and Silver Cloud II is a compact, vee unit (Bore 4.1," Stroke 3.6") made of aluminium alloy and with a capacity of 6230 c.c. It weighs no more than the 6 cylinder engine which it replaces, delivering greater torque over the entire speed range. Yet its smoothness and silence are such that there is little indication of the increased engine performance...air conditioning. The heating, demisting and refrigeration units are redesigned to give increased capacity and flexibility of control. Rear window demisters and press button window lifts are available."

In November 1960 a photograph was taken from the roof of the car, over the windscreen, on a wet, cobbled street at night, so that the bonnet and wings, covered with droplets of water, emerged from the bottom of the picture. The car seemed, in monochrome with distant lights from other cars on both sides of the road, to be facing the wrong way up a one-way street. But the lights of the cars in front were slightly smaller than those on the right, so it was probably a normal street. "Whatever the weather — full ventilation, air conditioning or heating ensure a journey in complete comfort for driver and passengers of the Rolls-Royce Silver Cloud II," began the copy, which concluded, after a brief description of the engine, transmission and steering, "An exceptionally high degree of safety is provided by three separate braking systems — two hydraulic and one mechanical,

The decision you will take alone

Not all top decision-makers yet own a Rolls-Royce. But those who do are markedly more determined to make up their own minds without advice from others.

This comes from our latest enquiry into the habits and attitudes of Rolls-Royce owners. Some of the other findings are equally significant and, perhaps, even more surprising. For example 78% of owners normally drive the car themselves. And 85% regard the car primarily as a business asset.

Your Rolls-Royce dealer and a test-drive in a Silver Shadow will show you why.

From the monocoque construction, the exceptionally smooth and flexible 6.2 litre V-8 engine, and automatic transmission with electrically operated gear selection; to the security of disc brakes on all four wheels operated by three separate hydraulic systems, and independent suspension with automatic height control.

Here is a luxurious saloon that offers a combination of comfort, smoothness and safety, workmanship, finish and quality of materials no other car can match. Yet it can show a clean pair of heels to most sports cars without raising its voice above a well-bred whisper. No other car can be driven so fast and so far with so little fatigue. And none depreciates as slowly.

All this the Rolls-Royce dealer will demonstrate and enlarge upon. Then he will leave you to make your decision— alone.

ROLLS-ROYCE the best car in the world

Rolls-Royce Silver Shadow I. By the late 1960s, many people who could afford a Rolls-Royce disliked it for being pompous, aristocratic or conspicuously old-guard. Others, conversely, liked it but feared that they could not live up to it. Hence this piece, one of a series of advertisements from Dorland Advertising built around a survey of owners that revealed, innocuously enough, that only 3 percent of owners had titles, that 85 percent saw their cars as business assets and that 78 percent drove themselves. The claim that owners were "markedly more determined to make up their own minds without advice from others" suggests an intended appeal to the small, independent businessman rather than to the professional who routinely takes expert advice before making important decisions. This particular car was used in several advertisements, and had a two-tone paint scheme just visible here. In later years many Shadows were hastily repainted white for wedding hire.

The whole is greater than the sum of its parts.

Some factors which distinguish the Rolls-Royce from ordinary motor cars:

A small piece off every crankshaft is both physically and chemically analysed.

The wheel nuts are made of heavy brass. They screw on clockwise on the right hand side, and anti-clockwise on the left hand side, to ensure that the nuts on both sides tend to tighten as the wheels turn.

The turning circle is only 38 feet. Both ways. In a single manoeuvre, a Rolls-Royce can be parked in a space only five and one-half feet longer than the car itself.

All rotating parts are dynamically balanced.

The fan blades are staggered to reduce aerodynamic noise.

Major assemblies, such as the final drive unit, are held together with numerous small bolts rather than a few large ones. This minimises the risk of leaks, and follows a principle laid down by Sir Henry Royce.

Three independent braking systems work simultaneously. Two of them are power-assisted.

The radio is a standard fitting. There are four speakers. Earthing strips in each wheel prevent tyre-generated static electricity.

The seats can be moved forwards, backwards, up, down and tilted. These actions are performed by electric servo motors. They can also be manually reclined.

Each circuit is individually fused. The fuses can be changed from the driver's seat.

Fourteen coats of finish are applied.

One central switch locks all doors.

The ride height is automatically maintained at the optimum. When passengers get in or out, this correction of height is quick; when the car is moving it is slow.

Refrigerated air conditioning is a standard fitting.

The facia veneer is mirror-imaged from the centre line.

With 6.75 litres, the engine provides more than adequate power.

The whole is greater than the sum of its parts.

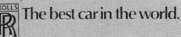 The best car in the world.

Rolls-Royce Motors Limited. Makers of the Rolls-Royce Silver Shadow and Bentley Four-Door Saloon, the Rolls-Royce Silver Shadow Long Wheelbase Saloon, the Rolls-Royce and Bentley Corniche Two-door Saloon and Convertible and the Rolls-Royce Phantom VI.

E

Rolls-Royce Corniche Convertible. "First, study the product you are going to advertise. The more you know about it, the more likely you are to come up with a big idea for selling it. When I got the Rolls-Royce account, I spent three weeks reading about the car and came cross a statement that 'at sixty miles an hour, the loudest noise comes from the electric clock.' This became the headline, and it was followed by 607 words of factual copy." So wrote David Ogilvy in 1983 about his famous advertisement for the Rolls-Royce Silver Cloud in America. In July 1971, Rolls-Royce in Britain used a similar approach for the Corniche by Mulliner Park Ward, which had taken over from the almost identical-looking Silver Shadow four months earlier.

acting independently and in concert." No Ford advertisement ever referred to things happening "in concert"—and if a humorist might remark that this was because, in a Ford, they rarely did, the tone of planned and deliberate action, its consequences accurately foreseen, embodied much of the appeal of the Silver Cloud, and the way in which, to many owners, it seemed to be liked to be driven.

And then, in the late 1960s, everything changed. In 1965, the Silver Shadow arrived with unitary construction, disc brakes, all-independent self-levelling suspension with hydraulics of frightening complexity, and tasteful but characterless styling. "It's a remarkable thing about Rolls that only its salesmen and customers are ever in the least bit pompous or reserved," said *Car*. "The boffins are as unstuffy, as talkative, as patient and as friendly as any in the industry. Even the chief stylist, John Blatchley, was disarmingly truthful when we challenged him about the new car's Farina-in-the-Fifties lines. Didn't he think the [Mercedes 600] had a bit more zing to it, a bit more personality? Maybe. Had he perhaps been at such pains to avoid date-prone gimmicks that he'd robbed the shape of any personality? Yes, but that was almost unavoidable; and in any case it grew on one. Which rival styles did he most admire? 'Oh! that Buick Riviera's just lovely….' Actually Blatchley is right about the Shadow's looks becoming more acceptable with time. Seeing it dodging about amongst London's traffic one is struck by its unobtrusive honesty of line."[6] The car was only seriously criticized, in the main, for its over-light and vague steering, for roll, and for poor roadholding, the tail being prone to breaking away at quite low speeds on wet roundabouts. The car was quickly improved.

Apart from the 1965 announcement, the Silver Shadow was most heavily advertised during 1968–71. The car was shown speeding along a country road, on an airfield, in the countryside, and outside that favourite Bentley venue of old, the factory. In 1968–69 it was sold openly to businessmen. Headlines and opening copy were arresting: "Why doesn't every successful man own a Rolls-Royce? 'Attitude of mind' would appear to be the answer…." "Decisions…decisions…decisions…. The Rolls-Royce owner has a mind of his own—and is unusually determined to make it up unaided…." "Apart from money, what do you need to own a Rolls-Royce? Something money can't buy: bigness in mind and outlook…." The copy described a survey of owners and their attitudes in which it had been discovered that 78 per cent of owners normally drove themselves, 97 per cent did not have a title, and 85 per cent regarded the car as a valuable business asset. In particular, owners were "highly independent thinkers. They form their own judgments. They make their own decisions. They are unusually demanding and critical…." Similar copy was used in each advertise-

ment and in some versions the owner's determination to make decisions unaided suggested a small businessman rather than someone successful in a wider context, but the point was clarified by the end of 1969: "Workhorse—One of the interesting findings of a recent survey into the habits and attitudes of Rolls-Royce owners was the extent to which the car is regarded as a business asset. No less than 85 per cent of owners saw the car primarily in this light. These are the men at the top…." It was a small point, but one worth making.

Similarly dramatic headlines continued in 1970, in a different style, as in April: "And now, the Rolls-Royce of cars. There's been the Rolls-Royce of watches. The Rolls-Royce of lawn mowers. For all we know, there may have been the Rolls-Royce of collar studs. Not that we are surprised that our name is taken to be synonymous with the best…." Which was a cue for the car's features and marque values: "Building the best car in the world is almost incidental. Our number one objective is to make a car to satisfy the needs of a very special, exacting sort of person. It must, without fail, take him absolutely anywhere he chooses to go. And leave him as it found him. It must reflect his standards of excellence; cater to his taste in comfort; satisfy his prowess as a driver. It has to be a business asset, a social asset, and personal asset. Without fuss and with very little effort…. Wouldn't you be surprised if you didn't get it all, and more, with a Rolls-Royce?" And wouldn't he have been surprised to find the copy, written in the language of the businessman rather than that of the engineer or aesthete, so similar to that used for some upmarket American cars before the Second World War?

In July, David Ogilvy's approach, too, came across the Atlantic in an advertisement for the two-door Silver Shadow: "What can you say about the best car in the world? …If you have a son, or a nephew, with a mechanical bent, an enquiring mind and an irritating habit of asking 'Why?' here are a few technological facts to blind him with…. The refrigerated air conditioning is designed to keep the temperature as you like it, no matter what it's like outside. Engineering thought shows in every detail. Right down to the wheel nuts which are threaded clockwise and anti-clockwise on opposite sides of the car. So that the heavy brass nuts tend to tighten as the wheels turn…. By the time he's old enough to own one, he'll be old enough to understand." The copy itself was not in the Ogilvy class—it was a little mundane, insufficiently quirky, its style too close to that for mainstream cars from British Leyland, for which Dorland Advertising were also agents—but Ogilvy's idea was still effective. It was a shame that his best line could only be used once.

19

Rover

"One of the world's best engineered cars"

The long arm of Raymond Loewy Associates reached out to the least likely of British car companies in September 1949, when Rover introduced its 75 (P4), a four-door saloon that looked very like the 1947 Studebaker designed in large part by Loewy. It replaced the stop-gap Rover 60 and 75 (P3) of 1948–49, whose style, with four or six side windows, dated back to 1938, when the Sixteen (16hp by the old RAC rating) had been advertised, quoting a review in *The Daily Telegraph*, as "The Rolls-Royce of Light Cars." The Sixteen and related Twelve and Fourteen were produced until the P3 took over in 1948, and were accompanied by the similarly pre-war Ten until 1947. In his self-designed 1951 book, *Never Leave Well Enough Alone*, Loewy proposed that MAYA — Most Advanced Yet Acceptable — should be a designer's credo: "Our desire is naturally to give the buying public the most advanced product that research can develop and technology can produce. Unfortunately, it has been proved time and time again that such a product does not always sell well. There seems to be for each individual product…a critical area at which the consumer's desire for novelty reaches what I might call the shock-zone. At that point the urge to buy reaches a plateau, and sometimes evolves into a resistance to buying…the smart industrial designer is the one who has a lucid understanding of where the shock-zone lies in each particular problem. At this point a design has reached what I call the MAYA…stage…. We might say that a product has reached the MAYA stage when 30 per cent (to pick an arbitrary figure) or more of the consumers express a negative reaction to acceptance."[1]

When the P4 was first conceived in 1947, Rover knew that British manufacturers would be competing with American designs in export markets and examined a number of American models, including two 1947 Studebaker Champion Regal DeLuxe four-door sedans. Rover's chief engineer, Maurice Wilks, decided to adopt the Studebaker's novel "three-box" styling, its centre-opening doors, its sloping boot lid and many other details. Wilks also added a "pass lamp" to the centre of the grille. (In the American market, where it was illegal, the lamp was shielded by a cover in which the number "75" was cut out for illumination from behind.) Wilks' ideas were translated into drawings by Rover's chief body designer, Harry Loker, and the body of one of the Studebakers was put on a Rover development chassis to create a "Roverbaker" test mule.[2] The Rover's inspiration was instantly identifiable in the production design.

Yet for most potential Rover buyers in Britain — if not in many export markets, where the 75 enjoyed a head start over equivalent cars from other countries — Rover's designers had passed through the MAYA stage into the territory of the more advanced than tasteful. By tradition, Rover customers were conservative. "I have found very few motorists who approve of the new body styling" said the car's reviewer in the *Birmingham Gazette*.[3] As Rover engineer and eventual engineering director of BL Cars, Charles Spencer (Spen) King recalled, "When the P4 came out there was a terrific 'anti' customer reaction. People stamped out of the [1949] Motor Show saying: 'I've had Rovers for years, my father's had Rovers for years, but I'm never going to buy one again if you're going to make motor cars which look like that.'"[4] But the 75 was rescued by its other qualities, not least its wood and leather trim and an overall aura of having been solidly, thoroughly and above all intelligently designed. "African walnut was used in Rovers for its straight grain and incredible stability. I 'found' a supply of this wood for my kitchen cupboards, and it's still there after 30 years!" recalled Rover's chief stylist from 1954 to 1981, David Bache.[5]

This attention to long-term durability was typical of the company and of the P4, which on both sides of the Atlantic was often called "the poor man's Bentley." It was built in updated form until May 1964, by which time the definitive Rover of the 1960s, the 2000 (P6), had been on sale for eight months. A bias towards engineering and a culture of trained and reflective intelligence permeated the firm: "I was the first stylist Rover had ever had," recalled Bache, who moved to the company from Austin in August 1953, "as Maurice Wilks had pretty much done it all himself. But he was quite sensitive and always appreciated nice quality things. He'd never ever order anyone to do anything. He would always suggest.... The difference between working at Austin and at Rover was absolutely like chalk and cheese. The Austin hierachy were, by comparison, roughnecks. At Rover, the quality and standard of the article were uppermost."[6] This philosophy was not surprising in a company which had worked with Frank Whittle's prototype gas turbine engines from 1940–43 and returned to the field in 1945, producing a number of experimental turbine cars, most notably the Rover-BRM prepared for the 1963 Le Mans 24-Hour race. Austin dabbled with a gas turbine-engined Sheerline saloon in the early 1950s, but BMC's Leonard Lord was wary. "You are not getting me in there with that ruddy thing. I'll stand and watch," he said, before eventually riding in the back.[7]

It was ironic that by following the Studebaker design of Loewy and Virgil Exner so closely Rover should have breached Loewy's own design philosophy more comprehensively than did any other British car manufacturer at the time.[8] Strategically, however, Wilks had been right to seek inspiration from the most modern car available as to do so allowed a long production run, which was essential for the profitability of a company as small as Rover. The controversy faded when Ford (1950), Vauxhall (1951), Austin (also 1951) and other British manufacturers brought out their own "three-box" designs, and in 1952 the P4 gained a conventional radiator grille and lamp arrangement. In 1955 David Bache gave the boot a generic English shape to increase its luggage capacity, and in 1957 he squared up the front wings to improve the car's "placeability" in traffic.[9] By now the design had become thoroughly integrated into the automotive establishment. Nevertheless, the experiment would not be repeated. When David Bache produced a radical design, much-lauded within Rover, for the car that would become

the 3-Litre (P5) of 1958, Maurice Wilks studied it at length and concluded, "That's a very beautiful model you've produced. I know everyone is most impressed with it. But we can't make it you know. And I'll tell you why we can't make it. It's a head-turner and the Rover Company doesn't make head-turners. We like to make vehicles which pass unobtrusively and are not noticed."[10]

If Rover's designs were often innovative — the 2000 of 1963 would look more innocuous than the first 75 but would be more advanced in its engineering — the company's postwar advertising (from C. Vernon & Sons until the end of 1956 and subsequently from F.C. Pritchard Wood and Partners) was never other than conservatively tasteful. The P3 of 1948 was "One of Britain's fine cars now made finer," and the main slogan continued until the mid-1950s. In the early 1950s Rover cars were sometimes promoted alongside the Land-Rover, which was produced in higher numbers: "To the casual glance two more dissimilar vehicles could not be imagined. Yet the stocky Land-Rover receives the same careful attention in machining and construction as does its elegant companion. And the Rover Seventy-Five, with all its grace, is as tough and sturdy as the Land-Rover. Fitness for purpose is the keynote of both" said a 1953 advertisement. The P4, with its deep-railed and heavy chassis, was certainly tough, as a result of which it was heavier than the 1947 Studebaker in a cheerful departure from another of Loewy's *dicta*: "Weight is the enemy."[11] In Rover's market, however, extra solidity and durability gathered extra sales.

While Studebaker's early post-war advertising adopted colour photography, Rover's artists produced some of the most attractive paintings of the early 1950s. Several showed the 75 in side view against dramatic cloudscapes and countryside, often without accompanying copy except for Rover's own address and continuing slogan, "One of Britain's Fine Cars." Longer copy appeared in 1955–56 and a restrained and quietly confident tone remained throughout the decade. A February 1960 advertisement for the six-cylinder Rover 100 was typical: "The Rover 100 replaces the highly-successful '90' and '105' models and is in fact a development of them. It has even more smoothness than the '90' and a performance comparable to that of the '105.' The Rover 100 is powered by the new Rover 2.6-Litre sloping head engine with a 7-bearing crankshaft first developed for the 3-Litre...." It cost £1538 4s 2d, which compared well with the Humber Super Snipe's £1453 and the £1579 of the flashier but less robust Jaguar 2.4 Litre, a car with a not-quite-respectable image which few Rover owners — many of them

---

Opposite: **Rover 110 (P4).** A final fling for Auntie, who was now available only in six-cylinder form, and with steel rather than aluminium doors. As so often with upmarket British cars, the Rover's styling grew more rather than less conservative with the passing years, and although the car is shown on the inevitable shingle, there is nothing racy about the picture or the copy. The body design, which in its original 1949–54 form had a more steeply sloping bootlid and low-set horizontal tail-lights, was inspired by Studebaker's 1947 Champion, but the Rover's interior — always a great selling-point — was strictly British-traditional except for a few modernist indulgences (rectangular instruments, push-button interior door releases, column-change) on early cars.

THE FIELD, *April 25 1963*

The ROVER 110 & 95 saloons quietly, luxuriously, travel far and fast

In recent years, no other cars of comparable price have been able to match the Rover 6-cylinder saloons for utter reliability, silent performance, and luxurious comfort. All the traditions of Rover engineering are here combined in motor cars that are a lasting pleasure to drive and be driven in.

ROVER 110 The more powerful replacement for the Rover 100. Very high cruising speeds and an all-round performance that belies its quiet looks. Basic price: £1,143.0.0. Plus P.T. £238.13.9. Total: £1,381.13.9.

ROVER 95 The six-cylinder replacement for the Rover 80. Swift, silent, and comfortable in the Rover tradition. The ideal introduction to Rover motoring. Basic price: £1,023.0.0. Plus P.T. £213.13.9. Total: £1,236.13.9.

ROVER—ONE OF THE WORLD'S BEST ENGINEERED CARS

The Rover Company Limited   Solihull   Warwickshire   London Offices and Showrooms: Devonshire House, Piccadilly   Makers of fine cars and the world-famous Land-Rover

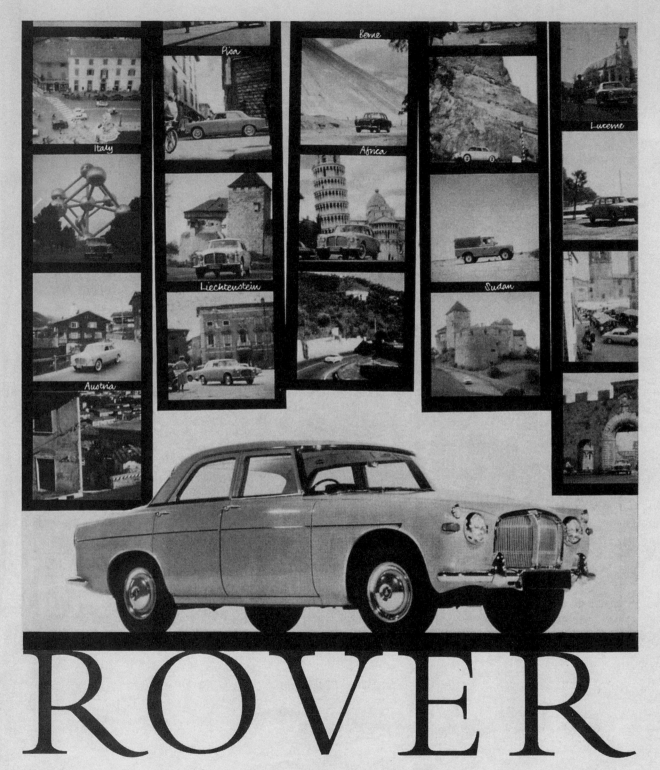

ROVER

It was born and bred to cross the frontiers of the world, this Rover 3-Litre. It combines the grace and comfort of a town carriage with the dash—and stamina—necessary for long-distance motoring. On the 3-Litre power steering is an optional extra. On all three Rover models—the 80, 100 and 3-Litre—front wheel disc brakes and overdrive are standard equipment.

The '80', £1,396.10.10d. The '100', £1,538.4.2d. The '3-Litre' with conventional gearbox, £1,783.5.10d., with automatic transmission £1,864.0.10d. (Prices include P.T.)

THE ROVER COMPANY LIMITED, SOLIHULL, WARWICKSHIRE. *Makers of fine cars and the world-famous Land-Rover.*

self-consciously pillars of their communities—would wish to be seen in, even if they acknowledged its technical merits.

In 1963 the last Rovers of the old style — the six-cylinder 110 and 95 — were promoted in an advertisement that in double-spread form showed a dark blue car on one page and small monochrome photographs with long copy on the other, while in the single-page version just the colour photograph appeared, with shortened copy above it. The old design had been extensively updated in detail and now cost either £1381 13s 9d as a 110 or £1236 13s 9d as a 95: "In recent years, no other cars of comparable price have been able to match the Rover 6-cylinder saloons for utter reliability, silent performance and luxurious comfort. All the traditions of Rover engineering are here combined in motor cars that are a lasting pleasure to drive and be driven in," said the copywriter, in the style of the independent road testers so often quoted in the company's earlier copy. Fortunately the real independent testers of the day agreed.[12]

The design of Rover's first monocoque body[13] was unobtrusive, even a little bland, and the 3-Litre became a favourite with government ministers and officials. It was slightly pompous in a way that the 75 and its derivatives, for all their weight[14] and centre-opening doors, never were. Rover tested the new car rigorously: "We used to split gearboxes in half," remembered test engineer Brian Terry, "I've done one right in the middle of the Coventry road…. This was with a 3.0-litre straight six while doing a performance-test type standing start — you know, 3500 revs and foot sideways off the clutch pedal. It just went bang and stood still. And the gearbox cracked straight down the centre where the sump plug was, it fell open, and all the gears fell out. It was rather fun!"[15] The result was "A fine achievement of Rover engineering: a long, low and wide car which handles with delightful delicacy," according to Rover's copy in May 1959, above a photograph of an olive green car on a sea shore with pleasure boats in the background.

The advertisement was one of several from 1958–59 that combined photographs rather than paintings with a layout similar to that of five years previously: in each piece the picture took up most of the page and included a slogan or short copy, while at the bottom of the page just the name of the car and Rover's address were given. A similar approach was used in parallel advertising for the earlier design. In February 1958 a cream and fawn car was shown simply with the words "Rover engineering has produced an outstanding range of cars." The only way to identify the model (a 105R with Roverdrive automatic transmission incorporating a torque converter and button-activated, vacuum-servo operated clutch for emergency low and reverse gears) was to look at the badge on the side of the bonnet. Backgrounds were usually simple and in this case just flat grass and sky which met at a horizon far beyond the car. A similar effect was achieved in monochrome advertisements, in which photographs of the cars were rendered in fine dots, like those of an ordinary picture greatly magnified, so that grass almost looked like coarse gravel. In these pieces copy was usually longer, and if the overall effect was unusual, even slightly strange, the result was immune to variations in paper or print quality. Even on poor paper the pictures retained a clarity lacking in more sophisticated illustrations blurred by indifferent reproduction.

In 1960, Rover's photography became more adventurous, as the 3-Litre was posed among a collection of the continental road signs its owner might encounter on exciting adventures abroad. In 1961, a conventional studio pose was accompanied by strips of photographs above it, like holiday slides, from Italy, Austria, Lucerne, Africa, and Brussels: "Rover — It was born and bred to cross the frontiers of the world…. It combines the grace and comfort of a town carriage with the dash — and stamina — necessary for long-distance motoring" said typical 1961 copy. In 1962 the slogan, "One of the world's best engineered cars" appeared in the marque's advertising and in the spring a dark blue 3-Litre paused beside a modern bridge: "The outstanding characteristics of the 3-litre are its comfort and spaciousness, and its silence of running almost regardless of speed" said the copy, quoting *Autocar*. In the summer a white car appeared at night in front of an important-looking office block, beneath the same quotation. The following year, a black 3-Litre Mk II rested in a forest, offering "High performance, remarkable luxury." 1964's advertising concentrated on a new Coupé model — in fact a four-door saloon with a different, lower, roofline — which was shown in more escapist contexts and settings. With "four armchair-comfortable, deeply-moulded individual seats, the front two reclinable" it was less an upmarket family car than a specialized businessman's express[16]: "100 m.p.h. armchair comfort in the Rover 3-Litre Coupé" promised an early headline; "Silent power in complete luxury" assured another; in October 1964 an owner could "Drive 200 miles effortlessly, chair a board meeting or two, drive back — in time for a show and a late steak!" In 1966, the promise of opulent comfort extended to the Mk III saloon. A glamorous woman, velvet-clad, and mink-wrapped, sat in the back seat: "Don't let the comfort fool you—this car tops 100." The 3-Litre, with an interior that was highly designed but not flamboyant, was successful and, as the 3.5 Litre with a V8 engine from 1967, con-

Rover 3-Litre (P5). Rover joined the trend towards advertising with an international flavour in 1960, but the reader of this colourful and imaginative piece was spared puns about cars roving around the world. The copy is restrained and brief, but nevertheless contrives for Rover a new, youthful image. The filmstrip theme was novel and clever, working particularly well with a large format (14" × 10" in this case). It was, in fact, so novel that any imitation would be too obviously just that, so Rover's series remained unique.

tinued until 1973. Nevertheless, the P4, said Spen King, "was a far better car than the bigger 3-litre P5," although, he added, the image that Rover had established as makers of solid, "middle-of-the-road" products helped to sell the Rover 2000 of 1963–77,[17] on which design work began in September 1956.

The Rover 2000, with the Triumph 2000, created a new market for sophisticated, medium-sized executive cars. In 1960, there was a hierachy of family saloons in Britain which began with bubble cars and ended with the large six-cylinder models from Austin, Ford and Vauxhall. Above this level, mainstream marques gave way to prestige saloons produced in smaller quantities by Daimler, Jaguar and Rover. The largest cars from BMC's luxury brands of Vanden Plas and Wolseley, together with Rootes' Humber Hawk and Super Snipe, bridged the gap. But when Triumph and Rover each introduced a 2000 model in 1963, the ground was cut from under both of the old categories. They survived for a few years, but their presence in the market diminished — literally and figuratively.

For Rover, the 2000 represented a departure from tradition: "The Rover 2000 was a conscious effort by Rover to change the image of their products. There was a worry in the company about what sort of car to do next as a replacement for the P4 and a decision was made to produce a cheaper, lighter car. There was a lot of discussion about this and it was decided to let the younger generation at Rover have a go…. As it turned out, the car sold between 750 and 800 per week throughout its life," recalled Spen King. A figure of 300 per week had been envisaged originally.[18] Early styling proposals were fairly outlandish and included features such as four-door pillarless construction (with which several British manufacturers experimented in the late 1950s, although the feature never reached production in Britain); a sloping nose with recessed, "bug-eye" headlamps in both single and double configurations on each side; a tail which in retrospect can be seen to anticipate Panhard, Dual-Ghia L.6.4 and Jensen C-V8 themes; and fins, which in initial (1957–58) clays looked like those of the 1960 Mercury Comet.[19] But the most obvious influence in the production car was that of Citroën. This was not in the use of base-unit construction, which Rover had conceived independently in 1953, but in the new car's rear pillars and the way in which the front doors met the bonnet at the base of the windscreen. The body construction conferred great safety and allowed easy replacement of the car's non-structural, bolt-on outer panels, at a small cost in weight and lost inches for passengers and luggage. Weight was reduced, on the other hand, by the use of aluminium boot and bonnet lids. "I…think the

Rover cage isn't only intrinsically safe. It gives the car an acoustic deadness that implies solidity which, in turn, engenders driver confidence and calmness of mind; which, in turn, produces safe driving. I'm certain of that," said long-term owner and former *Motor* deputy editor, Rab Cook in 1980.[20] Although the magazine did not find the 2000 as refined as earlier Rovers in 1963, it was impressed by the car from the outset: "From the point of view of ride we would put it in the top three amongst European cars irrespective of price…. One has the impression that it was planned by engineers who are enthusiastic drivers and by stylists who put function before decoration, and the result is something of an object lesson to other manufacturers."[21] Sensibly, the car was planned and promoted as a comfortable four-seater.

British advertising for the 2000 was confident and imaginative. In October 1963 a double-page spread showed a cream car on the beach and summarized its features on the opposite page: "Rover engineering takes motoring years ahead. Rover 2000. The new light 2-litre saloon with Grand Touring specification. Meet the car that demonstrates what creative engineering really means— the Rover 2000. This new O.H.C. 2-litre saloon combines independent front and de Dion rear suspension — base unit construction — 4-speed, all-synchromesh gearbox — disc brakes all round — and a lavish, 4-seat continental-style G.T. interior…. Rover — one of the world's best engineered cars." In 1964 the car was seen in continental locations ("Internationalist…Individualist…Rover 2000 sets the lead in fine cars for a generation to come!") and a competition career of four-and-a-half seasons between 1962 and early 1966 allowed the 1965 headline: "Monte Carlo Rally 1965 — 237 started, 22 finished all stages. After covering 3000 high-speed miles through rain, blizzard and snowbound mountain passes, a Rover 2000, driven by Roger Clark…and Jim Porter, was the first Touring Car home. In the whole Rally, its performance was excelled only by five cars, all in the G.T. (Gran Turismo) Category— an outstanding performance by these two fine drivers."[22]

Themes varied during the mid-1960s. A 1966 advertisement borrowed the title of Vance Packard's well-known 1957 critique of advertising, *The Hidden Persuaders*, for its own ends: "Hidden persuader in the absolute car…. A fact or two…. The lightweight high torque o.h.c. 2 litre engine. Pulls well? Sure. Top gear is virtually an overdrive. The concave pistons give smooth combustion, silent running. Top speed is 105 mph…. The most successful 2 litre car in Britain."[23] In 1967 the 2000 was promoted as an intelligent choice in headlines such as "Some people buy this car for its name— If you want a better reason, read on" and "If you

Opposite: **Rover 3-Litre Mk II Coupé (P5).** Affluent escapism was the main theme of a lavish advertising campaign which promoted the new coupé (really a semi-sports saloon) alongside the established (1958) 3-Litre saloon in the early 1960s. Rover's advertising combined imaginative photographs with a flair for compelling imagery which extended throughout copy for the 3-Litre saloon, the new 2000 (from 1963) and various types of Land-Rover.

Drive 200 miles effortlessly, chair a board meeting or two, drive back—in time for a show and a late steak!

Relax—and leave the crowd behind!

Everyone travelling by road wants swift, safe, *effortless* driving. There and back. Rover engineering created two thoroughbred cars to give this – the Rover 3-Litre Coupé (shown here) and Saloon. Both are Rover-engineered throughout, with a unique combination of power and luxury that makes a long road shorter, a long day less tiring. Each reflects the famous high standards of Rover engineering skill in design. In construction. In reliability. The Saloon has been proved in the world's toughest rallies. The Coupé (developed from the Saloon) is the fastest car in the Rover range. With low, sleek lines, it offers high power and individual luxury. Both cars have a silent, high-

performance 3-litre engine, rich interiors, superb roadholding, long life, *lasting* value See your Rover dealer. Choose the model *you* like. Enjoy fast, relaxed driving at its thoroughbred best in Rover 3-Litre Motoring! Coupé Manual Model (including overdrive) – £1,536.10.0 plus p.t. £321.13.4. Total £1,858.3.4. Automatic Model – £1,588.0.0 plus p.t. £332.7.11. Total £1,920.7.11. Saloon Manual Model (including overdrive) – £1,412.0.0 plus p.t. £295.14.7. Total £1,707.14.7. Automatic Model – £1,463.10.0 plus p.t. £306.9.2. Total £1,769.19.2.

ROVER

ROVER 3-LITRE MOTORING — ROVER QUALITY THROUGHOUT

The Rover Company Limited, Solihull, Warwickshire. London Office: Devonshire House, Piccadilly. MAKERS OF THE WORLD-BEATING ROVER 2000

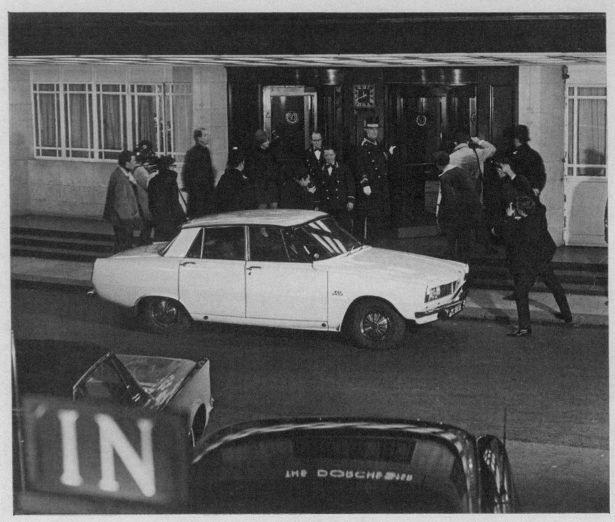

Some people buy this car for its name.

If you want a better reason, read on.

First we'll tell you what our car gives you. Then we'll tell you the name we gave it.

It gives you luxury.

Its scientifically designed seats are more comfortable than most armchairs. They certainly are better for you. On them is real leather where it matters most. On the floor is deep pile carpeting.

The engine is truly remarkable.

It has an advanced combustion chamber design and a racing-type overhead camshaft. You can have two versions. Quick. That's the single carburettor version. And quicker. That's the twin-carburettor model. Both sip petrol like misers. It is very quiet.

You'll soon get used to warning other cars that you're passing them. We're tempted to say that you could hear the clock ticking. But we give you a very quiet clock.

The maximum speed is way above the U.K. limit. Don't worry. We give you four-wheel disc brakes to restrain it. And unique all-round suspension that just swallows bumps and curves.

We designed safety into this car before safety was fashionable. It was recently awarded a special AA Gold Medal for safety.

You'll never have to pamper it.

After 3000 miles of torture-testing, the internationally famous "Car and Driver" motor magazine called it an "automotive milestone". Since then we've made some improvements.

So that may have been a bit extravagant.

It's too early to tell how long it will last you. But you could easily be still driving it in ten years' time.

In California it costs $4,198. And they're queueing for it. But don't let that scare you. Here it's only about £1,415. If that seems a fair price to you, we'll throw in its name free.

Rover 2000 T.C.

(Single Carburettor Manual or Automatic version available.)

The Rover Company Limited, Solihull, Warwickshire.
London office:
Devonshire House, Piccadilly.
Makers of fine cars, gas turbines and the world-famous Land-Rover

know one of Europe's Rover 2000 T.C. owners— You've got a shrewd friend." Refinement was highlighted in 1968, as two small children slept on the back seat: "When little things drop off at 70 mph you'll be grateful a Rover is still a Rover." Copy described the car's vibration-reducing "tuned harmonic damper" and de Dion rear suspension. The back seat appeared empty a month later as a distant sports car was seen through a rain-lashed rear window: "When you've moved on and left sports cars behind you'll thank goodness a Rover is still a Rover." Safety — always one of the car's selling-points— dominated 1969's advertising. "Are you driving a balloon?" asked a February headline beneath a picture of a balloon with a car drawn on it: "Is your car one in which only fractions of an inch of metal protect you in an accident? You could be about as safe as the air in a balloon. Frightening, isn't it? We build into every car safety features few other cars have. Like a safety cage that surrounds and protects you and your passengers. And a very strong bulkhead that is designed to prevent the engine penetrating the passenger compartment in the event of a head-on collision. Features that won for us an AA Gold Medal." The theme continued in 1970: "You can do it, but can your car?" asked one advertisement showing a wet country road with signs for a steep descent, floods, slippery surfaces and road works. In June 1969 a blue 2000 was shown in front view, its badges taped over. "A Rover by any other name would be competition.... We take extra time and extra care. Like giving every engine a complete bench test instead of just a brief check. And driving every car round our test track until we're completely satisfied. We build in special safety features too. Like a steel safety cage.... For these reasons, and more, Rover was chosen car of the year in North America, Europe and Australasia."

Rover withdrew from the United States in 1971, having sold comparatively few cars, but during 1965–67 the company produced some of the best safety-related advertising for any marque, domestic or imported, before or since. With the publication of Ralph Nader's *Unsafe at Any Speed* in 1965, the subject had become topical, as it had not been when last made the subject of a major automobile campaign (by Ford) in 1956. Perhaps the most ingenious Rover advertisement appeared in August 1965. The picture showed the White House with three Rovers, bumper to bumper, overhead: "To Whom it May Concern: Does Your Government Intend to Walk Until 1967?"— the cue being a government news release, "reported at length in a Times of New York dispatch" in which the General Services Administration had "drawn up a list of safety features that it will demand in the 38,000

1967 cars it will buy." Long copy described the Rover 2000's features and gave a full list of dealers from Mobile, Alabama to Worland, Wyoming. Rover invited the reader to fill in "Short Form 1776 AD" and to say how many 2000s he was interested in buying: (One? Two? 38,000?) Each one cost "$3800 East Coast, $3898 West Coast. Places in between cost in between."

1966–68 advertising pushed — even rammed — its point home. "Why is the owner of this Rover 2000 smiling?" asked a May 1966 headline above a sedan with a very bent front end. "Because he's alive." The engine had been deflected downwards; the steering column had collapsed; the front of the car had crumpled progressively; the seats, dashboard and glove boxes were properly padded and the car had disc brakes all round. "The stern fact is that very few cars have any of the safety features we have mentioned; and only the 2000 has all of them — and a good many more besides." Another 1966 advertisement showed the Rover and a light switch. "The Rover 2000 TC's *first* purpose is to be safe? For the same reason that a light switch, first of all, shouldn't electrocute you." The copy concluded: "In the recent furore over safety standards some spokesmen have pointed out that most accidents are caused by driver error. So? Is that an offense punishable by hurt or worse? And what of the innocents who aren't driving?" Advertising in February and March 1967 showed passengers in safety harnesses with the headlines, "How to get your wife to fasten her Rover 2000 safety harness: Tell her it drives men mad" and "How to get your husband to fasten his Rover 2000 safety harness: Tell him it's a Sam Browne belt and he looks like a World War 1 aviator." Some 1968 advertisements showed no car at all, but stood out by using white-on-black print: "Heaven can wait" began one, which described repeat purchases by Rover owners who had written off their cars but survived. Another asked: "It costs a little over $4000 to replace your crummy old second car with a Rover 2000. What do you figure it would cost to replace your wife and kids?" Long copy that pulled no punches, combined with quotations from independent road tests, made a convincing case. Unfortunately for Rover, the 2000 was too unusual, and insufficiently reliable under American motoring conditions, to sell well in the United States, even to the readers of the *Scientific American* where (among other magazines) these advertisements appeared. By 1968–69, however, domestic cars were being sold on their safety features, and it is possible that Rover's advertising contributed in a small way to injury reduction by encouraging the new climate in which the subject was taken more seriously than it had been.

Opposite: **Rover 2000 T.C. (P6).** Killing several birds with one stone: snobs are reassured that their decisions can be justified, while the rational are reassured that they will not be laughed at. The popularity of white as a car colour from around 1962 onwards allowed the photographer a nocturnal variation of the evergreen luxury hotel motif, and the 2000's image, more youthful than the 3-Litre's, makes the night-time excursion plausible. Taken together, these advertisements for the T.C. (see also overleaf) show the variation possible within a specified layout and overall (in this case upmarket-venue) theme.

The Field, June 6, 1967

GALERIE DU VILLAGE

If you know one of Europe's Rover 2000 T.C. owners

You've got a shrewd friend

Just 20 miles from England Rover 2000 T.C. is an exclusive imported car. And it takes a shrewd sort of man to separate the car from the glamour. Because this car has plenty of both. Internationally famous *Auto Visie* magazine called it "One of the best examples of a modern, handsome, manageable . . . high-class car which can be found today." And usually reserved *Berlingske Tidende* said, "This car is so wonderful, that it is . . . really beyond description." High praise. But is it justified? See for yourself.

Take a good look at its line: elegant, yet ruthlessly calculated for aerodynamic efficiency.

Now come inside. Look at its individual, deep-contoured seats; specially designed for restful high-speed driving. Notice the adjustable steering wheel; the cushioned trim; the real leather . . .

the hundred and one thoughtful Rover touches.

What about performance? T.C. means twin-carburettors. This car is fast. Yet with unique all-round suspension and crisp four-wheel disc brakes it is effortless to control. At any speed. And all the time you have the security of Rover's revolutionary deep-built safety.

Of course you may not want a car just for its features. You may like the glamour of an exclusive imported model. In that case there's just one more thing to say. Buy it here. You'll not only save money, you'll be making an investment

ROVER 2000TC
(Single Carburettor Manual or Automatic version also available)
The Rover Company Ltd., Solihull, Warwickshire.
Makers of fine cars, gas turbines and the world-famous Land-Rover.

Rover 2000 T.C. (P6). No doubt the patron of the Galerie du Village would have been pleased to see the Citroën influence in the styling of the popular 2000 saloon. The target market for this twin-carburettor car was younger than that for the more expensive Rover 3-Litre. The fad for imported cars was just getting under way at the time, and buyers were discovering the dynamic prowess of continental models. The 2000 was shown, by implication, to be at home in such company.

Take a Land-Rover and leave it for your wife to take Deborah to school, give Michael a driving lesson, convey half a ton of home growns to the church bazaar, cart home a crate of champagne for the baby's christening, collect the stranded speaker for this month's W.I. meeting. Now the only excuse you've got for missing the 8.25 this morning is that it isn't running.

Second Car? So who needs a first car!

Rugged chassis, 27 (rust-proof) functional body styles; four-wheel drive in eight forward and two reverse gears, petrol or diesel, over 80 optional extras, 120 pieces of specialised equipment. No wonder so many people take a Land-Rover. Rural dwellers can't do without them. Can you? From £710. Built by The Rover Company Limited, Solihull, Warwickshire. **LAND-ROVER**

Land-Rover Series II Station Wagon (88 in. wb). Land-Rover advertising usually showed the vehicle at work on farms or construction sites, or taking horseboxes, guns and dogs to sporting events. But while Land-Rovers were essential for farmers and for others who worked in the countryside (the Austin Gipsy was never a serious rival and most war-time Jeeps had worn out by 1960), a few advertisements targeted those commuters who lived in country deep enough for minor roads to be impassable in winter, but who for the rest of the year might be happy with a conventional estate car with good ground clearance — say, an Austin A60 or Morris Oxford — or perhaps even a second-hand Humber or Standard. This Station Wagon is therefore advertised as a year-round asset with a good dose of the snob appeal that would fuel the four-wheel-drive obsession of later years. The happy couple would, of course, be prevailed upon to tow everyone else out next winter, so it is just as well that they sound public-spirited here.

America's greatest influence on Rover's fortunes was with an engine—the light-weight, aluminium 3.5 Litre Buick V8.[24] Rover began work on the Buick engine early in 1965, and it was fitted into the 3-Litre body from 1967 (to create the Rover 3.5 Litre, or P5B) and into the 2000 body from April 1968 (creating the Three Thousand Five, as it was first called, or P6B). The Buick original "was a very nice piece of work" recalled test engineer Brian Terry, even if, after extensive detailed development—not least in the substitution of twin SU carburettors for the original Rochester four-barrel, which on hard corners shed petrol from the overflow causing the engine to die on one bank of cylinders—the Rover version was "very much changed from the American engine, far more than people realise, I think."[25]

Early British advertising showed the front of a red 3500 (as the car was called at the end of the advertisement) in the dark, with just the "V8" badge and part of the bumper visible. It was "The first car seriously to challenge the Rover 2000 in 5 years." The accompanying copy, at about 700 words among the longest of the decade for a single-page advertisement, quoted road tests, described features and, highlighted the engine: "Power flows from its new 3500cc engine as effortlessly as from a tidal wave. The road-holding attains new heights of achievement. The whole car acquires a character previously associated only with truly exotic machinery and unattainable sums of money." *Car* had reservations, finding the unpowered steering "as much as a strong man can deal with" on sharp turns taken fast, and considered acceleration from 0–60 in 13.5 seconds unspectacular compared with the 2000 TC's 16.3 seconds. The transmission—a Borg-Warner automatic—absorbed a good deal of the 184 gross bhp available, and a manual gearbox would eventually arrive in 1972. But *Autocar* managed 0–60 in 10.5 seconds and found the car durable on long-term test.[26] With the larger 3.5 litre V8 in October 1967, Rover emphasized refinement: "Rover announce the incredibly smooth new 184 bhp 3.5 litre V8. With apologies. Apologies to those who thought our 3 litre was the ultimate in smoothness. Because we now have to tell you to try our new 3.5 litre. It sets a completely new standard." *Motor* headlined its road test of the Coupé version "Power with pomp" and charged to 60 mph in 10.7 seconds compared with the 3 Litre's 15.8 seconds.[27] American advertising promoted the 3500 as the "Baby V8" which combined the best points of American and European cars with its own unique features. "To sum up," concluded a March 1970 advertisement, "Bigness in cars is a thing to be avoided, short of inconveniencing the passengers. The Rover 3500S is a splendid example of how, with ingenuity, this can be done without sacrificing any of the conveniences larger cars offer…test drive it, and we believe you'll see all the bigger V-8s for what they really are. Gross." If he read the advertisement, Raymond Loewy must surely have agreed—at least until he overheated in 105 degrees while several hundred miles from a Rover dealer.

20

(Reliant) Scimitar

"Join the GTE set!"

In 1961, Reliant[1] joined AC and BMW as a car manufacturer known for three wheelers and for specialized sporting cars. In 1968, the company became a true pioneer when it announced the fibreglass-bodied Scimitar GTE, a car with the style of sports coupe and the practicality — with a good proportion of the carrying capacity — of an estate car. During its development Reliant nicknamed it the "high performance estate," and the name was abbreviated by Lancia for the Beta HPE of 1975–84, designed within Lancia under Piero Castagnero. "The GTE created a totally different image," recalled its designer, Tom Karen, in 1986. "An ordinary estate has lots of glass all lined up around the greenhouse. With the GTE, we had the glass in the door, a thick pillar, then the rear glass over that rising waist-line whose area roughly matched that of the door glass. The result was balanced glass areas, not just a transparent box…. Actually, the first time I'd played with this type of rear end was back in 1963, and that thinking then led to the Robin…. Think of all the firsts on [the GTE]! It was the first sporting estate, for a start. It was also the first, for the same reason, to offer considerable luggage space. Then there was the rising waistline…. There was the kick-up on the rear of the roof. The split rear seats. The excellent aerodynamics — we didn't need spoilers or anything to overcome lift…. The whole thing gelled, and worked remarkably well. I can remember the launch very clearly — it was unbelievably exciting. We really didn't know what reaction to expect, and found people almost totally split — half loved it, half hated it. But it sure started a trend!"[2]

The GTE had no sports-estate ancestors to speak of. The Tornado Typhoon Sportsbrake of 1960, a kit car produced in very small numbers, could be counted only if ac-cidental resemblance in just one respect counts as ancestry. Certainly the idea that a sporting car should have a rear hatch was not new: the Aston Martin DB 2/4 and AC Aceca of the 1950s were well-known as, later, were the fixed-head Jaguar E-type (1961) and Triumph GT6 (1966). But these were not in any sense of the word estate cars, whereas the GTE was genuinely both a sports coupe and an estate car. The Volvo 1800ES (1971), Jensen GT (1975) and Lancia HPE all followed, as, from 1988, did an Eventer conversion of the Jaguar XJ-S by Lynx Motors International of Sussex. The Scimitar's closest equivalent was the Gilbern Invader estate car of 1971–72, built in Wales and developed, like the Reliant, from an earlier sports coupe. In most cases, as with other Gilberns, it was supplied partly assembled as a package of components in order to circumvent the Purchase Tax charged on complete new cars. But although the Gilbern was not a kit car by any normal meaning of the phrase and its fibreglass body was designed and built to a high standard, only about 105 Invader estates were ever made, while the more sophisticated Scimitar would continue until 1986, with 14,276 being built, compared with 473 Jensen GTs and 8078 of the Volvo. Internationally, the best known of the breed would be the Lancia, of which 71,258 were made.[3] The GTE would also inspire the Volvo 480 of 1987.

Reliant first became involved with sports cars in 1960, when the company arranged with Autocars Ltd. of Haifa in Israel to help set up a production plant there that would produce small cars and trucks. In that year, Itzhak Shubinski of Autocars visited the 1960 Racing Car Show and thought that a good sports car could be developed by combining an Ashley Laminates bodyshell with a chassis designed and produced by Leslie Ballamy for use in Ford Ten-based Debonair GT kit cars built at Tunstall, Stoke-on-Trent. The chosen body and chassis were well respected designs of their type from established manufacturers and would be extensively modified by Reliant before the car went into production. In the meantime the company produced a design study for the sports car and Ray Wiggin, Reliant's new assistant general manager who would soon become its managing director, visited Haifa with a wooden model and secured the order. The car would be powered by a 61 bhp, 1703cc Ford Consul engine and would be built from kits by Autocars and marketed principally to America's patriotic West Coast Jewish community. The Israeli company decided that the body would be most attractive to the American market if given a lengthened nose and huge chrome overriders, and prototypes were shown at the New York Motor Show in the spring of 1961. Autocars' production facilities took longer than expected to prepare, so the first 100 cars were built by Reliant, of which 98 were shipped to America for sale by Autocars. The Israeli company then agreed that Reliant could make and sell the design in England under the name of Sabre, so the two remaining cars from the original batch were converted to right hand drive; the new Reliant Sabre was announced in October 1961. Reliant subsequently sent a further 50 kits to Israel but in 1963, Autocars went into liquidation and the kits were impounded, where they remained until 1981.[4]

Early British advertising for the Sabre sold the car under the slightly contrived slogan, "swept motoring." "Reliant Sabre — Swept Motoring — a new sports car experience. New, exciting, different, the Reliant Sabre 1700 is everything a sports car should be — superb in the aerodynamic line of its fibreglass bodywork, startling in performance, magnificent in its luxurious comfort. Powerful front disc brakes for safe stopping, wide opening doors, wind-up windows — open car motoring with saloon car comfort." Beside the copy a simple monochrome photograph of the car appeared in a black circle. "It wasn't a very good car" recalled Ray Wiggin in 2001,[5] and commentors — and Americans — agreed, not least about the strange nose. The standard Sabre's Ford Consul engine gave a top speed of only 93 mph, and acceleration of 0–60 in 14.4 seconds was slow for any but the cheapest sports car. But it cost £1128 10s 7d or £1164 19s 9d with a hard top (plus £52 10s if an Alexander cylinder head and twin SU carburettors to give 90 bhp were specified) when an Austin-Healey 3000 Mk II cost £1202. Just 208 Sabres were made, of which 55 found homes in Britain, with most of the remainder going to mainland Europe. From 1962 a few were built with GT coupe bodywork in a style similar to that of the Ashley Sportiva. In the same year a version with a much more conventional and attractive nose and a 2553cc, 109 bhp Ford Zodiac engine was introduced and called the Sabre Six GT. Testing a GT in April 1964, *The Autocar* achieved 0–60 in 12.2 seconds and a top speed of 110.5 mph.[6] With a much better chassis, drivetrain and suspension than the 1961

original, the six-cylinder GT came first and second in its class in the 1963 Alpine Rally and was a greatly improved car, but only 75 were told, together with two six-cylinder open cars.

The most curious advertisement for the Sabre Six appeared jointly for "Reliant Motor Co. England" and "Autocars Co. Ltd. Israel," their names in the respective companies' chosen typefaces, in June 1964. There were three pictures. First was the "Sabra Sports Car. A dynamic sports car for the Israeli re-export market that combines exceptional performance with truly elegant design" — its overriders still firmly in place. Second was the "Sabre Six G.T. Derived from the 'Sabra', the 'Sabre Six' is a power-packed motor car designed for Great Britain to give effortless high speed cross country motoring with 'motorway' cuising at well over 100 m.p.h." And, finally, there was the "Sussita Station Wagon. A tough, good-looking station wagon designed for Israel to withstand…hard driving and give unrivalled performance and economy." It looked like a van version of a 1958 Datsun. In the middle of the advertisement, below the sports cars but above the Sussita and unconnected to the copy, were the words, "Israel's thriving motor industry."

If the average British motorist was baffled by the Sabre and by the advertisement, informed opinion thought that Reliant had developed Autocars' brief with remarkable speed and ingenuity, given its restrictions. Ray Wiggin was not about to give up sports cars. In 1954 the industrial designer David Ogle, a former Fleet Air Arm pilot who had graduated in industrial design from the Central School of Art in London, and who had subsequently worked for the radio and television manufacturers Murphy, formed his own company, Ogle Design, in Letchworth, Hertfordshire. He soon acquired a contract with Murphy's major rival, Bush, and became well known for his designs for the company. In 1959 he designed the Ogle 1.5 sports coupe (of which eight were built, based on the Riley One-Point-Five), and in 1962 he designed and began to produce the Mini-based Ogle SX1000, of which an estimated 66 were eventually made. And then, early in 1962, Boris Forter, the managing director of the cosmetics group Helena Rubenstein, commissioned a run of six sports coupes to be based on the Daimler SP250 chassis. David Ogle made some preliminary sketches.

In May 1962, however, Ogle was killed in an accident while returning from Brands Hatch in an SX1000, and Ogle's partner, John Ogier, asked Tom Karen, a naturalized Czech who had begun his career with Briggs and Ford and who in 1958 won a prestigious award for a four-seater sports car, to become the firm's managing director and chief designer.[7] Karen completed Ogle's initial sketches and a working prototype, called the SX 250, appeared at the 1962 Motor Show. A second car was completed early in 1963. Ogle originally hoped that Reliant would produce the SX1000, but Ray Wiggin declined. He loved the SX 250, however (as did William

Lyons when he saw it), and wondered if its body could be adapted to the Sabre GT chassis. It could: Karen modified the shell's substructure to suit, and the Scimitar GT was announced in time for the 1964 Motor Show with styling altered only slightly from the 1962 original.[8]

The Scimitar was distinctive without being eccentric, with a front very similar to that of the German Ford Taunus 17M of 1960, though the resemblance was rarely remarked upon as the Taunus was virtually unknown in Britain and the Scimitar, unlike the Ford, had four conventional headlamps in keeping with its character. "In those days cars had a lot of overhang, fins and awful things like that. This was completely different with a creaseline all round and a vestige of a spoiler—the first on a production car," recalled Karen.[9] Although its performance was respectable, with 120 bhp giving 117 mph and 0–60 in 10.1 seconds, the Scimitar's chassis continued to be developed and the car was updated in October 1966 with a 2994cc Ford V6 engine (and in 1967 with an alternative Ford V6 of 2495cc). Yet the Scimitar suffered from the patchy reputation of its ancestor, from the lack of the kind of marque heritage that mattered to many coupe buyers, and for its fibreglass bodywork, as many motorists were still prejudiced against the material. Between 1964 and 1970 only 1006 were sold, which made it a rare sight.[10] It might have benefited from more frequent and less understated advertising, too. "*One* word on the Scimitar GT—Unique" said a 1966 advertisement. "You would like to know more about beauty, power and luxury? Please write to Scimitar Division, Reliant Motor Company Limited, Tamworth, Staffordshire." True, the car was parked in a field with a girl looking beyond it into the far distance, but the copy seemed half-hearted. Tasteful understatement only really worked when the public already knew that there was something to understate; the reader's imagination, rather than doubt, then filled the gap.

The advertisement ran for six or eight months or so, and in 1967 the car was advertised by sports car specialists The Chequered Flag of Chiswick, west London as "a 2 plus 2 gran turismo car excelling in luxury, quality and elegance, outstanding performance (125 mph with 144 bhp)." Perhaps unwisely, the short copy concluded, "Very early delivery." The 3 litre version cost £1516 while the new 2.5 litre was only £1315. A 1968 advertisement was devoted to quotations from a *Motor* road test and was headlined with the editor's verdict, "Astonishing value for money." Owners' comments, reported the magazine, had been "probably the most uniformly favourable collection of owners' opinions we have yet received." Those who did encounter the car knew it as a good GT, but its rear seat room was very limited and its appeal was consequently specialized. In 1970 it was advertised as "the elusive GT." If the copywriter's point was that, in the Scimitar, desirable GT characteristics could at last be found, the copy could lead a reader with a certain mindset to wonder whether the Scimitar was deservedly rare. The word had not yet spread.

In 1965, however, a brighter future was prefigured by a show car produced by Ogle for the glass makers, Triplex. Based on the Scimitar GT, the Ogle GTS incorporated estate car bodywork with a short tailgate finishing just below the car's waistline and rear side windows made of bonded Triplex glass that curved into the roof. It was subsequently borrowed by Prince Philip, and attracted so much attention that he was not able to use it often. The car was later displayed for many years at the National Motor Museum in Beaulieu, Hampshire. The regular Scimitar, meanwhile, was selling slowly, and a version mocked up with a longer rear roofline did not convince Karen as being the solution to the car's slow sales. But when Karen returned from holiday in 1967, "there was one of those flashes from heaven. You know the sort of thing, lots of things you've been mulling over suddenly fall into place. We took that crude scale model, made from cardboard, plaster and foam, and reworked one half of it into what was basically the GTE form. Ray called in on his way back from the Motor Show in 1967 to look at various proposals, took one look at the model GTE, and that was it. Very few people have the boldness to take such an instant decision, but Ray did.... If you're going to quote me, mention the super relationship between Ray and myself. We've done a lot of work for Reliant over the years, and much of that was based on a direct dialogue between us. Ray is one in a hundred...."[11] There was, therefore, no direct link between the Ogle GTS and the GTE: "Tom Karen is quite adamant that it was not an evolutionary model towards the GTE," reported his interviewer, Mike McCarthy.[12] Nevertheless, Prince Philip's liking for the GTS anticipated the GTE's appeal: "The customers who bought the first GTEs were architects, surgeons, people like that who did not need a car with four doors so that they could take clients to lunch. The Design Council, in particular, panned it, but the GTE sold like mad."[13] It was launched in October 1968 for the Motor Show. It cost £1759, or £1823 with overdrive.

The GTE's popularity surprised even Reliant. In the spring of 1970, *Car* reported that there there was a six-month waiting list, and remarked, "Reliant sports cars are made only in very small quantities and are not heavily promoted in Britain or sold with any degree of push abroad. Nobody at the factory seems to be aware yet what a winner they have on their hands, or to see, as we think we can see, what formidable numbers they could make by pushing the product or raising the price. All of which, for those of us who feel convinced that a GTE is really the answer to the transportation problems of the young Briton on the move, and in view of the current delivery situation, is perhaps just as well."[14] The GTE was not completely unpromoted, however, and 1968's announcement advertising was spot-on. "Join the GTE set!" said the headline beneath a car shown outside an expensive London town house. The copy, sub-headed "Grand touring elegance plus estate versatility," expressed the point of the car simply and concluded, "Why didn't any-

JOIN THE GTE SET!

– with the new Scimitar GT E

Grand touring elegance *plus* estate versatility

The GTE set is the most exclusive in the country. *Only* Reliant offer the benefits of a grand tourer *and* a capacious estate in one luxurious car. The three litre version tops 120 miles an hour, yet returns an easy 25 miles to the gallon. And, there's seating for four adults with all their luggage.

Why didn't anyone think of a GT E before?

SCIMITAR GTE 3 Litre

Reliant Motor Company Limited
Tamworth, Staffordshire
Telephone: 0827 4151

one think of a GTE before?" That line was not unusual, but a product that lived up to it was. The GTE contained many details that appealed to an upmarket clientele, not least the split backrest of its rear seat, whose halves could be folded individually — a feature last seen in Harold Radford's Rolls-Royce and Bentley Countryman and Mini conversions. The car's positioning was consolidated when Princess Anne became a long-term owner and fan; she bought the last example made. An automatic version was announced towards the end of 1969 ("But that's not why it's unique…") and by 1972 the car was shown outside the obligatory stable with riding gear in the back: "Load-swallower GTE. Four seats. Not 2+2, four real seats. And a flat, full-width, estate-car-type luggage-deck. *And* 115 mph, whenever you want it. Remarkable…. This is an evolved, refined, extremely civilized car. There is, literally, nothing like it." The advertisement quoted *The Times*, for whom it was "the ideal car for the man who is reluctant to give up his sports car, but feels he must because of impending babies and push-chair paraphernalia." As a sporting, upmarket "lifestyle estate," it was arguably thirty years ahead of its time.

Opposite: (**Reliant**) **Scimitar GTE.** A stylish proto-yuppie conveyance which outlived subsequent rivals from Volvo and Jensen, the GTE started out in 1962 as a conventional-looking, Daimler V8-engined coupé by the industrial designer David Ogle, which Reliant put into production, Zephyr-powered, in 1964. This announcement advertisement wisely does not mention the glassfibre body (too many kit car overtones, however unfairly) or the "glue it, whack it and hope" quality of some of the interior trim. But it was as basically right as it looked, and people who liked it loved it.

21

Sunbeam

"For people with a ZEST for living"

"The car that has everything! Style — space — economy — speed with safety — It's new…from bonnet to boot! Look at the exquisite lines, the exciting new two-tone styling, the roomy interior. A brilliant 1.4 litre engine and overdrive on third and top gears give smooth acceleration up to speeds of around 90 mph…. Yes, the Sunbeam Rapier is a beautiful car in every way — and bred from a long line of Rally Champions." In the late 1950s the Rapier — described here in July 1956 — would become a rally champion in its own right, but the first version, introduced in October 1955 was a comparatively tame little hardtop, if unusual for that body style alone. It was also heavy (2360 lb.) for its 57.5 bhp, 1390cc engine and expensive at £1043 17s when a six-cylinder Ford Zephyr convertible cost £1036 7s. Cannily, Rootes introduced the Rapier ahead of the Hillman Minx on which it was based, so that the Minx would appear to have been inspired by the modern and upmarket two-door hardtop (or sports saloon, as it was usually called) rather than *vice versa*. The new Minx arrived in May 1956.

The Sunbeam name lent cachet to the new car as, however cynically used from 1938 onwards as part of the synthetic Sunbeam-Talbot compound marque, it was associated with some of the most glamorous racing, record-breaking and fast touring cars of the interwar years. Moreover, the early Sunbeam-Talbot 90 (1948–54) and very similar Sunbeam Mk III (1954–57) had been very well liked. But the first Rapier (retrospectively called the Series I)[1] was not truly sporting: its engine was hard-worked, its steering springy, its suspension roll-prone, its column-change cumbersome, and its roadholding, particularly at the back on wet roads, not good. In these respects it had not improved enough upon its semi-predecessor, the Hillman Californian

hardtop of 1953–55 (£780 5s 10d in its last season) to last long without further development.

But it did look good, thanks to Holden ("Bob") Koto and Clare Hodgman of Raymond Loewy Associates, who had devised the shape of the parent Minx in 1953. The Rapier, with its wraparound rear window, adopted the stylistic details, if not the overall proportions, of the 1953 Studebakers to which the Minx was more obviously related. And the Rapier was continually updated. In September 1956 it gained twin carburettors and an extra 4.5 net brake horsepower ("Now! More power, more zip…yet with generous m.p.g.") and an optional floor-mounted gear-change which was standardized for the Series II of February 1958. For the Series II, Tim Fry, the future co-designer of the Hillman Imp who had joined the Rootes styling department as an apprentice in 1953, devised tail fins: "The Rootes family wanted fins, to give the Rapier added visual length…. I must have sketched them out in 1956, one of the first things I did. We gave it painted headlight bezels, too, and a narrow painted side stripe…. [In original form] it did look rather dumpy. I also designed a lowered version of the old Sunbeam-Talbot grille…to give it a more upmarket apearance. It looked like a Minx before.[2] Kenneth Howes, who in 1957 joined Rootes from Ford Styling in Dearborn to become Assistant Chief Appearance Designer and as such to design the 1959 Alpine sports car, "completed the facelift on the front of the [Rapier] by designing the two side grilles."[3]

With the Series III of September 1959 the side flashes were made narrower and the side grilles were altered to include four rather than two bars each; the windscreen became deeper and wider; and the original square rear numberplate was replaced with a rectangular one. For the Series

IV of October 1963 the side flash was narrowed again so that from the doors forward it was simply a chrome strip; and the centre and side grilles were altered yet again to complement a new, less heavily domed, bonnet. Between February 1958 and October 1963 (Series II–IIIA), the Rapier was also available as a convertible. Mechanical changes included enlarged engines for the Series II (1494cc, 68bhp), Series IIIA of April 1961 (1592cc, 75bhp) and Series V of September 1965 (1725cc, 85bhp), and frequent improvements to the gearbox and its ratios and to the suspension, steering and brakes— including the adoption of front disc brakes (the first on a medium-sized British car) with the Series III. A walnut dashboard arrived at the same time, and the interior was further updated with the Series IV. The cumulative effect of so many alterations was to create, by 1965, a car very different from the 1955 original.

Rootes' advertising for the 1955–57 Series I was conventional for the Group and for its period. The car appeared in bright two-tone colour schemes such as red and beige, fawn and brown and—a favourite—black and yellow, which looked as dramatic in real life as in the paintings used in advertisements. A particularly natural-looking monochrome photograph was used in late 1957. For the Series II, paintings reappeared and Rootes emphasized the car's rally wins, beginning, in February 1958, with the Stuart Trophy awarded for being the first British car in the Monte Carlo Rally of that year, proudly displayed within mock laurels. More victories, such as "R.A.C. Rally — Outright Winner" and "1st & 2nd closed cars over 1300c.c.— Circuit of Ireland Rally" were added in successive versions of the same advertisement. [4] In September new artwork appeared in which the car sped stylishly through rough terrain. At the beginning of 1959, under the headline, "Record-breaking Rally Wins for the Sunbeam Rapier," the copywriter dispensed with the laurels—which were getting crowded—and told a picture story with small paintings which showed individual cars roaring to victory. Meanwhile a more conventional Rootes advertisement, running in parallel, showed the convertible with the hardtop, against a suburban backdrop rendered in pen and ink, in a smaller picture below. The copy was divided into "his and hers" paragraphs: "Men are enthusiastic about the power-plus 1½ litre 'Rallymaster' engine…. Women are enthusiastic about the dazzling good looks…exceptional comfort…. Stylish interior with rich carpeting…. Wide choice of contemporary colour schemes. Everybody's enthusiastic about owning the *individually styled* Sunbeam Rapier." The hardtop now cost £985 14s 2d, with the convertible at £1042 7s 6d. A Ford Zephyr convertible cost £1028 4s 2d while an open Hillman Minx cost £848 5s 10d.

Towards the end of 1960, a welcome testimonial came from Jack Brabham, who was shown beaming at the wheel: "It pays to buy a winner. There's nothing succeeds like success…. That's why you can have every confidence in the Rally-bred Sunbeam Rapier. I own one and its a great car…. A winner in every way." In 1961 conventional photographs returned — including, in May, an imaginative pairing of hardtop and convertible, seen from above — and Brabham's face appeared in a box at the foot of the page beside his testimonial. Early in 1961 he supported the Alpine, too, though by way of endorsement rather than testimonial as he did not seem to own one. By the end of 1961, conventional copy had reappeared in Rapier advertising although Brabham's face remained for a while. The new Series III was "For people with a zest for living." In pale blue with a dark blue flash and roof, sidelights glowing in the twilight, it was a glamorous car, and the glamour remained even in more informal, woodland settings during 1962: "For the man who wants all the speed off the mark, passing and climbing power, stability and sensitive handling of a sports car PLUS luxurious space and comfort, there is a special car…. In rally after rally, from the Monte Carlo to the Greek Acropolis, it has *proved* its performance, *proved* its reliability by winning top awards. If you really want to enjoy your driving, you must try the Rapier. Ask any Rootes dealer for a trial run." 1961–63 were the Rapier's glory years: its reputation was established and it was not yet outmoded. In later years it was advertised less often, and sales declined gently until the last Series V was produced in June 1967.

If the Sunbeam Rapier was a semi-successor to the old Hillman Californian, the new Alpine[5] sports car, launched at Cannes in July 1959, followed the Sunbeam-Talbot 90-based car of 1953–55 only in its name and number of seats. In 1992 the new model's designer, Kenneth Howes, recalled: "The Sunbeam Alpine was 100 percent my design. That sort of thing does not happen very often — being given the chance to design a sports car and to see it right through, unchanged, from clay model to mass production. It was a wonderful and exciting opportunity, one that I had been waiting for for years."[6] Howes had started his career in 1940 as a student engineer in the Swindon workshops of the Great Western Railway and, after qualifying as a chartered mechanical engineer, had joined Raymond Loewy's London office in 1948. When that office closed he moved to New York and thence, almost immediately, to South Bend, Indiana to work on Loewy's designs for Studebaker. In 1955 he left Raymond Loewy Associates to head a design group at Ford Styling in Dearborn. Two years later he was head-hunted by Rootes, who had already rejected an in-house proposal for a sporting car: "Other than [being required to use the Hillman Husky floorpan] I had a completely free hand. There was no restricting brief. I just went ahead and designed the car I wanted. I was never told I was producing a new version of the Sunbeam Alpine. It was looked on as a completely new car that would be a break from the past…. [Bernard Winter, Rootes' Head of Engineering who controlled the styling department] did not interfere in any way…."[7] Howes knew that the fins which were such a memorable part of his de-

for people
with a
ZEST
for living

THE IMPROVED SUNBEAM RAPIER

Once again Sunbeam makes an important move forward, with further refinements to the pace-making Rapier. There is a new, all-synchromesh gearbox for the 1.6 litre engine – giving silky smoothness to that famous Rapier thrust. And to match the smooth performance of the new gearbox, a modified front suspension for even better road holding. Now add to this the *ideal* driving position, with seat and steering wheel adjusting to your needs ; a light, self-adjusting clutch ; and servo-assisted brakes (disc in front). Then think . . . what other sports-car gives you saloon comfort ? What other luxury saloon gives you sports-car performance ? None but the Sunbeam Rapier. Drive one today.
£889.13.9 (inc. £154.13.9 p.t.)

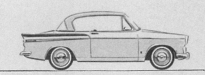

BY APPOINTMENT TO
HER MAJESTY THE QUEEN
MOTOR VEHICLE
MANUFACTURERS
ROOTES MOTORS LTD

ROOTES MOTORS LTD
LONDON SHOWROOMS AND EXPORT DIVISION: ROOTES
LIMITED DEVONSHIRE HOUSE PICCADILLY LONDON W1

sign would not be fashionable forever: "When I was working on [the original quarter-scale Alpine clay in 1957] Bernard Winter asked me how long fins would last. I said five years. Five years later they cut off the Alpine's fins! William Rootes had greeted the fins on the Alpine with enthusiasm."[8]

With a well-equipped interior, comparatively gentle suspension, an attractive optional aluminium hardtop (which included a wraparound rear window), and a 78bhp version of the Rapier's engine, the Alpine was well-received at £971 10s 10d as a "soft" alternative to the more vigorously sporting Austin-Healey 3000 (£1168), MGA 1600 (£940) and Triumph TR3 (£991). For Triumph TR3 owners, the Alpine's wind-up windows were louche, a first step along the way to the smooth-shaven decadence of, say, a Mercedes-Benz 190 SL (£2735)—but a few years later they would appear in Triumphs and MGs, too. Three hinged metal flaps concealed the lowered soft top to give a "flat deck" look to the open car. Like the Rapier, the Alpine was steadily developed through five Series[9] to become a "civilized sports car," as *Motor* called the Series V in 1966,[10] rather than simply a saloon in sporting guise. The Alpine continued until January 1968.

Alpine advertising, too, was gentler than that from Triumph or MG. In April 1961 the car was a shown on a cobbled street, top down, its fifty-something owners about to go on a trip. Neither looked dressed for a long or punishing journey. The Alpine was "sports classic.... There is nothing better in driving than putting the rally-bred Sunbeam Alpine through its paces. Here's pep, power...sensitive handling...flashing acceleration from the 1.6 litre engine...phenomenal stopping power from front disc brakes. If you want to enjoy going even more than arriving, the exciting Sunbeam Alpine is your car." In June the same couple appeared on one side of the page about to set off and, on the other side, speeding along a country road. Jack Brabham's endorsement accompanied both, and had been the subject of its own advertisement in January ("'It's a beaut,' says Jack Brabham"). For the international English-speaking market in mid-1962 the car was shown with whitewall tyres, its owners younger and more stylishly dressed: "The car with winning ways. This is the Sunbeam Alpine, winner of the Thermal Efficiency Cup at Le Mans 1961, winner of the Speed-Manoeuvrability Test in the Monte Carlo Rally 1962. Hits 60 in 13 seconds, hares round corners and stops from a 'ton' in next to no time." Competitive credentials established, the copy moved on to the car's strongest suit: "A winner on looks and comfort, too—especially with women. The roll-up windows mean a lady can let her hair down without getting windswept. While a snug-fitting soft-top (or optional hard-top) keeps warmth *in*, weather *out*...."

In early United States advertising, the $2595 Alpine was "Prettiest thing that ever kept a man waiting." For British buyers in 1964 the Series IV was "making the pace in the fast lane.... For sports performance with touring luxury, drive a Sunbeam Alpine." The rest of the copy was prosaic ("The modified compound carburettor needs no special tuning...") but the possible variations were extensive for a British sports car: a Sports Tourer (soft-top) model cost £853 8s 9d, and could be ordered with a hardtop, whereas the Gran Turismo Hardtop was just that—without a folded soft top beneath—at £913 17s 1d. Overdrive on top and third gears or Borg-Warner automatic transmission were available at extra cost. "This is the life!" began a June 1966 advertisement for the Series V, as an open model rolled through a bend on its whitewall tyres. In another picture, two small children played on the rear shelf: the Alpine was for the man who was slowing down, but who had not yet quite stopped. A year later the woman drove: "The trend is Alpine," confirming its reputation as a "ladies' car"—an image which by the mid-1960s genuinely reflected reality.

The "Alpine" that really caught enthusiasts' imagination was the Sunbeam Tiger of 1964, intended primarily for America but introduced to the British market in March 1965 at £1445 10s 5d. In October 1962, Jack Brabham and Stirling Moss, sharing an Alpine, took a respectable third place at the Riverside Grand Prix. In conversation afterwards with the West Coast manager in California for Rootes Motors Inc., Ian Garrad, Brabham wondered whether the car might just possibly take a V8.[11] Garrad asked his service manager, Walter McKenzie, to look for a suitable engine. McKenzie examined Chrysler, General Motors and Ford installations: the 260 cu. in. (4261cc) Ford would fit. Garrad then asked Carroll Shelby, who had created the AC Cobra with a similar engine, to devise a conversion. After much testing and modification, the car was shown to Rootes' directors in Britain and tested by the normally chauffeur-driven Sir William (Billy) Rootes, who then secured a supply of engines by contacting Henry Ford II and Lee Iacocca personally. The car was developed to its final production form by a team of engineers from Rootes and from Jensen of West Bromwich, who would build the car. As introduced the Tiger produced 168bhp (gross), giving 0–60 in 9.5 seconds, a standing-start quarter-mile time of 17 seconds and a top speed of 117 mph.[12] Later—especially modified—Tigers burned even brighter. (Equivalent figures for a 92.5bhp, 1725cc Alpine Series V GT were 13 seconds, 19 seconds and 96.3 mph.)[13] The Alpine managed 25.6 mpg overall, the Tiger 16.9 mpg. The early

---

Opposite: **Sunbeam Rapier Series IV.** By 1964, the Rapier had acquired a sporting image that distanced it from the now finless Minx. Action shots had long been used in Rapier advertising, but photographs took over from paintings in the early 1960s. "For people with a zest for living" was a long-running Rapier slogan. The intricacy of the chrome detailing, which extended even to the door catch, was impressive, but no amount of escapist copy could disguise the age of Rootes' increasingly outmoded product range.

SUNBEAM ✦ ROOTES

The trend is Alpine!

Now everyone with a taste for fashion is going for the Alpine! There's nothing like it for making you feel in line with the newest ideas! With its unique combination of Sunbeam sizzle and luxury touring comfort it's a natural! Things go smoother and swifter with the Alpine! 1725 cc engine develops 100 bhp. Acceleration is great, too.

Boot space is enormous for a sports car. There's 9.25 cubic feet for everything you're likely to need. You can't better this in the price area!

Cockpit comfort means every luxury for driver and passenger, with fully reclining seats. There is an occasional seat you can really use. And don't forget the full instrumentation and front disc brakes! Your Sunbeam dealer has an Alpine for you to try out now!

Recommended prices: Sports Tourer **£892** inc. p.t. GT Hardtop **£954** inc. p.t.

Optional extras—overdrive on third and top gears. Wire wheels.

To: Sunbeam-Talbot Ltd., Ryton-on-Dunsmore, Coventry. I am interested in purchasing a Sunbeam Alpine. Please send me literature and arrange for me to have a test drive. (I am over 18 years old.)

NAME

ADDRESS

SUNBEAM ALPINE

Tiger—subtlest of Q-cars with its chrome, Alpine hubcaps—was identified by thin stainless trim strips along its waistline. A Tiger II, with racing stripes and an "egg-crate" grille, was produced in small numbers during 1967 and was not marketed in Britain although a very few were converted to right-hand drive and remained in the country.

British Tiger advertising in the general media was infrequent and mild-looking, though Rootes were not shy about the car's performance. In April 1966 two photographs, side by side, each showed the car from above. In the first, the car sped towards the bottom of the page in a blur with the caption: "68 mph in second...." In the second it stood still, a woman at the wheel, her shopping on the back shelf behind the seats, with the caption, "20 in top." The copy elaborated: "It's not a mistake. The Tiger does toddle at 20 miles an hour in top gear.... But always ready to surge forward at your command without even a gear change.... It's got everything you expect in a sports car, with something you seldom get—docility. For all the 164 bhp developed by its V8 engine and 0 to 60 in 9.2 [*sic*] seconds, any housewife can take it shopping!" For all its appeal to enthusiasts, however, the shortlived Tiger was not a success.[14] George Bishop of *Car* found it, in effect, too slow for its engine capacity to qualify as a real high-performance car; too crude in its chassis; too under-tyred and under-braked to allow full use of the performance that it did offer; and too noisy and cramped for a gentleman's tourer. For what it could do, Bishop found it expensive.[15] In 1965 S.C.H. Davis was more charitable, finding the Tiger "truly a Sunbeam, a car with a fierce, animal character such as enthusiasts of earlier days loved.... Those who like this type of car are not worried by certain features which might disturb the 'A-to-B' motorists. Steering [always a weak point of the Alpine] is good if a little springy, the car holding its line on a fast curve as a good car should. There is a beautiful sound of mechanism doing its work well, which some may call a noise.... In all, the Tiger stands out as a car of character, a real sports car as befits a Sunbeam."[16] Like many cars of distinct and specialized character, the Tiger divided expert opinion.

Rootes had not finished with American themes, however, for in 1967 the Group announced a new Sunbeam Rapier,[17] based on the Hillman Hunter floorpan and mechanical elements but with styling remarkably like that of the 1965–66 Plymouth Barracuda. Yet according to stylist Roy Axe,[18] "It has often been suggested that the Rapier was influenced by the Barracuda but I can categorically say that we didn't know anything about the Barracuda when working on the Rapier. The first model had a roof very like the original Rapier's with a very large rear window."[19] The new, 2279 lb. car had a softer character than its namesake of the early 1960s, and at nearly fourteen feet, seven inches long was a foot longer, too. Its performance was good—0–60 took less than 14 seconds—but its road-holding was no better than its parentage implied. "What's the new deal to families bored by family cars?" asked Rootes in 1968, above a moody picture of a metallic blue Rapier against a black background, windows wound down to show its pillarless style and black vinyl interior, "The New British Dream. £1,323." As with the Humber Sceptre, the copy below was mainly a list of features.

In 1969, with imported cars taking ten per cent of the market, the Rapier was promoted as a GT car to tackle the European opposition: "If G.T. motoring is foreign to you, you'll want the British G.T. myth exploder—the Sterling Sunbeam Rapier." Copy was in the new "we-and-you" style, increasingly favoured by the mass-producers from 1967 onwards, which went down badly with some British motorists but was at least unstuffy: "There's no reason to look far to find real G.T. motoring. We'll bring it home to you with the exciting Sunbeam Rapier. It's got everything you'd expect from a car with its name.... You've got a close-ratio gear-box with sports type gear lever floor mounted between two shaped, adjustable front seats.... Servo assisted brakes will stop your grand tour just where you want."

The more powerful Rapier H120, developed by Holbay Racing Engines and fitted with a distinctive bootlid whose shape—ahead of its time—incorporated a subtle spoiler, arrived in December 1968. In 1969 it was advertised as "Today's Rapier H120. The vintage car of Tomorrow.... In the great tradition of Sunbeam.... The 110 b.h.p. H.120 has a top speed of up to 120 m.p.h. And the 1.7 litre engine with dual twin-choke, Weber carburettors takes it to 60 m.p.h. in around 11 secs.... The price is £1,503. Look upon it as an investment. Also the 100 m.p.h. Sunbeam Rapier, £1,242 and the new Sunbeam Alpine £1,085." By 1969 the "vintage" theme had become one of the minor standbys of car advertising; MG used it in Britain in 1964 and in America, with the "investment" angle, in 1965; and Mercedes-Benz would show a gull-winged 300SL in 1973. Chrysler's copy was optimistic, too, as *Autocar* managed just 105 mph in its H120 test car. "Up to" must have allowed for a very strong tailwind.[20] The new Alpine of 1969 was an unsporting but far from austere version of the Rapier with plain hubcaps and simpler equipment and with 78bhp rather than the Rapier's 88bhp or the H120's 105bhp. The Alpine's style and lack of pretension made in an appealing car, especially when seen

Opposite: **Sunbeam Alpine Series V.** One of the last advertisements for the Alpine, which was discontinued at the beginning of 1968 and was among the first of the civilized sports cars when introduced (with larger fins) in 1959. At a painting this illustration is unusual for 1967, but it anticipates a style of brochure photography that other marques would adopt in the 1970s, and the helicopter is very much of its period. The angled text recalled Crawfords' pre-war Chrysler campaigns and even a 1937 Ford advertisement for the V-8 "30," although "You can't better this in the price area" was an uncharacteristic piece of escaped sales-ese. Earlier Alpines and Rapiers had been promoted heavily with testimonials from the racing driver, Jack Brabham, whose name became familiar again in 1967–68 with the Brabham (Vauxhall) Viva.

in gold against Rootes' favourite black background: "Announcing the new Sunbeam Alpine. A pretty, expensive car that only cost £1,085. Pretty it is, expensive it isn't. When you pay £1,085 for a car you expect a certain amount. With the Alpine you get more"— and the copywriter was away with his list of features: "A line and finish that looks more like £2000.... Then to add to the expensive look there are things like a veneered facia. Centre console. All of this makes you feel good. We could tell you a whole lot more about the new Alpine. But we'd like you to see for yourself. Compare it with other cars at the price. We believe that if you see it you'll believe." Yet fewer than 50,000 of the Rapier family were sold between 1967 and 1976, which hardly made it a best-seller.[21] For many people it was just a little too big, a little too soft and a little too expensive for something so mass-produced in its character. For all its energy, the copy had not carried conviction that the Rapier was *better* than the continental GTs.

Much more appealing — though even less successful — was the Sunbeam Stiletto launched in October 1967. As one-time owner Graham Robson recalled, it "combined the fast-back style of the Hillman Imp Californian with the chassis and running gear of the Imp Sport, but was also treated to a four-headlamp nose style...reduced-camber front suspension and an upmarket interior featuring a unique dashboard, reclining front seats and a padded steering wheel rim. It was an attractive and good handling little car which never sold as well as it should have done." Only around 10,000 were built.[22] The name was probably a drawback: no-one without Rapiers always on their mind would think of a stiletto, first of all, as a dagger with a narrow blade; for most people it was a heel. The name, once heard, would lodge in a woman's mind and many women did like the car, which had a distinctly feminine character. Yet it was advertised to the group of men most likely, if forced by circumstances into a small saloon, to seek one with a masculine feel: "Zoom! The new Sunbeam Stiletto. For men whose wives think they've given up sports cars. Reassure your wife with a new Sunbeam Stiletto. Show her how luxuriously saloon it is.... Don't tell her it's got a race-bred Sunbeam Sports engine..." The disguise was a little too thorough, and it was discontinued in 1972.

22

Triumph

"Triumph put in what the others leave out"

The Triumph Herald was a breath of fresh air when it was announced in April 1959. As the second British small car with Italian styling—the Austin A40, introduced seven months earlier, had been the first—it revolutionized Standard-Triumph's image as a producer not only of interesting sports cars like the TR3A, but also of interesting saloons. The Herald's predecessor, which shared its 948cc engine, was anything but stylish. The Standard Ten was a homely thing, whose nature condemned it to be promoted with equally homely advertising. "Mr. Smith, our neighbour, took this photograph the day our Standard Ten arrived," said a proud—or at least cheerfully resigned—owner in March 1958. "We wouldn't be without our Standard Ten Companion," reflected Mother in June, as Father loaded a boat onto the roof, Mother herself stood behind the car with the oars, and two small children packed up a picnic basket with a conscientiousness beyond Dr. Spock's wildest dreams. Six weeks before the Herald's introduction, another family hugged the father who had bought a Standard Pennant: "Picture of a happy V.I.P. Not the sort who gets his name in the papers, but a man who is important to the people who matter to him. With his family around him, he's got everything he wants from life—plus that little bit more. A happy V.I.P...and the Standard completes the picture." In the United States, where the Standard name was practically unknown, the Companion was called the Triumph TR10 Companion and offered as a prize on television game shows such as *The Price Is Right*. At $1899, however, it sold slowly, as did the sedan.[1]

The Eight, Ten and Pennant range provided sound transport but lacked inspiration and proved resistant to updating. Styled by Vic Hammond under the supervision ("lift

that up a bit") of Walter Belgrove, the Eight had appeared in 1953, the Ten had joined it in 1954 and the Pennant of 1957–60 was all too obviously a stop-gap: "Ted Grinham came in one day and said he had just seen the Colin Neale Mk 2 Ford Consul with the peaked headlamps. He asked for a scale drawing of the...Eight and took a gold pencil out of his pocket, put a line along the side, added peaks at the front and back...and said, 'There you are. That's what I want', and walked out.... I did that chrome strip down the side under duress. Somebody had shown it to Ted Grinham and he said, 'Oh, that's nice, put it down the side.' Actually, there's a definite shape to it and it was put on upside down and nobody knew...."[2]

By early 1957, Belgrove and Grinham had left the company and Harry Webster, Standard-Triumph's inventive and resourceful chief engineer, knew that in-house proposals for the Ten's replacement, code-named Zobo, were inadequate: "We had tried and tried with all these styles in Coventry...and what we finished up with was a mechanical bathtub on wheels. I can't describe it as anything else. It looked dreadful...a 'zobo' is a Tibetan pack animal of indeterminate sex, half-way between a bull and a cow. Believe me, somehow or other that is what the lumpy thing looked like at first!"[3] Then, early in 1957, Webster met Giovanni Michelotti,[4] but even he struggled for several weeks with the "bathtub" prototype until Webster, calling in at Michelotti's studio while on holiday, asked him (in French, neither being able to speak the other's native language) what he would produce if given a free hand. Within minutes, he had sketched the eventual Herald,[5] and a silver and black coupe prototype arrived in Coventry on Christmas Eve, 1957.

The new body included small fins above chrome overriders, rather like those of a 1956 Chrysler but much more delicately proportioned, and would be produced in coupe and two-door saloon forms from April 1959,[6] as a convertible from March 1960,[7] as a (two-door) estate car from May 1961[8] and as a Courier van from February 1962. Early colour options included Targo Purple or Alpine Mauve, with matching interiors.[9] The expected sources could not supply monocoque bodies, so the Herald was designed around a backbone chassis, which allowed assemblers in export markets to build cars from completely knocked down (ckd) kits with minimal facilities. The Herald was assembled in India and subsequently developed there into the four-door Standard Gazel.[10] In Britain, Standard-Triumph made a feature of the chassis both in advertising and at the car's four-hour launch at the Albert Hall in London, where a car was dramatically assembled on stage in a much-rehearsed display that was repeated at launches in major world markets.[11] Unlike the body, Michelotti's interior was fairly characterless and austere, but a more British version was easily devised which included innovative details such as a dashboard in moulded fibre (which was was changed to wood for the Herald 1200 of 1961), adjustable steering wheel and seats, a recessed tray on the gearbox cover and a net in polythene-covered wire (like that used in washing-up racks) for small parcels. This interior, with its excellent driving position, would become one of the Herald's most popular features.

Triumph's advertising in the 1960s was among the most lively in Britain—even a little too lively. One 1961 advertisement read, "You are invited to hurl the new Triumph [Herald] 1200 at the nastiest corner you know…. If you really take it faster than you should, you may get a bit of tyre squeal. That's all." In the House of Lords, Lord Conesford considered the advertisement "an incitement to dangerous driving." Lord Chesham, replying for the Government, reminded the House that "the Government have no power to control the terms of commercial advertisements"—which at the time were comparatively unregulated. Standard-Triumph nevertheless withdrew the advertisement.[12] The Herald's swing-axle rear suspension was always controversial: with a transverse leaf spring of the right stiffness, set so that the wheels rested with a slight negative camber, it allowed relatively fast cornering for its day if the driver slowed and changed down before a bend and accelerated smoothly through it. "It steers impeccably, can be cornered extremely fast on a level keel without anxiety, and has excellent roadholding…it is a car which flatters an inexperienced or inexpert motorist, and should thereby contribute towards raising present-day standards of road safety," said *The Autocar*

of the coupe in May 1959, although a saloon tested in June was found to be "not as good."[13] Subsequent reports were less flattering, although individual cars varied and the suspension's effects could depend on tyres and road surfaces. One Herald 1200, abruptly cornered by a prospective Triumph customer, spun into a London news-stand (*via* a flower stall) on its demonstration run.[14]

In announcement advertising a happy couple welcomed the Herald. "It's a new experience in motoring!" exclaimed the slogan placed (unusually) in the centre of the page. At £702 7s 6d for a saloon and £730 14s 2d for a coupe, the Herald was not cheap when a 948cc Austin A40 de luxe cost £650 13s 4d and a similarly-engined Morris Minor 2-door de luxe cost £618 15s 10d. The Herald was therefore promoted on its equipment, which was good for a small car, and on its innovative features. One advertisement promised "Big insurance saving" in a special plan which took advantage of the straightforward repairs often allowed by the body's construction; another highlighted a turning circle of 25 feet which would be the centrepiece of many press, television and cinema advertisements for the Herald throughout its life; and a third—disingenuously—promised "Away with the grease gun!..The Triumph Herald means the end of greasing worries…. Normal greasing has at last been practically [sic] eliminated. The steering ball-joints require no lubricating whatever…." Read literally, the copy was true: the steering's top joints were ball-joints and they needed no lubrication (although replacement joints with grease nipples would become available) but the screw-threaded bottom joints did need regular lubrication with axle oil; without it they would wear, seize, and eventually cause wheels to become detached. And the only practicable way to administer the oil was with a grease-gun reserved for the job.

The 948cc engine of 1959–61 Heralds was small for the car, especially in the single-carburettor, 35.5 bhp form fitted to the standard saloon, so early in 1960 a saloon was shown in a dramatic line drawing, speeding along the M1: "Now you can enjoy the sensational Triumph Herald Saloon with all the verve, dash and liveliness of a twin-carburettor power unit." A box at the foot of the page gave performance figures for the new variant, which cost £737 15s 10d. In the same year, Drivers' World Championship winner Jack Brabham offered an 83bhp, Coventry Climax-engined Brabham Herald at just over £1000. His coupe of 1960 reached 60 mph in 10.8 seconds and a top speed of 102 mph; in 1962 the Brabham saloon was found to be a little slower.[15] The Herald's build quality was variable at first and early warranty costs were high, but the car improved and prices gradually became more competitive: by October 1964 a Herald 1200 cost

Opposite: **Triumph Spitfire 4 (Mk I).** Atmospheric, upmarket advertising for a popular sports car in 1965. It was comfortable by sports car standards, with wind-up windows in proper doors with external handles and independent rear suspension—although this was of the swing-axle type which was potentially lethal in inexpert hands. The bodywork was not very durable, and could flex and unlatch its doors when badly rusted, so that it was as well to keep the (optional) hardtop in place. Exports took priority, and early versions like this one, retrospectively called the Mk I and produced until December 1964, are very rare in Britain today.

The perfect two's-company car, the Triumph Spitfire, at dawn after an Oxford ball.

Black ties and Spitfire

Now you can buy a sports car with all the social graces—the Triumph Spitfire. It is elegant and fast. It is highly manoeuvrable (you can take it anywhere). It is classed with sports cars costing a great deal more.

The Spitfire is lithe, good-looking, aerodynamic. It sprints from 0-50 in 11 seconds—quickly reaches a top speed of 92 mph. For the extra-mercurial,

Triumph now offer three stages of tune. The most comprehensive gives the Spitfire a top speed of 107 mph.

A car for all seasons

To hold this energy in check the Spitfire has all-round independent suspension. Front-wheel disc brakes. And a 24-ft turning circle that makes it as parkable as a tea trolley.

Bad weather is no problem. The windows wind up. The hood keeps out wind and rain. (There's a hardtop available for the complete sybarite.) And inside there's comfort above and beyond the call of sports-car motoring.

Your Triumph dealer will arrange a free trial drive. No formality. The Spitfire doesn't stand on ceremony.

STANDARD ▮▮ TRIUMPH

A member of the Leyland Motor Corporation

£579 7s 1d compared with £575 10s 5d for a 1098cc, 2-door Morris Minor de luxe, and £575 10s 5d for an 1197cc Ford Anglia Super. The Herald would sell very well throughout the 1960s, and this was in no small part due to its advertising, which built on its genuine appeal as a good-looking, innovative and useful car. It was particularly popular with women, who did not usually drive it hard and who appreciated its light controls and "all-corners" visibility. The tight turning circle really did make town shopping easier, whatever the gender of the shopper.

In 1961, when Mather and Crowther took over the Standard-Triumph account from George Cuming Ltd., who had been Standard's agents since long before the Second World War, Triumph advertising acquired a distinctive look that would outlast the decade despite the account's being relinquished to Hobson Bates & Partners in 1966. In Mather and Crowther's chosen layout, a large photograph of the car in an optimized but realistic setting was placed above a witty headline and long, often humorously written copy which described the practical advantages of individual features. The layout would become all but universal in British car advertising by 1974. Successive advertisements built upon each other: "Following the strip cartoon and the TV soap opera the continuing theme finds new favour," remarked Michael Frostick, reviewing the campaign in 1970.[16] Headlines were imaginative, such as "Only a hovercraft has more independent suspension than a Triumph Herald" and "The Triumph Herald U-turns where other cars Y-turn" in 1964; "The Triumph Herald's bumpers are covered in rubber. Instead of dents" and "The Triumph Herald is founded on steel girders (like most things that are built to last)" in 1965; "Join the Triumph Herald round-in-one club (and U-turn in just 25-ft)" in 1966; and — best of all — "The girl gets dated. The Triumph Herald doesn't" in 1967, which made the most of the car's feminine appeal and of the fact that the convertible, shown with a girl outside Mary Quant's Brompton Road bazaar, was "the only modern low-price 4-seat open car on the market today."[17]

A light touch characterized cinema and television advertising, too. The driver of a Herald 12/50 spots a pretty girl and, naturally, performs a quick 25-foot U-turn and follows her: "In a Triumph Herald you can really follow your intuition," says the cheeky-chappie voiceover, "It's the most go-anywhere car in its class." The girl walks down some steps. The car follows, its driver focused on the girl's disappearing bottom. "Thanks to all-round independent suspension, the wheels soak up the bumps. While you soak up the scenery." Then her boyfriend appears. She stops; they kiss; retreat

seems a good idea: "There's a very quick gear-change too," says the voiceover, as the car reverses back up the steps. "It could only be the Triumph Herald. Ask your dealer for a trial drive."[18] In "Getaway in a Triumph Herald," a cloth-capped car thief steals a Herald and leads the police into a tight spot in which he can turn round but which confounds the police Wolseley. After a chase in which he scoots between obstacles which the Wolseley lumbers round or overshoots, he loses his pursuers and spots a small space between two parked cars. With a tight turning-circle, he can squeeze in. What he doesn't see is that one of the other cars is the police car. The Herald's features, such as "hairpin cornering," appear on the screen at the end.[19]

Home market advertising was not really needed for the Herald-based Triumph Spitfire,[20] yet the little sports car was not completely neglected. The Spitfire, like the Herald, was produced almost exactly as Michelotti designed it, except for the interior. It shared the Herald's swing-axle suspension and its manoevrability — not to mention the associations carried by sports cars everywhere, especially when red, as in June 1966: "Hairpins never trouble the Triumph Spitfire owner (though he may have to sweep them out of the cockpit). Without being the slightest bit ladylike, the Triumph Spitfire Mk 2 is a lady's car. Not that the ladies go much for actually *driving* them, but you do see a lot of very talented passengers. Now why? What makes the Spitfire such a homage-wagon? Possibly the way it's capable of reaching 90 mph with a deep, resonant purr — the sweet, unraucous sound of power…. Or maybe it's the deeply padded bucket seats which hold them masterfully in snug reassurance. But, you know what women are, probably they just like being seen in something that looks as if it came out of 'La Dolce Vita.' Not out of toyland. Or…wait a minute. Go to the mirror. Open your shirt, ruffle your hair. You don't think it's anything to do with the type of man that drives a Spitfire? Do you?"

The Spitfire's great advantage over the rival Austin-Healey Sprite and MG Midget (though not the MGB) was that a tall man could drive it more comfortably, so in theory "ladies" who liked their men tall preferred Spitfire drivers. But many six-foot Midget fans improvised, and in real life women often drove Spitfires themselves, usually in white, maroon or one of a number of shades of blue rather than red. The Spitfire was fun rather than macho, and its styling gave it a genteel sophistication, so that 1964's advertising could show it in Oxford at dawn as well as on a hairpin bend or streaming race track. The car appeared on a country road in 1965; in a London mews in 1968; and

Opposite: **Triumph Spitfire Mk II.** The great majority of Spitfires were exported and only a few advertisements for each Mark were published in Britain. The car was as popular in Australia and North America as in its home market, and it was a favourite in club events. This 1966 Australian advertisement, with a large photograph of the car at speed and smaller pictures of it from different angles, follows the general scheme of the home market catalogue and describes improvements over the Mk I. "A ride as soft as it's safe" could be taken the wrong way, as by saloon car standards it was harsh and gave a curious light wiggle on small bumps, though it was noticeably better than a rigid axle over rail crossings. Enthusiasts all over the world now restore them, performing miracles with heaps barely recognizable as cars, let alone as Triumphs.

Turn the new
TRIUMPH Mk II SPITFIRE
inside out...

...and find a power of difference!

Outside, only the aluminium grille and MK11 motif reveal the new Spitfire. (Why change beautiful lines?)

But inside . . .

An engine boosted to 67 b.h.p., with new high-lift camshaft, extractor exhaust, modified inlet manifolding, etc., and stronger, competition-bred clutch to cope with the extra zip. 0 to 50 under 10 secs., betters 19 secs. for standing quarter-mile, 96 m.p.h.

A cockpit fitted out in luxury, with deeper, softer, contoured

seats; upholstery in plush, two-way stretch vinyl; door-to-door carpets; black-trimmed waist rails, facia and windscreen surround; safety padded grab handle and parcel shelf leading edge.

A strengthened body and chassis, with steel girder members and panels reinforced at strain points to give greater rigidity. Tough, rattle-free construction and fixings.

A ride as soft as it's safe, with all-round independent suspension giving an even softer, safer ride by improvements to rear suspension. Fade-free, self-adjusting disc brakes.

A finish impeccable in detail, with immaculately-appointed engine compartment, bright with chrome and polished aluminium, sure-grip "Deerhide" steering wheel trim, chromed Spitfire MK11 on

boot lid, wheel trims. And, to let you sound off on new Spitfire value, uprated horns.

LE MANS, 1965. Fifty-one cars started, 14 finished. Two were Triumph Spitfires, 1st and 2nd in their class, 5th and 6th overall in the G.T. category, in company with 5 Ferraris, 2 Porsches, 1 Cobra, 1 M.G.B., 1 Austin Healey, 1 Iso Grifo, 1 Rover B.R.M.

TRIUMPH Mk II SPITFIRE

£1099

AUSTRALIAN MOTOR INDUSTRIES LTD. COOK STREET, PORT MELBOURNE. VIC. — OR YOUR NEAREST TRIUMPH DEALER

"among the birds and breeze," as the copywriter put it, in 1970. In March 1967, when the Spitfire became a Mk 3 and its front bumper was placed in front of the grille, it acquired a slightly French look, and a reader knowing no better might have expected a whirring overhead-camshaft engine and supple suspension in the style of, say, a Peugeot 204. No chance: underneath the continental style was a traditional English sports car, bumps, rattles and all, yet it offered good value at £751 10s 3d with a hardtop in February 1968, and even in mid-1970 "the fun runner" with "Roadhold...cat-sure and confident" cost only £886 3s 0d in the same form.

In 1961, Lord Conesford's objection to Triumph's exuberant copy had struck many as fussy and over-literal, but in 1965 the climate changed when Ralph Nader published *Unsafe at Any Speed*. The book gave Triumph's copywriters food for thought, as the Herald-based cars had the same kind of swing-axle rear suspension as the rear-engined Chevrolet Corvair which was the main object of Nader's invective, even if the Triumphs' stiffer springs, lighter weight and more favourable weight distribution made them less dangerous than the Corvair, the Renault Dauphine or the VW Beetle. In a patent application filed in May 1956, the former head of research and development at Chevrolet Division of General Motors, Maurice Olley, had remarked on the "potentially dangerous vehicle handling characteristics" bestowed by swing axles, but he had been ignored.[21] The dangers were also known to Triumph's engineers, who realized in 1958 that a "pivoting transverse leaf rear leaf spring would solve the problem completely — yet this was not adopted for the production chassis until the Spitfire Mk IV of 1970."[22]

Triumph had reason to be worried: threatened safety legislation that arose out of the culture of concern created by Nader's book would lead the TR7 of 1975 to be announced only as a hardtop. In the meantime (except in cars destined for the United States, which retained the TR4's rigid axle), the Triumph TR4A had a trailing arm rear suspension more sophisticated than the Spitfire's swing axles, and in February 1967 Triumph implicitly challenged Nader with the headline, "Safe at any speed — the Triumph TR4A." The copy continued: "There are two sides to safe driving. How safe are you? How safe is your car? If you are an aggressive fathead, the Triumph TR4A will not improve your safety rating. (Nor will any other car in the world.) But if you are a considerate driver, you will find the TR4A is among the surest-footed high-performance cars you can buy." There followed a sub-heading, "Speed for safety's sake" and justifying copy: "The top speed of the TR4A is neither here nor there. It is, in fact, about 40-mph more than our present limits here, so you had better save it for there." In the pic-

ture a car ran beside a light aircraft taking off: "TR4A finds a rare opportunity for exercise at full throttle, on the perimeter of an airfield," said the caption. The copy concluded irreproachably: "Safety, like other things, is what you make it. The TR4A invites you to make it your driving philosophy. See your Triumph dealer for a demonstration of the good sense of the TR4A." During 1967–68, Triumph made a marque-wide slogan of the theme: "Triumph puts you safely ahead."

Earlier TR advertising was more traditional, and emphasized the car's masculine appeal: "Why does the Triumph TR4 separate the men from the boys? ...A tough, lusty and very fast sports car. A man's car that has been proved over the world's most punishing rally courses.... Twenty minutes in a TR4 will how you just what a *real* sports car can do for a man. And vice versa." At £949 2s 6d for a hardtop model, it was almost practical, too. In 1965 the TR4A was "to give the man who drives hard a real ride for his money...for men who accept a thoroughbred's challenge. You?" With the six-cylinder TR5 PI of 1967, Britain's first fuel-injected production car, the appeal became more subtle: "Open up a whole new world of sports car driving in the TR5 PI," and a 1969 advertisement for the TR6 PI showed the car in front view — "Take a good look at the hot new TR6 PI while you've got the chance" — and then from the rear: "This is all you'll usually see."[23]

With the six-cylinder, 1596cc Vitesse introduced in May 1962 (and its 1998cc 2-Litre successor of October 1966), Triumph made the most of existing bodies and engines, and the old Herald rear suspension, much criticized by the press in this more powerful car, was eventually replaced for the Vitesse 2-Litre Mk II introduced in October 1968. The "Vitesse" name was a revival from the 1930s. The car's new small "six" was the same size externally as the two-litre engine used in the Standard Vanguard Luxury Six, and a two-litre Herald coupe with a new bonnet cleverly styled by Michelotti to accommodate the larger engine had been used by Harry Webster personally in 1960.[24] At £837 0s 3d in 1962, the Vitesse was the cheapest six-cylinder car in Britain, not fast (0–60 took nearly 17 seconds) or particularly economical (25mpg) for its weight (17.75 cwt), but much more refined than the Herald, and with a more modern sporting character than the Sunbeam Rapier or Riley One-Point-Five.

In 1962 the new Vitesse was "The smooth six...the supple six...the smart six...the safe six," and was targeted towards female motorists and men newly deprived of their sports cars: "Darling, you haven't lost a sports car, you've gained a Triumph Vitesse" said a January 1966 headline, as a proud father held twins while the mother, watched by a

Opposite: **Triumph Vitesse 2-litre.** A Vitesse with unusually good panel fit is posed in an upmarket setting in 1968. The choice of Harley Street as a backdrop was clever, suggesting wealth, discrimination, detail craftsmanship and perfectionism, as well as a certain snob value, in one go. The headline indicated the onset of knocking copy; until the mid-sixties, manufacturers had been reluctant overtly to compare each other's products in advertising, but such coyness was on the way out by 1968. Within a few years, names would be given.

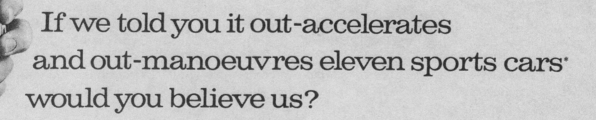

The Triumph 2-litre Vitesse...

If we told you it out-accelerates and out-manoeuvres eleven sports cars* would you believe us?

The Triumph Vitesse may be a four-seater, but it certainly doesn't act like one. In fact, 'Motor' calls it the sportsman's saloon. With its 2-litre, 95 b.h.p. engine she takes a mere 8.3 seconds to go from 0 to 50. But while surge is always there, noise never is. That's the beauty of six-cylinder motoring—you overtake so *quietly*.

Mind you, the Vitesse is far from being just a straight-stretch performer. On fast corners, for instance, independent suspension keeps the wheels tight down on the road. All four of them.

You get this same security when you touch the disc brakes. Or handle the light, positive steering which gives you that fantastic 25-foot turning circle. So when you park, you can slot the Vitesse in almost anywhere.

The price is equally impressive. For all this liveliness we ask just £838.15.7 for the saloon ; £883.0.7 for the convertible, purchase tax included. And a test drive, remember, costs nothing. How soon are you going to become a Vitesse man ? *Check the figures for yourself in 'Motor' Road Test Summaries.*

Standard-Triumph Sales Ltd, London Showrooms: Berkeley Sq. London W1. Grosvenor 6050   **Triumph puts you safely ahead**

concerned-looking Matron, got into the driving seat to leave the maternity hospital, where the Vitesse was "equally at home [as]….in the car-park at Brands Hatch," according to the caption. "New mothers will note the wide doors (which hold themselves open as they get in and out)" added the copy, side-stepping a small disadvantage of the Herald body, which was that the doors swung shut under their own weight unless pushed right open. The same was true of the Spitfire.[25] Sporting speed as well as character arrived in 1966. "New 2-litre Triumph Vitesse out-accelerates and out-manoevres eleven leading sports cars! Check the figures for yourself in 'Motor' Road Test Summaries" said a May 1967 headline, in comparative advertising which, as it did not name the sports cars, stopped short of direct knocking copy (which was unheard-of at the time). The theme continued into 1968. In April 1969 the 2-Litre Mk 2 was "The 2-seater beater" with "new wishbone independent rear suspension to make sure you're as safe on the corners as on the straight." It cost £972 6s 5d, or £1020 12s 6d as a convertible. Always too specialized to be a best-seller, the Vitesse sold best in its early years when GT versions of modern, mass-produced saloons had yet to become commonplace. In later years it became a respected enthusiasts' car in 2-Litre form and found a low-production niche until 1971.[26]

Even more specialized was the Triumph GT6,[27] a sporting fastback introduced in October 1966. "All the world wants the new Triumph GT6" said a January 1967 advertisement showing a white car on wire wheels disappearing into the sunset. The world outside the United States had to wait until January 1967 for deliveries, however, such was the demand for the car. With the engine of the Vitesse 2-Litre and a lift-up rear hatch, the GT6's character was quite different from that of the Spitfire on which it was based, and on this model the rear suspension was unquestionably lethal if the car were mishandled. On the other hand its price of £1158 5s 6d took it out of the price range — and perhaps, as a closed car, out of the fantasy range — of many careless and inexperienced drivers. In America the GT6 was advertised as "The fasterback with the fog-free window," an electric heating element underlining the model's un-sports-car-like completeness of equipment. In 1968 a GT6 Mk II arrived with improved rear suspension like that fitted to the Vitesse 2-Litre Mk 2, and with the Spitfire Mk 3's raised front bumper. "Our winning streak" said Triumph in May 1970, showing a red car whizzing past a blue display chassis, which offered "more sting, more cling." "Underlying all the glamour, there's Triumph engineering. *Safety* engineering," explained the copy, which mentioned the car's radial ply tyres,

anti-burst door locks, collapsible steering column and strong steel chassis. In a head-on accident (as the copywriter did not say), the other car might have to be the crumple zone.

Triumph's sporting reputation did much for the appeal of its modern saloons — the £1094 Triumph 2000 Mk 1 of October 1963,[28] and the £797, 1296cc Triumph 1300 of October 1965. The 1300 — in spirit a kind of British Lancia Fulvia berlina and unique in Britain, for a small luxury car, in not being based on a cheaper model — was Triumph's first and only front-wheel-drive design. A 1968 advertisement called it "The limousine with everything except limousine length"; in 1970 it was "The short answer to the limousine." Its styling, devised by Michelotti to echo that of the 2000, was settled by May 1963 and the car was initially envisaged as a replacement for the Herald 1200. But when the Herald proved unexpectedly popular and a car was need to fill the gap between it and the 2000, the 1300 was developed as a more upmarket, supplementary model. It continued until 1970 and evolved, with a new grille and tail, into the 1500 of 1970–73, and also, with rear-wheel drive, into the inexpensive Toledo of 1970–76. The 1500's style joined with the Toledo's rear-wheel-drive layout in the 1500TC and Dolomites of 1973–1980.[29] The 2000, meanwhile, inherited the six-cylinder engine of the Vanguard Luxury Six but none of that car's comparatively dour character, and the dated and uncertain associations of the Standard name ("elevated and upstanding" or "the opposite of de luxe"?), together with the positive success of "Triumph" since 1959, meant that the old marque was abandoned for good. The strategy worked, as the 2000 became fashionable[30] and was forever compared with the innovative, slightly more expensive (at £1265 9s 7d) — and only four-cylinder — Rover 2000 introduced at the same time.

The comparison was not lost on Triumph's copywriters, who in February 1967 referred to the Triumph 2000 as "the only car in this price range [then £1198] to be consistently bracketed with cars costing £150 more" in an advertisement whose headline marked the distance between genuine upper-middle market saloons and titivated versions of ordinary saloons: "When you realise that all-round independent suspension matters more than two-tone paint, you're ready for the Triumph 2000." The headline was backed up with a compliment from *The Times*: "Over Belgian pavé and unmade roads astonishingly fast and smooth progress was made, where the average family saloon would have become unbearably unstable." 1966–68 advertising for the 1300 quoted *Autocar* ("The Triumph 1300 is the best

---

Opposite: **Triumph 2000 Mk I.** The testimonial was an unusual form of advertising by 1968, and was more commonly found coming from a famous personality, as with the racing driver Jack Brabham's pieces for Sunbeam at the turn of the decade. The speaker here is not famous, but quality and mechanical competence are imputed to the car by his status, so that enthusiasm was bolstered with a measure of objectivity. There was more than a hint of Alfa 2600 Sprint in the rear wing line, although the front was distinctive enough, and was reflected in the design of the dashboard (imagine the headlights as instruments and the leading edge of the bonnet as dash padding). Triumph's advertising was notable for its excellent photography, which continued into the 1970s.

The Autocar, February 29, 1968

Lieutenant Commander Tim Hale keeps quiet about his nuclear powered submarine but he can't stop talking about his Triumph 2000

Tim Hale is first lieutenant aboard HMS Warspite, Britain's latest nuclear powered Hunter-killer submarine. When he isn't driving around in the Warspite, he's driving his Triumph 2000. And all in all he has quite a lot to say about it.

How long have you had the Triumph 2000?

'Let's see, it must be something like eighteen months now, I suppose. And I've done nearly 20,000 miles.'

What made you decide on the 2000?

'Well, this is the thing: I wanted a car which would get me about fast and comfortably, with enough room in it to chuck all my kit. The 2000 answers it. After all, I'm used to travelling in a pretty fast, sophisticated way at sea, why shouldn't I travel in the same way on land?'

And are you pleased with the car?

'Yes, very. As I say it's a comfortable car, reliable, with bags of oomph in it. When they were building Warspite up at Barrow-in-Furness, I did the odd week-end down to my home in Devon, and it was really nice to have a decent car. I used to get on a big road, put the needle on 70 and leave it there. And do you know, I never felt that engine being strained at all.'

What do you like best about the Triumph 2000?

'There are several things really. One, I can get the seat back far enough — I've got long legs; it's quiet to drive; and it's powerful enough to be able to get on with the job. Six cylinders make a lot of difference.'

How about the finish?

'The finish on the Triumph, I reckon is good. There's also quite a bit of metal behind it, so you can have the odd little scrape with a bumper and it doesn't show. I know it's only a tiny thing, but tiny things are important.'

Are you happy with the gearbox, the ratios?

'The gears I think are absolutely splendid. I didn't have the automatic deliberately, be-

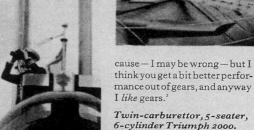

cause — I may be wrong — but I think you get a bit better performance out of gears, and anyway I *like* gears.'

Twin-carburettor, 5-seater, 6-cylinder Triumph 2000. Saloon £1,197.13.11, Estate £1,455.16.5, ex-works including PT. Optional overdrive £61.9.2, automatic drive £95.17.6.

TRIUMPH

TRIUMPH PUTS YOU SAFELY AHEAD

STANDARD-TRIUMPH SALES LTD.
LONDON SHOWROOM: BERKELEY SQUARE.
LONDON W1. PHONE: GROSVENOR 6050.

Triumph 2000. 6 cylinders, 90-BHP. 5 seater. Leather seating. 'Full-flow' ventilation system. All-independent suspension. Saloon £1,197.13.11. Estate £1,455.16.5. Ex works with p.t. Extras: overdrive or automatic.

When you realise an estate car can be lean, low and lovely, you're ready for the Triumph 2000 Estate

An estate car is not most people's idea of a *concours d'élégance* winner. But then the Triumph 2000 Estate is far removed from most people's ideas of an estate car.

It is quicker off the mark than most sports saloons. A car that moves from 0 to 50-mph in 10.7 seconds is very near the top of the league for acceleration. Even more useful, the Triumph 2000 Estate is phenomenally quick from 40-mph to 60-mph—and these are the critical speeds for safe overtaking.

And don't think that the beautiful swept lines of the Triumph 2000 have cramped its load-carrying style. With the rear seat folded flat there is 50 cubic feet of loadspace, and the loading platform has a maximum length of 5 ft 3¾ ins and a maximum width of 4 ft 6¼ ins.

This freighter with the lines of a greyhound has all the talents of the Triumph 2000 saloon. A six-cylinder engine ('effortless quietness no four-cylinder unit can equal'— *Sunday Times*). All-round independent suspension ('scrabbles round corners like a cat'—*Sunday Express*). Beautiful perforated leather seating and 'full-flow' ventilation (no comment—this speaks for itself).

See the new Triumph 2000 Estate at any Triumph dealer, and you'll realise why this slender beauty seduces strong men away from fastback coupés.

STANDARD-TRIUMPH SALES LTD.,
LONDON OFFICE AND SHOWROOM: BERKELEY SQUARE
LONDON W1. TEL: GROSVENOR 6050   **TRIUMPH**

small car currently available"; and "One of the safest cars available today"), the *Daily Mail* ("Car with the built-in everything") and the *Daily Mirror* ("Even in cars costing more than £4000 I have never tried more comfortable seats.") The last writer was not being fulsome or eccentric: the 1300's seats really were some of the best available as they were multi-adjustable for height, rake and reach, and were combined with a steering wheel that could be adjusted for rake and reach, too. "If you can't get comfortable in any of the 81 seat positions of the Triumph 1300," said a January 1967 headline beneath photographs of the seat and steering wheel in the most widely differing positions possible, "try adjusting the steering column." Long copy, in the form of a short article, highlighted the car's interior equipment and features such as its turning circle of 31 feet, which was remarkable for a front-wheel-drive car. It was allowed by the 1300's conventional, rather than transverse, engine layout and cannily arranged, slighly trailing, driveshafts.

Road testers generally admired the 1300, their main criticisms being of slightly heavy steering at low speeds and limited rear leg room. Folding window winders infuriated *Car* as being difficult to unfold and use in a hurry. A twin-carburettor model—in effect with the Spitfire Mk 3 engine—arrived in 1967. Curiously, one advertisement for the 1300 ran for almost two years between January 1968 and December 1969, the first version displaying a car on cobbles with the doors open under the quotation from the *Daily Mail*, while the second version used the same picture but re-located the headline and modified the copy. When the fashion for marque-wide slogans began to spread in the late 1960s, Triumph (by now openly "Leyland Triumph") followed 1967–68's "Triumph puts you safely ahead" with "Triumph put in what the others leave out" during 1969–70.

Meanwhile, the 2000 put pressure on Ford, Rootes and Vauxhall not only directly, by taking sales from their top-line models, but also indirectly, by making them appear unsophisticated. Rivals had "flapped about, renaming things Executives and God knows what; believe me, we've hurt 'em. And rightly so. Doing things out way, we've got to make the most of our ideas in the time it takes the opposition to tool up a copy," said Harry Webster.[31] As announced, the Triumph 2000 cost £1095 to the Rover 2000's £1265. Advertising was confident from the start: "The masterly new 6-cylinder Triumph 2000 introduces grand luxe motoring at a medium price" announced Standard-Triumph in October 1963. The car had been "built with one thought in mind. To make motoring the civilised pleasure it should be for the driver and for his passengers." Features were listed in detail from the outset, and in 1966 Triumph teased the big producers: "When you realise that seating five people in comfort is more civilised than packing in six, you're ready for the Triumph 2000." Many people were ready: sales of Austin Westminsters, Ford Zephyrs, Humber Hawks and Vauxhall Crestas were declining. In 1968 the 2000 was shown with an aircraft and an advanced submarine, whose pilot and commander also owned the car. The icing on Triumph's cake was provided by the 2000 estate car. Introduced in October 1965 and converted by Carbodies of Coventry from the saloon bodyshell, it was the most elegant mass-produced estate car of its time and attracted a very upmarket clientele who appreciated its nimbleness and delicate styling. It was as different as a station-wagon could be from the beast of burden that had been the equivalent Standard Vanguard. "Guide for lovers of fine things with special reference to the late-20th-cent. Triumph 2000 Estate Car" began an announcement headline beneath a car shown outside an antiques shop. "You will be pleased to discover that *craftsmanship* is still very much alive in the nineteen-sixties," concluded the copy.

One of the most unusual Triumph advertisements of the 1960s was not for a car, but for a concept. The Triumph XL90, a bubble-shaped people carrier in bronze and white, was envisaged with "such ideas as a 'sealed-for-life' engine/transmission unit. Pneumatic controls for suspension and brakes. Hand-grip steering. Ultrasonic screencleaning. Light-sensitive window tinting. And automatic guidance and speed control for fog and on motorways." The car looked like the kind of thing that might nowadays be imagined in long lines in an urban shuttle-rail service of the future, and for a late-1960s concept it looks surprisingly undated. To the copywriter it was "the shape of Triumph to come. And how it helps us put you safely ahead today." Pure concept cars had rarely been seen in day-to-day publicity since the 1950s, when Detroit conditioned the public to future styles by showing its dream cars in advertising. Many of the XL90's imagined features would come to pass, though sadly only two totally new production Triumph styles—the Stag of 1970 and the TR7 of 1975—would ever be introduced (the Acclaim of 1981–84 being essentially a Honda). Nevertheless a plastic-bodied Triumph TRX prototype of the 1970s, which took its name from a futuristic 1950 roadster by Walter Belgrove, shared something of the XL90's curvaceous and glassy style.[32]

Opposite: **Triumph 2000 Mk I Estate.** The "lifestyle estate" has been with us since the days of the wooden-(re)bodied second-hand Rolls-Royce, but the Triumph 2000, typical of the post-war breed with its tailgate sloping more gently than the average, was one of the first modern upmarket estates. (Rover had to make do, from 1969, with a handful of conversions by Panelcraft in a style which, from the rear, looked rather like Simca's 1501 wagon, albeit without that car's roll-down tailgate window). The Triumph was built by Carbodies, who were well-known in the 1950s for their convertible conversions of mass-produced saloon bodies, and for the FX4 London taxi. This advertisement is more convincing than Hillman's more obviously staged equivalent on a similar theme for the Super Minx estate, whose Singer Vogue derivative was, co-incidentally, assembled by Carbodies until its discontinuation in 1967, though apparently at no great profit to the company.

23

Vanden Plas

"Prestige without ostentation"

In 1947, production began of the first Austin Princess at the coachbuilders Vanden Plas in Kingsbury, north-west London. Carosserie Vanden Plas had been respected coachbuilders in Brussels since 1870 and in Antwerp from 1884, and had become known in England from around 1906. In 1913 the importer of Vanden Plas-bodied Metallurgique cars joined with the established British coachbuilder Warwick Wright and another coachbuilder with which it was already collaborating, called Theo Masui, to create Vanden Plas (England) Ltd. "Thus Wright obtained the means both to import Vanden Plas bodies and to manufacture them under licence."[1] In 1922 the company began to produce bodies for Bentley but went into receivership shortly afterwards following a general slump in trade, and, under new management, it moved to Kingsbury. In the 1930s Vanden Plas prospered, and produced bodies for Alvis, Talbot and Invicta among others, as well as for Bentley.[2] In June 1946 the firm became of subsidiary of Austin (and therefore, from 1952, of BMC), and in mid-1957 "Princess" replaced Austin as the post-war car's marque name. In 1960, Vanden Plas became a BMC marque name in its own right.

The Princess itself continued through Mk II and III versions until 1956, when an updated, full-width, Princess IV took over. Traditional in side profile with old-fashioned wing lines retained in faint outline on the body sides, the Princess IV was advertised during 1957–58 as "specially made for a well-defined group of people." Alas, that group defined itself rather too well for BMC, and the model was discontinued in 1959 after only 200 had been made, compared with 1910 of the 1947–56 originals.[3] In 1959 just the long-wheelbase Austin Princess 4-litre, introduced in 1952 and usually sold in Limousine form with a glass division, remained.

With its distinguished heritage, however, the Vanden Plas name was worth preserving, not least because a specially trimmed Austin A105 saloon of 1958–59, called the A105 Vanden Plas, had been very well liked. Originally conceived as a one-off for Leonard Lord's own use, this A105 cost £1475 2s, compared with £1235 17s for the standard A105, and it was inexpensively promoted by adapting an earlier advertisement for the regular model. A satisfying 500 were sold, and the car filled a niche between conventional six-cylinder big cars from BMC, Ford and Vauxhall and the more specialized sixes from Daimler, Jaguar, Humber and Rover.

By 1959 production plans were well advanced for the Austin A99 Westminster and Wolseley 6-99, and BMC's Leonard Lord had suggested that Vanden Plas should make an upmarket version of each.[4] Three months before the 1959 Motor Show, however, Lord changed his mind. "We had actually started assembly of both cars," recalled Vanden Plas managing director since 1954, Roland Fox, "when we had a phone call from Lord to say that he wanted us to cancel the Austin and Wolseley versions and make a Princess instead.... It was actually a brilliant idea...to associate a prestige name with a quality car that could be produced at an attractive price.... It meant we needed a new radiator grille. I suggested...that we make it a cross between a Bentley and an Alvis.... It eventually became the Vanden Plas 3-litre and it turned us into quite a big producer...we eventually got production up to a hundred a week."[5]

For all that the Princess 3-litre was indubitably a badge-engineered Austin, it was no mere sales department's confection: Vanden Plas still had its own works and its own craftsmen who completed the model from shells and drive-trains sent down from Cowley, where BMC finished some cars only when maximum capacity had been reached at Kingsbury. The coachbuilder fitted sound-deadening, special leather and wood trim and instruments, and applied the cars' unique paint schemes to a high standard. "Contrary to popular belief," said J. Eason Gibson of *Country Life* in 1964, "Vanden Plas is not just a name, with little behind it. In fact, the cars in their range are made from components delivered from parent BMC units...to their factory at Kingsbury in London."[6]

Yet the image of the car remained fragile. In a slightly tetchy review of the 4-litre R in 1967, Bill Hartley of *The Illustrated London News* thought BMC were trying too hard: "I would have thought it rather brash to describe a car as a "prestige" model, hinting that its ownership was a mark of one-upmanship and a status symbol."[7] But by 1967, the Princess had been promoted on its prestige — real or imagined — for six years, and advertising for the 3-litre Mk II of 1961–64 was much heavier than that for the original 3-litre of 1959–61.[8] In the spring of 1961, for instance, copy had been comparatively understated: "Vanden Plas Princess— the car in a thousand. Prestige without ostentation is the acknowledged stamp of a Vanden Plas Princess. Now there is a Princess 3-litre as well as the 4-litre [1952-style saloon and limousine]. It has all the qualities of its big-sister—coachbuilt interior...disc brakes, speed, comfort—and withal a style, a personality and a gracefulness which set it far above any comparable car."

A more overt preoccupation with status arrived with the Mk II during late 1961 and early 1962. An imaginary businessman spoke about his choice: "I thought of 50,000 miles before I chose our new [£1626] Princess. And that's only one thing our new car must be good for. Because of my job, it must be fast, roomy, and comfortable to the point of luxury. My wife drives quite a bit, so heavy cars are out— yet it must be sturdy, because we often holiday abroad. Price is an important factor. And finally, I don't want a car that absolutely everyone has." The "absolutely" revealed a nervy self-consciousness under the practical exterior. In another advertisement in the series, the aspirant's young wife kept up the pressure: "I could only dream we had a new Princess. In my family, when it comes to cars, MEN do the choosing. My husband says— without any prompting whatever from me— that the ideal car for us is a Princess 3-litre. It has (he declares) all the virtues...like being reasonably priced, fast, roomy, reliable and easy to drive. And (as he has left it for me to observe) it is very beautiful and luxurious indeed. If you stroked it, I think it might purr. Oh what a good thing I chose the husband I did!" As in America (notoriously) with Packard's 120 and Six in the 1930s, so in Britain with Vanden Plas nearly thirty years later: wives prodded their husbands sharply in the back and the most blatantly aspirational copy accompanied cars whose prestige was not *quite* assured. After all, the 3-litre Mk II resembled an Austin Westminster, and that car still looked like a large Austin

Cambridge. For the time being, the Rover 3-Litre, a much more sophisticated car both mechanically and socially, was safely out of range at £1880.

The trend peaked a year later: "What's he like? You can tell a lot from his Princess! For instance, the Princess 3-litre reflects his assurance; his dislike of ostentation; his own quiet good taste; his air of youthfulness— whatever his age in years. The Princess suggests, too, that he is a man of standing.... Finally, he's a bit of an individualist, this man. The Princess is not a car that 'absolutely everyone' has." With "absolutely everyone" now in quotation marks, the copy sound less effete than before, but what the advertisement really suggested was that a copywriter had curled up in front of the fire with *National Geographic* and studied Cadillac's advertising closely.[9] Visually, these Vanden Plas advertisements were uninspired, with one photograph of the car, without background, being used for several pieces. In October 1963, however, the 3-litre Mk II was photographed outside a large suburban house as a father in his business suit, shoes highly polished, opened the door for his little girl dressed in riding gear: "Think of a Princess in your family. You're thinking of changing your car. You're looking for one that matches your position in life. With more space. Think of a Princess.... Think and act. And you will soon own a Princess."

Between March and July 1964, extensive coverage was achieved by preparing a new advertisement in colour and monochrome versions and placing it every three or four weeks in upmarket magazines; subscribers to *Country Life* or *The Field*, for example, saw it five times over three months or so. The car's grille was highlighted while the copy emphasized features: "Many luxury cars cost more but few are better equipped than the Vanden Plas Princess." This was true, and the increasing confidence and flair of 3-litre advertising reflected the growing success of the car, of which 12,615 were sold, including 7900 of the Mk II.[10] By contrast, annual sales of the equivalent Austin A99 and A110 and Wolseley 6-99 and 6/110 were greatest in their early years. In 1964, the 3-litre Mk II was replaced by the slightly more upmarket Vanden Plas 4-litre R. At £1994 6s 3d, this new Princess fell under the all-important £2000 tax threshold for company cars but was a direct rival to the Rover 3-Litre Mk II, which was now slightly cheaper than the BMC car.[11]

The 4-litre R was an unusual concoction of updated 3-litre Mk II and Rolls-Royce engine which ended up as somehow rather less than the sum of its parts. In 1938 Rolls-Royce had begun to design a range of three engines—a "four" (B40), a "six" (B60) and an "eight" (B80)—of which a 4887cc version of the six was used in the 1955 Rolls-Royce Silver Cloud and Bentley S1. It powered both marques' cars until a V8 took over in 1959. Versions of the B40 and B60 were also used in post-war military vehicles. In 1958, an all-aluminium version of the basic B60 design, of 3909cc capacity, was developed for a proposed six-cylinder "small"

THE FIELD, June 11 1964

Many luxury cars cost more

but few are better equipped than the Vanden Plas Princess

Specification : 120 BHP, overhead-valve engine, top speed 100 mph. Twin S.U. carburettors. Dual exhausts. 3 speed gearbox with overdrive. Power assisted brakes, discs at front. Independent front suspension with anti-roll bar; rear trunnion-mounted leaf springs with anti-roll bar. Heater, demisters and fresh-air circulation. Twin fog lamps. Reversing lamp. Automatic gearbox and power assisted steering available as extras.

When you lean back in this big saloon you find that every seat has ample leg room, is super-comfortable, and rich with the subdued glow of English leather. Wide arm rests are provided, deep pile carpet, walnut picnic tables for passengers, and instruments recessed in a polished walnut fascia.

12 months warranty and backed by B.M.C. service

Vanden Plas Princess

3-litre (Mark II) Saloon £1346.12.11
Also available Princess 4-litre Saloon or Limousine £2840.2.11
VANDEN PLAS (ENGLAND) 1923 LTD., KINGSBURY, LONDON N.W.9
Personal Exports Division, 41-46 Piccadilly, London W.1

Bentley (the Burma) and for possible use in a new military vehicle. But the contract for that vehicle was cancelled, the Burma project was not continued and the engine, now designated FB60, appeared to have no immediate use.

During 1959–61 Rolls-Royce considered merging its Car Division and Diesel Engine Division with the commercial vehicle divisions of Leyland, or BMC, or bus makers ACV.[12] No merger took place, but Rolls-Royce remained in contact with BMC and was already associated with the Corporation to the extent that Pressed Steel at Cowley, who made bodies for several manufacturers including BMC, had built Standard Steel Rolls-Royce and Bentley bodies since 1946. Rolls-Royce also had a difficulty: the Silver Cloud II and equivalent Bentley S2 (both 1959–62) were not selling as well as had been hoped and the Cloud's replacement was taking longer than expected to develop. Meanwhile Rolls-Royce's chief designer, Frank Tarleton and its chief stylist since 1951, John Blatchley, liaised with BMC's Alec Issigonis and chief sylist, Dick Burzi. The possibility arose that a "small" six-cylinder Bentley could be developed from the Princess 3-litre, which at the time had just been introduced. The rear wings of the Vanden Plas could be modified to take Bentley S2 tail-lights, a Bentley grille could be fitted, and the FB60 Burma engine could replace the BMC original. Running prototypes of this concept (called "Java") were built, but Rolls-Royce abandoned the idea when the Cloud III and Bentley S3 (1962–65) were successfully introduced and the design of the eventual monocoque Silver Shadow and Bentley T1 began to take shape. BMC, however, thought many ideas in Java worth developing for a top-line car of its own, and Leonard Lord's successor, George Harriman, was particularly enthusiastic. A modified Vanden Plas 3-litre body, with cropped fins, horizontal tail-lights, more upright front and rear screens without the peaks of the 1959 style, fitted with the Rolls-Royce FB60 engine and with other structural and mechanical improvements, was introduced in August 1964.[13] The new car's styling was restrained, if a little lacking in character. Vertical tail-lights like those of the contemporary Alvis would have blended well with the new rear wing design to give the 4-litre R a more traditionally upmarket appearance at the rear to match its grille. The horizontal tail-lights were not quite similar enough to those of a Mercedes-Benz to banish thoughts of the Austin or Morris 1800.

The new car was well received. *Autocar* devoted much of its early test to describing the car's features and equipment, found the steering vague and lacking feel but the brakes very good, and concluded that "the refinement of the car justifies its inclusion in the £2000 price category." The magazine managed 0–60 in 12.5 seconds, a top speed of 109 mph and an overall fuel consumption of 14.8mpg.[14] For *The Field*, S.C.H. Davis found the collaboration represented by the car surprising: "The first announcement that the Vanden Plas Princess, the luxury car of [BMC's] range, was to be fitted with a Rolls-Royce engine left one momentarily dazed. The Princess seemed to have a niche of its own in any case, to be a big, comfortable car at a tempting price. That the change was right, however, cannot be doubted. The very fact of having a Rolls-Royce engine immediately evoked world-wide interest and gave the car prestige that will make all the difference to its future."[15]

Announcement advertising from Colman, Prentis & Varley Ltd. on the front cover of *Autocar* of August 21, 1964 showed a businessman looking into the open engine compartment of a two-tone green car: "What did the perfectionist find in the new Vanden Plas Princess 4-litre R? A Rolls-Royce engine." A monochrome version of the advertisement appeared in several newspapers and magazines between the car's announcement and April 1965, and in July was followed by a piece that was comparatively homely and modest: "The man who drives everybody's car gives his gold medal to the Princess with the Rolls-Royce engine. The most exclusive motoring award of the year — the John Critchard nod of approval — has gone to the Vanden Plas Princess R (John is the carriage attendant of the Dorchester Hotel and knows every luxury car.).... At £1,996 6s 3d incl. p.t. the Princess R is not a common car. But then the man who owns a Princess R is not a common man."

Unfortunately, as so often with BMC cars in their early years, the 4-litre R squandered its warm reception. First, its engine was insufficiently developed when the car was introduced. Secondly, initial sales projections were over-optimistic for the car's potential market and for its production facilities, as George Harriman's initial target of 200 cars a week overstretched both Vanden Plas (whose maximum practical capacity was about 120 cars a week) and Rolls-Royce, which had to employ inexperienced labour to produce enough engines. Leonard Lord changed the number of his own 4-litre R from BMC 1, "because wherever he took the car he was harrassed all the time by people wanting to complain about their own car."[16] Early engines in particular were unreliable. Hydraulic tappets that were slow to quieten down when the car was started were more of a nuisance than a mechanical liability, albeit that this was exactly the kind of fault that would dishearten someone buying a car for its Rolls-Royce engine. But water leaks and loose cylinder liners were more serious.

The word got around, and expensively hand-finished cars accumulated for so long on Oakley Aerodrome near

---

Opposite: **Vanden Plas Princess 3-litre Mark II.** Another close-up of a prestigious grille attached to a mass-produced body — in this case an Austin Westminster. Individuality was only surface deep, so the copywriter wisely concentrates on features rather than snob appeal. The lower picture, with a two-tone colour scheme and cream wheels, makes the car look more than ever like an ordinary late-1950s family hack, and does not do it justice. And, yes, a few of the grille bars are slightly bent!

What did the perfectionist find in the new Vanden Plas Princess 4-litre R?

Lift the bonnet of the new Princess R and you find 3·9 litres of Rolls-Royce engine.

This meticulously finished 6-cylinder engine, with its noiseless hydraulic tappets and a 7-bearing crankshaft, gives 175 brake horsepower and a velvet performance to a car already known for its smoothness.

Complementing the magic ease of this engine is the Borg Warner Model 8 automatic gearbox and Hydrosteer power-assisted steering. (*Assisted*, note, so that you lose none of the feel of the road.)

These refinements give an indication of the thoughtfulness which has gone into this car. Adjustable vents on the fascia admit constant fresh air. The reclining seats are operated by a precise winding handle. The rear springs are interleaved with rubber for smooth riding. Double belt drive to the waterpump, fan and dynamo underwrites the car's reliability.

Reading about the Princess R is a poor substitute for first-hand experience. The delights of this car only come to life on the road. See your Vanden Plas dealer. At £1,995 6s. 3d. tax paid, the new Princess R is not merely without equal. It has few challengers.

Vanden Plas (England) 1923 Ltd, Kingsbury, London NW9.

Personal Exports Division, 41-46 Piccadilly, London W1.

12 mths. warranty and backed by BMC service

The BRITISH Motor Corporation Ltd

Vanden Plas Princess 4-litre R. The best of all worlds, or an Austin Westminster with Rolls-Royce servicing costs? The engine was not the same as that fitted to Rolls-Royce cars, although it gave the car a more exotic flavour than that of the earlier 3-litre. To mention "adjustable vents on the fascia" which admitted "constant fresh air" was perhaps trying too hard for an announcement advertisement, even if the feature was as yet unusual: Ford's Aeroflow ventilation, talking piece of the 1964 Motor Show, was still a month away. Nor was it wise to show the car with the bonnet up — an image that might remain in the reader's mind long after the copy was forgotten, particularly as early examples proved troublesome. In later years BMW, to make a similar point, would photograph its engines close-up.

PRINCESS OUTSIDE VIP INSIDE!

Whenever you see a Princess 4-litre you can be sure someone "at the top" is around. For the Vanden Plas Princess 4-litre is pre-eminently the town carriage of Royalty, ambassadors, statesmen and many others who wield authority in a dozen different spheres.

They relish its smooth comfort, its impressive reliability and its air of quiet good taste. But perhaps the quality which any owner most appreciates in his Princess 4-litre is its prestige . . . prestige without a trace of ostentation.

VANDEN PLAS
PRINCESS 4-LITRE
Price £2150.0.0
plus £986.13.1 P.T. and surcharge

VANDEN PLAS
PRINCESS 3-LITRE
Price £1114.0.0
plus £511.16.5 P.T. and surcharge

Vanden Plas Princess 3-LITRE & 4-LITRE

Vanden Plas (England) 1923 Ltd., Kingsbury Works, Kingsbury, London N.W.9. Personal Exports Division : 41-46, Piccadilly, London W.1

434

Vanden Plas Princess 4-litre. "Prestige without a trace of ostentation"…Not only must the plutocrat show off, but he must also demonstrate that he is beyond showing off! The aim was not, of course, to convince the mass of ordinary motorists who knew a pompous limousine when they saw one, but the owner might be fooled by the copy just long enough to sign the cheque. The car was a success within its limited market, and became a favourite of the funeral trade, so mere mortals could ride in it after all.

Aylesbury that "it seems that more than one repeat purchaser was incensed to find that their new car bore an earlier chassis number than the one they had just traded in."[17] Small faults sometimes went uncorrected because BMC and Vanden Plas each imagined the other to be primarily responsible for inspection of complete cars. "The crux was that Vanden Plas...just saw itself as a trimmer and took no real responsibility for anything other than the bits it stuck on," recalled engineer Jim Lambert, whom BMC sent to Kingsbury, "There was thus no real sign-off by Engineering before the cars went to the customer.... I virtually lived at Vanden Plas for several months, and we eventually got it right. I even went to Smiths for a clock with a more regular tick. But...the reputation of the car had been ruined, and even if it had had gold-plated door handles people wouldn't have wanted one."[18]

An advertisement published between December 1965 and June 1966 showed a two-tone black-over-lilac car in Harley Street. "Men who have arrived, arrive in the Princess with the Rolls-Royce engine. It is not so surprising that successful men should choose the Vanden Plas Princess R. They are demanding people, and in this beautiful car they find the highest skills of the coachbuilder and the engineer perfectly matched." By this time the car was generally reliable, but sales were so low that the copywriter still had to write "should choose" rather than "have chosen." In July, 1964's photograph of the car outside the Dorchester reappeared: "Vanden Plas luxury. Rolls-Royce power, for less than £2,000. That's BMC creative engineering. This is something greater than a very great car.... This is the flexibility and freedom to think wider and plan without restraint. It's the 'know-how' that marries the finest with the finest. And keeps the cost reasonable. So step inside the 'Princess R'— and let Vanden Plas surround you with the superlative in luxury and craftsmanship. With hand-rubbed walnut and deep-tufted carpets...." Cunningly, the number plate of the car had been changed from a 1964 "B" registration to a special-looking, touched-in number in the old style. In its last years the 4-litre R was rarely advertised and early in 1968, with production running only at about four cars a week, the model was discontinued. 6555 had been made.[19]

The most successful Vanden Plas cars of the 1960s were rarely advertised. From 1956–59 the Princess Mk III ("Incomparable Princess...for particular people") and Princess IV ("Luxury...but in good taste") had been promoted quite extensively, and during that period at least four different advertisements appeared for the long-wheelbase saloon and limousine. "Austin's Princess...it's the only name possible!" claimed BMC in a March 1957 headline, a few months before the car's marque name was changed to Princess and only three years before it became Vanden Plas. But by the early 1960s the large car had established its niche, and 1962's slogan, "Princess outside — VIP inside!" spoke the truth, even if the VIP was sometimes an undertaker or, in the case of hearse conversions, deceased. Although old-fashioned, this car largely sold itself until it was discontinued in May 1968 after a respectable 3344 or so had been built.[20] It was replaced by the Daimler DS420, which was built by Vanden Plas around a body developed from that of the Jaguar Mk X (420G from 1966). British Leyland closed the Vanden Plas factory at Kingsbury in 1979, but the Daimler limousine remained in production until as late as 1992.

The biggest-selling Vanden Plas of the 1960s— a car that only the British would think to make — was a top-line version of the Morris 1100. Inspired by a one-off commissioned by Fred Connolly, whose leather was used in existing Vanden Plas cars among others, it was announced in October 1963 and became available at the very end of the year. By mid-1965 it cost £925 18s 9d when a Ford Zephyr 6 was £889, an Austin A110 Mk II, £998 and a four-door Morris 1100 de luxe, £644. "It's not cheap. But if you can buy it, you should enjoy it" said Small Car.[21] A 1275cc Princess 1300 arrived in the autumn of 1967 and was built alongside an updated 1100 (Mk II) before that car was discontinued in the spring of 1968. The 1300 was produced until May 1974. A successful and much-loved model, so pleasing intrinsically that its pretension inspired amusement, even affection, rather than contempt, it hardly needed to be advertised at all.[22] True, the grille looked incongruous on a car so small and low, but the interior trim was genuinely of good quality and not specified, or built, down to a price. 43,741 were made, and today the model remains in demand among collectors across the world.

24

Wolseley

"Buy wisely — buy Wolseley"

In 1957, Wolseley began to break with a tradition. From the late 1930s until 1955–56, most Wolseley advertising had been aimed at the businessman with an impression to make and a social position to consolidate. The cadences of Wolseley copy were affectedly middle-aged and lent themselves easily to parody, especially by the young. In 1955, for example, the owner of a four-cylinder 4/44 invited a 6/90-owning friend to agree that "both cars have something which has always been characteristic of Wolseleys—a kind of quiet distinction—which is difficult to explain but conveys a lot to one's friends." In real life the car could be taken to convey almost anything, including—given a significant part of the 6/90's market—that its owner liked to be mistaken for a policeman. A perennial difficulty with aspirational copy was that in order to convince the reader that the product would make him look successful, the copywriter had to use language that no successful person would ever use about himself. The danger with such an approach was that the target market would remain unconvinced while younger readers— the potential buyers of the future—would be put off the marque for good. In fact criticism by *The Autocar* of the early 6/90's gear-change, brakes and other details cost its designer his job.[1]

In January 1957, however, Wolseley's advertising retreated from social competition towards more cheerful, private satisfactions with "Selective, Automatic Control"— known elsewhere as Manumatic transmission. Small pictures of the 4/44's similar-looking successor, the 15/50, and of a 6/90 Series II, were accompanied by drawings of a man playing an organ, an old-timer in cravate and soft hat throwing what looked like a small music stand over a bridge into a river, and a girl with a wreath round her neck, an urn

in her hand, and a happy smile which suggested that the contents of the urn had not died penniless. The object heading towards the river and presumably also in the urn was a clutch pedal, rendered over-scale for effect.[2] "Two-pedal motoring with Wolseley…" began the copy, "No doubt exponents of the modern mighty organ are happy with lots and lots of pedals, but then, they don't have to brake hard or take violent evasive action—at least one would think not—the music is popular enough. Now with the motorist it's different, there's always the unexpected to cope with, so we take the view that some simplification of control is a step in the right direction…." The Manumatic cost £50 and conventional automatic gears on a 6/90, £172 10s: "Both these systems make experts of us all…. 'Selective Automatic' calls simply for the manipulation of a gear lever, 'Automatic' does everything but select your route—yes we admit there's still room for progress, but we keep going ahead." True, the copy was a little heavy-footed and avuncular, although it anticipated the automatic route selection that would arrive with satellite navigation forty years later, and during 1958–60 Wolseley advertising sometimes reverted to antediluvian type. Yet lightheartedness had filtered through, and this advertisement was built around a tangible feature.

In April 1957, BMC introduced the first small Wolseley since the pre-war-style Ten of 1939–48.[3] The Wolseley 1500 (or Fifteen Hundred, as it was called in 1957–58 advertising) was only twelve feet, eight inches long and combined a relatively large, 1489cc, engine with high gearing by British standards and a comparatively low weight of 2060 lb. The new car had been developed from from a Morris 1200 prototype, styled by Dick Burzi, which had been intended to replace the Morris Minor and was considered for production as late as the beginning of 1957. But in 1955 Alec Issigonis had returned to BMC from Alvis, and the 948cc Morris Minor 1000, introduced in the autumn of 1956, seemed likely to sell strongly until new Issigonis designs could take over. The Morris 1200 was therefore developed into the upmarket, compact Wolseley 1500 and Riley One-Point-Five for the British home market and small-scale export, and into the 1958 Morris Major and Austin Lancer for Australia. The Wolseley 1500 was announced in April 1957 at £796 7s and the Riley arrived in November at £864 17s. The Wolseley was also made in Australia from the autumn of 1957. [4]

The 1500 was the last Wolseley not to be derived from a production Austin or Morris, and it appealed both to owners of existing large Wolseleys seeking something smaller in retirement and to younger, more sporting motorists moving up from mainstream small saloons. The latter, in particular, liked its floor-mounted gearchange, lively performance (0–60 in 24.4 seconds and a top speed of 77.5 mph), and 35mpg economy. The 1500 was more agile, as well as £102 cheaper, than a Singer Gazelle and £12 cheaper even than the Austin A55 Cambridge, which shared its engine. Moreover, the car did not look or feel like an upmarket Morris: it was was attractively styled inside with a wooden dashboard and door cappings and upmarket details such as chrome-rimmed dashboard switches. As in earlier Wolseleys, BMC had used wood, leather, chrome and different plastics imaginatively. "Here, indeed, is high quality at the right price" said The Autocar.[5]

Announcement advertising was confident and factual: "Now…performance and style with economy—The car you've always wanted! Brilliantly styled and engineered, the new Fifteen Hundred is designed for the motorist who likes to travel economically, comfortably yet swiftly. With a high top gear and a big engine, performance is exciting, but runnings costs are amazingly low—44 m.p.g. at 35 m.p.h. Features include: 1,500 c.c. O.H.V. engine. 4-speed gearbox. Independent front suspension. Rack and pinion steering. Powerful brakes. Luxury 4-seater body. A compact, thrifty, high performance car with traditional Wolseley luxury." The car was shown in profile in two-tone paint beneath drawings of the interior, boot compartment and floor-mounted gear-change—the latter an increasingly popular feature as the fad for column-changes waned. In a 1958 advertisement, potential buyers were illustrated, catalogues in hand, telephoning their dealers: "Sensational car…sensational success. The unprecedented demand for the [1500] is a measure of how closely this amazing car approaches the popular ideal." Separate blocks of copy described individual features. By June 1959, road testers had reported on the car, and ad-

vertising quoted eight of them under the headline, "Here's what the men who drive them all say about the Wolseley '1500.'" After a detrimmed Fleet model had been announced in January 1959 at £746 17s,[6] traditionally Wolseley references to commercial life reappeared, yet without the pretension of earlier years: "No better buy for business—and pleasure too!"

This lively new tone filtered up to copy for the larger Wolseley 15/60 announced in December 1958[7] and to a lesser extent to that for the six-cylinder 6–99 introduced in August 1959.[8] The copywriter trawled the dictionary for Wolseleyish words but the message was straightforward in January 1959: "Farina links line with luxury for you. Styled by Farina, mentor of fashion in cars, the new 15/60 combines exquisite line with luxury and the technical excellence of Wolseley engineering. Sleek yet capacious, swift yet economical, this fascinating…. Wolseley is designed expressly for modern conditions and to satisfy the particular requirements of the more discriminate." Or "discriminating," as old Wolseley hands doubtless growled between puffs of their pipes. The 15/60 was a sturdy car, heavier and less agile than the 1500 but with the same engine, and good value at £991. For doubters the advertisement included small drawings of the interior layout, boot and dashboard. In later headlines the 15/60 was "Fashioned for the fastidious" and "Just heavenly" (from a female motorist) "But down-to-earth in price" (from a man). The Pinin Farina styling was mentioned every time. By 1960 the car was "Every inch a Wolseley—every mile a joy…. Only experienced 15/60 owners really know the pleasure of driving this delightful car. But you, too, can thrill to the immediate response at the accelerator pedal"—if not at the steering, which had an inch or two of free play even when new.

With the 6–99, the copywriter's tone was more sober, as in March 1960: "The most significant advance yet in better-class motoring. Engineered by Wolseley and styled by Farina, the new [£1255] 6–99 goes right ahead of contemporary values to provide, for a moderate price, not only exceptional luxury, but a performance that is quite remarkable. Riding comfort, stability and superb handling combine with abundant power to produce what is undoubtedly the finest Wolseley of all." In June, the car was "[a]mong the world's high performance cars but on its own in luxury value." As with the 15/60, small drawings showed features such as "Robust front suspension. Disc brakes." The Autocar found that these made faint noises from time to time but were otherwise excellent. In the autumn of 1961, the 15/60 and 6–99 were updated to become the 16/60 and 6/110.[9] With cropped fins[10] and a revised interior the 16/60 represented good value

---

Opposite: **Wolseley 1500 Mk III.** The "car versus train" theme had been popular in automobile art and advertising between the wars, following several well-publicized races, and its appearance here suggests a deliberate appeal to the older motorist. The copy is modest, but few other advertisers of the 1960s invited readers to "hanker" after performance, or anything else. There is an undercurrent of impoverished gentility, as if the car is being targeted towards those used to high-quality cars but no longer able to afford them.

1½ litre performance and WOLSELEY luxury for only £729.15.3 (inc. P.T.)

The compact lively economical
WOLSELEY 1500

- 1,500 c.c. O.H.V. engine. Four-speed gearbox with central floor gear change.
- Overall length under 12 ft. 8 in. Easy to park, fits the smaller garage.
- Luxuriously finished four-seat interior with walnut veneer fascia. Safety glass all round. Provision for seat belts. Heater and screen washer standard.
- 36 m.p.g. (vide *The Motor*).

BUY WISELY—BUY WOLSELEY
TWELVE MONTHS' WARRANTY and backed by BMC service

W213

There's something different about the Wolseley '1500'. Compact and beautifully finished too, but that's not all. Take a look under the bonnet at the 1½ litre O.H.V. engine. Try out the performance which this high power-to-weight ratio gives you . . . lively get-away, quiet running at high speeds, economy and lasting reliability. If you're 'sold' on the convenience of the smaller car yet still hanker for full-size performance and a touch of luxury then buy the Wolseley '1500'.

The Wolseley '1500' is available in two versions, Fleet Model £530 plus £199.15.3 P.T. Family Model £550 plus £207.5.3 P.T.

W OLSELEY-A LUXURIOUS WAY OF MOTORING

WOLSELEY MOTORS LTD., COWLEY, OXFORD

London Showrooms: 12 Berkeley Street, W.1 · Overseas Business: Nuffield Exports Ltd., Oxford and 41-46 Piccadilly, London, W.1

The Field, November 19, 1964

Combined operation
(for the 2 car family)

You can buy this elegant Wolseley 6/110 Mk. II and the superb little Hornet for your wife, both for the price you might expect to pay for a 3 litre car of any other make. Two luxurious cars for the price of one. You don't have to buy them both unless you wish.

TWELVE MONTHS' WARRANTY and backed by B.M.C. Service

THE BRITISH MOTOR CORPORATION LTD.

Either Wolseley adds up to the finest luxury value money can buy.

Your Wolseley dealer will be delighted to give you a demonstration of any of the following models:

✻ Hornet Mk. II, 1500 Fleet, 1500 Family, 16/60 (manual or automatic).

✻ 6/110 Mk. II (manual with or without overdrive, or automatic).

✻ The Hornet is now fitted with B.M.C.'s exclusive Hydrolastic suspension system.

✻ The 6/110 Mk. II gives 3 litre luxury and high performance. Interior features include reclining front seats and folding picnic tables in the rear compartment.

BUY WISELY – BUY
WOLSELEY

WOLSELEY MOTORS LIMITED. (Sales Division) LONGBRIDGE, BIRMINGHAM.

Overseas business: Nuffield Exports Ltd., Oxford.
Personal Exports Division: 41-46 Piccadilly, London W.1.
W. 236/C

at £993 compared with an Austin A60 at £854, and was advertised as a medium-sized luxury car, "surpassing all previous luxury value." In May 1962, the 6/110 was claimed to offer "value-for-money unmatched in the 3-litre class." As the Wolseley then cost £1266 compared with the Humber Super Snipe's £1444 and the Rover 3-Litre's £1772, the claim was justified.

As the decade advanced, Wolseleys were advertised with large, often colourful paintings against prestigious or dramatic backdrops such as modern houses, airports, docks and boatyards (16/60), expensive urban locations and "Oxbridge" colleges (1500), office blocks and cityscapes (6/110) or up-market domestic settings (Hornet). Headlines were impressionistic such as "Line…luxury…" and "Passport…two weeks…" (15/60); "Social Call…second car…" and "Compact…convenient…" (1500); and "Company car…incomparable value…" (6/110). In 1962–63 the 1500 was "compact, lively, economical," while the 16/60 was "Luxuriously practical—a car that satisfies" and offered "family motoring at its most luxurious." The copy beneath the headlines and pictures was in the established new Wolseley style. The cars were shown in paintings throughout, almost always with people in them or nearby. Photography would arrive in 1964, largely disappear again in 1966, and reappear for good in 1967. 1964's photographs were realistic, with cars in colours that blended into backgrounds which, in the new medium, appeared in authentic detail. In 1965 a two-tone brown and beige 6/110 complemented the country house behind it; in 1967 a 16/60 in cream and dark blue was set off by the craggy outcrops of a highland scene. At Motor Show time in October 1964, the whole range was shown on a beach: "Motoring on a different plane…. The commonplace is not for the Wolseley owner. His zest for life, appreciation of refinement and ability to relax are rewarded in this luxurious marque. For him the sparkling performance of B.M.C. engine power, the comfort of real leather and deep pile carpets."

In October 1961 the Wolseley range expanded as far down as it would go with the Hornet, a Mini to which Dick Burzi had added a traditional grille, extra chrome trim and an extended boot. At £672 it was slightly cheaper than its similar-looking sister, the £694 Riley Elf, which arrived at the same time. The interiors included wooden trim around the instrument binnacle of the Hornet and across the dashboard of the Elf. Leather seats soon became available. Both cars lasted until 1969 and were updated to Mk II form, with 998cc rather than 848cc engines, in January 1963, and to Mk III form in October 1966, when they gained push-button door handles and winding windows three years before those features appeared on regular Minis.[11] From 1964 Hydrolas-

tic suspension was fitted to all Mini saloons including the Hornet and Elf. A high-performance Viking Hornet Sport, a convertible created in the manner of the Minis produced since mid-1963 by Crayford Engineering, was offered by Viking Performance Ltd. of Suffolk from the beginning of 1964.[12] In 1966 Crayford converted 57 Hornets for the food manufacturers, Heinz, who in a competition called the "Greatest Glow on Earth" gave them away to buyers of Heinz products who "successfully matched up a variety of Heinz soups with a variety of picnic menus. If, for example, you considered that the best accompaniment to Liver Sausage Salad was Cream of Green Pea, you simply ticked the appropriate box and popped it in the post, together with copious quantities of Heinz labels."[13] *Small Car* recalled the first Hornet as having been beyond the pale, "among the ugliest, most uncomfortable and least desirable cars ever offered to the great British public,"[14] but the magazine's disdain for badge engineering had developed into a severe allergy by 1964 and there was nothing intrinsically bad about the car. From 1963 onwards the Hornet developed a stable niche.

The Hornet and Elf were sold by different BMC dealers, and some of them idly wondered whether the target market—affluent housewives and metropolitan girls-about-town—ever realized that the car was based on the Mini. In fact they usually did and, as the Mini itself became fashionable, were untroubled. Riley copy was coy at first, but no subterfuge was attempted by Wolseley: an early advertisement in *Homes and Gardens* was headed "Wonderful, wonderful Wolseley Hornet" and promised "All the proved advantages of B.M.C. mini-motoring plus Wolseley luxury." In a 1963 advertisement the Hornet was advertised neutrally as a conventional small car: "Whether you need a family car, a business car or a second car you certainly buy wisely when you buy a Wolseley Hornet," but most later advertising showed the little car with women at the wheel and copy to suit. In April 1964 "Her errands were never easier. Running the children to school—quick, safe and in roomy comfort. Shopping in the village—no parking problems, so nippy in traffic and what ingenious use of luggage space. Taking friends out to tea—smart and luxuriously equipped with refinements like real leather upholstery." In November 1964 the prospective 6/110 owner was encouraged to buy "the superb little Hornet for your wife." The theme continued in a long-running advertisement within a 1966–67 series which showed cars against painted collages of items characteristic of the places where they would be used: "In the hopping, shopping, bargain-grabbing bustle of the High Street you'll be glad you chose a Wolseley Hornet—effortless to drive,

Opposite: **Wolseley 6/110 Mk II.** Rich couples are wooed with a big saloon, whose name reflected its Austin A110 parentage. Increasing prosperity made two-car ownership a possibility for the well-off, and desirable to metropolitan couples who had decided to sample the country, provided that neither would be trapped there. The husband is expected to buy and choose both cars, and the point is made unusually explicitly for 1964. But this is Wolseley territory, a corner of the automotive globe where modern ideas are not adopted lightly.

WOLSELEY 16/60

Family motoring at its most luxurious

What luxury to have ample space for the whole family. A 19 cu. ft. boot that easily takes all the luggage. Spacious seating that gives the children enough elbow room to enjoy even the longest journeys, and for their safety childproof locks. And what a joy to have such easy handling, lively acceleration and smooth yet economical cruising.

Yes, the Wolseley 16/60 automatic with real leather upholstery, pile carpets and polished woodwork makes motoring a real pleasure. £760.10.0 plus £159 P.T. The 16/60 with manual gear change costs £692.10.0 plus £144.16.8 P.T.

BUY WISELY —BUY WOLSELEY

TWELVE MONTHS' WARRANTY and backed by BMC Service

WOLSELEY – A LUXURIOUS WAY OF MOTORING

WOLSELEY MOTORS LIMITED
COWLEY, OXFORD

Overseas Business: Nuffield Exports Limited, Oxford.
Personal Exports Division, 41-46 Piccadilly, London, W.1.

W229/C

558

Wolseley 16/60. Authentic late-fifties advertising from Wolseley in 1964, albeit with slightly more modern clothes and minimal elongation. The house is a period piece, too, with its central chimney, horizontal picture windows and Venetian blinds— a surprisingly modern choice for a Wolseley owner, although BMC were keen to portray the car as a successful businessman's model rather than a Harold-and-Hilda potterer for Sunday afternoons. The 16/60 had a luxurious interior and various upmarket touches, such as those popular sixties selling points, zero-torque door catches that gave a quality "k-donk," lending showroom appeal and reminding older buyers of coachbuilt saloons.

THE FIELD. *March 31 1966*

In the hopping, shopping, bargain grabbing bustle of the High Street you'll be glad you chose a Wolseley Hornet—effortless to drive, economical to run and easy to park.

BACKED BY BMC SERVICE—Express, Expert, Everywhere
BUY WISELY—BUY *Wolseley* HORNET

£578.10.10. inc. P.T.

THE **BRITISH** MOTOR CORPORATION LIMITED

WOLSELEY MOTORS LIMITED (SALES DIVISION), LONGBRIDGE, BIRMINGHAM · Overseas Business: BMC Export Sales Limited, Birmingham Personal Exports Division: 41-46 Piccadilly, London W 1

Wolseley Hornet Mk II. If the successful professional man was urged in 1964 to buy a "superb little Hornet for your wife," eighteen months later she chose it for herself. The appeal is to the middle-class housewife (few married women had careers in 1966), and shopping is implied to be fun, rather than a tedious necessity. The signs in the background —"self-service," "delicatessen"— and the wire shopping basket all indicate developments in British consumerism that would later be taken for granted, except the (snobbish) furriers, which would be about as politically incorrect as you could get in later years. In 1966 the food manufacturers Heinz gave away 57 Hornet convertibles, specially converted by Crayford Engineering of Westerham in Kent, to entrants in a national competition who successfully matched different Heinz soups with items on a picnic menu. Each car was fitted with numerous extras including a picnic case, Max Factor make-up compartment and tartan rug. Remarkably, 42 of these cars have been traced.

Retreat. Go now to your lakeside haven.
To sleepy days lounging
in small, clinker-built boats,
the shelter of hills.
To suppers of freshly caught trout.
A world away from it all —
your world.
Like the Wolseley 18/85 —
One of the good things of life.

Wolseley 18/85. Extra powerful 4 cylinder engine. Four speed gearbox.
Front-wheel drive. Disc brakes at front. Hydrolastic® suspension.
Power-assisted steering. Exceptionally spacious interior and boot.
Wolseley luxury. Price £1081 16s. 1d. inc. £236 16s. 1d. P.T. With
automatic transmission £98 7s. 10d. extra inc. £21 7s. 10d. P.T.

BRITISH
LEYLAND
WOLSELEY

economical to run and easy to park." In this as in others of the series, the copy was short and presented in a modish sans-serif typeface. In 1968, when the social whirl became just too exhausting, the Hornet owner could "exchange the racket of suburbia for soft leather seating and door to door carpeting" in "a world away from it all."

The "world away from it all" series of 1967–68 was the last major campaign from Longleys & Hoffman before Dorland Advertising took over in the summer of 1969 with a much more generically British Leyland style. The 1967–68 campaign included every Wolseley model and featured landscapes of a kind captured beautifully in paintings for Riley, Singer, Rover and others during the 1950s but generally neglected since. A two-tone black and cream 6/110 Mk II, for example, was photographed at some distance and height among bracken and heather; the Hornet appeared beside a bubbling stream; a white Wolseley 1300 rested between trees in a forest; an 18/85 in rich, metallic dark purple stood on exposed ground with mountains in the far distance; and in another piece the same car was seen beside a lake against a similar, probably Scottish, backdrop. A 1969 advertisement showing a blue 1300 Mk II against spectacular Highland scenery was published in two versions. In the first, the copy simply described the car and listed its features and specifications. In the second, statistics were banished to small print and made way for elegaic, escapist copy: "Take the high road. Up and above the soft patchwork of hedge-bordered fields. To the blithe hills, the rolling summit of sky. A world away from it all — your world. Like the Wolseley 1300 Mk II. One of the good things of life."[15] It was almost a shame to mention the car.

Opposite: **Wolseley 18/85 Mk I.** Even Wolseley joined the ranks of escapists in 1968, although the escape was introverted and recuperative, towards "a world away from it all." The appeal, as ever, is to the older male buyer, and the way of life which Wolseley had so long sought to represent fitted uneasily into the modern world. The car itself was essentially a Morris/Austin 1800, with proportions that could never be described as elegant. Unsurprisingly, there was an automatic version, with a rather stiff right-hand selector on the dashboard. By 1975 that illuminated badge, highlighted in the marque's final advertisements, would be no more.

The Field, October 19, 1961

How luxurious can an Austin Seven get?

Most people are very nicely satisfied thank you with *any* Austin Seven. Others want the earth. The new Austin Super Seven has been designed for them. It's got everything any other Austin Seven's got–high m.p.h. (70), high m.p.g. (50), large space inside (for seating four adults), small space outside (for parking in eleven feet). *And it's got much more. Here's what.*

INSIDE New duotone trim in subtly blending colour-choices. Sound insulation to hush the engine to a gentle purr. Fuller cushions for greater comfort: thick new carpets. New oval-shaped instrument panel, including both oil-pressure and water-temperature gauges. And many many more extras.

OUT New duotone palette of brilliant colours to choose from. Much more dashing fine-mesh grille. It's altogether a gayer, brighter car. Add up the list of improvements when you see the new model at your Austin dealer. Price: £405 plus £186.17.3 Purchase Tax and surcharge.

GET INTO AN AUSTIN AND OUT OF THE ORDINARY

NEW AUSTIN SUPER SEVEN
THE AUSTIN MOTOR COMPANY LIMITED · LONGBRIDGE · BIRMINGHAM

By Appointment to
Her Majesty The Queen
Motor Car Manufacturers
The Austin Motor
Company Limited

Backed by BMC 12-month
warranty and BMC service

Austin Super Seven. The earliest (1959–61) Minis sold slowly as middle-class buyers thought them utilitarian while the less well-off, who could ill afford to lose money on experimental purchases, preferred the similarly priced, 100E Anglia-derived, Ford Popular, a known and sturdy quantity, easily serviced at home, and with a boot big enough to take the family's luggage on holiday. BMC made the Mini more habitable in 1961, however, and sales took off once the type's qualities became more widely known. The original "Se7en" name gave way to "Seven" (as here) and was dropped completely in January 1962. This is an early, tentative foray into the humorous advertising which would characterize Mini promotions in the 1970s.

The Field, January 25, 1962

WHEN EXPERTS MEET—THERE'S A **ZEPHYR**

Competitor and spectator alike are proud to own Ford's splendid Zephyr. For this is a *motorist's* car, brilliantly designed and brilliantly built to give any-road, any-conditions satisfaction. The sturdy 6-cylinder engine, with or without automatic transmission, gives reassuring acceleration and a steady drive at all speeds from traffic-jam creep to an open-road gallop that tops 90 mph. The finely furnished interior promises luxury motoring for six without squashing or squeezing: power disc brakes are now standard on front wheels.

FROM £941.17.3 (£645 + £296.17.3) AUTOMATIC TRANSMISSION OR OVER-DRIVE OPTIONAL EXTRAS. CONVERTIBLE MODEL ALSO AVAILABLE.

ZEPHYR FROM *Ford* OF BRITAIN

Ford Zephyr Mk II. "I know he's late, Freddie, but once he gets onto averages he goes on for hours." Ford appealed, with a sly snobbery, to the sporting man in 1962, confident that the Zephyr's rally successes of the late 1950s would have impressed him. The copy could not be more different from 1960's for the Zodiac: it is sober and masculine, and matches the subdued colour scheme. Like Vauxhall, Humber and others who had to sell dated designs until well into the 1960s, Ford largely abandoned garish pastel shades in favour of a more restrained idiom. The front disc brakes had been optional since 1960, and, in the kind of feature-for-feature competition that would intensify in the 1960s, Vauxhall offered them on the rival Velox and Cresta from late 1961. This Zephyr, with its Consul and Zodiac brethren, was the first British Ford to feature a fuel filler behind the rear number plate.

THE FIELD, *October 4 1962*

New from Ford...the small car with a big difference!
CONSUL
CORTINA

Making small-car history...

With the new Consul Cortina, the economy is small-car; its costs are truly small-car and it gives up to 40 m.p.g. But from then on, what a difference! Not only is the Cortina big-car roomy and big-car stylish ... it has real big-car ruggedness. And power to spare, besides. Like Cortina quality, Cortina reliability is also built in. Solid. Prove all this as Ford did, drive it. Then you'll agree: it's the small car with a big difference.

Enjoy small-car savings...BIG-car everything else!

Brilliantly reliable 1200 cc engine, developed from famous race-and-rally winning Anglia unit · 0-60 mph get-aways in 26 secs through four-speed, all synchromesh gear box · Top speeds in the high seventies · Yet up to 40 m.p.g. Generous 5-seater roominess · Impressive international styling with all-round panorama vision · Big-car ruggedness, proved over thousands of testing miles on cruel pavé surfaces · Every 5000 miles or 'twice a year' service · Low-cost Ford servicing facilities available everywhere · Privilege hp/insurance rates · Only Ford could have brought Europe this new kind of small car — the result of their unrivalled engineering experience all over the world.

| 2-door Standard model from only | £639.0.3 (tax paid) | De Luxe model illustrated from only £666.10.3 (tax paid). 4-door versions coming soon. A wide range of fine accessories and options available. **CONSUL CORTINA FROM FORD OF BRITAIN** |

612

Ford Consul Cortina Mk I. An announcement advertisement for a new kind of medium-sized car, meticulously costed so that it could be sold cheaply, yet profitably. The car's name, which wags pointed out was Latin for kettle, but which was taken from the resort of Cortina d'Ampezzo, lent the necessary glamour and Euro-chic. Yet while the car's orientation was European (reflected in sales brochures), this studio shot is in the American style, showing the Cortina's balanced proportions. A real achievement was the car's light weight in relation to its size, particularly as this did not make it fragile or unusually rustprone. In America the Cortina, at $1600 in October 1962, was marginally undercut by its German Ford rival, the front-wheel-drive Taunus 12M, at $1500, although only a few hundred 12Ms actually arrived in the U.S. Even fewer entered Britain.

When you get a sudden, mad urge to go nowhere in particular...burn up the miles...feel the whip of the wind. Is it love, fate — or a slight touch of the compulsive, highly contagious MGB's? Is yours a restless, driving, nagging, aching, yearning, longing to proceed immediately to your nearest MG showroom? Why fight it? Remember: MGB drivers never travel alone. MGB £855.5.0.

Backed by BMC Service — Express, Expert, Everywhere. The M.G. Car Co. Ltd., Sales Division, Longbridge, Birmingham. Overseas Business: B.M.C. Export Sales Ltd., Birmingham & Piccadilly, W 1

MGB Sports. The restraint of the 1950s was discarded in MG copy of the mid-sixties, and, even if it appears overdone to modern eyes, it was effective at the time. The photograph deliberately focuses on the happy female passenger, and the implication would be made more explicit in the 1970s with such headlines as "Your mother wouldn't like it" and "You can do it in an MG." Orange was a favourite colour for all of them and, best of all, the wit was good-humoured rather than grimly post-modern-ironic. In the 1960s a copywriter could smile without looking over his shoulder.

*No problems in crowded Kensington
for the Triumph Herald 13/60*

The cosy parker.

Lots of new cars have come along since the Triumph Herald first came on to the road.

But when it comes to parking, the Herald 13/60 still runs rings round them all. Which shows you what a great idea it was in the first place.

Its turning circle is a midget 25 feet. And it slots comfortably into parking spaces only 3 feet longer than itself.

That's what Triumph engineering is all about. Clever, practical engineering ideas that help you get more out of a car.

Of course, the Herald isn't what it was.

All along the line it's been continuously improved.

The Triumph Herald 13/60 has racy new looks. And a zoomy new 1300 engine, delivering 27% more power. (0-50 is a brief 12 seconds.)

Which brings you some very handy benefits: Less gear changing. Safer overtaking. Faster acceleration.

New seats that make 200 miles seem like 20. More leg room for the people in the back. Front discs and heater are standard.

And servicing is every 6,000 miles.

Which, for most people, means once a year.

All the old virtues which have made the Herald a living legend are still there. Steel girder chassis. Crunchless rubber bumpers. All-independent suspension.

And, of course, it's still that legendary cosy parker.

Herald 13/60 £763·8·7. Convertible £822·3·7. Estate £841·15·3. Ex-works including purchase tax.

Standard-Triumph Sales Ltd, Coventry. Tel: OCO 3-75511

 TRIUMPH

Triumph put in what the others leave out

417

Triumph Herald 13/60. The Herald had been in production for a decade when this advertisement appeared in 1969. The car was a popular individualist, particularly with women in the home counties, but impending obsolescence meant that it was no longer fashionable. Enter the inevitable worthy virtues, which included a remarkable turning circle. This driver's Kensington neighbours own a Jaguar E-type and Vauxhall Victor respectively, the latter about to receive a thump from the Herald owner, who should be looking at his nearside front wing, or to his rear, but not at his front wheel! The layout of this piece, with a photograph, witty headline and blocks of copy below, would dominate car advertising in the 1970s.

Punch, March 25 1959

Have the lot, guv!

The night is young and hearts are
high. The dinner was excellent,
the dancing delightful, the girl divine
and the car a Dauphine. What
more could anyone want!

"Have the lot, guv?"

"My friend, I've <u>got</u> the lot."

RENAULT DAUPHINE

Fully assembled by RENAULT LIMITED · WESTERN AVENUE · LONDON · W.3

Renault Dauphine. Renault, well-known adepts at public relations and advertising, sold an estimated 60–70,000 Dauphines in Britain between 1956 and 1965. The majority were imported, but sizeable numbers were built up from kits at the company's London assembly plant in Acton. For a while it was Britain's hightest-selling foreign car, and publicity included Britain's first major single-model television campaign as well as colourful and imaginative print advertising. Attractive, light and cheap to run, the Dauphine was adopted by London's early minicab operators and, if rust took most British Dauphines off the road by 1975, the car's reputation never suffered in Britain as it did in America, where 6-volt electrics, fragile fibre timing wheels, rustproneness, erratic service and a general unsuitability for high-speed cruising, not to mention competition from domestic compacts and the Volkswagen, drastically reduced the model's sales from approximately 91,000 in 1959 to fewer than 30,000 in 1962. A few dozen Dauphines survive in Britain.

◆

Part Three

Imported Marques

Britain Embraces the World

◆

Faced with a high unit cost of £796, as well as, perhaps, some prejudice against a foreign car, the strategy of the advertising agents [C. Vernon & Sons] was like that of Henry VII, who turned adversity to his advantage: it made a virtue of the 'difference' and 'foreignness' of the Dauphine in justification of its price. Since the advertising was aimed at people with higher incomes, it presented the Dauphine as an elegant, feminine, chic French car associated with Paris models and young people in happy situations.

— Ralph Harris and Arthur Seldon, *Advertising in Action*, 1962.

25

Volkswagen, Renault and Citroën

Special Cases

As continental marques long established in Britain, where they had factories until July 1961 and February 1966 respectively, Renault and Citroën were unusual among importers, and the Volkswagen, an early leading import, was unique. In August 1955, *Motor Trader* asked plaintively, "Why is West Germany's Volkswagen cutting into British export sales to the extent that it is? Practically half the Swedish market has been lost to it. We are told that it outsells all other cars in five European markets and that stiff import duties have been imposed on it by Belgium, France and Italy as a measure of self-protection. On August 5 the millionth car was produced at the Wolfsburg works which, in 1946, was a shambles. Now nearly 1,200 vehicles a day are being produced and 50 per cent are going for export. How does it happen?" The magazine went on to describe how the car was produced, sold and serviced. By December 1959, the British concessionaires, V.W. Motors Ltd., were importing about 8000 Volkswagens a year. In the summer of 1961 the magazine devoted a supplement to the marque.[1]

The great strengths of the Volkswagenwerk were the reliability of its car and the excellence of the service network on which it insisted—characteristics in which many British manufacturers fell short. According to Robert Braunschweig, editor of the Swiss journal *Automobil Revue*, which was published in French and German and read throughout Europe, "The very export successes of the first post-war years created problems which later turned against the British firms; whereas the scarcity of cars in general made sales very easy, their quality and durability [were] not always entirely satisfactory. Non-British products, with which these cars were replaced in the early fifties, did not, of course, suffer from these defects. Even today the after-effect of this first

post-war period has not been overcome entirely in certain markets." Having tried mainland European and American marques *faute de mieux*, motorists became highly attached to them: "This is the reason why no better warranty exists for future success than goodwill accumulated in past years, and there is hardly a more difficult task than to reconquer markets which have been lost. Even in the United States of America the situation is hardly different. Although the American public may be more capricious, and shift its allegiance for very superficial reasons, not a manufacturer has been known to get away with a product which did not give full satisfaction over a prolonged period.... Public acceptance of a car in free export areas is based upon [1] a good reputation of earlier products hailing from the firm concerned; [2] a close network of distributors, agents and service stations; [3] generous interpretation of warranty claims; [4] regular advertising."[2] "Free export areas" eventually included Britain, and in the long term Braunschweig's criteria would apply to British cars in their home market as well as abroad.

Braunschweig listed forty cars and their principal competitors, and by 1957 the competition was strong: the Volkswagen competed against the Ford Prefect, Morris Minor and Standard Ten; and the Hillman Minx and Vauxhall Victor faced rivals from DKW, Fiat, Ford, Goliath, Opel, Panhard and Simca. The six-cylinder British Fords and Vauxhalls, and the Standard Vanguard, were compared with the Mercedes-Benz 180, the Opel Kapitän, the Renault Frégate and the V8-engined Simca Vedette Versailles. If the Frégate was a thoroughly uninspired car with a tendency to jam its steering-column gear-change on Alpine passes,[3] the Vedette had a lively character surprisingly different to that of the

Zephyr. The Mercedes-Benz was considered excellent by any standard.

Articles which described why motorists in export markets had deserted British manufacturers naturally led many British readers to wonder whether they should do the same. But in the short term British car makers benefited from a local loyalty to the home product and, in the early post-war years, from an aversion to anything German. Such feelings, combined with import duties and a general resistance to novelty whatever its origin, tended to limit sales of the Volkswagen in particular. "In our family, no one drove German cars," recalls the biographer and social historian, Ruth Brandon, "If my mother caught sight of a Mercedes or a Volkswagen she would shudder and say, 'Horrible thing!' I hated the savagery in her voice, the vindictive unforgivingness. And most of all my own inability—dimmed now, but in some degree active—to detach myself from these feelings.... My father drove a succession of severely patriotic vehicles: a Standard 9, followed, as business improved, by a pair of stately Triumph Renowns.... British to the core. As was the last car of my childhood, an elegant dark grey MG Magnette...."[4] A similar reaction would reduce sales of Japanese cars to older British motorists until the 1980s.

At the end of the Second World War, the British motor industry notoriously dismissed the Volkswagen as a design undeserving of resurrection, at least in England. Billy Rootes did not want to build it in England or in Germany, and Vauxhall was similarly dismissive. The Americans, Australians and French did not want it either, even if not all who examined the design were blind to its technical merits. In later years it became conventional to assume that Britain had missed a unique opportunity to absorb a future rival and to expand its own motor industry to mainland Europe. A minority, however, disagreed, considering that the British would not have built, developed, marketed or supported the car as thoroughly as was necessary for it to secure the success that it achieved in German hands. The Volkswagen's appeal in world markets, self-regenerating once its reputation had become established, was founded on virtues that, as Braunschweig implied, the British car industry did not consistently nurture. Even if "what-ifs" about the past can never be proved empirically, it is probably fair to say that Volkswagen benefited not only from the work of remarkable individuals during 1945–55, but also from cultural and psychological conditions that did not obtain elsewhere, and which were essential to its survival. On this view the Volkswagen was a goose that would not have laid any golden eggs outside the very particular habitat that was its homeland, where it became a focus of a post-war national aspiration that concentrated the minds and hearts of all connected with its development and manufacture. If the company was slow to abandon the Beetle's layout after its design, with the passing of rear-engined cars in general, had become irrecoverably obsolescent, that did not negate the earlier achieve-

ment. Where ruggedness and simplicity were paramount, it survived: although the Beetle ceased to be produced in Germany in 1978, it was built in Mexico until July 2003.[5]

In the 1950s, the Volkswagen polarized opinion all over the world. "It is extraordinary how much controversy rages around the little Volkswagen," wrote S.C.H. Davis in 1958, "On the one hand there are those who rave about its slim, modern line; on the other are the unbelievers, who refer to it as having the appearance of an in-growing toe nail. Some allege fantastic performance which others deny. There is no half-measure of opinion.... I think this is a very interesting little car which has the air of good workmanship one has come to expect from Germany."[6] Moreover, it was comparatively inexpensive: in the spring of 1958 a saloon de luxe cost £758 17s, which was just £10 10s more than a basic ("Special") Hillman Minx and nearly £40 less than a Renault Dauphine (£796 7s). For many British motorists the Volkswagen's extra cost compared with a two-door Morris Minor de luxe (£651 12s) or a Standard Super Ten (£653 17s) was more than adequately compensated by its durability and the advantages of an air-cooled engine.

The Volkswagen had champions from the start, especially Bill Boddy, the editor of *Motor Sport* who "first became aware of [the car] when Army personnel who had used military versions in the field, or who had seen the first production saloons, wrote to *Motor Sport* about it. At this time the specification of the Beetle was regarded as highly unconventional, and therefore to be regarded with suspicion by British car users.... Only those less staid in their technical thinking accepted the VW."[7] Beetles trickled into Britain from 1947, and were officially imported from 1953 until German production ceased. In 1954 a de luxe saloon cost £689 12s 6d, a Volkswagen Microbus de luxe £1276 2s 6d. Boddy bought his first Beetle in 1955, and found the company's customer relations service "as efficient as it was unpretentious."[8] The VW's handbook of ninety pages or so was notably clear and comprehensive, and included an elegant and colourful cutaway illustration of the car in side view showing its main features and mechanical layout. There was also humour in small cartoons: things to check before using the car included fan belt tension (illustrated with two children playing tug-of-war), tyre pressures (with a small boy bowling a tyre along the road), brake efficiency (with a cowboy on his horse stopping suddenly) and the amount of fuel in the tank (with a chef bearing a large tureen).

Volkswagen conformed to the fourth of Braunschweig's 1957 criteria—"regular advertising"—too. In Germany the car was not heavily advertised in the ordinary sense until the Opel Kadett arrived in the early 1960s. Before then, announcements of production and sales records (which were also published in export territories) were generally thought sufficient, and they constituted advertising of a kind. But in Britain the car was advertised by the agents Downtons Ltd.

from October 1953; by Havas Ltd. from October 1957; and then, famously, by Doyle Dane Bernbach from 1968, beginning a long association between the agency and Volkswagen in Britain. In 1988, Tony Taylor, group account director for Volkswagen at DDB Needham (as the agency had become) said of advertising for the new Passat, "What we've done with the Passat comes out of a long-term campaign — we're actually celebrating 20 years of working with VW. So its not a question of starting with a completely blank sheet of paper, we started way back with the Beetle."[9] The 1988 television campaign, in which the new car was dropped through seven feet onto the studio floor, referred to past Volkswagens, including the Beetle. Doyle Dane Bernbach had advertised Volkswagens in America since 1959 in a famous series that deliberately pitched the car against the planned obsolescence[10] and commensurate advertising styles of American cars of the day. Best-known were the advertisement that captioned the car "Lemon" because "the chrome strip on the glove compartment is blemished and must be replaced," and the piece that, after the moon landing, showed a model of the lunar module instead of a car: "It's ugly, but it gets you there."[11]

Early British advertising for the car was, by comparison, conventional. "See the internationally famous Volkswagen with these new features," said a 1957 Motor Show advertisement, "The VW has a host of new features. In addition to those shown [wider front and rear screens and a larger glove compartment] are larger windscreen wipers, improved interior trim, a platform-type accelerator pedal.... No wonder there are now nearly 2,000,000 VWs on the roads of the world." In 1958–59 the marque's advertisements became more imaginative and were at first astonishingly diverse. A painting in a European style of a few years earlier, impressionistic renderings, and close-up photographs of small components all appeared within a year of each other. In 1959–60 the marque settled down to a coherent campaign, "The car that owes its success to the man in the street," in which Volkswagens were depicted naturalistically by photographer Pamela Chandler in places such as Covent Garden, a market-place and a busy street. For copy these advertisements carried just the VW logo and the slogan, "The best value in the world."[12] During 1961–67, Volkswagen advertising concentrated on the car's economy, service back-up, durability and imperviousness to the weather, and reflected the themes and copy styles used by Doyle Dane Bernbach in the United States. "Weather beaten" said one headline. "The car that always comes second" said another, piously, because "It's the Volkswagen Service that comes first." A 1964 advertisement showed unblemished parts of a parked VW such as a tail-light, a door hinge and a windscreen rubber and asked, "What stays out all day, all night, summer & winter, yet doesn't grow old?" In 1965 a horse pulled a cart on which lay a damaged radiator, hoses, water pump and centre driveshaft, all of them "parts a Volkswa-

gen never needs." British advertisements from Doyle Dane Bernbach in 1968–69 sometimes had American counterparts. "In 1953, it was the Volkswagen that looked funny" said a May 1969 piece that showed the car with a Standard Eight, a Ford Prefect and a Hillman Californian. In America the car had been seen with 1949 cars from Tucker, Packard, DeSoto, Studebaker and Hudson: "Where are they now?"

By 1970, however, for all of its virtues and continual development, the Beetle was old-fashioned, and the VW 1500 (1961–65) and subsequent 1600 fastback (1967–73), modern-looking but similarly rear-engined, were never really popular in Britain, although many more fastbacks were seen than 1500 saloons.[13] The VW 411 of 1968–72 was the last rear-engined Volkswagen car, and was advertised in Britain as "a Volkswagen for people who can't afford to be seen in a Volkswagen." Styled by Brooks Stevens[14] with a slightly nose-up stance and (at first) large oval headlamps, it looked ungainly. Some people found the off-set pedals of the right-hand-drive car uncomfortable. The 411's handling was better than that of the Beetle, but like all rear-engined cars it was too sensitive to cross-winds and too light in its steering unless a heavy load were carried in the boot. The engine was accessible from above only through a hatch (in the ordinary sense) beneath the rear window which gave an effective opening no deeper than a couple of planks of wood. "Not an easy car to service yourself," decided *Motoring Which?* in April 1971.[15] In July the same magazine summarized the particular advantages of the Beetle as "quite good reliability; fairly quiet high-speed cruising; difficult to steal from; good instruments and minor controls; good bumpers" and its particular disadvantages as "uncomfortable; noisy at low speed; rather poor heating; badly affected by side winds; poor pedal layout; heavy fuel consumption; poor guarantee; tedious daily checks." The poor guarantee was a surprise to many readers, even if optimists could argue elliptically that a long guarantee was needed only for a car that was likely to break down. The magazine thought the car tested — a 1302S ("1600 Super Beetle") — expensive at £975, although a basic Volkswagen 1200 cost a more reasonable £783. By contrast, the Hillman Avenger (Plymouth Cricket in America) cost between £903 for a de luxe and £1137 for a GT.[16] The 411's price proved contentious both in its home market and abroad, as traditional Volkswagen virtues made up a lower proportion of a car's appeal once it became comparatively expensive. In Britain a four-door 411 cost £1282 even in 1969.

In the late 1950s and early 1960s, the Beetle had one rival in particular, both in Britain and, more briefly and to a lesser extent, in the United States. This was the Renault Dauphine, whose name otherwise referred to the wife of the eldest son of the ruler of the Dauphiné region (especially the son of Louis XIV) or, less esoterically, to a female dolphin. Renault had initially intended to call the car the Corvette, until someone remembered the Chevrolet sports car.[17] During 1959, *Motor Trader* carried an advertisement showing a

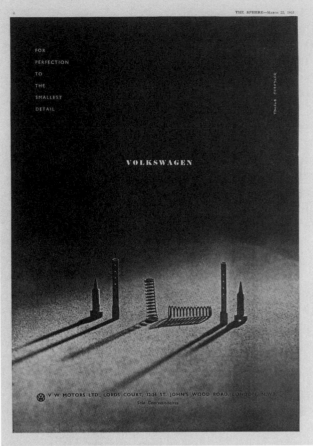

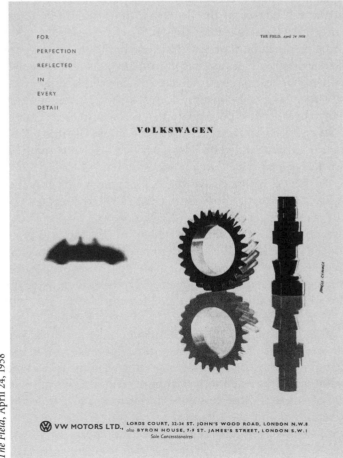

Dauphine at the bottom of the page while above it, descending vertically, were the large letters "L.S.D." representing the colloquial (usually spoken) abbreviation of pounds, shillings and pence. "Lots to be gained by Selling the Dauphine," said the copywriter, using the letters in successive copy lines. Such an advertisement could not, of course, have appeared ten years later. In the same magazine, Renault crowed: "Dauphine sales put Renault in the lead. Renault Limited are now the leading importers of cars into the United Kingdom. The Dauphine outsells all other foreign cars in this country. Dauphine world beater!" At this time, early in 1960, the Dauphine was at the height of its popularity and it briefly took 3.5 percent of the small car market. Renault's sales network, meanwhile, had expanded during 1957 and 1958 from under 200 dealers to 750 or so, many of which held exclusive franchises.[18] It seemed an act worth getting in on. Renault's advertising budget for the car in Britain was substantial, too. As Ralph Harris and Arthur Seldon recounted in a detailed analysis of Renault's campaign in 1962, serious advertising for the Dauphine began in 1957, and in that year 1700 cars were sold against an advertising expenditure of £44,200. In 1958, 2700 cars were sold against a budget of £76,600, and in 1959 the figures were 10,000 cars and £131,100. In 1960, 21,500 cars were sold and expenditure on Dauphine advertising extended to £277,200, of which press advertising amounted to £161,000, television advertising to £79,500 and general production costs for both, together with dealer literature and dealer advertising material, to £36,700. By contrast, only 12,997 German cars of all types were sold in Britain in 1960.

The Dauphine campaign was devised by C. Vernon & Sons, who had been Renault's advertising agents since long before the Second World War and would remain with the company throughout the 1960s. In its first year, Dauphine advertising "was directed chiefly to readers of the Class A publications (*The Times, Daily Telegraph*, the higher quality Sunday newspapers, 'glossy' periodicals, etc.)," but in 1958 "[t]he advertising 'message' was gradually extended down the income scale to embrace more widely bought national dailies (*Daily Mail, Daily Express*), and the appeal developed the subsidiary themes of economy (45 mpg), comfort (independent four-wheel suspension) and safety

('steady as a rock at 70 mph')." In 1959, a "60-second television advertisement won a diploma at the 1959 Cannes Film Festival and was used by the parent company in other countries."[19] Television advertising had been used from the beginning of the campaign in 1957. As Harris and Seldon remarked in 1962, "The strategy of the company in selecting a single model as the spearhead for its penetration of an overseas market appears to have been of decisive importance. It is similar to that successfully employed by Volkswagen and contrasts sharply with some British efforts in [mainland] Europe which are dispersed over too many models and modifications."[20]

The Dauphine was the first post-war Renault to be sold in Britain in significant numbers. A handful of Frégates and few hundred of the tiny, 747cc Renault 4CV (1946–61) appeared on British roads in the 1950s, and that car had loyal devotees, but at £599 13s 4d at the end of 1954, when a Ford Prefect cost £560 14s 2d, the 4CV (or 750 as it was called in Britain) was very much an "alternative" choice. Upper-middle-class francophiles generally preferred the much larger Citroën Light Fifteen (£971 10s 10d). Both models were assembled in Britain — the Citroën at Slough, where it received uniquely British trim, Lucas semaphore indicators and other details; the Renault at the company's assembly plant at Acton in west London, which was expanded during 1958–59. Renaults of many kinds had been available in Britain before the Second World War, but none had sold in large numbers. In 1960, however, 2000 Dauphine kits would be assembled at Acton, and 15,000 Dauphines would be imported between January and May of that year.[21]

The Dauphine was announced — or rather, its announcement was announced — at the beginning of February 1956: "New Renault to be Announced in Spring. Renault are to market in the early spring an additional model, intermediate between the 750 [4CV] and the Frégate, to be known as the Dauphine..." — and a picture of the car was shown on a sunny beach, complete with its distinctive "spider" wheels, inherited from the 4CV, whose rims were attached to their discs by five bolts. By the middle of March the car had been presented in Paris and could described in detail in Britain, where it would cost £769 7s.[22] The price later rose to £796 for 1957 before falling to £759 in June 1958, to £717 in April

---

Opposite: **Volkswagen (1200).** Doyle Dane Bernbach became famous for ground-breaking Volkswagen advertising in America from 1959, and in Britain from the late 1960s. Yet in the latter market the agency inherited an existing tradition of quiet iconoclasm established by Havas Ltd., under whom, astonishingly, all four of these advertisements appeared within 11 months during 1958–59. The themes of ubiquity, durability and meticulous engineering are, and would remain, Volkswagen staples, but none of the advertisements is itself characteristic of the period. Pamela Chandler's beautiful close-up photographs — not to mention the accompanying copy and layout — are decades ahead of their time, although the typeface of "Volkswagen" is a survivor from German pre-launch publicity of 1938. The modest copy and highly stylized illustrations of the last advertisement recall British and German (particularly Adler) advertising of the late 1930s. The family scene, by contrast, is very much in a continental style of 1950–55. It was also used in America under the earnest headline, "The money we save driving this sensible car will do lots of good for our children." Volkswagens began to trickle into Britain after 1947 and official imports began in 1953, helped by the car's remarkable durability and a notably efficient service operation, under which — as elsewhere in the world — dealers were required to have extensive stocks of spares before cars could be sold. Volkswagens made up the majority of imported German cars in 1958–59, supplemented by a few Borgwards, Mercedes, German Fords and DKWs, the occasional V8-engined BMW or privately imported Opel, and a steady stream of what Leonard Lord of BMC characteristically called "bloody awful bubble cars," which he was determined to defeat with the Mini.

1959 and to £690 in May 1960. At twelve feet, eleven inches long and five feet wide, the Dauphine was not particularly small by British standards but it was extremely light at about 1400 lb., and its features included a spare wheel stored within a lockable tray under the raised centre part of the front bumper. The number plate was attached to the front of the tray, and the whole device, which was claimed to allow the wheel to act as a shock absorber in an impact, was patented.[23] Another innovation was a Ferlec electro-magnetic automatic clutch developed by S.A.F Ferodo in Paris, which was announced for the 4CV at the beginning of 1955 and which cost £38 5s on the Dauphine. As with Lockheed's Manumatic in Britain, the clutch, in normal use, was operated by a switch in the gearlever.[24]

As two rear-engined small cars produced in huge numbers in their homelands (the millionth Dauphine being built in 1960, the two-millionth in 1963), the Dauphine and Volkswagen De luxe were comparable in many respects, and by February 1960, with the Dauphine pacing the Volkswagen, they were identically priced in Britain at £717. A Birmingham accessory manufacturer even produced chrome-and-enamel key-chains, with miniature cars, for each.[25] But the markets for the two cars, whilst overlapping, were not identical. While the Volkswagen was aimed more towards value-conscious couples and small families who needed reliability and durability above all else, the Dauphine was a pretty four-door car aimed in particular towards affluent and fashion-conscious women. This targeting was reflected in early purchasing patterns and, indeed, in the cars' colours: the Volkswagen was usually seen in sober shades, many of them dark or semi-metallic or both, while the characteristic colour of the early Dauphine in Britain was bright red, which was otherwise not usually seen, except on sports cars, until the Vauxhall Victor appeared in 1957.

Renault were forever aware of the competition from Volkswagen, and early advertising prepared the necessary ground. "Renault — The leader of the French Automobile Industry" announced a June 1957 advertisement between two large aerial photographs of the company's Paris headquarters and of the new factory at Flins (beside the Seine, 25 miles west of Paris), "the most modern in Europe." In August the car took centre stage while the copy moved into Volkswagen territory: "RS/GB = A first class reason for buying Renault. Wherever you go in Britain, you can relax when you go by Renault. For there is now a complete national network of Renault Service agents, ready and willing to meet your every need, with a first-class after-sales service. In fact, Renault Service is all over Great Britain! A full list of these service agents may be had on request from Renault Ltd., Western Avenue, London, W.3."

Two contrasting advertisements appeared in October 1957. The first, with a simple monochrome drawing and the theme "So much extra in the Renault Dauphine" listed features under the headings, "Extra Comfort," "Extra Driving Ease," "Extra Safety and Security" and "Extra Long Life." By contrast, a parallel advertisement showed a watercolour painting of a red Dauphine being driven at speed against a golden backdrop, a magnificent swan flying overhead: "Renault Dauphine — Her elegance, power and smoothness in movement make it a sheer delight to drive a Dauphine. Few cars indeed can boast so fine a performance with such economy." The claim was fair, too: in 1959 a Dauphine tested by The Autocar gave nearly 41 mpg overall, and 58 mpg at a steady 30 mph. With only 845cc and 31 bhp the Dauphine was not fast, however: 0–60 took 43.9 seconds and the car's top speed was only 65 mph; wide gaps between the car's three speeds did not help. Extra power arrived with the tuned (37.5 bhp), four-speed Gordini Dauphine in 1958 and its successor, the 40 bhp Dauphine Gordini of 1960, which became available in de luxe form in 1961 at £797 5s 10d compared with the standard Gordini's £749 2s 6d. In 1962 a Ruddspeed performance conversion, at £104 10s fitted, gave 42 bhp, 0–60 in 15.6 seconds and a top speed of 86 mph for an average fuel consumption of 30 mpg or so.[26]

In 1958 advertising, Renault's appeal to women became much more overt. A short series published in Vogue, The Sphere and other upmarket magazines showed fashionable women in French-looking "model" poses, as in February: "Recherchée (something rather special). Just look at those lines! Now there's a beautiful model. L'élégance française… chic is the word for the Renault Dauphine, a car you'd be proud to own. She not only looks good — she is good. She drives like a dream, with real power at your command. She's easy on the petrol as well as on the eye — and she's smooth as silk for driving in town. Give the Dauphine a closer look. She makes driving a real pleasure in every way." A small drawing of the car appeared at the bottom of the page. "Sensationelle (something rather special)" promised a June advertisement, "With natural French flair for fashion, this Paris model creates an atmosphere of charm, elegance and delight wherever she goes. And no wonder — for she's a Renault Dauphine, the most sprightly and exciting of Continental cars. Do you remember how she won the Monte Carlo Rally against all comers? Swift on the open road and oh, so easy on the petrol, she makes driving a real pleasure, even in town!" If one could hear the copywriter's feet clump-clumping heavily through the silk (how many women would remember anything as happening "against all comers"?) the point was still made: the Dauphine was not an earnest *phut-phut* like the Volkswagen. Many future copywriters, too, would write about small cars as if they were people, occasionally referring to a car as "she" or, more often, using its type name as the name of a person, without "a" or "the" before it. Many people thought the Dauphine one of the best looking cars in the world.

In 1959–60 Dauphine advertising was essentially conventional, as Harris and Seldon implied, but it was still imaginative within the conventions of its type. "The 1959

Dauphine turns all heads!" said smiling his-and-her faces in October 1959, "She turns all heads with her looks and wins all hearts with her performance." In a May 1960 advertisement, multicoloured posters in the style of a western saloon-bar bill-board described features such as "Taxi-type turning circle" and "7 sparkling colours"—a novel approach which, with its deliberate visual clutter, typified a kind of conservative wackiness that was a staple of lighthearted advertising for many kinds of products for a year or two. Like other car manufacturers, Renault adopted colour photographs, such as June 1959's studio shot of a red Dauphine that appeared with a drawing of a Hansom cab into which photographs of the occupants had been cleverly integrated: "Ah, me dears, remember the clip-clop leisurely days when two wheels and one horsepower was considered fast? Nowadays everybody wants these here new-fangled horseless carriages. Mind you, if you really do need another pair of wheels and a heap more power, they do say the Dauphine is newer-fangled than most."

The Dauphine craze did not last, however. Fewer than 4000 French cars were sold in Britain during 1961 (compared with approximately 4,100 in 1958, 14,400 in 1959 and more than 38,000 in 1960), and Renault's advertising expenditure declined sharply during 1961–63. "[I]f the peak success of 1960 has not been maintained," concluded Harris and Seldon in 1962, "such ups and downs demonstrate that even the best advertising cannot triumph over market forces that were in part aroused by competition from the Dauphine."[27] The steady advance of the Volkswagen continued, and a broadly similar number of Beetles were imported in 1961 as in 1960. For all its chic in 1958–60, and although (as advertising proudly boasted during 1958–60) it won the 1958 Monte Carlo Rally, the Renault was not especially durable. Its engine lasted longer under British conditions than it did in the United States, but its bodywork rusted badly, "though no worse than the [earlier Renault] 4CV or certain other contemporary small cars," recalled J. Dewar McLintock.[28] The Dauphine shared the Volkswagen's suspension layout, however, and consequently its tendency to oversteer and, in extreme circumstances, roll over. "Sideways...effects are always more interesting with a rear-engined car but on the other hand, rear-wheel traction is good because of the weight over the axles. What all this adds up to is that if you corner violently, breakaway will come in suddenly and you have to have exceptionally good reactions to correct the slide and avoid disaster...for some reason any disasters with Dauphines seemed to attract more attention than with the Volkswagen.... One good thing about the car was that if you were so unfortunate as to roll it, you had a good, strong turret top to take the crunch."[29] A great many Dauphines were rolled, including, eventually, a pale blue car with leather upholstery and chrome-plated wire wheels presented to the Queen and the Duke of Edinburgh when they visited the French Renault plant at Flins in 1957, which

in the late 1960s was used as a staff hack at Buckingham Palace. The Aerostable suspension of 1960 onwards, in which air-filled rubber bags supplemented the standard springs, only partly cured the problem, and by then the damage to the car's reputation in Britain had been done. By the time of the 1964 Motor Show, only the Gordini was listed.

The Dauphine's image was additionally undermined in quite a different way in June 1961, when Welbeck Motors Ltd. of west London bought 500 Dauphines for conversion into the country's first minicabs. In order to attract passengers needing longer runs out of central London, the minicabs would normally charge a flat rate of a shilling (12d) a mile and would not charge for empty running. Fitted with meters, Pye radio communication equipment and instantly recognizable advertising panels, the cars were stated not to be in competition with London's famous black cabs, but London's taxi drivers saw the development very differently. "In the early days," recalled McLintock, "there were many savage battles between the established licensed cabbies and the freebooting newcomers; and that the latter should use Renaults was a little ironic, since such wide use was made of Renault taxis in the formative years of the legitimate taxi companies."[30] In the short term, Welbeck Motors' choice of car was good for Renault, who sold several hundred extra cars. But even if few London cabbies ever mistook "civilian" Dauphines for the distinctively painted minicabs, the dispute tarnished the Dauphine's image for many middle-class buyers. The London sophisticates who had been targeted in 1957–59 were often extremely loyal to the black cabs which they used during the week, and it was not every woman who felt that she could laugh off cabbies' jokes or absent-minded attempts by travellers to get into the back and hitch a ride. And many aspirational motorists, too, would avoid a car, whatever its merits, that was known as a minicab. In the meantime the capricious chic market was becoming enchanted by the Mini and, to a lesser extent, by the Triumph Herald.

The retreat of the Dauphine in Britain coincided with an even sharper decline in the United States, where for a short time it had been the second best-selling imported car after the Volkswagen. That decline, caused by a combination of recession, the passing of the fashion for imported cars other than the Volkswagen, the advance of the domestic American "compacts" and the Dauphine's own fragility under American motoring conditions, was so catastrophic that thousands of Dauphines rusted in import parks. Small British sedans fell out of favour in the United States almost as quickly. In February 1961, Renault announced that its Acton assembly plant, where the Renault models most popular in Britain had been built for decades, would be closed in July, and would be replaced by a huge new spare parts depot.[31] In January 1962 a Coventry member of Parliament accused Renault of "dumping" cars at Southampton following the American recession. The accusation was denied by

Renault U.K.'s managing director, Jean Ordner, who stated that "every Renault imported into Britain during the past five years has been specifically ordered and built for sale in Britain and could not be sent elsewhere."[32] In September 1962, Renault reduced the trade discounts available to its 600 remaining British dealers while retail prices of the Dauphine and Floride were also reduced. "Keeping our advertising, temporarily, to a minimum, we present now, for the whole of the Renault range, a price list that would otherwise become practicable only after a long series of customs adjustments," said Ordner.[33] The new prices anticipated reductions in import tarriffs that were expected to follow negotiations within Europe.

Renault's was a sharp retrenchment in Britain as elsewhere, but by the mid-1960s the company was recovering strongly. True *chic* was achieved with the Floride, a sporty-looking 2+2 inspired by the Volkswagen Karmann-Ghia, intended primarily for the American market and based mechanically on the Dauphine at first and subsequently — as the Caravelle — on the Renault R8 introduced in 1962. The car's genesis was complicated but its styling made it instantly attractive to fashionable Europeans and to a few European car enthusiasts in the United States. Its fins were very subtle, being canted outwards by just a few degrees,[34] and a moulded-in side spear, which opened downwards behind the door into a chrome-straked air intake in front of the rear wheel and upwards onto the rear deck, was distinctive and anticipated the side sculpture of the 1960 Volvo P1800 coupe for which Frua[35] was partly responsible. The Floride's recessed headlamps, an innovation on a mass-produced European car though lightly anticipated by the twin-headlamp layout of the regular 1958 Packards, became a feature of many cars of the 1960s, including the MGB and Michelotti's design, produced in October 1960, for the Triumph Spitfire.[36]

Of the beautiful Renault for beautiful people, McLintock remarked twenty years later, "The ladies loved the Floride and Caravelle, which looked at once impudent and opulent, as well as being essentially French, even if designed bodily by an Italian. It was no hardship for Brigitte Bardot to sit prettily at the wheel of a Floride when asked to do so by the Renault PR boys, and she made a wonderful picture."[37] What was good enough for Brigitte was good enough for Britons, and in the summer of 1961 two advertisements showed the car with a glamorous couple. In the first advertisement a dinner-jacketed smoothie helped his companion into a gold convertible, while in the second a white coupe rested between trees in the afternoon sun against a Mediter-

ranean coastline. The copy was the same for both: "Not for ordinary folk — The Renault Floride is the most beautiful car in the world and quite one of the most desirable. It has all the attributes of a dream car — yet has the virtue of being real. It brings to its owner a sense of satisfaction that is beyond all words. The Floride is exclusively on sale through Renault dealers. In three models: Convertible, Fixed head coupe, or Convertible with removable hard top." It cost £1191 as a convertible or £1212 as a coupe, which was expensive for an 845cc, 36 bhp car that could only just manage 73 mph and 0–60 in 24 seconds, but perhaps less than outrageous for the Floride's looks and comparative luxury. The Volkswagen Karmann-Ghia was comparable at £1272 (coupe) or £1433 (convertible). That other continental glamourpuss, the Volvo P1800 coupe, cost a ferocious £1948 at the end of 1961, which was not far short of the Jaguar E-type (£2160 or, as a fixed-head, £2262). The closest British equivalent to the Floride was the Ford Consul Capri, which appeared on the home market at the beginning of 1962 at £916 and which, like the Renault, was advertised in white with glamorously dressed couples. The "co-respondent" market was never large, either literally or figuratively, yet the Floride and its advertising lent glamour to the Renault name and fuelled a growing middle-class perception, from which all continental marques benefited, that foreign cars were glamorous and exciting.

In 1962, a pair of advertisements for the updated coupe and convertible — now called the Caravelle and Floride S respectively — appeared in which the Caravelle took centre stage. In June the new coupe was photographed at ground level outside a picturesque farmhouse; in August it appeared in an open field, silhouetted against the sunset, in a style of photography that would become popular in the late 1960s. Yet with slotted wheels, filled-in air intakes and a new, steeply sloping rear window, the Caravelle lacked something of its predecessor's dream-car look, even if a 956cc, 51 bhp engine, disc brakes, a stiffened floorpan and improved suspension made it, objectively, a better car. The copy, used for both advertisements, was more practical, too: "Caught in a rare moment of repose — This is one of the two new Florides at rest. No ordinary cars, these. Extra muscle in their big new engines. Extra thrust to match their new bold look. Extra stopping power in their four-wheel disc brakes. There's luxury, new-found space and a host of those out-of-the-ordinary features that make for prestige…find for yourself how excitingly it turns form into performance." By 1965, with 1108cc, *Autocar* achieved 0–60 in 17.6 seconds and a top speed of 89 mph, which in a rear-engined car with low-

Opposite: **Renault Floride.** Italian-styled sporting derivatives of small saloons were popular across Europe and, as imports, in America during the late 1950s and early 1960s. VW's Beetle-based Karmann-Ghia and Triumph's Herald-derived Spitfire by Michelotti were probably the best known, but the Floride, developed from the economical if sometimes fragile Dauphine, caused a minor sensation when revealed in Paris in 1958, and it was subsequently promoted by Brigitte Bardot. The car was not fast (845cc, 36 bhp) or, with swing axles and a rear engine, particularly safe, but as one of the most glamorous non-specialist cars of its period it justified lavish advertising. Needless to say, sports car traditionalists thought it beneath contempt — but did Monsieur care?

NOT
for
ordinary folk

The Renault Floride is the most beautiful car in the world and quite one
of the most desirable. It has all the attributes of a dream car—yet has the
virtue of being real. It brings to its owner a sense of satisfaction that
is beyond all words. The Floride is exclusively on sale through Renault
dealers. In three models: Convertible, Fixed head coupé, or Convertible
with removable hard top. **RENAULT ▸FLORIDE**

RENAULT LTD WESTERN AVENUE LONDON W3 • SHOWROOMS: 54 BROMPTON ROAD SW3

Clan-carrier

Big on people room, big on luggage room, big on performance.
The one small thing is the price.

Nobody's made an elastic-sided car yet. But for sheer stretchability the new Renault 4 comes close.

It holds a family of five in easy comfort. It takes a mountain of luggage – even the pram.

And it's the easiest car to load – for five reasons. Four of them are its easy-to-enter doors.

The fifth reason is also a door. The whole back opens and gives you the room to pack in a baby elephant – or a baby giraffe if you get the sun-roof model.

The new Renault 4 is sturdily and sternly practical – built for family motoring without fuss.

You can treat it rough. The tough box-frame chassis and torsion bar suspension don't mind punishment. The Renault 4 takes rugged country in its stride. And you don't feel a thing.

Economy is built-in too. The Renault 4 never needs grease, water or anti-freeze. Servicings are almost nil. And you get 40-45 to every gallon (many owners claim even more).

And the really big feature is the small price. It includes fully synchromesh gearbox, heater/demister, screen-washer, full underspray, childproof safety locks, courtesy light and . . .

STOP PRESS—NEW LUXURY FOR '67. New tailored-for-comfort seats and door upholstery. All in stitched grained leathercloth.

New 18" deep rear parcel shelf. Instantly removable when you want full estate car capacity.

New dashboard with all controls at your fingertips.

Price of this small miracle is £543.15.8. (inc. P.T.). Post the coupon now for all the details we couldn't get into this ad.

RENAULT 4

To: Renault Ltd, Western Avenue, London, W3
Please send free brochure and list of nearest dealers.

Name_____

Address_____

_____

CL.2

Main West End showrooms 77 St. Martins Lane WC2

geared steering was, for most people, fast enough. As the car weighed only 1800lb or so unladen, it could still manage 30 mpg, driven normally, or 40mpg on gentle long runs.[38] It had become, like other Renaults, sensible.

In the early 1960s Renault did not advertise heavily, but from the introduction of the Renault 4 in 1961, front-engined, front-wheel-drive models began to take over from the old Dauphine. The last rear-engined Renault 1100 (called the Renault 10 in America) was sold in 1971. In many ways the Renault 4 was a Citroën 2CV for the conventionally minded, as it shared the Citroën's high ground clearance, tenacious road-holding and prodigious but harmless roll while offering full-width bodywork, a metal roof, a full-depth tailgate, a water-cooled 845cc engine and, from 1967, a four-speed gearbox. It was practical, capacious and as ideal for the English countryside as for that in France. "In spite of import duties the price [£581 for a 4L in 1962] is competitive with domestic vehicles and...offers something outside the British range with which to impress the neighbours," said *Small Car* in 1964.[39] Advertising for the Renault 4 took off from 1966 onwards, when the little car's platform chassis was photographed with a family and its luggage in place: "Clan-carrier.... Nobody's made an elastic-sided car yet. But for sheer stretchability the new Renault 4 comes close." The tailgate was a novelty at the time, too: "The whole back opens and gives you the room to pack in a baby elephant — or a baby giraffe if you get the sun-roof model."

Sturdy practicality and rustic whimsy became major themes of Renault 4 advertising during 1969–70, and the car was targeted towards the affluent middle classes. In January 1970 a group of musicians loaded their recording equipment into the back: "Renault 4: for people who take a lot on." In March the car was shown alone in a double garage, the family's skis just visible on a home-made rack behind: "We bought our Renault 4 as a second car and it ended up as our first car." Renault implied snob-value, too, as in December, when the Marquis of Bath was shown with five Renault 4s that he used around his estate: "Owners of very large estates may need more than one Renault 4," said the copywriter. Features included "No greasing. The Renault 4 is greased for life. And no sudden death duties, either. 'The cars are very reliable and the few spares I've needed are always in stock'," confirmed the Marquis, who signed off: "In my opinion it would be difficult to find a car that does so much, so cheaply, as the Renault 4." The most convincing kind of testimonial always came from someone who liked the car for the same reason that an average reader would buy it.

The Renault 16, introduced in 1965 and widely available (and widely road tested) in Britain from early 1966,[40] was advertised as "an entirely new breed of car...designed to be more than a saloon, more than an estate car. It represents the most remarkable contribution to automobile engineering for years." Such a claim was usually a sign of desperation, but the world's first mass-produced medium-sized, front-wheel-drive, five door family hatchback was spacious, a little controversial in its looks, especially inside (though the controversy largely faded by 1970) and heavy in its steering, but very comfortable and, with multi-adjustable seats, versatile too. Its steering-column gearchange was surprising in such a modern car, but was found to be good of its type. "The shape of 2 cars in one," as a 1968 headline called it, was advertised with realistic colour photographs of the car on country roads or, in the case of the more usual monochrome advertisements, against no background at all. Little was characteristically "sixties" about Renault 16 advertising — Renault's layouts, type-faces, cut-out coupons and, by 1969, drawings of seating positions were all more typical of the following decade. Headlines were confident: "Few estate cars are as fast. Few other GTs are as comfortable. Few other saloons carry as much luggage," said a 1970 advertisement for the 102 mph 16 TS. "Spend fifteen minutes in the Renault 16 before you spend £1500 on a two litre" said another headline in the same year.

There was no greater contrast than that between British advertising for the Renault 16 and Renault's 1966 American advertising for the rear-engined Renault 10, in which the company was still apologizing for the Dauphine. After a prolonged period of self-abasement, Renault began a 1967 advertisement, "No more apologies," before describing the new car and how it had been improved, and concluding, "We made sure the automobile would just plain stand up. In short, we made sure that we would never have anything to apologize for again. And so help us, we never will." They never did — but the ground was never made up, either. In England, by contrast, Renault were in a strong position as its cars were, for a European country, standard-sized, and the Dauphine, though ephemeral, never acquired the reputation for hopeless fragility that dogged it in the United States. The Renault 1100, as the Renault 10 was called in Britain, sold fairly well as a brisk, light and economical alternative to heavier and more firmly sprung British small cars. "There's a supple difference" said a 1968 headline below a maroon car speeding down the inevitable country lane (maroon being a favourite colour with Renault at the time). "Some family cars make two hundred miles feel like 2000. But not the luxurious Renault 1100. Because its supple seats are scientifically designed to overcome the nasty side of travel — the pins and needles. And the cramp." Which was

Opposite: **Renault 4.** Another striking advertisement from Renault, in a very different genre. The R4, introduced in 1961, was the company's first modern car with its front-mounted engine, front-wheel drive, a lift-up tailgate and, amusingly but harmlessly, a wheelbase slightly longer on one side than the other to accommodate the rear suspension's torsion bars. The body-on-platform construction allowed advertisers to show a natural cutaway of a kind impracticable with a conventional monocoque. The copy is ahead of its time with an unforced, practically-minded informality more typical of the 1970s.

What makes the big Renault 16 an entirely new breed of car?

The experts all agree that the Renault 16 is an entirely new breed of car. It's designed to be more than a saloon, more than an estate car. It represents the most remarkable contribution to automobile engineering for years.

Perhaps the most remarkable thing about this car is the seats. There are seven different ways to arrange them. From the ultimate in armchair comfort for five, the Renault 16 can be quickly altered to give 42 cu. ft. of carrying space.

The Renault 16's good design doesn't stop with the seating. There's independent all-round suspension with extra long torsion bars to give you the smoothest, road-hugging ride. There's the luxury of air conditioning. There's a 1½ litre aluminium engine that does well over 80 m.p.h. at an economical 30 plus to every gallon. And there's much more besides.

Still need convincing? Then what about test driving the new Renault 16? After an hour at the wheel the only thing that's liable to disappoint you is going back to your present car. Still, you can soon put that right.

Price £868.5.8.
Grand Luxe £918.13.7 (both inc.p.t.)

Test drive it once and find out.

For free brochure and list of Renault dealers, post to: Renault Limited, Western Avenue, London W3.
Main West End Showrooms: 77 St. Martin's Lane, London WC2.

Name

Address

RENAULT 16

much more than could be said of the seats in the BMC 1100 in any of its marques.[41] To British motorists, comfort, practicality and innovation were French small cars' great selling points.

Too much innovation, however, made motorists nervous. In 1926 Citroën opened a British manufacturing plant at Slough, where cars were built with many locally sourced parts until 1966. But while the mechanically advanced and conservative-looking Citroën Light Fifteen (the British version of the Onze Légère *Traction Avant*) found a small but steady market in the early post-war years, by 1955 most of Slough's production went to the right-hand-drive export markets of Australia, New Zealand, Rhodesia and South Africa.[42] The Citroën 2CV was built at Slough from 1953–64, but only 752 of these cars attracted buyers in Britain.[43] The 2CV would become fashionable only after 1974, after which well over 100,000 were were sold in the years up to 1990, when imports ceased.[44] At £598 7s in 1956, the Slough-built 2CV, with an engine of 425cc, cost as much as an 1172cc Ford Prefect (£593 17s), and was much too slow, noisy and crude-looking to appeal to mainstream motorists. Its virtues, acknowledged by engineers and lauded by those who tried the car, remained largely unknown. A 1956 advertisement promised: "55 miles to the gallon! — and independent suspension. This is the car to make all car designers revise their thinking! The 2 C.V. not only gives you at least 55 miles on a gallon of low grade fuel, but incorporates a revolutionary system of 4 wheel independent suspension." The claims were true, and road testers generally gave the 2CV excellent reviews, but this was irrelevant to the suburban conformist for whose neighbours the sound of an air-cooled 2CV being driven at maximum capacity — as it always was— had little appeal.[45] The car was anglicized with the Bijou of 1960–64, a 2CV with a neat little fibreglass hardtop body designed by the stylist of the Lotus Elite, Peter Kirwan-Taylor. At £596 2s 6d in 1961, the Bijou represented good value for such an up-to-date look — which reflected that of the DS — but as a car it was still much too slow: The *Autocar* achieved a top speed of 50.3 mph and a 0–40 time of 31.3 seconds.[46] The Bijou was a liability on British roads, and only 211 were sold.[47] The gloriously Gallic 602cc Citroën Ami 6 of 1961, with its fiercely reverse-raked rear window and heavily sculpted nose, was a favourite of its designer Flaminio Bertoni, and in France the Ami was promoted with delightful brochure photography. In England, "the world's most comfortable medium-sized car" was imported complete rather than assembled at Slough, and remained a minority

taste: just 95 (including 57 Breaks, or station wagons) were sold in Britain between 1961 and 1966.[48] Like other Citroëns, the Ami would become more popular in Britain in the 1970s.

In Britain in the 1960s the best-known — and by far the most widely advertised — Citroën was Bertoni's famous DS, of which 6737, including 3838 of ID derivatives, were built and sold by Citroën at Slough during 1956–66 at a rate of a few hundred a year.[49] Early DS copy was rhapsodic, as in April 1958: "The car that has driven a gap in the English language. How can a lover describe his beloved? How does a mother describe her child? We are faced with the same inadequacy of language when we try to tell you of the superlative qualities of the Citroën D.S.19.... It's beyond praise because praise, spoken, sung, or exquisitely rhymed can only present a pale shadow of the magic of a car that takes you, as you slide under the steering wheel, ten years into the future." The copy listed the car's most unusual features, such as its hydro-pneumatic suspension, four-wheel disc brakes, hydraulically assisted steering, hydraulically operated gearbox, front-wheel drive and excellent all-round visability. The DS was also—as the copywriter did not say—one of the most comfortable cars in the world in which to ride in the back, as the wide rear pillar allowed a measure of privacy while the wrapped-round rear window and thin side pillars let in light by which to read a newspaper or write letters— the latter being possible, on ordinary roads, in virtually no other car at the time.[50] Small print at the very bottom of the page mentioned the similar-looking but hydraulically simpler (and therefore, to some motorists, less frightening) ID19, available in France from May 1957 and in Britain from March 1958. Neither model was cheap: an ID19 cost £1498 compared with the £1726 asked for the DS19, while a Humber Super Snipe was £1494 and a Rover 3-Litre cost £1764. This was very much upper-middle-class territory where admiration of unusual design, however well informed and genuine, did not always translate into sales.

An advertisement in *Motor Trader* alerted Citroën dealers to Slough's press campaign: "Superlative Citroën — They've only to drive it to be sold on it. ['Sold' was printed like a windscreen sticker, held between fingers and thumb.] That's the message of the impressive national press advertising campaign from April onwards in important newspapers and magazines including: *Sunday Times — Tatler — Punch — Financial Times — Country Life — Autocar — Motor — Economist — The Queen — Lilliput*. Strong advertising support for Citroën dealers is already appearing in the press. Angled in the right way and to the right people it's

---

Opposite: **Renault 16.** The hatchback invasion begins. This car, the first medium-sized non-utility five-door hatchback apart from occasional adaptations of saloons by coachbuilders, made most British cars look old-fashioned when it appeared in 1965, and only in 1969 would Britain respond in kind with the Maxi. The R16's seats had four positions—normal; "holiday," in which the entire rear seat was moved forward by six inches to increase luggage space; "bulky goods," in which the rear seat cushion pivoted forwards while the backrest was raised and strapped horizontally so that goods could pass underneath; and "shooting brake," in which the whole rear seat and parcel shelf were removed. Additional positions were possible on the Grand Luxe. Citroën's mid-1960s advertising in Britain was generally unremarkable and less interesting, as advertising, than Renault's; this would change in the 1970s.

Country Life, April 24, 1958

The Illustrated London News, May 13, 1967

Citroën DS19 and Safari. Rhapsodic copy for the most remarkable four-door car of its period. It was assembled from a combination of French and British components at Slough until 1966 and subsequently imported complete from France. The operation was small-scale — 590 cars were built in 1958; 1960's total of 2154 was a high point; and the Safari was quite rare, 779 being built between 1960 and 1966. This 1967 advertisement for the Paris-built Safari was therefore aimed a small, largely upper-class market, so perhaps the humour lay only in the incongruity of where, rather than if, tea would be taken. Over the years, the DS greatly expanded the wider public's imagination of what a car could be, and it was partly responsible for mainstream motorists' growing impression, only partly justified, that the most interesting cars were made abroad. DS sales suddenly took off after 1970 and some striking advertisements were produced for it during 1971–74. In the meantime advanced and sophisticated advertising for the car came not only from France, but also from the Swiss, whose clear photography and imaginative illustration complemented the car's futuristic lines to great effect in the early 1960s.

going to sell the Citroën D.S.19 (and, of course, the I.D.19) as it's never been sold before." The announcement appeared several times throughout the year and Citroën's advertising expenditure for the model was broadly equivalent to that of a smallish indigenous producer, such as Daimler.

In its 1958 Motor Show advertisement, Citroën concentrated on the ID19: "One new and brilliant Citroën after another…and each one 10 years ahead of its time. What car comes near the new and brilliant Citroën? Answer: only another new and brilliant Citroën…. Don't just keep up, get ten years ahead with a Citroën." The copy was accompanied by bullet-pointed features and, to underline the point, by two identical line drawings representing the DS and the ID. In the early 1960s, Citroën's advertising concentrated on the Safari, describing it in 1964 as a "unique luxury estate car. An 8-seater…or 8 feet of flat floor with 13 cwt. loading," with a special trick allowed by the suspension: "Unlike other

estate cars, it always runs at the same height from the ground and remains perfectly level, whatever the weight carried." In addition, the brakes were "weight-compensated…automatically compensate themselves, front and rear, if the load varies, so that full braking efficiency is maintained automatically at all times." The Safari could be justified on practical as well as aesthetic grounds. By contrast, the DS21 Pallas, the most luxurious of the breed, was shown in 1967 in Curzon Street in London, outside "C.F. Trumper — Hairdresser by appointment to the late King George VI." "Why is this car such a snip for £2,000?" asked the headline. The copy described the car's suspension, its finger-tip clutchless gearchange, its power steering and braking, its automatically self-levelling headlamps and the advantages of the body style: "Like it or not, it's aerodynamically perfect. So that the faster you drive the firmer the air pressure presses you down onto the road. (Which gives you the Citroën road holding, magnifique!).” At a time when some family cars actually rose a little at speed, either at the front or at the rear, or both, this was a worthwhile feature.

From 1968, the DS was advertised regularly in colour — usually in dark blue during 1968–69 — with photography that made the best of the cowled twin headlamps which were a feature of the model from September 1967. On some models the inner headlamps swivelled with the steering to illuminate the corner around which the driver was turning. “Advance and be recognized” said one headline, with a DS shown in wide-angle front view against the sunset. A small picture at the bottom showed a hand writing out a cheque for what was now a less expensive car, comparatively speaking, at £1420 in its cheapest form. In March 1969, the DS was “The advanced car at the retarded price,” which killed a number of birds with one stone and, in the guise of a mechanical pun, delivered a swift kick to the shins of the lumbering opposition. Safety was emphasized: in November 1968 the car was parked on sand under the headline, “There’s safety in numbers,” which introduced 42 safety features, the last of which was that “the price of safety starts at £1420.” Some of these features were Citroën staples, like front-wheel drive; others were details held in common with many other cars, such as “safety design door handles,” while a few were very much selling-points of 1968 rather than of 1958, such as “engine and boot compartments...specially designed to absorb shock on impact.” American DS advertising also concentrated on safety: in a June 1968 advertisement the car was surrounded by twelve diagrams of components such as a suspension globe, a brake caliper, the body monocoque, and the brake pressure distributor. The approach was in a tradition of “Don’t just tell — show!” advertising that dated at least as far back as J. Stirling Getchell’s campaigns for Plymouth in the 1930s.

Comfort remained a selling-point, too, particularly as many medium-sized cars of the late 1960s were more cramped in the back than their higher-built predecessors of ten years earlier. In April 1969, the camera pointed through an open rear door into a tan interior. It was a rainy day and a toddler was perched with her fluffy rabbit on the far end of the back seat. “A few words about the new Citroën that will be of great comfort to you” began the copy, before de-

scribing the interior padding and suspension. In 1971, oil paintings showed a red DS with sailing boats in the background (“Haven of peace and quiet two seconds from the sea”) and a white Safari that was leaving — inevitably — a country estate (“Spacious rural retreat with miles of drive”). The artwork rescued the advertisement from cliché. Photography returned in 1972, when a Citroën D Special was shown on a country road (“The greatest invention since the car”) and a Pallas appeared in a meadow at dawn with its owners in the far distance (“A Citroën DS owner only falls in love twice”). In 1974 a metallic green DS, photographed in a studio under subdued lighting, was surrounded by labels indicating the features that improved its economy: “The aerodynamic Citroën DS has the right figure for today. 26.9 mpg DIN.” It was very much an advertisement of its time and, when more and more people were choosing continental cars, gave progressives an excuse to buy, at last, the car that they had coveted for fifteen years.

With the Citroën, as with other continental models, buyers asked, either openly or by implication: “It’s different, but is it better?” There were two ways of answering the question. The first was to say that a car was better than the indigenous opposition because it had demonstrable features — like independent rear suspension, disc brakes or interior equipment — that the opposition lacked, or that it performed, in one way or another, better than its competitors. Gadgets could be counted and speeds could be measured. The second approach was to claim that the car was qualitatively better. Relevant qualities ranged from the subjective feeling of contentment experienced by an owner through knowledge of a car’s exclusivity or marque heritage to semiobjective qualities such as ride comfort and character — the latter arising out of a combination of characteristics such as gearing, engine sound, handling, the smell of the interior plastics, and so on. In the Citroën’s case “different” was in many respects “better,” even if in some ways the car was quite ordinary: it’s engine was an old-fashioned in-line four, and the car’s build quality was not unusually good, although the hydraulic equipment was designed and built to extremely fine tolerances and was usually reliable. For a four-door car, however, it remained uniquely desirable.

26

Alfa Romeo to Wartburg

Importers Spread Their Wings

While Renault, Citroën and Volkswagen were special cases among early post-war importers, others followed in increasing numbers. Of remaining European marques, the principal advertisers during most of the 1960s were Mercedes-Benz, Alfa Romeo, Lancia, BMW, Peugeot, Fiat and Volvo, more or less in that order at first, although advertising expenditures varied from year to year, as did the degree of concentration on particular cars and in individual media over time. In any one year the apparent rank order of the marques varied according to the season and the newspapers and magazines considered.[1] Datsun and Toyota entered the fray in 1968. During the early 1960s, few importers could afford extensive campaigns and colour advertising was consequently rare, as were unusual typefaces, layouts, settings and visual effects. Simple photographs and unpretentious copy sufficed in most cases. Half-page and quarter-page advertisements in upmarket magazines were common; double-spreads virtually unknown. In retrospect, therefore, many British advertisements for mainland European cars are more interesting for the cars they depict than as advertising. But there was one extraordinary exception to all of these trends in the five-page colour advertisement placed by Lancia in *Country Life* in the summer of 1965, which showed the whole Lancia range and featured some exceptional photography. It was a beautiful catalogue, superbly presented, describing cars full of interesting technical and design features. Only in such a setting could the Lancia Flavia Zagato look even remotely plausible as a production car. The advertisement certainly outclassed others of the period and confirmed the marque's reputation to readers who might have ignored earlier monochrome advertisements for individual models.[2]

In the meantime, Mercedes-Benz produced some striking colour advertisements, very similar to the marque's advertising in West Germany, throughout 1959, before adopting a more indigenous and somehow less forbidding approach, mainly in black and white, for the "fintail" saloons and their coupe and convertible derivatives in 1961–63. Mercedes' obvious advantage over everyone else, and a necessary one given its prices, was quality. The marque's 1959 campaign stressed the theme above all else, advertising individual models as examplars of the marque in this respect as much as for their particular features. In each advertisement the copy was divided into a short article at the top of the page while shorter, more general copy about Mercedes-Benz appeared below, under its own headline, within the deep blue background against which each model advertised, whatever its colour, was painted. This lower copy was similar in each advertisement and was introduced by headlines such as "Quality to be experienced," "Quality — your constant companion," "Any way you look at it — Quality!" and "Enjoy this quality." In April 1959 a red 220S (£2393 17s) was shown from above: "Rely on quality. Wherever you go, and no mat-

Opposite: **Mercedes-Benz 300SE Convertible.** "Ask your local dealer for a trial run"—but in a car costing over £6000 (or ten Ford Anglias) the run would probably be short, and the price is not mentioned here. Owners included the actor Peter Sellers, who bought the 1962 Earls Court Motor Show car and kept it for just over a year; lesser mortals settled for a 220SE convertible at around £4500. True cheapskates saved a further £4–500 and bought open Aston Martin DB4s. The Convertible was, of course, a supremely glamorous car, and, although advertisements for it were rare and hardly necessary, it lent sparkle to the marque's "fintail" saloons, from 190 to (occasionally) 300SE, which accounted for most Mercedes sales in Britain, as elsewhere.

L U X U R Y

Words can't adequately describe the full magnificence of a Mercedes-Benz. An illustration helps, of course, such as the one above of the superb 300SE Convertible. But the only realistic way to judge a Mercedes is to see one and try it for yourself. Admired and respected wherever you go, the Mercedes symbolizes perfection and the ultimate in sophistication. As an example of superb automobile engineering, it is unsurpassed. As a means of transport, it offers the high quality and luxury that reflect the fine taste and refinement of its fortunate owner. For style, performance and sheer technical perfection the Mercedes is undoubtedly ruler of the road. Test-drive one. It will confirm the difference that great engineering makes.

ASK YOUR LOCAL DEALER FOR A TRIAL RUN

300SE COUPE. A majestic 3-litre with independent air suspension 4-wheel disc brakes, automatic gearbox, power steering and fuel injection engine.

220SE SALOON. A 6-cylinder fuel injection engine. All independent suspension. Powerful, fade-free brakes. Exceptional comfort and performance. Daimler-Benz automatic gearbox an optional extra.

SUPERB AS A CAR — WITH SERVICE TO MATCH

MERCEDES-BENZ

MERCEDES-BENZ (GREAT BRITAIN) LIMITED, GREAT WEST ROAD, BRENTFORD, MIDDLESEX
Head Office, Distribution and Service Dept. Tel: ISLeworth 2151 *Export Dept.* 10 Albemarle Street, London W.1. Tel: HYDe Park 3351
COUNTRY-WIDE NETWORK OF DISTRIBUTORS AND SERVICE AGENTS · WRITE OR 'PHONE FOR DETAILS

THE FIELD, with which is incorporated *Land and Water* and *The County Gentleman*, is published every Thursday, price 2s. 0d., by THE HARMSWORTH PRESS LTD., 8, Stratton Street, London, W.1, Thursday, May 9, 1963. Printed by GALE & POLDEN LTD., 28, Craven Street, London, W.C.2, and Aldershot, Hampshire. PRINTED IN GREAT BRITAIN, and registered as a newspaper for transmission in the United Kingdom and to Canada by magazine post. Entered as second class matter at the Post Office, New York, N.Y. March 1897.

ter how many miles you cover, the reliability of a Mercedes-Benz guarantees you relaxation and safety. The three-pointed star is a symbol of Mercedes-Benz quality and precision...."

In June 1959, a white 300SL hardtop (£5313 12s 6d) appeared below a short story: "A really fast answer. The door had hardly been closed beside him when Mr. Kragg tried to slip out again. But — too late! As if shot from a gun he sped away. He had only his ignorance to blame. Mr. Kragg had simply asked the automobile salesman the top speed of a smart touring sports car. About 150 mph? He could not believe that. The salesman insisted on proving his statement and nothing could stop him...." This was not an English scene; but that was its appeal. In August, a dark blue 300d four-door hardtop (£5101 2s 6d) was described as the chosen transport for "Paul Glueck, a Hamburg businessman who wanted to drive overland to Persia and India, and then to visit the Far East" and who drove his car over 22,500 miles before returning home. "Whether on wild mountain roads or scorching desert, he always knew that his Mercedes-Benz 300 was a safe and luxurious haven." Only a small handful of the model were ever sold in Britain, but their reputation helped Mercedes sell quite a few thousand fintails over the next few years. In 1960, the 220 cost £2249 and the 220SE, £2690.

In the late 1960s, Mercedes-Benz stressed the marque's international credibility and, in July 1966 with the new 250SE, capitalized on its frequent appearances in thrillers: "'Eighteen minutes after first light. Empty sky. On the deserted runway the white Mercedes waited, waited....' You've read it in novels, seen it in films. Countless times. Countless places. A street in Istanbul. Château on the Loire. Submerged garage in Belgravia.... Always that Mercedes, waiting, cruising, surging. Power? Success? Why Mercedes? Isn't it because the world of Mercedes is a world of its own? An escape from things that don't go right to things that do? Satisfy curiosity now...." And then there was the Mercedes-Benz 600, hardly a car in need of advertisement, but proof, if proof were needed, of the marque's technical supremacy. In August 1967 a dark blue 600 was shown in front view. The scenery behind looked suspiciously German, as it could have been if the picture was simply a reversed image of a left-hand-drive car on the right of the road, with the image of the number plate (MB — 600, in the German style) added afterwards: "Imagine floating over the road on a cushion of air — yet retaining perfect control under all conditions." The copy described the marque's air suspension, introduced in 1961, "just one example of the engineering excellence that has been a tradition at Daimler-Benz for eight decades — ever since the company's founders invented the automobile." No English modesty there. Efficiency and technology dominated most of the year's copy; headlines such as "If you like people who deliver sooner rather than later...you'll like the Mercedes 300 SEL" and "Imagine an engine with a built-in brain that increases power by 15 per cent — and actually reduces

fuel consumption" (for fuel injection) were representative. August 1968's "When you've reached the level of the new 280SE something more than prestige begins" put the technology to social as well as practical use. In 1970, the 280SE sedan and 250CE Coupe were photographed in the rain beside Chepstow Racecourse and the polo ground at Cowdray Park above the single copy line, "Steal a little thunder." And in March 1968 that enduring luxury sports car, the 280SL, "the car men (and women) dream about," appeared under the headline, "Come glide with me." Many are still gliding nearly forty years later.[3]

Lancia was an engineer's marque in quite a different sense, producing cars of very high quality with a delicacy of styling and engineering foreign to Mercedes — although Mercedes robustness was foreign to them, too. Lancias' propensity to rust would become notorious and, though real, would be much exaggerated in the late 1970s, with the result that most motorists became impermeable to advertising for the marque, and brochures, by 1980, carried silver stickers advertising anti-rust warranties.[4] But for twelve years or so from the early 1960s, Lancia built up its sales and reputation with uniquely appealing cars that were often imaginatively advertised. Wisely, the marque did not try to be all things to all drivers.

A few Lancias had entered Britain in the 1950s, yet although the marque appeared in the price lists it is not recorded[5] as being advertised between May 1956 and March 1961. It took a determined effort to run an Appia (£1689 in 1958), Aurelia (£3346) or Flaminia (£3751) during those years, albeit that Lancias had never been cars to be bought on a whim and, anyway, rewarded involvement. But in the spring of 1961 a new concessionaire was appointed to handle a new model, the Flavia sedan[6] — a modern, well-finished, comfortable and refined car with a water-cooled flat-four engine. It was plain and boxy compared with European rivals such as the Peugeot 404, and its four headlamps looked like the afterthought that they were, but a roomy interior in a mid-Atlantic style included many enjoyable details, such as switches arranged in a semi-circular bank to the right of the steering wheel (on a right-hand drive car) and small map bins ahead of the doors. The last feature survived even on late Beta Coupes of the early 1980s. The Flavia was not fast, however: *The Autocar* achieved a top speed of 93 mph and 0–60 in 18.7 seconds, and concluded: "Because of its price the Lancia Flavia is a somewhat exclusive one-and-a-half in this country — a car for the connoisseur. It sets a standard in certain important respects which is bound to give some other manufacturers food for thought, showing what can still be done with a four-cylinder engine and steel springs. The workmanship and detail finish suggest that it is intended as a lasting possession."[7]

In April 1961 Lancia Concessionaires Ltd. advertised the Flavia in upmarket maagzines and in the motoring press, and adapted a regular advertisement to appeal for dealers in

Motor Trader: "Back in Britain now! …For several years this famous Italian marque has been absent from the British market. Now it is back, spear-pointed by the brilliant new 1½-litre Flavia. With six seats, and disc brakes all round, this new model—the first-ever Italian front-wheel-drive production car—raises the curtain on a country-wide advertising campaign. Lancia Sales and Service Agencies are now being arranged for the whole Lancia range; exclusive-territory rights are available in many areas. Enquiries are urgently invited from well-established concerns with adequate display and service facilities." In *The Autocar*, the equivalent conventional advertisement announced that "a few left-hand-drive models are available now; right-hand-drive in the last week of May. £2,125 including Tax"—and modified the trade advertisement's invitation: "To the Motor Trade: Exclusive-territory rights are available in many areas; enquiries will be welcomed from well-established concerns with adequate service facilities." Later in April the price had been rounded up to £2126, though by the end of the year the Flavia would be more expensive, at £2188, than an open E-type Jaguar (£2160).

The Flavia's price was difficult to argue for, but later in 1961 a car was photographed cornering at speed and the copywriter came out fighting: "There are two kinds of motor car you can buy for over £2000—The Obvious (more and more of them make them more and more obvious!) [or] The Lancia Flavia (we cannot promise more than 73 during the rest of this year)." In the spring of 1963 the same photograph appeared above the headline, "If 401 people want to buy this Lancia it's one customer too many"—the "supply of Lancia Flavias" being only 400 for the year. "The overall impression is of a car finished with minute care. You won't, for instance, find the false glitter of chrome on the body trim. The trim on the Lancia Flavia is of stainless (and peel-less) steel…." And it now cost only £1760. By October 1963 the car was being sold on the fact of its exclusivity as much as for its features, with which other manufacturers were quickly catching up. A Flavia was seen from behind through the windscreen of a following car. The copy took the form of a conversation: "What's that car, Proctor?" "A Lancia Flavia, sir." "A Lancia, eh? You don't see many of those about." It turned out that the chauffeur's previous employer had bought one. "'Proctor, he'd say, 'I'll take the Lancia today.' Well sir, I could understand his Lordship's feelings. The Lancia is a beautiful car. A gentleman's car. But a chauffeur who never gets a chance to drive is a contradiction in terms. That is why I resigned my position, sir." "Yes, I see. Do you happen to know where the Lancia showrooms are?" "In Mayfair, sir. Albemarle Street. And sir, do you happen to have a friend who wants a chauffeur?" It was amusing in a Woosterish kind of way—and it was also modern, since extended conversation, as distinct from occasional exclamations and exchanges, had not appeared before in post-war British car advertising. Conversational slices-of-life,

often transferring to print from television advertising, would appear for many products in the 1970s and 1980s. The Lancia advertisement, meanwhile, had a curiously timeless quality; because its theme was so un-ordinary, the reader had already made the imaginative leap away from everyday life when he read it. As a result, the piece seemed less affected than most aspirational copy.

The theme was developed in 1964. A large saloon—its badges removed but still obviously a coachbuilt Bentley or Rolls-Royce—was seen from behind in a stable garage. The space beside it was empty. "Why is the Lancia never at home?" asked the headline. "They found that one car wasn't enough. So, being well-to-do people, they bought a Lancia Flavia. And now they don't find much use for the other car. The Lancia is like that. It has the most winning ways. Everything about it is different from other cars." The copy described the car's engine, its brakes, its interior and its comfortable ride. "So why is the Lancia never at home? It's too much fun to drive." Coupe and convertible variants were easier to promote. The Flavia Convertible (by Vignale) was shown in two pictures. "Is Gran Turismo only for due?" asked the caption to the first, in which the car sped along a main road. "Lancia says no, it's for quattro" said the second caption, beneath a photograph of the car at rest. The Flavia Coupe (By Pininfarina) was "Grandissimo Turismo!" in a 1964 advertisement in *Country Life*, while in *The Autocar* enthusiasts were addressed in a very different style: "Six questions to answer before you do something foolish"— "*How good a driver are you*? The Lancia Flavia [Coupe] is not for conventional, inexperienced or fuddy-duddy drivers. *Have you ever driven on a circuit or in a rally*? You will need a touch at least of professional dedication to enjoy this car. If you are not stirred by the glamour of the international motoring world, much of the Lancia's quality will escape you. *Do you like changing your car*? Lancia built this car for people to whom ownership is a bit of a love affair. Its life expectation is long, and its attractions increase with familiarity. So it's not a car to be given up quickly. *Are you conscientious*? A Lancia can't be carelessly treated. Servicing may take a couple of days and require a visit to a Lancia agent many miles from home. You will want to keep it washed and polished. And you will certainly be reluctant to let others drive it…."

The appeal of the Flaviasport by Zagato, that curious sports coupe with side windows behind the doors which curved into the roof and a rear window hinged to open electrically from its bottom edge, was even more specialized. In 1964 it was shown in front view, photographed from the ground with light behind the car. The headline quoted F. Scott Fitzgerald: "The very rich are different from you and me…" and the copywriter elaborated: "The very rich have very different standards from the not so rich. Different values, too. They don't have to ask how much something costs before they buy it; only how good it is. And, for the very rich,

The Field, April 20, 1961

FLAVIA 'CON AMORE'

Always fresh, always willing, always
responsive, always at hand – Flavia. Always ready to give you
pleasure – to drive. Feel yourself sink into those deep-cushioned seats
as she leaps forward, fast and safe, through those four gears,
too delightful to be automatic. Feel her grasp the road, round bends,
through traffic. Touch her disc brakes, immediate, safe.
Try Flavia – you'll want her, as your own.

 flavia

BY LANCIA

£2,126 (Inc. Tax)

LANCIA CONCESSIONAIRES LIMITED

Head Office (Service and Spares): Lancia Works, Alperton, Middlesex (ALPerton 2155)

Here NOW at 16 ALBEMARLE STREET, LONDON, W.1 (HYDe Park 7166)

good must be very good indeed. So, Lancia asked the Italian designer Zagato to design a sports car that the very rich might buy today.... There are faster cars. Not many but a few. There are cars as comfortable, and as much fun to drive. But there is no other car in the world today that has quite this combination of dash and dignity and engineering brilliance. That's why the Flaviasport costs £2,736." By April 1965, the car's name had changed slightly. A 110 mph speedometer, unidentified but recognizable to enthusiasts as coming from a Triumph Spitfire, was captioned, "You can do 100 m.p.h. in a car costing £700."[8] Or, "In the Flavia Zagato (£2,734) you can do it without your wife losing her hat, her hairpins, her temper or her nerve.... When Lancia decided to bring out a fast car, they thought, in typical Italian fashion, about women; both as passengers and drivers.... The Flavia Zagato is one of the few cars in which you cruise at very high speeds, for 500 miles on end, without anxiety or exhaustion.... For those who can afford it, £2,734 seems little enough to pay for a quiet, but interesting life."

And then there was 1965's five-page advertisement which described "The remarkable legacy of Signor Vincenzo Lancia.... A large, glossy car of supreme elegance, most probably drawn up outside a palatial entrance: in simple terms, that is the legacy which Vincenzo Lancia left to the world. The remarkable thing about it, however, is not so much the car, but the fact that it exists today." The short essay which followed was illustrated with close-up photographs of details such as the quarterlight of a Flaminia Supersport and the instruments of a Flavia Zagato, together with more conventional advertising shots of different Flaminias, Flavias and Fulvias, all nine models of which were lined up in a row at the bottom of the centre double-spread with their specifications and prices. The marque's appeal was then broadened later in 1965 by a single-page colour advertisement for the Fulvia coupe, shown in grey on a cobbled square: "If you ever felt like flirting with those rare, expensive Lancias, meet their little sister Fulvia." A few years later the car was shown in a very modern-looking picture surrounded by white horses: "One name stands out from the herd."

Sadly, Lancia stood out a little too far to be profitable in the long term and sales fell worldwide in the late 1960s. The debt-ridden company was taken over by Fiat in October 1969, and subsequent Lancias, though inherently interesting, suffered from a perception that they were essentially "alternative Fiats." Detailing deteriorated although the market for cars of such high quality as earlier Lancias was never

large enough to allow their production to be consistently profitable. If the price were lowered so that more could be sold, each made no money. If the price were raised, so that each car would in theory be profitable, too few cars were sold to make the theory a reality, or to fund the development of new models. Only a few of the special Flavias by Vignale, Pininfarina and Zagato had come to Britain; the Zagato in particular was a collector's piece of which only a handful were sold.

If the Lancia appealed to connoisseurs, Alfa Romeo produced sporting cars for motorists who appreciated advanced engineering but could not spend days learning about or tending it. Not that the Alfa Romeo 2600 Berlina (£2271 in 1963) found many British buyers, but the Giulia sedan, less exquisitely detailed than a Lancia Flavia but more immediately attractive, found a ready audience: "We could write you a book about the new right-hand drive Alfa Romeos. About their power. About their speed and safety at speed" said a 1963 advertisement which showed a car about to accelerate towards the reader down a black strip bearing the name of the marque. In 1964, Alfa Romeo used white-on-black copy and illustrations to draw attention to cars like the Giulia 1600 Spider in a distinctive series of advertisements that were as effective as any colour advertising. "Why on earth don't Alfa Romeo make their 2-seater, 5 forward gear, 110 mph, Farina body, 106 bhp, 1600cc, disc-brake, bobby-dazzling, tarmac-eating, bend-hugging, kiss-the-girls-and-make'em-cry Spider with right hand drive?" asked an April 1964 advertisement above a Spider seen head-on. "They do"! said the reply at the bottom. Other models shown in the series included the Giulia Sprint G.T. ("What is it that flies, glides, shimmers, purrs and overtakes? Test drive an Alfa Romeo and see!") and the 2600 Sprint ("A very distinguished car. Take a very distinguished test drive in it"). "Prrroww!" announced the importers in huge letters in 1967, "Here is the new Alfa Romeo 1300 GT. If you have £1650 in the bank—unbank it now!" The similar-looking 1750 GTV of 1969 was for "when the Sunday drivers have all gone home," while a 1750 Berlina, similarly proportioned to the Giulia but smoother in its details, was shown at an Italian wedding: "The Italians are crazy about women and fast cars. That's why they marry them. No-one cried at Sig. Mastroni's wedding. Except for the Conte de Nuovarini and that was from laughing too much. After the wedding, Sig. Mastroni sold his sports car, and bought a family car. His idea of a family car is a fast car that 5 people can enjoy together. So he bought an Alfa Romeo 1750."[9] All were loved by enthusiasts, and the

Opposite: **Lancia Flavia Berlina.** Very much a car for the gentleman-engineer who could both afford and enjoy its high quality and front wheel drive, the £2126 Flavia was, by purely utilitarian criteria, arguably the poorest-value mid-size family saloon on the market in 1961; a four-door Cortina 1500 De-Luxe cost only a little over £600 two years later. And the Lancia, though well built, was probably more, rather than less, rust-prone than the Cortina in the British climate. Import taxes exacerbated the natural price difference, of course, but the Flavia was really a car for the kind of man who, a decade earlier, would have chosen a Riley RMA or Jowett Javelin (or even a pre-war Aprilia) over a Wyvern or Consul—for the driving experience and the sense that designer and owner both appreciated engineering undertaken, at least in part, for its own sake.

For those with taste and the money to indulge it – the Alfa Romeo Giulia S.S. A 2-seater coupe of immense distinction…with the kind of acceleration and road-holding that you expect from an Alfa…with a 1570 cc, 129 bhp engine and a top speed over 125 mph…with twin choke carbs, disc brakes, 5 forward gears and a body shape that says, clearly, 'Bertone'. The price is £2394.1.3 including tax. Expensive? Of course! What else would you expect a hand-built Alfa to be? □ To arrange for a test drive with your nearest dealer, get in touch with: Alfa Romeo (G.B.) Limited, 164, Sloane Street, London, W.1. Tel: BELgravia 7746/7/8. **ALFA ROMEO**

Hand built….and decidedly expensive

1966–70 Spider, with its distinctive, tapering tail and a public profile raised by an appearance in *The Graduate*, gathered a small upper-middle-class market to itself in the late 1960s and 1970s.

If the most distinctive advertising for Alfa Romeo appeared in the early part of the decade, the reverse was true of BMW: only in the late 1970s did BMW advertising take on the appearance and flavour that would serve the marque well during the twenty years that followed. But BMW's modern reputation — necessary for that advertising to work — began to grow when the four-door 1500 saloon arrived in Britain in the early 1960s and when the 1600 Coupe joined it in 1966. The 1600, really a sports saloon, would develop into the almost identical-looking 2002 of 1968. Earlier BMWs — the "Baroque angel" V8s, the highly specialized 503 coupe and convertible and 507 sports car, and the BMW 700, made no serious impression on the market, although the Michelotti-styled, rear-engined 700, as a saloon, coupe or convertible, appealed to some sporting enthusiasts. But *Small Car* gave the 1500 a rave review in 1963, headlining its test of an olive green, German-registered example "£1376 worth of *worth*," adding, in a slightly contrived attempt to fit the subject to the title (as it then was) of the magazine, "Who says Borgward built the last German quality small car?" Tester Jerry Sloniger concluded presciently, "Old BMW fans can amuse themselves driving one every day with pleasure and dreaming about a twin-carb version, dieted roughly 500 lb. and carving the heart right out of the 1.6 class. Meanwhile the product as it is remains one of the most pleasant road cars we know. All it takes is money...."[10] "Graduate to a BMW" said a half-page advertisement in April 1965 for the 1800 with the same bodywork, its copy consisting of a dozen flattering quotations from an independent road test.

Sloniger's day-dream came true in 1967 with the "Internationally acclaimed BMW 1600 Coupe," which "sets new standards for family cars: speed 102 mph; 0–50 in 7.2 seconds; 30 mpg; ...exceptional road-holding; out-of-this-world visibility." In 1968 the car was shown outside the Royal Courts of Justice on The Strand, a distinguished-looking barrister in wig and gown about to get in. "Successful men choose BMW — Since its introduction in the U.K., the sporty BMW 1600 Coupe has been proclaimed an outstanding success not only here but throughout the world...." If the copy was dull, the car was not, and a January 1969 advertisement for the new 2002 was livelier. A car was shown on a bend at speed, the picture clinically clear: "What's a 113 mph family coupe doing in a 70 mph country? Keeping plenty of safety in reserve." Copy full of figures concluded with the slogan, "...for the sheer joy of driving unbeatable BMW." In 1969, the 2002 was shown side-by-side with the 2000, which shared the body of the earlier 1500 and continuing 1800: "Switch on...the going is fast." The best-known BMW advertisement of the period appeared in the summer of 1968, when a 2002 was shown in the driving mirror of another car: "Move over...from out of nowhere, a speck appears in your rear-view mirror, grows instantly larger, and you see the famed blue-and-white medallion on the bonnet. That's a BMW 2002 bearing down on you and you'd best...move over" — in the sense of moving over from an existing car to a BMW, of course.[11] There was no British equivalent to the 2002 and the larger BMW 2800 of 1970 was sold not only as a sporting saloon, but as a glamorous one: "The 125mph dream car — For the man who can please himself."

Individual imported marques began to adopt distinct styles of advertising in late 1960s, and in 1969 British advertising from Fiat, hitherto homely and largely from the London distributor, Jack Barclay Ltd., conformed to an international campaign in which Fiat was portrayed as automotive provider to the world, even where the settings and copy were local. The Fiat 124 saloon and 124 Sport Coupe were seen in the distance against beautiful Irish scenery. "You are free," said one piece for the Coupe. "Cast your worries aside. It is undemanding. It is only a car. Functional. Sound and enduring. An asset." In another piece the same model was shown on a beach: "Don't fall in love — It's only a car. And true love has other meanings. All you have to do is drive it. Relaxed. Confident." With the 124 saloon, the reader was invited to "Just say: It's mine. It will serve you well in the heat of summer and the snows of winter. Always there. Precise. Efficient."[12] In an advertisement targeted towards enthusiasts, the little rear-engined Fiat 850 Coupe, one of the prettiest cars of its period, was shown with a red 124 Sport Coupe in the odd setting of a large car park: "These are the cars that steal the scene behind the scenes. The fast Fiats. The GTs that get the drivers to the circuits. The 90 m.p.h. Fiat 850 Coupe is Britain's lowest priced 2 + 2 GT. The Fiat 124 Coupe is a full 4-seater GT which does 105 m.p.h. Test drive one at your Fiat dealer — he's listed in the new Yellow Pages — and you'll know what makes these goers such stoppers!" They cost £916 3s 8d and £1477 11s 5d respectively. In 1970 a red 850 Coupe was seen, bizarrely as it seemed at first, beside an old steam train carrying tourists. The venue was explained by a small caption "...then I dashed up the valley to meet them after their ride." The copywriter added, "This is the one. The one that gets away. The most appealing fastback this side of a thousand pounds.

Opposite: **Alfa Romeo Giulia S.S.** In the 1970s, many importers would match each other and the home product model for model — Alfa's own Alfasud, although only latterly a hatchback and with a character all its own, competed in a market crowded with cars and buyers. Not so with the unique Sprint Speciale, however, produced at a rate of a few hundred a year for a specialized market which sought something much less obvious than the surprisingly unaerodynamic Jaguar E-type. This advertisement's white-on-black style, shared with other Alfas in 1964–5 and later taken up by Ford with the Mexico, was a novelty in the mid-1960s. The insect deflector just behind the bonnet of this car suggests serious sporting intent.

You've seen it. Now handle it. At your Fiat dealer...." And if this was wacky-snappy copy in the Vauxhall style, another range advertisement, related graphically but with conventional copy, showed "Europe's widest range of cars"—a dozen or so—in a field with a flock of sheep. BMC's range was wider, but was spread among several marques.

Other continental saloons became fashionable too. Auto Union, hitherto known for small, two-stroke cars, passed in 1964 from Mercedes-Benz, who had owned it since 1958, to Volkswagen, under whom the Audi name was revived in 1965 with a new model, officially called the Auto Union Audi, but latterly known as the Audi 72 to distinguish it from subsequent versions with different engines. This was an updated Auto Union F102 with a 1695cc, four-cylinder engine designed by Mercedes Benz instead of the F102's two-stroke. The first Audi 100 appeared in 1968, and although in 1969 it was still called the Auto Union Audi, by 1970 "Auto Union" had been dropped. "Motor safer: own yourself the 100LS" said a March 1970 headline, which was followed later in the month by "Motor easier: own yourself the 100LS" and in July by "Motor cooler: own yourself the 100LS." It was the car with which Audi created the brand identity on which its long-term reputation would be founded.

In January 1959, advertising began for the Volvo 122S (Amazon), which had been sold by the Brooklands Motor Company from November 1958 at £1399 1s 10d, and which was the first Volvo to be officially imported into Britain. In a small black and white advertisement in 1961, the 122S was described as "New for the fortunate few..." and in 1962 it offered "whispering power for the fortunate few." It gained its reputation for safety and robustness quickly, and by 1964 it was taking on a long-term identity with the slogan, "Be sure...be fast...be safe," which was echoed by Saab, early in 1966, with "Go swift — go safe — go Saab." This suggested a rivalry that did not really exist, as the Saab was still (just) a small two-stroke, and the characters of the marques remained different: the Volvo was more conventional in its engineering and in its image than the Saab, even after the Saab 99 ("Big brother is here!") began to arrive in reasonable numbers in 1970. Meanwhile, a V4-engined 96 appeared later in 1966, and in April 1968 it was shown with a muffled grandmother about to get in: "Have Saab gone power mad? The Saab is made by the company that designs and builds one of the world's best supersonic jet fighters. So we talk a lot about power and rapid acceleration.... But we're not power mad, we also say that there's no safer car on the road than the Saab V4.... Power we like — plus safety!" In 1970 the 96 was shown with small pictures of a jet fighter, of a Saab rally car and of a body shell: "Saab 96: the plane-maker's contribution to safer driving." Build quality was a Volvo feature, too, as in May 1967 with the new Volvo 144, "created in Sweden with all the care in the world." In June, Volvo showed a red 144 and a picture of an open ashtray: "Who wants a car with engineered ashtrays? The same people who want a 115 BHP engine, a dual-circuit brake system, seats designed by an orthopaedic surgeon and rally-proved suspension." Two more long-term marque images were becoming entrenched.

Peugeot, by contrast, occupied middle ground between the individualistic Citroën and the high-performing BMW and Volvo. As as the most conservative of French marques, Peugeot was probably closest to Audi in its immediate appeal although its robustness, like that of Mercedes-Benz, was legendary in mainland Europe and in Africa. "A car worthy of a trial," said Peugeot in a tiny quarter-page advertisement in *Country Life* in 1964, "One of the best made cars in the world.... Everywhere people who appreciate quality go Peugeot." Full-page advertisements began to appear regularly in 1968, when photographs of the front, back and sides of a 404 estate car were arranged into the flat form of a cut-out-and-fold model: "Cut round the dotted line and find out what a really great estate car looks like," invited the copy. In May 1969, the 204 and 404 estate cars were shown in small pictures beside a jumble of road signs and a man walking against the rain with an umbrella with the headline, "The times you wish you had a Peugeot." In November, details of the Peugeot 504, a newcomer the previous year, appeared in a sober advertisement headed, "We've come a long way since 1889." It was one of the most sensible and image-free cars of its era.

But it was not cheap, and for some motorists in the 1960s, as with buyers of Ford Populars ten years earlier, the most sensible car was the cheapest new one. In the early 1960s, Skoda advertised regularly in *Practical Motorist*, as in May 1965: "More for your money makes Skoda supreme! ...Skoda Octavia costs £529.19.11 yet all the 'extras' are there!" That, in a nutshell, was the appeal of the front-engined Octavia, an attractive if old-fashioned car whose shape had first been seen in 1954, and of the "Newest and greatest Skoda 1000MB" shown in a smaller picture alongside. Both were swing-axled and both handled dreadfully, the 1000MB more so because of the weight in its tail, but English motoring conditions showed up the designs' weakness as those in Czechoslovakia did not; on rough ground the Octavia,

Opposite: **Volvo 221/222 Estate Car (Amazon).** There is nothing in this unassuming advertisement to suggest that the Volvo is not just another ephemeral late-1960s import. Who, in 1967, would want a car introduced ten years previously with a grille design inspired by a Chrysler two years older still? The advertisement's theme was also, to put it kindly, tried and tested. Yet the car was tried and tested too, in difficult conditions, and it was one of the toughest and longest-lasting models of its period. For more than 30 years, Volvo estates were bought for their safety and durability (a lifespan of 20 years was not uncommon) and although you had to be fairly prosperous to afford a new one, the less well-off sought them out secondhand. They had to be scrapped eventually, of course, but even then one could still open the doors with several cars piled on top.

The down-to-earth

and up-to-town estate car

Some estate cars are down-to-earth. Others are up-to-town. The Volvo Estate is both. A luxury 5-seat town *and* country car.

But first of all it's down-to-earth. To start with, at £1,280 it costs less than any other quality estate car. And it's tougher. Made to stand up to the most punishing roads in the world. Built with reinforced rear springing that's been supplemented with progressively-acting hollow rubber springs to carry big, heavy, suspension-torturing loads. And to make sure that even with the spacious fully-carpeted cargo space crammed, it sacrifices nothing in safety and roadholding.

Bulky, awkward shapes are no problem either. The rear doors divide horizontally to give extra carrying space and make loading easier.

And the Volvo Estate is no slow-coach. That 85 B.H.P. engine delivers a lot of power. Even fully loaded, it gives you high average speeds, nippy overtaking, and good acceleration.

But we didn't just make it a great Estate. We really went to town on making it a luxurious city car. We made it look sleek and feel sleek, too. We had an orthopaedic surgeon design the fully-reclining front bucket seats and the bench seat for 3 behind.

There's thermostatically controlled fresh air heating and ventilation to cope with every quirk of the British climate. And even with the seat belts on, you can reach all the controls easily.

Like we say. The Volvo Estate is a down-to-earth car. Even when it's up-to-town.

The Volvo Estate is also available with a 100 B.H.P. engine. And remember, only Volvo, with its great safety and reliability record, can give you a year's free comprehensive insurance with reduced premiums thereafter!

Contact your Volvo dealer; he will be pleased to arrange a test drive.

VOLVO ESTATE CAR
Created in Sweden with all the care in the world

For the address of your local dealer please write to: VOLVO CONCESSIONAIRES LTD., P.O. Box 7, Tower Ramparts, Ipswich. LONDON SHOWROOM: 26B ALBEMARLE ST., W.1.

with its good ground clearance and large wheels, fared well. The extras—courtesy lights, a radiator blind, reclining front seats, comprehensive toolkit and others—were listed at the bottom of the advertisement. The 1000MB, meanwhile, was a good-looking car by the standards of its rear-engined type. "If you've got money to throw around on a new car, throw less of it around on a Skoda" said another advertisement. "A Skoda is a small car for people with big families and strictly middle-sized incomes. It isn't a TC, a GT, a fastback or a sooped-up, whooped-up anything. It's just a family saloon that will cost you less to buy, less to run and won't let you down." It would run on two-star petrol and, of course, came with many features, "all in the basic model so you don't pay a penny more for them…only someone with more money than sense buys a car without weighing up what it's going to give him for the money he lays out. And you've got more sense than that, haven't you?"

From 1966 the Skoda was rivalled by the Russian Moskvich 408 saloon at £679, "Year's best family motoring bargain." Front-engined and over-powered, it handled as one would expect from a car four feet, ten inches high with a tracks of four feet or so. The styling, generic-saloon *circa* 1960, suggested a reskinned Standard Vanguard. *Motor* found it "the nearest approach to paradise attainable by the motorist who enjoys doing his own servicing" with an instruction manual that was "exceptionally comprehensive."[13] It sold slowly at first but sales of the updated 412 took off in 1972–73, before safety complaints, not least about passenger-impaling interior equipment, condemned it in 1975 to the history books and to happy collectors of motoring oddballs. Traditionally-minded motorists, reared on cars of the 1930s and 1940s, who neither cornered fast nor trusted garages, found the 408 useful enough, and a former owner of a Standard Ensign estate car wrote to *Motor*, in the summer of 1966, about the usefulness of an imported, right-hand-drive Volga Universal, a large, sturdy and elegant station wagon in the 1955 style. His article was printed alongside the test of the Moskvich.[14] More common than the Moskvich but less so than the Skoda was the three-cylinder, two-stroke, Wartburg Knight, a 1966 successor to the Wartburg 312 ("Luxury in everything except price") of which over a thousand had been imported between 1964 and 1966. Where the 312 had been attractively curvaceous—a little like a four-door Volkswagen Karmann-Ghia—the Knight was inoffensively square. Early advertising, under the heading "No one gives you this much car for £620" was exactly as expected.

In pre-Datsun days, extras-as-standard were not exclusively an Eastern European specialism, however: "NSU *give* you a clock" was one of the more surprising headlines of 1963, when the instrument was shown in the middle of the page with the car—a Prinz 4, costing £549 19s 10d—at the bottom. Simca, long known for its rear-engined 1000, adapted the theme as it moved towards front-wheel drive

and enlightenment with the Simca 1100 hatchback in 1967: "From £759 the new Simca 1100 is a lot of motor car…. Don't take our word—Test drive a Simca." Other advertisements for the car quoted favourable reviews from broadsheet newspapers and motoring magazines, and in December 1967 blocks of copy headed "Versatility, "Comfort" and "Performance" were keyed into a photograph of the car, seen from behind. In 1970 the Simca was shown between cones on a marked track: "Try the road-holding of the Simca 1100 GLS." A second picture showed an empty track with some cones knocked down: "Try the road-holding of its competition."

The Daf, by contrast, in which ease of driving was paramount and motion, if not speed, was achieved with a continuously variable belt-driven transmission, was targeted exclusively to women. "The Daf was meant for YOU" said a 1961 advertisement showing the little saloon being pursued by a crowd of line-drawn children and their dog, "The Daf gives you independence as no other car can…. Its wonderful Variomatic transmission does away with gear-changing completely. Press the accelerator to go, press the brake pedal to stop—that's all there is to do!" In 1965 the Daf was shown outside a country house, a Facel Vega in the background, abandoned by its owner who was getting into the little car. "I thought he bought it for me!" said a woman standing on the doorstep, hands on hips, looking cross enough to break Daf drive-belts with her bare hands. In 1966 the car was "For the lady of the house—Husbands can be thoughtful. Especially when they buy you a Daf—the fully-automatic car thoughtfully designed for you. No gears! Just an accelerator and brake…. Time for school? Forget the formality—pile in the kids and let's go! Now—the shopping. Easy, responsive steering and a tight turning circle…. Rush hour. Relax in your Daf and let the rest of the crowd waggle their gear levers and thump their clutches like maniacs. Your Daf will get pretty dusty…. But you're a woman with things to do, places to go. Let your husband clean it while you cook the Sunday dinner!" Above the copy was a simple photograph of the car with a heart and arrow drawn in the dust on the door.

Two groups of cars were advertised infrequently during the 1960s: the exotic sports cars and the small Japanese saloons. Importers of exotics had small budgets and advertisements in general media could only sell a few cars. Nevertheless, George Abecassis of InterContinental Cars Ltd. at Walton-on-Thames in Surrey, who imported the Facel Vega, placed at least four attractive monochrome pieces in up-market magazines during 1960–62. In April 1960 the effortlessly glamorous HK500 (£4467), "Low, powerful, beautiful…fabulous in performance and luxury trim—the world's fastest touring car" appeared in a traditional country-house-at-night setting to offer "sheer, unbeatable power as sedately controlled as a Sunday school," while in October it was shown from above, golfers and their bags behind. "Take a good look at Facel Vega (when it moves it's difficult to fol-

The Field, April 20, 1961

What a car is this Facellia from France! A taut little beauty with typical Gallic verve!

The Facellia will make news wherever it is motored. This car is the latest example of outstanding engineering from Facel Vega, makers of high-precision jet engine components and the fabulous HK500, the world's fastest touring car. For instance, the Facellia has recently taken 1st and 3rd places in its Gran Turismo class in this year's Monte Carlo rally: won outright the R.A.C. Open Challenge Trophy for safety and comfort.

This is only the beginning of achievement for a car that is the outcome of intense French study of every major metallurgical and mechanical development of the past fifteen years.

Consider the specification of Facellia: 4 cylinder twin overhead camshaft unit of 1.6 litres, built strictly to racing practice. Develops 115 b.h.p. at 6,400 r.p.m. Twin choke carburettor,

Facel Vega is here...
NOW COMES FACELLIA
new smaller sister to the fabulous HK500

5 bearing crankshaft. All synchromesh box. 4 wheel Dunlop servo discs. Classic chassis and suspension, structured to last indefinitely.

Now consider the performance: 115 m.p.h. maximum, 0-60 m.p.h. in 11.4 seconds. 28 m.p.g. driven hard. Fabulous road-holding from ideally balanced suspension. Extraordinary stopping power. *Even the handbrake holds firmly on a gradient of 1 in 3.*

See the Facellia with drophead or detachable hardtop in the two-plus-one seat, two-plus-two seat, and full four seater versions. Current deliveries are now to British specification for finish and fittings. This makes the Facellia range the most luxurious and most comprehensively equipped

sports cars ever offered to the British public.

The Company that imports the Facellia and the bigger Facel Vega into Britain is InterContinental Cars Limited of Egham, Surrey. Telephone the Managing Director, George Abecassis, at Egham 4181 and talk Facellia. Talk specification... talk performance... he will tell you all you want to know. His demonstration and after-sales service set a standard unique in the business... you will have the personal attention of Abecassis himself or one of his highly trained team of ex-racing men. Abecassis will tell you frankly that pound-for-pound on performance and pleasure the Facellia is modestly priced at £2,508 tax paid.

Regular deliveries of the new Facellia are now arriving from France. They are collected from Lydd Airport by InterContinental Cars Limited, sole concessionaires in Britain for Facel Vega.

Facel Vega Facellia. "Develops 115 bhp at 6,400 rpm" — but not for long, as the Facel-developed twin overhead cam engine proved so unreliable that it took the company into receivership in 1962 and out of car production entirely in 1964. The worst of the problems had been solved by the time that British imports began in 1961, and many breakdowns could have been avoided with careful running-in and maintenance. Yet although the Volvo engined Facel III of 1963 was completely reliable, the damage had been done and the final Facel 6 version, fitted (except for one BMW-powered example) with an Austin-Healey 3000 engine sleeved down to 2.7 litres, was not officially imported; just 26 were made. Approximately 25 Facellias were sold in Britain by former racing driver George Abecassis alongside the larger, generally reliable, and undisputedly glamorous V8 models (an HK500 is seen here on the left). The aeronautical theme of this advertisement was popular at the time, and its use here to show cars arriving, rather than simply posed or going on holiday with their owners, is a neat touch.

low)." In 1961, the camera captured the HK500's dashboard as it purred through the rain, wipers a-blur, the driver's left hand on the huge steering wheel. If the wheel, from this angle, suggested an Austin Cambridge, the dashboard was in the best Facel pretend-aircraft style. "Out of the common market" said the headline, "a truly international piece of engineering...the pride of France and the most luxurious car in Britain." A subsequent Facel II was "the quiet sensation," and the Facellia of 1961, unreliable though it proved to be, was nothing if not elegant. By 1964 there was the Iso Rivolta, "Mailed fist...velvet glove," and in 1967 the copywriter adopted David Ogilvy's famous line: "At 163 mph in the Iso Grifo, the loudest noise you can hear is a well known Italian racing car trying to keep up." Porsche, on the other hand, preferred inexpensive quarter-pages containing short quo-

tations from independent road tests. Sometimes no car appeared at all. Anyone likely to buy a Porsche knew what it looked like.

This was not true of most Japanese cars in 1965, which, except for the Austins and Hillmans produced with British help in the 1950s, were not taken seriously by most motorists. Thoughtful commentators, however, knew better: in July 1965, Stuart Griffin, writing in *Car*, pointed out that Japan produced 32.6 per cent more cars—1,702,469 of them — in 1964 than in 1963, and the potential within the Japanese domestic market, where only one in 204.2 people then owned a car, suggested that economies of scale would operate to the advantage of Japanese exporters in the future. Griffin concluded, "English growingly aware of the fact there is a threat mounting from Japan still do not know too much

The Field, October 21, 1965

Daihatsu BERLINA
The car with 'Extras' that are fitted as 'Standard'

Daihatsu created the BERLINA for those who dream of sports car beauty and excitement, yet must look for family comfort and safety. The BERLINA is a combination of these desirable features from the sheen on the plush bucket seats to the family-safe, two-door construction. And the BERLINA is within your price range . . . a compact car masterpiece at a price you can afford.

● Front reclining seats ● 90% stainless steel fittings ● Small high-performance engine (797c.c. 41 b.h.p.) ● Complete chassis ● Car radio, semi-automatic aerial, cigarette lighter, wheel trims, electric clock, etc.

and lots more

£799 INCLUDING PURCHASE TAX

Estate car version **£789** including purchase tax

See it at our Showrooms, or post coupon for brochure and address of nearest Distributor.

Please send me Descriptive DAIHATSU brochure and address of nearest Distributor.

NAME ....

ADDRESS ....

DUFAY (B'HAM) LIMITED
175-177 GREAT PORTLAND ST., LONDON, W.1   (F)

Daihatsu Compagno Berlina and Toyota Corona. The Daihatsu looks harmless enough, and it was— neither the handful of Compagnos imported nor their maker did Britain's car industry any damage in the 1960s, as this car, first produced in 1963, was frenetic, cramped and overpriced. But the "extras as standard" theme of the advertisement made it the prototype for hundreds of later pieces for Japanese cars which, in the 1970s, would persuade family motorists seeking reliability and comfort on a budget to desert domestic brands. Daihatsu would return with the more mainstream Charade in 1977. Among the pioneers of the mid-1960s, the Toyota Corona had greater success, being praised for its build quality, equipment and low price, although the suspension and brakes were not good by 1966 European standards and the styling was controversial. The need to grease 18 nipples every 3000 miles, 1950s-style, put many off, while reassuring others of the car's engineering integrity! This advertisement has a pioneering flavour, introducing the make and calling for additional dealers. Curiously, the contemporary *Statistical Review of Press Advertising* records the earlier Toyopet Tiara as having been advertised briefly in Britain during 1961 and 1963 (by Toyota of Japan rather than by a British importer), although it is unlikely that any were sold: only two new Japanese cars were sold in Britain in each of those years, compared with 1230, most of them Coronas, in 1966. Many British motorists were initially reluctant to buy Japanese cars, whether through patriotism, suspicion of novelty or memories of the Second World War, but increasingly changed their minds after breaking down once too often in the local product. Sales took off in the early 1970s.

The Field, June 9, 1966

THE FIELD, *June 9 1966*

FLEXIBILITY
SPEED
POWER

£777

JAPANESE STYLE

Toyota Corona. From Japan's largest motor manufacturers the fantastically flexible Toyota Corona 1500. On the open road-90 m.p.h. in top gear with real flexibility-Japanese style. And you've only to look at Toyota's deep, deep acrylic enamel finish to guess that here is a car at last that puts you in a different class in de-luxe 1500 cc motoring. Smooth, quiet-as-a-whisper motoring even at the highest cruising speed.

Self adjusting brakes, electric windscreen washers, dual-speed wipers, dual-speed heater blower and four sealed beam headlamps are only a few of Toyota's many luxury features-and every single item is checked and double checked before leaving the factory. So much attention to detail, so thoroughly well made. Toyota Corona -Japan's most exciting new export!

TOYOTA CORONA 1500 SALOON £777 INC. P.T.
TOYOTA CORONA 1500 STATION WAGON £829 INC. PT.

A FEW AREAS STILL AVAILABLE FOR SELECTED DEALER APPOINTMENTS

Post this coupon today for illustrated brochure and name of your nearest dealer.

NAME _____

ADDRESS _____

FIW.

TOYOTA CORONA

A PRODUCT OF JAPAN'S LARGEST MOTOR MANUFACTURERS

SOLE CONCESSIONAIRES IN U.K

MOTOR IMPORTS CO. LIMITED
7 GRESHAM ROAD, LONDON S.W.9 TEL: REDPOST 2438

TOYOTA MAIN DEALERS

Ballard, **Abergavenny** . Avon Filling Stn., **Avonmouth** . Auto Sales, Bilston . Flights, **Birmingham, 6** . K & S Motors, **Bolton** . Swanmore Gge., **Bournemouth** . Car Distributors, **Cardiff** . Tyre Care, **Chatham** . Gloucestershire Motors, **Cheltenham** . Autosales, **Cirencester** . Drovers, **Darlington** . Motorway Sales, **Derby**   E. S. Longstaff, **Edmonton** . Lynchford Car Sales, **Farnborough** . Central Gge., **Ferndown** . Kent Auto Panels, **Folkestone** . Mynd House Motors, **Gloucester** . Fredrick Motors, **Gorleston-on-Sea** . Gaiety Gge., **Grimsby** . Stanleys Motors, **Hounslow** . Miles, **Hull** . West End Motors, **St. Helier, Jersey** . Francis Motors, **Leicester** . Autocars Ltd., **London, S.W.2** . Autocars Ltd., **London, S.W.9** . Autocars Ltd., **London, S.W.16** . Bakers Service Stations, **London, E.7** . Wrights, **Lowestoft** . Schenk Motor Engineering, **Manchester** . Fairgreen Motors, **Morden** . Taylor & Blacklock, **Newcastle-on-Tyne** . Nevile Johnson, **Belfast, N. Ireland** . Flewitts Gge., **Nottingham** . Hays, **Plymouth** . W. M. Beesley, **Preston** . Dennis Waldron, **Redditch** . Harmer Car Sales, **Redhill** . Baker Motors, **Rochdale** . Newmans, **Salisbury** . Fox's Gge., **Sevenoaks** . Portland Autos, **Sheffield** . Shipley Motor Services, **Shipley** . Kingsley Gge., **Smethwick 40** . Criterion Gges., **Southampton** . Marymead Motors, **Stevenage** . Bealdslow Motors, **St. Leonards-on-Sea** . Allam Motor Services, **Stoneleigh** . Philip Bright, **Torquay** . Frank Senier, **Wakefield** . E. H. Welling, **Watford** . Lesfield Motors, **Warrington** . Dennis Bircher, **Wellington** . Stonebridge Service Stn., **Willesden** . Chiltern Autos, **Wokingham** . E. S. Longstaff, **Woodford** . Hylton Rd. Gge., **Worcester** .

The Field, May 12, 1966

The Field, August 19, 1965

Ford Mustang Hardtop and (AMC) Rambler Classic 770. All kinds of American cars could be seen on British streets in the 1960s, from surviving, locally-assembled pre-war Chryslers named after improbable London suburbs to post-war cars imported individually by American servicemen, celebrities, embassy officials and enthusiasts. But there were very few of any particular model, and, as sales of a given type would be low and models changed every year, they were infrequently advertised. Among the best known were the Mustang and the Rambler, the former combining power and style with a useful compactness, while the Rambler, especially in Station Wagon form, offered space and comfort with restrained styling in a combination unavailable within Europe. But it was no cheap car for everyman: £1876 would buy two Vauxhall Crestas. Although nothing was remarkable about this advertising as advertising, it makes a striking contrast with American copy for the same cars, which in their homeland were comparatively inexpensive.

of the surging automobile industry, about what models come out under what name-brands, in what categories…there is rising competition on the horizon in the none too distant future for British manufacturers at home and abroad."[15] In the short term, the Daihatsu Compagno Berlina "which everyone including our printer kept mistaking for Daihatus" was the first Japanese model to be sold in Britain. "I remember that it arrived for test [by *Autocar*] on July 8, 1965," recalled Stuart Bladon, "just two days after my son was born. I saw an ominous problem looming: great-granny was coming down to inspect the new baby, and I would have to meet her at the station with this horrid little Japanese car. Was it really so frightful? Well, we all thought so; and I believe that my road test made it plain, even though people always used to say they had to read between the lines to get at the truth about cars we had tested."[16] It was, however, well equipped and well built, and a hundred or so cars were imported. More significant was the Toyota Corona announced at the London Motor Show in 1965, when, according to another *Autocar* tester of the time, Martin Lewis, "the British public got its first look at a proper Japanese motor car. And little did it or the rather complacent British motor industry realize just what lay in store." Re-acquainted with the model in 1985, Lewis recalled asking where the indicator switch was: "Well, would you think of tipping the semi-circular horn [ring] to left or right to make the indicators work? And that noise of the repeater: it sounded just like a ping-pong ball bouncing down a long flight of wooden stairs."[17] But on this occasion *Autocar* had left open the possibility that many more cars could follow, if initial imports "meet with success."[18]

Japan's tentative entry into the British market was her-

alded by suitably modest advertising, but in 1968–69 Datsun campaigned strongly with pictures of dark red and light blue cars speeding along the world's freeways and clambering over rough ground. The pictures for the Datsun 1600 seemed to have been chosen from an international collection for right-hand-drive markets, and an international flavour, albeit occasionally with references lost on (or uninteresting to) British readers distinguished early Datsun advertising. "Two rather remarkable family sedans" said an October 1968 advertisement, with copy that began, "Even the glove compartment has enough room for 2,000 gilt-edged Nissan stock. So spacious is DATSUN that 5 P.M. sized people are cozy and comfy for hours (Or two adults, one child and two active Russian wolfhounds. The amazing economy of DATSUN 1000, in particular, allows you to indulge in whatever whims for wolfhounds you may have.) Careen [*sic*] in the new DATSUN 1600 along dual carriageways at 100 mph! (If you can get away with it.)…" Not that the reader would be likely to get away with it for long by 1968, any more than would copywriters of later years. Launching a new marque was always difficult, so trans-national whimsy that did not really fit any national culture, but did not offend it, was the safest bet in the short term, as was a certain Dad-at-the-disco lightheartedness. In November, a dark red Datsun 1000 was shown outside a boutique: "If she's not a Penny Pincher why'd she buy the DATSUN 1000? You'd have to ask her. But we do know that this very finicky lass is never in the red. Sure, she insisted on the smart new DATSUN. And got it. But we can't vouch for who bought it." It was, as the copy explained, stylish, sporty, responsive, "Dashing, daring and desirable…. It just occurred to us. Maybe you're a penny pincher and just don't care about such things. Even then, though, this new marvel probably will be your next car. The new DATSUN 1000 5-passenger sedan by Nissan, auto leader of the Orient."

Traditional themes were attempted, too, as when two 1600 saloons were seen side by side in woodland: "Love at first sight — A cheery 'hello' in a sunny forest glade. A conversation that's not really so accidental. After all, people who've been around know who's right for them pretty quickly. They can tell by the car a person drives, for example. Anyone who drives a DATSUN has a sense of style…." In 1969 the small Datsun was captioned "The cars that launched a thousand ships." The copy explained, "They're Datsuns and they're international (Nowadays that's kind of rare.) But then also unusual is the high performance for the low price. Small wonder our cars go places. Like Iceland, Turkey, Canada. In fact any one of the hundred countries to which Datsun cars are shipped. (An exercise that's involved well over a thousand launchings)…Datsun. The International Car." In 1969, ruggedness was emphasized in headlines such as "Amazes the Tough Guys!" and "How come that lady's driving the winner of the Safari Rally?" It was all a long, long way from the world of the Austin A40 and the Ford Consul Classic.

Conclusion

For all the good design and for all the excellence of the new copy, an uncertainty is to be felt. Nobody seems to know quite what does in fact sell a motor-car.... Are all the myths exploded? Do the vague dreamlike figures sailing Walter Mitty-like in the azure blue backgrounds of the new sports car really sell anything, or is the name and address of the local dealer set in some long forgotten type in the local paper all that we really need? Will we not soon go out and buy a car with the same lack of emotion with which we at present go out and purchase a new saucepan? Or is the converse true, that in a world getting forever more drab, this is the last bastion of personal excitement, the last flash left in our ever less exciting pan?

— Michael Frostick, Advertising and the Motor-car, 1970

Thirty-five years ago, no-one quite knew what sold a car (or motor-car, as the phrase, less often heard today, then was), and today we are are only slightly further forward. True, we have ideas about the subject: we know that if a car is truly, comically bad, it will not sell for long, however it is advertised; but few very bad cars are produced today, even if we allow that people differ in what they take "bad" to mean. Are we no further forward because we are at all unintelligent, or lazy, or because circumstances conspire against us? Arguably not: although these things might contribute to our uncertainty, they are not responsible for it. We will never truly know — as opposed to guess, or suspect, or reasonably surmise — what sells cars because what was true in 1970 still applies — each type of car is unique, as is each purchaser and each moment when a purchase is made. Even an individual model "changes" over time as it becomes comparatively different against new competition. It is not so much that the goalposts are moving, but that the purchase of a car requires so many pre-conditions to be satisfied: there are, as it were, many pairs of goalposts receding into the distance, each affecting the others in complicated ways that seem random even when they are not. The history of British car advertising suggests no *reliable* correlation between a car's advertising and its success.

In truth, no certain prediction can be made about any-thing affected simultaneously by so many factors as is the success of an advertisement. Human and circumstantial uniqueness ensure that we cannot determine scientifically, by experiment, the outcome of many simple variables even in ordinary life. If the actual probability of anything that happens is, necessarily, one hundred per cent because there is only one real world, the predictive probability of an imagined future is a different thing. Philosophers write volumes on the problem; advertising agents know it in their bellies: the old joke still applies, that even if fifty per cent of advertising is found to work, no-one never knows exactly which fifty per cent. So while research can limit unpredictability, it cannot eliminate it. That is why advertising can be nerve-shredding for its practitioners and one reason why it is so endlessly fascinating to the rest of us, the hidden persuaded.

Do we now buy cars as unemotionally as we buy saucepans? The saucepan manufacturer might think that Frostick's analogy begs the question, but for most people buying a new car *is* still an event. People usually only have one car, or perhaps two; and the car is still an aspirational purchase. It is enjoyed for itself — its looks, its feel, its speed, its practical benefits, for the places it can take its owner — and for what it says about that owner: most new "executive" cars are much too dull to be worth their prices except as social clothing, worn as if to say, "Please let me belong." Such

"For pity's sake, John, buy the wretched thing."

We'd like you to test drive a Jaguar XJ6.
But first we ought to warn you that it can
be a very persuasive experience.
So you might start out with no more than
a hankering for the car and finish up well
and truly bowled over by it.
However if you're willing to take the risk
ring 020-334-2121-Ext 132 and we'll arrange
for a car to be brought round to your house.
But take your wife, too.
So you'll both be in the same boat.

Jaguar XJ6

One drive is worth a million words.

1972 Jaguar XJ6. Jaguar advertising was imaginative and informal at the turn of the decade, showing the car as a source of private contentment as much as a means of public display. Unlike some luxury cars, the XJ6 was genuinely enjoyable to drive, being very low and stable as well as powerful, and a long waiting list formed when it was announced.

The Illustrated London News, August 1977

Country Life, April 19, 1973

With 500,000 in the world, how can the 'Z' remain so exclusive?

Only a limited number of people in Britain were lucky enough to take delivery of a new Datsun 260Z last year.

Which may seem strange when you realise that the Safari–winning 'Z' is the biggest selling sports car in the world, with over 500,000 already in enthusiastic hands!

The problem is to produce enough Z's to meet demand in 130 countries, from America to Saudi Arabia.

And no wonder the 'Z' is in demand! As a specialist, high performance car, with beefy power and the civilised comfort of a luxury saloon, it really is a unique and remarkable car.

It has a 2.6 litre, straight six OHC engine that pushes out 150 b.h.p.; a close-ratio 5-speed gearbox; fat high speed radials on handsome alloy wheels; huge power-assisted brakes; precise rack and pinion steering; independent suspension all round. If you want to drive hard – and well – the 'Z' will suit your mood perfectly.

As a rugged competition car, the 'Z' has proved itself in rallies and races in every part of the globe, including TWO outright victories in the incredible East African Safari! If you want to hurtle side-ways through the African bush, the 'Z' is built to take all the punishment you can give.

On the other hand, this car is equally at home in Mayfair or Knightsbridge. You won't be using all the power, but you *will* be enjoying all the luxury. Comfortable cloth upholstered bucket seats for two, or four people, push-button radio with electric aerial and stereo cassette player; a heated rear window that is really a vast opening hatchback, a cockpit array of instruments and controls, with a four mode wiper system, central fusebox and much more.

Two versions of the famous 'Z' are now available – the Sports two-seater and the 2+2, which really does have room for four adults.

Both cars will top 120 mph and both, remarkably, are quite capable of giving 30 to the gallon, although 25/26 is more likely in everyday motoring.

This year, you could join the limited number of people in Britain who will take delivery of the fabulous Datsun 260Z – and become one of the knowledgeable enthusiasts who have made the 'Z' the world's best selling sports car.

If you like the sound of a world-tested 2.6 litre six-cylinder OHC engine in a luxury executive Saloon or Estate Car, ask your dealer about the 260C.

The Saloon will cosset you in luxury, from its electrically operated windows to its stereo cassette player; the Saloon and Estate (with 75 cu. ft. of luggage space!) will give you power steering, power assisted brakes and 100 m.p.h. performance with Datsun reliability and economy.

It's easy to see why Datsun's six cylinder cars are in such demand the world over, a demand that's never easy to satisfy.

DATSUN U.K. LIMITED, DATSUN HOUSE, NEW ROAD, WORTHING, SUSSEX. TEL: WORTHING 68561. **DATSUN**

Life is full of unnecessary pleasures.

Toyota build a motor car as if your life style depended on it.

Take the Corolla 1200 Coupé.

A twin carb 83 bhp (gross) engine puts it unsquarely in the sporting class.

However, what makes the fast life more than bearable are the little luxuries that go with it.

Like head-high reclining seats,

radial tyres, tinted glass, two-speed windscreen wipers, tachometer and push button AM radio.

Imagine being that chic.

Corolla 1200 Coupé. One of the Toyota Collection.

Toyota (GB) Limited, 120 Purley Way, Croydon, Surrey CR0 4XJ. 01-681 1921

1973 Toyota Corolla 1200 Coupe and 1977 Datsun 260Z. Famously popular saloon and sports cars from the leading Japanese marques in Britain during the 1970s. The Corolla was a world-wide success. Although the Datsun 240Z was the world's best-selling sports car, relatively few, as this advertisement implies, reached Britain. This 260Z is a 2+2.

Punch, June 19, 1974

1974 Chrysler 2-Litre. Designed in Britain, this car was originally intended to be a Humber (with British V6) in Britain and a Simca (with Simca engine) in France, but the Humber was cancelled early in 1970 while the four-cylinder Simca version was launched in France as the Chrysler 180 later in the year. The 2-Litre version followed in 1972. The smaller, similar-looking Hillman Avenger (sold as the Plymouth Cricket in America) was a much greater success in Britain. This advertisement is typical of large family car advertising in the 1970s: the photograph is realistic (even the weather is typically British and overcast), while the style is snappy, with short sentences and part-sentences in the language of estate agency or the hotel brochure. The double-page spread, which allowed the car to be shown in as large a scale as possible, was most effective in the centre of a staple-bound magazine (as here), where the gutter between the pages was virtually eliminated.

CHRYSLER

A quiet introduction to 2-Litre motoring.

Even as you're forming your first impressions, you'll be reassured by the Chrysler 2-Litre.

Because everything about your initial introduction inspires confidence.

From the outset, its quiet ride creates an atmosphere of comfortable calm.

As do the contoured, deeply upholstered seats. Which recline in the front and offer a cushioned central armrest in the back.

And hold you as surely and comfortably as the Chrysler 2-Litre holds the road.

A quietly confident air is enhanced by carpeting which extends from door to door.

While your equilibrium is subtly secured by servo-assisted disc brakes both front and rear.

In fact, everything you appreciate the first time you drive the Chrysler 2-Litre is something you'll come to appreciate more as time goes by.

Because it's a very genuine car.

Which won't need an overdraft's worth of option packs, or the addition of a vinyl roof (which is standard on the 2-Litre) to bring it up to your expectations.

Nor do we offer any such options.

Since everything, except your own personal choice of accessories, is included as standard.

So, as the snags start to emerge from other cars you may have considered, it's worth

remembering that the Chrysler 2-Litre you buy is the same as the car you see advertised, or drive at your Chrysler Dealer.

And, these days, that may even be something worth shouting about.

CHRYSLER 2-LITRE

The Illustrated London News, February 1974

Your very own piece of motoring history: £3,823.

Back in 1964, before we'd even begun to think about the NSU Ro80, we built a car unlike any other before it.

Powered by a completely new kind of engine that worked with a circular movement rather than up and down, it was the world's first rotary driven car.

In action, its rotary engine proved as impressive as it had appeared on paper: almost totally free of mechanical vibration. And unusually silent, producing only a low turbine-like noise when cruising at speed.

We felt that such an entirely new approach to the internal combustion engine demanded an equally different approach to the design of the car it would drive.

Hence, we designed a car from scratch: the NSU Ro80. Which took its place in motoring history as the world's first mass production car to be powered by the twin rotor Wankel engine.

Neither is it just our opinion that the Ro80 represents an important step forward for the motor industry.

The National Motor Museum at Beaulieu recently added the Ro80's Wankel engine to its collection, alongside such notable company as the 1909 Rolls Royce Silver Ghost; the 1930 Bentley 4½ litre; the 1938 Lagonda V12. And the record breaking 1961 Bluebird.

The NSU Wankel engine as fitted to the first rotary powered saloon car in the world, the NSU Ro80. Presented to the National Motor Museum, Beaulieu by Audi NSU (GB) Ltd.

But unlike these cars, you don't have to go out of your way to see the NSU Ro80. Any Audi NSU dealer will be only too pleased to show it to you.

After which, you may want to add this particular piece of motoring history to your collection too.

AUDI NSU

If you want a better car, think about it.

The price shown is the manufacturer's recommended retail price, including VAT and special car tax. The price may be subject to currency surcharge.
Customer Information Dept., Audi NSU (GB) Ltd., Quadrant House, Church Street, Dunstable, Bedfordshire. Tel: 0582 603171. Export enquiries to 95 Baker Street, London W.1. Tel: 01-935 0088. A member of the Thomas Tilling Group.

1974 NSU Ro80. Headline, photograph, body copy, marque name and logo, snappy pay-off—these were the standard ingredients of car advertising in Britain during the 1970s. The car itself was very much an individual, although it was Mazda, rather than NSU, who made the rotary engine durable. Approximately 37,200 were produced between 1967 and 1977, and present-day specialists can make the engine run reliably over much higher mileages than were possible in 1974. The Ro80's styling was remarkably advanced—compare it with that of, say, Vauxhall's FD Victor, introduced in the same year—and the advertisement, too, is now a piece of motoring history. It is a brave advertising theme, however, as the reader might well "think about it," decide that contemplating history is safer than making it, and buy a Rover or small Mercedes instead.

Price: £1,863.76 inclusive of car tax, VAT and extras pack. (Seat belts, number plates and delivery extra).

We'd like to put a little light in your life.

The Wolseley is the only car in the world with its name up in lights.

But that's not its only distinction.

When it was built in 1895, it was the very first British car.

Later, Winston Churchill owned a Wolseley.

So did the Duke of Windsor.

Drive today's Wolseley Six and you can see why.

You'll enjoy vivid performance from a powerful six cylinder engine, reminiscent of the legendary Wolseley 'Silent Six'.

There's the sumptuous and spacious interior you'd expect from the marque.

The walnut fascia, rich pile carpet and deeply-cushioned seats show that dignity and style haven't disappeared from modern motoring.

Judge a Wolseley Six for yourself.

At the very least, we can guarantee it'll put a little light in your life.

Wolseley Six The only car in the world with its name up in lights.

Wolseley

1974 Wolseley Six. A very late advertisement for Wolseley, a marque by now aimed quite openly at the elderly. It disappeared in 1975 following sales of a few thousand Wolseley models of Leyland's new wedge-shaped 18–22 saloon, introduced in scarcely distinguishable Austin, Morris and Wolseley forms in March 1975 and renamed Princess across the range six months later. But if the appeal is specialized, the layout, as with NSU, is conventional, and for a few years in the 1970s there was remarkable uniformity of approach in British car advertising.

Country Life, December 9, 1976

"Sit in one of the new Minis, you feel ten feet tall."

When we showed Eric Sykes a new Mini® Clubman 1100 he took a bit of convincing that it was a Mini.

The new contoured seats threw him. And the wall-to-wall carpeting. The new, easy-to-get-at controls didn't look like the last Mini Eric had seen.

And the fact that the new Minis are quieter, with an improved suspension for a smoother ride made it hard to convince him he really was in one of the most famous cars in the world.

But we did it in the end.

You see, the Mini's celebrated fuel economy hasn't changed. Neither has the larger than life feeling you get when you slide behind the wheel.

Try feeling ten feet tall at your Austin or Morris showroom. It's a great feeling. Ask Eric Sykes.

Welcome back to a better Mini.

From Leyland Cars. With Supercover.
® 'Mini' is a Registered Trade Mark of Leyland Cars.

1976 Mini Clubman. "Mini" became a marque in its own right in 1969, and the squared-up Clubman was introduced in the same year. Light-hearted endorsements were a regular occasional theme in mid-1970s advertising: actor and comedian Eric Sykes was the tallest, while other Mini-loving celebrities included Twiggy and the selection of models who gathered round another Clubman ("Top models. And why they wear Minis"). Petula Clark, meanwhile, endorsed the Chrysler Sunbeam hatchback.

The Illustrated London News, April 1976

1976 Princess 2200 HLS. The great selling-points of Japanese cars in the 1960s and 1970s were reliability and "extras as standard," neatly brought together in a 1979 Toyota advertisement that showed a hand holding a cigarette lighter with the headline, "On a Toyota Cressida, if it comes off in your hand, it's supposed to." But if the overall reliability of British cars would remain hopeless for several years by comparison, some, like this Princess, were well equipped and imaginatively advertised.

themes have endured, and among cars of the 1960s the aspirational versions of ordinary models seem the most dated today, the most endearingly "period." A Rolls-Royce Silver Cloud is enjoyed in the twenty-first century for much the same reasons as it was enjoyed in 1955, or 1965. The same is true of an old sports car. But the emotions of the man who achieved a kind of contentment in a Riley 4/Seventy Two that he thought would elude him in a Morris Oxford are more difficult to recapture: the distinction between the Morris and the Riley was written in a language of associations that we have lost. The enthusiast enjoys both cars, but in a different way to the man who sat on the same leather before him, forty years ago. His involvement is self-conscious as his predecessor's was not. His history is different and so, therefore, is his experience. He alone knows what happened next.

In British car advertising what happened next was, comparatively speaking, conformity. Graphically, the typical advertisement of 1980 was quite similar to that of 1970, whereas the 1960s, as Frostick implies, were years of great change in styles of copy, layout and illustration, as well as in the cars themselves. The wilder fancies of 1960 did not come about: the gas turbine was mass-produced by neither Rover nor Chrysler, and the Wankel rotary engine became almost entirely a Mazda specialism, Citroën M35 and Birotor notwithstanding. The story of the NSU Ro80 is especially poignant. "In 1978 the Ro80 may have a little competition" said a 1968 advertisement, "We've spent seventeen years developing this car. For the next ten our competitors will be wondering how.... This [advertisement] has been just a glimpse of the future. There's more to the Ro80. Much more. Enough to make you despair over cars as they are today.... It'll be another ten years before the others catch up." By 1974, the car was being advertised as "your very own piece of motoring history" and three years later it was just that. In the meantime, copy for conventional cars gradually became more sophisticated, and enduringly enjoyable advertisements were produced for Jaguar, MG, and the Mini in particular. The hatchback, meanwhile, took over from the small saloon as the car for the people; who, for everyday use, would choose a Renault Dauphine over a Renault 5?

Some day, you'll settle down with a nice, sensible girl, a nice, sensible house and a nice, sensible family saloon.

Some day.

The race-proven 1493cc engine with twin SU carbs, taking you effortlessly from 0-60mph in 11.9 seconds and to a top speed of over 100mph.
82lb/ft torque at 3000rpm.
Rostyle sports wheels with radial tyres.
Four speed all synchromesh gearbox.

Rack and pinion steering. Full sports car instrumentation.
And all those top-down runs with various close friends, snug in the reclining seats.
Some day, you'll look back on all these things with a smile. If you treat yourself to an MG Midget now.

MG MIDGET

This page and opposite: **1978 MG Midget** (*left*), **1980 Triumph TR7 Drophead** (*below*), and **1985 Reliant Scimitar SS1** (*opposite page*). Farewell from the traditional post-war British sports car. This MG advertisement shared its headline with others in a well-known series for the last Midgets and MGBs, and is well remembered in its own right. The nice, sensible girl of the future would probably not be tall, however, as the driver would struggle to fit comfortably in the car if much over 5' 9." The TR7, derided by old-time TR enthusiasts when introduced as a two-seater, fixed-roof coupe in 1975, developed a good following late in life, although the conscious archaism of "Drophead" was risky, as it reminded older motorists of what the TR7 patently was not, while encouraging younger buyers to dismiss the car as one for the buffer zone, even if the buffers would not be seen dead in it. The copywriter is obviously conscious of the dilemma, even if it is beyond his power, as messenger, to solve it. A V8-engined (TR8) version was produced for export, of which just a handful found their way onto the British market. Other advertisements for this, the last open-topped Triumph, took more confident advantage of the controversial shape — one piece showed the car as a rocket, pointing upwards, ready for take-off. The bumpers, required by safety laws, were generally considered ugly, albeit less so than those of the MG.

The Scimitar SS1 was Giovanni Michelotti's last project before his death in 1980, the clay model being finished by his long-term assistant, Tateo Uchida. It was traditional in conception but specialized by default, by virtue of a production rate of only a few hundred a year. It looked odd and leaked, but the fussy eventual styling, developed from Michelotti's original proposal, disguised variable panel fit and allowed shut lines to be conveniently placed between the plastic body panels. If the copy is modest, the illustration is quietly inspired, with a theme and compass design that suggest the 1930s. (By contrast, an English Chrysler advertisement of 1937 had shown a car on a compass with a seventeenth-century look, its points labelled "appearance," "comfort," "performance" and "economy.") In 1989, the traditional front-engined, steel-bodied, four-cylinder sports car returned with the Mazda Miata or MX-5, from a country whose entire motor industry sold just one car in Britain in 1960.

93 million miles.

The TR7 is now available with a little extra headroom.

The TR7 is now open.
In fact it's the first launch of a major new British open-top two-seater in years. So it will no doubt come in for a fair amount of scrutiny from the sports car fraternity.
And since the fraternity is known for a degree of traditionalism, we fully anticipate a few raised eyebrows among the older members.

True, the performance is well up to the TR standard. Indeed, with 5 gears, 2 litres of power and a top speed of 114 mph, it's not just the lack of a roof that makes your hair stand on end.
But where, we hear them ask, are the other distinguishing marks of the great British open two-seater?
Where, for instance, are the

noise and vibration so loved by the purists? Why, in this car, when you want to have a word with your passenger, you scarcely need to raise your voice, let alone bellow.
And what's happened to that time-honoured sports car austerity? With deep, comfortable seats, thick carpets, speakers built into the doors and all that interior space, we can

already hear the purists tut-tutting.
Gone, too, are the hours that you used to spend fighting to put the hood up or down. In the TR7 Drophead one person can do the job in less than 60 seconds.
Even so, we reckon the car's performance is going to win over the traditionalists in the end.
For once you're on the road with

the tachometer needle edging up and the wind in your hair, you know you're driving a thoroughbred TR.
Its wind-cheating shape and taut suspension make it stick to the road like superglue, even on the tightest of bends.
The new TR7 Drophead is now appearing at your local showroom in a range of shockingly untraditional

colours and metallic finishes.
If you're still young enough to appreciate the sky for a roof and the thrill of the open road, we strongly suggest a test drive.
If not, why are you still reading this? Better go for a test drive just in case.

The new TR7 Drophead.
Jaguar Rover Triumph

TRIUMPH

THE GETAWAY CAR

The Scimitar SS1 gets you away in style. Gets you away in comfort. With crisp performance, impeccable road manners and high standards of reliability and economy.

Styled by Michelotti and built by a new technology process, the body is rustproof, knock resistant and inexpensive to repair.

And the spacious interior with its deep,

velour faced seats and relaxed driving position is designed for comfort.

Power is provided by well proven 1300cc or 1600cc overhead camshaft engines. The 1600cc, shown here, achieves 110mph, 0-60 in 9.6 secs. and 46mpg at a constant 56mph. The SS1 gets you away from the humdrum.

From just a little under £7000.

SCIMITAR·SS1
RELIANT·TAMWORTH·ENGLAND

If it were the stripes only, we might as well have sold you a Zebra.

Sunseeker. Alpine cool.
1442 ccs hot.
0-60 in around 13 seconds.
Into the wide blue up to 102mph.
Alpine Sunseeker £4222*

**Chrysler Alpine Sunseeker.
A real beast – and it ain't no Zebra.**

ALPINE

Price includes Car Tax, VAT and front inertia reel seat belts. Excludes delivery and number plates. *Prices correct at time of going to press.

CHRYSLER
UNITED KINGDOM

1979 Chrysler Alpine Sunseeker. The 1970s, and the advent of the hatchback in particular, saw the arrival of the special editions, "being sale-boosters in times of recession, and used…in the same way as school-children dream up improbable reasons for an extra half-holiday," as Michael Sedgwick put it in 1983. But copywriters were in a quandary: do you emphasize the essential benefits of the design, in which case — why the special edition? Or do you emphasize the special edition, in which case the reader will ask, "but is the actual car any good?" The strategy was most effective when worthwhile extras were included in an established and popular model sold at a special low price; this advertisement was striking, but was perilously close to being an in-joke.

The Geographical Magazine, December 1980

Efficient engineering plus adrenalin.

What leaps from 0-60 mph in just 8.6† seconds, rushes on up to 113 mph and clings to the road like a competition car, yet returns an almost unbelievable 40.9 mpg at a steady 56 mph** and requires less maintenance than most family saloons?

Answer: Ford's astonishing new XR3.

Tuned for the eighties.

The XR3 story began four years ago, just when the fuel crisis had really begun to bite.

That's when Ford went to work on a new front wheel drive Escort.

The target they set themselves was to design a car that would cost even less to run than its predecessor. But perform as well or even better.

The sports derivative of this new Escort, designated the XR3, was to become

the purest expression of that ideal – the epitome of the fast, high efficiency hatchback.

High power. Low service costs.

The heart of the XR3's exhilarating performance is its brand new high efficiency engine, a triumph of elegantly simple design.

With an aluminium cylinder head, hemispherical combustion chambers, high lift overhead camshaft, twin choke carburettor and breakerless ignition, it produces no less than 96 bhp from only 1.6 litres.

Even more important from the point of view of running costs, the new engine is very straightforward to service. It only needs a major service every 12,000 miles, with an interim service at 6,000.

Efficient shape. Light weight.

It's the XR3's strikingly efficient shape that releases the engine's full potential.

Thanks to a deep front air dam, the fairings round the wheels and that big dished rear spoiler, it has a drag coefficient of only 0.375.

Equally vital to acceleration and fuel economy, computer technology has kept the car's weight to a minimum without sacrificing strength.

Limpet-like roadholding. Businesslike cockpit.

The pleasure of driving this refined little machine is sharpened by its phenomenal roadholding.

Suspension is independent all round with pressurised gas filled shock absorbers and supple coil springs, ventilated disc brakes and rack and pinion steering. And the car squats low and wide on those beautiful alloy wheels with

their advanced ultra low profile tyres.

Deeply contoured bucket seats provide a businesslike driving position. The steering wheel is small, the pedals broad and firm, and the gear change short and crisp.

A nice touch, the rev counter is positioned in its housing so that the red line is at the top.

And here's another example of the technology that's gone into the car, a new electronic module activates an array of warning lights which allow you to check oil level, brake pad wear, radiator and screen wash levels without leaving your seat.

Best of all, this red blooded sports car can carry four people comfortably and has a load capacity of 48.7 cu ft with the back seat folded.

So at £5123* it's totally practical, not just a rich man's toy.

If you'd like something to stir the adrenalin, ask your dealer to arrange an XR3 demo.

*Max. price at 14th November, 1980. Seat belts, car tax and VAT included. Delivery, number plates and head restraint seats at extra cost. †Ford computed figures.

**Gov. fuel economy figures – mpg (litres/100km): Constant 56 mph (90 kms): 40.9 (6.9). Constant 75 mph (120 km): 31.7 (8.9). Simulated urban cycle: 27.7 (10.2).

FORD ESCORT **XR3** *Ford*

1980 Ford Escort XR3. Alloy wheels, spoilers, sports seats and steering wheel — and the beginnings of technophilia with a graph and plenty of figures. With such a hatchback, who needed a sports car or a less practical, traditional coupe? The advertisement and the car heralded the preoccupations of the 1980s.

With such cars, continental marques became commonplace, and "buying foreign," by 1980, had ceased to be daring or aspirational. Was it unpatriotic to decline a Morris Ital? In the 1980s, technology and aspiration came together in a relationship which has not yet run its course, although the increasing resistance of luxury car buyers to models whose interiors remind them too much of office life, now that computers and mobile telephones are all but universal, suggests that new emphases and combinations of past themes may yet emerge.

Appendix 1

Year Letter Suffixes of Car Number (License) Plates

During the 1960s, the United Kingdom had a car registration system under which cars were registered by local authorities according to an overall scheme determined nationally. In many cases, numbers were allocated to dealers in batches, with the result that different models of a given make sold by the same dealer on the same day often carried successive numbers. Before 1963, and in some areas until 1965 (see below), a car's registration number was made up from of a group of letters and a group of numbers (usually three of each), with the last two letters indicating where the car was registered. This remained the case after the new suffix letters arrived. Thus, for example, the "PA" of Ford Consul Classic 672 MPA indicates a car registered in Surrey, the "EA" of Jensen C-V8 701 KEA indicates a car registered in West Bromwich, and Hillman Super Minx JLC 262D was registered in London. Once allocated, a registration number (and registration plates) normally stayed with a car throughout its life wherever in the country it was based.

In 1963, year letters, or suffixes, were introduced, beginning with the letter "A." However, not all 1963 cars were registered with an "A" suffix and not all 1964 cars received a "B," as the use of year letters by local authorities become compulsory only with the "C" suffix in 1965. Until 1967, suffix letters changed in January, but, as this caused a new-year rush of car buyers seeking the latest suffix for 'one-upmanship' and anticipated resale value, the changeover month was altered in 1967 to August.

Finally, the actual design of number plates changed in the late 1960s. Until the last few months of 1967, a number plate was made from black or silver letters and numbers fitted to (or stamped in) a black plate. After October 31, 1967 reflective number plates, with black digits on a white (front) or yellow (rear) reflective background, became available. These increased in popularity and became compulsory equipment on all cars first registered on or after January 1, 1973.

Year suffixes from 1963—1971 are as follows (*Note*: an 'I' suffix was not used):

1963 (some areas)	A
1964 (some areas)	B
1965	C
1966	D
January 1, 1967–July 31, 1967	E
August 1, 1967–July 31, 1968	F
August 1, 1968–July 31, 1969	G
August 1, 1969–July 31, 1970	H
August 1, 1970–July 31, 1971	J

For further information about the history of car registration in Britain, see Philip Riden, *How to Trace the History of Your Car* (2nd ed.) (Merton Priory Press, 1998); and Dave Moss, *Number Plates* (Shire Publications Ltd., 2003).

Appendix 2

United Kingdom Purchase Tax Rates for Four-Wheeled Passenger Cars

Purchase Tax (p.t.) was levied on new cars between 1940 and 1973 and, at different rates, on commercial vehicles until 1959. By altering the rate of tax, a government could benefit from, and affect, the demand for new cars. The tax was abolished in April 1973, after which Car Tax and VAT were charged instead. Purchase tax rates were changed as follows:

October 1940. Purchase Tax introduced at 33⅓ % on a car's wholesale price, defined as ⅚ of the tax-excluded recommended retail list price.

June 1947. Increased to 66⅔ % on cars with a retail value of more than £1,280; other cars remain at 33⅓ %.

April 1951. Increased to 66⅔ % on all cars (subsequent rates applied to all four-wheeled cars irrespective of size or retail price).

April 1953. Reduced to 50 %

October 1955. Increased to 60 %

April 1959. Reduced to 50 %

July 1961. Increased to 55 %

April 1962. Reduced to 45 %

November 1962. Further reduced to 25 %

July 1966. Increased to 27½ %

March 1968. Further increased to 33⅓ %

November 1968. Increased again to 36⅔ %

July 1971. Reduced to 30 %

March 1972. Further reduced to 25 %

April 1973. Purchase tax on cars replaced by a combination of Car Tax of 10 % on the wholesale price (defined as before), plus VAT of 10 % on the total. The total tax charged was equivalent to a purchase tax rate of 23 %. VAT was a new tax on several goods and services introduced on April 1, 1973. The original rate of 10 % was reduced on July 29, 1974 to 8 %, reducing the combined taxes equivalent to purchase tax charged on cars from 23 % to 20.4 %.

Source: Compiled from figures provided by the Society of Motor Manufacturers and Traders (SMMT) in *The Motor Industry of Great Britain*, 1974 ed., pp. 335–336.

Appendix 3

The Value of the Pound 1958–1970
Compared with Its Value in 2001

The following figures indicate how many 2001 pounds (£) would be needed to make up the value of a pound on the date given, together with the rate of inflation for the year. (Thus in 1959, for example, a pound was worth 13.63 times its value in 2001, and inflation during 1959 was 0.9 %). Figures are rounded up to two decimal points.

Date	Comparative multiplier	Price inflation
1958	13.75	2.7 %
1959	13.63	0.9 %
1960	13.50	1.1 %
1961	13.13	2.9 %
1962	12.63	3.6 %
1963	12.44	1.8 %
1964	12.00	3.5 %
1965	11.44	4.9 %
1966	11.00	3.8 %
1967	10.75	2.6 %
1968	10.25	4.7 %
1969	9.69	5.6 %
1970	9.19	5.9 %

Note: Before a decimal currency (with 100 pence, or "p," in a pound) was adopted in Britain in February 1971, there were twelve pence (d) in a shilling (s) and 20 shillings in a pound (£). The "d," for pence, originally stood for "denarius," a Roman silver coin whose name was used in England for the silver penny. Prices were written in units of diminishing value, e.g., £862 12s 6d.

Source: Figures calculated from data in Patsy Richards, *House of Commons Research Paper 02/44: Inflation: The Value of the Pound 1750–2001* (House of Commons Library, 2002)

Appendix 4

The Value of the U.S. Dollar Against the Pound: Exchange Rates, 1958–1970

Date	£ per $	$ per £
1958	0.3569	2.802
1959	0.3572	2.800
1960	0.3567	2.803
1961	0.3562	2.807
1962	0.3568	2.803
1963	0.3575	2.797
1964	0.3584	2.790
1965	0.3568	2.803
1966	0.3584	2.790
1967	0.4194	2.384
1969	0.4166	2.400
1970	0.4178	2.393

Source: Figures in the first column provided by, and in the second column calculated from, exchange rates given in the *United Nations Statistical Yearbook, 1963 ed.*, pp. 516–517; *1970 ed.*, p. 567; and *1972 ed.*, p. 604. (UN, 1963–72). The comparable figures for 1999 are 0.618 and 1.618: *ibid., 2001 ed.*, p. 831.

Appendix 5

UK Car Production, Registrations, Exports and Imports, 1958–1970

Date	Production	New registrations*	Exports	Imports	New regns. less imports	Imports as % of new regns.
1958	1,051,551	566,319	483,877	10,940	555,379	1.9
1959	1,189,943	657,315	568,846	26,998	630,317	4.1
1960	1,352,728	820,088	569,916	57,309	762,779	7.0
1961	1,003,967	756,054	370,758	22,759	733,295	3.0
1962	1,249,426	800,239	544,792	28,610	771,629	3.6
1963	1,607,939	1,030,694	615,827	48,163	982,531	4.7
1964	1,867,640	1,215,929	679,383	65,725	1,150,204	5.4
1965	1,772,045	1,148,718	627,567	55,558	1,093,160	4.8
1966	1,603,679	1,091,217	556,044	66,793	1,024,424	6.1
1967	1,552,013	1,143,015	502,596	92,731	1,050,284	8.1
1968	1,815,936	1,144,770	676,571	102,276	1,042,494	8.9
1969	1,717,073	1,012,811	771,634	101,914	910,897	10.1
1970	1,640,966	1,126,824	690,339	157,956	968,868	14.0

*New registrations include imports. *Note*: the figures for new registrations exclude cars supplied to the Isle of Man and to the Channel Islands, but include those supplied to Northern Ireland. These figures also include small numbers of certain used vehicles, "such as ex-W.D. [War Department] stock and those imported after use overseas without having been previously registered in the United Kingdom."

Source: First four columns: *The Motor Industry of Great Britain 1971*, pp. 12, 53, 163, 321 (SMMT, 1971); last two columns calculated from these figures.

Appendix 6

Imports of Cars from Selected Countries, 1958–1973

Date	France	W. Ger.	Italy	USA	Can.	Sweden	Czech.	U.S.S.R.	E. Ger.	Japan
1958	4,101	5,555	824	201	205	54	49	None	None	None
1959	14,412	8,223	3,042	269	330	458	188	4	None	None
1960	38,257	12,997	4,475	326	448	413	255	40	None	1
1961	3,763	13,229	1,713	229	519	1,661	1,735	5	2	2
1962	6,597	9,415	2,890	135	172	2,521	946	None	None	2
1963	10,588	12,235	5,749	306	647	3,657	3,211	25	None	2
1964	13,865	17,171	12,635	300	739	4,070	2,621	26	441	15
1965	13,695	18,043	4,873	284	465	4,414	2,145	25	372	168
1966	17,256	20,127	9,375	368	286	4,957	1,333	298	369	1,230
1967	23,065	34,738	17,262	480	85	8,110	2,509	192	1,585	1,422
1968	23,274	26,405	24,238	375	102	8,184	909	793	1,518	5,788
1969	26,199	23,246	22,247	282	39	10,095	814	None	928	2,676
1970	47,217	39,227	26,037	315	42	15,156	1,554	249	954	4,291
1971	84,607	68,141	41,836	287	17	23,407	3,187	835	1,415	16,969
1972	128,711	86,226	57,596	551	13	34,294	8,243	4,976	3,146	67,860
1973	140,192	85,734	56,960	966	24	34,884	10,058	10,345	5,078	97,338

Source: SMMT: *The Motor Industry of Great Britain (1959–1974 eds.)*

Appendix 7

Exports of Cars to Selected Markets, 1958–1970

Date	USA	Canada	Australia	N.Z.	S. Africa	Sweden	Denmark	Norway	Irish Rep.	Switzerland
1958	152,543	45,423	56,231	23,202	43,862	20,422	7,212	2,571	17,939	3,399
1959	208,143	73,001	46,172	22,529	26,535	20,023	11,852	2,547	19,536	4,468
1960	131,808	91,315	50,998	24,426	39,895	13,639	10,429	6,887	25,005	5,567
1961	30,519	45,893	19,697	26,101	20,407	12,550	10,527	7,738	22,389	9,764
1962	73,658	38,811	46,088	31,695	35,421	20,113	26,321	10,616	26,913	16,198
1963	68,509	13,902	56,764	43,506	54,531	23,203	21,149	10,506	30,383	22,092
1964	79,116	35,051	65,119	46,032	68,940	24,349	24,657	11,602	36,643	25,608
1965	69,929	31,888	45,572	41,617	47,951	31,779	19,786	11,846	29,061	27,369
1966	83,729	30,578	41,175	34,707	47,178	15,222	25,534	13,280	28,389	22,582
1967	70,766	24,923	27,298	27,210	41,299	10,271	28,882	13,777	30,875	23,135
1968	97,069	43,354	51,717	27,079	35,685	13,489	31,148	12,362	36,230	27,322
1969	103,691	50,332	48,854	36,437	46,082	14,432	39,939	12,292	32,423	34,585
1970	76,891	21,640	44,961	37,646	44,002	11,963	32,083	10,468	32,960	31,100

Date	France	W. Germany	Austria	Italy	Belgium	Netherlands	Portugal	Japan
1958	2,433	4,058	4,052	992	7,794	10,131	1,829	571
1959	2,869	5,307	4,740	1,329	13,701	11,393	2,654	917
1960	6,246	6,565	3,110	4,810	18,514	14,800	2,030	983
1961	14,708	5,598	4,357	12,475	17,473	12,622	3,821	710
1962	33,330	9,866	8,407	23,006	23,889	15,743	5,096	789
1963	36,390	8,471	11,710	37,881	34,543	24,885	5,879	2,211
1964	30,769	6,836	11,035	10,010	34,778	33,458	7,088	2,654
1965	27,374	6,627	11,979	9,098	36,152	36,869	12,007	2,542
1966	21,152	6,290	12,299	4,940	32,221	23,106	12,668	2,723
1967	11,140	9,979	11,501	3,180	40,166	22,830	12,702	2,051
1968	21,867	18,895	17,455	39,306	52,856	11,679	16,393	1,719
1969	18,378	14,324	20,103	52,497	54,994	11,977	21,446	1,730
1970	5,856	14,977	27,761	53,472	53,173	15,389	18,362	1,781

Source: SMMT: *The Motor Industry of Great Britain (1959–1971 eds.)*

Appendix 8

Leading Automotive Advertisers, January–May 1968

Marque	*Expenditure (£)*	*Other products*	*Expenditure (£)*
Ford	366,150	Esso oil & petrol	477,700
Hillman	317,533	Castrol oil	419,349
Vauxhall	214,976	Dunlop tyres	300,690
BMC	169,782	Shell petrol	295,729
Fiat	147,776	National petrol	205,009
Triumph	139,782	Michelin tyres	204,461
Volkswagen	106,746	BP petrol	189,551
Renault	98,130	Goodyear tyres	116,250
Volvo	63,690	India tyres	98,919
Mercedes-Benz	56,361	Mobil oil	95,756

Source: Compiled from figures in "Spotlight on Automotive Advertising," *Advertising*, July/August 1968, p. 22.

Appendix 9

Division of Advertising Expenditure by Media Category, January–May 1968

	British cars (£)	Imported cars (£)
Provincial newspapers	430,200	177,000
National daily papers	405,700	206,900
Colour supplements	245,300	91,200
General weeklies	185,300	75,600
TV	177,700	None
General monthlies	95,300	18,700
National Sunday papers	80,000	99,100
London evening papers	42,400	24,200
Trade & technical press	18,500	5,500
Women's monthly magazines	10,900	4,600
Total	1,691,300	702,900

Note: Press advertising expenditure for British cars during the first half of 1968, including June, was the 5th highest among the top 20 product groups, behind Cigarettes, Department and Variety Chain Stores, Direct Mail Order Houses and Air Travel and Transport. Press advertising expenditure for imported cars was 15th highest, behind Carpet and Floor Coverings and ahead of Gas. No cars featured among the top 20 product group expenditures on TV advertising during this period. Combined press and TV expenditure for British cars, at £2,016,700, was the 16th highest among the top 20 product groups, behind Cleansers (Abrasive and Chemical) and ahead of Paints and Stains. Imported cars did not feature in this top 20, in which the first two places went to Chocolate Confectionery (£5,226,000) and Cigarettes (£4,944,600). Cigarettes were not advertised on TV.

Source: Compiled from figures in "Spotlight on Automotive Advertising," *Advertising*, July/August 1968, pp. 9, 20, 21.

Appendix 10

Car Manufacturers' and Importers' Advertising Agencies, 1958–1970

The advertising agencies of car manufacturers and importers were listed in the *Statistical Review of Press Advertising* (see *Appendix 11A* below) and its successors from July 1932 until December 1966; from September 1968 until May 1969; and from October 1969 to December 1970. Agencies were not listed after December 1970. Where a new agency was instructed during a period in which listing temporarily ceased (i.e. January 1967–August 1968 or June–September 1969) the date of first listing (usually September 1968 or October 1969; sometimes later if advertising for the car was intermittent) is given below, and is marked with asterisk*.

Many imported marques were advertised before 1958, and where this is the case the date of first listing is given in square brackets. Where advertising for a marque began during 1958, or ended before the end of 1970, the month of first and/or last listing is given in round brackets. Thus a marque first listed in April 1958 and last listed in March 1970 would be marked "(4/58–3/70)" whereas one first advertised in March 1957 and last advertised in 1973 would be marked "[3/57 —] (1958–1970)." Some marques and models were officially imported in very small numbers but not advertised in the ordinary way, although their availability was well known to readers of the small ads in *The Autocar*, *The Motor*, *Motor Sport* and other motoring journals. Marques and models not officially imported or advertised were occasionally seen on the road when individual cars were imported for Motor Show display or for road testing by magazines, or were brought in by dealers to order, by private individuals working in Britain or returning from abroad or — not least — by domestic manufacturers for evaluation. Many of these cars subsequently changed hands between motoring enthusiasts. Some marques, such as Fiat and Opel, were advertised in the Republic of Ireland (Eire) before they were advertised in Britain.

The dates on which agencies for individual marques changed should be read as approximate dates only, especially during the period prior to 1967 when the *Statistical Review* and its successors were published quarterly rather than monthly. Changes recorded as having occurred at the ends of year quarters are likely in some cases to have taken place during, rather than at the end of, the last quarters for which they are listed. In addition, an advertisement published early in the currency of a new agency might have been prepared by its predecessor: for example, Hobson, Bates and Partners are recorded as having taken over the Triumph account in or around October 1966, but some Triumph Herald advertisements listed in reliable contemporary sources as having been prepared by Ogilvy and Mather Ltd. continued to be published in the early months of 1967.

The agency for a marque newly listed was not always known immediately. In many cases the first known agency is likely to have been used from the marque's first importation or, if British, its beginning, but this might not always be the case. Similarly, where the agency for a new marque is at first not known, and the marque is subsequently listed as advertising directly, this could mean either that direct advertising was employed from the beginning or — as was not unknown — that the marque tried an agency before deciding to advertise directly. Advertisers occasionally changed agencies only to change back again within a short time.

Marques that shared an agency were invariably either members of the same corporate group or not in effective competition with each other. Some marques were advertised and sold directly by their manufacturers or dealers without an advertising agency's being involved. Agencies' names are occasionally given in abbreviated form, although names have been cross-checked and expanded to their full form wherever possible. The names of several agencies changed following merger, expansion, contraction or reorganization.

Marque	*Agencies until December 1970***
AC (1958–1970)	7/57–11/64: Wilkes Brothers & Greenwood; 12/64–1970+ : A.T.A. Advertising.
Alfa Romeo (4/61–1970)	4/61–12/62: (Not known); 1/63: Charter advertising; 1/64: George Cuming Ltd.; 9/68*-1970+: Colman, Prentis & Varley.
Alvis (1958–1970)	7/50–1970+: John Haddon & Co. (*Note*: the last Alvis was completed in September 1967.)
Armstrong Siddeley (1958–9/60)	7/53–9/60: Dolan Ducker, Whitcombe & Stewart Ltd.
Aston Martin (1958–1970)	4/50–5/62: Dudley Turner & Vincent Ltd.; 6/62: Eric Garrott Associates; 7/67–1970+: Holmwood Advertising Ltd.
Austin (1958–70)	10/55–3/66: Colman, Prentis & Varley Ltd.; 4/66: S.H. Benson Ltd.; 9/68: Cogent Elliott (except Austin 1300 and Austin 3-Litre: Dorland Advertising Ltd.; 10/69*–1970+: S.H. Benson Ltd. (See also *British Motor Corporation* and *British Leyland*, below.) (*Note*: S. H. Benson Ltd. were also Austin's agency from 7/38–9/55.)
Austin-Healey (1958–12/68)	10/55–3/66: Colman, Prentis & Varley Ltd.; 4/66–12/68: S.H. Benson Ltd.
Auto-Union DKW (including Audi from 1965) (4/59–1970)	4/59: Downtons Ltd.; 4/62: (Direct advertising); 1/63: Goble & Bone; 10/65: Papert, Koenig & Lois Ltd.; 9/68*: John Haddon & Co.
Bentley (1958–1970)	10/33: Dorland Advertising Ltd. (See also *Rolls-Royce & Bentley*, below.)
British Motor Corporation (BMC) (1958–4/68)	4/54–3/66: Service Advertising Co. Ltd.; 4/66–4/68: Dorland Advertising Ltd. (See also *British Leyland*, below.)
British Leyland (BMLC): (5/68–1970)	9/68*-1970+: Dorland Advertising Ltd. (*Note*: some British Leyland advertising combined complementary marques and models, e.g. Austin and Morris versions of the same design under the "Austin-Morris" marque name and different ranges of Minis, especially after "Mini" replaced Austin and Morris as the cars' marque name in late 1969.)
British Leyland (BLMC) *exceptions to above*:	5/69: Prestige advertising: Pritchard Wood, Partners; 11/69: Prestige advertising: Wasey, Pritchard, Wood & Quadrant; 10/69*-1970+: BLMC Minis: S.H. Benson Ltd.; BLMC Unipart: 12/69–1970+: Lovell & Rupert Curtis; BLMC Gauntlet used cars: from 6/70: Longleys & Hoffman.
BMW [1/57 —] (as BMW Isetta to 6/63; as BMW to 1970) (1958–70)	1958: (Not known); 1/61: Haig McAlister Ltd.; 4/63: Walkley Hodgson; 7/65: Richards, Marshall & Fairburn; 1/66–1970+: Smee's Advertising Ltd.
Bond (as Sharp's Commercials Ltd., Preston, Lancashire to 12/63; as Bond Cars Ltd., Preston, Lancashire to 1970) (1958–1970)	7/55–12/61: (Direct advertising); 1/62: G. Street & Co. Ltd.; 1/64: Modern Advertising Ltd.; 1/65: Connell, May & Steavenson; from 6/70: Clarendon Advertising. (*Note*: agency given as not known before 7/55, so direct advertising could have been used from marque's first listing as an advertiser in 12/50.)

Borgward [7/53 —]
(1958–9/61; 3/63–4/64)

10/53–9/61: J. Willis Advertising; 3/63–4/64: (not known). (*Note*: Borgward production ended in 1961.)

Bristol (1958–1970)

1/55–9/61: Crane Publicity (as Crane Advertising Ltd. from 1/61); 10/61–1970+: Norman Davis Ltd.

Checker Marathon (3/66 only)

3/66: Digby Wills Ltd.

Chevrolet [4–7/56]
(1/59–12/60; 4/63–1970)

1/59: R.S. Caplin Ltd.; 4/63–1970+: Bernard Hodgson Advertising Ltd. (as Bernard Hodgson-Frost Smith from 7/66).

Chrysler [10/46 — 9/47, 7/56 — 11/56] (2/63–1970)

2/63: Silver Advertising Ltd.; 4/66–1970+: Young & Rubicam. (*Note*: listed as imported by Simpsons Motors (Wembley) Ltd., Salmon St., London SW9 to 11/65; then by Chrysler Motors Ltd., Mortlake Road, Richmond, Surrey from 5/66.)

Chrysler (Aus) (1967–1970)

9/68*-1970+: Young & Rubicam.

Chrysler UK (1970)

From 9/70: Foote, Cone & Belding Ltd.

Citroën [1945 —] (1958–1970)

1/55–4/59: Napper, Stinton, Woolley Ltd.; 5/59: Modern Advertising Service Ltd.; 1/65: Connell, May & Steavenson; 9/68*: London Prog. Advertising; 1/69–1970+: Connell, May & Steavenson.

Citroën & Panhard combined (10/58–2/59, 10/63)

10/58–2/59: Napper, Stinton, Woolley Ltd.; 10/63: Modern Advertising Service Ltd.

Coronet 3-wheeler (1958 only)

1958: Tibbenham Ltd.

Daf (3/61–1970)

3/61: Holmwood advertising; 1/64: Osborne-Peacock Co.; 10/65: K.S. Advertising Ltd.; 1/66: Chesney, Good & Associates; 9/68*–1970+: Burrows Hayman Associates.

Daihatsu (10/65–4/68, 1/69)

10/65: A.P. Services Ltd.; 1/69: McConnell & Co. Advertising.

Daimler (1958–1970)

10/44–12/60: London Press Exchange Ltd.; 1/61: Nelson Advertising Service; from 1/70: Benton & Bowles.

Daimler & Jaguar combined (11/62–1970)

11/62: Nelson Advertising Service; from 1/70: Benton & Bowles.

Datsun (10/65–1970)

10/65: Standard Advertising Agency; 6/68*-1970+: Park, Monico, Nicolls & Bluff.

Dodge (9/63 only)

9/63: Batten, Burton, Durstine & Osborn Ltd.

Facel Vega (8/58–3/65)

8/58–3/65: (Direct advertising)

Fiat (1/58–1970)

From 1/58: Alan Betts Ltd.; 7/58: (not known); 4/59–1970+: Crane Publicity Ltd: (as Crane Advertising Ltd. from 1/61, as Field & Crane Ltd. from 7/65, as Crane, N.C.K. Ltd. from 1/66, as Crane, Norman, Craig from 9/68*, as Norman, Craig & Kummel from 2/69).

Ford (1958–1970)

10/46–12/60: Rumble, Crowther & Nicholas Ltd.; 1/61: London Press Exchange Ltd.; 11/66: Collett Dickenson Pearce; 9/68*: J. Collings & Partners (*Note*: This intermission is not confirmed in COP's own agency history); 4/69–1970+: Collett Dickenson Pearce.

Ford (Germany) (11/59–1970)	11/59: Rumble, Crowther & Nicholas Ltd.; 1/61: London Press Exchange Ltd.; 10/68*–1970+: Collett Dickenson Pearce.
Ford (Australia) (8/67–1970)	8/67–1970+: (Not known).
Frazer-Nash (12/63 only)	12/63: (Direct Advertising) (*Note*: The last Frazer-Nash car was made in 1957).
Gilbern (10/65–1970)	10/65–1970+: (Direct advertising).
Glas (10/65 only)	10/65: (Direct advertising).
Goggomobil [7/57–] (1958–60)	7/57–9/57: (Not known); 10/57: S. F. & Partners Ltd.; 10/59–12/60: K.S. Advertising Ltd.
Gordon 3-wheeler (3/60 only)	3/60: S. C. Peacock Ltd.
Gordon-Keeble (10/64–3/65)	10/64–3/65: Freeman, Mathes & Milne.
Heinkel Cabin Cruiser [1/57 —] (1958–3/61)	1/57–9/59: Auger & Turner Ltd.; 10/59: McConnell & Co. (Advertising) Ltd.; 4/60–3/61: Powell Advertising.
Hillman (1958–1970)	1/46–3/62: Basil Butler Co. Ltd.; 4/62: Butler & Gardner Ltd.; 9/68*–1970+: Foote Cone & Belding Ltd.
Honda (3/67–1970)	9/68*: D. Williams & Partners; 12/68–1970+: K.M.P. Partnership.
Humber (1958–1970)	1/46–3/62: Basil Butler Co. Ltd.; 4/62: Butler & Gardner Ltd.; 4/64: Erwin Wasey, Ruthrauff & Ryan Ltd. (as Erwin Wasey Ltd. from 10/64); 9/68*–1970+: Foote Cone & Belding Ltd.
Iso (4/64–11/66, 4/67) (intermittently)	4/64–67: Osborne-Peacock Co. Ltd.; 4/67: (not known).
Jaguar (1958–1970)(from 4/34–12/44 as S.S.)	4/34–12/69: Nelson Advertising Service; from 1/70: Benton & Bowles.
Jensen (1958–1970)	4/55–9/63: Longleys & Hoffman; 10/63: Baker-Dorset Associates; 1/65: K.S. Advertising Ltd.; 4/66: Chesney, Good and Associates Ltd.; 1/69: Papert, Koenig, Lois; from 1/70: Forsyth & Marketing Improvements.
Lagonda (9/61–6/63)	4/50–9/61: Dudley Turner & Vincent Ltd.; 5/62–6/63: Eric Garrott Associates. (*Note*: no Lagonda advertising listed 7/57–8/61.)
Lancia [1/49; from 10/53 intermittently] (3/61–70)	3/61: (Not known); 4/61: Cecil Turner Ltd.; 4/62: Collett Dickenson Pearce & Partners Ltd.; 7/66: Griggs Lander Associates; 9/68*: Dunn-Meynall, Keefe.
Lotus (7/60–1970)	7/60: (Direct advertising); 7/63–1970+: Industrial Publicity Service.
Marcos (4/65–1970)	4/65–1970+: T.C. Bench Ltd.
Maserati (4/63–1970)	4/63: Direct Advertising; 4/64: Sells Ltd.; 10/65: Richards, Marshall & Fairburn Ltd.; 1/66: Smee's Advertising Ltd.; from 12/70: Connell, May & Steavenson.
Mazda (1/67–1970)	10/68*: Detsu Advertising; 10/69*–1970+: Napper Stinton Woolley.

Mercedes-Benz [9/53 —] (1958–1970)	From 1/58: Mason-Peacock Ltd.; 4/59: Downtons Ltd. (as Downton, Dixon W. & C. W. from 4/65); 1/66: London Prog. Advertising Ltd.; 7/66: Downtons, Dixons, W. & C. W. (as Downton-Dixon from 9/68*); 9/68*–1970+: Garland-Compton (as Compton U.K. Partners from 2/70).
Messerschmitt [11/54 —] (1958–9/61, 4–7/63)	From 1/58: Mason-Peacock Ltd.; 7/58–9/61: Hausmann Advertising: 4–7/63: Hausmann, Langford & Partners.
MG (1958–1970)	10/44–12/60: Saward Baker & Co. Ltd.; 1/61: City & General Advertising Ltd.; 1/66: Saward Baker & Co. Ltd.; 9/68*: Brunning Advertising & Marketing; 1/69: Saward Baker & Co. Ltd.; 10/69*–1970+: Dorland Advertising.
Morgan (1958–1970)	1/38–3/63: S. D. Toon & Heath Ltd.; 4/63: Granville Lang & Partners; 1/66: Langford Smedley Advertising; from 3/70: G. C. Smedley Associates.
Morris (1958–1970)	10/34–1970+: Dorland Advertising Ltd. (*Note*: Morris dealer advertising 9/68–11/68: Cogent Elliott.)
Moskvich (10/65–1970)	10/65: Charter Advertising; 10/69*: Hampshire House; from 1/70: Allardyce & Hampshire.
NSU Prinz (10/58–7/67)	10/58: Leggett Nicholson & Partners Ltd.; 4/62: Burnett Nicholson; 7/63: (Direct advertising); 4/64: Wood & Webster Ltd., 4/65: Mayfair Advertising Ltd., 9/68–1970+: Park, Monico, Nicolls & Bluff.
NSU (6/67–1970)	9/68*–1970+: Park, Monico, Nicolls & Bluff.
Oldsmobile [4/56–11/57 intermittently] (1–2/60)	1–2/60: R. S. Caplin Ltd.
Opel (10/67–1970)	9/68*–1970+: McCann-Erickson Advertising.
Panhard (10/58–5/65)	10/58: Napper, Stinton, Woolley Ltd.; 7/60: Modern Advertising Service Ltd. (*Note*: this agency took over Citroën and combined Citroën and Panhard advertising in 4/59. The apparently delayed change for Panhard alone might be a mistake or might indicate continued use of existing advertisements. The Panhard marque was discontinued by Panhard's owners, Citroën, in 1967.)
Peugeot (10/58)	10/58: (Not known); 1/61: (Direct Advertising); 1/62: David Pilton Advertising Ltd.; from 8/70: Roe Compton Ltd.
Plymouth (1968–3/70)	10/68*–3/70: Young & Rubicam.
Pontiac (10–12/59, 1/63–12/65, 5/68, 5–7/70)	10/59: (Direct advertising); 1/63–7/70: B. Hodgson-Frost Smith.
Porsche (1/60–1970)	1/60: (Not known); 7/61: (Direct advertising); 10/64: David Pilton Advertising Ltd.; 1/65: (Direct advertising); 1/66: David Pilton Advertising Ltd.; from 8/70: (Direct advertising).
Princess (1958–70)	10/57–6/65: Colman, Prentis & Varley Ltd.; 7/65: Davidson, Pearce, Berry & Tuck Ltd.; 7/66–1970+: S.H. Benson Ltd. (*Note*: Princess was first listed separately from Austin in 10/57.)
(AMC) Rambler (5/63–1970)	5/63: Webster Ridgway & Partners; 10/63–1970+: Baker-Dorset Associates.

Reliant Regal 3-wheeler (1958–12/62); Reliant (1/63–1970)	1958: Clinton-Wall; 1/63: Ripley, Preston & Co., 3/64: Maurice G. Parker; 4/64: Ripley Preston & Co. and Maurice G. Parker (*Note*: it is possible that Maurice G. Parker joined Ripley Preston & Co. in March 1964 to promote the new Scimitar coupe while Ripley Preston & Co. continued to advertise the three-wheelers); 9/68*: Monarch Advertising; 10/69*: Clifford Bloxham & Partners; from 6/70: Clarendon Advertising.
Renault [1945 —] (1958–1970)	7/32 (possibly earlier)-1970+: C. Vernon & Sons (*Note*: the *Statistical Review* was first published in 10/32, giving data from 7/32.)
Riley (1958–11/69)	10/32–6/60: Dixon's West End Advertising Agency Ltd.; 7/60: Saward Baker & Co. (*Note*: Riley marque discontinued October 1969, although new cars still being sold by dealers in 1970. Non-dealer advertising ceased some time between 5/69 and 10/69. Dealer advertising only in 10/69 & 11/69; none in 12/69.)
Rolls-Royce (1958–1970)	10/39–1970+: Dorland Advertising Ltd.
Rolls-Royce & Bentley combined (1958–70)	10/39–1970+: Dorland Advertising Ltd.
Rootes Group (1958–8/70)	10/43–3/62: Basil Butler Co. Ltd.; 4/62: Butler & Gardner Ltd.; 9/68*–8/70: Foote, Cone & Belding.
Rover (1958–1970)	1/57–1970+: F.C. Pritchard Wood & Partners (as Wasey, Pritchard, Wood & Quadrant from c. summer 1969.)
Saab (11/60–1970)	11/60: Glover's Advertising Ltd.; 4/62: Glover-Pethick Advertising Ltd.; 4/63: Brunning Advertising & Marketing Ltd.; 3/69–1970+: Norman, Craig & Kummel.
Simca [10/53 —] (1958–1970)	1/56–6/58: Alan Betts Ltd.; 7/58: (not known); 7/59: Young & Rubicam Ltd.; 5/61: Batten, Burton, Durstine & Osborn Ltd.; 4/63: London Prog. Advertising Ltd.; 1/69–1970+: Young & Rubicam.
Singer (1958–5/70)	10/54–6/61: S.D. Toon & Heath Ltd.; 7/61–5/70: Erwin Wasey, Ruthrauff & Ryan Ltd. (as Erwin Wasey Ltd. from 10/64; as Wasey, Pritchard, Wood & Quadrant from c. summer 1969.)
Skoda (7/58–70)	7/58: Auger & Turner Ltd. (as Auger, Turner, Baratte from 10/61); 1/62: Major & Co. (Advertising) Ltd.; 10/66: Alfred Pemberton Ltd.; 11/68–1970+: George Cuming Ltd. (*Note*: Skoda listed as previously advertised by agents Rapid of Prague from 4/55 and intermittently, either by unknown agents— possibly Rapid — or directly, since 4/50.)
Standard (1958–12/64)	7/32 (if not earlier) -12/60: George Cuming Ltd.; 1/61–12/64: Mather & Crowther Ltd. (*Note*: The last Standard car was made in May 1963.)
Studebaker [7/55] (5–11/63)	5/63: (Direct advertising); 7–11/63: London Prog. Advertising Ltd.
Sunbeam (1958–9/70)	10/53-c. 8/68: Erwin Wasey, Ruthrauff & Ryan Ltd. (as Erwin Wasey Ltd. from 10/64); 9/68*–9/70: Foote Cone & Belding Ltd.
Toyota Toyopet Tiara (10–12/63)	10–12/63: (Not known).
Toyota (11/64 only)	11/64: Nikkatsu Advertising.

Toyota (10/65–1970)   10/65: Mayfair Advertising Ltd.; 1/66: Major & Co. (Advertising) Ltd.; 9/68*–1970+: Lonsdale, Crowther Ltd.

Trident (10/69–1970)   10/69–1970+: (Direct advertising)

Triumph (1958–1970)   3/46–12/60: George Cuming Ltd.; 1/61: Mather & Crowther Ltd. (as Ogilvy & Mather Ltd. from 10/65); 10/66–1970+: Hobson, Bates & Partners.

Trojan 200 bubble car   1/62–2/65: Smee's Advertising.
(1/62–2/65)

TVR (7/65–1970)   7/65–1970+: Leighton Advertising Ltd.

Vanden Plas   See *Princess*, above.

Vauxhall (1958–1970)   1/33–9/66: W. S. Crawford Ltd.; 10/66–1970+: Masius, Wynne-Williams.

Volkswagen [7/53 —]   10/57-c. 8/68: Havas Ltd.; 9/68*–1970+: Doyle, Dane, Bernbach.
(1958–70)

Volvo (1/59–1970)   1/59: (Not known); 4/60: Bernard Hodgson Advertising Ltd., 7/66: Bernard Hodgson-Frost Smith; 9/68*: Napper, Stinton, Woolley Ltd.; 10/69*–1970+: Geer, Dubois.

Wartburg (5/64–1970)   5/64–1970+: Napper, Stinton, Woolley Ltd.

Wolseley (1958–1970)   4/38-c. 9/69: Longleys & Hoffman (as H.C. Longley Ltd. to 3/54); 10/69*–1970+: Dorland Advertising.

*If not earlier: see the *Introduction*, above.

**Manufacturers' and importers' agencies were not listed after December 1970: see the *Introduction*, above.

Appendix 11

Contemporary Estimates of Advertising Expenditures by Marque and Model

11A: Press Advertising, 1958–1970

The following figures are calculated from and summarize selected monthly data given in a variety of formats (all very different from that adopted here) in the quarterly *Statistical Review of Press Advertising* until December 1962; its successor quarterly *Statistical Review of Press and T.V. Advertising* until December 1966; and monthly successors *Monthly Statistical Review of Press, T.V., Outdoor and Radio Advertising; Statistical Review; Advertising Statistical Review*; and *ASR — Advertising Statistical Review* between January 1967 and December 1970. From early 1971, the journal was published in a much reduced form as a research document of stapled or ring-bound sheets, with estimated expenditures for particular products or groups of products becoming available to individual subscribers by arrangement. The journal continued at least until 1975.

The estimates in the *Statistical Review* and its successors (which covered thousands of products and services, of which cars represented a very small proportion) were calculated by analyzing every month about 100,000–120,000 (sometimes over 170,000) advertisements in individual issues of 1000–1200 national, daily, evening and local newspapers, general and trade magazines and specialist publications. Advertising rates could, of course, be discovered by ordinary inquiry. In March 1969, the figures were stated as representing "about 82 % of the current [Advertising Association] estimates for Press display (including trade and technical display, but excluding production costs and financial and classified advertising)." The proportion of car advertising "caught" was probably higher than this average,

which also took into account more ephemeral and specialized products and those of purely local interest. The expenditures given are nevertheless likely to be lower than total advertising costs as they do not take into 100 percent of press advertising or account for agency fees or origination expenses. However, as they cannot take into account any private arrangements — especially discounts — that might have been negotiated between manufacturers, importers or dealers and those who accepted their advertising, the estimates below might in some cases be higher than actual costs. For example, the expenditures for Renault advertising during 1958 and 1959 are estimated at £82,288 and £125,451 respectively, whilst a 1962 source analyzing Renault's advertising for Dauphine, its major product at the time (the 4CV and Frégate being sparsely advertised and the Floride, though a highlight of the 1958 Motor Show, not entering production until May 1959), gives Dauphine press advertising expenditures for these years as £58,000 and £82,500, excluding production costs.* As estimates, however, the figures below nevertheless enable present-day historians, enthusiasts and researchers to make useful comparisons between different marques' relative advertising expenditures and between expenditures for cars and other goods. Except in a few cases requiring clarification or correction, marque and model names are given in the forms originally presented.

The format, as well as the title, of the *Advertising Statistical Review* and its successors changed several times during the late 1960s, as a result of which figures are not available for the period June-September 1969. Advertising expenditures for these four months are therefore not listed below, and "none known" in any entry for 1969 below should be taken only to mean that no advertising is *recorded* as having been placed during January-May and October-December of that year. The total estimated annual expenditures in *Appendix 11C* below do, however, include figures for June, August, and September 1969, with only that for July having to be estimated by the author from the figure for the previous July and the general trend over the year. Secondly, the proportion of actual expenditures which the journal claimed to "catch" declined during 1969 — to about 60 % by December — so figures for the last months of 1969 should be considered low estimates by comparison with those for early 1969 and for 1958–68.

Figures for 1958–66 include both pure marque, advertising (called "marque advertising" below) and advertising bearing dealers' names (called "dealer advertising" below). From January 1967 onwards these expenditures were differentiated, and they are identified below as 'M' and 'D' respectively within each marque section. Where post-1966 dealer advertising expenditures are given for models in aggregate while — as happened with many marques from 1967 onwards— parallel marque advertising expenditures are given for those models individually, the dealer and model expenditures are shown in separate sections, with individual models listed in order of introduction of basic type. Some individual advertisements showed combinations of models (such as estate cars or front-wheel-drive ranges) or combinations of a company's marques (such as Austin and Morris 1100s or Hillman and Sunbeam Imps) and advertisements of this kind were often published in parallel with conventional advertising for individual models. Some models were combined only for individual advertisements or for a short series, after which they were once again advertised individually. Combined and single model advertisements are listed separately below where originally differentiated.

Finally, between January 1960 and December 1962, several marques whose advertising expenditures were very small (amounting to a combined monthly average of £290) were not listed individually but were grouped together in the category of "other advertisers." For this reason some marques that seem to disappear over one or more quarters during 1960–62 might in fact have continued to have been advertised on a small scale and be included within the "other advertisers." By contrast, several small manufacturers and importers only ever advertised intermittently and many marques and models did not exist, or were not imported, or were not advertised, over the whole of the 1958–70 period. Some appeared only for a single month. Many manufacturers advertised certain models regularly throughout their years of production while promoting others less regularly.

Each year's entry below for a marque or model gives (1) the months during the year in which the marque or model was advertised; (2) the highest monthly expenditure for that year; and (3) the average monthly expenditure for the other months of the year during which the marque or model was advertised, rounded up or down to the nearest pound (£). These averages, calculated by the author from the monthly figures, sometimes conceal wide variations between individual months' expenditures and do not include zero figures for the months in which advertisements did not appear. The total advertising expenditure for a marque or model during a year can be calculated by multiplying the average figure given by the number of months to which it applies and then adding the highest monthly figure. Thus, for example, in 1958 AC advertised in January, May, July, October, November and December; their highest expenditure, at £580, was in October; and the average of their five remaining monthly expenditures was £152. AC's estimated advertising expenditure for 1958 was therefore £580 + (5 × £152) = £1,340, equivalent (see *Appendix 3* above) to £18,425 at 2001 values.

*Ralph Harris and Arthur Seldon. *Advertising in Action.* London: Hutchinson/Institute of Economic Affairs, 1962, pp. 240–243.

AC (marque and dealer advertising differentiated from 1967): 1958: (1, 5, 7, 10–12 [10: 580]; 152); 1959: (1–5, 8–12 [10: 748]; 94); 1960: (4, 6–11 [10: 703]; 148); 1961: (1–6, 10–12 [3: 348]; 146); 1962: (none known; possibly among combined "other advertisers" with very small expenditures— see after *Wolseley*, below); 1963: (October only: 379); 1964: (9, 12 [9: 445]; 56); 1965: (October only: 613); 1966: October only: 583); 1967: (M: 2, 10 [10: 847]; 26 / D: none known); 1968: (M: 7, 10 [10: 628]; 252 / D: 4, 10 [10: 68]; 20); 1969: (M: October only: 514 / D: 4–5 [4: 218]; 42); 1970: (M: October only: 705 / D: September only: 15).

Alfa Romeo (marque and dealer advertising differentiated from 1967): 1961: (4–8, 10–12 [4: 130]; 125); 1962: (4–12 [10: 421]; 107); 1963: (1–12 [10: 4,827]; 900); 1964: (1–12 [10: 8,643]; 3,015); 1965: (1–12 [10: 5,867]; 3,308); 1966: (1–12 [3:

4,123]; 2,072); 1967: (M: 1–11 [6: 5,311]; 1,059 / D: 1–12 [5: 3,785]; 1,030); 1968: (M: 2–12 [5: 3,671]; 2,340 / D: 1–12 [5: 4,215]; 987); 1969: (M: 1–5, 10–12 [3: 14,823]; 3,509 / D: 1–5, 10–12 [10: 5,751]; 1,809); 1970: (M: 1, 4–12 [7: 5,890]; 3,110 / D: 1–12 [9: 5,095]; 1,522).

Alvis (marque and dealer advertising differentiated from 1967): (*Note*: the last Alvis passenger car was completed on September 29, 1967): 1958: (2, 6, 10–12 [10: 2,717]; 221); 1959: (3–12 [10: 3,402]; 1,084); 1960: (1–12 [10: 3,409]; 597); 1961: (1–12 [10: 1,239]; 384); 1962: (4–12 [5: 1,098]; 415); 1963: (1–12 [10: 1,927]; 237); 1964: (2–12 [10: 536]; 195); 1965: (1–11 [10: 981]; 252); 1966 (1–11 [7: 1,016]; 338); 1967: (M: none known / D: 1–2, 4–5 [4: 57]; 15); 1968: (M: none known / D: July only: 2); 1969: (none known); 1970: (M: none known / D: (1–12 [10: 100]; 61).

Armstrong-Siddeley (*Note*: the last Armstrong-Siddeley passenger car was made on September 6, 1960): 1958: (1–12 [10: 10,543]; 1,197); 1959: (1–12 [4: 5,278]; 1,887); 1960: (1–9 [3: 3,373]; 703).

Aston Martin (marque and dealer advertising differentiated from 1967): 1958: (4–11 [6: 974]; 538); 1959: (1–6, 8–11 [6: 1,214]; 253); 1960: (10–11 [11: 456]; 3); 1961: (3–10 [10: 290]; 171); 1962: (1–8 [5: 907]; 191); 1963: (2–12 [10: 2,806; 527); 1964: (1–12 [12: 915]; 128); 1965: (1–12 [9: 4,930]; 1,447); 1966: (1–12 [2: 1,270]; 356); 1967: (M: none known / D: 1–12 [7: 2,657]; 486); 1968: (M: 4–12 [7: 2,361]; 1,372 / D: 1–12 [1: 426]; 168); 1969: (M: 1–5, 10–11 [2: 744]; 239 / D: 1–5, 10–12 [10: 1,889]; 245); 1970: (M: 4, 7, 11 [7: 454]; 145 / D: 1–12 [7: 990]; 282).

Austin, 1958–66 (marque and dealer advertising): 1958: (1–12 [10: 41,276]; 16,110); 1959: (1–12 [1: 64,384]; 18,614); 1960: (1–12 [10: 60,351]; 14,470); 1961: (1–12 [11: 47,625]; 18,462); 1962: (1–12 [11: 30,672]; 17,980); 1963: (1–12 [9: 58,351]; 16,330); 1964: (1–12 [10: 68,596]; 21,435); 1965: (1–12 [10: 26,303]; 14,828); 1966: 1–12 [11: 20,769]; 14,557).

Austin dealer advertising, 1967–70: 1967: (1–12 [10: 10,451]; 6,665); 1968: (1–12 [10: 10,288]; 5,095); 1969: (3–5, 10–12 [4: 27,266]; 8,344); 1970: (1–12 [10: 9,029]; 4,325).

Austin: individual models and combinations of models (marque advertising): Austin A60: 1967: (2–4, 10–12 [3, 4 + 11: each 103]; 73); 1968: (1–3 [3: 1,049]; 420). Austin A40: 1967: (July only: 103); 1968: (February only: 2). Austin A.110: 1967: (4–5 [5: 542]; 362); 1968: (May 1968: 72). Austin 1100 saloon: 1967: (2, 5–7 [2: 6,140]; 239); 1968: (4–6, 9, 11 [6: 1,508]; 620); 1969: (2–3 [2: 323]; 222); 1970: (6: 2,050). Austin 1300 saloon: 1968: (7–12 [9: 1,534]; 529); 1969: (1–4 [3: 11,431]; 3,984); 1970: (October only: 3,850). Austin 1800: 1967: (1–2, 5–6, 8–12 [9: 952]; 488); 1968: (1–12, 5–10, 12 [2: 953]; 418); 1969: (1–5, 12 [4: 10,097]; 1,041); 1970: (June only: 3,500). Austin 3-Litre: 1968: (10–12 [11: 16,699]; 5,750); 1969: (1–2, 11 [2: 4,080]; 1,990); 1970: (4–7, 9 [5: 13,668]; 4,261). Austin Maxi: 1969: (4–5 [5: 49,467]; 47,330); 1970: (4, 6–8, 10–12 [7: 30,451]; 14,320).

Austin dealer service: 1962: (11–12 [11: 390]; 252).

Austin-Healey (marque and dealer advertising differentiated from 1967): 1958: (1–12 [5: 14,175]; 1,048); 1959: (1–12 [12: 2,431]; 678); 1960: (1–12 [7: 13,982]; 1,586); 1961: (1–12 [3: 7,034]; 978); 1962: (1–12 [4: 7,872]; 1,169); 1963: (1–12 [10: 1,376]; 553); 1964: (1–12 [12: 5,102]; 871); 1965: (1–12 [5: 1,377]; 549); 1966: (1–12 [3: 784]; 446); 1967: (D: 1–8, 11–12 [5: 216]; 56); 1968: (D: 2, 7–8, 12 [7: 117]; 25).

Austin-Healey: individual models (marque advertising): Sprite: 1967: (2–12 [12: 545]; 165); 1968: (1–12 [3: 610]; 254); 1969: (1–3, 5 [1: 372]; 254). Austin-Healey 3000: 1967: (1–4, 6, 9 [4: 314]; 107).

Auto Union DKW (marque and dealer advertising differentiated from 1967): 1959: (4–12 [11: 1,644]; 875); 1960: (1–12 [7: 1,772]; 807); 1961: (1–12 [5: 2,940]; 942); 1962: (1–12 [3: 787]; 300); 1963: (1–12 [6: 1,012]; 323); 1964: (1–12 [2:

607]; 207); 1965: (1–12 [7: 676]; 191); 1966: (1–12 [3: 8,887]: 2,122); 1967: (M: 2–10, 12 [5: 6,158]; 1,044 / D: 1–12 [5: 6,558]; 1,412); 1968: (M: 1–12 [3: 10,062]; 2,094 / D: 1–12 [3: 3,273]; 588); 1969: (M: 3–5, 11 [11: 5,548]; 1,637 / D: 1–5, 10–12 [5: 3,313]; 380); 1970: (M: 2–9 [4: 7,838]; 3,919 / D: 1–12 [6: 2,119]; 1,315).

Bentley (marque and dealer advertising differentiated from 1967) (see also *Rolls-Royce and Bentley combined*, below): 1958: (1–12 [4: 3,769]; 622); 1959: (1–6, 8–12 [10: 5,033]; 251); 1960: (1–3, 10–12 [12: 5,872]; 1,261); 1961: (1–7, 9–12 [9: 3,336]; 563); 1962: (1–9 [6: 103]; 41); 1964: (1–12 [6: 82]; 36); 1964: (1–12 [4: 151]; 52); 1965: (1–4, 6–12 [8: 69]; 24); 1966: (2–3, 5–6, 8 [6 + 8: each 127]; 3); 1967: (M: 1,6 [6: 127]; 5 / D: 3, 7–8, 10–11 [11: 131]; 8); 1968: (M: none known / D: 1–7 [6: 54]; 15).

Berkeley: 1958: (1–12 [5: 186]; 97); 1959: (2–5, 8, 10–12 [10: 718]; 100); 1960: (1–9 [4: 1,305]; 217).

British Motor Corporation [BMC]: (marque and dealer advertising differentiated from 1967) (*Note*: the British Motor Corporation merged with Leyland to form British Leyland in 1968; the merger was announced on January 17, 1968. For individual BMC ranges, see separate sections below); 1958: (1–12 [10: 27,056]; 11,311); 1959: (1–12 [10: 53, 114]; 5,755); 1960: (1–12 [10: 49,934]; 9,729); 1961: (1–12 [10: 74,240]; 15,901); 1962: (1–12 [10: 85,435]; 14,734); 1963: (1–12 [10: 85,789]; 20,376); 1964: (1–12 [10: 78,306]; 27,922); 1965: (1–12 [10: 80,659]; 28,326); 1966: (1–12 [10: 87,061]; 28,434); 1967: (M (full range): 1–12 [10: 61,894]; 10,088 / D: 1–12 [3: 17,767]; 9,039); 1968: (M (full range): 1–4 [2: 7,769]; 3,393 / D: (1–4 [2: 8,505]; 6,433).

BMC: individual models and combinations of models (marque advertising): Estate car range: 1967: (September only: 353). BMC Mini saloons: 1967: (1–5, 7–12 [1: 20,752]; 1,175); 1968: (1–4 [1: 15,000]; 7,777). BMC 1100 saloons: 1968: (January only: 18,150). BMC 1100 Countryman and Traveller estate cars: 1967: (April only: 7,854). BMC 1300 saloons: 1967: (10, 12 [10: 14,055]; 252); 1968: (3–4 [3: 579]; 43). BMC Mini and 1100 saloons: 1967: (7–8 [8: 10,250]; 4,400). BMC Austin/Morris 1800: 1967: (2–3, 7–9 [3: 26,156]; 10,791); 1968: (2–4 [2: 1,522]; 391).

BMC: other products and services (marque advertising): BMC Service: 1958: (1–12 [8: 156]; 79); 1959: (1–12 [12: 801]; 447); 1960: (1–12 [3: 6,332]; 1,585); 1961: (1–12 [2: 2,457]; 1,748); 1962: (1–12 [1: 1,087]; 694); 1963: (1–12 [11: 1,405]; 775); 1964: (1–12 [5: 13,566]; 1,771); 1965: (1–12 [11: 1,468]; 904); 1966 (1–12 [4: 1,374]; 986); 1967: (1–12 [11: 3,573]; 993); 1968: (1–4 [4: 8,948]; 937). BMC Used car warranty: 1958: (December only: 106). BMC Used cars: 1960: (11–12 [12: 8,134]; 5,302); 1961: (1–3 [1: 660]; 337). BMC (unspecified): 1967: (2, 11 [11: 900]; 450).

British Leyland (marque advertising): 1968: full car range: 5–12 [10: 40,685]; 3,866); 1969: (1, 3, 5, 10, 12 [5: 30,455]; 7,627); 1970: (4–8, 10 [5: 34,369]; 4,505).

British Leyland group dealer advertising (marque advertising): 1968: (5–12 [10: 14,668]; 6,012); 1969: (1–5, 10–12 [3: 8,491]; 5,452); 1970: (1–12 [10: 11,501]; 3,184).

British Leyland prestige advertising: 1968: (5–6, 10, 12 [5: 31,446]; 1,777); 1969: (2–5, 10 [5: 730]; 61); 1970: (1, 10 [1: 900]; 680).

British Leyland: individual models and combinations of models (marque advertising): Estate car range: 1968: (6–7, 9–10 [9: 702]; 432). Mini saloons: 1968: (5–6, 8, 10–12 [10: 2,810]; 866); 1969: (1–5, 11–12 [31,140]; 8,176); 1970: (1–6, 9–12 [4: 43,496]; 10,131). Minis and estate cars: 1970: (5, 7–8, 11 [5: 15,017]; 2,439). Austin/Morris 1100 saloons: 1968: (May only: 782); 1969: (May only: 1,436); 1970: (4–9 [5: 18,145]; 11,945). Austin/Morris 1300 saloons: 1968: (June only: 50); 1969: (10–12 [10: 59,854]; 11,757); 1970: (1–9, 11 [3: 39,203]; 6,377). Austin/Morris 1100 and 1300 saloons: 1968: (7, 10 [10: 523]; 255); 1969: (10–12 [10: 1,730]; 972); 1970: (1–3, 6–12 [3: 31,083]; 5,093). Austin/Morris 1800: 1968: (10–11 [10: 523]; 76); 1969: (none known); 1970: (4, 6–9 [9: 16,971]; 10,094).

British Leyland: other products and services (marque and dealer advertising): Service: 1968: (M: 5–12 [9: 3,190]; 1,353 / D: none known); 1969: (M: 1–2 [1: 484]; 66 / D: none known); 1970: (M: June only: 406 / D: none known). Unipart (parts): 1969: (M: December only: 4,157 / D: December only: 1,566); 1970: (M: 1–12 [8: 13,627]; 2,137 / D: 1–12 [6: 565]; 94). Gauntlet used cars: 1970 (M: 6–7 [6: 41,592]; 3,069 / D: 6–12 [10: 14,747]; 9,887).

BMW and **Isetta** (marque and dealer advertising differentiated from 1967) (*Note*: advertiser given as Isetta (GB) Ltd. to 6/63; as BMW Concessionaires (England) Ltd. from 7/63): 1958: (1–12 [5: 1636]; 630); 1959: (1–12 [4: 2,161]; 906); 1960: (1–12 [6: 1,005]; 588); 1961: (4: 6,380); 827); 1962: (1–12 [12: 751]; 1963: (1–12 [10: 779]; 304); 1964: (1–12 [7: 2,643]; 981); 1965: (1–12 [10: 4,600]; 1,448); 1966: (1–12 [3: 8,498]; 2,074); 1967: (M: 1–7, 9–11 [10: 8,186]; 1,527 / D: 1–12 [10: 3,104]; 829); 1968: (M: 1–12 [2: 7,450]; 2,181 / D: 1–12 [9: 3,962]; 1,181); 1969: (M: 1–5, 10–12 [12: 5,838]; 2,003 / D: 1–5, 10–12 [5: 2,937]; 1,111); 1970: (M: 1–11 [10: 15,570]; 4,539 / D: 1–12 [10: 6,190]; 2,338).

Bond (marque and dealer advertising differentiated from 1967): 1958: (1–12 [11: 1,310]; 433); 1959: (1–12 [11: 716; 298); 1960: (1–12 [4: 868]: 350); 1961: (1–12 [5: 967]; 531); 1962: (1–12 [4: 2,319]; 565); 1963: (1–12 [5: 1,879]; 487); 1964: (1–12 [4: 3,971]; 587); 1965: (1–12 [4: 2,636]; 659); 1966: (1–12 [5: 4,252]; 639); 1967: (M: 5–7 [6: 1,324]; 178 / D: 1–12 [5: 894]; 263); 1968: (M: 2–3, 5–7, 11–12 [6: 3,161]; 552 / D: 1–2, 4–10, 12 [10: 1,175]; 367); 1969: (M: 1, 4–5, 10–11 [10: 5,623]; 1,635 / D: 1–5, 10–12 [5: 635]; 162); 1970: (M: 1–2, 6–8 [1: 650]; 165 / D: 1–12 [6: 2,843]; 200).

Borgward: 1958: (1–4, 6–12 [10: 796]; 144); 1959: (1–12 [10: 1,434]; 207); 1960: (1–12 [10: 1,934]; 540); 1961: (1–9 [3: 771]; 190); 1962: (none known; possibly among combined "other advertisers" with very small expenditures—see after *Wolseley*, below); 1963: (3–4, 6–8 [3: 177]; 77); 1964: (1–4 [1: 13]; 5).

Bristol (marque and dealer advertising differentiated from 1967): 1958: (3–4, 8–10 [8: 752]; 19); 1959: (2–5, 8, 10, 12 [10: 375]; 39); 1960: (4–9 [7: 204]; 119); 1961: (7–12 [10: 1,068]; 183); 1962: (1–9 [8: 68]; 32); 1963: (5–6, 9–10 [10: 711]; 215); 1964: (10–11 [10: 585]; 25); 1965: (October only: 741); 1966: (8, 10–11 [10: 369]; 19); 1967: (M: none known / D: 2–3, 6–12 [10: 800]; 305); 1968: (M: none known / D: 3, 9–11 [10: 937]; 96); 1969: (M: 1,9–10 [10: 153]; 94 / D: 4–5, 10 [10: 367]; 193); 1970: (M: none known / D: 3, 10 [3 + 10: each 95]).

Checker Marathon: 1966 (March only: 363).

Chevrolet (marque and dealer advertising differentiated from 1967): 1959: (1–6, 8–11 [3: 424]; 59); 1960: (1–12 [5: 215]; 144); 1961–62: (none known; possibly among combined "other advertisers" with very small expenditures—see after *Wolseley*, below); 1963: (4–5, 12 [5: 665]; 290); 1964: (1–12 [6: 3,053]; 837); 1965: (1–12 [3: 1,828]; 350); 1966: (1, 3, 5–7, 9–12 [5: 219]; 43); 1967: (M: 2, 10–11 [2: 180]; 168 / D: 1, 3–4, 7 [3: 292]; 48); 1968: (M: none known / D: May only: 17); 1969: (M: none known / D: 4, 10, 12 [10: 208]; 82); 1970: (M: none known / D: May only: 88).

Chrysler (U.S.) (marque and dealer advertising differentiated from 1967): 1963: (2–3, 5, 11 [3: 132]; 22); 1964: (5–6, 10 [10: 857]; 55); 1965: (6, 8, 10–11 [10: 337]; 39); 1966: (5, 7–8, 10, 12 [7: 6,385]; 1,654); 1967: (M: March only: 1,299 / D: 3, 7 [3: 35]; 30); 1968: (M: 1, 3, 6, 10 [1: 556]; 302 / D: 10–11 [10: 60]; 13); 1969: (M: 5, 12 [12: 2,420]; 380 / D: none known); 1970: (2–3 [2: 475]; 380 / D: 1, 8–9 [1: 456]; 124).

Chrysler (Australian) (marque and dealer advertising): 1967: (M: 2, 4–7, 9–10 [2: 957]; 640 / D: 1–2, 4–10 [5: 759]; 274); 1968: (M: 4–6, 8, 11 [6: 2,511]; 378 / D: 1–11 [3: 5,209]; 492); 1969: (M + D: none known); 1970: (M: none known / D: 4–5, 7–8 [5: 360]; 85).

Chrysler (UK) dealer advertising (for earlier corporate advertising, see *Rootes Group*, below): 1970: (9–12 [10: 3,376]; 1,138).

Citroën (marque and dealer advertising differentiated from 1967): 1958: (1–10, 12 [10: 3,510]; 1,244); 1959: (1–12: [10: 4,758]; 1,636); 1960: (1–12 [5: 1–12 [5: 9,335]; 2,603); 1961: (1–12 [4: 6,987]; 2,154); 1962: (1–12 [4: 7,963]; 1,566); 1963: (1: 3,792]; 1,726); 1964: (1–12 [4: 4,849]; 1,583); 1965: (1–12 [10: 11,406]; 2,307); 1966: (1–12 [5: 7,190]; 3,044); 1967: (M: 2–7, 9–12 [4: 12,560]; 5,177 / D: 1–12 [3: 1,856]; 765); 1968: (M: 1–6, 9–12 [10: 9,884]; 2,154 / D: 1–12 [5: 3,625]; 983); 1969: (M: January only: 677 / D: 1–5, 10–12 [10: 1,948]; 1,114); 1970: (M: see individual models, below / D: 4–5, 7–8 [5: 360]; 85).

Citroën: individual models and combinations of models (marque advertising): Citroën car range: 1969: (November only: 1,280); 1970: (3–7 [4: 4,635]; 436). D Series range: 1969: (2–5, 10–12 [12: 3,678]; 676); 1970: (3–12 [5: 3,196]; 973). Safari estate car: 1970: (August only: 240). Ami 8: 1969: (11–12 [11 + 12: each 1,200]); 1970: (2, 4, 6 [4: 8,516]; 1,687). Dyane: 1969: (2–5, 11 [2: 7,765]; 4,738); 1970: (4–6 [5: 6,215]; 2,086).

Citroën and **Panhard** combined advertising (*Note*: Citroën took over Panhard in 1955; the last Panhard was built in 1967): 1958: (10–11 [11: 2,001]; 338); 1959: (February only: 107); 1960–62: (none known; possibly among combined "other advertisers" with very small expenditures—see after *Wolseley*, below); 1963: (October only: 19).

Coronet (3-wheeler): 1958: (1–12 [5: 100]; 54).

Daf (marque and dealer advertising differentiated from 1967): 1961: (3–6, 10–12 [5: 876]; 282); 1962: (1–3, 10 [10: 264]; 51); 1963: (1–12 [10: 473]; 124); 1964: (1–12 [4: 7,560]; 144); 1965: (1–12 [2: 2,760]; 830); 1966: (1–12 [10: 8,446]; 2,099); 1967: (M: 1–2, 5–10 [1: 3,770]; 500 / D: 1–12 [10: 2,081]; 1,132); 1968: (M: 1–10 [9: 7,916]; 873 / D: 1–12 [10: 1,934]; 726); 1969: (M: 1–5, 10–11 [3: 10,437]; 4,056 / D: 1–5, 10–12 [10: 1,205]; 692); 1970: (M: 1–5, 7–10 [3: 13,415]; 6,655 / D: 1–12 [10: 1,873]; 726).

Daf cars and commercial vehicles (marque advertising): 1970 (November only: 624).

Daihatsu (marque and dealer advertising differentiated from 1967): 1965: (10–12 [10: 289]; 106); 1966: (1–3, 6–7, 10–11 [7: 273]; 62); 1967: (M: March only: 10 / D: 1–2, 10–12 [10: 113]; 52); 1968: (M: none known / D: 1–2, 4 [2: 28] 23); 1969: (M: none known / D: January only: 108); 1970: (none known).

Daimler (marque and dealer advertising differentiated from 1967): 1958: (1–12 [7: 5,948]; 158); 1959: (1–12 [3: 4,094]; 1,326); 1960: (1–12 [7: 6,463]; 2,521); 1961: (1–12 [10: 7,898]; 3,460); 1962: (1–12 [4: 33,922]; 1,872); 1963: (1–12 [10: 10,117]; 2,262); 1964: (1–12 [10: 8,376]; 2,582); 1965: (1–12 [10: 8,387]; 2,333); 1966: (1–12 [10: 22,027]; 2,132); 1967: (M: 1, 3–7, 9–12 [10: 24,957]; 1,442 / D: 1–12 [10: 6,054]; 2,077); 1968: (M: 1, 3–7, 9–11 [6: 10,195]; 3,889 / D: 1–12 [10: 2,026]; 980); 1969: (M: 3–5, 10–11 [10: 23,661]; 8,517 / D: 1–5, 10–12 [10: 3,199]; 1,388); 1970: (7–8, 10–11 [7: 11, 260]; 3,880 / D: 1–12 [9: 865]; 418).

Daimler and **Jaguar** combined (marque and dealer advertising differentiated from 1967): 1962: (11–12 [11: 227]; 22); 1963: (1–12 [3: 878]; 263); 1964: (1–12 [4: 507]; 202); 1965: (1–12 [10: 1,220]; 269); 1966: (1–12 [2: 1,172]; 249); 1967: (M: 4, 8 [8: 2,540]; 33 / D: 1–12 [10: 1,037]; 442); 1968: (M: October only: 104 / D: 1–12 [11: 1,256]; 467); 1969: (M: April only: 54 / D: 1–5, 10–12 [10: 644]; 450); 1970: (M: 7, 10 [10: 2,332]; 20 / D: 1–12 [10: 1,182]; 682).

Daimler and **Lanchester** combined (*Note*: could be either marque or dealer advertising for spares and service; the last Lanchester was produced in 1956): 1963: (1–12 [3 + 8: each 5]; 4); 1964: (1–5, 7–12 [1, 5, 7 + 12: each 5] 4); 1965: (1–11 [4, 7 + 10: each 5]; 4); 1966: (6–7 [6 + 7: each 4]).

Datsun (marque and dealer advertising differentiated from 1967): 1965: (October only: 240); 1966: (July only: 240); 1967: (M: 5, 7 [7: 675]; 350 / D: none known); 1968: (M: 6–12 [10: 5,424]; 2,092 / D: 10–12 [11: 470]; 368); 1969: (M: 1–5, 10–12 [3: 12,394]; 4,468 / D: 1–5, 10–12 [3: 1,773]; 584); 1970: (M: 2–10 [4: 4,233]; 1,739 / D: 1–12 [10: 1,959]; 607).

Dodge: 1963: (September only: 4).

Facel Vega: 1958: (8–10, 12 [10: 313]; 132); 1959: (4–5, 10–11 [10: 612]; 144); 1960: (2, 4, 10–11 [10: 1,600]; 445); 1961: (2, 4–5, 10–11 [4: 989]; 321); 1962: (none known; possibly among combined "other advertisers" with very small expenditures—see after *Wolseley*, below); 1963: (3–4, 10 [10: 309]; 155); 1964: (October only: 340); 1965: (March only; 18).

Fiat (marque and dealer advertising differentiated from 1967): 1958: (1–12 [3: 1,606]; 475); 1959: (1–12 [5: 3,057]; 1,180); 1960: (1–12 [11: 5,888]; 2,106); 1961: (1–12 [4: 2,186]; 109); 1962: (1–12 [5 + 6: each 4,258]; 2,447); 1963: (1–12 [5: 5,310]; 3,415); 1964: (1–12: [5: 15,232]; 8,381); 1965: (1–12 [3: 16,322]; 5,348); 1966: (1–12 [3: 21,865]; 7,295); 1967 (M: 1–4, 9–12 [1: 17,669]; 8,564 / D: 1–12 [6: 19,296]; 8,170) 1968: (M: 1–12 [3: 40,574]; 9,419 / D: 1–12 [3: 15,274]; 5,379); 1969: (M: 2–5, 10 [2: 6,330]; 4,183 / D: 1–5, 10–12 [3: 12,629]; 4,108); 1970: (M: February: 428 / D: 1–12 [5: 11,364]; 4,456).

Fiat prestige advertising: 1969: (2, 4–5, 11–12 [12: 7,216]; 2,305); 1970: (1, 3–6, 9–12 [3: 11,320]; 1,967).

Fiat: individual models and combinations of models (marque advertising): Fiat range: 1969: (2–3, 5 [3: 23,940]; 1,680); 1970: (March only: 19,245). Estate car range: 1967: (7–12 [9: 964]; 412); 1968: (August only: 186). Fiat 500 and 600: 1967: (5–6 [6: 5,514]; 3,490); 1968–69: (none known); 1970: (September only: 3,450). Fiat 500L: 1970: (4–6 [5: 9,800]; 2,625). Fiat 850 saloon: 1967: (5–7 [5: 3,674]; 332). Fiat 850 (model/s not specified): 1969: (2–5 [3: 8,168]; 3,152); 1970: (4–6 [4: 3,300]; 2,013). Fiat 850 and 124 coupes: 1969: (3–5 [5: 3,304]; 1,295). Fiat 124 saloon: 1967: (5–7 [6: 8,887]; 6,703); 1968: (none known); 1969: (2–5 [3: 6,391]; 4,810); 1970: (5, 9–10 [5: 10,420]; 2,979). Fiat 125: 1969: (3–5 [3: 9,067]; 2,432); 1970: (4–5, 9 [5: 11,250]; 2,898). Fiat 128: 1970: (4–6, 8–9 [4: 27,339]; 3,417).

Ford, 1958–66 (marque and dealer advertising): 1958: (1–12 [10: 63,604]; 29, 515); 1959: (1–12 [10: 157,479]; 34,621); 1960: (1–12 [10: 135,776]: 45,410); 1961: (1–12 [6: 126,194]; 52,557); 1962: (1–12 [4: 178,137]; 60,015); 1963: (1–12 [10: 225,745]; 63,299); 1964: (1–12: [4: 154,374]; 61,100; 1965: (1–12 [10: 124,423]; 56,042); 1966: (1–12 [4: 144,728]; 50,399).

Ford dealer advertising, 1967–70 (models not differentiated): 1967: (1–12 [10: 24,911]; 15,802); 1968: (1–12 [1: 41,235]; 10,142); 1969: (1–5, 10–12 [2: 34,157]; 7,486); 1970: (1–12 [10: 32,098]; 9,305).

Ford: combined car and commercial vehicles: 1967: (M: none known / D: 6, 9–10 [10: 115]; 18); 1968: (M: none known / D: July only: 7); 1969: (M + D: none known); 1970: (M: 1, 4, 10, 12 [1: 2,112]; 327 / D: none known).

Ford ranges, 1967–70 (marque advertising): Full car range: 1967: (1–6, 9–12 [9: 12, 474]; 2,461); 1968: (2–3, 10–12 [12: 33,180]; 602); 1969: (10–11 [10: 38,608]; 2,511); 1970: (2, 12 [2: 12,110]; 168). Estate car range: 1967: (4, 9 [9: 443]; 200). Saloons (described as "various," otherwise unspecified): 1967: (10–11 [10: 3,472]; 55); 1968: (1,10 [10: 30,929]; 440). Estate cars ("various," as above): 1967: (2–3,

10 [2: 8,546]; 1,079); 1968: (October only: 23); 1969: (January only: 51).

Ford: individual models and combinations of models, 1967–70 (marque advertising): Anglia saloons: 1967: (1, 3–4, 6–7 [1: 17,459]; 6,341). Anglia estate cars: 1967: (1–2 [2: 4,600]; 4,400). Anglia and Corsair saloons: 1967: (January only: 115). Corsair saloons: 1967: (1–9 [1: 30,731]; 10,962); 1968: (4, 6–11 [9: 23,596]; 8,877). Corsair and Cortina saloons: 1967: (3–5 [4: 1,898]; 1,185). Cortina, Corsair, Zephyr and Zodiac saloons: 1967: (March only: 11,050). Cortina saloons and estate cars: 1969: (4–5, 10 [4: 22,648]; 6,200); 1970 (Mk III): (10–11 [11: 36,215]; 24,000). Cortina saloons: 1967: (1–7, 9–11 [9: 25,283]; 6,660); 1968: (1, 4–5, 8–12 [11: 46,987]; 7,638); 1969: (1–3, 5, 10–12 [1: 65,006]; 14,747); 1970 (Mk II): (1–2, 5–7, [2: 21,962]; 15,388); 1970 (Mk III): (10–11 [10: 159,293]; 9,753); Cortina estate cars: 1967: (2–3, 8 [2: 15,753]; 501); 1968: (8–10 [8: 10,610]; 4,087). Cortina Lotus: 1967: (M: 3–6 [3: 1,969]; 1,269 / D: July only: 160). Zephyr and Zodiac saloons: 1967: (9, 12 [9: 5,000]; 15). Zephyr saloons: 1967: (1–2, 10–12 [10: 62,640]; 16,878); 1968: (7–10 [8: 27,299]; 8,087). Zephyr police car: 1967: (March only: 60) (*Note*: Vauxhall Cresta police car advertised April, 1967). Zodiac saloon: 1967: (3–4, 6, 9–11 [9: 15,760]; 2,866); 1968: (3, 5 [5: 1,700]; 507); 1969: (November only: 10,375). Executive saloons: 1967: (1, 11 [11: 19,803]: 350). GT 40: 1968: (4–6 [5: 9,606]; 2,012); 1969: (none known); 1970: (3–5, 7–10, 12 [each month: 80]). Escort saloons and estates: 1970: (1, 3, 4 [1: 15,772]; 10,705). Escort saloons: 1968: (1–6, 8, 10–12 [1: 105,948]; 10,055); 1969: (4, 10–11 [10: 41,149]; 980); 1970: (1–7, 9–10, 12 [4: 58,338]; 13,997). Escort estate car: 1968: (3–5 [3: 16,605]; 6,949). Capri: 1969: (2–6, 10 [2: 132,308]; 9,800); 1970: (2–5, 9–10 [3: 53,477]; 13,408).

Ford Service (marque and dealer advertising differentiated from 1967): 1963: (2–11 [10: 10,817]; 874); 1964: (1–12 [4: 1,614]; 501); 1965: (1–12 [9: 24,070]; 1,415); 1966: (1–12 [9: 15,253]; 1,170); 1967: (M: 1–12 [10: 17,619]; 1,634 / D: 1–12 [11: 4,255]; 970); 1968: (M: 2–7, 10–11 [3: 6,000]; 583 / D: 1–12 [11: 2,764]; 1,171); 1969: (M: 1–2, 4–5, 11 [11: 20,404]; 401 / D: 2–5, 10–11 [3: 1,532]; 542); 1970: (M: 1, 10, 12 [1: 257]; 73 / D: 1, 3–8, 10–12 [11: 3,726]; 315).

Ford parts: 1970: (M: 2–4 [2: 11,347]; 5,733 / D: 3–5 [3: 238]; 240).

Ford A1 Used Vehicle Plan (marque and dealer advertising differentiated from 1967): 1963: (2–3, 5–6, 10, 12 [3: 13,148]; 2,054); 1964: (3–8, 11–12 [3: 15,621]; 2,063); 1965: (3–5, 9–11 [9: 7,035]; 2,737); 1966: (3–7, 9–11 [4: 3,035]; 854); 1967: (M: 9–11 [9: 8,574]; 309) / D: 9–12 [9: 14,854]; 7,315); 1968: (M: 1–3, 9, 11–12 [3: 13,645]; 4,425 / D: 1, 4–10 [4: 13,563]; 9,018); 1969: (1–2 [1: 14,094]; 10,290 / D: 1–5, 10–12 [1: 7,455]; 3,130); 1970: (M: 2–4 [2: 10,929]; 3,320 / D: 1–12 [10: 3,803]; 1,914).

Rentaford (known only as dealer advertising in 1967; therefore might have been dealer advertising in earlier years): 1962: (1–12 [1: 3,263]; 269); 1963: (1–9, 11–12 [1: 243];

88); 1964: (1–7, 9–12 [12: 737]; 69); 1965: (1–12 [1,753]; 178); 1966: (1–5, 7–12 [9: 204]; 84); 1967: (1–10, 12 [4 + 5: each 154]; 46).

Ford Visit Europe Plan: 1967: (2, 5, 7–12 [10: 760]; 333); 1968: (2–12 [3: 870]; 587); 1969: (2–5, 12 [3: 1,144]; 476); 1970: (2–4, 6–9 [7: 1,018]; 546).

Ford Film Library: 1967: (7, 9–10 [7: 130]; 84); 1968: (8–11 [9 + 11: each 96]; 48); 1969: (1, 4–5 [each month: 96]).

Ford Sports Club: 1968: (4–10, 12: [7: 5,125]; 925); 1969: (1–5, 10 [1: 240]; 137); 1970: (May only: 628).

Ford (U.S. & Canada) (marque and dealer advertising differentiated from 1967): 1960: (1–12 [4: 976]; 248); 1961–66: (none listed separately); 1967: (M: June only: 6 / D: 2, 5, 7 [5: 16]; 3 / D with Australian Ford: August only: 203); 1968: (M + D: none known); 1970: (M: 4–5, 10, [10: 1,210]; 493 / D: none known).

Ford (Australia) (marque and dealer advertising): 1967: (M: 8–9 [8: 684]; 480 / D: none known); 1968: (M: 2–3, 10 [10: 1,006]; 480 / D: October only: 138); 1969: (M: none known / D: February only: 13); 1970: (M: 5, 7, 9–10 [5: 715]; 320 / D: none known).

Ford (Aus. and Germany): 1970: (M: February only: 220 / D: none known).

Ford (Germany) (marque and dealer advertising differentiated from 1967): 1959: (11–12 [11: 2,352]; 95); 1960: (1–12 [3: 995]; 290); 1961: (1–12 [4: 1,352]; 142); 1962: (1–12 [4: 349]; 138); 1963: (1–12 [5: 216]; 68); 1964: 1–4, 6–7, 10–11 [6: 210]; 99); 1965: (2–12 [10: 278]; 69); 1966: (1–12 [7: 441]; 116); 1967: (M: 1–2, 10 [10: 23]; 14 / D: 3–5, 9–10 [5: 54]; 19); 1968: (M: none known / D: 4, 7, 10–11 [10: 58]; 28); 1969: (M: November only: 504 / D: October only: 28); 1970: (M: 5, 7, 10 [5: 745]; 374 / D: 3–4, 10 [3: 100]; 32).

Frazer-Nash: 1963 (December only: 25).

(Meadows) Frisky: 1958: (9–12 [10: 726]; 195); 1959: (1–10, 12 [3: 306]; 104); 1960: (4–5, 7 [5: 264]; 26).

Gilbern (marque and dealer advertising differentiated from 1967): 1965: (10–12 [10: 313]; 94); 1966: (1–12 [4: 398]; 103); 1967: (M: 1, 4, 8 [4: 88]; 46 / D: 2–7, 9–12 [4: 54]; 39); 1968: (M: 4, 6–12 [6: 529]; 252 / D 1–5, 7, 10 [10: 95]; 49); 1969: (M: 1, 4, 10–12 [10: 939]; 249 / D: 1, 10 [10: 135]; 6); 1970: (M: 3–4, 6–11 [7: 631]; 375 / D: 1–6, 8–10 [9: 221]; 57).

Glas: 1965: (October only: 88).

Goggomobil: 1958: (1–12 [10: 552]; 103); 1959: (1–12 [10: 915]; 120); 1960: (1–12 [10: 346]; 116).

Gordon 3-wheeler: 1960: (March only: 119).

Gordon-Keeble: 1964: (10–12 [10: 1,190]; 396); 1965: (1–3 [1,302]; 120).

Heinkel Cabin Cruiser: 1958: (1–12 [3: 568]; 188); 1959: (1–12 [3: 273]; 155); 1960: (1–12 [6: 649]; 189); 1961: (1–3 [1: 234]; 77).

Hillman: 1958: (1–12 [9: 28,279]; 9,525); 1959: (1–12 [9: 30,550]; 3,673); 1960: (1–12 [3: 21,572]; 4,107); 1961: (1–12 [10: 42,224]; 10,559); 1962: (1–12 [10: 23, 467]; 7,617); 1963: (1–12 [5: 68,717]; 13,592); 1964: (1–12 [2: 65,344]; 32,097);

1965: (1–12 [5: 57,656]; 27,839); 1966: (1–12 [3: 62,397]; 23,072).

Hillman dealer advertising, 1967–70 (models not differentiated): 1967: (1–12 [1: 23,034]; 7,149); 1968: (1–12 [9: 9,657]; 5,249); 1969: (1–5, 10–12 [10: 9,725]; 3,757); 1970: 1–12 [2: 38,937]; 4,230).

Hillman: individual models and combinations of models, 1967–70 (marque advertising): Super Minx Estate Car: 1969: (April only: 261) (*Note*: this almost certainly refers to the "Arrow" type of Hillman Estate Car (see below); the Super Minx was discontinued in 1967). Imp saloons: 1967: (1–12 [9: 15,350]; 2,517); 1968: (1–3, 5 [2: 20,630]; 8,645); 1969: (3–4, 10 [10: 17,688]; 444). Imp and Sunbeam Imp Sport: 1967: (5–7 [6: 15,379]; 5,553). Californian: 1968: (February only: 3,615). Husky: 1967: (4, 6 [4: 1,568]; 55). Hunter saloons: 1967: (1–2, 4–7, 9–12 [9: 12,435]; 852); 1968: (1–5, 7–8, 10, 12 [12: 45,996]; 5,950); 1969: (1–5, 10 [3: 15,034]; 5,736); 1970: (1–3, 6, 10 [10: 20,120]; 6,346). Minx saloon ("Arrow" type): 1967: (1–8, 12 [1: 14,975]; 5,378); 1968: (1–5, 9–12 [5: 17,991]; 7,837); 1969: (1–5, 12 [5: 27,505]; 7,377). Hillman Estate Car ("Arrow" type): 1967: (4–7, 9–10, 12 [4: 4,857]; 706); 1968: (1, 3, 5, 8 [5: 780]; 246). Hillman GT saloon ("Arrow" type): 1969: (October only: 21,948); 1970: (3–5 [5: 5,355]; 774). Hillman Avenger saloons: 1970: (2–6, 8, 10–11 [2: 102,429]; 9,604).

Honda: 1967: (M: 3–4, 8–10 [10: 1,546]; 515 / D: 1–12 [3: 1,603]; 529); 1968: (M: 2–12 [7: 10,665]; 3,463 / D: 1–12 [5: 2,355]; 1,143); 1969: (M: January only: 5,406 / D: 1–5, 10–12 [10: 1,075]; 641); 1970: (M: none known / D: 1–12 [6: 2,013]; 392).

Honda 230 & 600 (marque advertising): 1969: (2–4 [2: 9,528]; 2,090).

Hondamatic: 1970: (M: 2, 7, 9 [2: 1,200]; 285 / D: 2, 4, 7–8 [8: 44]; 33).

Humber, 1958–66 (marque and dealer advertising): 1958: (1–12 [10: 24,600]; 2,524); 1959: (1–12 [10: 16,272]; 2,447); 1960: (1–12 [10: 19,666]; 2,857); 1961: (1–12 [6: 12,491]; 3,872); 1962: (1–12 [9: 16,723]; 3,545); 1963: (1–12 [1: 30,119]; 3,945); 1964: (1–12 [10: 13,487]; 2,139); 1965: (1–12 [9: 15,346]; 2,853); 1966: (1–12 [6: 18,228]; 8,092).

Humber dealer advertising, 1967–70: 1967: (1–12 [9: 10,093]; 395); 1968: (1–12 [6: 735]; 278); 1969: (1–5, 10–12 [5: 319]; 121); 1970: (1–5, 7–10, 12 [4: 230]; 101).

Humber: individual models and combinations of models (marque advertising): Humber range: 1967: (1–3 [1: 290]; 73). Hawk: 1967: (May only: 216). Imperial: 1967: February only: 88). Sceptre Mk II saloon (Hillman Super Minx type): 1967 (2–8 [5–358]; 149). Sceptre Mk III saloon ("Arrow" type): 1967: (9–11 [9: 28,333]; 519); 1968: (1–12 [3: 4,112]; 1,234); 1969: (1–3 [2: 9,273]; 3,328); 1970: (February only: 215).

Iso Rivolta: 1964: (4, 10, 12 [4: 957]; 99).

Iso sports car (unspecified: either Rivolta or Grifo, or both): 1966: (5–8, 11 [6: 405]; 154); 1967: (April only: 220).

Jaguar (marque and dealer advertising differentiated from 1967): 1958: (1–12 [10: 35,122]; 4,496); 1959: (1–12 [10: 52,287]; 4,531); 1960: (1–12 [10: 32,823]; 9,146); 1961: (1–12 [10: 50,440]; 9,278); 1962: (1–12 [10: 35,656]; 7,628); 1963: (1–12 [10: 40,992]; 9,634); 1964: (1–12 [10: 58,735]; 5,942); 1965: (1–12 [10: 41,340]; 7,902); 1966: (1–12 [10: 37,085]; 12,893); 1967: (M: 1–12 [10: 35,430]; 11,882 / D: 1–12 [9: 8,793]; 3,047); 1968: (M: 1–12 [9: 61,989]; 9,200 / D: 1–12 [10: 10,363]; 2,539); 1969: (M: 1–5, 10–12 [10: 23,759]; 5,889 / D: 1–5, 10–12 [4: 1,548]; 902); 1970: (M: 1–12 [6: 31,673]; 6,946 / D: 1–12 [2: 2,343]; 892).

Jensen: (marque and dealer advertising differentiated from 1967) 1958: (3–7, 9–10, 12 [5: 281]; 142); 1959: (2–12 [5: 778]; 213); 1960: (4–9 [4: 334] 152); 1961: (4–6 [6: 277]; 116); 1962: (10–11 [10: 868]; 9); 1963: (2–5, 7, 10–12 [7: 404]; 67); 1964: (2–12 [10: 872]; 280); 1965: (1–12 [7: 3,660]; 757); 1966: (1–12 [10: 4,720]; 945); 1967: (M: 4, 10 [10: 1,688]; 110 / D: 1–6, 8–12 [1: 551]; 140); 1968: (M: 3, 8, 10 [3: 437]; 164 / D: 1–7, 9–12 [10: 888]; 279); 1969: (M: 2–5 [5: 3,092]; 1,009 / D: 1–5, 10–12 [2: 1,856]; 754); 1970: (M: none known / D: 1–12 [1: 1,702]; 345).

Lagonda: 1961: (9, 11 [9: 569]; 278); 1962: (5–6 [5: 223]; 205); 1963: (June only: 12).

Lancia (marque and dealer advertising differentiated from 1967): 1961: (3–12 [10: 3,367]; 1,502); 1962: (1–12 [5: 2063]; 450); 1963: (1–12 [10: 1,636]; 727); 1964: (1–12 [9: 2,310]; 939); 1965: (1–12 [3: 2,341]; 879); 1966: (1–3, 5–7, 9–12 [10: 1,801]; 137); 1967: (M: 1–12 [5: 2,528]; 1,166 / D: 1–12 [10: 547]; 135); 1968: (M: 2–7, 9–12 [10: 3,233]; 1,121 / D: 1–12 [10: 693]; 263); 1969: (M: 1–5, 10–11 [10: 7,324]; 2,544 / D: 1–5, 10–12 [11: 736]; 237); 1970: (M: 3–6, 8, 10–12 [11: 8,295]; 2,689 / D: 1–12 [9: 592]; 175).

Lea-Francis (Lynx): 1960: (October only: 275; the car attracted no orders).

Lotus (marque and dealer advertising differentiated from 1967): 1960: (7–12 [7: 946]; 339); 1961: (1–3, 10–12 [12: 286]; 149); 1962: (1–12 [10: 2,244]; 537); 1963: (1–12 [9: 1,817]; 705); 1964: (1–12 [8: 1,659]; 918); 1965: (1–12 [10: 2,467]; 1,318); 1966: (1–12 [5: 2,174]; 1,232); 1967: (M: 1–12 [6: 3,925]; 1,003 / D: 1–12 [6: 1,640]; 751); 1968: (M: 1–12 [10: 1,599]; 8,222 / D: 9: 1,786]; 662); 1969: (M: 1–5, 10–12 [10: 9,562]; 2,045 / D: 1–5, 10–12 [10: 1,454]; 680); 1970: (M: 1–12 [1: 10,901]; 2,936 / D: 1–12 [4: 2,454]; 960).

Marcos (marque and dealer advertising differentiated from 1967): 1965: (4–8 [4: 597]; 177); 1966: (3, 5, 10–11 [3: 70]; 32); 1967: (M: 3–4 [3: 147]; 87 / D: 1, 4–6 [4: 170]; 22); 1968: (M: none known / D: 1–2, 4–5, 8–12 [8: 194]; 55); 1969: (M: 10, 12 [12: 144]; 39 / D: 1–5, 10–12 [4: 339]; 167); 1970: (M: 6–8 [7: 581]; 315 / D: 1–12 [9: 1,162]; 196).

Maserati (marque and dealer advertising differentiated from 1967): 1963: (4–5, 7–11 [10: 699]; 54); 1964: (3–4, 10–11 [4: 125]; 59); 1965: (1, 3–12 [10: 733]; 126); 1966: (1–3, 7, 10–11 [10: 90]; 63); 1967: (M: 8, 10, 12 [10: 457]; 93 / D: 6, 9 [6 + 9: each 31]); 1968: (M: 3–4, 7, 9, 11 [7: 160]; 18 / D: 2, 4, 6–10 [each month: 8]); 1969: (M: March only: 36 / D: 1–3, 5, 10–12 [3: 103]; 35); 1970: (M: April only: 9 / D: 1–6, 10–12 [10: 63]; 18).

Mazda cars and trucks: 1965: (12–12 [12: 450]; 280); 1966: (1–10, 12 [12: 615]; 252).

Mazda cars: 1967: (M: 1, 5, 7, 10 [each month: 265] / D: none known); 1968: (M: 1, 3, 5, 8 [each month: 380] / D: none known); 1969: (M: 10–12 [10: 514]; 185 / D: October only: 48); 1970: (M: 2–10 [4: 2,372]; 980 / D: 3–12 [7: 1,349]; 653).

Mercedes-Benz (marque and dealer advertising differentiated from 1967): 1958: (1–12 [7: 6,086]; 1,476); 1959: (1–12 [9: 4,495]; 1,927); 1960: (1–12 [7: 3,064]; 1,488); 1961: (1–12 [10: 5,546]; 2,962); 1962: (1–12 [9: 5,572]; 2,767); 1963: (1–12 [2: 8,861]; 4,657); 1964: (1–12 [7: 18,186]; 10,337); 1965: (1–12 [6: 26,179]; 15,453); 1966: (1–12 [10: 17,294]; 10,132); 1967: (M: 1–12 [9: 19,202]; 7,521 / D: 1–12 [5: 5,397]; 2,469); 1968: (M: 1–12 [6: 17,035]; 6,139 / D: 1–12 [5: 5,936]; 2,699); 1969: (M: 1–5, 10–12 [11: 14,996]; 5,700 / D: 1–5, 10–12 [5: 3,607]; 1,348); 1970: (M: 1–11 [7: 18,413]; 7,524 / D: 1–12 [6: 7,167]; 2,827).

Messerschmitt bubble car: 1958: (1–12 [6: 915]; 238); 1959: (1–12 [5: 430]; 213); 1960: (1–12 [5: 448]; 212); 1961: (1–9 [5: 262]; 98); 1962: (none known; possibly among combined "other advertisers" with very small expenditures— see after *Wolseley*, below); 1963: (4–7 [4 + 5: each 80]; 60).

MG, 1958–66 (marque and dealer advertising): 1958: (1–12: [10: 3,435]; 2,044); 1959: (1–12 [2: 14,784]; 2,397); 1960: 1–12 [10: 4,499]; 2,636); 1960: (1–12 [10: 4,499]; 2,636); 1961: (1–12 [7: 12,016]; 2,514); 1962: (1–12 [10: 17,046]; 3,666); 1963: (1–12 [4: 4364]; 2,382); 1964: (1–12 [5: 9,162]; 3,801); 1965: (1–12 [10: 5,481]; 3,131); 1966 (1–12 [8: 5,148]; 3,246).

MG dealer advertising, 1967–70: 1967: (1–12 [6: 2,137]; 1,334); 1968: (1–12 [10: 1,734]; 1,072); 1969: (1–5, 10–12 [3: 1,837]; 1,163); 1970: (1–12 [3: 2,080]; 501).

MG: individual models and combinations of models, 1967–70 (marque advertising): MG range: 1967: (4, 7, 10–11 [11: 220]; 94); 1968: (5, 11–12 [11: 4,712]; 347); 1969: (1–3 [1: 4,433]; 2,539); 1970: (none known). Magnette Mk IV: 1967: (1, 3 [1: 1,318]; 189). Midget: 1967: (3, 5–7, 12 [5: 278]; 136); 1968: (1, 3–4, 6–9 [3 + 4: each 3,857]; 883); 1970: (3–7 [5: 6,448]; 748). MGB: 1967: (1–11 [4: 4,912]; 1,866); 1968: (1–3, 5–6, 9 [3: 328]; 87); 1969: (February only: 262); 1970: (3–9 [4: 7,812]; 3,132). MGC: 1967: (10, 12 [10: 3,447]; 180); 1968: (3–7, 10 [5: 4,706]; 561); 1969: (October only: 299). MG 1100: 1967: (1–2, 4, 6–7, 9 [6: 4,142]; 2,248). MG 1300: 1968: (1–3, 5–9 [7: 3,823]; 1,199).

Morgan (marque and dealer advertising differentiated from 1967): 1958: (1–10, 12 [10: 418]; 53); 1959: (2–6, 8, 10–12 [10: 465]; 70); 1960: (1, 3, 5–7, 10–11 [3: 916]; 195); 1961: (3–12 [10: 552]; 77); 1962: (1–12 [10: 386]; 81); 1963: (2–7, 9–10, 12 [10: 887]; 102); 1964: (1, 4–11 [10: 400]; 130); 1965: (1, 3–11 [10: 333]; 119); 1966: (1, 3–12 [10: 557]; 169); 1967: (M: 2–7, 9–11 [10: 360]; 110 / D: 1–11 [10: 182] 18); 1968: (M: 1–12 [10:

1,734]; 1,072 / D: 3–7, 9–10 [9: 593]; 166); 1969: (M: 1–5, 10–12 [3: 1,837]; 1,163 / D: 1, 3–5, 10–11 [10: 658]; 113); 1970: (M: 3–11 [10: 589]; 145 / D: 4–10 [5: 274]; 101).

Morris, 1958–66 (marque and dealer advertising): (1–12 [4: 13,621]; 8,358); 1959: (1–12 [3: 37,184]; 9,697); 1960: (1–12 [10: 23,066]; 10,125); 1961: (1–12 [10: 26,924]; 11,407); 1962: (1–12 [8: 79,263]; 11,853); 1963: (1–12 [1: 21,198]; 8,748); 1964: (1–12 [1: 33,217]; 11,562); 1965: (1–12 [9: 14,482]; 8,933); 1966: (1–12 [3: 24, 762]; 11,624).

Morris dealer advertising, 1967–70: 1967: (1–12 [3: 8,041]; 5,428); 1968: (1–12 [10: 5,226]; 3,602); 1969: (1–5, 10–12 [10: 9,371]; 3,210); 1970: (1–12 [10: 6,228]; 2,893)

Morris: individual models and combinations of models, 1967–70 (marque advertising): Morris full car range: 1967: (3, 12 [12: 1,461]; 19); 1968: (1, 9, 12 [1: 229]; 50); 1969: (1–2, 4–5 [5: 108]; 69). Morris Mini, 1100 and 1300: 1967: (10–11 [11: 635]; 480); 1968: (December only: 4,493); 1969: (1–3 [1: 2,569]; 918); Minor 1000 saloon: 1967: (2, 6, 10 [Each month: 110]); 1968: (May only: 74). Oxford Series IV saloon: 1968: [3–6, 11 [11: 12,798]; 493). Morris Mini saloons: 1967: (2, 4, 6, 8, 12 [12: 60]; 26). Morris 1100 saloon: 1967: (1–5, 10 [1: 5,780]; 74); 1968: (6–12 [8: 1,459]; 588); 1969: (February only: 74). Morris 1300 saloon: 1969: (3–5, 10 [4: 14,830]; 2,753). Morris 1800: 1967: (1–4, 6–9 [7: 969]; 330); 1968: (1–4, 7–11 [9: 1,782]; 982); 1969: (1–5, 10 [4: 9,439]; 1,136).

Moskvich (marque and dealer advertising differentiated from 1967): 1965: (10–12 [10: 457]; 111); 1966: (1–2, 4–12 [8: 1,074]; 237); 1967: (M: 3–5, 7, 10 [10: 1,430]; 361 / D: 1–10, 12 [10: 802]; 61); 1968: (M: 1–2, 5–8, 10–12 [5: 3,225]; 362 / D: 2–12 [6: 618]; 76); 1969: (M: 1–5, 10–12 [2: 1,022]; 322 / D: 1, 3–5, 10–11 [10: 1,054]; 386); 1970: 4, 10 [10: 654]; 192 / D: 1–12 [10: 1,807] 200).

NSU Prinz (to July 1967) and NSU (from June 1967) (marque and dealer advertising differentiated from 1967) 1958: (October only: 776); 1959: (1, 5–12 [10: 2,695]; 357); 1960: (1–12 [4: 1,309]; 567); 1961: (1–12 [10: 1,050]; 422); 1962: (1–12 [3: 2,191]; 980); 1963: (1–12 [10: 4,118]; 1,575); 1964: (1–12 [10: 3,618]; 1,302); 1965: (1–12 [7: 3,648]; 1,479); (1–12 [3: 1,424]; 848); 1967 NSU Prinz: (M: 1–2, 4–5, 7 [5: 1,691]; 513 / D: 1–5, 7 [5: 2,188]; 642); 1967 NSU: (M: 6, 9–10, 12 [9: 540]; 202 / D: 6, 8–12 [6: 2,359]; 1,462); 1968: (M: 1–12 [6: 8,377]; 728 / D: 1–12 [5: 2,506]; 1,256); 1969: (M: 1–5, 10 [3: 12,179]; 2,725 / D: 1–5, 10–12 [10: 2,817]; 1,361); 1970: (M: 1–5, 7–8, 10–12 [4: 13,178]; 2,253 / D: 1–12 [5: 7,443]; 2,884).

Oldsmobile: 1960: (1–2 [2: 150]; 114).

Opel: 1967: (M: October only: 416 / D: 10–12 [10: 840]; 531); 1968: (M: 2–6, 8–11 [5: 4,559]; 2,042 / D: 1–12 [10: 2,203]; 889); 1969: (M: 2–5, 10–12 [10: 14,003]; 4,596 / D: 1–5, 10–12 [10: 2,918]; 1,519); 1970: (M: 2–12 [3: 12,979]; 2,044 / D: 1–12 [10: 7,028]; 3,191).

Panhard: 1958: (10–11 [10: 558]; 52); 1959: (4–6, 8–12 [5: 2,308]; 57); 1960: (1–9 [5: 1,968]; 678); 1961: (1–11 [1:

2,807]; 406); 1962: (4–8, 10 [6: 800]; 258); 1963: (1–5, 7, 10–11 [10: 62]; 13); 1964: (3–7, 9–10 [5: 522]; 186); 1965: (1–2, 5 [5: 20]; 10).

Peugeot (marque and dealer advertising differentiated from 1967): 1958: (10–12 [10: 1,171]; 134); 1959: (1–12 [10: 2,765]; 323); 1960: (1–12 [10: 3,043]; 828); 1961: (1–12 [10: 1,480]; 611); 1962: (1–12 [10: 2,487]; 735); 1963: (1–12 [4: 2,788]; 907); 1964: (1–12 [10: 2,452]; 914); 1965: (1–12 [4: 2,870]; 958); 1966: (1–12 [4: 4,509]; 871); 1967: (M: 2–6, 10 [3: 3,090]; 1,589 / D: 1–12 [6: 1,048]; 437); 1968: (M: 3–12 [4: 3,769]; 635 / D: 1–12 [4: 1,141]; 307); 1969: (M: 1–5, 10–12 [10: 2,815]; 1,194 / D: 1–5, 10–12 [10: 906]; 448); 1970: (M: 1–10 [7: 3,072]; 937 / D: 1–12 [10: 1,707]; 553).

Plymouth: 1968: (M: 2–6, 10 [2: 689]; 472 / D: 3, 6 [6: 198]; 38); 1969: (M: 4–5, 10–11 [10: 1,784]; 705 / D: April only: 2,365); 1970: (M: none known / D: 1, 3 [3: 35]; 32).

Pontiac (marque and dealer advertising differentiated from 1967): 1959: (10, 12 [10: 246]; 87); 1960–62: (none known; possibly among combined "other advertisers" with very small expenditures—see after *Wolseley*, below); 1963: (1–7, 9–12 [5: 276]; 79); 1964: (2–5, 8 [5: 208]; 129); 1965: (2–5, 8, 10, 12 [10: 47]; 19); 1966–67: (none known); 1968: (M: none known / D: May only: 58); 1969: (none known); 1970: (M: none known / D: 5, 7 [5 + 7: each 88]).

Porsche (marque and dealer advertising differentiated from 1967): 1960: (1–12 [4: 148]; 142); 1961: (1–12 [6: 366]; 181; 1962: (1–12 [6: 466]; 181); 1963: (1–12 [5: 299]; 207); 1964: (1–12 [6: 434]; 216); 1965: (1–12 [10: 507]; 283); 1966: (1–12 [10: 568]; 314); 1967: (M: 1–12 [10: 429]; 137 / D: 1–12 [6: 133]; 57); 1968: (M: 1–12 [5: 266]; 130 / D: 1–8, 10–12 [6: 355]; 82); 1969: (M: 1–5, 10–12 [10: 359]; 216 / D: 1–5, 10, 12 [5: 258]; 66); 1970: (M: 1–5, 7–12 [10: 628]; 240 / D: 1–12 [6: 191]; 81).

Princess (marque and dealer advertising): 1958: (2–7, 10–12 [11: 3,159], 807); 1959: (1–6, 8–11 [10: 1,696]; 706); 1960: (1–6, 8–12 [6: 1,941]; 816); 1961: (1–12 [11: 5,888]; 3,142); 1962: (1–12 [3: 7,231]; 2,543); 1963: (1–12 [1: 3,030]; 1,494); 1964: (1–12 [8: 34,090] 1,995); 1965: (1–12 [1: 2,977]; 1,901); 1966: (1–12 [3: 16,155]; 5,440); (no marque advertising known after 1966).

Princess dealer advertising, 1967–70: 1967: (1–12 [2: 484]; 170); 1968: (1–6, 9–10 [4: 84]; 32); 1969: (1–2 [1: 42]; 11); 1970: (1, 8, 12 [12: 28]; 24).

(AMC) Rambler (marque and dealer advertising differentiated from 1967): 1963: (5–12 [7: 691]; 305); 1964: (1–12 [4: 878]; 475); 1965: (1–12 [11: 1,275]; 373); 1966: (1–6, 8–11 [5: 1,770]; 619); 1967: (M: 2–8, 10–11 [2: 657]; 361 / D: 1–11 [7: 416]; 133); 1968: (M: 1–2, 5–8, 10 [5: 2,199]; 395 / D: 2–7, 10 [7: 199]; 103); 1969: (M: 1, 4–5, 11–12 [1: 729]; 361 / D: 2, 10 [10: 29]; 8); 1970: (M: 1–6 [2–4: 570] 423 / D: 2–5 [5: 181]; 72).

Reliant Regal 3-wheeler (*Note:* Reliant Sabre not listed, but possibly included in 1961–63 figures for 3-wheeler or among "other advertisers" with very small expenditures—

see after *Wolseley*, below): 1958: (1–12 [2: 636]; 411); 1959: (1–12 [6: 774]; 374); 1960: (1–12 [11: 1,074]; 607); 1961: (1–12 [10: 1,277]; 854); 1962: (1–12 [12: 1,937]; 1,621).

Reliant cars & 3-wheelers (marque and dealer advertising differentiated from 1967): 1963: (1–12 [1: 3,189]; 1,157); 1964: (1–12 [11: 2,767]; 1,657); 1965: (1–12 [1: 5,291]; 3,413); 1966: (1–12 [1: 4,611]; 2,887); 1967: (M: 1–12 [9: 2,225]; 760 / D: 1–12 [4: 3,213]; 1,899); 1968: (M: 1–12 [10: 3,594]; 1,556 / D: 1–12 [10: 3,223]; 1,942); 1969: (M: 1–5, 10–12 [11: 9,471]; 1,704 / D: 1–5, 10–12 [3: 1,919]; 865); 1970: (M: 1–12 [3: 18,875]; 3,482 / D: 1–12 [10: 2,068]; 1,019).

Renault: marque and dealer advertising, 1958–66: 1958: (1–12 [10: 12,570]; 6,338); 1959: (1–12 [10: 23,470]; 9,271); 1960: (1–12 [4: 32,632]; 20,219); 1961: (1–12 [5: 33,084]; 10,889); 1962: (1–12 [10: 25,418]; 6,437); 1963: (1–12 [4: 21,434]; 10,178); 1964: (1–12 [4: 29,190]; 10,656); 1965: (1–12 [9: 30,055]; 11,925); 1966: (1–12 [2: 40,767]; 19,346).

Renault car and van: 1961: (September only: 421); 1962: (February only: 73); 1963 (2–6, 12 [5: 2,574]; 596).

Renault dealer advertising, 1967–70: 1967: (1–12 [6: 10,039]; 6,370); 1968: (1–12 [5: 10,249]; 5,841); 1969: (1–5, 10–12 [11: 14,517]; 7,440); 1970: (1–12 [5: 21,174]; 7,664).

Renault: individual models and combinations of models, 1967–70 (marque advertising): Renault car range: 1969: (3, 10–12 [10: 1,097]; 574); 1970: (2–4, 7, 10, 12 [10: 592]; 133). Renault 4: 1967: (1–6, 8–12 [11: 9,413]; 3,172); 1968: (1–2, 4–5, 9–12 [11: 6,556]; 3,016); 1969: (1–5, 10–12 [10: 15,577]; 5,061); 1970: (1–6, 9–12 [10: 8,505]; 3,770). Renault 8 Gordini: 1967: (2, 10, 12 [10: 5,310]; 859); 1968: (1–2, 4–5, 9–10 [2: 2,758]; 847); 1969: (2–3 [2: 3,267]; 100). Renault 8S: 1969: (2–3, 5: [3: 4,431]; 1,028). Renault 8–1100: 1967: (1–6, 9–12 [9: 10,561]; 3,180); 1968: (1–7, 9–12 [11: 10,531]; 3,025); 1969: (1–5 [2: 11,620]; 5,131). Renault 10 (*Note:* Renault 8–1100 above called Renault 10 in some markets outside Britain); 1969: (10–11 [11: 5,518]; 4,670); 1970: (1–5, 9–11 [2: 7,400]; 3,426). Renault 16: 1967: (1–6, 9–11 [9: 7,523]; 3,716); 1968: (1–6, 9–12 [5: 6,080]; 3,450); 1969: (1–5, 10–12 [11: 13,420]; 6,114); 1970: (1–5, 9–11 [11: 11,133]; 5,678). Renault 6: 1969: (11–12 [11: 26,920]; 9,058); 1970: (1–2, 4–6, 11–12 [11: 12,045]; 4,049). Renault 12: 1970: (5–7, 10–12 [5: 21,053]; 5,637).

Riley, 1958–66 (marque and dealer advertising): 1958: (1–12 [6: 4,959]; 1,835); 1959: (1–12 [4: 13,259]; 1,864); 1960: (1–12 [7: 8,429]; 2,230); 1961: (1–12 [10: 3,629]; 1,681); 1962: (1–12 [6: 9,609]; 3,255); 1963: (1–12 [5: 3,350]; 2,168); 1964: (1–12 [3: 13,132]; 2,849); 1965: (1–12 [10: 6,230]; 2,159); 1966: (1–12 [10: 4,126]; 2,136).

Riley dealer advertising, 1967–70 (*Note:* Riley marque discontinued in October, 1969): 1967: (1–12 [5: 946]; 594); 1968: (1–12 [11: 728]; 496); 1969: (1–5, 10–11 [5: 645]; 297); 1970: (January only: 163).

Riley: individual models, 1967–69 (marque advertising): 4/Seventy-Two: 1967: (1–3, 7, 9, 12 [12: 1,659]; 394). Riley Elf: 1967: (3–6, 10–12 [4: 2,420]; 1,575); 1968: (1, 3–7,

9–11 [5: 2,256]; 693); 1969: (February only: 410). Kestrel: 1967: (1, 4–7 [7: 2,567]; 1,246); 1968: (1–12 [7: 3,035]; 797); 1969: (1–4 [3: 2,990]; 1,927). (*Note*: advertising from October 1968 listed as for the Kestrel was almost certainly for its similar replacement, the Riley 1300 Mk II): Riley 1300 Mk II: 1969: (May only: 814 — but see above).

Rolls-Royce (marque and dealer advertising differentiated from 1967): 1958: (1–12 [10: 4,947]; 557); 1959: (1–6, 8, 10–12 [8: 5,556]; 1,291); 1960: (1–12 [11: 5,798]; 315); 1961: (1–12 [9: 7,869]; 747); 1962: (1–12 [10: 5,727]; 1,124); 1963: (1–4, 6–12 [3: 446]; 97); 1964: (1–12 [5: 587]; 167); 1965: (1–12 [10: 13,056]; 162); 1966: (1–12 [10: 8,750]; 463); 1967: (M: May only: 184 / D: 1–12 [10: 382]; 108); 1968: (M: 3–6, 9–10 [9: 6,842]; 3,521 / D: 1–12 [3: 2,756]; 439); 1969: (M: 1, 3–5, 10 [3: 6,336], 2,311 / D: 1–5, 10–12 [3: 2,229]; 655); 1970: (M: 3–7, 9–10 [9: 11,677]; 3,334 / D: 1–12 [7: 3,058]; 687).

Rolls-Royce and **Bentley** combined advertising (marque and dealer advertising differentiated from 1967): 1958: (1–12 [5: 650]; 426); 1959: (1–12 [9: 3,767]; 762); 1960: (1–12 [7: 2,419]; 1,771); 1961: (1–12 [1,984]; 981); 1962: (1–12 [10: 2,426]; 517); 1963: (1–12 [11: 674]; 414); 1964: (1–12 [5: 1,394]; 417); 1965: (1–12 [10: 5,489]; 381); 1966: (1–12 [10: 1,617]; 321); 1967: (M: none known / D: 1–12 [9: 895]; 317); 1968: (M: none known / D: 1–12 [2: 2,268]; 567); 1969: (M: none known / D: 1–5, 10, 12 [3: 1,719]; 319); 1970: (M: November only: 440 / D: 1–12 [10: 2,091]; 607).

Rootes Group: marque and dealer advertising, 1958–66: 1958: (1–12 [10: 36,294]; 872); 1959: (1–12 [10: 31,200]; 1,945); 1960: (1–12 [10: 45,595]; 6,372); 1961: (1–12 [12: 11,977]; 3,214); 1962: (1–12 [10: 22,868]; 3,166); 1963: (1–12 [10: 40,856]; 3,240); 1964: (1–12 [10: 39,038]; 2,986); 1965: (1–12 [10: 39,064]; 4,731); 1966: (1–12 [10: 18,683]; 3,603).

Rootes Group dealer advertising, 1967–70: 1967: (1–12 [10: 9,809]; 2,762); 1968: (1–12 [10: 15,378]; 4,028); 1969: (1–5, 10–12 [10: 10,479]; 5,154); 1970: (1–8, [7: 2,582]; 850).

Rootes Group full car range (marque advertising) (*Note*: for later corporate advertising see *Chrysler (UK)*, above): 1967: (1, 5–6, 10–11 [10: 27,186]; 957); 1968: (5, 10, 12 [10: 9,660]; 4,042); 1969: 4, 10–12 [11: 40,734]; 11,491); 1970: (1, 4–5 [4: 14,355]; 2,154).

Rootes Group: individual models and combinations of models, 1967–70 (marque advertising): Imp saloon range: 1968: (5–6, 10–12 [10: 28,073]; 10,451); 1969: (1–5, 10–12 [11: 61,962]; 4,645); 1970: (1–2, 4, 6 [6: 14,724]; 7,098).

Rootes Specialized Service (marque and/or dealer advertising to 1966, but listed only as marque advertising from 1967): 1961: (1–12 [6: 4,221]; 1,227); 1962: (1–12 [2: 4,220]; 793); 1963: (1–12 [10: 426]; 91); 1964: (1–12 [10: 1,568]; 688); 1965: (1–12 [2: 2,808]; 1,829); 1966: (1–12 [1: 3,428]; 2,040); 1967: (1–12 [5: 2,704]; 1,407); 1968: (1–12 [3: 3,934]; 2,127); 1969: (1–2, 4 [4: 257]; 72).

Rootes Overseas Delivery Plan (marque advertising) 1967: (*Note*: Plan not listed before 1967, but might be in-cluded in earlier, undifferentiated, Rootes marque and dealer advertising: see above); 1967: (1–8, 10, 12 [8: 521]; 282); 1968: February only: 380).

Rootes Used Cars (marque advertising): 1969: (3–5 [3: 36,612]; 18,450).

Rootes (Scotland): 1962: (listed August only: 471); 1964: (listed August only: 32).

Rover (marque and dealer advertising differentiated from 1967): 1958: (1–12 [10: 16,353]; 5,766); 1959: (1–12 [9: 22,526]; 5,499); 1960: (1–12 [10: 29,531]; 3,642); 1961: (1–12 [10: 25,438]; 6,709); 1962: (1–12 [9: 19,521]; 7,894); 1963: (1–12 [10: 91,737]; 7,358); 1964: (1–12 [10: 23,818]; 6,970); 1965: (1–12 [10: 55,648]; 13,279); 1966: (1–12 [10: 32,086]; 9,594); 1967: (M: 1–11 [10: 22,744]; 8,681 / D: 1–12 [2: 6,488]; 3,303); 1968: (M: 1–7, 9–12 [4: 19,947]; 10,128 / D: 1–12 [4: 9,623]; 3,147); 1969: (M: 1–5, 10–12 [10: 19,305]; 8,669 / D: 2–5, 10–12 [2: 4,726]; 2,684); 1970: (1–12 [10: 34,059]; 13,921 / D: 1–12 [10: 5,627]; 1,756).

Rover and **Land-Rover** combined advertising (marque and dealer advertising differentiated from 1967): 1958: (1–12: [11: 458]; 195); 1959: (1–12 [7: 884]; 230); 1960: (1–12 [10: 414]; 181); 1961: (1–12 [10: 827]; 406); 1962: (1–12 [4: 732]; 322); 1963: (1–12 [5: 933]; 217); 1964: (1–12 [8: 399]; 182); 1965: (1–12 [3: 667]; 281); 1966: (1–12 [3: 317]; 163); 1967: (M: April only: 297) / D: 1–3, 5–12 [2: 384]; 259); 1968: (M: 3, 10 [10: 29]; 9 / D: 1–12 [10: 393]; 205); 1969: (M: none known / D: 1–5, 10–12 [10: 848]; 204); 1970: (M: 9, 12 [9: 4,770]; 270 / D: 1–12 [9: 439]; 90).

Saab (marque and dealer advertising differentiated from 1967): 1960: (11–12 [12: 823] 297); 1961: (1–12 [11: 5,807]; 548); 1962: (1–12 [11: 6,086]; 1,446); 1963: (1–12 [2: 3,391]; 809); 1964: (1–12 [4: 6,545]; 1,192); 1965: (1–12 [4: 3,145]; 1,333); 1966: (1–12 [9: 6,484]; 1,420); 1967 (M: 3–5, 7–12 [3: 4,620]; 1,992 / D: 1–12 [10: 1,513]; 587); 1968: (M: 2–12 [10: 8,615]; 1,725 / D: 1–12 [6: 1,641]; 608); 1969: (M: 2–4, 10–12 [11: 11,411]; 3,588 / D: 1–5, 10–12 [10: 1,219]; 525); 1970: (M: 2–8, 10–11 [11: 14,231]; 1,756 / D: 1–12 [10: 1,867]; 532).

Scootacar: 1958: (11–12 [11: 297]; 32); 1959: (1–12 [12: 519]; 147); 1960: (1–12 [3: 447]; 241); 1961: (1–9 [1: 583]; 177); 1962: (1–9 [1: 216]; 45).

Simca, 1958–66 (marque and dealer advertising: 1958: (1–12 [10: 1,050]; 177); 1959: (1–12 [10: 4,330]; 675); 1960: (1–12 [5: 8,930]; 2,379); 1961: (1–12 [5: 10,363]; 986); 1962: (1–12 [6: 8,806]; 305); 1963: (1–12 [10: 3,315]; 1,344); 1964: (1–12 [3: 9,962]; 2,578); 1965: (1–12 [4: 8,421]; 2,352); 1966: (1–12 [4: 9,881]; 3,355).

Simca dealer advertising, 1967–70: 1967: (1–12 [12: 4,767]; 1,652); 1968: (1–12 [10: 3,416]; 1,174); 1969: (1–5, 10–12 [12: 1,839]; 1,170); 1970: (1–12 [10: 4,910]; 1,332).

Simca car range, 1967–70 (marque advertising): 1967: (1, 10–11 [10: 3,822]; 141); 1968: (4–6, 10–12 [10: 3,084]; 334); 1969: (1–5 [5: 622]; 190); 1970: (2–4 [2 + 3: each 120]; 110).

Simca: individual models and combinations of models,

1967–70 (marque advertising): Simca 1000 saloon: 1967: (1–8, 12 [12: 2,347]; 128); 1968: (none known); 1969: (4, 11–12 [12: 4,813]; 288); 1970: (1–5, 9–10, 12 [9: 9,260]; 3,299). Simca 1301 saloon: 1970: (October only: 5,730). Simca 1301 and 1501 saloons and estate cars: 1967: (1–8, 10–12 [10: 2,689]; 205); 1968: (3, 5–6 [6: 314]; 92); 1969: March only: 251). Simca 1501 Estate Car: 1967: (3–7, 9–11 [3: 201]; 61); 1968: (1, 3, 5, 7, 11 [11: 720]; 14); 1969: December only; 791); 1970: (1–4, 9–11 [11: 4,175]; 527). Simca 1100: 1967: (11–12 [11: 3,406]; 3,237); 1968: (5–6 [5: 226]; 60); 1969: (5, 10–12 [11: 6,024]; 1,578); 1970: (1–7, 10–12 [11: 7,480]; 2,464). Simca 1204 Special: 1970: (10, 12 [10: 2,626], 1,555).

Singer, 1958–66 (marque and dealer advertising): 1958: (1–12 [9: 7,734]; 4,052); 1959: (1–12 [9: 10,271]; 3,687); 1960: (1–12 [10: 7,016]; 1,491); 1961: (1–12 [7: 24, 522]; 2,115); 1962: (1–12 [10: 12,389]; 4,713); 1963: (1–12 [9: 15,631]; 2,715); 1964: (1–12 [10: 49,481]; 10,573); 1965: (1–12 [9: 21,506]; 9,229); 1966: (1–12 [19,210]; 9,614).

Singer dealer advertising, 1967–70 (*Note*: Singer marque discontinued in April 1970): 1967: (1–12 [1: 7,423]; 3,517); 1968: (1–12 [10: 4,422]; 2,029); 1969: (1–5, 10–12 [3: 1,263]; 587); 1970: (1–5 [1: 732]; 103).

Singer: individual models and combinations of models, 1967–70: Singer range: 1968: (5–6, 10 [10: 17,365]; 7,925). Chamois: 1967: (2–8 [5: 12,748]; 3,279); 1968: (August only: 7,125). Vogue saloon ("Arrow" type): 1967: (4–9 [5: 1,735]; 364); 1968: (none known); 1969: (11–12 [11: 3,630]; 2,970); 1970: (January only: 2,035). Vogue Estate Car: 1967: (4–6, 10–12 [5: 4,824]; 332); 1968: (3, 6, 8 [6: 16,544]; 316). Chamois and Vogue saloon and Estate Car: 1967: (1–2, 5 [1: 525]; 483). Gazelle saloon ("Arrow" type): 1967: (1–7, 10 [10: 8,100]; 3,839); 1968: (1, 5, 8 [5: 1,800]; 450); 1969: (2–5 [4: 16, 537]; 7,665).

Skoda (marque and dealer advertising differentiated from 1967): 1958: (1–9, 11–12 [8: 565]; 206); 1959: (1–12 [4,777]; 179); 1960: (1–12 [10: 1,331]; 551); 1961: (1–12 [3: 1,484]: 760); 1962: (1–12 [2: 669]; 235); 1963: (1–12 [10: 6,182]; 1,446); 1964: (1–12 [6: 6,470]); 1965: (1–12 [4: 5,205]; 1,854); 1966: (1–12 [4: 8,867]; 2,130); 1967 (M: 3–11 [1: 1,602]; 681 / D: 1–12 [10: 3,362]; 1,552); 1968: (M: 2–11 [9: 4,172]; 931 / D: 1–12 [6: 2,497]; 1,697); 1969: (M: 1–5, 10–12 [3: 1,263]; 587 / D: 1–5, 10–12 [3: 1,062]; 576); 1970: (M: 4–6 [4: 2,668]; 704 / D: 1–12 [5: 2,287]; 481).

Standard, 1958–64 (marque and dealer advertising) (*Note*: the Standard marque was discontinued in May 1963): 1958: (1–12 [4: 22,921]; 12,264); 1959: (1–12 [1: 5,873]; 2,768); 1960: (1–12 [7: 9,076]; 4,890); 1961: (1–12 [5: 6,867]; 1,214); 1962: (1–12 [9: 701]; 206); 1963: (1–11 [2: 15,230]; 1,326); 1964: (5, 10, 12 [12: 61]; 8).

Standard and **Triumph**: 1958: (1–12 [10: 37,108]; 4,165); 1959: (1–12 [10: 73,802]; 3,248); 1960: [10: 32,543]; 2,664); 1961: [10: 28,287]; 1,788); 1962: [5: 20,810]; 2,034); 1963: (1–12 [11: 3,979]; 1,601); 1964: (1–12 [10: 1,958]; 917); 1965: (1–12 [9: 2,474]; 1,023); 1966: (1–12 [1: 1113]; 720).

Standard-Triumph dealer advertising, 1967–68: 1967: (1–12 [1: 571]; 272); 1968: (1–8 [8: 155]; 49).

Standard-Triumph Stanparts (marque advertising) 1967–70: 1967: (1–11 [5 + 7: each 79]; 58); 1968: (1–12 [5: 254]; 100); 1969: (1–5, 10–12 [5: 325]; 167); 1970: (1–9 [1: 176]; 129).

Stirling: 1958: (October only: 101).

Studebaker: 1963: (5, 7, 9–11 [10: 650]; 293).

Sunbeam: 1958–66 (marque and dealer advertising): (1–12 [2: 14,872]; 3,645); 1959: (1–12 [18,073]; 3,514); 1960: (1–12 [10: 10,712]; 3,649); 1961: (1–12 [6: 13,349]; 3,917); 1962: (1–12 [1: 10,616]; 2,804); 1963: (1–12 [3: 10,334]; 1,921); 1964: (1–12 [5: 9,567]; 2,117); 1965: (1–12 [4: 11,041]; 2,969); 1966: (1–12 [10: 12,461]; 1,420).

Sunbeam dealer advertising, 1967–70: 1967: (1–12 [5: 3,636]; 689); 1968: (1–12 [5: 1,349]; 859); 1969: (1–5, 10–12 [10: 3,132]; 450); 1970: (1–10, 12 [7: 847]; 300).

Sunbeam: individual models and combinations of models, 1967–70 (marque advertising): Imp Sport (*Note*: see also Hillman: individual models and combinations of models, above; and *Hillman Imp and Sunbeam Imp Sport* in *Hillman*, above): 1967: (1–9 [1: 11,015]; 1,989); 1968: 1–3, 5–8 [1: 10,367]; 1,375); 1969: (1–5 [2 + 3: each 1,748]; 1,154). Stiletto: 1967: (10, 12 [12: 462]; 457); 1968: (3–10 [4: 851]; 395). Rapier: 1967 (Series V): (6–7 [6 + 7: each 216]); 1968 (fastback "Arrow" derivative): (1, 4, 6–7, 9–11 [4: 16,940]; 5,145); 1969: (1–4 [3: 14,560]; 5,490); 1970: (1, 5 [5: 3,630]; 2,209). Alpine Series V (sports): 1967: (5–8 [5: 6,148]; 445); 1968: (none known; Series V sports dropped early in 1968); Alpine ("Arrow" derivative, introduced October 1969): 1969: (October only: 17,989); 1970: (November only: 15).

Toyota Toyopet Tiara: 1961: (10, 12 [10: 240]; 140); 1963: (October only: 265).

Toyota (marque and dealer advertising differentiated from 1967): 1964: (November only: 450); 1965: (10–12 [11: 551]; 401); 1966: (1–12 [7: 3,492]; 1,548); 1967: (M: 1–12 [7: 2,317]; 994 / D: 1–12 [10: 1,850]; 890); 1968: (M: 1–12 [4: 3,916]; 1,363 / D: 1–12 [10: 1,293]; 552); 1969: (M: 1–5, 10–12 [10: 6,006]; 1,979 / D: 1–5, 10–12 [10: 1,789]; 516); 1970: (1–12 [3: 2,101]; 1,079 / D: 1–12 [10: 746]; 245).

Trident (marque advertising): 1969: (October only: 105); 1970: (3, 10 [10: 105]; 75).

Triumph, 1958–66 (marque and dealer advertising): 1958: (1–12 [7: 4,122]; 928); 1959: (1–12 [5: 37,578]; 5,885); 1960: (1–12 [8: 31,329]; 8,897); 1961: (4: 62,126]; 13,440); 1962: (1–12 [2: 46,064]; 17,855); 1963: (1–12 [3: 60,064]; 19,133); 1964: 1–12 [1: 83, 386]; 34,713); 1965: (1–12 [2: 63,006]; 31,544); 1966: (1–12 [2: 84,987]; 38,289).

Triumph dealer advertising, 1967–70: 1967: (1–12 [3: 13,656]; 8,799); 1968: (1–12 [10: 12,927]; 5,175); 1969: (1–5, 10–12 [10: 8,684]; 3,933); 1970: (1–12 [5: 14,690]; 4,947).

Triumph car range, 1967–70 (marque advertising): 1967: (11–12 [11: 571]; 266); 1968: (1, 3–4, 6–10 [3: 6,896]; 377); 1969: (1–5 [1: 158]; 61); 1970: (October only: 189).

Triumph: individual models and combinations of models, 1967–70 (marque advertising): Herald saloons: 1967: (1–12 [2: 47,736]; 6,274); 1968: (1–4, 7, 9, 11–12 [11: 26,717]; 4,675); 1969: (1–5, 10–12 [2: 35,522]; 12,164); 1970: (1–4, 8–10 [10: 16,993]; 4,144). Herald Convertible: 1967: (2–3, 11 [2: 2,233]; 997). Herald Estate Car: 1967: (3–4 [3: 902]; 798). Herald saloons and Estate Car: 1967: (1–3, 5–7 [5: 11,823]; 2,968); 1968: (2–6, 8–9 [6: 11,027]; 3,107); 1969: (April only: 55). Vitesse saloon: 1967: (2, 4–6 [5: 2,577]; 2,100); 1968: (1–6, 8, 10–11 [10: 4,568]; 1,029); 1969: (2–5 [3: 4,206]; 1,623). Triumph TR4: 1967: (1–10 [10: 7,278]; 1,499). Triumph TR5: 1968: (5–6, 8 [5: 428]; 203); Triumph TR6: 1969: (January only: 6,767). Triumph Spitfire: 1967: (1–2, 4–7 [1: 6,797]; 1,738); 1968: (2–6 [4: 4,912]; 1,859); 1969: (none known, but see *Introduction, para 3,* above); 1970: (5–9, 11 [8: 12,697]; 2,610). Triumph GT 6: 1967: (1–4, 7–9 [8: 1,330]; 647); 1968: (4–5, 7, 9–10 [9: 6,923]; 1,551); 1969: (none known, but see *Introduction* above); 1970: (4–5, 7–8 [5: 8,269]; 974). Triumph 2000 saloon: 1967: (1–5, 7, 11–12 [3: 37,547]; 10,073); 1968: (1–10, 12 [5: 10,859]; 5,101); 1969: (3–5, 10–11 [4: 16,438]; 4,172); 1970: (4–5, 7 [5: 9,178]; 3,079). Triumph 2000 Estate Car: 1967: (2, 9 [2: 665]; 35); 1968: (1, 4 [1: 621]; 122). Triumph 2.5 P.I.: 1968: (October only: 10,559); 1969: (1, 3, 5, 10–12 [10: 15,067]; 4,928); 1970: (1–5, 12 [4: 13,773]; 6,967). Triumph 1300: 1967: (1–8, 10–12 [11: 20,052]; 7,204); 1968: (1–9, 11–12 [11: 10,648]; 4,360); 1969: (1–5, 10–12 [20: 429]; 9,086); 1970: (1–2, 5, 7–8, 10 [2: 10,587]; 6,895). Triumph 1500: 1970: (9–12 [11: 27,654]; 6,168). Triumph Toledo: (9–12 [11: 26,824]; 9,929). Triumph Stag: 1970: (6–7 [6: 23,948]; 1,705). Triumph XL90 (futuristic concept, produced as model): 1967: (July only: 523); 1968: (3, 7 [3: 150]; 8).

Triumph (unspecified): 1967: (1, 3–4, 8 [4: 490]; 55).

Trojan 200 bubble car: 1962: (1–12 [3: 4338]; 521); 1963: (1–12 [4: 6391]; 645); 1964: (1–7, 9, 12 [3: 1,470]; 146); 1965: (February only: 10); 1966: (April only: 60); 1967–68: (none known); 1969 (dealer advertising): (December only: 152). (*Note*: Trojan car production ceased early in 1965, although engines continued to be made after that date).

TVR (marque and dealer advertising differentiated from 1967): 1965: (July only: 28); 1966: (4–12 [4: 307]; 113); 1967: (M: 1–2, 4–5, 8–9, 11–12 [1: 336]; 36 / D: 1, 3–5, 9 [4: 168]; 42); 1968: (M: 1–3 [1 + 2: each 24]; 21 / D: 3, 5–11 [9: 190]; 58); 1969: (M: November only: 76 / D: 1–3, 10–11 [11: 136]; 20); 1970: (M: 4, 8–12 [4: 271]; 178 / D: 1, 4, 8–10 [9: 298]; 57).

Unicar: 1958: (3–12 [4: 695]; 274); 1959: (1–2 [2: 74]; 47).

Vanden Plas: See *Princess*, above.

Vauxhall, 1958–66 (marque and dealer advertising): 1958: (1–12 [10: 49,682]; 20,775); 1959: (1–12 [2: 41,777]; 19,671); 1960: 1–12 [8: 46,677]; 22,937); 1961: (1–12 [9: 81,870]; 20,344); 1962: (1–12 [10: 62,348]; 20,560); 1963: (1–12 [9: 115,614]; 20,954); 1964: (1–12 [10: 132,335]; 28,117); 1965: (1–12 [10: 86,402]; 40,049); 1966: (1–12 [10: 70,934]; 36,086);

Vauxhall dealer advertising, 1966–70: 1967: (1–12 [6: 23,127]; 10,428); 1968: (1–12 [10: 20,217]; 10,068); 1969: (1–5, 10–12 [3: 18,580]; 8,330); 1970: (1–12 [10: 29,810]; 8,643).

Vauxhall full car range, 1967–70 (marque advertising): 1967: (3, 10–12 [10: 6,380]; 1,267); 1968: (4, 6, 8, 10, 12 [8: 450]; 72); 1969: (2, 5, 10–12 [5: 2,900]; 481); 1970: (1–2, 4–9 [7: 4,145]; 829).

Vauxhall: individual models and combinations of models, 1967–70 (marque advertising): Viva saloons: 1967: (1–12 [9: 26,330]; 6,564); 1968: 1–12 [10: 71,080]; 15,038); 1969: (1–5, 10–12 [2: 65,616]; 17,445); 1970 (HB): (1–9 [2: 72,040]; 13,922); 1970 (HC) (10, 12 [10: 114, 319]; 2,441). Viva estate cars: 1967: (6–11 [7: 17,459]; 6,792); 1968: (2, 6 [2: 3,195]; 54); 1969: (5, 11–12 [12: 18,794]; 3,465); 1970: (1, 3 [1: 6,934]; 3,005). Viva saloons and estate cars: 1969: (4, 10–11 [4: 19,495]; 8,108; 1970: (January only: 4,070). Victor saloons: 1967 (FC): (1, 4–8 [4: 6,383]; 3,205); 1967 (FD): (10–12 [10: 37,094]; 13,967); 1968: (1–12 [11: 16,360]; 6,255); 1969: (1–5, 10–11 [10: 30,073]; 12,053); 1970: (1–7, 10–12 [6: 26,609]; 12,755). Victor Estate Car: 1967 (FC): (January only: 64); 1968 (FD): (5–12 [5: 26,617]; 3,369); 1969: (2–4 [2: 1,142]; 350); 1970: (none known). Ventora: 1968: (2–6, 8, 10–12 [2: 17,566]; 4,037); 1969: (1, 3–5, 10 [5: 3,647]; 1,424); 1970: (1–2, 4, 12 [12: 15,040]; 4,715). Cresta saloons: 1967: (1–10, 12 [5: 11,746]; 2,864); 1968: (11–12 [11: 1,550]; 1,294); 1969: (2–5 [3: 2,424]; 1,128); 1970: (none known). Cresta police car: 1967: (April only: 180) (*Note*: Ford Zephyr police car advertised March 1967). Viscount; 1967: (1–5, 7, 9–11 [4: 6,789]; 2,425); 1968: (1, 7, 11–12 [1: 340]; 508); 1969: (1–2 [1: 380]; 330); 1970: (none known). Cresta and Viscount: 1967: (December only: 3,640).

Vauxhall (unspecified): 1967: (September only: 13); 1968: (4–6 [5 + 6: each 308]; 115); 1969: (May only: 98); 1970: (1–2, 11 [2: 2,851]; 421).

Vauxhall and **Bedford** combined advertising, 1958–67 (marque and dealer advertising): 1958: (1–12 [5: 9,955]; 530); 1959: (1–12 [10: 1,051]; 449); 1960: (1–12 [6: 10,741]; 938); 1961: (1–12 [11: 3,173]; 1,115); 1962: (1–12 [4: 2,625]; 872); 1963: (1–12 [11: 2,375]; 1,062); 1964: (1–12 [6: 2,742]; 1,292); 1965: (1–12 [11: 2,389]; 1,470); 1966: (1–12 [1; 2,432]; 1,339); 1967 (marque only): (January only: 110).

Vauxhall and **Bedford** combined dealer advertising, 1967–70: 1967: (1–12 [9: 6,628]; 1,209); 1968: (1–12 [1: 2,279]; 1,304); 1969: (1–5, 10–12 [1: 2,346]; 1,040); 1970: (1–12 [7: 1,488]; 511).

Vauxhall and **Bedford** Service, 1967–69 (marque advertising): 1967: (2–5, 7–12 [10: 846]; 194); 1968: (1–9, 11–12 [7: 769]); 1969: (1–3, 5 [2: 262]; 133); 1970: (none known, but advertising for service might be included in unspecified Vauxhall advertising above, or have transferred to dealer advertising for 1970).

Vauxhall and **Bedford** used vehicles, 1963–65 (marque advertising): 1963: (3–4, 6, 10–11 [3: 12,761]; 661); 1964: (1–6, 8, 10–12 [4: 8,274]; 2,535); 1965: (1–2, 4, 6–8, 10–12 [11: 2,389]; 306); 1966: (1–4, 6 [1: 1,217]; 56).

Vauxhall and **Bedford** Quality Tested used vehicles (marque and dealer advertising): 1966 (M +/or D: October only: 54); 1967: (M: 2, 4, 6, 8–12 [10: 90]; 53 / D: 9–12 [10: 2,842]; 1,376); 1968: (M: 1–6, 8–11 [1: 111]; 59 / D: 1–12 [12: 1,662]; 770); 1969: (M: 2, 5, 11 [5: 65]; 32 / D: 1–5, 10–12 [1: 3,254]; 1,109); 1970 (M: none known / D: 1–12 [12: 1,662]; 770).

Volga: 1963: (December only: 251); 1964: (1–3, 5–8 [1: 266]; 63); 1965: (10–11 [10 + 11: each 88]); 1966: (1–4 [3: 32]; 16).

Volkswagen (marque and dealer advertising differentiated from 1967): 1958: (1–12 [10: 2,338]; 955); 1959: (1–12 [12: 7,529]; 1,026); 1960: (1–12 [9: 13,460]; 5,533); 1961: (1–12 [6: 10,923]; 6,733); 1962: (1–12 [3: 18,865]; 8,901); 1963: (1–12 [3: 24,375]; 10,313); 1964: (1–12 [9: 27,310]; 14,839); 1965: (1–12 [9: 36,094]; 12,713); 1966: (1–12 [3: 32,431]; 16,545); 1967: (M: 1–12 [3: 28,090]; 10,549 / D: 1–12 [3: 8,968]; 5,731); 1968: (M: 1–12 [10: 25,622]; 12,779 / D: 1–12 [10: 7,903]; 4,008); 1969: (M: see individual models, below / D: 1–5, 10–12 [5: 6,780]; 3,159); 1970: (M: see individual models, below / D: (1–12 [10: 8,803]; 3,686).

Volkswagen: individual models and combinations of models, 1969–70: Volkswagen range: 1969: (October only: 32,725); 1970: (4, 10 [4: 15,453]; 5,500). Volkswagen saloons (unspecified): 1969: (2–4 [2: 38,293]; 19,863); 1970: (2–3, 5–7 [3: 11,237]; 5,380). Volkswagen 1200 (Beetle): 1970: (2–3, 5–7 [3: 11,237]; 5,380). Volkswagen 1500 (Beetle): 1969: (3–5, 11–12 [5: 60,692]; 7,070). Variant and Fastback (1600): 1970: (5–6 [5: 9,500]; 4,500). Volkswagen 411: (2, 4 [2: 75]; 24).

Volvo (marque and dealer advertising differentiated from 1967): 1959: (1–12 [11: 767]; 200); 1960: (1–12 [10: 9,433]; 806); 1961: (1–12 [10: 8,046]; 2,538); 1962: (1–12 [10: 7,052]; 3,334); 1963: (1–12 [11: 12,012]; 4,774); 1964: (1–12 [3: 10,120]; 5,625); 1965: (1–12 [3: 9,494]; 4,668); 1966: (1–12 [7: 10,819]; 5,821); 1967: (M: 1–12 [4: 11,646]; 4,977 / D: 1–12 [10: 5,916]; 4,974); 1968: (M: 1–12 [3, 9,300]; 6,330 / D: 1–12 [10: 8,298]; 4,890); 1969: (M: 1–5, 10–12 [3: 9,862]; 6,689 / D: 1–5, 10–12 [2: 8,746]; 6,037); 1970: (M: 1–7, 9–12 [3: 11,484]; 6,100 / D: 1–12 [10: 10,955]; 5,529).

Wartburg (marque and dealer advertising differentiated from 1967): 1964: (5–12 [10: 1,249]; 686); 1965: (1–12 [8: 957]; 222); 1966: (1–12 [10: 2,225]; 584); 1967: (M: 2–12 [6: 1,019]; 626 / D: 1–12 [3: 2,053]; 731); 1968: (M: 1–11 [4: 1,322]; 649 / D: 1–12 [10: 3,207]; 913); 1969: (M: 2–5, 10–12 [3: 937]; 391 / D: 1–5, 10–12 [10: 2,855]; 934); 1970: (M: 3–7 [3: 1,313]; 802 / D: 1–12 [3: 905]; 258).

Wolseley, 1958–66 (marque advertising): 1958: (1–12 [12: 21,730]; 5,245); 1959: (1–12 [1: 17,744]; 4,944); 1960: (1–12 [7: 8,412]; 4,792); 1961: (1–12 [3: 14,762]; 7,239); 1962: (1–12 [5: 13,468]; 5,521); 1963: (1–12 [4: 7,586]; 4,383); 1964: (1–12 [6: 29,981]; 6,753); 1965: (1–12 [10: 9,242]; 5,283); 1966: (1–12 [5: 6,939]; 3,762);

Wolseley dealer advertising, 1967–70: 1967: (1–12 [5: 10,571]; 1,389); 1968: (1–12 [2: 1,782]; 896); 1969: (1–5, 10–12 [1: 2,269]; 438); 1970: (1–12 [3: 363]; 223).

Wolseley: individual models, 1967–70 (marque advertising): Wolseley 16/60: 1967: (1–3, 10–11 [10: 1,472]; 145); 1968: (3, 5–6 [5: 1,234]; 27). Wolseley 6/110: 1967: (2–5, 7, 10, 12 [4: 5,726]; 900); 1968: (1–2 [2: 252]; 70). Wolseley 1100: 1967: (3–6 [5: 4,714]; 2,997). Wolseley 1300: 1968: (1–3, 7 [2: 3,919]; 1,527); 1969: (2–5 [5: 9,580]; 2,889); 1970: (8–9 [9: 4,890]; 40). Wolseley 18/85: 1967: (5–12 [5: 8,391]; 1,253); 1968: (1–12 [4: 5,238]; 1,424); 1969: (1, 4–5 [1: 1,884]; 460); 1970: (5–10 [8: 11,968]; 3,412).

Other advertisers, January 1960 — December 1962 (*Note:* The figures for each year show (1) the numbers of advertisers in this category during each quarter; (2) the highest combined monthly expenditure by these advertisers for the year; and (3) their average monthly total in this category for the year. From January 1963 onwards, expenditures were given for individually for all advertisers, as above): 1960: (1–3/60: 7; 4–6/60: 11; 7–9/60: 9; 10–12/60: 11; [10: 603]; 222); 1961: (1–3/61: 9; 4–6/61: 11; 7–9/61: 14; 10–12/61: 13; [7: 656]; 411); 1962: (1–3/62: 16; 4–6/62: 7; 7–9/62: 7; 10–12/62: 11; [10: 521]; 152).

11B: Television Advertising, 1955–1970

The following figures are calculated from and summarize data given in a variety of forms, all very different from that below, in the *Statistical Review of TV Advertising,* published twice each year from 1956–58 and quarterly from 1959–62; and the quarterly (1963–66) later monthly (1967–70) journal, *Statistical Review of Press and T.V. Advertising* and its successors (see *Appendix 11A,* above). Estimated monthly expenditures were given from October 1958 onwards; prior to October 1958 expenditures were given for undivided periods of six months. The figures throughout were high estimates which did not take into account any discounts offered to advertisers; these discounts have been estimated at up to 40%, compared with the prices given on television companies' rate cards, in the medium's first few years: see Walter Taplin. *The Origin of Television Advertising in the United Kingdom* (Pitman & Sons Ltd., 1961), pp. 5–6. For example, Renault spent £28,900 on television advertising space in 1959*, which is just over 68% of the £42,400 estimated by the *Statistical Review.* Towards the end of 1969, the analysis of television advertising was confined to the London region, with the results being extrapolated to take into account advertising in other regions. Actual national expenditures for any cars known from other sources to have been advertised disproportionately in London during 1969 will therefore have been lower than the figures given. As with press advertising, figures for June-September

1969 are unfortunately not available, although (see below) relatively few car advertisements are likely to have been broadcast during this four-month period.

The modern reader is immediately struck by how few car advertisements were broadcast during the 1960s, even if some, such as Renault's pioneering campaign for the Dauphine, Vauxhall's early advertising for the Viva, and Standard-Triumph's humorous commercials for the Herald, which highlighted its very small turning circle, are still remembered by car enthusiasts today. Cars were advertised quite frequently on television in the late 1950s, as were oils and accessories, commercial vehicles, motor scooters and caravans. In the second half of 1961, however, there was a sudden decline in television car advertising. Not a single car advertisement was broadcast in the Motor Show month of October 1961, and only occasional advertisements were screened during the following few years. Tim Bell, who founded the advertising agency, Saatchi and Saatchi with the Saatchi brothers in 1970, recalls that "there was little…car advertising in the sixties, due to the secret cartel agreement between the manufacturers, and virtually no spirit advertising for the same reason": see Tim Bell, *The Agency Viewpoint 3*, in *British Television Advertising: The First 30 Years*, ed. Brian Henry (Century Benham, 1986), p. 441. The scope for car advertising was, however, quite limited by modern standards, as there was only one commercial television channel — ITV — during the 1960s. It began broadcasting in the London area on September 22, 1955, and the different regional companies making up the ITV network together achieved virtually complete national coverage by September 1962. Approximately 8.2 million homes could receive ITV in 1960, rising to approximately 17 million in 1970. Colour arrived on the non-commercial BBC2 in July 1967, and on ITV just a few weeks before the end of the decade, on November 15, 1969. In 1969 there were about 200,000 colour televisions in British homes (out of a total of approximately 18 million sets), and about 14 million colour televisons (out of a total of 20 million or so) in use by 1980: see Brian Henry, *The History*, ibid., pp. 24–25, 122.

The figures below are presented in the same way as those for press advertising in *Appendix 11A* above, except that all monthly expenditures over £500, and the two highest monthly expenditures where one or more is less than £500, are given in each case. All advertising is pure marque (rather than dealer) advertising except where otherwise identified, and advertisements for individual marques and models came from the same agencies as were used for their press advertising except for Vauxhall television advertisements of 1960–61. Marque and model headings are given in their original forms, so advertising for a particular model should be considered alongside that for the marque as a whole and for other models in the range. Commercial vehicles are not included except, perhaps, in *Standard products*, as the Standard range included light vans and pick-ups. The specific dates of advertisements recorded as having been broadcast during the six-month periods from September 1955 to September 1958 are not known.

*Ralph Harris and Arthur Seldon. *Advertising in Action*. London: Hutchinson/Institute of Economic Affairs, 1962, pp. 240–241.

Austin: 9/55–3/56: (18,289); 4/56–9/56: (16,549); 10/56–3/57: (7,458); 1958: (October only: 1,045); 1959: (1, 3, 7–8, 10 [1: 4,849; 7: 6,340; 8: 1,200]; 188); 1960: (August only: 257); 1961: (1–4, 6–9 [1: 2,664; 2: 7,240; 3: 5,600; 4: 6,470; 7: 660; 8: 780]; 165); 1962: (none known); 1963: (4, 9, 10–12 [4: 10,208; 9: 8,046]; 120); 1964: (1–7 9–12 [2: 12,993; 10: 11,338]; 91); 1965: (1–3, 6–8, 11–12 [2: 13,791; 12: 1,128]; 209); 1966: (1, 3–5, 10 [1: 444; 5: 10,608]; 24); 1967–70: (none known).

Austin and **Austin-Healey**: 5/58–9/58: (7,700).

Austin Seven (Mini): 1960: (5–6 [5: 13,821; 6: 1,186]).

Austin Seven (Mini) & **Morris** Mini-Minor: 1961: (March only: 3,210).

British Motor Corporation (BMC), 1956–67: 4/56–9/56: (1,100); 10/56–3/57: (2,200); 1958: (October only: 294); 1959: (none known); 1960: (10, 12 [10: 660; 12: 1,152]); 1961: (1–2, 4–5 [1: 6,294; 2: 6,010; 4: 2,314; 5: 1,038]); 1962–1963: (none known); 1964: (April only: 71); 1965: (1, 3–5, 10 [1: 1,090; 10: 80]; 26); 1966: (September only: 74) 1967 (M: none known / D: January only: 32).

British Leyland (BLMC), 1968–70: Full range: 1969: (October only: 9,524); Gauntlet used cars: 1970: (M: June only: 54,464 / D: June only: 16,650).

Chevrolet: 1964: (4–5 [4: 145; 5: 50]).

Citroën: 1959: (October only: 275); 1960–1963: (none known); 1964: (May only: 108).

Daf: 1966: (October only: 47).

Daimler: 1964: (2–5 [3: 120; 4: 110]; 38); 1965: (none known); 1966: (April only: 80).

Daimler and **Jaguar** combined advertising: 1964: (June only: 65); 1965: (October only: 64); 1966: (1, 3, 10 [1 + 10: each 32]; 8). 1967 (M: none known / D: January only: 56).

Datsun 1970: (M: July only: 3,364).

Fiat: 1961: (4–5 [4: 7,375; 5: 1,715]); 1962–1963: (none known); 1964: (2–4, 11–12 [2: 36; 11: 70]; 19); 1965: (3, 6–7, 10, 12 [6: 303; 12: 225]; 19); 1966: (January only: 90); 1967: (M: none known / D: 1–2 [1: 130; 2: 105]).

Ford: 9/55–3/56: (10,786); 4/56–9/56: (2,010); 10/56–3/57: (10,007); 4/57–9/57: (165); 10/57–3/58: (6,425); 4/58–12/58: (none known); 1959: (3, 4, 7–11 [3: 12,816; 4: 2,530; 7: 2,492; 8: 5,236; 9: 12,704; 10: 18,031; 11: 805]); 1960: (10–12 [10: 660; 12: 1,840] 240); 1961: (April only: 20); 1962: (March only: 1,690); 1963: (2–10, 12 [4: 4,855; 5: 4,806; 6: 995; 7: 2,299; 8: 2,494; 9: 3,077; 10: 3,340]; 15); 1964: (2–6, 9–12 [3: 1,247; 2 + 9: each 140]; 73); 1965: (1–6, 9–12 [2: 505; 3: 8,227; 4: 6,461; 5: 2,207]; 65); 1966: (2, 4, 6, 8–10 [2: 398; 4: 1,535]; 138).

Ford Consul Cortina: 1962: (9–11 [9: 35,075; 10: 555]; 180).

Ford Estate Cars: 9/55–3/56: (1,950).

Ford Motor Service: 4/58–9/58: (13,295); 1959: (April only: 9,230).

Ford Motor Show: 1958: (October only: 10,475).

Ford: individual models, 1967–70 (marque advertising): Cortina saloons: 1967: (March only: 4,560); Corsair saloons: 1967: (4–5 [4: 3,755; 5: 1,330]); Capri: 1969: (February only: 80,214).

Ford dealer advertising, 1967–70: 1969: (3–5 [3: 953; 4: 2,274; 5: 1,218]).

Ford A1 Used Vehicle Plan: 1963: (5, 8 [5: 1,468; 5: 10]); 1964–65: (none known); 1966: (3, 5 [3: 456; 5: 90]); 1967–68 (None known): (M: none known / D: April only: 284).

Heinkel: 1960: (October only: 330).

Hillman (see also *Hillman Minx*, below): 10/56–3/57: (4,367); 4/57–9/57): (none known); 10/57–3/58: (6,660); 10/58: (2,400); 12/58: (58); 1959: (March only: 12); 1960–1962: (none known); 1963: (11–12 [11: 312; 12: 24]); 1964: (1–3, 5–7, 9–12 [2: 790; 3: 483]; 78); 1965: (1–6, 8–12 [1: 1,896; 2: 2,409; 3: 4,245; 4: 18,066; 5: 10,240]; 125); 1966: (1–6, 10–12 [1: 1,272; 3: 65,047; 4: 957]; 44).

Hillman Minx: 4/56–9/56: (4,561); 10/56–1960: (none known, but see *Hillman*, above); 1961: (January only: 480).

Hillman: individual models, 1967–70 (marque advertising): Imp saloons: 1968: (2, 3, 5 [2: 72,354; 3: 44,667; 5: 53,651]). Minx 1500 saloon ("Arrow" type): 1967: (March only: 94). Avenger saloons: 1970: (2–3 [2: 52,948; 3: 36,131]).

Hillman dealer advertising, 1967–70: 1967: (January only: 233); 1968: (February only: 8,325).

Isetta: (10–12 [10: 450; 12: 1,225] 450); 1960: (1–2, 4, 6, 8, 10 [6: 288; 10: 160]; 90).

Jaguar: 9/55–3/56: (165); 4/56–1962: (none known); 1963: (9–12 [10: 75; 12: 60]; 30); 1964: (1–4, 6–9 [2 + 4: each 45; 1, 6, 7 + 9: each 30]; 15); 1965: (1–5, 11 [5: 80; 11: 72]; 25); 1966: (2, 11–12 [2 + 11: each 56; 12: 40]); 1967: (M: none known / D: February only: 40).

Lotus: 1967: (M: June only: 90).

Mercedes-Benz: 1964: (6–10 [8: 708; 9: 392]; 108); 1965: (2–7, 9–10 [2: 216; 3: 384]; 40); 1966: (October only: 30).

Messerschmitt: 1959: (May only: 300).

MG: 4/56–9/56: (438); 10/56–1964: (none known except *MG Magnette*, below); 1965: (9–10 [9: 80; 10: 10]); 1966: (July only: 10); MG Magnette (Mk III): 1959: (July only: 740).

Morris: 9/55–3/56: (17,940); 4/56–9/56: (850); 10/56–3/57: (11,227); 4/57–1958: (none known); 1959: (3, 7 [3: 4,828; 7: 600]); 1960–1962: (none known except individual models below); 1963: (10–12 [10: 510; 11: 390]; 250); 1964: (1–5, 8–12 [2: 530; 12: 1,042]; 240); 1965: (2–4, 7, 10–11 [2: 816; 3: 2,184; 11: 615]; 240); 1966: (1, 4–5, 7–11 [7: 88; 10: 55]; 23).

Morris (individual models): Mini-Minor: 1960: (6–8 [6: 3,625; 7: 1,300]; 75); 1961: (January only: 7,024); Minor

1000: 1961: (3–4 [3: 2,275; 4: 4,440]); Oxford Series VI: 1961: (2–4 [2: 3,000; 3: 5,040; 4: 1,290]).

NSU Prinz: 1959: (October only: 300); 1960–1963: (none known); 1964: (9–10 [9: 2,593; 10: 670]); 1965: (October only: 26); 1966: (May only: 210).

Reliant cars and 3-wheelers: 1965: (May only: 40).

Renault (see also *Renault Dauphine*, *Renault Service* and *Renault Dauphine Service*, below): 4/57–9/57: (2,565); 10/57–3/58: (4,865); 10/58: (2,000); 11/58: (1,710); 12/58: (1,510); 1959: (1–7, 9–12 [1: 1,368; 2: 2,742; 3: 7,461; 4: 5,689; 5: 4,561; 6: 9,094; 7: 2,820; 9: 1,210; 10: 2,809; 11: 2,822; 12: 1,832]; 1960–1962 (none known); 1963: (August only: 264); 1964: (3–9 [3: 27,321; 4: 48,674; 5: 16,728]; 179); 1965: (1–5, 11 [4: 780; 5: 859]; 251); 1966: (none known).

Renault Dauphine (see also *Renault*, above): 1960: (1–3, 7 [1: 9,770; 2: 13,059; 3: 17,752; 7: 5,635]); 1961: (2–6, 12 [3: 52,235; 4: 35,960; 5: 27,143; 6: 1,675]; 210); Renault Service: 4/58–9/58: (1,596); 10/58–1960: (none known); 1961: (July only: 231); Renault Dauphine Service: 1960: (4–6 [4: 11,458; 5: 3,213; 6: 36,648]).

Riley: 9/55–3/56: (350); Riley One-Point-Five: 1959: (August only: 600).

Rolls-Royce: 1969: (M: 4–5 [4: 162; 5: 256]).

Rootes Group: 1960: (October only: 660); 1961–1963: (none known); 1964: (4, 7–10, 12 [7: 51; 10: 100]; 16); 1965: (1–4, 6, 11 [2: 129; 6: 44]; 12); 1966: (5–6 [5 + 6: each 9]).

Rootes Imp saloon range: 1968: (M: June only: 29,211); 1969: (1, 10–11 [10: 9,524; 11: 58,141]).

Rootes Group dealer advertising: 1967: (January only: 17).

Rover: 1964: (October only: 26); 1965: (July only: 28).

Saab: 1966: (1–2, 4–7, 10–12 [4: 45; 6: 469]; 11).

Simca: 1959: (6–8: [6: 1,036; 7: 1,305; 8: 2,121]); 1960: (5, 11 [5: 138; 11: 783]); 1961–1963: (none known); 1964: (2, 5–8, 11 [5: 141; 6: 993]; 49); 1965: (none known); 1966: (November only: 15); Simca car range: 1967: (4–5 [4: 250; 5: 1,750]).

Singer: 1964: (October only: 26); 1965: (2, 6–7, 10 [2: 210; 10: 1,035]; 10); 1966: (4, 8, 11 [4: 100; 8: 300]; 15).

Standard: 4/56–9/56: (3,431); 10/56–3/57: (55); 10/57–3/58: (3,665); Standard cars & Ferguson tractor: 10/57–3/58: (2,940); Standard products: 9/55–3/56: (550); Ensign: 4/58–9/58: (300); Vanguard: 1958: (October only: 1,000); Standard & Triumph: 1960: (October only: 660).

Stirling: 1958: (October only: 735).

Sunbeam: 1959: (January only: 275).

Sunbeam-Talbot: 9/55–3/56: (110).

Toyota: 1970: (M: July only; 5,362).

Triumph (see also *Standard & Triumph*, above; and *Triumph Herald*, below): 4/56–9/56: (248); 10/56–1962: (none known); 1963: (September only: 328); 1964: (11–12 [11: 39,918; 12: 172]); 1965: (1–2, 4–5, 7, 10 [1: 35,869; 2: 501]; 35); 1966: (5, 11 [5: 13; 11: 80]).

Triumph Herald: 1959: (October only: 1,426); 1960: (September only: 410); 1961: (April only: 8,277).

Triumph dealer advertising, 1967–70: 1967: (February only: 20).

Vauxhall: 9/55–3/56: (3,900); 10/56–3/57: (10,143); 4/57–1958: (none known); 1959: (February only: 6,283); 1960 (5, 10 [5: 16; 10: 2,828: both direct advertising); 1961; (September only: 19,498: direct advertising); 1962: (June only: 423); 1963: (9–12 [9: 21,616; 10: 3,510; 11: 627]; 12); 1964: (5–8, 10–11 [5: 246; 11: 173]; 57); 1965: (2–6, 8–12 [2: 1,245; 3: 3,802; 4; 6,232; 5; 3,354; 8: 642; 11: 737]; 307); 1966: (1–10, 12: [2: 805; 4: 1,053; 5: 1,646; 9: 29,363; 12: 3,932]; 174).

Vauxhall: individual models, 1967–70: 1967: (5–7, 10–12 [5: 530; 10: 1,000]; 320); 1968: (1–2 [1: 800; 2: 750]); 1969: (none known); 1970 (HC): (October only: 93,074). Victor saloons: 1967: (5–8, 11–12 [5: 1,180; 6: 1,980; 7: 600; 8: 860;

9: 2,110; 12: 550]); 1968: (1–4 [1: 1,310; 2: 1,000; 3: 1,780; 4: 880]); 1969: (May only: 464). Viscount: 1967: (5–11 [5; 1,290; 7: 560; 10: 760]; 320); 1968: (February only: 450).

Volkswagen: 1960: (8–9, 11 [8: 68; 11: 45]; 20); 1961: (3–5 [3: 470; 4: 512]; 34); 1962–1963: (none known); 1964: (2–4, 7–9 [2: 280; 3: 584]; 17); 1965: (August only: 366); 1966: (4–6, 10 [4: 3,920; 5: 6,944]; 55).

Volkwagen dealer advertising, 1967–70: 1967: (1–2 [1: 143; 2: 272]).

Volvo: 1965: (11–12 [12: 233]; 12); 1966: (5–11 [9: 1,570; 10: 325]; 24); 1967–68: (none known); 1969: (M: none known / D: May only: 247).

Wolseley 15/60: 1959: (August only: 600).

11C: Approximate Total Monthly Press Advertising Expenditures, 1958–1970, and Television Expenditures, 1955–1970

The figures in the table below are calculated from and summarize those given in *Appendix 11A* and *Appendix 11B* above. The combined expenditures of the undifferentiated "other advertisers" of 1960–62 referred to in the *Introduction* to *Appendix 11A* above, amounting to an average of £290 per month, have been divided equally between British and imported cars. Corrections to original figures notified in subsequent issues of the *Statistical Review* in its various forms have been incorporated. Known original mistakes, such as the mis-categorization of a new marque as British or imported, or the accidental inclusion of car manufacturer's parallel motorbike line, have been corrected.

	British cars (£)	Imported cars (£) (including British-built Citroën, Isetta & Renault)	Total (£)
1955–1958 (TV only)			
9/55–3/56	54,040	No known TV	
4/56–9/56	32,812	No known TV	
10/56–3/57	45,457	No known TV	
4/57–9/57	165	2,565	
10/57–3/58	19,690	4,865	
4/58–9/58	21,295	1,596	
10/58	16,949	2,000	
11/58	No known TV	1,710	
12/58	58	1,560	
Total	190,466 (av. 58,605 p.a.)	14,296 (av. 4,399 p.a.)	204,762 (av. 63,004 p.a.)
1958 (press only)			
January	149,794	11,265	
February	147,255	11,821	
March	184,986	13,080	
April	162,029	11,491	
May	239,486	9,893	
June	124,037	16,369	
July	129,761	16,908	
August	72,752	6,663	
September	180,293	15,128	

October	416,399	31,520	
November	213,276	15,842	
December	156,227	8,508	
Total	2,176,295	168,488	2,344,783

1959

January	164,313 (+ 5,124 TV)	14,155 (+1,368 TV)	
February	186,288 (+ 6,283 TV)	16,560 (+ 2,742 TV)	
March	209,145 (+ 17,742 TV)	28,561 (+ 7,461 TV)	
April	176,752 (+ 11,760 TV)	27,319 (+ 5,689 TV)	
May	173,205 (No known TV)	28,895 (+ 4,861 TV)	
June	91,266 (No known TV)	14,594 (+ 10,130 TV)	
July	80,595 (+ 7,860 TV)	9,561 (+ 4,125 TV)	
August	162,304 (+ 7,636 TV)	10,229 (+ 2,121 TV)	
September	238,920 (+ 12,704 TV)	20,504 (+ 1,210 TV)	
October	573,759 (+ 19,752 TV)	53,699 (+ 3,834 TV)	
November	178,718 (+ 985 TV)	28,999 (+3,272 TV)	
December	97,235 (No known TV)	23,536 (+3,057 TV)	
Total	2,332,500 (+ 89,846 TV)	276,612 (+ 49,870 TV)	2,609,112 (+139,716 TV)

1960

January	132,777 (No known TV)	31,839 (+ 9,920 TV)	
February	118,871 (No known TV)	38,932 (+ 13,659 TV)	
March	181,806 (No known TV)	51,716 (+ 17,752 TV)	
April	202,026 (No known TV)	75,386 (+ 11,499 TV)	
May	209,366 (+ 13,837 TV)	77,686 (+ 3,351 TV)	
June	187,337 (+ 4,811 TV)	66,006 (+ 36,936 TV)	
July	212,988 (+ 1,300 TV)	41,314 (+ 5,635 TV)	
August	172,845 (+ 332 TV)	18,474 (+ 86 TV)	
September	207,237 (+ 2,700 TV)	43,029 (+ 20 TV)	
October	538,699 (+ 5,723 TV)	61,787 (+ 490 TV)	
November	204,389 (+ 240 TV)	20,411 (+ 828 TV)	
December	186,716 (+ 2,992 TV)	14,159 (No known TV)	
Total	2,555,057 (+ 31,935 TV)	540,739 (+ 100,176 TV)	3,095,796 (+ 132,111 TV)

1961

January	219,969 (+ 16,462 TV)	40,841 (No known TV)	
February	244,727 (+ 16,250 TV)	36,608 (+ 210 TV)	
March	279,063 (+ 16, 125 TV)	58,007 (+ 52,705 TV)	
April	363,613 (+ 22,811 TV)	73,703 (+ 43,847 TV)	
May	214,930 (+ 1,038 TV)	80,468 (+ 28,892 TV)	
June	315,019 (+ 180 TV)	52,765 (+ 1,675 TV)	
July	200,308 (+ 660 TV)	26,039 (+ 231 TV)	
August	104,044 (+ 780 TV)	16,370 (No known TV)	
September	221,701 (+ 19,648 TV)	26,053 (No known TV)	
October	445,784 (No known TV)	44,766 (No known TV)	
November	251,527 (No known TV)	28,529 (No known TV)	
December	186,110 (No known TV)	14,337 (+ 210 TV)	
Total	3,046,795 (+ 93,954 TV)	498,486 (+ 127,770 TV)	3,545,281 (221,724 TV)

1962

January	182,963 (No known TV)	24,476 (No known TV)
February	260,379 (No known TV)	35,483 (No known TV)
March	293,195 (+ 1,690 TV)	48,911 (No known TV)
April	376,379 (No known TV)	53,727 (No known TV)
May	291,517 (No known TV)	58,097 (No known TV)
June	191,915 (+ 423 TV)	50,849 (No known TV)
July	120,053 (No known TV)	24,213 (No known TV)
August	181,461 (No known TV)	14,462 (No known TV)
September	267,667 (+ 35,075 TV)	26,856 (No known TV)
October	510,921 (+ 555 TV)	58,087 (No known TV)
November	285,724 (+ 190 TV)	31,970 (No known TV)
December	137,170 (No known TV)	10,464 (No known TV)
Total	3,099,344 (+ 37,923 TV)	437,595 (No known TV)	3,536,939 (+ 37,923 TV)

1963

January	258,840 (No known TV)	23,928 (No known TV)
February	239,977 (+ 1,200 TV)	55,185 (No known TV)
March	365,789 (+ 6,155 TV)	67,920 (No known TV)
April	295,519 (+ 15,063 TV)	75,444 (No known TV)
May	324,827 (+ 6,274 TV)	77,912 (No known TV)
June	163,656 (+ 995 TV)	58,046 (No known TV)
July	109,583 (+ 2,299 TV)	40,617 (No known TV)
August	84,777 (+ 2,504 TV)	19,612 (+ 264 TV)
September	252,824 (+ 33,439 TV)	36,971 (No known TV)
October	696,310 (+ 7,510 TV)	76,511 (No known TV)
November	304,074 (+ 1,539 TV)	49,374 (No known TV)
December	167,003 (+ 451 TV)	23,998 (No known TV)
Total	3,263,179 (+ 77,429 TV)	605,518 (+ 264 TV)	3,868,697 (+ 77,693 TV)

1964

January	366,045 (+ 635 TV)	52,994 (No known TV)
February	353,891 (+ 14,558 TV)	64,831 (+ 366 TV)
March	388,149 (+ 2,489 TV)	100,011 (+ 27,905 TV)
April	404,218 (+ 823 TV)	116,846 (+ 48,843 TV)
May	406,606 (+ 852 TV)	110,214 (+ 17,027 TV)
June	288,711 (+ 391 TV)	100,160 (+ 1,187 TV)
July	204,561 (+ 216 TV)	71,516 (+ 572 TV)
August	176,011 (+ 109 TV)	48,723 (+ 790 TV)
September	258,893 (+ 406 TV)	70,927 (+ 3,294 TV)
October	698,949 (+ 11,827 TV)	113,636 (+ 730 TV)
November	306,749 (+ 40,180 TV)	49,373 (+ 94 TV)
December	157,470 (+ 1,743 TV)	33,864 (No known TV)
Total	4,010,253 (+ 74,229 TV)	933,095 (+ 100,808 TV)	4,943,348 (+ 175,037 TV)

1965

January	389,014 (+ 39,076 TV)	43,234 (+ 219 TV)
February	394,810 (+ 19,626 TV)	81,448 (+ 621 TV)
March	371,698 (+ 18,720 TV)	119,215 (+ 747 TV)
April	271,080 (+ 31,047 TV)	124,247 (+ 855 TV)
May	315,427 (+ 16,033 TV)	92,214 (+ 859 TV)

June	280,213 (+ 851 TV)	86,398 (+ 345 TV)
July	227,566 (+ 158 TV)	54,823 (+ 29 TV)
August	140,140 (+ 1,338 TV)	38,606 (+ 366 TV)
September	341,534 (+ 572 TV)	93,017 (+ 60 TV)
October	617,949 (+ 1,960 TV)	139,133 (+ 80 TV)
November	314,546 (+ 2,415 TV)	43,827 (+ 242 TV)
December	169,486 (+ 1,871 TV)	34,235 (+ 458 TV)
Total	3,833,463 (+ 133,667 TV)	950,397 (+ 4,881 TV)	4,783,860 (+ 138,548 TV)

1966

January	314,370 (+ 1,938 TV)	76,089 (+ 102 TV)
February	338,254 (+ 1,277 TV)	106,463 (+ 12 TV)
March	391,767 (+ 65,939 TV)	151,247 (No known TV)
April	452,301 (+ 3,810 TV)	130,002 (+ 3,965 TV)
May	358,597 (+ 12,480 TV)	114,913 (+ 7,291 TV)
June	317,432 (+ 339 TV)	91,999 (+ 529 TV)
July	182,196 (+ 173 TV)	78,106 (+ 38 TV)
August	198,395 (+ 373 TV)	43,019 (+ 10 TV)
September	281,029 (+ 29,543 TV)	95,892 (+ 1,570 TV)
October	633,491 (+ 618 TV)	121,851 (+ 499 TV)
November	262,768 (+ 216 TV)	74,125 (+ 85 TV)
December	151,417 (+ 4,059 TV)	27,492 (+ 12 TV)
Total	3,882, 017 (+ 120,765 TV)	1,111,198 (+ 14,113 TV)	4,993,215 (+ 134,878 TV)

1967

January	333,250 (+ 481 TV)	95,383 (+ 130 TV)
February	330,423 (+ 332 TV)	119,515 (+ 105 TV)
March	344,010 (+ 4,560 TV)	150,548 (No known TV)
April	300,924 (+ 3,755 TV)	158,712 (+ 250 TV)
May	307,931 (+ 6,815 TV)	172,107 (+ 1,750 TV)
June	326,491 (+ 3,185 TV)	134,887 (No known TV)
July	222,557 (+ 1,540 TV)	71,638 (No knownTV)
August	144,853 (+ 1,750 TV)	39,943 (No known TV)
September	371,942 (No known TV)	100,121 (No known TV)
October	601,541 (+ 1,760 TV)	151,889 (No known TV)
November	277,294 (+ 2,560 TV)	89,438 (No known TV)
December	158,674 (+ 1,000 TV)	48,147 (No known TV)
Total	3,719,890 (+ 27,738 TV)	1,332,328 (+ 2,235 TV)	5,052,218 (+ 29,973 TV)

1968

January	356,246 (+ 2,110 TV)	81,494 (No known TV)
February	280,599 (+ 74,554 TV)	126,255 (No known TV)
March	254,606 (+ 46,541 TV)	179,241 (No known TV)
April	276,969 (+ 880 TV)	145,823 (No known TV)
May	342,889 (+ 53,651 TV)	170,095 (No known TV)
June	296,133 (+ 29,211 TV)	132,768 (No known TV)
July	192,334 (No known TV)	108,090 (No known TV)
August	182,500 (No known TV)	74,507 (No known TV)
September	371,932 (No known TV)	103,956 (No known TV)
October	546,350 (No known TV)	173,469 (No known TV)
November	311,635 (No known TV)	103,157 (No known TV)
December	277,362 (No known TV)	48,501 (No known TV)
Total	3,689,555 (+ 206,947 TV)	1,447,356 (No known TV)	5,136,911 (+ 206,947 TV)

1969

January	270,329 (+ 101,246 TV)	78,656 (No known TV)
February	386,343 (+ 80,214 TV)	190,544 (No known TV)
March	404,995 (+ 953 TV)	286,882 (No known TV)
April	438,900 (+ 2,720 TV)	163,076 (No known TV)
May	348,138 (+ 1,938 TV)	217,788 (+ 247 TV)
June	419,241 (+ 2,051 TV)	129,159 (No known TV)
July*	213,494* (TV not known*)	138,342 (TV not known*)
August	239,926 (No known TV)	90,951 (No known TV)
September	283,194 (No known TV)	102,619 (No known TV)
October	586,979 (+ 19,048 TV)	196,324 (No known TV)
November	330,447 (+ 58,141 TV)	172,645 (No known TV)
December	173,500 (No known TV)	85,455 (No known TV)
Total	4,095,486* (+ 266,311 TV)	1,852,441 (+ 247 TV)	5,947,927 (+ 266,558 TV)

*Figures for July not available. These estimates assume that expenditure increased to the same extent in July 1969 over July 1968 as during the rest of the year as a whole. It is also assumed that there was no TV expenditure in July.

1970

January	184,719 (No known TV)	78,161 (No known TV)
February	429,012 (+ 61,273 TV)	140,818 (No known TV)
March	379,655 (+ 36,131 TV)	213,520 (No known TV)
April	421,538 (No known TV)	236,705 (No known TV)
May	385,483 (No known TV)	269,315 (No known TV)
June	388,684 (+ 71,114 TV)	129,721 (No known TV)
July	278,838 (No known TV)	102,501 (+ 8,726 TV)
August	212,243 (No known TV)	45,094 (No known TV)
September	190,550 (No known TV)	144,832 (No known TV)
October	624,494 (+ 93,074 TV)	207,656 (No known TV)
November	304,097 (No known TV)	158,463 (No known TV)
December	164,344 (No known TV)	68,705 (No known TV)
Total	3,963,657 (+ 261,592 TV)	1,795,491 (+ 8,726 TV)	5,759,148 (+ 270,318 TV)

Appendix 12

Ages and Incomes of Owners of New Fords in 1963

	Anglia	Cortina	Classic	Zephyr 4	Zephyr 6	Zodiac
Sample	504	394	291	263	345	367
	%	%	%	%	%	%
Age:						
16–24	4	5	5	2	3	1
25–34	21	18	21	16	17	17
35–44	26	34	26	37	34	35
45–54	23	27	27	32	28	26
55–64	14	13	13	11	14	12
65 & Over	3	3	1	2	2	4
Not stated	9	—	7	—	2	5
Income (£) (ABC1 = 1,000 +)						
Under 1,000	25	24	16	13	5	4
1,000–1,500	35	36	30	32	17	10
1,500–2,000	13	16	23	22	23	17
2,000–3,000	5	8	10	13	20	21
Over 3,000	3	2	5	6	20	22
Not stated	19	14	16	14	15	26
HJI* under 1,000 (C2DE**)	30	28	19	15	6	3
HJI over 1,000 (ABC1**)	70	72	81	85	94	95

*Household Joint Income (excluding the section of the sample whose income is not stated)
**Approximate categorizations, with conventional socio-economic categories converted to income bands.

The researchers concluded: "From these figures it is clear that the primary market for all models is among ABC1 households, of which there are approximately 5 million in the UK. And within these households, we believe our prospective purchaser to be primarily the man…[A]iming at this target audience of ABC1 men on a national basis entails the use of mass media which also penetrate deeply into C2DE households…. Comparing the [favourable qualitative attributes of press and

TV advertising] we conclude that although Press scores highest in terms of coverage and cost, its lead over TV is roughly equalled by the creative advantages and IMPACT of TV."

Source: The London Press Exchange Ltd. (Market Research Office). *Ford Motor Company Ltd: Draft of An Appraisal of Mass-Media for Passenger Car Advertising.* London: London Press Exchange Ltd., 1963. (History of Advertising Trust: HAT Archive).

Notes

Dates are given in the European form of day/month/year; i.e., 4/3/64 = March 4, 1964, rather than April 3, 1964.

Preface

1. In 1951 the population of the United Kingdom was estimated at 50.2 million, compared with 57.8 million in 1991 and 59.8 million in 2000: Jil Matheson and Penny Babb (eds.) *Social Trends No 32 (2002 edition)*. London: National Statistics/The Stationery Office, 2002, p. 28.

Part One — 1. Austin

1. For the background to the merger between Austin and the Nuffield Organization (which contained the Morris, M.G., Riley and Wolseley marques), and for the model ranges which followed, see Graham Robson. *The Cars of BMC*. Croydon: Motor Racing Publications Ltd., 1999, pp. 9–24 and 276–280. For a summary of many reasons for BMC's decline in the 1960s and for the nationalization of British Leyland in 1975, see also Dale Drinnon. "Signposts on the highway to hell." *Practical Classics*, August 2003, pp. 72–77. At the time of writing the Austin marque name is dormant and is owned by MG Rover.

2. See, for example, *Small Car*, January 1964, pp. 36–43 (1100s) and April 1964, pp. 45–53 (A60 Cambridge and sisters). For original 1961–63 BMC publicity films for the corporation and its products, reissued on videotape, see British Motor Industry Heritage Trust (BMIHT). *The Factory Films: The Original BMC Films*. Gaydon, Warwickshire: BMIHT, 2001.

3. The car is known to have been sketched and costed, and what is believed to be prototype was discovered in a scrapyard in 1990: see David Knowles. *MG: The Untold Story*. London: Windrow & Greene, 1997, p. 96. The car combined a conventional "Mini" rear with an MG grille in the manner of the Riley Elf and Wolseley Hornet, but would have competed with the Mini Cooper.

4. I.e. the "B" series engine first used in the M.G. Magnette ZA and ZB of 1953–58, and subsequently in models within the Austin, Morris, M.G., Riley and Wolseley marque ranges. This engine looked like that of the earlier Austin A40s of 1947–54 and was designed by the same team, but only a few parts were interchangeable: see Robson, *The Cars of BMC*, pp. 281–992; and Lindsay Porter. "The A, B — and D of Austin Engines." *Thoroughbred & Classic Cars*, February 1985, pp. 64–67. For the earlier Austin Devon and Somerset, see Stewart J. Brown and David Whyley. *Austin: The Counties Years*. Newbridge, Midlothian: Arthur Southern Ltd./The Austin Counties Car Club, 1992, pp. 11–17 and 36–42. For the career of Austin and BMC engine designer Eric Bareham, see Lindsay Porter. "Designer in the Shade." *Thoroughbred & Classic Cars*, June 1985, pp. 30–32.

5. See Jon Pressnell. *Morris Minor: Exploring the Legend*. Yeovil, Somerset: Haynes, 1998, pp. 74–84. See also Pedr Davis. "BMC/British Leyland Down Under." *Thoroughbred & Classic Cars*, March 1983, pp. 60–63 and 84; Jeff Daniels. "Leyland Might Have Beens." *Thoroughbred & Classic Cars*, October 1981, pp. 78–80; and Theodore Gillam. "Wizards of Aus." *Practical Classics*, De-

cember 2000, pp. 54–59 (covering Australian BMC and British Leyland cars from 1958–74).

6. For the advertising agents responsible for particular campaigns, see *Appendix 10*, pp. 330–336, above.

7. For summaries of the life and work of Alec Issigonis (1906–88) see, for example, Tony Dawson. "Father of the Mini." *Classic and Sports Car*, January 1985, pp. 31–34; Christie Campbell. "Sir Alec Issigonis and the Making of the Mini." *Thoroughbred & Classic Cars*, September 1979, pp. 16–19 (interview); Ronald Barker. "Issigonis." *Car*, December 1988, pp. 134–141 (tribute by distinguished motoring journalist and personal friend); Jonathan Wood. "Issigonis." *Thoroughbred & Classic Cars*, December 1988, p. 83 and January 1989, pp. 46–47 (extended obituary).

8. Barney Sharratt. *Men and Motors of 'The Austin'*. Yeovil, Somerset: Haynes, 2000, p. 127. Kay Petre's appointment received wide publicity beyond the motoring journals: see, for example, Courtenay Edwards. "Trends in Car Design" in *Daily Mail Ideal Home Book 1956*. London: Associated Newspapers Ltd., 1956, pp. 200–204 (includes photographs of a quarter-scale clay and full-size mock-up of the A40/A50 Cambridge under construction). For Kay Petre's career, see John Bullock. *Fast Women: The Drivers who Changed the Face of Motor Racing*. London: Robson Books, 2002, pp. 137–178. Between April 1953 and March 1960 over 20,000 Austin Somersets and Cambridges were built in Japan by Nissan, and the agreement under which they were made was crucial to Nissan's development and eventual autonomy: see Peter Grimsdale. "Announcing the 1953 Nissan Austin." *Thoroughbred & Classic Cars*, July 1991, pp. 58–61; Barney Sharratt. "Letter from Tokyo." *Thoroughbred & Classic Cars*, August 1994, pp. 96–100; Barney Sharratt. "Austin's Rising Son." *Thoroughbred & Classic Cars*, March 1995, pp. 72–76 (with interview with ex-Nissan MD, Teiichi Hara). Isuzu produced the Hillman Minx under a similar arrangement between 1955 and 1963: see Giles Chapman. "Rootes of an Empire." *Classic and Sports Car*, January 1997, pp. 92–96 (interview with Rootes' Ken Middleton, who oversaw the arrangement and ensured its success). An original 1954 Austin publicity film for the A40/A50 Cambridge, "I am a Car," has been re-issued by BMIHT on videotape with parallel cinema advertisements: see *Austin in the Fifties: The Original Austin Films*. Gaydon, Warwickshire: BMIHT, 2001.

9. For the A40 see, for example, *The Autocar*, 19/9/58, pp. 390–396; 8/7/60, pp. 56–59 (Countryman); *The Field*, 6/11/58, p. 843; 22/2/63, p. 347; *The Motor*, 7/3/62, pp. 154–157; 13/3/63, pp. 196–199; *Motor Trader*, 24/9/58, pp. 358–360; *Small Car*, May 1963, pp. 39–44 (with Ford Anglia and Morris Minor).

10. Barney Sharratt. *Post-war Baby Austins A30 — A35 — A40*. London: Osprey Publishing Ltd., 1988, p. 20.

11. Sharratt, *Men and Motors of 'The Austin'*, p. 164. The Farina family had established a body building concern in Turin in 1905, and the design company Carrozeria Pinin Farina was created by Battista Pinin Farina in 1930. In 1961 the name Pinin Farina was changed by decree to the single word, Pininfarina.

12. See the Bibliography, pp. 386–387, below.

13. See *The Autocar*, 16/1/59, pp. 68–71; 6/3/59, pp. 343–346; 20/1/61, pp.

100–103 (Countryman estate car); 6/11/64, p. 1007 (used car test); *Country Life*, 10/12/59, p. 1155.

14. Sharratt, *Men and Motors of 'The Austin'*, p. 167. For Farina's original Cambridge proposal, see *ibid.*, p. 166; or Anders Clausager. "Italian Dressing." *Classic and Sports Car*, July 1991, pp. 105–108. For the history of the range, see also Giles Chapman. "Oxbridge Blues." *Classic and Sports Car*, June 1986, pp. 86–87.

15. Michael Sedgwick and Mark Gillies. *A-Z of Cars 1945–1970 (2nd ed., revd. Jon Pressnell)*. Bideford, Devon: Bay View Books, 1993, p. 27. An A60 with automatic transmission was available, as was a diesel engine in the A60 or Oxford from November 1962. Total production of all derivatives of this style was over 850,000, with the Austin the most popular. For the A60, see *The Autocar*, 13/10/61, pp. 576–578 (with other BMC "Farina" cars); 9/5/68, pp. 14–16 (long-term assessment with Wolseley 16/60); *Automobile Engineer*, December 1962, p. 517 (diesel engine); *The Illustrated London News*, 3/2/62, p. 198 (Countryman estate car); 11/8/62, p. 230; *The Motor*, 13/12/61, pp. 778–782. The A55 Mk II was 14' 10" tall, 5' high and 5' 3.5" wide. The A60 was more powerful than the A55 Mk II (61 bhp versus 53 bhp) and faster (80.4 mph versus 78 mph and 0–60 in 19.8 seconds versus 23.6), with greater engine capacity (1622cc versus 1489cc), wheelbase (100.25" versus 99.25") and tracks (4' 2.5" versus 4' 0.87" at the front and 4' 3" versus 4' 1.87" at the rear): *Autocar*, 13/12/61 and 6/3/59: see this *Note* and sources in *Note 13*, above.

16. For the A99, see *The Autocar*, 14/8/59, p. 5; 21/8/59, pp. 49–53; 25/9/59, pp. 263–266; 19/5/61, p. 817A (estate car conversion by Windsor Motor Co.). For the later A110, see *The Autocar*, 10/7/64, pp. 72–76 (A110 Mk II); *The Field*, 20/9/62, p. 541. See also Mike Taylor. "Choice: BMC's 3.0-litre saloons reviewed." *Thoroughbred & Classic Cars*, July 1984, pp. 106–108. 15,162 A99s and approximately 26,100 of the A110 were sold: Sedgwick and Gillies, *A-Z of Cars*, p. 27.

17. For the Mini's evolution in the 1960s, see Chris Rees. *Complete Classic Mini 1959–2000*. Croydon: MRP Publishing Ltd., 2003, pp. 7–82; and Graham Robson. "Magic Mini." *Thoroughbred & Classic Cars*, September 1989, pp. 106–114. For the restoration of the oldest Mini surviving in its original form, see Jon Pressnell. "An Obsession with Originality." *Classic and Sports Car*, October 1991, pp. 82–85. For Mini production methods as surviving into the 1990s, see Gavin Conway. "Making History." *Classic and Sports Car*, October 1996, pp. 132–137. See also *The Autocar*, 28/8/59, pp. 93–97; 20/10/61, pp. 663–666 (Cooper); 10/9/65, pp. 497–502 (Cooper); 16/10/69, pp. 78–79 (Clubman); *Automobile Engineer*, August 1959, pp. 302–305 (general description); April 1961, pp. 125–134 (drivetrain); May 1961, pp. 162–171 (suspension, steering and brakes) and 188–191 (cluster gear machining); June 1961, pp. 210–217 (body design and electrical equipment); January 1962, pp. 30–31 (Moulton rubber suspension); *Country Life*, 21/12/61, p. 1589 (Cooper); 1/8/63, p. 275 (Cooper S); *The Field*, 19/7/62, p. 121 (Ogle Mini-G.T.); *The Illustrated London News*, 3/9/60, p. 408; 7/12/63, p. 966; *The Motor*, 7/8/63, pp. 36–41; *Motor Trader*, 26/8/59, pp. 58–60; 11/11/59, pp. 204–207; 3/5/61, p. 148 (aftermarket extras, including wheel spats/fender skirts); *Practical Motorist*, August 1964, p. 1348 (Speedwell Amal GT conversion); *Small Car*, June 1963, pp. 39–41 (with Hillman Imp); October 1963, pp. 35–45 (test of range); January 1965, pp. 17–19 (interview with Sir Alec Issigonis).

18. See *The Motor*, 1/5/63, pp. 65–66.

19. Mike Taylor. "Built to Order." *Thoroughbred & Classic Cars*, June 1984, pp. 38–40 (interview). In fact the idea to produce the de Ville came from Graham Arnold, later sales director for Lotus, who had been "drafted into the company by the parent group chairman, Fritz Swain." The cars were painted in the colours of customers' Rolls-Royces at the suggestion of Peter Reynolds, managing director of the company's Rolls-Royce and Bentley Division: see Graham Arnold. "Devil De Ville." *Classic and Sports Car*, September 1990, p. 22.

20. Giles Chapman. "Harold Radford." *Classic and Sports Car*, March 1986, pp. 78–79 (interview).

21. *Small Car*, October 1964, pp. 24–27. See also *Country Life*, 21/1/65, p. 121; *The Field*, 28/1/65, p. 177. Although Harold Radford recalled Peter Sellers as a customer for the Radford Mini, Sellers' original Hooper car is described in *The Motor* (see *Note 18*, above) as having "sham caning applied by Hooper's heraldic artist Geoff Francis."

22. See *Autocar*, 24/7/69, pp. 10–13 (Austin 1300); *Car*, July 1970, pp. 62–69 (Austin 1300 with Ford Escort, Hillman Avenger and Vauxhall Viva); *Country Life*, 7/11/63, p. 1209; *The Motor*, 11/9/63, pp. 62–63; 18/9/93, pp. 54–59; 30/7/66, p. 54 (Innocenti 1100); 29/10/66, pp. 117–119 (Countryman estate car); 21/10/67, pp. 170–172 (1100 and 1300 Mk 2); *Small Car*, January 1964, pp. 36–43 (test of Austin, Morris, MG and Vanden Plas versions). See also Mike Taylor. "Badge Engineering." *Thoroughbred & Classic Cars*, October 1989, pp. 106–109; Andrew Everett. "The One That Got Away." *Your Classic*, July 1994, pp. 42–49. Three Austin 1100 convertibles are believed to have been built by Jensen from Coun-

tryman estate cars: see *Thoroughbred & Classic Cars*, August 1993, p. 40. Six Morris 1300 convertibles and six MG 1300 convertibles were built by Crayford: see *Thoroughbred & Classic Cars*, January 1990, p. 128.

23. See Sharratt, *Men and Motors of 'The Austin'*, pp. 180–187; and Clausager, "Italian Dressing," pp. 106–107.

24. See *Road & Track Road Test Annual 1969*, pp. 33–35. For a colour illustration of the America, see *Autocar*, 16/5/68, p. iii. Approximately 16,391 Americas were sold in the United States in 1969, 13,634 in 1970, 6550 in 1971 and 1010 in 1972: *Standard Catalog of Imported Cars 1946–2002 (2nd ed., updated Mike Covello)*. WI: Krause Publications, 2002, pp. 107–108. The Austin America was also sold in Canada and Switzerland, and approximately 59,000 were built: Robson, *The Cars of BMC*, pp. 95–96. An adaptation of the Austin 1300 with restyling by Michelotti to the front and rear to produce a conventional saloon body was built in Spain as the Austin Victoria and Austin Victoria Deluxe; a similar car was produced in Australia and South Africa, and was known as the Austin Apache: see "Odd Triumph." *Thoroughbred & Classic Cars*, December 1988, p. 115; and Clive White. "Variations." *Classics*, October 1997, pp. 68–74.

25. See Lorenzo Ramaciotti. *Pininfarina Solitaires*. Milan: Automobilia, 1989, pp. 128–131; *Autocar*, 21/11/68, pp. 50–51 (1800 and similar 1100 prototypes); *Motor*, 19/10/68, (page unknown) (advertisement showing Pininfarina 1800).

26. Danny Hopkins in "Staff Car Sagas." *Practical Classics*, August 2003 and *passim*. For the development of the 1800 and 3-Litre, see Sharratt, *Men and Motors of 'The Austin'*, pp. 188–196. See also Clausager, "Italian Dressing," p. 107; Jon Pressnell. "Land Crab." *Classic and Sports Car*, January 1986, pp. 92–93; "Tasmanian Devil?" (author unknown) *Thoroughbred & Classic Cars*, June 1992, p. 81 (Australian Austin Tasman and Kimberley variants). A prototype Vanden Plas 1800 with a rear very like that of a Simca 1301 or 1501 was built but not produced in series: see Brian Smith. *Vanden Plas Coachbuilders*. London: Dalton Watson Ltd., 1979, p. 282; and Michael Ware. "Prototype Vanden Plas 1800." *Thoroughbred & Classic Cars*, September 1993, p. 31 (shows car as surviving). See also *Autocar*, 16/10/64, pp. 753–758; 23/10/64, pp. 868–872; 11/7/68, pp. 11–15 (Mk II); 31/7/69, pp. 8–10 (general review of estate cars including Crayford); *Country Life*, 5/11/64, p. 1209; *The Field*, 10/12/64, p. 1309; *Motor*, 30/7/66, pp. 45–46; 29/10/66, pp. 105–110; *Small Car*, November 1964, pp. 50–57.

27. Sharratt, *Men and Motors of 'The Austin'*, p. 193 (interview with Ted Price of Fisher & Ludlow, who built the 1800 body). Approximately 340,868 Austin 1800s, Morris 1800s and Wolseley 18/85s were built between 1964 and 1975: Sedgwick and Gillies, *A-Z of Cars*, pp. 27, 144, 231.

28. See Jon Pressnell. "It's No Barge!" *Classic and Sports Car*, January 1994, pp. 94–99 (interviews with BMC personnel involved). See also *Autocar*, 5/12/68, pp. 10–14; *Country Life*, 5/6/69, p. 1444; *Motor*, 21/10/67, pp. 145–149.

2. Ford

1. An analysis of figures published in 1959 by the Society of Motor Manufacturers and Traders (SMMT) shows that Ford and BMC respectively held approximately 26 percent and 42 percent of the British car market in 1958: Anders Clausager. "The Swinging Sixties" in Nick Georgano, Nick Baldwin, Anders Clausager and Jonathan Wood. *Britain's Motor Industry: The First Hundred Years (ed. Nick Georgano)*. Yeovil, Somerset: Haynes, 1995, p. 163. The market shares during 1965–1970 of Ford and those marques of the later British Leyland which in 1965 constituted BMC were: 1965: 26 percent (BMC: 36 percent); 1966: 25 percent (35 percent); 1967: 25 percent (29 percent); 1968: 27 percent (30 percent); 1969: 27 percent (30 percent); 1970: 27 percent (29 percent): *ibid.*, p. 164 (figures rounded to nearest 1 percent). During the same period Rootes and Vauxhall alternated in third and fourth places, each with shares of around 9 percent-13 percent: *ibid.* The fortunes of Ford *of* Britain as an semi-autonomous organization should nevertheless be distinguished from those of Ford *in* Britain, considered as a branch of the international company. The British company, which had been only partly controlled from America, was wholly taken over by its American parent in January 1961 while continuing with a measure of practical independence. The British operation was decentralized during the decade as it outgrew its original Dagenham base; and the formal creation of Ford of Europe in 1967 followed Anglo-German co-operation between Dagenham and Cologne in the development of the Transit van announced in 1965.

2. David Burgess-Wise. *Ford at Dagenham: The Rise and Fall of Detroit in Europe*. Derby: Breedon Books, 2001, p. 142. David Burgess-Wise was Manager of Ford's European Corporate History Office from 1986–1991.

3. In the event the last Popular 100E was made in June 1962; 126,115 were

built: Martin Rawbone. *Ford in Britain: A History of the Company and the Cars.* Yeovil, Somerset: Haynes, 2001, p. 68.

4. Jonathan Wood. *Ford Cortina Mk 1 1962–66; 1200, 1500, GT, Lotus.* London: Osprey Publishing Ltd., 1984, p. 25. Terence Beckett joined Ford in 1950 as a management trainee after graduating in engineering and economics, and would become Ford of Britain's chaiman in 1976.

5. Burgess-Wise, *Ford at Dagenham*, p. 142. As to the contrast between management styles at Ford and BMC/BL see, for example, Jonathan Wood. "Wheels of Misfortune." *Thoroughbred and Classic Cars*, July 1988. pp. 93–95; "Barber and BL" *Thoroughbred & Classic Cars*, August 1988, pp. 20–23.

6. Burgess-Wise, *Ford at Dagenham*, p. 159. The appointment was made shortly before the launch of the Cortina and represented a considerable change of public image. As Burgess-Wise recalls, "Colonel Buckmaster [who had joined Ford shortly after leaving Eton in 1929 and managed the Ford-France's Paris office in the 1930s] ran the French section of the Special Operations Executive, which organized resistance against the occupying German forces": *ibid.*, p. 86. Sir Patrick Hennessy felt, however, that "Buckmaster was too grand, and that as a consequence, Ford's public image was flagging": *ibid.*, p. 159.

7. Tony Dron. "After Henry: Walter Hayes." *Thoroughbred & Classic Cars*, January 1995, p. 49 (interview).

8. See *Appendix 10 and Appendix 11A*, pp. 330–349, above.

9. Burgess-Wise, *Ford at Dagenham*, p. 151. For a brief history of Kirksite and an account of its advantages and disadvantages, see Bill Munro. *Carbodies: The Complete Story.* Marlborough, Wiltshire: The Crowood Press Ltd., 1998, p. 48.

10. James Ensor. *The Motor Industry.* London: Financial Times/Longman, 1971, p. 88.

11. Richard Truett. "I Did it My Way." *Classic and Sports Car*, September 1989, p. 83 (interview).

12. *Ibid.*, p. 79. Roy Brown was Chief of Design for Ford of Great Britain from 1960–1965. See also Thomas E. Bonsall. *Disaster in Dearborn: The Story of the Edsel.* Stanford, California: Stanford University Press, 2002.

13. Burgess-Wise, *Ford at Dagenham*, p. 12. The factory had previously been used to make tramcars, and Trafford Park was Britain's first trading estate: *ibid.*, p. 13.

14. *Ibid.*, p. 14.

15. To 4173 during January-July 1930 and 2974 during January-July 1931, against combined sales of other makes of 12hp to 24hp models of 58,805 and 47,074 in the same periods: see Sam Roberts. *Ford Model Y: Henry's Car for Europe.* Dorchester: Veloce, 2001, p. 26.

16. Briggs was not simply a Ford satellite, however, and made bodies for, *inter alia*, Austin, Jowett, the Rootes Group and Standard. When, after the death of Walter O. Briggs in America, it seemed likely that Chrysler would buy the American company and so gain control of the Briggs in England, Ford bought the Dagenham operation to secure its body supply: Burgess-Wise, *Ford at Dagenham*, pp. 128–129. The factory at Trafford Park closed in December 1931.

17. Wood. *Ford Cortina Mk I*, p. 18.

18. David Burgess-Wise's description: Burgess-Wise, *Ford at Dagenham*, p. 125. 155,340 103E Populars were made: Rawbone, *Ford in Britain*, p. 298. Far too many turned over in adverse conditions and when drivers had to take evasive action. The author's father, who used one in the early 1950s, recalled finding it very unstable compared with post-war designs. For the story of the design from 1937–59, see Jonathan Wood. "At Eights and Tens." *The Automobile*, January 2004, pp. 33–37. The 1937 design was by Ralph Roberts, chief stylist at Briggs Motor Bodies and formerly of LeBaron, where he had been "responsible for Stutz's middle-market Blackhawk bodies. Walter Briggs, a former manager of Ford's body plant, had set up his Detroit-based mass production body business in 1909, and in 1926 he acquired LeBaron for its repository of bright young talent": *ibid.*, p. 34.

19. See David Venables. "Maurice Gatsonides." *The Independent*, 22/12/98 (obituary). For the Consul, Zephyr and Zephyr Zodiac Mk 1 see, for example, Graham Robson. "1951–56 Consul and Zephyr: Doing it for England." *Collectible Automobile*, December 2003, pp. 8–17.

20. Approximately 660,000 saloons and 16,300 convertibles were built: see Michael Sedgwick and Mark Gillies. *A-Z of Cars 1945–1970 (2nd ed., revd. Jon Pressnell).* Bideford, Devon: Bay View Books, 1993, p. 73. The convertibles, including a Zodiac model, were built by Carbodies of Coventry and were introduced in October 1956: see Munro. *Carbodies*, pp. 57–60 (Mk I) and 89–91 (Mk II). 1957 prices for the Mk II range extended from from £818 17s (basic Consul) to £1,310 17s (Zodiac Convertible). A Zephyr cost £916 7s. For road tests of the Mk II see, for example, *The Autocar*, 3/6/60, pp. 900–903 (Consul); *Country Life*, 12/9/57, p. 506 (Zephyr estate car); 17/11/60, p. 1181 (Zephyr); *The Field*, 27/9/56, p. 551 (Consul); 19/7/56, p. 123 (Zephyr); 26/1/61, p. 169 (Zephyr estate car); 1/8/57, p. 205 (Zodiac Automatic). Aftermarket styling accessories

included Styla-Fins, Styla Spinners and imitation wire wheel covers from K.F. Ward Ltd. of Birmingham in 1958 and, in 1961, a "continental kit" from H. & J. Quick Ltd. of Manchester. Many other accessories were available from various companies. Large, sheet-steel fins and headlamp hoods for the Zephyr and Zodiac Mk 1 were sold in 1958 by D.F. Lott & Co. of London. These made a black car look like a startled bat, and were not popular.

21. Lavinia Wellicome, Curator of Woburn Abbey: personal communication. Nevertheless, Woburn's owner, the Duke of Bedford, bought a Zodiac estate car, although the purchase is not known to have been connected with Ford's publicity. For photographs of this car (a "highline" model built before February 1959) outside Woburn Abbey, see Richard Wildman and Alan Crawley. *Bedford's Motoring Heritage.* Stroud, Gloucestershire: Sutton Publishing Ltd., 2003, p. 103. In America, a Zodiac cost $2321 (at port of entry) in 1956: *Standard Catalog of Imported Cars 1946–2002 (2nd ed., updated Mike Covello).* WI: Krause Publications, 2002, pp. 318–322. See also Martin Rawbone. "The Abbott Fords." *Thoroughbred & Classic Cars*, November 1987, pp. 52–54. For the wider Abbott story, see also Jon Mullins. "E.D. Abbott—The South's Finest?" *Classic and Sports Car*, June 1987, pp. 87–91.

22. Burgess-Wise, *Ford at Dagenham*, p. 137.

23. See, for example, the car shown in David Minton. "The First Meritocrats." *Classic Car Mart*, August 2003, pp. 8–14. See also Michael Allen. *Consul, Zephyr, Zodiac, Executive.* Croydon: Motor Racing Publications Ltd., 1990, p. 80.

24. "Continental coachwork: A Discussion of Some of the More Interesting Features of Bodies Built by Italian and Swiss Coachbuilders." (Author unknown) *Automobile Engineer*, April 1955, pp. 158–162.

25. This 1962 design, based on the Daimler SP250, was developed into the Reliant Scimitar coupes of 1964–70: see Brian Long. *Daimler V8 S.P. 250.* Godmanstone, Dorset: Veloce, 1994, pp. 121–123.

26. Burgess-Wise, *Ford at Dagenham*, p. 135.

27. *Ibid.*, p. 139.

28. *Ibid.*, p. 141; and see The Editors of Collectible Automobile. "1960–67 Ford Anglia: Angle By Engel." *Collectible Automobile*, February 2000, pp. 85–87.

29. *The Autocar*, 2/10/59, pp. 284–287. For a description of the car, see *ibid.*, pp. 292–296. For the development of the "Kent" design of engine used in the Anglia and subsequent British Fords see, for example, Jonathan Edwards. "'Kent'—The Engine From Essex." *Old Motor*, June 1980, pp. 26–30.

30. "Know What You Sell: No. 4—Ford Anglia." *Motor Trader*, 20/1/60, p. 81.

31. "Home Truths: Austin A40, Ford Anglia, Morris Minor." *Small Car*, May 1963, pp. 39–44. See also *Small Car*, November 1963, pp. 24–33 ("Giant Test" of standard and de luxe Anglia saloons and estate cars, and of 1198cc Super saloon).

32. 1,083,960 Anglia saloons and estate cars were built between 1959 and November 20, 1967, when production ended: Sedgwick and Gillies, *A-Z of Cars*, p. 74.

33. Wood. *Ford Cortina Mk I*, p. 43. For tests of the Anglia estate car see, for example, *Autocar*, 13/8/65, pp. 303–308; *The Field*, 5/4/62 (page unknown); *Practical Motorist*, June 1962, pp. 1086–1087.

34. See *The Autocar*, 25/9/59, p. 241 (Popular); 4/12/59, pp. 743–746 (Popular); *Country Life*, 29/12/60, p. 1606 (Prefect); *Motor Trader*, 7/10/59, p. 8 (Prefect). 126,115 of the Popular 100E and 38,154 of the Prefect 107E were sold: Sedgwick and Gillies, *A-Z of Cars*, pp. 73–74.

35. A famous declaration by the Conservative politician Harold Macmillan in 1959, the year of his election as Prime Minister, often rendered as "You've never had it so good."

36. See Burgess-Wise, *Ford at Dagenham*, pp. 140–141; Rawbone, *Ford in Britain*, p. 71; and Barney Sharratt. "The Slug Trail." *Thoroughbred & Classic Cars*, March 1994, pp. 92–97. For the first Consul Classic clay, see Kris Bubendorfer. *The New Zealand Ford Consul Capri and 315 Owners' Magazine*, www.mcs.vuw.ac.nz.

37. See Burgess-Wise, *Ford at Dagenham*, pp. 150–151; and Wood, *Ford Cortina Mk 1*, pp. 27–33. But it seems that the name nevertheless arose innocently: according to David Gay, Product Tuning Coordinator for Ford UK Styling from 1958 to 1969, "...the code name 'Archbishop' was...given to the...Mk 1 Cortina by N.F. ('Bow-tie') Harris, head of Product Planning. Three studios (Ford Cologne, USA and the UK) each produced styles which the management reviewed. [The 'Cardinal'] was in line with other [US] model projects, each with a code-name using US birds! 'Bow-tie' Harris misunderstood this concept and assumed an ecclesiastical context—hence his choice of 'Archbishop'": David Gay. "Archbishop's Name was for the Birds." *Practical Classics* (letter), May 2004, p. 21.

38. See *The Autocar*, 16/6/61, p. 947; 23/6/61, pp. 987–989 and 996–200; *Automobile Engineer*, June 1961, p. 222–223; *The Field*, 6/7/61, p. 37; *Motor Trader*, 24/5/61, pp. 236–238. 84,694 109E (1340cc) and 26,531 116E (1498cc) Consul

Classics were built: Sedgwick and Gillies, *A-Z of Cars*, p. 74. There were no station wagons except for 17 two-door saloons converted for the Kenyan police by coachbuilders Cassini and Hughes in Nairobi: Bubendorfer, *www.mcs.vuw.ac.nz.*

39. Burgess-Wise, *Ford at Dagenham*, p. 151.

40. For a photograph of filming in progress, see Giles Chapman. *The Worst Cars Ever Sold in Britain*. London: Sutton/WH Smith, 2001, p. 41.

41. Burgess-Wise, *Ford at Dagenham*, p. 151.

42. Rawbone, *Ford in Britain*, pp. 69–70.

43. *Motor Trader*, 20/9/61, p. 319.

44. *Standard Catalog of Imported Cars 1946–2002 (2nd ed., updated Mike Covello)*, pp. 323–324.

45. *Small Car*, June 1963, pp. 20–23 (test in Germany with VW Karmann-Ghia 1500). The contemporary Opel Rekord coupe was even more exaggeratedly long-tailed than the Capri but rather high-sided and far less rakish. See also *The Motor*, 10/1/62, pp. 925–927 (1340cc); 27/2/63, pp. 127–128 (GT); *Practical Motorist*, September 1962, pp. 50–51 (1340cc). 18,716 Consul Capris were made, including 7573 with the 1498cc engine, of which 1767 were GTs: see Sedgwick and Gillies, *A-Z of Cars*, p. 74; and Giles Chapman. "Capricious Coupe." *Classic and Sports Car*, April 1986, pp. 58–59.

46. For an early prototype, see Chapman, *The Worst Cars*, p. 41. For a later prototype, still with the original roofline but with different trim, see Rawbone, *Ford in Britain*, p. 99.

47. Burgess-Wise, *Ford at Dagenham*, p. 151.

48. See Giles Chapman. "Blue oval cult." *Classic and Sports Car*, April 1989, pp. 62–64. 25 Capris were used in development work for the Mechamatic gearbox. The extra performance of the Capri GT was not matched by its handling and stability, however: see *Small Car*, October 1963, pp. 50–51 (road test). For a description of the earlier (Hobbs) version of the transmission as fitted by Daimler to prototype Lanchester Sprites during 1954–55, see John Box. "Spritely to the End." *Thoroughbred & Classic Cars*, January 1996, pp. 90–93.

49. See *The Motor*, 19/9/62, p. 266; *Motor Trader*, 26/9/62, p. 547. 500 are believed to have been sold in Germany during 1962–1963: see Cersten Richter. *cersten.de/bynumbers/didyou.htm.*, 1999.

50. Iain Ayre. "Profile: Charles Thompson." *Ford Heritage*, Winter 1995, pp. 33–36.

51. For these sketches, see Allen, *Consul, Zephyr, Zodiac, Executive*, p. 104.

52. For the clay and the full-size mock-up, see Burgess-Wise, *Ford at Dagenham*, p. 135.

53. Burgess-Wise, *Ford at Dagenham*, p. 154.

54. For this proposal, see Rawbone, *Ford in Britain*, p. 100; and Martin Rawbone. "Z Cars." *Classic and Sports Car*, September 1986, pp. 74–77. For Thompson's ideas for the Frua car's grille and his rendering of some of Engel's ideas (which anticipate some production Lincolns and Mercurys of the early 1960s), see Allen, *Consul, Zephyr, Zodiac, Executive*, pp. 104–108.

55. For a sketch, *circa* 1959, by Charles Thompson with "Consul" nameplate and with vertical rather than canted fins, see Ayre, "Profile: Charles Thompson," p. 35.

56. Bonsall. *Disaster in Dearborn*, pp. 173–174.

57. Truett, "I Did It My Way," p. 81.

58. *Ibid.*, p. 83.

59. Graham Arnold. "Devil De Ville." *Classic and Sports Car*, September 1990, p. 22. For the original mock-up in ice blue with flush door handles and for the black, six-window prototype of the Zodiac Mk III, see Rawbone, "Z Cars," p. 75. For the black four-window Zodiac prototype, see Rawbone, *Ford in Britain*, p. 101.

60. *Motor Trader*, 18/4/62, p. 105. See also *Autocar*, 10/4/64, pp. 668–672 (Zephyr 6); 9/4/65, pp. 713–718 (Zodiac Executive); 24/9/65, p. 622 (used Zodiac); *Country Life*, 21/6/62, p. 1529 (Zodiac); 29/7/65, p. 283 (Zodiac Executive); *The Field*, 19/4/62, p. 779 (Zodiac); 13/12/62, p. 1241 (Zephyr 4); 22/8/63, p. 361 (Zephyr 4 automatic); 29/7/65, p. 259 (Zodiac Executive); *The Motor*, 18/4/62, pp. 399–402 (Zodiac); 2/5/62, pp. 494–497 (Zephyr 4) and 514–515 (range); 17/10/62, p. 437 (Hooper Zodiac); *Small Car*, June 1964, pp. 31–37 (Zephyr 4 with Fiat 1500L).

61. Geoff Owen. *Turning Back the Clock: The Life and Times of a Motor Trader*. Croydon: Fitzjames Press/MRP, 2000, pp. 172–173.

62: 106,810 of the Zephyr 4 were sold, together with 107,380 of the Zephyr 6 and 77,709 Zodiacs: Sedgwick and Gillies, *A-Z of Cars*, pp. 75–76. 4350 estate cars were built: David Burgess-Wise. *Complete Catalogue of Ford Cars in Britain*. Bideford, Devon: Bay View Books, 1991, p. 44.

63. Rawbone, *Ford in Britain*, p. 77. See also Wood, *Ford Cortina Mk 1*, pp. 27–63.

64. For the mock-up, painted ice blue, see Martin Rawbone. "Ford Cortina: Birth of an Institution." *Classic and Sports Car*, October 1992, pp. 104–106; or Rawbone, *Ford in Britain*, p. 102.

65. Rawbone, *Ford in Britain*, p. 79.

66. Ayre, "Profile: Charles Thompson," p. 35.

67. Jonathan Wood. "Archbishop to Cortina." *Thoroughbred & Classic Cars*, August 1983, pp. 10–11.

68. *Ibid.*, p. 11.

69. See Wood, *Ford Cortina Mk 1*, p. 73. See also *Autocar*, 10/1/64, p. 71 (automatic); 6/3/64, pp. 420–424 (Super automatic); 11/9/64, p. 523 (Crayford); 24/12/65, pp. 1344–1345 (Willment-developed GT); 11/9/64, pp. 508–510 (overview); 23/10/64 (1965 models); 8/1/65, pp. 58–62 (GT); *Automobile Engineer*, October 1962, pp. 372–373 (announcement); February 1963, pp. 61–63 (Super and Lotus); *Car*, August 1965, pp. 40–46 (1200 and VW 1200); *Country Life*, 23/7/64, p. 237 (Super automatic); *The Field*, 27/9/62, p. 589 (2-door 1200); 11/4/63, p. 666 (Super); 23/5/63, p. 981 (estate car); 19/9/63, p. 541 (GT); *The Motor*, 26/9/62, pp. 292–295 (2-door de Luxe); 23/1/63, pp. 980–990 (Super and Lotus); 3/7/63, pp. 44–47 (GT); 30/10/63, pp. 46–49 (estate car); 17/9/66, pp. 35–37 (Lotus Cortina); *Motor Trader*, 26/9/62, pp. 542–543 (announcement); *Small Car*, August 1963, pp. 32–39 (GT with Vauxhall VX4/90).

70. Burgess-Wise, *Ford at Dagenham*, pp. 160–161. For the story of the 1964 rally, see Graham Robson. "The Light Fantastic." *Ford Heritage*, January 1997, pp. 74–76.

71. In addition to the factory models, 42 Cortina Mk 1 convertibles were built by Crayford Auto Developments of Westerham in Kent, of which between 12 and 20 were sold in Britain while 30 formed a taxi fleet in Bermuda. A few, probably two, Crayford Lotus Cortina convertibles were also built: Martyn Morgan-Jones. "All Cut Up" [Crayford story]. *Classics*, November 2002, pp. 46–51; and Rawbone, *Ford in Britain*, p. 123. In addition to the convertibles, 19 cabriolets without rear quarter windows were built by Karl Deutsch in Germany to Crayford's specifications.

72. 331,095 Corsairs and 149,263 Mk IVs were built: Burgess-Wise, *Complete Catalogue of Ford Cars in Britain*, pp. 48–51 and 56–58.

73. Ayre, "Profile: Charles Thompson." p. 36.

74. For details of individual models, see *Autocar*, 10/12/65, pp. 1227–1232 (V4 GT); *Car*, July 1965, pp. 40–45 (1498cc with Vauxhall Victor 101); *Country Life*, 19/12/63, p. 1700 (1498cc); 20/1/66, p. 124 (V4); 30/3/67, p. 743 (2000E); *The Field*, 28/11/63, p. 1113 (1998cc); 16/12/65, p. 1317 (V4 GT, by S.C.H. Davis); 31/3/66 (V4 GT, by Lord Strathcarron); *Motor*, 2/10/63, pp. 93–104 (1498cc range); 19/3/66, p. 49 (estate and convertible); 7/1/67, pp. 15–17 (2000E). For the development of the V4 or "Essex" engine, see Jonathan Wood. "An Engine Called Essex." *Thoroughbred & Classic Cars*, February 1995, pp. 100–103. See also P. Waring. "Essex Man Writes." (letter elaborating on above article from personal experience of design and manufacture). *Thoroughbred & Classic Cars*, November 1995, p. 93.

75. Truett, "I Did It My Way," p. 83.

76. Ensor, *The Motor Industry*, p. 86. Geoffrey Pattie, account director at Collett Dickenson Pearce and the agency's joint managing director during 1969–72, recalls: "...in 1966 we had the opportunity to make a presentation to the Ford Motor Company who 'thought' they wanted a corporate campaign...[Ford's] existing advertising was designed to conform to strict rules about the preferred angles from which particular cars were to be photographed, the size of the logo in relation to the size of the advertisement and so on and so on. Only people in key positions seemed to be aware that Ford's problem was their image.... We made the presentation at the beginning of November 1966. The fact that Ford had asked for a corporate campaign made it clear to us that they were worried about their image...Although we pitched for a corporate budget, Ford gave us the entire passenger car account.": Geoffrey Pattie. "The Judo Solution" in John Salmon and John Ritchie (eds). *Inside Collett Dickenson Pearce*. London: B.T. Batsford, 2000, pp. 52–55. Imaginative advertising resulted: see the text and notes 79–99, below.

77. The Mk IV was quickly nicknamed "the slider": Ensor, *The Motor Industry*, p. 88. See also *Autocar*, 15/8/68, pp. 41–44 (Zephyr V4); 30/1/69, pp. 14–16 (Coleman-Milne Zodiac limousine); 2/10/69, pp. 2–7 (with Vauxhall Cresta); *Car*, May, 1966, pp. 23–27 (Zephyr and Zodiac V6s); August 1966, pp. 43–49 (with Vauxhall Cresta); *Country Life*, 19/5/66, p. 1285 (Zodiac); 18/12/69, p. 1670 (Zephyr V6 estate); *Motor*, 23/4/66, pp. 55–60 (Zodiac); 22/4/67, pp. 15–20 (Zephyr V6). In 1968, 25 cars with Ferguson four-wheel drive and anti-lock brakes including 22 for the Home Office were built for evaluation by the Transport Road Research Laboratory and police forces: see *Thoroughbred & Classic Cars*, April 1993, pp. 58–63; *Classic Cars*, November 1997, pp. 104–105; *Ford Heritage*, January 1997, pp. 48–52.

78. Ensor, *The Motor Industry*, p. 88. "Substantially" did not mean "sufficiently," however: nearly 50,000 MK IVs were produced in 1966, but only 18,406 in 1967; 24,744 in 1968; 19,828 in 1969; 18,925 in 1970; and 17,758 in 1971: Martin Rawbone. "The Dagenham Lincoln." *Ford Heritage*, March 1996, pp. 78–92. Production ended in December 1971.

79. When the pound was devalued against the dollar in 1968, Ford prepared

for up to 50,000 orders through American dealers. This figure was never reached, but sales of over 16,000 British Fords in 1967, nearly 23,000 in 1968 and approximately 21,500 in 1969 represented a fourfold increase over the previous general trend: see *Standard Catalog of Imported Cars 1946–2002 (2nd ed., updated Mike Covello)*, pp. 323–326.

80. See Paul Clark. "The E Experience." *Thoroughbred & Classic Cars*, July 1984, p. 66. Annual 1600E sales were: 1967: 2524; 1968: 11,385; 1969: 17,807; 1970: 17,501—which, added to kits supplied to other European Ford factories, amounted to a total of 58,582: *ibid.*, p. 66.

81. Rawbone, *Ford in Britain*, p. 123. See also *Autocar*, 16/5/68, pp. 11–15 (1300 de luxe); 25/7/68, pp. 19–23 (GT estate); 20/2/69, pp. 26–28 (1500 Automatic, long-term test); *Car*, November 1966, pp. 24–26 (range); February 1967, pp. 38–45 (1300, with Vauxhall Viva HB de luxe); *Country Life*, 1/12/66, p. 1483 (1300); 3/8/67, p. 283 (Cortina Lotus); 1/8/68, p. 298 (Savage); 14/11/68, p. 1288 (GT estate); *The Illustrated London News*, 16/11/68, p. 35 (Savage); *Motor*, 23/9/67, pp. 1–30 (Cortina supplement; various models and background) and pp. 63–68 (1600 test); 21/10/67, pp. 175–176 (1600E).

82. About 1100 Cortina Savages were sold: see Jeremy Walton. "Savage Mood." *Classic and Sports Car*, February 1986, pp. 43–45 (interview with the Savage's creator, Jeff Uren).

83. In the eight years up to 1965, spending on basic necessities such as food, drink and tobacco rose by 12 percent, while spending on cars rose by 300 percent: Ensor, *The Motor Industry*, p. 16.

84. See Chris Harvey. "After Anglia." *Car*, March 1986, p. 144; and Michael Allen. "Ford Escort Mk 1." *Thoroughbred & Classic Cars*, April 1993, pp. 34–42. See also *Autocar*, 28/3/68, pp. 3–4 (estate cars); 6/6/68, pp. 11–15 (Twin Cam); 16/10/69, pp. 124 (GT); *Car*, February 1968, pp. 35–37 (range); July 1970, pp. 62–69 and 87 (1300 Super with Vauxhall Viva, Hillman Avenger and Austin 1300); *Country Life*, 9/1/69, p. 72 (Twin Cam); *The Illustrated London News*, 27/1/68, p. 34 (range).

85. See Mike McCarthy, Jeremy Walton and Martin Buckley. "The Car You Always Promised Yourself?" *Classic and Sports Car*, May 1987, pp. 69–77.

86. "Capri 1600" (author unknown). *Road & Track Road Test Annual 1971*, p. 24.

87. Mike Taylor. *Ford Capri: 'The Car You Always Promised Yourself'*. Marlborough, Wiltshire: The Crowood Press Ltd., 1995, p. 35–59. For colour illustrations of early mock-ups, see Rawbone, *Ford in Britain*, p. 111.

88. Ensor, *The Motor Industry*, pp. 19–20.

89. *Ibid.*, p. 20.

90. See Taylor, *Ford Capri*, p. 7. Ford's official advertising agencies during 1969 are recorded in the *Advertising Statistical Review* as being J. Collings & Partners to March 1969 and Collett Dickenson Pearce thereafter.

91. Ensor, *The Motor Industry*, p. 20.

92. Taylor, *Ford Capri*, p. 45.

93. See *Appendix 11B*, p. 351, above.

94. Ensor, *The Motor Industry*, p. 21.

95. *Ibid.*, p. 21.

96. *Car*, February 1969, pp. 21–23. See also *Autocar*, 13/2/69, pp. 10–15 (1600GT); 10/7/69, pp. 8–12 (2000GT); 31/7/69, p. 13 (Crayford 3 litre engine conversion); 4/9/69, pp. 34–39 (2000 GT with Sunbeam Rapier H120); 16/10/69, p. 89 (Crayford convertible); 30/10/69, pp. 20–24 (3000GT XLR); *Car*, May 1969, pp. 56–61 (1600GT with Triumph Vitesse Mk 2); *Country Life*, 22/5/69, p. 1315 (1600GT); 8/1/70, p. 99 (3000GT XLR). Abbott of Farnham announced a Capri convertible at the 1969 Motor Show but, although 50 orders were taken, only seven cars were built: Rawbone, "The Abbott Fords," p. 54. Thirty-four cabriolets were subsequently built by Crayford: Rawbone, *Ford in Britain*, p. 123.

97. *Homes and Gardens*, January 1970, p. 84.

98. Burgess-Wise, *Complete Catalogue*, p. 64.

99. See Michael Frostick. *Advertising and the Motor-car*. London: Lund Humphries, 1970, p. 132. A second advertisement used the same copy with a picture of a silver-grey GT 40 parked on tarmac. This was one example of the way in which Collett Dickenson Pearce improved Ford's image: see Pattie, "The Judo Solution," pp. 52–53 and 55.

3. Hillman

1. From 1927, the brothers had been sole agents for Hillman in Britain and abroad, and both firms were under the practical control of the Rootes family from 1928 onwards. Whether Rootes took over Humber and then merged with Hillman, or acquired an interest in Hillman and then in Humber, remains unclear. But the two companies certainly merged at the end of 1928, and it "seems to be agreed…that Rootes had complete control and that Humber Ltd. was a

wholly owned manufacturing subsidiary from 1932": Graham Robson. *Cars of the Rootes Group*. Croydon: Motor Racing Publications Ltd., 1990, pp. 9–27. See also John Bullock. *The Rootes Brothers: The Story of Motoring Empire*. Yeovil, Somerset: Patrick Stephens Ltd., 1993, pp. 9–53; and "Rootes Review." *The Autocar*, 28/11/68, pp. 51–64.

2. Robson, *Cars of the Rootes Group*, p. 9.

3. *Ibid.*, p. 27. For the story of the Rootes Group and Chrysler in the 1960s see, for example, Stephen Young and Neil Hood. *Chrysler: A Corporation in Transition*. New York: Praeger Publishers, Inc., 1977, pp. 73–135.

4. F.T. Poulton. "This Plan Got 100 per cent Dealer Co-operation." *Business*, June 1931, pp. 282–283.

5. Bullock, *The Rootes Brothers*, pp. 54–60.

6. *Ibid.*, p. 59. For an inside story of Rootes public relations in the postwar years as recalled by the Group's PR chief at the time, see also John Bullock. "Scoop!" *Thoroughbred & Classic Cars*, January 1994, pp. 100–105.

7. Robson, *Cars of the Rootes Group*, p. 17.

8. See John Pressnell. "Fry's Impish Delights." *Classic and Sports Car*, March 2000, pp. 122–126. In December 1955 Billy Rootes objected to Studebaker's use of the Hawk name, which in the United States, Canada and elsewhere was registered to the Group and had been used since 1945 on the smaller Humbers. Studebaker-Packard's counsel replied that the work "hawk" would always be used as part of a compound name. There the matter rested until the Studebaker Hawk arrived in 1960; Rootes objected again, and that car became the Gran Tourismo Hawk for 1962. But the Studebaker did not survived beyond 1964, while the Humber Hawk remained in production until 1967: see Richard Langworth. *Tiger, Alpine, Rapier: Sporting Cars from the Rootes Group*. London: Osprey, 1982, pp. 56–57. For the 1953 Studebakers, see Michael Lamm. "Fashionably Late: The Story of the 1953–55 Studebaker." *Collectible Automobile*, February 2000, pp. 8–21. For the clay model of the Minx styled by Holden ("Bob") Koto and Clare Hodgman of Raymond Loewy Associates in London and for the model, originally badged "Hillman," that was developed into the Humber Hawk Series I of 1957, see Barney Sharratt. "Loewy's Man in London." *Thoroughbred & Classic Cars*, April 1996, pp. 88–92 (interview with former colleague of Clare Hodgman under Raymond Loewy, Tucker Madawick). For Madawick's earlier career, see Jim Farrell. "Tucker Madawick: Universal Designer." *Collectible Automobile*, June 2000, pp. 72–80 (interview). For the work of Loewy's London office, including designs for Rootes cars before and after the Second World War, see Patrick Farrell. "A Triple Start: 1937, 1947, 1969 — Loewy London 1934–1990." in Angela Schönberger (ed.). *Raymond Loewy: Pioneer of American Industrial Design*. Munich: Prestel-Verlag, 1991, pp. 161–171.

9. Barney Sharratt. "Roy of the Rootes." *Thoroughbred & Classic Cars*, May 1995, pp. 62–66. John Bullock recalls, "[A]s the wing line in elevation had to be retained [from the original four-headlamp proposal], small 'half moon' parking and turn signal lights were mounted above the headlamps which, though the subject of some criticism, were at least original." Bullock, *The Rootes Brothers*, p. 211.

10. See Mike Worthington-Williams. "Chrysler Casualty?" *Classic and Sports Car*, September 1984, p. 16.

11. For the Zimp, see *Small Car*, January 1965, pp. 20–23; A. Hitchcock. "Zimp Memory." *Classic and Sports Car*, December 1984, p. 12; Mike Worthington-Williams. "Hillman Zimplicity." *Classic and Sports Car*, October 1986, p. 18; and Mike McCarthy. "Zig Zag." *Classic and Sports Car*, December 1997, pp. 132–135. For the Zagato Mini, see *Automobile Engineer*, January 1962, p. 20.

12. For the "Series" Minxes, see *The Autocar*, 4/9/59, pp. 132–135 (Easidrive automatic transmission); 4/8/61, p. 163 (Minx 1600, Series IIIC); 11/8/61, pp. 195–197 (Series IIIC with Perkins diesel engine); 24/1/64, pp. 156–160 (Series V automatic); 24/7/64, pp. 160–163 (Rootes 1592cc model range); *Automobile Engineer*, May 1960, pp. 191–198 (Easidrive described); *Country Life*, 19/9/57, p. 552 (Series I convertible with Alexander performance conversion); *The Field*, 15/8/57, p. 285 (Series 1 Estate car); 16/9/57, p. 541 (Series II "Jubilee"); 13/2/64, p. 293 (Series V); 28/10/65, p. 877 (Series VI); *The Motor*, 6/6/62, pp. 703–706 (Series IIIC); 4/9/63, pp. 56–58 (Series V); 6/11/63, pp. 52–57 (Series V); 27/11/63, pp. 48–51 (Husky Series III); *Motor Trader: Service Supplements* to issues of 30/9/59, 30/12/59 and 27/1/60 (Easidrive); *Small Car*, August 1964, pp. 42–52 (Series V with Triumph Herald 12/50); May 1964, pp. 24–81 (Husky Series III with Skoda Octavia).

13. For the Super Minx, see *The Autocar*, 6/10/61, pp. 518–521; 14/2/64, pp. 296–300 (convertible); 27/11/64, pp. 1114–1118 (Mk II); *Automobile Engineer*, August 1962, p. 307 (convertible); *Car*, February 1966, pp. 42–47 (Mk IV with Ford Corsair V4); *Country Life*, 3/5/62, p. 1038; 14/5/64, p. 1196 (Mk III); *The Field*, 1/5/62, p. 889; 9/8/62, p. 314 (estate car); 31/1/63, p. 193 (estate car); *The Motor*, 14/3/62, pp. 194–197; 4/7/62 (convertible); 17/10/62, pp. 445–446 (Mk II); 2/4/66, pp. 21–26 (Mk IV); 3/9/66, pp. 15–20 (Mk IV); 15/9/67, pp. 14–18 (Mk IV); *Motor Trader*, 4/10/61, pp. 14–15; 4/7/62, p. 9 (convertible); 7/11/62 (Italian Super Minx); *Small Car*, September 1963, pp. 20–30 (Mk II range).

14. For the estate car, see Bill Munro. *Carbodies: The Complete Story*. Marlborough, Wiltshire: The Crowood Press Ltd., 1998, pp. 115–117.

15. *Small Car*, April 1963, pp. 8–9.

16. Nick Georgano, Michael Sedgwick and Bengt Ason Holm. *Cars 1930–2000: The Birth of the Modern Car*. New York: Todtri, 2001, pp. 369–370.

17. David Henshaw and Peter Henshaw. *Apex: The Inside Story of the Hillman Imp*. Minster Lovell, Oxfordshire: Bookmarque Publishing, 1999, p. 6.

18. *Ibid.*, p. 8.

19. Barney Sharratt. "The Slug Trail." *Thoroughbred & Classic Cars*, March 1994, pp. 92–97. When Saward later accepted an invitation to return to Ford, Ron Wisdom designed subsequent Imp variants: *ibid*.

20. Henshaw and Henshaw, *Apex: The Inside Story of the Hillman Imp*, p. 15.

21. Pressnell, "Fry's Impish Delights," p. 125.

22. See *The Motor*, 8/5/63, pp. 81–85. See also *The Autocar*, 24/9/65, pp. 611–612 (Super Imp); 22/10/65, pp. 849–852 (Super Imp); *Country Life*, 6/6/63, p. 1326; 6/1/66, p. 36 (Super Imp); *The Field*, 20/6/63, p. 1181; *Motor*, 5/3/66, pp. 49–54; 21/1/67 (Californian); *Small Car*, February 1964, pp. 33–41 (with Vauxhall Viva). See also Kevin Blick. "Little Wonder." *Classic and Sports Car*, December 1983, pp. 62–63.

23. Michael Sedgwick and Mark Gillies. *A-Z of Cars 1945–1970* (2nd ed., revd. Jon Pressnell). Bideford, Devon: Bay View Books, 1993, pp. 89, 182, 193.

24. Robson, *Cars of the Rootes Group*, p. 35.

25. Henshaw and Henshaw, *Apex: The Inside Story of the Hillman Imp*, p. 60.

26. Robson, *Cars of the Rootes Group*, p. 35.

27. Barney Sharratt, "The Slug Trail," p. 93.

28. See Mike McCarthy. "Day of the Hunter." *Classic and Sports Car*, February 1993, pp. 54–59.

29. See Sedgwick and Gillies, *A-Z of Cars*, pp. 90, 96, 183.

30. See *Motor*, 3/6/67, pp. 13–18. See also *Autocar*, 12/9/68, pp. 12–13 (Mk II and Singers); 21/8/69, pp. 2–6 (Hunter Mk II); 2/10/69, pp. 16–17 (GT); *Car*, October 1966, pp. 28–29 (Hunter); March 1967, pp. 43–47 (Hunter with Morris 1800); May 1968, pp. 34–36 (Hunter Mk II with Ford Cortina Mk II and Vauxhall Victor FD); *Motor*, 15/10/66, pp. 11–15 and 27–32 (Hunter); 28/1/67, pp. 20–21 (Minx); 7/10/67, p. 76 (Hunter Mk II).

31. David Burgess-Wise. *Ford at Dagenham: The Rise and Fall of Detroit in Europe*. Derby: Breedon Books Publishing Company Ltd., 2001, pp. 167–168.

32. Robson, *Cars of the Rootes Group*, p. 141.

33. Bullock, *The Rootes Brothers*, p. 238.

34. *Ibid.*, p. 238.

35. At the time of writing the Hillman marque name remains dormant and is owned by Peugeot.

4. Morris

1. See Ray Newell. "A Million Minors." *Thoroughbred & Classic Cars*, February 1986, pp. 40–42. For the early history of Morris production at Cowley, near Oxford see, for example, Graham Robson. "A-Z of Cowley." *Thoroughbred & Classic Cars*, January 1993, pp. 94–97. For personal recllections of William Morris (later Lord Nuffield), see Rodney Walkerley. "William Morris…Viscount Nuffield, the Irritable Tycoon, 1877–1963." *Thoroughbred & Classic Cars*, November 1977, p. 25. See also Jon Pressnell. "Morris Dies." *Classic and Sports Car*, January 1984, p. 4. The Morris marque was discontinued at the end of 1983.

2. At the time of writing, no national advertisement specifically for the Traveller is believed to have been published, although the Traveller was illustrated in Morris range advertisements in the 1950s and in BMC's 41-model line-up of October 1965. For some Morris Minor catalogues and advertisements, mainly from the 1950s, see Ray Newell. *Morris Minor: The First 50 Years*. Bideford, Devon: Bay View Books Ltd./Morris Minor Owners Club, 1997, pp. 38–45. For comprehensive illustrations of Morris Minor catalogues (as distinct from advertisements), see Jon Pressnell. *Morris Minor: Exploring the Legend*. Yeovil, Somerset: Haynes, 1998, pp. 70–73 and 105–108. For a breakdown of Minor production figures, see Tony Dron. "All-time Greats: Morris Minor." *Thoroughbred & Classic Cars*, July 1996, pp. 76–83.

3. Of 987,364 Minors built by November 12, 1960, 479,525 were exported. 101,246 went to Australia; 52,431 to the USA (mostly in the late 1950s); 35,432 to the Republic of Ireland (Eire); 34,639 to South Africa, 34,216 to New Zealand; 29,538 to Canada; 25,375 to Sweden; 20,356 to Holland; 16,405 to Malaya, and 14,213 to Denmark: *The Autocar*, 6/1/61, pp. 37–38. For the Minor, see also *The Autocar*, 8/5/64, pp. 876–880 (1098cc four-door); *The Field*, 13/9/56, p. 463 (803cc Traveller), 25/10/56, p. 751 (948cc four-door); 13/8/59, p. 277 (948cc convertible); 2/3/61, p. 399 (948cc four-door); *The Motor*, 9/1/63, pp. 882–885 (1098cc four-door).

4. The production car lost some of the prototype's sleekness. For illustrations of the Wolseley prototype and of the production Morris Six and Oxford, and for the story of their derivation from the Minor's design, see Ray Newell. "Forgotten Classics?" *Thoroughbred & Classic Cars*, February 1989, pp. 46–49. See also Graham Robson. *The Cars of BMC*. Croydon: Motor Racing Publications Ltd., 1999, pp. 135–144. For a proposed replacement for the Six based upon the Oxford Series II but fitted with an upright grille, see Jon Pressnell. "Oxford Circus." *Classic and Sports Car*, April 1991, pp. 105–106. For the Oxford Series II-IV and related Isis, see Mike Taylor. "Morris Motors." *Thoroughbred & Classic Cars*, October 1988, pp. 64–67; and Brian Palmer. "Oxford Revisited." *Popular Classics*, May 1992, pp. 24–29. For the Minor's design and development, see Paul Skilleter and Ray Newell. "Morris Minor: The Thomas Papers." *Thoroughbred & Classic Cars*, June 1988, pp. 45–61 (inside story of the Minor revealed by papers of Morris managing director from 1937, Miles Thomas); Barney Sharratt. "Morris Men." *Thoroughbred & Classic Cars*, April 1994, pp. 92–96 (interviews with the Chief Road Tester at Cowley, Joe Gomm and with Morris Motors Development Engineer and BMC Suspension Engineer, Cyril Hodgkins); and Christy Campbell. "Birth of the Morris Minor — Thirty Years On." *Thoroughbred & Classic Cars*, July 1978, pp. 45–61 (interview with Sir Alec Issigonis).

5. For many decades the Oxford Series III continued in production in India as the Hindustan Ambassador: see Peter Stevens. "Indian Summer." *Car*, April 1991, pp. 122–125. For the 1948–54 Oxford MO, see Jon Pressnell. "Rural Charmer." *Classic and Sports Car*, February 1996, pp. 92–95.

6. *Small Car*, May 1963, pp. 39–44. Drink-drive laws were introduced in Britain in January 1966 and the first breathalysers arrived in 1967.

7. See *The Autocar*, 8/5/59, pp. 681–684; 20/3/64, pp. 520–524; *Automobile Engineer*, April 1959, pp. 145–146; *Country Life*, 11/6/59, p. 1333; 19/10/61, p. 901 (Series VI); *The Field*, 26/3/59, p. 581; 15/12/60, p. 1219 (Traveller); 8/7/65 (page unknown) (Series VI); *The Motor*, 22/5/61, pp. 74–77 (Series VI); *Motor Trader*, 25/3/59, pp. 344–345; *Small Car*, April 1964, pp. 45–53 (Series VI with Austin, MG, Riley and Wolseley sister cars).

8. See John Heselwood, "All About 'The Mighty BRICK': History of the Mini in Australia." Queensland: Mini Owners' Club Inc., *www.coopers.itgo.com*; and *www.miniownersclub.com*.

9. See *The Autocar*, 16/9/60, pp. 408–410 (Traveller); 23/9/60, pp. 466–469 (Traveller); 22/9/61, pp. 430–432 (Super and Cooper); 14/8/64, pp. 314–317 (Cooper 1275 S); *Country Life*, 7/3/68, p. 544 (Mk II); *The Field*, 20/10/60, p. 737 (Traveller); 21/9/61, p. 535 (Cooper); 8/2/62, p. 251 (Cooper); *The Illustrated London News*, 12/9/59, p. 254 (Cooper); *The Motor*, 24/4/63, pp. 54–57 (Cooper S). See also Chris Rees. *Complete Classic Mini 1959–2000*. Croydon: MRP Publishing Ltd., 2003, pp. 7–82.

10. In 1950 Alan Lamburn, A.M.I.Mech.E., M.S.A.E. designed a car with a transversely mounted, 500cc, twin-cylinder, four-stroke, air-cooled engine, in which "[t]he crankcase, which also forms the housing for the transmission and final drive and the common oil sump for the engine and transmission, is an aluminium die-casting" as the design was described in *The Autocar* in September 1952. Later in 1952 Lamburn wrote to Issigonis at Alvis asking if the firm might be interested in his idea; Issigonis mentioned in his reply that he had read the article in *The Autocar* with great interest. It is not known whether Issigonis was influenced by the article when designing the Mini: see *The Autocar*, 5/9/52, pp. 1094–1097; and Jonathan Wood. "Small Miracle." *Thoroughbred & Classic Cars*, April 1984, pp. 86–89. Issigonis had joined Alvis in 1952 and returned to BMC at the end of 1955. For BMC economy car proposals in the 1950s, see Barney Sharratt. *Post-war Baby Austins A30— A35— A40*. London: Osprey Publishing Ltd., 1988, pp. 143–157.

11. See Malcolm McKay. "Smart Alec." [*Thoroughbred &*] *Classic Cars*, October 1997, pp. 124–128 (examination of recently discovered Issigonis papers auctioned by Christie's).

12. See Malcolm McKay. "Rubber Radical." *Thoroughbred & Classic Cars*, June 1995, pp. 73–76 (interview with Alex Moulton). An updated Mini (the "9X") was designed by Alec Issigonis and completed in 1968, but did not reach production: see Jon Pressnell. "Thoroughly Modern Mini." *Classic and Sports Car*, August 1998, pp. 158–163.

13. *The Motor*, 25/9/63, pp. 57–60 (12,000 mile report). See also *Automobile Engineer*, September 1962, pp. 328–337 (explanation of suspension by Alex Moulton); October 1962, pp. 370–372; *Country Life*, 24/11/66, p. 1386 (Traveller estate car); *The Motor*, 22/8/62, pp. 116–119; *Motor Trader*, 15/8/62, pp. 260–261; *Small Car*, January 1964, pp. 36–43 (test of Austin, Morris, MG and Vanden Plas 1100s). For a recent comparison of the Morris 1100 with the Morris Minor, see Jon Pressnell. "Back to Front." *Classic and Sports Car*, September 2003, pp. 106–111.

14. These films have recently been re-issued on videotape by the British Motor Industry Heritage Trust (BMIHT) at Gaydon, Warwickshire. For non-British advertising for the 1100, see *www.elevenhundred.com*.

15. See *Autocar*, 1/5/69, pp. 14–17 (1800S Mk II); *Country Life*, 17/7/69, p. 160; *Car*, March 1967, pp. 43–47 (with Hillman Hunter); September 1969, p. 73 (1800 modified by Taurus Performance Tuning); *The Field*, 8/8/68, p. 293 (Mk II); *Motor*, 2/7/66, pp. 23–28.

16. Barney Sharratt. *Men and Motors of 'The Austin': The Inside Story of Car Making at Longbridge*. Yeovil, Somerset: Haynes, 2000, p. 213.

17. *Ibid.*, p. 219. The Ital was the last Morris and, at the time of writing, the Morris marque name remains dormant and is owned by MG Rover.

5. Reliant

1. *Small Car*, January 1964, pp. 53–57.

2. See Andrew Nahum. "Tamworth Manifesto." *Thoroughbred & Classic Cars*, June 1985, pp. 96–98. See also Elvis Payne. "The Reliant Regal Mk 1— Mk VI." *www.3wheelers.com/regal.html*. This site includes details of subsequent Reliants and much information about three-wheelers in general.

3. The *1962 Scooter & Three Wheeler Yearbook* listed five three-wheelers in addition to the Reliant and Bond Minicar Mk G. These were the Frisky (Family Three, with Villiers or Excelsior engine); the Isetta (Standard, Plus and Superplus); the Messerschmitt (KR200); the Scootacar (Standard, De Luxe and De Luxe Twin); and the Trojan (200). These marques lasted respectively until 1964, 1963, 1964, 1965 and 1965.

4. Malcolm Bobbitt. *Bubblecars and Microcars*. Marlborough, Wiltshire: The Crowood Press Ltd., 2003, p. 84.

5. Mark Dixon. "Plastic Fantastic." *Practical Classics*, March 2001, pp. 44–49 (including interview with Ray Wiggin).

6. *Car*, November 1965, p. 43; *Small Car*, January 1964, p. 56.

7. *Ibid.*, p. 55; and *1962 Scooter & Three Wheeler Year Book*, pp. 73–75 (Regal Mk VI road test).

8. See *Autocar*, 20/6/68, pp. 35–39 (estate car); *Motor*, 12/11/66, pp. 33–38 (saloon).

9. Approximately 2600 Rebels were made, of which about 850 were exported: see *The Defiant Reliant, freespace.virgin.net/maureen.hayton/rebel/rebelhome.htm*. For Reliants generally, see Daniel Lockton. *Rebel Without Applause: The Reliant Company: Vol 1: From Inception to Zenith*. Minster Lovell, Oxfordshire: Bookmarque Publishing, 2003.

6. Singer

1. John Bullock. *The Rootes Brothers: Story of a Motoring Empire*. Yeovil, Somerset: Patrick Stephens Ltd., 1993, p. 199.

2. Graham Robson. *Cars of the Rootes Group*. Croydon: Motor Racing Publications Ltd., 1990, p. 90; and Kevin Atkinson. *The Singer Story*. Godmanstone, Dorset: Veloce Publishing Plc., 1996, pp. 207–232. For publicity drawing dealers' attention to newspaper advertising for the Hunter, see *Motor Trader*, 19/10/55, p. xlvii or 26/10/55, p. xv.

3. Bullock, *The Rootes Brothers*, p. 197. For details of the takeover and of prior negotiations, see *Motor Trader*, 21/12/55, pp. 413–414; 28/12/55, p. 433; 4/1/56, pp. 3–4; and Atkinson, *The Singer Story*, pp. 230–232.

4. An excellent example of this car is displayed at the Museum of British Road Transport in Coventry.

5. For the production Roadster of 1939–55, see Bill Haverley. "Fifties Modern." *Thoroughbred & Classic Cars*, June 1986, pp. 70–71. 18,666 complete SM1500 saloons and 542 rolling chassis were built between 1947 and 1954; Hunter production (1954–56) amounted to 4750 cars: Michael Sedgwick and Mark Gillies. *A-Z of Cars 1945–1970 (2nd ed., revd. Jon Pressnell)*. Bideford, Devon: Bay View Books, 1993, p. 180. For the story of the SM1500 and fibreglass SMX, see Giles Chapman. "Roadster to Nowhere." *Classic and Sports Car*, August 1988, p. 94. An SMX roadster survives at the museum of the British Motor Industry Heritage Trust (BMIHT) in Gaydon, Warwickshire. See also Jon Pressnell. "Middleweight Knockout." *Classic and Sports Car*, August 2003, pp. 150–153 (Hunter with Wolseley 4/50); and Mike Worthington-Williams. "Spotlight on Singer." *Classic Car Mart*, March 1994, pp. 36–39.

6. See Edward Briant. "My Grandfather's Hand." *Thoroughbred & Classic Cars*, October 1994, p. 115; and Singer S.M. Series Catalogue 112/D/50 [1950]. For the life and work of Harold Connolly, see Louis Connolly (ed.). *The Motoring Art of Harold Connolly*. Southsea, Hampshire: Icon Publications, 2003.

7. See *The Motor*, 23/1/57, pp. 1006–1009. See also *The Field*, 14/2/57, p. 245; *Motor Trader*, 26/9/56, p. 350; 3/10/56, pp. 4–5; and John Pressnell. "Tail Ender." *Classic and Sports Car*, December 1997, pp. 120–125 (Gazelle Series 1 with Series IIIC). See also Stuart Bladon. "Went the Day Badly." *Thoroughbred*

& Classic Cars, November 1984, p. 83 (story of a 1958 road test of a Gazelle Mk IIA convertible that did not go as planned).

8. Robson, *Cars of the Rootes Group*, p. 52.

9. See *The Autocar*, 17/3/61, pp. 415–418 (Mk IIIB); 15/5/64, pp. 930–934 (Mk V); *The Field*, 9/8/62, p. 281 (Mk IIIC); 9/4/64, p. 693 (Mk V); *The Illustrated London News*, 7/3/64, p. 370 (Mk V Automatic).

10. Bernard Lovell. *The Story of Jodrell Bank*. London: Oxford University Press, 1968, pp. 243–244. For photographs of the telescope, see also *www.jb.man.ac.uk/public/story/mk1.html*.

11. See *The Autocar*, 22/9/61, pp. 438–441; 2/10/64, p. 659B (Mk III); *Automobile Engineer*, September 1961, pp. 352–353; *Country Life*, 5/10/61, p. 758; *The Field*, 2/11/61, p. 825; *The Illustrated London News*, 19/8/61, p. 310; *Motor Trader*, 26/1/61, pp. 94–95; *The Motor*, 16/5/62, pp. 596–597 (estate car).

12. Bill Munro. *Carbodies: The Complete Story*. Marlborough, Wiltshire: The Crowood Press Ltd., 1998, p. 117.

13. David Henshaw and Peter Henshaw. *Apex: The Inside Story of the Hillman Imp*. Minster Lovell, Oxfordshire: Bookmarque Publishing, 1999, p. 68.

14. *Small Car*, March 1965, pp. 50–55 (Chamois tested with Fiat 850). See also *The Autocar*, 18/12/64, pp. 1254–1258; 30/1/69, pp. 18–22 (Mk II); *The Illustrated London News*, 3/7/65, p. 36; *Motor*, 19/11/66, pp. 25–27.

15. *Small Car*, March 1965, p. 50.

16. See *Autocar*, 30/1/69, pp. 26–28; *The Illustrated London News*, 4/2/67, p. 38.

17. *Homes and Gardens*, July 1969, p. 82.

18. Atkinson, *The Singer Story*, p. 249. At the time of writing the Singer marque name remains dormant and is owned by Peugeot.

19. The following Singers were produced from 1956–70: Gazelle Mk I: 4344; Gazelle Mk II: 1582; Gazelle Mk IIA — IIIB: 40,516; Gazelle Mk IIIC: 15,115; Gazelle Mk V: 20,022; Gazelle Mk VI: 1482; Vogue I: 7423; Vogue II: 20,021; Vogue III: 10,000; Vogue IV: 10,325; Chamois: 40,678; Chamois Sport: 4149; Chamois Coupe: 4971; "Arrow" Vogue: 47,655; "Arrow" Gazelle: 31,482: Sedgwick and Gillies, *A-Z of Cars*, pp. 180–183.

7. Standard

1. For microcars of the period see, for example, Malcolm Bobbitt. *Bubblecars and Microcars*. Marlborough, Wiltshire: The Crowood Press Ltd., 2003. For a description and explanation of the Laycock de Normanville overdrive, see Graham Robson. "Going into Overdrive." *Thoroughbred & Classic Cars*, June 1993, pp. 64–65.

2. See, for example, *Sport & Country*, 17/4/57, p. 352. This report mentioned that "the body design comes from the Italian firm, Vignale, of Turin." The car was also illustrated in *The Autocar*, 31/5/57, p. 740. At that time no plans had been announced for Frisky production.

3. Harry Webster. "Harry's Game." *Classic and Sports Car*, November 1990, pp. 60–65 (article assembled from interview tapes).

4. *Ibid.*, p. 61; see also Graham Robson. *Triumph Herald and Vitesse: The Complete Story*. Marlborough, Wiltshire: The Crowood Press Ltd., 1997, pp. 34–40.

5. See Jonathan Wood. "High Standards." *Thoroughbred & Classic Cars*, October 1986, pp. 99–103; Kevin Desmond. "Tyrant of Genius." *Classic and Sports Car*, February 1986, pp. 80–81; and Graham Robson and Richard Langworth. *Triumph Cars: The Complete 75-Year History*. London: Motor Racing Publications Ltd., 1979, pp. 9–157.

6. Barney Sharratt. "Raising the Standards." *Thoroughbred & Classic Cars*, May 1996, pp. 96–100.

7. 184,799 of the Vanguard Phase I were sold between 1947 and 1952: Michael Sedgwick and Mark Gillies. *A-Z of Cars 1945–1970 (2nd ed., revd. Jon Pressnell)*. Bideford, Devon: Bay View Books, 1993, p. 185.

8. See Sharratt, "Raising the Standards," p. 99. 85,047 Phase II cars, including 1973 diesels, were built from 1952–55: Sedgwick and Gillies, *A-Z of Cars*, pp. 184–185.

9. *The Field*, 19/1/56 (page unknown). See also *The Autocar*, 30/7/54, pp. 153–156 (Phase II diesel); 14/10/55, pp. 533–554 (Phase III); 26/4/57, pp. 551–553 (Phase III estate car); 21/7/61, p. 97 (used 1958 Phase III); 31/8/56, pp. 286–289 (Sportsman); *Country Life*, 1/10/53, p. 1056 (Phase II); 11/10/56, p. 776 (Sportsman); *The Field*, 3/1/57, p. 29 (Phase III estate car); 11/10/56, p. 639 (Sportsman); 7/11/57 (Ensign); *The Illustrated London News*, 4/8/56, p. 204 (Phase III); *The Motor*, 28/5/52, pp. 566–568 (Phase IA); 15/8/62, pp. 74–77 (Ensign); *Motor Trader*, 5/9/56, pp. 250–252 (Phase III estate car and Sportsman). For the contemporary smaller Standards (Eight, Ten and Pennant), see Mike McCarthy. "Standard Fare." *Classic and Sports Car*, September 1993, pp. 103–106.

10. Barney Sharratt. "Loewy's Man in London." *Thoroughbred & Classic Cars*, April 1996, pp. 88–92.

11. *Ibid.*, p. 91.

12. *Ibid.*, pp. 91–92. One proposal was a highly attractive styling model for the Austin A30 by Holden ("Bob") Koto, working under Loewy: see Barney Sharratt. *Men and Motors of 'The Austin'.* Yeovil, Somerset: Haynes Publishing, 2000, p. 110.

13. *Ibid.*, p. 92. See also Jim Farrell. "Tucker Madawick: Universal Designer." *Collectible Automobile*, June 2000, pp. 72–80 (interview).

14. Quoted in Sharratt, "Raising the Standards," p. 99. For the model, see Sharratt, "Loewy's Man in London," p. 90.

15. For the Ford/Simca design see, for example, Jon Pressnell. "Simca Takes Flight." *Classic and Sports Car*, September 1995, pp. 102–107. Simca bought the ailing Ford-France in July 1954; the new Vedette, still badged as a Ford, was announced at the Paris Show of that year.

16. Very few Vedettes entered the country. The only right-hand drive 1956 Simca Vedette Versailles known to survive in Britain was found by the author in a Sussex scrapyard in 1996 and subsequently rescued by longstanding Vedette enthusiast Guy Maylam: see *Classic Car Mart*, January 1998, p. 76. Until the early 1990s, post-war American cars discarded in the 1950s and 1960s by visiting servicemen could still be found, with British cars of a similar age and all far beyond restoration, at Prior's Scrapyard at Yaxham, Norfolk: see Liz Turner. "Tin Mine!" *Classic and Sports Car*, November 1986, pp. 42–44.

17. 901 Sportsmans were built between August 1956 and March 1958, and a further 61 cars (including 28 estate cars) were built with later Vanguard Vignale bodies and Sportsman trim during 1959–60: David Bowers. "Fell Runner." *Triumph World*, April/May 2003, pp. 52–54 (Sportsman restoration). Two Sportsmans were sent to the United States as demonstration models: *ibid.* The following other Vanguards were produced: 1955–58 Phase III saloon and estate car: 37,194; 1957–61 Ensign saloon: 18,852; 1962–62 Ensign De luxe saloon and estate car: 2318; 1958–61 Vignale Vanguard saloon and estate car: 26,276; 1960–63 (Vignale) Vanguard Luxury Six: 9953: Sedgwick and Gillies, *A–Z of Cars*, pp. 186–188. The regular Vanguard Phase III was updated for 1957 with an improved interior, hooded headlamps and chrome trim strips along the sides of the car; larger bumpers arrived for 1958. An Australian-assembled Phase III, with extra chrome and three-tone paint schemes, called the Vanguard Spacemaster Phase III, was launched in March 1956. It was updated in 1957 with unique trim and colours and in 1958 gained small fins on the rear wing tops above the tail-lights. Australians were also offered Vanguard vans and pick-ups, or "utes," with similar styling but separate chassis frames: see "Strine Standards." *Classic and Sports Car*, July 1992, p. 37; and "History: Australian Assembly." *Standard and Triumph Car Club of NSW*, www.users.bigpond.com/spacemaster1/oz.html.

18. Robson, *Triumph Herald and Vitesse*, p. 86.

19. S.C.H. Davis in *The Field*, 18/6/59, p. 1181. See also *The Autocar*, 20/2/59, pp. 268–271; 24/2/61, pp. 294–297 (Luxury Six); *Country Life*, 22/1/59; *The Field*, 17/11/60 (Luxury Six); 9/2/61, p. 255 (Luxury Six estate car); *The Illustrated London News*, 3/1/59, p. 38; 4/2/61, p. 200 (Luxury Six estate car); *Motor Trader*, 22/10/58, pp. 138–140 (Vignale Vanguard and Ensign); *Practical Motorist*, September 1961, pp. 56–57 (Luxury Six estate car). See also Jon Pressnell. "Vanguard's Last Voyage." *Classic and Sports Car*, February 1997, pp. 86–90; and Simon Goldsworthy. "High Standards." *Practical Classics*, September 2003, pp. 34–39.

20. For the code flags from A–Z, see Peter Kemp (ed.) *The Oxford Companion to Ships and the Sea*. Oxford: Oxford University Press, 1988, pp. 966–967.

21. For the story of a one-off Ensign built in 1959 with a Triumph 2.2 litre engine as suggested by Colin Chapman, see Peter Garnier. "Non Standard." *Thoroughbred & Classic Cars*, May 1984, pp. 27–29.

22. *Motor*, 21/1/67, p. 76.

23. Graham Robson. *Triumph 2000 and 2.5 PI: The Complete Story*. Marlborough, Wiltshire: The Crowood Press Ltd., 1995, p. 78.

24. *Ibid.*, pp. 19–63.

8. Vauxhall

1. Jeremy Dixon, *The Guardian*, 26/4/00.

2. Kenneth Ullyett. *The Vauxhall Companion*: London: Stanley Paul, 1971, p. 115.

3. Dixon, *The Guardian*, 26/4/00.

4. Or aesthetic rather than functional: see L.J.K. Setright. *Drive On! A Social History of the Motor Car*. London: Granta Books, 2003, p. 385.

5. They were naive in this, however, given that many artists and designers had eclectic tastes and enthusiastically, if selectively, embraced and developed

vernacular idioms. In England the relationship between social class, education, aspiration and ideas of "good taste" has always been complex: see, for example, Stephen Bayley. *Taste: The Secret Meaning of Things*. London: Faber and Faber, 1991, pp. 3–71. For an American perspective on longstanding general critiques of consumerism that have influenced patterns of consumption on both sides of the Atlantic, see Michael Schudson, "Delectable Materialism: Second Thoughts on Consumer Culture." in David Crocker and Toby Linden (eds.) *Ethics of Consumption: The Good Life, Justice and Global Stewardship*. Littlefield, Maryland: 1998, pp. 249–268.

6. Maurice Platt. *An Addiction to Automobiles*. London: Warne, 1980, p. 143. Nevertheless, Graham Robson records that Jones "was required to take direction from the Chevrolet studio under the able Clare MacKichan": Graham Robson. "1957–61 Vauxhall Victor: Pontiac's British Cousin." *Collectible Automobile*, June 2003, p. 67. The extent to which such direction was given in practice, and whether it was ever given directly or was always conveyed *via* Vauxhall's management, are not stated. Maurice Platt, M.Eng., F.I.Mech.E., M.S.A.E. became technical editor of *The Motor* in 1923 and joined Vauxhall in 1937.

7. Geoffey Charles. "Vauxhall Formula for Best Sellers." *The Times*, October 21, 1967.

8. Vauxhall Motors Ltd., *Vauxhall Cars since 1903 (revd. ed.)*. Luton: Vauxhall Motors Ltd., 1977, p. 18. General Motors bought 80 percent of Opel stock in March 1929 and increased the proportion to 100 percent by October 1931. In 1938 Opel produced 115,000 cars to Vauxhall's 32,224: Gerald Palmer. *Auto-Architect: The Autobiography of Gerald Palmer*. East Horsley, Surrey: Magna Press, 1998, pp. 83–84. For the Cadet, see the advertisement on p. 7, above. For the history of Vauxhall generally, see Len Holden. *Vauxhall Motors and the Luton Economy, 1900–2002*. Bedfordshire: The Bedfordshire Historical Record Society/The Boydell Press, 2003; and David Burgess-Wise. *Vauxhall: A Century in Motion 1903–2003*. Oxford: Vauxhall Motors Ltd./CW Publishing, 2003 (the latter available at the time of writing exclusively from Vauxhall Heritage Services Ltd. at www.vauxhallheritage. com).

9. "The Vauxhall Velox Model E." *The Motor*, 11/6/52, p. 632. In general outline the E-type looked like the 1949 Chevrolet, although the Vauxhall's rear wing line was much less pronounced than the Chevrolet's. The E-type's tail-lights and surrounding panelwork were unique and intriguingly sculpted. Both E-types were economical for their size, a fact highlighted in advertisements.

10. The 1957 Victor was 13' 10.5" long, 5' 2" wide and 4' 11" high with a 98" wheelbase and front and rear tracks of 4' 2." It weighed 2191lb. Its 4-cylinder, overhead valve, 1507cc engine, based on that of the earlier Wyvern, gave 52 bhp (gross) at 4200 rpm and 84.5lb/ft of torque at 2400 rpm: see *The Autocar*, 21/6/57, p. 862. Drive was through a leaf-sprung "live" rear axle and three-speed gearbox with column change and synchromesh on all forward gears. Carburation was by downdraught Zenith. Clutch release was hydraulic. Front suspension was by coil springs and wishbones. Performance figures given in *The Motor*, 6/4/57, p. 156 (and *The Autocar*, 21/6/57, p. 862) are: top speed: 72.5 mph (75); 0–50: 18 secs (18.6); 0–60: 28.1 secs (29.8); overall fuel consumption: 30.6 mpg (30.1). Claims in announcement advertising of a top speed of "over 75 mph" and a 0–50 time of 14.5 seconds continued to be published at least until September 1957. See also *The Autocar*, 1/3/57, pp. 272–275 (new model announcement); Michael Allen. *British Family Cars of the Fifties*. Yeovil, Somerset: G.T. Foulis/Haynes, 1985, pp. 167–173; Alan Earnshaw and Robert Berry. *Vauxhall Cars 1945–1964 (2nd ed.)*. Cumbria: Trans-Pennine Publishing, 2001, pp. 14–17.

11. *The Times*, 8/2/57. Rivals included the 1172cc Ford Prefect deluxe at £631 7s, the 1390cc Hillman Minx Special at £748 7s (and de luxe at £773 17s), the 1489cc Austin A50 Cambridge at £772 7s, the 1489cc Morris Cowley 1500 (a stripped Oxford Series III of which only 4623 were built compared with 58,117 equivalent Oxfords) at £779 9s and the larger, 1703cc Ford Consul at £781 7s: *ibid.*

12. *Ibid.*

13. Ray Legate. *Salute the Victor: 40th Anniversary of the F Model*. Trinity Publications/Classic Car Mart, 1997, pp. 5–7.

14. Platt, *An Addiction to Automobiles*, pp. 169–170.

15. *Ibid.*, p. 168.

16. Very few 1958–60 Rekords came into Britain as the car was not officially imported, although the author saw a good example in characteristic light yellow on the road in York, in the north of England, as late as 1990. The marque was advertised in the Republic of Ireland (Eire) from 1959. The 1958-style Rekord (P1), with panoramic front and rear screens, was sold in the United States by Buick dealers ("German Made...American Style..."), with the Victor being imported from September 1957 and sold by Pontiac dealers. The larger Opel Kapitän, rarely seen in the U.S. and, except for the odd example, not imported into Britain, was restyled with a panoramic windscreen and similar rear window in a 1958 ("keyhole tail-light") update of a 1954 body which had already been improved slightly for 1955–58. The design of the centre part

of the 1955–58 Kapitän's dashboard anticipated that of the 1957 Victor: see Jeremy Satherly. "Jahwohl Mein Kapitän." *Classic Car Mart*, September 1997, pp. 64–69. No convertible Victor was ever produced (although at least one enthusiast has subsequently converted a Victor 101 saloon), but in Germany in 1959, Autenrieth of Darmstadt made a few hand-crafted and individually detailed Rekord P1 convertibles with extended doors and lavish interiors at approximately twice the price of the standard car. From 1958 onwards, Opels generally had slightly more severe lines than the equivalent Vauxhalls. From 1975, new Vauxhall and Opel body designs were essentially shared while differing in frontal styling and other details.

17. See *The Motor*, 5/3/58, pp. 171–173 (announcement of estate car and Newtondrive).

18. *Country Life*, 31/7/58, p. 237; *The Motor*, 6/3/57, pp. 156–159; *The Field*, 6/6/57, p. 915; 9/10/58, p. 651; 9/4/59, p. 671; 28/12/61, p. 1305.

19. *The Autocar*, 21/6/57, pp. 859–862. For a contemporary analysis of Vauxhall body production processes, see *Automobile Engineer*, January 1959, pp. 31–38.

20. See Platt, *An Addiction to Automobiles*, pp. 172–174.

21. Frans Vrijaldenhoven, letter to *Collectible Automobile*, October 2003, p. 4.

22. Platt, *An Addiction to Automobiles*, p. 176.

23. Mike McCarthy. "Back in Time to Beaulieu." *Classic and Sports Car*, October 1991, p. 100.

24. See Graham Robson. "1958–62 Vauxhall Victor, Lost in the Shuffle." *Collectible Automobile*, June 1994, pp. 85–87; Graham Robson. "1957–61 Vauxhall Victor: Pontiac's British Cousin." *Collectible Automobile*, June 2003, pp. 64–72.

25. *The Times*, 1/1/58.

26. See *The Autocar*, 22/1/60, p. 154. For illustrations of the Envoy, see Earnshaw and Berry, *Vauxhall Cars 1945–1964 (2nd ed., 2001)*, p. 17 (F-type) and pp. 36–37 (FB). Victors exported to the United States were Supers rather than standard models: *Standard Catalog of Imported Cars 1946–2002 (2nd ed., updated Mike Covello)*. WI: Krause Publications, 2002, p. 808. For British cars assembled and sold in Mexico, including the Vauxhall Victor, see Nicholas Manning. "Mexican English." *Thoroughbred & Classic Cars*, December 1993, pp. 100–101.

27. *The Autocar*, 27/2/59, p. 310.

28. See *Modern Publicity 1961/62*. London: Studio Books/Longacre Press Ltd., 1961, p. 77.

29. Platt, *An Addiction to Automobiles*, p. 172. The 1958 Cresta was 14' 9.5" long, 5' 8.5" wide and 4' 10" high with a 105" wheelbase and front and rear tracks of 4' 6." It weighed 2646lb: see *The Autocar*, 2/5/58, p. 660.

30. One such car, with a 6" × 2" hole in the rear wing, was used by the magazine *Practical Motorist* for a feature on body repairs: see F. Jakeman. "Filling the Gap." *Practical Motorist*, May 1965, p. 993.

31. Quoted by Daimler historian Brian Long from *Driving Member*, the magazine of the Daimler and Lanchester Owners Club in Brian Long. *Daimler V8 S.P. 250*. Godmanstone, Dorset: Veloce, 1994, pp. 18–19. In 1958 Daimler considered adapting the PA body and fitting it with a V8 engine and luxurious interior to make a Daimler saloon. Although a running prototype was built, the project did not proceed far: *ibid.*, pp. 15–20.

32. See *Thoroughbred & Classic Cars*, December 1988, p. 108. See also *The Autocar*, 15/5/59, pp. 716–719 (test of same car). The only known surviving "three window" Friary estate was found in a parlous state by enthusiast John Ankerman in 1988: see *Your Classic*, February 1990, pp. 24–30. For a test of the original Cresta PA, see *The Autocar*, 2/5/58, pp. 657–660. For a detailed description and photographs of completely original, low-mileage 1959 Cresta saloon, see *Popular Classics*, June 1996, pp. 6–10.

33. In 1958, 142,933 new cars were registered in Britain in the 1400cc-1600cc capacity groups compared with 64,958 in the 2100cc-2700cc capacity groups, which included the PA and its main rivals: see Society of Motor Manufacturers and Traders (SMMT). *The Motor Industry of Great Britain 1959*. London: SMMT, 1959, pp. 38–39. The Cresta was distinguished externally from the Velox mainly by stainless trim around the side windows and gutters, full wheel covers, badges (including a freestanding bonnet badge) and, in many cases, two-tone paint. Inside, it was fitted with more luxurious trim and equipment. A Vauxhall publicity photograph of a Cresta was used in an advertisement for "Silver Fox" stainless steels: see *Punch*, 14/1/59 (page unknown).

34. See Jim Williams. *Boulevard Photographic: The Art of Automobile Advertising*. WI. Motorbooks International, 1997, pp. 18–68. For typical studio photographs of the Cresta PA, see Earnshaw and Berry, *Vauxhall Cars 1945–1964 (2nd ed., 2001)*, p. 28. In the first edition of this book, the authors recall that, in the early 1990s, "literally at the 24th hour," a great number of Vauxhall's publicity photographs, now preserved, were rescued by the company's Director of Supply from a skip: *ibid. (1st ed., 2000)*, p. 9.

35. See *The Autocar*, 21/8/59, p. 45 (new model announcement); 10/6/60, pp. 933–936 (test of Velox). For 1961 models, see *The Autocar*, 19/8/60, pp. 263–266 (new model announcement); 16/9/60, pp. 416–418 (test of Cresta). See also *Country Life*, 27/10/60, p. 975; *The Illustrated London News*, 3/12/60, p. 1021 (1961 Cresta); *Automobile Engineer*, December 1960, pp. 525–531 and January 1961, pp. 2–8 (detailed description of Hydra-matic transmission); March 1961, pp. 95–97 (installation of air conditioning in Velox). For 1962 models, see *Country Life*, 8/3/62, p. 544 (Velox); *The Field*, 1/2/62 (Cresta); *The Motor*, 14/2/62, pp. 47–50 (test of Velox); *Practical Motorist*, October 1961, pp. 172, 175 (descriptions of Hydra-matic and Overdrive-equipped Crestas). A total of 173,604 PA models were built: Vauxhall Motors Ltd. *Vauxhall Cars since 1903 (revd. ed.)*, p. 34.

36. This model received welcome publicity when a 2.6 litre Friary estate was bought by the Queen. Approximately 1600 Friary PAs were built, compared with 5643 Ford Consul, Zephyr and Zodiac Mk II estate cars by coachbuilders E.D. Abbott Ltd. of Farnham, Surrey: Martin Rawbone. "The Abbott Fords." *Thoroughbred & Classic Cars*, November 1987, pp. 52–54. For the wider Abbott story, see also Jon Mullins. "E.D. Abbott — The South's Finest?" *Classic and Sports Car*, June 1987, pp. 87–91.

37. Nick Walker. *A-Z of British Coachbuilders 1919–1960*. Bideford, Devon: Bay View Books, 1997, pp. 116–117. Martin Walter's Dormobile estate car was initially offered as a conversion to customers' 1956 models: see Earnshaw and Berry, *Vauxhall Cars 1945–1964 (2nd ed., 2001)*, pp. 12–13. For a contemporary description of the car see, for example, *Country Fair*, April 1957, pp. 65–67. The 1957 Velox Dormobile (which cost £1112, and was listed as a standard model in the Vauxhall range) was distinguished from the 1956 version by a different two-tone paint scheme and a smoother design of fibreglass tailgate, which acted as the roof of a custom-made tent when camping. The bench seats pivoted on metal frames which allowed them to be converted into a bed. Few Dormobiles were made; a two-tone blue example seen by the author in Essex in 1985 was then the only known survivor. In April 1959 the rival Ford Zephyr and Zodiac Farnham estate cars cost £1099 0s 10d and £1198 4s 2d respectively.

38. Platt, *An Addiction to Automobiles*, p. 180.

39. *Ibid.*, pp. 179–180.

40. The new car could reach 60 mph in 18.2 seconds; its top speed was 80mph: see *The Motor*, 4/12/63, pp. 48–53. Total FB production between September 1961 and October 1964 amounted to 328,642 cars: Vauxhall Motors Ltd. *Vauxhall Cars since 1903 (revd. ed.)*, p. 35.

41. *Country Life*, 19/3/64, p. 654.

42. *Small Car*, April 1963, pp. 43–45.

43. The engine gave 81 bhp (gross) and a 0–60 time of 16.4 seconds: *Small Car*, April 1963, pp. 43–45. See also *The Autocar*, 15/9/61, pp. 395–40 (new model announcement); 8/11/61, pp. 596–599 (test of saloon); 24/11/61, pp. 896–899 (test of estate car); 7/2/64, pp. 244–248 (test of 1594cc estate car); *Automobile Engineer*, October 1961, pp. 389–391 (new model announcement); *The Motor*, 20/3/63, pp. 228–231 (test of De Luxe estate car); 11/9/63, p. 71 (announcement of 1594cc models); 4/12/63, pp. 48–53 (test of 1594cc saloon).

44. The flash was originally shown in brochures with parallel sides; on production cars it moved slightly up the car and was stepped behind the rear door. In 1963, a few months before the car was updated alongside the other Victors, it resumed its original shape while staying in its existing position.

45. The two cars were tested together in a "giant test" in 1963: See *Small Car*, August 1963, pp. 32–39. See also *The Autocar*, 20/10/61, pp. 657–658 (new model announcement); 26/6/64, pp. 1240–1244 (test); *Country Life*, 24/5/62, p. 1246; *The Motor*, 24/1/62, pp. 990–992 (preview and driving impressions); 16/5/62, pp. 592–595 (test); *Practical Motorist*, October 1962, pp. 160–161 (short test). For the VX 4/90's rally history and brochure illustrations, see *Classic and Sports Car*, June 1994, pp. 82–85.

46. With their hardware and framework, doors were expensive to design and tool up, and resemblance lent marque identity. The new sixes (which gave 113 bhp gross) were much larger than the Victors at 15'2" long × 5'10" wide (Victor: 14'5" × 5'4"): *The Motor*, 3/10/62, pp. 336–339, 341–342 (new model announcement and article by Maurice Platt). See also *Automobile Engineer*, October 1962, p. 378; *The Field*, 30/1/64, p. 193; *Motor Trader*, 3/10/62, pp. 12–13.

47. See *The Motor*, 16/10/63, pp. 215–216. Some Radford Crestas "were also produced for military use as 'staff cars', and a batch were still being exported to the Middle East as late as the spring of 1965": Earnshaw and Berry, *Vauxhall Cars 1945–1964 (2nd ed., 2001)*, p. 46. The Radford Cresta's "Executive" moniker was adopted by Ford in 1965 for its super-luxury Zodiac: Graham Arnold. "Devil De Ville." *Classic and Sports Car*, September 1990, p. 22. In July 1965, three months before the range was replaced, a two-door "Wellington" hearse conversion was announced by hearse specialists Coleman-Milne Ltd. of Bolton, Lancashire: See *The Autocar*, 16/7/65, p. 132.

48. *Motor*, 14/5/66, pp. 43–47 (test). See also *The Autocar*, 5/3/64, pp. 466–470 (test of estate car); 1/10/65, pp. 637–642 (test of VX 4/90); *Country*

Life, 28/4/66, p. 1051 (estate car); *Motor*, 21/1/67, pp. 60–64 (24,000 mile report); *Car*, July 1965, pp. 40–45 (two-car test with Ford Corsair). 233,263 FCs were made between October 1964 and August 1967, including 13,449 of the VX 4/90: Michael Sedgwick and Mark Gillies. *A–Z of Cars 1945–1970 (2nd ed., revd. Jon Pressnell)*. Bideford, Devon: Bay View Books, 1993, p. 214.

49. James Ensor. *The Motor Industry*. London: Financial Times/Longman, 1971, p. 109.

50. *Small Car*, February 1964, pp. 30–32. See also *Autocar*, 17/12/65, pp. 1284–1289 (SL90); 6/11/64, pp. 977–981 (test of Bedford Beagle estate car); *Country Life*, 28/11/63, p. 1416; *The Field*, 24/6/65, p. 1189 (SL); *The Motor*, 2/10/63, pp. 83–88 (new model announcement); 23/10/63, pp. 84–89 (test).

51. Sedgwick and Gillies, *A–Z of Cars*, pp. 215–216.

52. Ensor, *The Motor Industry*, pp. 110, 112. See also *Autocar*, 22/10/65, pp. ii–vii (new model announcement); 19/11/65, pp. 1076–1081 (test of Cresta de Luxe with Powerglide); *Car*, August 1966, pp. 43–49 (test of Cresta de Luxe with Ford Zephyr V6); *Country Life*, 16/6/66, p. 1608 (Cresta); 23/2/67, p. 412 (Viscount); *The Field*, 24/11/66 (Viscount); *The Illustrated London News*, 16/3/66, p. 32 (Cresta); *Motor*, 3/9/66, pp. 27–32 (test of Viscount); and Earnshaw and Berry, *Vauxhall Cars 1945–1964 (2nd ed., 2001)*, pp. 52–56. For a comparison of Crestas PA, PB and PC, see *Classic and Sports Car*, March 1995, pp. 78–83.

53. Vauxhall originally hoped for sales of 100,000 a year: Geoffrey Charles. "More new 1968 models for the Motor Show." *The Times*, 16/10/67. In the event, 212,362 FDs, including VX 4/90 and six-cylinder Ventora variants, were sold between October 1967 and March 1972: Sedgwick and Gillies, *A–Z of Cars*, pp. 214–216. See also *Autocar*, 2/10/69, p. 25 (announcement of VX 4/90); *Car*, March 1968, pp. 40–41 (test of Ventora); May 1968, pp. 34–36 (test with Ford Cortina and Hillman Hunter); *Country Life*, 22/2/68, p. 418 (Victor 2000); 5/12/68, p. 1489 (Victor 2000 estate car); 28/3/68, p. 735 (Ventora); *The Field*, 18/4/68, p. 749 (Victor 2000); *Motor*, 21/10/67, pp. 155–163 (description of Victor FD). Gerald Palmer, who joined Vauxhall as Assistant Chief Engineer — Passenger Cars in January 1956 and retired in 1972, found "some satisfaction in [Vauxhall's] decision to develop a rear suspension related to my design for the [1953–57 Riley] Pathfinder fifteen years before": Palmer. *Auto-Architect*, p. 83.

54. Anders Clausager. "The Swinging Sixties." in Nick Georgano, Nick Baldwin, Anders Clausager and Jonathan Wood. *Britain's Motor Industry: The First Hundred Years (ed. Nick Georgano)*. Yeovil, Somerset: Haynes, 1995, p. 167. See also *Autocar*, 15/2/68, pp. 11–29 (test of estate car); *Car*, February 1967, pp. 38–45 (test of 1159cc model with Cortina 1300); April 1968, pp. 20–21 (test of GT); July 1970, pp. 62–69, 87 (test of 1159cc Viva with Escort and other rivals); *Motor*, 10/12/66, pp. 23–28 (test of 1159cc model); 29/7/67, p. 28 (Brabham). See also Robert Berry and Alan Earnshaw. *Vauxhall Cars 1965–1984*. Cumbria: Trans-Pennine Publishing/Vauxhall Heritage Services, 2001, pp. 5–15; and Russ Smith. "Vauxhall Viva GT." *Popular Classics*, February 1995, pp. 32–33.

Part Two — 9. The "Bond Bombshell" and Other Specialists

1. See pp. 237–240, above.

2. For Bristols since 1946 see, for example, Martin Buckley. "Souls of Discretion." *Classic and Sports Car*, May 1996, pp. 116–122. Bristol production in the 1960s was as follows: 406 (1958–61): 181; 407 (1961–63): 88; 408 (1963–65): 83; 409 (1965–67): 74; 410 (1968–69): 79; 411 (1969–76): 287: *ibid.*, p. 121. For individual models, see also *The Autocar*, 6/10/61, pp. 533–536 (407); *Country Life*, 14/3/63, p. 558 (407); *The Field*, 8/3/62, (page unknown) (407); *The Motor*, 25/9/63, p. 38 (408).

3. A total production of 979 was made up as follows: Cobra 260: 75; Cobra 289: 571; AC 289: 27; Cobra 427/428: 306: Michael Sedgwick and Mark Gillies. *A–Z of Cars 1945–1970 (2nd ed., revd. Jon Pressnell)*. Bideford, Devon: Bay View Books Ltd., 1993, pp. 7–8.

4. See John Mclellan. "Accent on AC." *Thoroughbred & Classic Cars*, September 1983, pp. 46–48 and October 1983, pp. 22–23 [p. 22]. For AC generally, see John Mclellan. "A Family Affair." *Thoroughbred & Classic Cars*, October 1985, pp. 24–27 and November 1985, pp. 42–45. For the AC Ace, of which 465 of the 693 built were fitted with Bristol engines (the remainder having AC or Ford Zephyr engines), see Tony Dron. "AC Ace." *Thoroughbred & Classic Cars*, November 1994, pp. 6–14. For a comparison of the AC 428 with the Bristol 410 and Jensen Interceptor, see Matthew Carter. "Back to Back." *Classic & Sports Car*, July 1988, pp. 45–51; and for the AC 428 see also Mick Walsh. "AC's High." *Classic and Sports Car*, November 1986, pp. 48–51. For the history of Frua including recollections of those who knew him see, for example, Giles Chapman. "Frua: The Man and his Line." *Classic and Sports Car*, April 1987, pp. 118–122.

5. *Car*, December 1966, pp. 24–25.

6. McLellan, "Accent on AC," [October 1983] p. 22.

7. See *The Autocar*, 16/10/59, pp. 380–383. See also *The Field*, 31/12/59, (page unknown).

8. For the different Graber and Park Ward styles, see Jon Pressnell. "Swiss Rolls." *Classic and Sports Car*, March 1994, pp. 62–66. For the Park Ward cars, see also Richard Sutton. "Eternal Triangle." *Classic and Sports Car*, April 1989, pp. 82–87; and Brian Palmer. "Dying Breed." *Thoroughbred & Classic Cars*, February 1987, pp. 112–115.

9. Martin Buckley. "Star Gazing." *Classic and Sports Car*, September 1989, pp. 64–67 (interview with Geoff Harris, Star Registrar of the Armstrong Siddeley Owners' Club). See also *The Autocar*, 11/9/59, pp. 181–184; *Country Life*, 3/9/59, p. 183; *The Field*, 27/2/58, p. 363 (Sapphire); *The Illustrated London News*, 6/6/59, p. 990.

10. See Kevin Brazendale. "Moggie Way." *Sports Car Monthly*, December 1985, pp. 52–55; Kurt Oblinger. "The Mod: Morgan Plus 4 Plus." *British Car*, June-July 1998, pp. 30–33.

11. Morgan's continuity of design and manufacture is unique. Introducing a book of Morgan advertisements prepared by Morgan historian and concours judge Ken Hill in 1996, Charles Morgan wrote: "The best advertising I expect to see is a Morgan driver enjoying himself in one of our cars, or, even better, a whole family enjoying their Morgan and treating it as an essential part of the fun they need in their lives": see Ken Hill. *Morgan: The Art of Selling a Unique Sports Car*. London: Blandford Press/Cassell, 1996. The book is highly recommended. See also Ken Hill. "Morgan's Magic." *Thoroughbred & Classic Cars*, July 1984, p. 47 (brief history of the company). For contemporary assessments of Morgan cars see, for example, *Autocar*, 12/9/68 (Morgan Plus 8 with Rover V8 engine); *The Motor*, 25/4/62, pp. 430–431 (4/4 with Triumph TR3 engine).

12. With 948cc, the Sprite managed 0–60 in 23.7 seconds and a top speed of 84.1 mph. Being only 11' 5.25" long and 4' 5" wide, the car felt much faster than it was; fewer sports cars provided more fun per mile-per-hour. See *The Autocar*, 6/2/59, p. 192 (performance conversion by Downton Engineering Ltd. of Salisbury, Wiltshire and lightweight moulded bonnet with headlights in the front wings rather than inboard of the wings on the bonnet, as on the standard car); 20/11/59, pp. 655–658; *Automobile Engineer*, July 1960, pp. 272–280 and August 1960, pp. 312–316 (description); *The Field*, 18/12/58, p. 1209. For the successors of the "Frog-eye" see, for example, *The Autocar*, 13/3/64, pp. 462–465 (Mk III with equivalent M.G. Midget Mk II); 10/4/69, pp. 50–55 (Mk IV with Triumph Spitfire Mk 3); *The Field*, 29/6/61, p. 1309 (Mk II); 14/11/63, p. 929 (Mk II, 1098cc); *The Motor*, 5/12/62, pp. 718–721; 9/9/67, pp. 25–30 (Mk IV); 14/10/67, pp. 95–99 (Mk IV with Triumph Spitfire Mk 3 and Honda S800); *Road & Track Road Test Annual 1969* [1968 test], pp. 23–28 (Mk IV with Datsun 1600, Fiat 850 Spider and Triumph Spitfire Mk 3); *Small Car*, October 1964, pp. 49–56 (Mk III with Triumph Spitfire). See also Jon Pressnell. "Best Buy: Austin-Healey Sprite and MG Midget." *Classic and Sports Car*, March 1998, pp. 114–122; and Arnold Wilson. "Midget Italian." *Thoroughbred & Classic Cars*, April 1991, pp. 106–109 (Innocenti Spider, based on Midget Mk III).

13. For big Healeys see, for example, *The Autocar*, 28/8/59, pp. 105–107; 22/12/61, pp. 1038A–1038D (3000 Mk II); 12/3/64, pp. 1132–1136 (3000 Mk III Convertible); *Automobile Engineer*, July 1959, pp. 270–272 (3000 Mk I); *Country Life*, 24/12/59, p. 1256 (3000 Mk I); *The Field*, 10/10/57, p. 629 (100-Six); 5/10/61, p. 629 (3000 Mk II); *The Illustrated London News*, 1/12/62, p. 902 (3000 Mk II); *The Motor*, 10/4/63, pp. 60–63 (3000 Mk II).

14. For the Elan see, for example, *Autocar*, 21/8/64, pp. 360–364; *Country Life*, 4/11/64, p. 1218; *The Field*, 27/8/64, p. 445; *The Illustrated London News*, 5/9/64, p. 356; *Motor*, 10/9/64, pp. 47–48.

15. See *Autocar*, 21/3/68, pp. 11–16 (+ 2 Special Equipment model).

16. The Gilbern was well regarded by enthusiasts and a much better car than its ingredients, baldly stated, suggested. Commercially, however, it was always vulnerable to others' economies of scale and to the prices charged by mainsream manufacturers for components, which kept Gilbern's own costs, and therefore its prices, comparatively high: see Jon Pressnell. "Chasing the Dragon." *Classic and Sports Car*, August 1994, pp. 89–91 (Gilbern GT of 1959–67, and interview with co-founder Bernard Friese); Brian Palmer. "Test Match." *Thoroughbred & Classic Cars*, July 1991, pp. 14–21 (comparison of Gilbern Genie — the Invader's similar-looking predecessor of 1966–69 — with 1971 Marcos GT, 1969 TVR Tuscan, 1971 Lotus Europa and 1966 Reliant Scimitar GT). Gilbern production amounted to about 277 GTs, 197 Genies and about 603 Invaders. The last Invader — the Mk III — was only available factory-built. Gilbern production ceased in 1973.

17. For contemporary views of the Bond Equipe, see *The Autocar*, 3/1/64, pp. 12–15 (GT); 9/7/65, pp. 59–64 (GT 4S); 8/5/69, pp. 15–17 (Equipe 2 Litre Convertible); *The Field*, 3/2/66, (page unknown) (GT 4S); *The Motor*, 22/5/63, pp. 66–67 (GT); 13/11/63, pp. 44–47 (GT); 13/8/66, pp. 47–48 (GT and GT 4S as used cars); 26/8/67, pp. 13–15 (Equipe 2 Litre); 11/11/67, pp. 17–22 (Equipe 2 Litre); *Practical Motorist*, January 1965, p. 547 (GT 4S). See also Tony Beadle. "There and Then." *Triumph World*, February/March 1998, pp. 36–39 (restored GT 4S). 451 GTs, 2505 of the GT 4S and 1432 Equipe 2 Litres were built: Sedgwick and Gillies, *A–Z of Cars*, p. 37.

10. Aston Martin and Lagonda

1. *The Autocar*, 13/10/61, pp. 584–587; 18/9/64, pp. 558–562. See also *Autocar*, 15/8/68, pp. 34–37 (DB6); 21/8/69, p. 32 (DB6 Mk 2 announcement); *Country Life*, 15/12/66, p. 1653 (DB6); *Motor*, 8/1/66, pp. 27–32 (DB6 Vantage). See also Mike McCarthy. "Gran Turismo." *Classic and Sports Car*, September 1983, pp. 33–35 (DB4 and Ferrari 250 GTE compared).

2. *The Field*, 4/6/64, p. 1125 (DB5).

3. Mark Hughes. "Forgotten Lagonda." *Classic and Sports Car*, November 1990, pp. 88–93.

4. *Ibid.*, p. 91. "Although *The Autocar* and *The Motor* published technical descriptions at the [October] 1961 launch, neither magazine ever carried out a road test": *ibid.*, p. 88. For a short test see, however, *The Field*, 30/11/61, p. 1109.

5. For contemporary estimates of advertising expenditure, see *Appendix 11A*, pp. 339, above.

6. Aston Martin DB production was: DB4 and DB4 GT (1958–63): 1115; DB4 GT Zagato (1960–63): 19; DB4 Drophead Coupe (1961–63): 70; DB5 (1964–65): 1021, including Drophead Coupe; DB6 (1965–70): 1567; Volante (drophead coupe) (1965–71): 215; DBS (1967–72): 860; DBS V8 (1969–72): 405: Michael Sedgwick and Mark Gillies. *A-Z of Cars 1945–1970* (2nd ed., revd. Jon Pressnell). Bideford, Devon: Bay View Books Ltd., 1993, pp. 20–22.

7. Some might think that "exciting retailers" struck an off note. But if one wanted to avoid the word "dealers," was there a more natural, alternative single word? Would a phrase like "car suppliers" or "suppliers of exciting cars" have been better? If the description was too specific it would narrow the field so much as to be unconvincing. "Retailers" suggested comparison with retailers of glamorous products other than cars. Not, perhaps, an easy call.

8. The team shown were: Mike Loasby, Dick Hickling, Harold Beach, Cyril Honey, William Towns, Dudley Gershon, A.S. Heggie, Roy Bamford, Tadek Marek, Dick Shaw, Alan Crouch and Bert Thickpenny. For the DBS, see *Autocar*, 10/10/68, pp. 66–71 (test); 2/10/69, pp. 21–24 (DBS V8 description). For the DBS V8, see Roger Bell. "Iron Fist." *Supercar & Classics*, September 1991, pp. 32–39; Tony Dron. "Aston Martin DBS & DBS V8." *Thoroughbred & Classic Cars*, November 1995, pp. 17–24.

9. Mike Taylor. "Townscape." *Thoroughbred & Classic Cars*, July 1986, pp. 60–63 (interview with DBS designer, William Towns). See also Martin Buckley. "William Tells." *Classic and Sports Car*, October 1992, pp. 73–75 (interview with William Towns). Towns was with Aston Martin from 1966 until 1969, and subsequently styled the Aston Martin Lagonda of 1976.

11. Bentley

1. For contemporary assessments of the Bentley S1, see *Rolls-Royce*, note 5, p. 373, below.

2. Rolls-Royce did not normally reveal horsepower figures, but the chief engineer of the Rolls-Royce Car Division, Harry Grylls, under whom the engine was designed by Jack Phillips and his team, revealed the figure of 178bhp in a 1963 paper read before the Institution of Mechanical Engineers (which incorporated the Institution of Automobile Engineers), *The History of a Dimension*: see Graham Robson. "Classic Engines: The 25 Year Career of the Rolls-Royce V8." *Thoroughbred & Classic Cars*, December 1984, pp. 84–86. For the history of the 1946–55 Bentleys and Rolls-Royces generally see, for example, Martin Nutland. *Rolls-Royce Silver Wraith, Silver Dawn & Silver Cloud; Bentley Mk VI, R-Series & S-Series*. Godmanstone, Dorset: Veloce Publishing Plc.,1997. See also Jon Pressnell. "Chancellor or Chairman." *Classic and Sports Car*, February 1994, pp. 52–59 (Silver Cloud 1 with Mercedes 300d four-door hardtop); Mike Walsh. "Heavenly Cloud?" *Classic and Sports Car*, November 1984, pp. 65–71; and Giles Chapman. "The Image Architect." *Classic and Sports Car*, December 1996, pp. 110–115 (interview with John Blatchley).

3. Production figures have been given as follows: Silver Cloud I (1955–59): 2238; Bentley S1 (1955–59): 3072; Silver Cloud II (1959–62): 2417; Bentley S2 (1959–62): 1865; Silver Cloud III (1962–65): 2044; Bentley S3 (1962–65): 1286: see Mark Hughes. "Best Buy: Bentley S3." *Classic and Sports Car*, March 1993, pp. 42–53. For more detailed production figures, including those for cars with coachbuilt bodies on Silver Cloud and Bentley 'S' Series chassis, see Nutland, *Rolls-Royce Silver Wraith et. al.*, pp. 167–172. Details of individual chassis are available from the relevant car clubs and specialist publications.

4. See *Appendix 11A*, p. 339, above.

5. For the early system, see Nutland, *Rolls-Royce Silver Wraith et. al.*, pp. 46–54.

6. David Ogilvy. *The Unpublished David Ogilvy*. London: Sidgwick & Jackson, 1988, pp. 164–165.

7. In reality the drum brakes could fade a little in hard use, as was probably unavoidable on a 4500 lb. car with automatic transmission, and the gearbox-driven servo did not provide enough assistance during repeated applications at low speed, but with twin hydraulic systems and mechanical back-up for the rear wheels the brakes were most unlikely to fail.

8. *The Field*, 5/9/63 (page unknown).

12. Daimler

1. Norah Docker. *Norah: The Autobiography of Lady Docker*. London: W.H. Allen, 1969, p. 13.

2. For the "Docker Daimlers" and related events see, for example, Mike Lawrence. "King and Queen of Daimler." *Classic and Sports Car*, April 1992, pp. 156–161. See also Brian Palmer. "Stardust." *Thoroughbred & Classic Cars*, November 1983, pp. 64–67 (1951 car); Brian Smith. "Dockers' Daimlers." *Thoroughbred & Classic Cars*, pp. 34–36; Martin Buckley. "Daimler's Queen of Excess." *Classic Cars*, May 1999, pp. 103–106.

3. For the Daimler Continental, now beautifully restored by Duncan Saunders, see Giles Chapman. "Daimler's 'Continental'." *Classic and Sports Car*, January 1995, pp. 88–91.

4. Docker, *Norah*, p. 108. The name was suggested by the price. For the Conquest see, for example, Charles Herridge. "Dance with a Daimler." *Classic and Sports Car*, September 1990, p. 80–85 (Conquest Century restoration). 4568 of the Conquest saloon, and 4818 of the faster but similar-looking Conquest Century, were built between 1953–56 and 1954–58 respectively. The other Conquest models were a saloon-based convertible called the Coupé (1954–55; production estimated at 234), a Roadster (1953–55; 65 built), and a New Drophead Coupé based on the Roadster (1955–57; 54 built): see Michael Sedgwick and Mark Gillies. *A-Z of Cars 1945–1970* (2nd ed., revd. Jon Pressnell). Bideford, Devon: Bay View Books, 1993, pp. 49–50.

5. *Ibid.*, pp. 49–50. 1955's announcement advertising adapted a painting of the earlier Regency and illustrated the dashboard, vanity case, suitcases and picnic case.

6. For the early promotion of the fluid flywheel, see John Speed. "Fluid Flywheel on Film." *Thoroughbred & Classic Cars*, December 1983, pp. 84–87 (personal account of promotion to dealers by Daimler's publicity assistant of the time.) For the history of Daimler generally see, for example, Jonathan Wood. "Detailing Daimler." *Thoroughbred & Classic Cars*, November 1988, pp. 72–77. To change gear on a fluid flywheel-equipped car, select the desired gear and then depress and release the gear-change pedal (which is where a clutch pedal would usually be). A gear can be selected long in advance of when it is needed, and then engaged quickly with the pedal. The car will stop on the footbrake, or accelerate, in any gear, although acceleration will be slow if a low gear (first or second) is not selected and engaged before pulling away. Care should be taken to ensure that the gear is properly selected (on the right-hand quadrant) before the pedal is used, and that the pedal is used with a firm and smooth action and only as recommended in the car's manual. (It must not, for instance, be used as a clutch.)

7. See *The Autocar*, 2/10/59, pp. 303–306. See also *The Autocar*, 25/9/59, pp. 250–255 (description); *Automobile Engineer*, October 1959, pp. 384–386; December 1962, p. 515 (retractable hardtop conversion by Anthony H. Croucher Ltd.); *The Field*, 7/5/59, p. 877; 12/3/62, p. 569. For the history of the SP250 (originally called the Daimler Dart until Chrysler Corporation, with whom "Dart" was registered as a Dodge trademark, objected), see Brian Long. *Daimler V8 S.P. 250*. Godmanstone, Dorset: Veloce Publishing Plc., 1994.

8. See Sedgwick and Gillies, *A-Z of Cars*, p. 50; and Jonathan Stein. *British Sports Cars in America 1946–1981*. Pennsylvania: Automobile Quarterly Publications, 1993, pp. 34–37.

9. Two cars were built, of which one survives: see Malcolm McKay. "Lyons' Dart." *Thoroughbred & Classic Cars*, March 1994, pp. 36–42.

10. An attempt to adapt the old steel tooling by adding sections of Kirksite, however, proved a false economy as the resulting panels had to be extensively lead-loaded and finished by hand. In late 1961 production was taken over by Jaguar: see Bill Munro. *Carbodies: The Complete Story*. Marlborough, Wiltshire: The Crowood Press Ltd., 1998, pp. 83–97 and 113–115.

11. The Majestic stayed in production until 1962; 1490 were built: Sedgwick and Gillies, *A-Z of Cars*, p. 50. See also *The Illustrated London News*, 4/4/59, p. 590.

12. See *The Autocar*, 23/10/59, pp. 490–491 (announcement); 12/5/61, pp. 772–775 (test); *Country Life*, 15/2/62, p. 354; *The Field*, 14/2/63, p. 285; 10/9/64, p. 533; *The Illustrated London News*, 14/4/62, p. 600. See also Martin Buckley. "Daimler's Dragster." *Classic and Sports Car*, June 1992, pp. 56–61.

13. *Car*, January 1968, pp. 45–50 (with Rover 3.5 Litre Coupé). An estimated 5700 of the 1966–69 Sovereign were build compared with an estimated

9600 of the equivalent Jaguar 420 from 1966–68: Sedgwick and Gillies, *A-Z of Cars*, p. 104.

14. See Long, *Daimler V8 S.P. 250*, pp. 14–20 and 110–114.

15. *The Field*, 12/11/64, p. 997. See also *Automobile Engineer*, October 1962, pp. 374–375; *The Motor*, 17/4/63, pp. 44–49. This magazine achieved 0–60 in 13.5 seconds and a top speed of 109.5 mph. In addition, see Peter Nunn. "Daimler's Dark Horse." *Classic and Sports Car*, February 1983, pp. 29–30 (buyer's guide). A manual gearbox became available as an option in 1967.

16. Sedgwick and Gillies, *A-Z of Cars*, p. 51.

13. Humber

1. For this advertisement see, for example, *Motor*, 16/9/67, pp. 47–49. For the postwar Humbers generally see Tony Freeman. *Humber: An Illustrated History*. London, Academy Books, 1991, pp. 53–114; and Mark Dixon. "Crown Jewels." *Practical Classics*, March 2000, pp. 30–35. At the time of writing the Humber marque name is dormant and is owned by Peugeot.

2. Graham Robson. *Cars of the Rootes Group*. Croydon: Motor Racing Publications Ltd., 1990, p. 150. Australians were offered a version of the 180 with a 3.5 litre or 4 litre Valiant engine called the Chrysler Centura, one of a number of British family cars of the 1950s onwards fitted with in-line six-cylinder engines for the Australian market: see, for example, Jon Pressnell. "Travellin' Man." *Classic and Sports Car*, June 1991, pp. 80–87. For a test of the police-equipped Super Snipe Estate Car without power steering see *Country Life*, 3/6/65, p. 1372. Tester J. Eason Gibson noticed in particular that the steering was heavy and that, with rubber mats inside, the car was noisier than the standard model.

3. Recalled by Stephen Lewis of the Post-Vintage Humber Car Club in 1987 following conversations with Rootes test drivers of the day. See Stephen Lewis. "Hot Humbers." *Thoroughbred & Classic Cars*, April 1987, p. 115. It is believed that a total of twelve V8s were built of which six were prototypes and six pre-production cars, ten being Super Snipes and two being Imperials. At least one Super Snipe had left-hand drive, and at least one V8-engined Humber Sceptre (which managed 128 mph but which was long ago cut up) was also built. Chrysler rather than Ford V8 engines were adopted and, of the Chrysler engines, at least one was a V8 of 318 cu. in. rather than the more common 273 cu. in. A late pre-production V8 was only about four miles per hour faster than a standard Super Snipe Series V with overdrive, with 0–60 taking about four seconds less in the V8, and fuel consumption was worse: see test engineers' data sheets reproduced in Freeman, *Humber: An Illustrated History*, pp. 97–99; and see Dixon, "Crown Jewels," p. 32; Michael Worthington-Williams. "What Might Have Been." *Classic and Sports Car*, January 1987, p. 16 (1966 Imperial with the smaller Chrysler V8); Michael Worthington-Williams. "Rare Humber." *Classic and Sports Car*, August 1987, p. 22 (recollections of Chrysler-engined Imperial owned by Alex Sayer, husband of former Rootes employee); Mike Taylor. "Don Tarbun." *Thoroughbred & Classic Cars*, February 1987, pp. 102–107 (interview with Rootes development engineer); Robson, *Cars of the Rootes Group*, p. 146. One pre-production Imperial V8 was used by Sir Reginald Rootes personally: Dixon, "Crown Jewels," p. 32.

4. Freeman, *Humber: An Illustrated History*, p. 102.

5. *Ibid.*, p. 102.

6. From Basil Butler Co. Ltd. (as Butler & Gardner Ltd. from the spring of 1962). Erwin Wasey, Ruthrauff & Ryan Ltd. (as Erwin Wasey Ltd. from October 1964) took over Humber advertising in or around April 1964.

7. The four-cylinder Hawk and six-cylinder Super Snipe were, after all, comparatively low-production models. The Hawk sold most strongly in its early years: 15,539 of the Series I were sold in 1957–59 compared with 6813 of the Series 1A, 7230 of the 1960–62 Series II, 6109 of the 1962–64 Series III, 1746 of the 1964–65 Series IV and 3754 of the Series IVA of 1965–67: Martin Buckley. "Just What the Doctor Ordered." *Classic and Sports Car*, January 1993, p. 101. It is likely that after October 1958 the Super Snipe took potential sales from the Hawk since many buyers were as loyal to the marque as to individual models. Of Super Snipes, 6072 of the 1958–59 Series I were sold, compared with 7175 of the 1959–60 Series II, 7257 of the 1960–62 Series III, 6495 of the 1962–64 Series IV, 1907 of the 1964–65 Series V and 1125 of the 1965–67 Series VA: *ibid.*, p. 101. 1907 of the Imperial were made between 1964 and 1967: *ibid.*, p. 101; and Michael Sedgwick and Mark Gillies. *A-Z of Cars 1945–1970 (2nd ed., revd. Jon Pressnell)*. Bideford, Devon: Bay View Books, 1993, p. 96. Estate cars were made in comparatively small numbers; for instance only about 800 of the Super Snipe Series II Estate Car were built: Martin Buckley. "Loaded with Style." *Classic Cars*, February 2004, pp. 80–84 (Series II sampled with comparable estate cars).

8. See, for example, "Frank Wootton." *Classic and Sports Car*, October

1998, p. 11 (obituary); and "Cars on Canvas." *Classic and Sports Car*, December 1998, pp. 32–33 (profile of work).

9. See *The Autocar*, 31/5/57, pp. 736–739 (new model announcement); and Freeman, *Humber: An Illustrated History*, p. 84 (publicity photographs). See also *The Field*, 20/6/57, p. 1003. For the 1957–67 Hawk and Super Snipe in general, see Buckley, "Just What the Doctor Ordered," pp. 98–101.

10. For a photograph of the body under construction at British Light Steel Pressings Ltd. see *Automobile Engineer*, June 1960, p. 233. By contrast the monocoque Rover 3-Litre, announced in September 1958, was 15' 6" long, 5' 10"wide and weighed approximately 3500 lb. (Sources varied according to the exact version and the running fluids such as oil, water and fuel included.)

11. Martin Buckley. "William Tells." *Classic and Sports Car*, October 1992, pp. 73–75 (interview with William Towns). Towns moved to Rover in 1963 and to Aston Martin in 1966.

12. These were made in England in 1953 by Clare Hodgman of Raymond Loewy Associates who, with Holden ("Bob") Koto, came over from America. Loewy's London office had closed in 1951: see Barney Sharratt. "Loewy's Man in London." *Thoroughbred & Classic Cars*, April 1996, pp. 88–92. For the 1952–57 Humber Super Snipe see, for example, Jon Pressnell. "Judge for Yourself." *Classic and Sports Car*, August 1996, pp. 78–81.

13. See Bill Munro. *Carbodies: The Complete Story*. Marlborough, Wiltshire: The Crowood Press Ltd., 1998, pp. 115–117.

14. *Motor Trader*, 1/10/58, pp. 6–7. See also *Country Life*, 21/5/59, p. 1154 (estate car).

15. *The Field*, 26/2/59, p. 271. For the latter emblem see Freeman. *Humber: An Illustrated History*, p. 83.

16. For the Series II, see *The Autocar*, 16/10/59 (new model announcement, with Hawk Series IA); *Automobile Engineer*, November 1959, pp. 433–434; *The Illustrated London News*, 5/3/59, p. 410 (estate car).

17. The backdrop was so impressionistic that another Humber in the background looked not just vaguely, but exactly, like a 1955 Chevrolet.

18. From 1960–66: see Dixon. "Crown Jewels," p. 34.

19. See *The Autocar*, 16/6/61, pp. 962–965 (Series III); 23/10/64, pp. 835–837 (Imperial); 11/6/65, pp. 1161–1166 (Imperial); *Automobile Engineer*, October 1962, pp. 373–374 (Series IV); *The Field*, 9/3/61, p. 455 (Series III estate car); 19/8/65, p. 401 (Imperial); *The Illustrated London News*, 19/11/60, p. 916 (Series III); 3/11/62, p. 724 (Hawk Series II Estate car); 1/10/66, p. 41 (Imperial); *The Motor*, 14/11/62, pp. 617–620 (Series IV).

20. Thrupp and Maberly had been founded in 1760 and were taken over by Rootes Ltd. in 1925, several years before the Rootes brothers bought Humber or Hillman. Before the Second World War the coachbuilder continued to build bodies on other manufacturers' chassis, but after 1945 it built bodies— mainly for two-door and luxury cars— solely for the Group. Its factory in Cricklewood, north London was closed and sold in August 1967. Some super-luxury Super Snipe limousines were built by Harold Radford from early in the model's run. Radford also offered a Countryman conversion at a cost of about £800–£850 over that of the standard car, depending upon the equipment ordered.

21. *Small Car*, December 1963, pp. 24–33 (test with Riley 4/72; the magazine found the Humber to be the better car). See also Doug Blain. "Is Stick-on Prestige Costing Britain Too Dear?" *Small Car*, September 1963, pp. 8–9; *The Motor*, 16/1/63, p. 936.

22. See the cars illustrated in Freeman, *Humber: An Illustrated History*, p. 100.

23. Mike Taylor, "Don Tarbun," p. 107.

24. At 2455 lb. with a full fuel tank, compared with the Rapier's 2289 lb. with a half-full tank: see *Automobile Engineer*, February 1963, p. 63 (Sceptre); and *Autocar*, 24/7/64, pp. 170–174 (Rapier). The Rapier tank could hold a maximum of ten gallons: *ibid.*

25. A sceptre, by contrast, is defined by *Chambers English Dictionary* as "a staff or baton borne as an emblem of kingship."

26. See *Country Life*, 4/7/63, p. 35; *The Field*, 28/2/63, p. 373; *The Illustrated London News*, 2/3/63, p. 322; and *Small Car*, December 1963, pp. 24–33. See also *Autocar*, 24/9/65, (page unknown) (announcement of Mk II); *The Motor*, 16/1/63, pp. 935–938 (new model announcement); 19/6/63, pp. 48–51 (road test); 4/6/66, pp. 32–37 (buyers' spot check); 16/4/66, pp. 21–26 (Mk II road test).

27. Although Rootes were known to study individual American models closely and the resemblance is far too close to be co-incidental, it would not have been known to most Sceptre buyers as very few 1958–60 Chevrolets had been sold in Britain.

28. 28,996 of the 1963–67 Sceptre were sold, including 11,985 of the Mk II. The Mk II was introduced in September 1965 with the Super Minx bonnet and a revised, horizontal, grille. It was discontinued in the summer of 1967: Sedgwick and Gillies, *A-Z of Cars*, p. 96.

29. For photographs of the Sceptre Mk III, including the interior, see Free-

man, *Humber: An Illustrated History*, pp. 104–107. See also *Country Life*, 23/11/67, p. 1362; *Motor*, 16/9/67, pp. 20–21 (new model announcement); 28/10/67, pp. 53–58.

30. Dixon, "Crown Jewels," p. 34.

31. 43,951 were sold between September 1967 and February 1976: Sedgwick and Gillies, *A–Z of Cars*, p. 96.

14. Jaguar

1. For the Mk VII–IX see, for example, *The Field*, 3/7/58, p. 35 (Mk VIII); 18/5/61, p. 999 (Mk IX). See also Richard Sutton. "Jaguar Mk VII, VIII, IX." *Classic and Sports Car*, August 1990, pp. 68–75; and Paul Skilleter. "Significant Seven." *Thoroughbred & Classic Cars*, March 1987, pp. 36–41; Laurence Meredith. "Tale of a Swinging Cat." *Thoroughbred & Classic Cars*, November 1994, pp. 91–96 (Mk VIII restoration).

2. *The Autocar*, 10/4/57, pp. 326–329. See also *Automobile Engineer*, November 1959, pp. 420–421 (Mk 2); *The Autocar*, 2/10/59, pp. 289–291 (Mk 2 announcement); 17/4/69, pp. 36–39 (Jaguar 240). In addition, see Stuart Bladon. "Went the Day Badly." *Thoroughbred & Classic Cars*, February 1984, p. 33 (enjoyable inside story of original 2.4 litre road test by *The Autocar*); and Martin Buckley. "Cat Among the Pigeons." *Classic and Sports Car*, March 1991, pp. 32–37 (story of the Mk 1 2.4 litre with brochure illustrations and test of surviving car).

3. William Lyons joined with Blackpool sidecar manufacturer William Walmsley in 1922 to form the Swallow Sidecar Company, which from 1926 also produced attractive bodies for several popular car chassis. The company moved to Coventry in 1928 and in October 1931 announced the first (Standard-powered) S.S. Cars (S.S. I and S.S. 2). The partners established S.S. Cars Ltd. in 1933 in order to concentrate on producing complete cars, which from October 1935 were called Jaguars. William Walmsley left the company shortly afterwards and in March 1945 S.S. Cars' name was changed to Jaguar Cars Ltd. (for the obvious reason). In mid-1945 Jaguar started to produce its own 2½ and 3½ litre engines on tooling bought from Standard, who continued to supply 1½ litre engines until 1948. Jaguar's own new engine appeared in the XK 120 of 1948 and subsequently in the Mk VII saloon of 1950, which was developed through the Mk VIIM (1954), Mk VIII (1957) and Mk IX (1958) until it was superseded by the Mk X (later, Mk 10) of 1961. The 2.4 litre Mk I, Jaguar's first monocoque car, appeared in 1955, and a 3.4 litre version was introduced in 1957. It acquired disc brakes within a few months. The XK 120 was followed successively by the XK 140 (1955), the XK 150 (1957) and the E-type (1961–74). For the story of the XK engine see, for example, Graham Robson. "XK X-Ray." *Thoroughbred & Classic Cars*, July 1983, pp. 50–53.

4. Andrew Whyte. "The Lyons Line Lives." *Motor*, 6/9/80, pp. 36–40 (interview with Sir William Lyons).

5. The Mk X was Britain's widest saloon at 6' 4" wide. It was 16' 10" long but only 4' 6.5" high. It weighed approximately 4200 lb.: see *The Autocar*, 13/10/61, pp. 568–573 (announcement); 9/10/64, pp. 696–701 (4.2 litre); 16/10/64, pp. 759–763 (4.2 litre automatic); 8/10/65, pp. 689–693 (4.2 litre with overdrive); *Country Life*, 13/6/63, p. 1385; *The Field*, 18/7/63, p. 129; *The Motor*, 20/11/63, pp. 50–55 (with overdrive). See also Stuart Bladon. "Went the Day Badly." *Thoroughbred & Classic Cars*, March 1988, p. 61 (story of Mk 10 road test); Robert Davies. "'G' for Grand'." *Thoroughbred & Classic Cars*, June 1988, pp. 106–108 (420G of Jaguar — particularly XK — engineer, Claude Baily); Richard Sutton. "Coventry Conflict." *Classic and Sports Car*, January 1985, pp. 42–45 (420G with Daimler Majestic Major); "Buyer's Guide: Jaguar 420G." *Classic and Sports Car*, October 1998, pp. 144–145 (authors not known). A total of 24,282 were sold between 1961 and 1970, including 5763 of the 420G from 1966: Michael Sedgwick and Mark Gillies. *A–Z of Cars 1945–1970* (2nd ed., revd. Jon Pressnell). Bideford, Devon: Bay View Books Ltd., 1993, pp. 103–104. A few (18 of the Mk 10 and 24 of the 420G) were built in limousine form with a glass division: *ibid.*, p. 104. Estimated production of other Jaguars is as follows: Mk 2 and 240/340 (1959–69): 90,640; S-type (1963–68): 24,900; and 420 (1966–68): 9600: *ibid.*, pp. 102–104.

6. For the S-type, see *Autocar*, 19/3/65, pp. 561–566 (3.8 litre with overdrive); *The Field*, 21/5/64, p. 1029; *The Motor*, 2/10/63, pp. 74–81 (announcement).

7. See *Appendix IIA*, p. 343, above.

8. For the E-type, see *The Autocar*, 17/3/61, pp. 402–404 and i–v (announcement, including cutaway diagrams); 24/3/61, pp. 453–456 (road test — fixed-head coupe); 14/5/65, pp. 953–958 (4.2 litre fhc); *Country Life*, 23/3/61, p. 662; 15/4/65 (4.2 litre roadster); 26/5/66, p. 1330 (2 + 2); *The Field*, 15/6/61, p. 1191; 2/9/65, p. 485 (4.2 litre roadster). See also Philip Porter. "Sooth Sayer." *Classic and Sports Car*, November 1987, pp. 88–91 (interview with Jaguar aerodynamicist Malcolm Sayer); Stuart Bladon. "E-type Experience." *Thoroughbred & Classic Cars*, July 1991, pp. 24–29 (tester of original E-type on restored and improved model).

9. For the 420 see, for example, *Autocar*, 18/12/69, pp. 23–24 (used car test); *Country Life*, 22/6/67, p. 1618; *Motor*, 6/5/67, pp. 15–20 (road test); and James Taylor. *Jaguar S-type and 420: The Complete Story*. Marlborough, Wiltshire: The Crowood Press Ltd., 1996, pp. 99–122.

10. *Autocar*, 12/6/69, pp. 8–15. See also *Country Life*, 11/12/69, p. 1613; Graham Robson. "XJ6 Classic Choice." *Thoroughbred & Classic Cars*, August 1991, p. 40–48; Richard Sutton. "Lyons' Pride." *Classic and Sports Car*, November 1986, pp. 96–103. For a recent comparison of the XJ6 with the Mk 2, S-type and 420, see Paul Hardiman. "Compact Pussycats." *Classic and Sports Car*, January 2002, pp. 82–87.

11. *Road & Track Road Test Annual 1971* (1970 test), pp. 66–68.

12. Andrew Whyte. "XJ6." *Thoroughbred & Classic Cars* (*Jaguar Supplement*), October 1986, pp. 10–12 (story of development and launch). For Jaguars generally see past and present issues of the magazine *Jaguar World Monthly* (formerly *Jaguar Quarterly* and *Classic Jaguar World*).

15. Jensen

1. *The Motor*, 24/7/63, pp. 46–49. See also *The Field*, 25/2/65, (page unknown) (C-V8 Mk 2); *Motor Trader*, 10/10/62, p. 67 (announcement). The C-V8 Mk 1 gave 305 bhp and an overall fuel consumption of 16.3 mpg; equivalent figures for the Mk 2 were 330 bhp and 13.2 mpg. The Mk 1 cost £3392 7s 1d when tested by *The Motor* in July 1963; the Mk 2 cost £3491 4s 7d in April 1965.

2. *Autocar*, 16/4/65, pp. 751–756 (manual car).

3. *Car*, December 1966, pp. 29–31. Torqueflite automatic transmission was fitted, as was a Powr-Lok differential. The C-V8 was available with a manual gearbox from the contemporary Chrysler truck range. The gearchange was therefore slow, so that the automatic car had faster acceleration. Only three manual cars were built: Keith Anderson. *Jensen*. Yeovil, Somerset: GT Foulis/Haynes Publishing, 1989, p. 112.

4. Cited in Giles Chapman. "Family Planning." *Classic and Sports Car*, March 1988, pp. 27–33.

5. By contrast, the Ferguson R5 prototype estate car, on which the four-wheel-drive and anti-lock braking systems used in Jensen C-V8 FF prototype of 1965 and in the Interceptor-based FF of 1966 were developed, was an ugly car, but it was ugly by default; its looks did not matter. For the Ferguson R5 prototype see, for example, *Motor*, 20/8/66, pp. 15–24. For the C-V8 FF, with a wheelbase four inches longer than that of the standard C-V8 but otherwise looking almost identical to that car, see *Autocar*, 15/10/65, pp. 743–745.

6. Anderson, *Jensen*, p. 109. For the career of Eric Neale, who left Jensen in 1966, see Mike Taylor. "Artist Designer." *Thoroughbred & Classic Cars*, December 1985, pp. 12–15 and January 1986, pp. 12–14.

7. The P66 was intended to be £1200 or so cheaper than the C-V8 and a replacement, in effect, for the Austin-Healey 3000. It was expected to be built primarily for the American market. For the P66 Interceptor coupe prototype, now restored in its original metallic olive green, see Glen Waddington. "Intercepted." *Classic Cars*, September 2002, pp. 88–93.

8. Giles Chapman. "The Good Life." *Classic and Sports Car*, September 2003, pp. 134–139 (interview with Tony Good). "The 'press fleet' was a C-V8 parked in the street": *ibid.*, p. 136.

9. The prototype had aluminium rather than fibreglass bodywork: see Malcolm McKay. "Jensen 541 Restored." *Thoroughbred & Classic Cars*, January 1994, pp. 72–78 (restoration of prototype by Russ Grief). See also Martin Buckley. "Flexible Friend." *Classic and Sports Car*, July 1996, pp. 119–123 (surviving 541R). For contemporary assessments of the 541 see, for example, *Country Life*, 13/10/55, p. 803 (541); *The Field*, 5/7/56, p. 35 (541); *The Illustrated London News*, 4/3/61, p. 368 (541S).

10. Two convertibles were built of which one survives, which was owned for a while by longstanding Jensen enthusiast Lord Strathcarron: see Giles Chapman. "Keeping the Family Jewel." *Classic and Sports Car*, May 1993, pp. 110–113 (convertible restoration). In 1962 a Jensen 541S was fitted with a Chevrolet V8 engine by Donald Healey: see Ian Young. "Healey's Hod-Rod." *Thoroughbred & Classic Cars*, February 1995, pp. 62–66. For a modern comparison of the 541 and C-V8, see James Elliott. "Caned and Able." *Classic and Sports Car*, February 1999, pp. 130–137. For a comparison of the C-V8 with the rival fibreglass-bodied Gordon-Keeble GK1, see Richard Heseltine. "Hybrids Revisited." *Classic and Sports Cars*, February 2004, pp. 114–119. A single Jensen C-V8 Coupe Cabriolet on a wheelbase 9" longer than that of the standard car was built during 1964–65.

11. This complicated contract proved difficult for all parties and in 1963 Volvo moved assembly and finishing of the P1800 to Sweden, where it was renamed the 1800S: see, for example, Dave Selby. "Volvo/Jensen: The Uneasy Alliance." *Classic Car Weekly*, 16/4/03, p. 35 (examination of original Jensen company documents). Pressed Steel continued to build the bodies until 1968, when the tooling, too, was shipped to Sweden. For the original 1949–57 Interceptor, see Alastair Clements. "There Once was an Ugly Duckling…" *Classic and Sports Car*, January 2001, pp. 126–131.

12. C-V8 production was as follows: Mk 1 (1962–63): 68; Mk II (1963–65): 250; Mk III (1965–66): 181: see Michael Sedgwick and Mark Gillies. *A-Z of Cars 1945–1970* (2nd ed., revd. Jon Pressnell). Bideford, Devon: Bay View Books Ltd., 1993, p. 106. The gross profit per car was £800: Mike Taylor. "The Death of Jensen." *Classic and Sports Car*, May 1983, pp. 57–59.

13. Chapman, "The Good Life," p. 136.

14. Sedgwick and Gillies, *A-Z of Cars*, p. 102. The Interceptor and FF achieved 0–60 mph in 7.3 secs. and 8.4 secs., and top speeds of 138.5 mph and 130 mph respectively: *Motor*, 4/2/67, pp. 13–18 (Interceptor); *Autocar*, 28/3/68, pp. 11–16 (FF).

15. *Car*, December 1966, pp. 29–31.

16. *Autocar*, 18/3/68, pp. 11–17.

17. *Autocar*, 4/9/69, pp. 22–26. See also *Autocar*, 25/1/68, p. 54 (Jensen company reorganization); 16/5/68, pp. 34–36 (Interceptor in Switzerland); *Country Life*, 9/5/68, p. 1243 (Interceptor); 16/4/70, p. 871 (Interceptor); *Motor*, 15/10/66, pp. 23–25 (Interceptor and FF announcement); 4/2/67, pp. 13–18 (Interceptor).

18. Chapman, "The Good Life," p. 136.

19. Jon Pressnell. "Go well — go Kjell." *Classic and Sports Car*, September 2000, pp. 146–151.

20. Chapman, "The Good Life," p. 137.

21. For the S-V8, see *Autocar*, 16/8/00, pp. 46–51 (road test); and for the SV Automotive car see, for example. Tony Dron. "The Tragic Tale of the Jensen S-V8." *Telegraph Motoring*, 14/6/03, p. 5.

16. MG

1. "MG — The Great British Sports Car" said the slogan of the time at the bottom of the page. This advertisement, showing a orange, K-registered MGB roadster, is reproduced in Nick Georgano, Bengt Ason Holm and Michael Sedgwick. *Cars 1930–2000: The Birth of the Motorcar.* New York: Todtri Book Publishers, 2001, p. 699.

2. The Magnette Mk IV remained in production until April 1968. According to Graham Robson, 9650 of the Mk III were sold in the financial year 1959–60 although sales then fell to "2000–3000 a year, and could not be persuaded to better that. In 1966–67, only 869 Mk IVs were built, and this dropped to a mere 327 in 1967–68": Graham Robson. "The Maligned Magnettes." *MG Enthusiast*, April/May 1986, pp. 41–44.

3. *The Motor*, 3/10/62, pp. 322–324; and *The Field*, 28/3/63, p. 577. In October 1964 the four-door available in Britain cost £714 9s 7d compared with the £611 15s 5d charged for an equivalent Morris 1100 De Luxe. See also *Autocar*, 17/10/68, pp. 110–114 (two-door MG 1300 Mk II); *The Motor*, 20/3/63, pp. 86–89 (road test); *Motor Trader*, 3/10/62, pp. 14–15; *Practical Motorist*, August 1964, pp. 1342–1343; *Small Car*, January 1964, pp. 36–43 (test with the four other BMC 1100s); January 1965, pp. 52–59 (test with Renault R8 1100). 124,860 of the 1100 and 32,549 of the 1300 were built between 1962 and 1973; the 1100 and 1300 overlapped during 1967–68: see Michael Sedgwick and Mark Gillies. *A-Z of Cars 1945–1970* (2nd ed., revd. Jon Pressnell). Bideford, Devon: Bay View Books Ltd., 1993, pp. 134; and Graham Robson, *The Cars of BMC*. Croydon: Motor Racing Publications Ltd., 1999, pp. 197–202.

4. All four were designed more or less in parallel by Gerald Palmer. For post-war MGs generally, see Robson, *The Cars of BMC*, pp. 171–202. See also Malcolm Green. *MG: Britain's Favourite Sports Car.* Yeovil, Somerset: Haynes Publishing, 1998; David Knowles. *MG: The Untold Story.* London: Windrow & Greene, 1997. For the ZA and ZB Magnette and related BMC cars, see Gerald Palmer. *Auto-Architect: The Autobiography of Gerald Palmer.* East Horsley, Surrey: Magna Press, 1998, pp. 47–64. For the ZA/ZB saloons, see also Graham Robson. "1953–58 MG Magnette: Adding Attraction." *Collectible Automobile*, October 2002, pp. 26–35; Anders Clausager. "Magnette ZA/ZB Series and Wolseley 4/44 and 15/50." *Classic and Sports Car*, February 1991, pp. 78–84. For all of the post-war MG saloons, Y-type to 1100, see Martin Buckley. "Old faithfuls…" *Classic and Sports Car*, October 1989, pp. 120–125.

5. See, for example, *The Autocar*, 26/11/54, pp. 849–852 (road test). See also *Automobile Engineer*, May 1955, pp. 179–190 (detailed description).

6. *Country Life*, 10/9/59, p. 243. See also *The Autocar*, 6/2/59, pp. 185–188;

10/4/59, pp. 546–548; *The Illustrated London News*, 7/3/59, p. 416; *The Field*, 12/2/59, p. 283; *Motor Trader*, 4/2/59, pp. 126–127.

7. For the Magnette Mk IV see, for example, *Small Car*, April 1964, pp. 45–53 (test with the other "Farinas." The magazine's Mk IV managed 85 mph, 0–60 in 19.3 seconds and 25.1 mpg. With two people the car weighed 2884 lb. compared with the 2702 lb. of the Austin Cambridge. The twin-carburettor engine gave 68 bhp.

8. For the Midget Mk I and its sister, the Austin-Healey Sprite Mk II (both 1961–64) see, for example, John Pressnell. "Abingdon's Orphans." *Classic and Sports Car*, May 1993, pp. 115–119. See also "Sprite/Midget: Classic Choice." (Author(s): not stated) *Thoroughbred & Classic Cars*, May 1991, pp. 40–47.

9. Robson, *The Cars of BMC*, p. 179. Just 2111 Twin-Cams were produced during 1958–60, compared with 98,970 of other MGAs from 1955–62; 152,528 Midgets (Mk I-III) from 1961–74; 334,768 MGB roadsters (Mk I-II) from 1962–71; 113,042 MGB GTs (Mk I-II) from 1965–71; 4542 six-cylinder MGC roadsters from 1967–69 and 4457 MGC GTs during the same period: see Sedgwick and Gillies, *A-Z of Cars*, pp. 132–135.

10. BMO 541B in red with a white roof.

11. In the style of 1939–40 Nash advertising in the United States.

12. For a detailed account of the MGB's development, see David Knowles. *MGB, MGC & MGB GT V8.* Osceola, WI: MBI Publishing Company, 2000. For American MGB advertising see *ibid.*, pp. 164–176. For the Belgian Coune MG coupe, see Richard Heseltime. "Brussels Snout." *Classic and Sports Car*, November 2003, pp. 100–103; Hein Schoone. "Belgian MGB." *Thoroughbred & Classic Cars*, December 1988, pp. 56–58; Giles Chapman. "Ich bin ein Berlinette." *Your Classic*, April 1992, pp. 62–63.

13. For information about the MG Sports Sedan including about 30 advertisements and relevant MG bibliography, see Michael Carnell. *www.palmettobug.com/mg1100/main.htm.*

14. These cars are described in some detail in Mike Covello (ed.). *Standard Catalog of Imported Cars 1946–2002 (2nd ed.).* Iola, WI: Krause Publications, 2002, pp. 570–576.

15. For a 1957 account of advertisers' quest to encourage consumers to seek status through cars and other products, see Vance Packard. *The Hidden Persuaders.* London: Penguin Books, 1991, pp. 45–53 and 106–115. The subject has spawned a fascinating literature which will, arguably, continue to expand for as long as humans, like other primates, live in flexible hierarchies within which social position has psychological and physiological effects without direct relation to immediate basic needs. For intellectuals who would have everyone opt out of consumer (including automotive) display, the *caveat* entered by Leo Rostin in 1963 is perhaps salutary: "The sad truth seems to be this: that relatively few people in any society, not excluding Periclean Athens, have reasonably good taste or care deeply about ideas. Fewer still seem equipped — by temperament and capacity, rather than education — to handle ideas with both skill and pleasure…. Intellectuals seem unable to reconcile themselves to the fact that their hunger for more news, better plays, more serious debate, deeper involvement in ideas is not a hunger characteristic of many. They cannot believe that the subjects dear to their hearts bore or repel or overtax the capacities of their fellow citizens." Leo Rostin. "The Intellectual and the Mass Media: Some Rigorously Random Remarks" in John S. Wright and Daniel S. Warner. *Speaking of Advertising.* New York, 1963: McGraw-Hill Book Company Inc., 1963, p. 176. For a summary of the life and work of Vance Packard (1914–1996) see, for example, *The Times*, 24/12/96 (obituary).

17. Riley

1. There were also low-production drophead coupe (RMD) and roadster (RMC) derivatives.

2. For the story of these Rileys see, for example, Jon Pressnell. "Diamond Life." *Classic and Sports Car*, August 1987, pp. 76–83. For the history of Riley generally from 1896 to 1957, see also Malcolm McKay. "Life of Riley." *Thoroughbred & Classic Cars*, July 1996, pp. 104–108. For pre-war ancestors of the 1½ Litre RMA and RME, see Jonathan Wood. "Riley 12/4." *The Automobile*, February 2004, pp. 24–28.

3. See Gerald Palmer. *Auto-Architect: The Autobiography of Gerald Palmer.* East Horsley, Surrey: Magna Press, 1998, p. 61. See also Brian Palmer. "Engineered With Style." *Thoroughbred & Classic Cars*, January 1992, pp. 102–106 (interview with Gerald Palmer). See also John Mclellan. "The Table Talk of Cecil Cousins." *Thoroughbred & Classic Cars*, January 1985, pp. 56–59 (interview with Cecil Cousins, MG works manager at Abingdon, where the Pathfinders were built). Late in 1956, a leaf-spring rear suspension system was adopted, although the early failures were almost certainly caused by inaccurate welding of the Panhard rod bracket to the chassis by chassis builders John

Thompson, who decided to weld the chassis on wooden trestles rather than by using the jig supplied: see Christopher Balfour in Palmer, *Auto Architect*, p. 62.

4. D.P. Crownshaw. "The 'Humpfinder'." *Classic and Sports Car*, February 1986, p. 12. The faults with the Pathfinder were classically of the kind in which, if just one of parties involved had done better, the trouble would not have occurred. The Pathfinder's steering — a cam and lever system rather than the earlier cars' rack and pinion — was not precise, but unlike the early brakes and Panhard rod it was not prone to trouble. Long-term owners of good Pathfinders have spoken very highly of the design as a whole: see Christopher Balfour in Palmer, *Auto-Architect*, p. 62 (owners' views). See also Charles Herridge. "Finding New Friends." *Classic and Sports Car*, November 1992, pp. 54–58 (preserved Pathfinder prepared by Chris Nixon for Monte Carlo Challenge).

5. Malcolm McKay. "The Man Who Designed the MGB." *Thoroughbred & Classic Cars*, December 1992, pp. 30–36 (interview with Don Hayter).

6. Did the copywriter accidentally leave out "combine" before "speed"? For Lockheed's advertisement and the test by *The Autocar* of the Two-Point-Six, see *The Autocar*, 20/12/57, front cover and pp. 983–986. Only 2000 were sold compared with 5152 Pathfinders. The Two-Point-Six cost the same as the outgoing Pathfinder —£1411 7s.

7. See Jon Pressnell. "The Minors That Might Have Been." *Classic and Sports Car*, April 1994, pp. 94–97; Jon Pressnell. "Major Upset." *Classic and Sports Car*, July 1986, pp. 56–59; and Jon Pressnell. *Morris Minor: Exploring the Legend.* Yeovil, Somerset: Haynes, 1998, pp. 74–84. For the Wolseley 1500, see pp. 267–269, above.

8. The 1489cc engine produced 68bhp and the car weighed 2104 lb.(See Anders Clausager. "Riley & Wolseley 1.5 and 1500." *Classic and Sports Car*, June 1990, pp. 84–92.

9. For details of Riley models from 1945 to 1969, see Graham Robson. *The Cars of BMC.* Croydon: Motor Racing Publications Ltd., 1999, pp. 203–222.

10. See *The Autocar*, 25/8/61, pp. 180–283; *Country Life*, 11/9/58, p. 538; *The Field*, 5/12/57, p. 1063; 6/4/61, (page unknown), (Mk II). See also Mike McCarthy and Peter Nunn. *Classic and Sports Car*, November 1983, pp. 82–84 (test with Sunbeam Rapier); and Brian Palmer. "Test Match." *Thoroughbred & Classic Cars*, March 1990, pp. 14–23 (test with Wolseley 1500 and other contemporary medium-sized saloons).

11. Michael Sedgwick and Mark Gillies. *A-Z of Cars 1945–1970 (2nd ed., revd. Jon Pressnell).* Bideford, Devon: Bay View Books Ltd., 1993, p. 164. Production of other Rileys was as follows: 4/68 (1959–61): 10,940; 4/72 (1961–69): 14,151; Elf (1961–69): 30,912; Kestrel and 1300 (1965–69): 21,529: *ibid.*, pp. 164–165.

12. *Country Life*, 13/8/59, p. 28. See also *The Autocar*, 24/4/59, p. 624–625 (announcement); 4/3/60, pp. 382–385 (road test); 3/3/61, pp. 323–324 (Riley Riviera — performance conversion with wire wheels and lowered fins and suspension by Wessex Motors Ltd. of Salisbury); *Motor Trader*, 29/4/59, pp. 120–121.

13. The readings were genuine; the speeds correspond to third gear.

14. For the 4/Seventy Two see, for example, *Small Car*, December 1963, pp. 24–29 (test with Humber Sceptre); April 1964, pp. 45–53 (test with equivalent Austin A60 Cambridge, Morris Oxford, MG Magnette Mk IV and Wolseley 16/60); *The Motor*, 28/2/62, pp. 118–121.

15. See, for example, *The Motor*, 10/7/63, pp. 46–49 (Mk II). See also Mark Gillies. "Given the Boot…" *Classic and Sports Car*, November 1984, pp. 86–87; and Chris Rees. *Complete Classic Mini 1959—2000.* Croydon: Motor Racing Publications Ltd., 2003, pp. 151–157.

16. See *Autocar*, 1/10/65, pp. 632–634 (announcement of Riley Kestrel and Wolseley 1100).

17. The subsequent — and very shortlived — Riley Kestrel 1100 Mk II was so-called to distinguish it from the earlier Riley Kestrel, which, although an 1100 in fact, was simply called the "Riley Kestrel." For details of these models, see Robson, *The Cars of BMC*, pp. 219–222. The Riley marque name is now dormant and is owned by BMW.

18. Rolls-Royce

1. David Ogilvy. *Ogilvy on Advertising.* London: Prion Books Ltd., 1995 [1983], p. 11. The advertisement is shown on p. 10.

2. *Ibid.*, p. 216.

3. David Ogilvy. *Confessions of an Advertising Man.* London: Pan Books, 1987 [1963], pp. 127–128. Ogilvy was nevertheless surprised to discover that the theme was not original. Charles Brower of the agency Batten, Barton, Durstine & Osborn wrote to him citing an advertisement for the American luxury car makers Pierce-Arrow written by Brower in 1933: "The only sound one can

hear in the new Pierce-Arrow is the ticking of the electric clock.": Stephen Fox. *The Mirror Makers.* London: Heinemann, 1990, p. 237.

4. Whether Ogilvy's position was truly coherent, how far he stuck to his own precepts, and whether any philosophy of advertising can be devised to cover all products and circumstances has been much and enjoyably debated.

5. *The Field*, 30/1/58, p. 197. See also *The Autocar*, 3/4/59, p. 491 (Drophead Coupe by Mulliner in the style of the Silver Cloud I); 13/5/60, pp. 772–775 (Silver Cloud II); *Automobile Engineer*, September 1959, pp. 348–350 (Silver Cloud II and Bentley S2); *Car*, July 1965, pp. 32–33 (comparison by Laurence Pomeroy of older and recent Rolls-Royces with each other and with the Humber Imperial); *Country Life*, 14/11/63, p. 1272; *The Field*, 9/5/57, p. 743 (Bentley S1); 13/8/64, p. 361 (Silver Cloud III); *The Motor*, 17/10/62, pp. 438–439 (Silver Cloud III and Bentley S3); 21/8/63, pp. 38–43 (Silver Cloud III).

6. *Car*, December 1965, pp. 38–39. See also *Autocar*, 8/10/65, pp. ii-vii and 699–703 (description); 16/1/69, pp. 50–52 (production processes); *Country Life*, 9/10/69, p. 915; 18/3/71, p. 625 (Corniche); *The Field*, 19/10/67, p. 723; 15/10/70, p. 731. 16,717 of the Silver Shadow I, including 2776 of a long wheelbase model, were built between 1965 and 1977: Michael Sedgwick and Mark Gillies. *A-Z of Cars 1945–1970 (2nd ed., revd. Jon Pressnell).* Bideford, Devon: Bay View Books Ltd., 1993, pp. 168–169.

19. Rover

1. Raymond Loewy. *Never Leave Well Enough Alone. (2002 ed.) [1951]* Baltimore, Maryland: John Hopkins University Press, 2002, pp. 277–280. This is a curious work, part manifesto, part autobiography and part corporate advertisement. The final shape of the Studebaker was by Virgil Exner, working with Loewy's ideas.

2. James Taylor. *Rover P4: The Complete Story.* Marlborough, Wiltshire: The Crowood Press Ltd., 1998, pp. 16–22, 39. See also Graham Robson. "Rover P4 (1949–64)." *Thoroughbred & Classic Cars*, October 1991, pp. 48–56.

3. Cited in Taylor, *Rover P4: The Complete Story*, p. 32.

4. See Jon Pressnell. "One Eye to the Future." *Classic and Sports Car*, January 1997, pp. 80–84.

5. Matt White. "Rover's Model Man." *Thoroughbred & Classic Cars*, March 1995, pp. 52–56.

6. *Ibid.*, p. 53.

7. Barney Sharratt. *Men and Motors of 'The Austin.'* Yeovil, Somerset: Haynes Publishing, 2000, p. 83.

8. The 1948 Austin Atlantic was slightly less controversial as it was more closely related to cars which Austin had already introduced and was a specialized model within a wide product range. It also marked less of a departure from customers' expectations of the particular marque — which was also true of the 1947 Singer SM1500.

9. Rover engineer and designer Gordon Bashford recalls: "Harry Loker had an eye for a line, but he used to have quite terrific arguments with Maurice Wilks. The early P4s had a sloping boot and a small rear window — Maurice Wilks was adamant that this was what he wanted. Harry said he'd regret it, and a few years later we were changing the car to have a higher boot and a bigger rear window": Jon Pressnell. "Quietly Does It." *Classic and Sports Car*, December 1991, pp. 91–95 (interview with Gordon Bashford).

10. White, "Rover's Model Man," p. 54. "Of course, I was absolutely floored. We had to retract and do something much less exuberant," recalled Bache: *ibid.*, p. 54. For photographs of styling models for the 3-Litre, see *ibid.*, p. 55.

11. From a paper which Loewy presented to the Society of Automotive Engineers in 1942: see Loewy, *Never Leave Well Enough Alone*, p. 307. For a discussion of automobile styling, including that of the 1947–50 Studebakers, see *ibid.*, pp. 305–320.

12. See, for example, *The Autocar*, 12/8/60, pp. 234–237 (100); *Country Life*, 25/2/60, p. 385 (80); *The Illustrated London News*, 2/4/60, p. 572 (80 and 100); *The Field*, 28/8/58, p. 381 (105S).

13. See *The Autocar*, 21/8/59, pp. 54–57; 1/12/61, pp. 937–940 (automatic); 15/5/64, p. 946 (convertible by Panelcraft); 13/11/64, pp. 1022–1026 (automatic); *Automobile Engineer*, February 1960, pp. 44–50 (body/chassis); March 1960, pp. 84–93 (engine, transmission and rear axle); April 1960, pp. 126–133 (suspension, steering, brakes and electrical equipment); October 1962, pp. 375–377; January 1963, pp. 10–11; *Country Life*, 14/12/61, p. 1536; 1/11/62, p. 1111; *The Illustrated London News*, 3/3/62, p. 349; 11/3/63, p. 746; *The Field*, 24/5/62, p. 1045; 1/12/60, p. 1115; 14/3/63, p. 469 (Coupé); *The Motor*, 3/10/62, pp. 318–321; 19/3/66, pp. 19–24; *Motor Trader*, 24/9/58, pp. 356–357.

14. A 1960 Rover 100 weighed 3444 lb.: see *Autocar*, 12/8/60, p. 237.

15. James Taylor. "Behind the Scenes." *Thoroughbred & Classic Cars*, October 1984, pp. 80–82 (interview).

16. 7983 3-Litre Coupés were made between 1964–67 compared with 40,558

saloons: Michael Sedgwick and Mark Gillies. *A-Z of Cars 1945–1970 (2nd. ed., revd. Jon Pressnell)*. Bideford, Devon: Bay View Books Ltd., 1993, p. 172. A total of 130,312 Rover P4s (60, 75, 80, 90, 95, 100, 105R, 105S and 110) were made: *ibid.*, pp. 170–171. For a comparison of the Coupé with the Vanden Plas 4-litre R, see Jon Pressnell. "Royal Pretender." *Classic and Sports Car*, July 1993, pp. 60–65.

17. Mike Taylor. "Rover Years." *Thoroughbred & Classic Cars*, June 1986, pp. 15–18 (interview with Spen King).

18. *Ibid.*, p. 16.

19. See *Motor*, 21/1/67, pp. 68–71; White, "Rover's Model Man," p. 54; James Taylor. "P6 Prototypes." *Thoroughbred & Classic Cars*, September 1991, pp. 56–62; Pressnell, "Quietly Does It," pp. 92–93.

20. Rab Cook. "A Tales of Two Thousands." *Thoroughbred & Classic Cars*, August 1980, pp. 18–20. For the P6 generally, see James Taylor. *Rover P6 1963–1977*. Croydon: Motor Racing Publications Ltd., 1993. See also Graham Robson. "Rover P6 Classic Choice." *Thoroughbred & Classic Cars*, November 1990, pp. 120–128.

21. *The Motor*, 9/10/63, pp. 106–111. See also *Car*, February 1969, pp. 49–55 (Triumph 2.5PI with 2000 TC); *Country Life*, 21/11/63, p. 1350; 6/6/68, p. 1538 (P6 BS mid-engined sports prototype); *The Field*, 16/9/63, p. 573; 19/12/63, p. 1265; *The Illustrated London News*, 2/11/63, p. 749; 4/11/67, p. 34 (Zagato Rover TCZ); *The Motor*, 5/2/66, pp. 13–16 (24,000 mile report); 1/10/66, pp. 26–32 (2000 TC).

22. See James Taylor. "Rover's Tale." *Thoroughbred & Classic Cars*, March 1996, pp. 78–81 (interview with service crew member Lou Chaffey).

23. 208,875 of the 2000, 2000 SC and 2000 TC, excluding completely knocked down (ckd) kits of parts for assembly abroad, were made between 1963 and 1973: Sedgwick and Gillies, *A-Z of Cars*, p. 172.

24. For the story of the engine's development for the Buick, see *The Autocar*, 23/9/60, pp. 461–463 (analysis by Karl Ludvigsen).

25. James Taylor, "Behind the Scenes," p. 82. See also *Autocar*, 15/8/68, pp. 28–30 (story of the engine's development for the Rover).

26. See *Autocar*, 28/8/69, pp. 33–35; *Car*, May 1968, pp. 19–21.

27. *Motor*, 7/10/67, pp. 59–64. See also *Car*, January 1968, pp. 44–50; *Country Life*, 21/3/68, p. 676; and Martin Buckley. "True Brits." *Classic and Sports Car*, July 1994, pp. 82–82 (3.5 Litre with Rolls-Royce Silver Cloud III).

20. (Reliant) Scimitar

1. See pp. 102–105, above.

2. Mike McCarthy and Martin Buckley. "Fit for a Princess." *Classic and Sports Car*, February 1986, pp. 65–71 (interview with Tom Karen). For a more recent interview with Tom Karen, see Richard Heseltine. "Man from Ogle." *Classic and Sports Car*, April 2001, pp. 145–147.

3. Brian Long. *Lancia: From Alpha to Zeta and Beyond*. Stroud, Gloucestershire: Sutton Publishing Ltd., 1999, p. 212. For a comparison of the Lancia, Jensen, Scimitar, Volvo and Jaguar see Brian Palmer. "Antiques Roadshow." *Thoroughbred & Classic Cars*, July 1994, pp. 14–22. For the Gilbern Invader see, for example, John Williams. "Estate Invader." *Thoroughbred & Classic Cars*, May 1991, pp. 90–94.

4. See Mike Laurence. "To Sharpen a Sabre." *Classic and Sports Car*, August 1990, pp. 78–83; Richard Heseltine. "Cut and Thrust." *Classic and Sports Car*, May 2002, pp. 146–151; Jonathan Wood. "Retro." [on Reliant's sporting cars] *Thoroughbred & Classic Cars*, October 1985, p. 19. Alan Williams. "Sabra Cadabra: The Story of Reliant's Prototype Sports Car." *Old Car*, January 1989, pp. 22–29 (surviving prototype). See also *The Field*, 28/6/62, p. 1303; *The Motor*, 21/2/62, pp. 80–83; *Motor Trader*, 4/10/61, p. 2 (announcement). In 1989 11 Sabras were known to remain including 10 in the U.S., of which two were beyond restoration: Williams, "Sabra Cadabra," p. 28. Autocars was taken over in 1974 by Rom Carmel, who discontinued the Sabra marque and produced cars under its own name until 1981. Reliant supplied components to Autocars until 1967.

5. Mark Dixon. "Plastic fantastic." *Practical Classics*, March 2001, pp. 44–49.

6. See *The Autocar*, 3/4/64, pp. 616–620. See also *Country Life*, 13/8/64, p. 415.

7. Mike McCarthy. "Ogle This." *Classic and Sports Car*, January 1996, pp. 100–102 (interview with Tom Karen). The 1958 award was first prize in the Institute of British Carriage and Automobile Manufacturers (IBCAM) awards.

8. The remaining four SX250s were never built. For the story of the SX250, see Giles Chapman. "Daimler Conquest." *Classic and Sports Car*, June 1998, pp. 156–159. For later versions of the Scimitar GT see *The Autocar*, 19/9/68, pp. 34–38 (2.5 litre V6); 18/8/69 (3 litre V6: long-term assessment); *Motor*, 16/9/67, p. 19 (2.5 litre V6 announcement).

9. Chris Harvey. "Cutting a Dash." *Thoroughbred & Classic Cars*, September 1986, pp. 59–64. See also Bob Murray. "Coupe De 'Glass." *Classic and Sports Car*, July 1994, pp. 67–71. Taunus 17Ms for the United States also had four conventional headlamps, but few were imported.

10. Michael Sedgwick and Mark Gillies. *A-Z of Cars 1945–1970 (2nd ed., revd. Jon Pressnell)*. Bideford, Devon: Bay View Books Ltd., 1993, p. 158.

11. McCarthy and Buckley. "Fit for a Princess," pp. 65–66.

12. *Ibid.*, p. 65.

13. Harvey, "Cutting a Dash, p. 59.

14. *Car*, March 1970, pp. 68–69. See also *Autocar*, 16/10/69, p. 137 (brief impressions); *Country Life*, 24/9/70, p. 764; *The Illustrated London News*, 20/9/69, p. 27. In addition, see Mark Hughes. "Best Buy: Scimitar GTE." *Classic and Sports Car*, August 1995, pp. 74–83; Malcolm McKay. "Starter Classic: Reliant Scimitar GTE." *Classic and Sports Car*, February 2004, pp. 134–137.

21. Sunbeam

1. See, for example, *The Autocar*, 3/6/60, p. 910 (used Series I); 11/9/59, pp. 173–174 (Series III); 24/7/64, pp. 170–174 (Series IV); *The Field*, 6/12/56, p. 1087 (Series I); 27/3/58, p. 567 (Series II hardtop); *Motor*, 26/11/66, pp. 23–28 (Series V); *Motor Trader*, 16/9/59, p. 135 (Series III). For the story of Sunbeam from 1887 to the 1977 Chrysler Sunbeam hatchback, see Jonathan Wood. "Sunbeam." *Thoroughbred & Classic Cars*, October 1985, pp. 113–117. A prototype Rapier was mistaken for a forthcoming Minx by an amateur photographer a few months before the car was introduced. When editors telephoned Rootes' PR chief, John Bullock, to ask about the pictures he could quite truthfully say that no new Hillman was planned for the year, and offered a free Minx to each editor if the "scoop" pictures proved to be of a Hillman. The pictures were not published—but the editors kicked themselves, to put it mildly, when the car was announced as a Sunbeam: see John Bullock. *The Rootes Brothers: Story of a Motoring Empire*. Yeovil, Somerset: Patrick Stephens Ltd./Haynes Publishing, 1993, pp. 205–207.

2. John Simister. "Sunbeam Rapier Series I-V." *Classic and Sports Car*, December 1990, pp. 75–82; Mike McCarthy and Peter Nunn. "Mid-Field Middleweights." *Classic and Sports Car*, October 1983, pp. 82–84 (Series IIIA compared with Riley One-Point-Five); See also Jon Pressnell. "Fry's Impish Delights." *Classic and Sports Car*, March 2000, pp. 122–126 (interview with Tim Fry); and "Mixed Doubles." *Classic and Sports Car*, June 1993, pp. 60–66 (C & S writers compare Rapier Series II with Alfa Romeo Giulietta, Borgward Isabella TS Coupe, Riley One-Point-Five and Volvo PV544).

3. Barney Sharratt. "Alpine Design." *Thoroughbred & Classic Cars*, November 1992, pp. 80–85 (interview with Kenneth Howes). See also Richard Langworth. *Tiger, Alpine, Rapier: Sporting Cars from the Rootes Group*. Osprey Publishing Ltd., 1982: p. 90–92.

4. For the Sunbeam Rapier's rallying history, see Langworth, *Tiger, Alpine, Rapier*, pp. 51–73. For the story of a remarkable Rapier restoration, see Dale Drinnon. "Nobody Wanted It, Nobody Loved It." *Practical Classics*, July 2003, pp. 39–43 (Series III convertible of Ted Welch). For the rescue and restoration of a lightweight Rapier Series III race car, one of two built by Rootes' Competition Department and shipped the United States in 1960, see David Parrott. "Sunbeam's American Racer." *Thoroughbred & Classic Cars*, March 1994, pp. 62–67. These cars were featured in *Motor Life*, February 1961: *ibid*. Rapier production was as follows: Series 1 (10/55–2/58): 7477; Series II (2/58–9/59): 15,151; Series III (9/59–4/61): 15,368; Series IIIA (4/61–10/63): 17,354; Series IV (10/63–9/65): 9700; Series V (9/65–6/67): 3759: Simister, "Sunbeam Rapier Series I-V," p. 77.

5. See Mike Taylor and Richard Sutton. "Soft Option." *Classic and Sports Car*, March 1985, pp. 67–73; Graham Robson. "Alpine: Classic Choice." *Thoroughbred & Classic Cars*, June 1991, pp. 40–47; Mark Hughes. "Sunbeam Alpine." *Classic and Sports Car*, May 1993, pp. 58–63. For the story of the Alpine's development generally, see Chris McGovern. *Alpine: The Classic Sunbeam*. London: Gentry, 1980. For the fastback Harrington Alpine, see Martin Buckley. "Brighton Belle." *Classic and Sports Car*, November 1995, pp. 92–95 (earliest known survivor, a Type A, with fins); and Giles Chapman. "Close Coupe." *Classic and Sports Car*, December 1998, pp. 37–41 (Type B, without fins, with MGB Berlinette by Jacques Coune of Brussels).

6. Barney Sharratt, "Alpine Design," p. 84.

7. *Ibid.*, p. 82.

8. *Ibid.*, p. 84. The Alpine was assembled by Bristol Siddeley Engines Ltd. in Coventry until the spring of 1962: see Graham Robson. *Cars of the Rootes Group*. Croydon: Motor Racing Publications Ltd., 1999, pp. 103–130.

9. Alpine production and Series introductions were as follows: Series I (1494cc, to 10/60): 11,904; Series II (1592cc, 10/60–2/63): 19,956; Series III

(1592cc, with new hardtop, 3/63–1/64): 5863; Series IV: (1592cc, with reduced fins, 1/64–9/65): 12,406; Series V (1725cc, 9/65–1/68): 19,122: Michael Sedgwick and Mark Gillies. *A-Z of Cars 1945–1970 (2nd ed., revd. Jon Pressnell).* Bideford, Devon: Bay View Books Ltd., 1993, pp. 191–192; and Mark Hughes, "Sunbeam Alpine," p. 59.

10. See *Motor,* 23/7/66, pp. 25–30 (Series V GT). See also *The Autocar,* 14/8/59, pp. 6–7 (Series I announcement); 21/8/59, pp. 60–62 (Series I detailed description); 2/12/60, pp. 969–972 (Series II); 17/1/64, p. 103 (Series IV); 22/5/64, pp. 984–988 (Series IV automatic); 24/9/64, p. 633 (used Series II hardtop); *Automobile Engineer,* August 1959, pp. 307–309 (Series I); *The Field,* 8/9/60, p. 419 (Series I); 9/5/63 (page unknown) (Series III hardtop); 12/3/64, p. 477 (Series IV automatic); 2/12/65, p. 1198 (Series V); *The Motor,* 20/3/63, pp. 235–236 (Series III); 25/9/63, pp. 50–53 (Series III); *Small Car,* December 1963, pp. 56–59 (Series III).

11. Jonathan Wood. "The Tiger Story." *Thoroughbred & Classic Cars,* February 1983, pp. 62–65 (interview with Ian Garrad). For the Tiger's development and production history, see further Tony Dron. "Sunbeam Alpine and Tiger." *Thoroughbred & Classic Cars,* January 1996, pp. 74–82; Mike Taylor. "Don Tarbun." *Thoroughbred & Classic Cars,* February 1987, p. 102–107 (interview with Rootes development engineer Don Tarbun); and Langworth, *Tiger, Alpine, Rapier,* pp. 120–139. See also Mike Taylor. *Tiger: The Making of a Sports Car.* Yeovil, Somerset: Haynes, 1991. In addition, see William Carroll's *Tiger — An Exceptional Motor Car* and Norman Miller's detailed study, *The Book of Norman*: Dron, "Sunbeam Alpine and Tiger," p. 78.

12. *Autocar,* 30/4/65, pp. 855–860.

13. *Motor,* 23/7/66, pp. 25–30.

14. A little over 7000 Tigers were built, of which approximately 5100 were sent to America. (Precise production figures are analyzed in the specialist literature.) Approximately 80 percent of all Alpines and Tigers combined were exported, mostly to America: Dron, *Sunbeam Alpine and Tiger,* p. 78.

15. *Car,* February 1967, pp. 54–55.

16. *The Field,* 15/4/65, p. 693.

17. See *Autocar,* 25/1/68, pp. 11–16; 10/10/68, pp. 77–80; *Country Life,* 25/4/68, p. 1048. In January 1968 the Rapier cost £1208 2s 11d.

18. Axe became Chief Stylist in 1967 after Chrysler had taken control of the Group and in 1969 was appointed Director of Design UK. In 1981, he became Director of Automotive Product Design at Chrysler in the United States: Barney Sharratt. "Roy of the Rootes." *Thoroughbred & Classic Cars,* May 1993, pp. 62–66.

19. *Ibid.,* p. 65.

20. *Autocar,* 9/1/69, pp. 28–33. See also *Autocar,* 4/9/69, pp. 34–39 (H120 with Ford Capri 2000GT); *The Illustrated London News,* 28/6/69, p. 32. For the Alpine, see *Autocar,* 16/10/69, p. 87 (brief announcement).

21. 46,206 of all types (Rapier, H120 and Alpine) were sold: Sedgwick and Gillies, *A-Z of Cars,* pp. 193–194. For the story of the range, and in particular the H120, see John Simister. "Sharpening the Sword." *Classic and Sports Car,* August 1991, pp. 86–90.

22. Robson, *Cars of the Rootes Group,* pp. 128–129. See also *The Illustrated London News,* 27/7/68, p. 32; *Motor,* 7/10/67, p. 74 (announcement). The other regular production Sunbeam Imps were the Sunbeam Imp Sport (1966–70) and the Sunbeam Sport (1970–66), the latter with four headlamps like the Stiletto but otherwise very similar to the Singer Chamois Sport of 1966–70. Production of these two other Sunbeams has also been estimated at approximately 10,000: Robson, *Cars of the Rootes Group,* pp. 128–129. The Sunbeam marque name is now dormant and is owned by Peugeot.

22. Triumph

1. See Michael Cook. *Triumph Cars in America.* St. Paul, MN: MBI Publishing Company, 2001, pp. 30–39. Small numbers of 948cc and 1147cc Heralds were sold in the U.S. during the early 1960s. The 1960–61 948cc car suffered from being underpowered, whereas the six-cylinder Sports Six (Vitesse) convertible of 1962 was too expensive at $2499 (when the Herald convertible cost just $1949) and by the end of 1962 had been reduced by $150: *ibid.,* p. 74. For all Triumph cars in Britain, see past and present issues of the magazine *Triumph World.* See also generally Jonathan Stein. *British Sports Cars in America 1946–1981.* Pennsylvania: Automobile Quarterly Publications, 1993, pp. 118–125.

2. Barney Sharratt. "Raising the Standards." *Thoroughbred & Classic Cars,* May 1996, pp. 96–100 (interview with Vic Hammond). For the story of the small Standards, see also Mike McCarthy. "Standard Fare." *Classic and Sports Car,* September 1993, pp. 102–106.

3. Graham Robson. *Triumph Herald and Vitesse: The Complete Story.* Marlborough, Wiltshire: The Crowood Press Ltd., 1997, p. 35–36.

4. The opportunity to meet came by chance, in what Graham Robson has understandably called "a miracle"; see pp. 117–118, above. For Standard-Triumph's own proposal, see Robson, *Triumph Herald and Vitesse,* pp. 35–36 (model) and Jonathan Wood. "Enter the Herald." *Thoroughbred & Classic Cars,* May 1983, pp. 99–91 (drawing, within first part of interview with Harry Webster); and Jonathan Wood. "Herald Triumph." *Thoroughbred & Classic Cars,* June 1983, pp. 78–80 (conclusion of interview).

5. For a comparison of earlier sketches based on "Zobo," and the sketch of what would become the Herald, see Graham Robson. "Hark, the Herald Angle." *Classic and Sports Car,* October 1986, pp. 77–78. *Note:* Of these four sketches the date of the top one is unknown, the middle two are dated 22/8/57 and the last, unmistakably showing the shape of the Herald, is dated 6/9/57: see "Harry's Game." *Classic and Sports Car,* November 1990, pp. 60–65 (extracts from interview tapes accompanied by bottom three sketches). Webster visited Michelotti on 5/9/57 and returned to Coventry on 6/9/57. For a fascinating insight into Michelotti's work, accompanied by 35 illustrations of design studies, models and prototypes including a Herald hatchback, see Malcolm McKay. "Drawing on Inspiration." *Classic Cars,* April 1998, pp. 92–99 (interview with Giovanni Michelotti's son, Edgardo Michelotti, in Turin).

6. See, for example, *The Autocar,* 24/4/59, pp. 617–621; *Automobile Engineer,* May 1959, pp. 181–183; September 1960, pp. 352–362 (detailed description of chassis, body and engine); October 1960, pp. 392–402 (detailed description of transmission, suspension, steering, brakes and electical equipment); *Motor Trader,* 22/4/59, pp. 94–95. The coupe was updated with ribbed rear quarter panels in June 1960 and discontinued in October 1964. A stripped Herald S arrived in February 1961; in April 1961 all models except the "S" gained a 1147cc engine in April 1961 to became Herald 1200s (with a new wooden dashboard); the Herald 12/50, a supplementary model with 51bhp engine and a folding sunroof, arrived in March 1963; the "S" disappeared in January 1964; the Courier van, moribund since late 1964, was discontinued entirely in 1966; and the Herald 13/60, with an updated bonnet and the Triumph 1300's 1296cc engine, arrived in August 1967. The last 1200 was made in May 1970 and the last 13/60 in May 1971. Kits of the 948cc Herald continued to be exported until 1973: see Mike Costigan. *Complete Guide to Triumph Herald and Vitesse.* Bideford. Devon: Bay ViewBooks Ltd., 1992, pp. 10–21.

7. See, for example, *The Autocar,* 11/3/60, pp. 416–417; *Motor Trader,* 16/3/60, p. 290.

8. See, for example, *The Autocar,* 19/5/61, pp. 815–816; *Motor Trader,* 24/5/61, p. 240.

9. See Costigan, *Complete Guide,* p. 24. The book gives detailed model-by-model specification changes and is recommended to any reader restoring a surviving car.

10. The Gazel's door layout was similar to that of a British four-door prototype: see Shyam Krishnamachari. "Triumphs of India." *The Courier [the magazine of the Triumph Sports Six Club],* February 2003, pp. 58–62.

11. This event took much planning and practice: see Robson, *Triumph Herald and Vitesse,* pp. 64–67. A film of the launch has been reproduced on videotape with cinema advertisements and other films issued to dealers: see British Motor Industry Heritage Trust (BMIHT). *Triumph Herald: The Original Triumph Films.* Coventry: BMIHT, 2001. Additional publicity was gained with a proving run from Cape Town to Tangier, which was made the subject of a book and of a film included in this videotape. See also Robson, *Triumph Herald and Vitesse,* pp. 52–59.

12. See *Motor Trader,* 21/6/61, p. 341; and *House of Lords Official Report (Hansard), Fifth Series — Vol. CCXXXII, 7th volume of session 1960–61 [12/6/61–7/7/61],* June 14, 1961, cols 177–179. The advertisement first appeared on May 28, 1961 and Standard-Triumph had decided to withdraw it as from June 8, 1961. Lord Conesford recommended that similar future advertisements be precluded by legislation: "Is [my noble friend]…aware that the company may derive great profit from this disreputable advertisement? I am advised that it makes the strongest possible appeal to nitwits, and, in the expert view of advertisers, nitwits form quite a large proportion of the purchasers of motor cars." Lord Chesham replied, "I think we are accustomed to a certain (shall we say?) overstatement in advertisements, and that the public as a whole tend to regard 'incitements', as my noble friend calls them, of this kind with a certain amount of reserve....I do not believe, however nit-witted the public may be in responding to advertisements, that a very large number are so nitwitted as to…obey an alleged incitement of this kind. I think people have more sense than that. The company have apparently recognised the undesirability of this advertisement by withdrawing it, and I do not think there is very much more we need do about it": *ibid.,* cols. 178–179.

13. *The Autocar,* 1/5/59, pp. 647–650 (coupe); 5/6/59, pp. 823–826 (saloon). See also *The Autocar,* 9/9/60, pp. 372–375 (convertible); 14/4/61, pp. 589–592 (1200); 7/3/68, pp. 27–31 (13/60 convertible); *Automobile Engineer,* May 1961, p. 187 (1200); *Car,* May 1969, pp. 38–39, 71 (Herald as example of swing-axled

car); *Country Life*, 24/9/59, p. 366 (coupe); *The Illustrated London News*, 25/3/61, p. 518 (convertible); 6/5/61, p. 772 (1200); 2/6/62, p. 910 (1200 convertible); *The Field*, 21/5/59 (page unknown) (coupe); 2/6/60, (page unknown) (convertible); 20/4/61, p. 781 (1200 convertible); 17/8/61, p. 313 (1200 estate car); 6/6/63, p. 1073 (12/50); *The Motor*, 18/9/63, pp. 61–64 (12/50); 17/12/66, pp. 15–18 (developments since 1959); *Motor*, 21/10/67, pp. 167–168 (Herald 13/60); *Motor Trader*, 12/4/61, p. 37 (1200); *Practical Motorist*, January 1965, pp. 534–535 (Herald 12/50).

14. See John Macartney. *In the Shadow of My Father*. Gloucestershire: John Macartney, 1998, p. 160 (first-hand recollection of the salesman).

15. See Malcolm McKay. "The Herald That Jack Built." *Thoroughbred & Classic Cars*, May 1996, pp. 60–64.

16. See Michael Frostick. *Advertising and the Motor-car*. London: Lund Humphries, 1970, p. 136. At the time of writing, the original guard book containing Mather and Crowther advertisements for Triumph is preserved at the History of Advertising Trust (HAT Archive) at Raveningham in Norfolk, England.

17. The Morris Minor convertible was hardly modern and the Rootes convertibles—Minx, Super Minx, Gazelle and Rapier—had long gone.

18. BMIHT, *Triumph Herald: The Original Triumph Films*. The voiceover sounds very like the actor Richard Briers. 525,767 Herald saloons, coupes, convertibles and estate cars were built between 1959 and 1971: Michael Sedgwick and Mark Gillies. *A-Z of Cars 1945–1970 (2nd ed., revd. Jon Pressnell)*. Bideford, Devon: Bay View Books Ltd., 1993, pp. 202–203.

19. See BMIHT, *Triumph Herald: The Original Triumph Films*.

20. For the Spitfire generally, see James Taylor. *Triumph Spitfire and GT6: The Complete Story*. Marlborough, Wiltshire: The Crowood Press Ltd., 2000. See also *Autocar*, 16/5/68, pp. 48–49 (Mk 3); 10/4/69, pp. 50–55 (Mk 3 with MG Midget); *Country Life*, 21/10/63, p. 1142 (Mk 1); *The Field*, 22/11/62, p. 1049 (Mk 1); *The Illustrated London News*, 2/2/63, p. 176 (Mk 1); *Homes and Gardens*, May 1970, p. 152 (Mk 3); *The Motor*, 17/10/62, pp. 440–443 (new model announcement); 18/3/67, pp. 16–17 (Mk III); 14/10/67, pp. 95–99 (Mk 3 with Austin-Healey Sprite and Honda S800); *Road and Track Road Test Annual 1969*, pp. 23–28 (1968 test of Mk 3 with Austin-Healey Sprite, Datsun 1600 Sports and Fiat 850 Spider); *Small Car*, November 1963, pp. 48–50 (Mk 1); *October* 1964, pp. 49–56 (Mk 1 with Austin-Healey Sprite); May 1965, p. 33 (Mk 2). Many of these articles also appear in published compilations. 148,482 Spitfires Mk 1–3 were built between 1962 and 1970: Sedgwick and Gillies, *A-Z of Cars*, p. 204.

21. Ralph Nader. *Unsafe At Any Speed: The Designed-in Dangers of the American Automobile*. New York: Grossman Publishers, 1965, p. 41. Olley, an Englishman, had worked for Rolls-Royce from 1912 and, when that company's Springfield venture was abandoned, moved to Cadillac in 1930. He subsequently did much work for General Motors on suspension and stability, and in 1937 was seconded to Vauxhall from Detroit: see Maurice Platt. *An Addiction to Automobiles*. London: Frederick Warne: 1980, pp. 102–117.

22. Robson, *Triumph Herald and Vitesse*, p. 47. "I really don't know why we didn't adopt it at that stage" recalled Maurice Lovatt, then a young project engineer at Standard-Triumph: *ibid.*, p. 47.

23. For these 1962–67 advertisements, see Bill Piggott: *Triumph TR — TR2 to 6: The Last of the Traditional Sports Cars*. Yeovil, Somerset: Haynes Publishing, 2003, pp. 85, 106, 110, 113, 131. For the Triumph TRs generally see, in addition, Chris Harvey. *TR for Triumph*. Yeovil, Somerset: Oxford Illustrated Press/Haynes Publishing, 1983. See also *Autocar*, 28/5/65, pp. 1053–1058 (TR4A IRS); 4/4/68, pp. 11–16 (TR5 PI); *Automobile Engineer*, September 1961, pp. 353–354 (TR4); *Country Life*, 11/7/63, p. 90 (Dove GTR4 fastback); 25/5/67, p. 1331 (TR4A); *The Field*, 14/9/61, p. 477 (TR4); *The Motor*, 11/7/62, pp. 876–879 (TR4 hardtop); *Motor Trader*, 6/9/61, pp. 250–252 (TR4 announcement).

24. See Robson, *Triumph Herald and Vitesse*, pp. 85–100, 127–141. See also *The Autocar*, 17/9/65, pp. 535–540; *Automobile Engineer*, June 1962, pp. 230–231; September 1962, p. 377; *Car*, May 1969, pp. 56–61 (2-Litre Mk II with Ford Capri 1600GT); *The Illustrated London News*, 3/8/63, p. 184; *The Motor*, 30/5/62, pp. 671–675; 23/4/66, pp. 85–86; 16/9/67, pp. 23–28 (2-Litre); *Motor Trader*, 30/5/62, pp. 382–383; *Small Car*, March 1964, pp. 31–39 (with Sunbeam Rapier Series IV).

25. The check straps could occasionally break, and the man who wished to stay on good terms with female passengers replaced them quickly. In either car the door could inflict a painful blow to a leg...

26. 31,261 of the 1600 are recorded as built from 1962 to 1966, compared with 10,830 of the 2-Litre Mk 1 of 1966–68 and 9,121 of the 2-Litre Mk 2 from 1968 to 1971: Sedgwick and Gillies, *A-Z of Cars*, p. 203. But see also Robson, *Triumph Hearld and Vitesse*, pp. 203–205 (1600: 31,278; all 2-Litres: 19,952). The Vitesse was only made as a saloon and convertible, apart from one prototype estate car, a few saloons converted, semi-officially, into estate cars by the company's London service department, and perhaps one coupe.

27. See Taylor, *Triumph Spitfire and GT6*, pp. 42–58. See also *Autocar*, 3/4/69, pp. 6–10 (road test); *The Field*, 16/11/67, (page unknown); *Motor*, 15/10/66, pp. 16–20 (announcement); 29/10/68, pp. 75–80 (road test); *Road & Track*, November 1966, p. 84 (short test). 15,818 of the GT6 Mk 1 and 12,066 of the GT6 Mk II were built: Sedgwick and Gillies, *A-Z of Cars*, p. 206.

28. For the Triumph 2000 Mk 1, see Graham Robson. *Triumph 2000 and 2.5PI: The Complete Story*. Marlborough, Wiltshire: The Crowood Press Ltd., 1995, pp. 39–100; Bill Munro. *Carbodies: The Complete Story*. Marlborough, Wiltshire: The Crowood Press Ltd., 1998, pp. 118–125, 140–142 (estate car); and David Evans. "The Space Race." *Classic and Sports Car*, June 2003, pp. 144–147 (estate car with Volvo 222 estate car). See also *The Autocar*, 10/1/64, pp. 66–70; 6/2/69, pp. 14–19 (2.5PI); 16/10/69, pp. 82–85 and 132–135 (Mk II); *Car*, February 1969, pp. 49–55 (2.5PI with Rover 2000TC); January 1970, pp. 68–73 (2000 Mk II with Vauxhall VX 4/90 (FD)); *Country Life*, 13/2/64, p. 336; *The Field*, 16/1/64, p. 113; *The Motor*, 16/10/63, pp. 120–126 (announcement); 21/5/66, pp. 21–26 (estate car); 10/9/66, pp. 17–20; 26/11/66, pp. 15–20 (automatic).

29. After a short interval the Dolomites were succeeded by the Triumph Acclaim of 1981–84 which was based upon the Honda Civic and was the last Triumph. At the time of writing the Triumph marque name is dormant and is owned by BMW. For the 1300, see Richard Langworth and Graham Robson. *Triumph Cars: The Complete 75-year History*. London: Motor Racing Publications Ltd., 1979, pp. 232–270; and James Taylor. "Triumph 1300/1500 and Dolomite." *Thoroughbred & Classic Cars*, September 1993, pp. 80–88. See also *Autocar*, 15/10/65, pp. ii-viii *et. seq.*, *Car*, March 1966, pp. 27–37 (including interview with Harry Webster); *Country Life*, 20/8/70, p. 465 (Toledo and 1500); *The Field*, 28/4/66, p. 793; *Motor*, 18/2/67, pp. 15–20.

30. 129,675 of the 2000 and 2.5PI Mk 1 were built between 1963 and 1970, and 148,350 of the 1300 were built between 1965 and 1970, including 35,342 of the 1300TC: Sedgwick and Gillies, *A-Z of Cars*, pp. 204–205.

31. Harry Webster, quoted in *Car*, March 1966, p. 27.

32. For the XL90 advertisement see, for example, *The Illustrated London News*, 1/7/67 (page unknown). For the TRX see, for example, "Prototriumph." *Thoroughbred & Classic Cars*, January 1987, p. 112. The Stag, however, began as a development of the 2000: see, for example, James Taylor. "High Hopes." *Thoroughbred & Classic Cars*, February 1992, pp. 74–80 (includes material from the Michelotti archives). For the TR7 see, for example, Mike McCarthy and Martin Buckley. "Customer Developed." *Classic and Sports Car*, March 1986, pp. 67–73. See also Harvey, *TR for Triumph*, pp. 48–61, 108–119.

23. Vanden Plas

1. Nick Walker. "Vanden Plas—From Coachbuilder to Manufacturer." *Classic Car Mart*, July 1996, pp. 67–69. The Kingsbury works was closed by British Leyland in 1979: see Brian Smith. "Another Coachbuilder Closes." *Thoroughbred & Classic Cars*, May 1979, pp. 27, 71 (story of closure and history). See also Brian Smith. "Vanden Plas Coachbuilders." *Thoroughbred & Classic Cars*, May 1980, pp. 54–57 (post-war history in detail).

2. *Ibid.*, p. 68. See generally Brian Smith. *Vanden Plas Coachbuilders*. London: Dalton Watson Ltd., 1979.

3. Michael Sedgwick and Mark Gillies. *A-Z of Cars 1945–1970 (2nd ed., revd. Jon Pressnell)*. Bideford, Devon: Bay View Books, 1993, pp. 24–26.

4. See Smith, *Vanden Plas Coachbuilders*, p. 270. See also *Motor Trader*, 16/4/58, p. 82 (new model announcement).

5. Barney Sharratt. *Men and Motors of 'The Austin'*. Yeovil, Somerset: Haynes, 2000, p. 168. The 1959 3-litre cost £1396 10s 10d and the 3-litre Mk II of 1961–64 was announced at £1625 16s 5d. Automatic transmission, which was widely fitted, cost an £70 extra in 1959 and £74 extra in 1961. The equivalent 1959 Austin A99 and Wolseley 6-99 cost £1149 and £1255 respectively, while the 1961 Austin A110 and Wolseley 6/110 were priced at £1270 and £1343 respectively (prices rounded to nearest pound). One two-door saloon, and seven of a Countryman estate car with a split tailgate were also built: see Michael Ware. "The only one?" *Thoroughbred & Classic Cars*, September 1992, p. 18 (2-door); and Michael Ware. "Sister to a Royal Princess." *Thoroughbred & Classic Cars*, October 1993, p. 38 (Countryman). See also Martin Buckley. "Loaded with Style." *Classic Cars*, February 2004, pp. 80–85 (Countryman tested with comparable estate cars). In 1965 the hearse makers Woodall Nicholson of Halifax built a 4-litre R estate car with a single-piece tailgate and squared up rear door windows which the Queen used at Balmoral: see Giles Chapman. "Heavenly Bodies." *Classic and Sports Car*, February 1987, pp. 68–69. Harold Radford produced a 4-litre R estate car with a more steeply sloping tail: see Mike Taylor. "Built to Order." *Thoroughbred & Classic Cars*, June 1984, pp. 38–40.

6. *Country Life*, 17/9/64, p. 712 (test of Princess 4-litre R).

7. *The Illustrated London News*, 18/2/67, p. 32 (4-litre R). For the 3-litre see, for example, *The Autocar*, 16/10/59, p. 379 (new model announcement); 11/11/60, pp. 843–846 (road test); *Country Life*, 7/9/61, p. 512; *The Field*, 17/10/63, p. 723 (Mk II); *The Illustrated London News*, 3/6/61, p. 948. See also Victor Norwood. "Your Cars." *Thoroughbred & Classic Cars*, October 1961, p. 35 (reader's 1964 Mk II).

8. See *Appendix 11A*, under *Princess*.

9. See advertisements in the *National Geographic* of 1955–59. The suggestion is not entirely fanciful as, while many American magazines were imported into Britain at this time, the *National Geographic* was particularly widely distributed and reached an older, middle-class audience. This Vanden Plas advertisement (published in various magazines between November 1962 and March 1963) is especially close to a Cadillac advertisement in the *National Geographic* of February 1959, which can also be seen in Yasutoshi Ikuta. *Cruise O Matic: Automobile Advertising of the 1950s (2000 ed.)*. San Francisco: Chronicle Books, 2000, p. 102. For collectors using other sources, the advertisement shows a dark orange 1959 Sedan de Ville, with the front of the car highlighted separately.

10. Sedgwick and Gillies, *A–Z of Cars*, p. 211.

11. For a comparison of the two cars, see John Pressnell. "Royal Pretender." *Classic and Sports Car*, July 1993, pp. 60–65.

12. See John Mullins. "Fallen Princess." *Classic and Sports Car*, September 1983, pp. 40–41.

13. Small Rolls-Royces and Bentleys based on the Austin/Morris 1800 or 3-Litre body were also contemplated: see John Pressnell, "Royal Pretender," pp. 61–62; and Ian Rimmer. "BMC's Rolls-Royce" *Thoroughbred & Classic Cars*, December 1987, pp. 88–90 (showing design studies and early Java prototype). For a summary of the 4-litre R's specification, see "Buyer's Guide: Vanden Plas 4-Litre R." *Classic and Sports Car*, March 1997, pp. 132–133. For modern driving impressions, see "Test Match." *Thoroughbred & Classic Cars*, January 1990, pp. 86–95 (with Alvis TF21, Ford Zodiac Executive, Humber Super Snipe, Rover 3-Litre and Jaguar S-type 3.4).

14. *Autocar*, 28/8/64, pp. 406–410. See also *Autocar*, 21/8/64, pp. 350–355 (new model announcement and description).

15. *The Field*, 24/9/64, p. 633.

16. Recollection of Leonard Lord's daughter, Pauline: see Sharratt, *Men and Motors of 'The Austin'*, p. 170.

17. *Ibid.*, p. 170. See also *Autocar*, 1/1/65, pp. 12–16; *Country Life*, 26/11/65, p. 1447; *The Field*, 30/9/65, p. 665; and see Martin Buckley. "Cloud Cover." *Classic Cars*, March 2003, pp. 76–78 (comparison with Rolls-Royce Silver Cloud III); and "Fact File: Vanden Plas Princess." *Classic and Sports Car*, April 1995, pp. 92–93.

18. John Pressnell, "Royal Pretender," pp. 62–63.

19. Sedgwick and Gillies, *A–Z of Cars*, p. 211.

20. *Ibid.*, p. 210. See also *The Motor*, 11/4/62, pp. 350–353 (road test).

21. *Small Car*, April 1965, pp. 51–53.

22. Sedgwick and Gillies, *A–Z of Cars*, p. 211.

24. Wolseley

1. See Gerald Palmer. *Auto-Architect: The Autobiography of Gerald Palmer*. East Horsley, Surrey: Magna Press, 1998, p. 73. Even in the 1930s, commentators found Wolseley copy overstated. One advertisement showed a limousine driving away from a castle under the headline, "An Englishman's home...." *The Advertising World* harrumphed, "Perhaps to the taunt of snobbery we might add patriotism, and call this type of appeal snob-patriotism, which sounds even worse....Copy is no less distasteful. It follows on from the caption '...and here is his state coach....' This type of stuff continues, later on actually refers to the comforts of the inside of the car. What happens about holding the road at high speeds, acceleration in second, results on exacting runs, is not referred to. As a potential buyer of a car in this class, I would have liked to have known. Besides, when I get that castle, I might want a bigger car than this": *The Advertising World*, March 1937, pp. 41–42.

2. A story is told that a man once managed to sell an Austin A50 Cambridge with Manumatic transmission by attaching a clutch pedal and spring to the pedal box. The system was not popular when new and even less so secondhand, although it was thoughtfully designed and some examples worked well for many years. It was available on the 15/50 for under two years from the end of 1956. For the story of the 4/44 and 6/90, both designed by Gerald Palmer alongside the MG Magnette ZA and ZB (1953–58) and Riley Pathfinder (1953–57), see Palmer, *Auto-Architect*, pp. 47–64, 71–76. For post-war Wolseley cars generally, see also Graham Robson. *The Cars of BMC*. Croydon: Motor Racing Publications Ltd., 1999, pp. 223–248. See also Brian Palmer. "Engineered with Style." *Thoroughbred & Classic Cars*, January 1992, pp. 102–106 (interview with Gerald Palmer).

3. The first Wolseley cars were built between 1896 and 1898 by Herbert Austin, works manager of the British branch (in Birmingham) of the Wolseley Sheep Shearing Co. which had been founded in Sydney, Australia by Irish-born Frederick Wolseley in 1887. Wolseley died two years later and in 1904 Austin left to form his own company. By 1914 Wolseley was one of Britain's largest car companies, but in 1926 it went bankrupt and was bought personally by William Morris in 1927. In 1935 Morris sold the company Morris Motors Ltd. From the late 1930s Wolseley cars shared many components, particularly bodies, with equivalent Morrises. Eight, 10, 12, 14, 18 and 25hp cars of pre-war style were reintroduced in 1945–46 and were all succeeded by the Morris Oxford-based 4/50 of 1948–53 and Morris Six-based 6/80 of 1948–54. The 1250cc Wolseley 4/44 arrived in 1952 and was replaced by the similar-looking 1489cc 15/50 in 1956, and the 2639cc 6/90 was introduced in 1954. The 15/50 and 6/90 were discontinued in 1958 and 1959 respectively.

4. See Jon Pressnell. "The Minors That Might Have Been." *Classic and Sports Car*, April 1994, pp. 94–97; Jon Pressnell. "Major Upset." *Classic and Sports Car*, July 1986, pp. 56–59; and Jon Pressnell. *Morris Minor: Exploring the Legend*. Yeovil, Somerset: Haynes, 1998, pp. 74–84. See also Anders Clausager. "Riley & Wolseley 1.5 and 1500." *Classic and Sports Car*, June 1990, pp. 84–92. 103,395 of the 1500 were made between 1957 and 1965 compared with 39,568 of the more sporting Riley One-Point-Five during the same period: Michael Sedgwick and Mark Gillies. *A–Z of Cars 1945–1970 (2nd ed., revd. Jon Pressnell)*. Bideford, Devon: Bay View Books Ltd., 1993, pp. 164, 230. For the Riley One-Point-Five, see pp. 212–218, above.

5. *The Autocar*, 31/5/57, pp. 743–746. See also *The Autocar*, 27/2/59, p. 298 (Arden performance conversion); *The Field*, 15/1/59, p. 115.

6. See *Motor Trader*, 16/12/59, p. 371.

7. See *The Autocar*, 13/5/59, pp. 387–390; *The Field*, 12/3/59, p. 471; 29/12/60, p. 1301; *Motor Trader*, 24/12/58, pp. 380–382.

8. See *The Autocar*, 14/8/59, pp. 23–26; *Automobile Engineer*, July 1959, pp. 272–274; *Country Life*, 26/11/59, p. 975; *The Illustrated London News*, 7/1/61, p. 38.

9. See, for example, *The Illustrated London News*, 7/9/63, p. 362.

10. Wolseley's advertising agency since 1938, Longleys & Hoffman, preparing artwork before the car was announced, was caught out by the late deletion of a proposed chrome embellishment on the rear door crease where the fin ended, which also appeared in some publicity photographs: see Graham Robson. *The Cars of BMC*. Croydon: Motor Racing Publications Ltd., 1999, p. 235. For the 16/60 and sister cars from Austin, Morris, MG and Riley, see *Small Car*, April 1964, pp. 45–53 (giant test).

11. For the development of the Elf and Hornet, see Chris Rees. *Complete Classic Mini 1959–2000*. Croydon: Motor Racing Publications Ltd., 2003, pp. 151–158. See also *Autocar*, 9/10/64, pp. 727–728 (Taurus performance conversion of Mk II); *The Field*, 3/3/66, (page unknown) (Mk II); *The Illustrated London News*, 6/6/64, p. 918; *Practical Motorist*, August 1964, pp. 1336–1337 (Mobil Economy Run at 60.67 mpg).

12. See *Autocar*, 17/1/64, pp. 122–123. 28,455 Hornets and 30,912 Elves were made between 1961 and 1969: Sedgwick and Gillies, *A–Z of Cars*, pp. 165 and 231.

13. Zoë Harrison. "Heinz Hornet 57." *Restoring Classic Cars*, August 1989, pp. 58–63. Equipment included a make-up compartment with Max Factor accessories; a Brexton picnic hamper containing a tea/lunch set, vacuum flasks, food boxes, tableware and tablecloth; an electric kettle with a socket in the boot; two insulated picnic cabinets in the rear of the car; and a woollen tartan picnic rug. For surviving cars see, for example, *Thoroughbred & Classic Cars*, March 1993, p. 30; *Classic and Sports Car*, September 2003, p. 29; and *Classic and Sports Cars*, October 2003, p. 26.

14. *Small Car*, April 1964, pp. 16–19 (recalling early car in test of Viking Hornet Sport). The magazine's assault on badge engineering began in an article called, "Is stick-on prestige costing Britain too dear?" in September 1963; 62 variations on nine high-selling family cars were counted, ranging from de luxe editions to low-production convertibles and station wagons to models bearing the badges of what were now derivative marques, such as Wolseley.

15. For later Wolseley models see, for example, *Autocar*, 15/10/65, pp. 747–750 (Wolseley 1100, based on the Morris 1100, introduced in 1965 and made as a 1300 until 1973, with the 1100 continuing until 1968); 18/9/69, pp. 6–10 (18/85, based on the Austin 1800, introduced in 1967 and made until 1972, with a six-cylinder version, the Wolseley Six, continuing until 1975); 12/6/69, pp. 31–32 (18/85, 12,000 mile report); *Country Life*, 12/10/67, p. 902 (18/85); *Motor*, 17/6/67, pp. 19–24 (18/85). The Wolseley marque

name became dormant in 1975 and at the time of writing is owned by MG Rover.

Part Three — 25. Volkswagen, Renault and Citrön

1. *Motor Trader*, 17/8/55, p. 179; 2/12/59, pp. 292–293; 21/6/61, *supplement*. The article of December 2, 1959, was accidentally alarmist, stating that "U.K. consumption, at some 18,000 a year, represents just over a week's output" of the Wolfsburg plant (which was stated as 3200 units a day). According to the Society of Motor Manufacturers and Traders, however, 8223 cars were imported from West Germany in 1959 (see *Appendix 6*, above). The vast majority of these were Volkswagens. The published literature on the early years of the Volkswagenwerk is vast, but see, by way of introduction, Laurence Meredith. "Diamond Beetles." *Thoroughbred & Classic Cars*, May 1991, pp. 98–102 (summary of the Beetle's history); and Lindsay Porter. "Vorsprung Durch..." *Thoroughbred & Classic Cars*, October 1986, pp. 66–69 (interview with Ivan Hirst, who put the VW factory back on its feet during 1945–47 and stayed until 1949, appointing Heinz Nordoff as his deputy in 1947). Nordoff began work on January 1, 1948 and control was progressively handed over to German management. For all of the rear-engined Volkswagens and for the early history of the company under Major Ivan Hirst (1916–2000) and company chairman Dr. h.c. Heinz Nordoff (1899–1968), see Joachim Kuch. *Volkswagen Model History: Boxer-Engined Vehicles from Beetle and Transporter to 412.* Yeovil, Somerset: Haynes, 1999. This book is also published in the United States by Robert Bentley Inc. under the title *Volkswagen Model Documentation* (1999), and in Germany by Motorbuch Verlag as *Volkswagen Modellgeschichte, Band 1* (1998).

2. Robert Braunschweig. "International Prospects for British Cars." *The Autocar*, 31/5/57, pp. 773–775. See also Richard Langworth. "Lost Opportunity." *Thoroughbred & Classic Cars*, March 1984, pp. 38–43.

3. Even in England, the land of many doubtful column-changes, the Frégate's was thought tricky: see, for example, *The Field*, 25/9/58, p. 557.

4. Ruth Brandon. *Auto Mobile: How the Car Changed Life.* London: Macmillan, 2002, pp. 196–197. For the Volkswagen story see *ibid.*, pp. 197–216.

5. See, for example, David Rennie. "End of the Road for Hitler's 'People's Car'." *The Daily Telegraph*, 12/7/03, p. 15.

6. *The Field*, 10/4/58, p. 659. See also *Autocar*, 1/5/69 (*Special Supplement: Focus on Volkswagen*); *Car*, August 1965, pp. 40–46 (1200 with Ford Cortina 1200 Mk 1); *The Field*, 11/9/58, p. 459 (Microbus); *The Motor*, 3/4/63, pp. 60–65 (1300); 16/7/66, pp. 21–26 (1300).

7. William Boddy. *VW Beetle: Type 1 & The New Generation.* London: Osprey, 1999, p. 72.

8. *Ibid.*, p. 85.

9. Tony Taylor. "Dropping In." *Motor*, 21/5/88, p. 57.

10. For the original meaning of "planned obsolescence," see *Note 14*, below.

11. For the background to the American campaign and for illustrations of over 250 of the agency's Volkswagen advertisements of 1959–78, including 30 or so from Britain and several from other European countries, see Alfredo Marcantonio, John O'Driscoll and David Abbott. *Remember Those Great Volkswagen Ads?* London: Booth-Clibborn Editions, 1993.

12. For examples of this and other British campaigns, see Daniel Young. *Advertising the Beetle 1953–1978.* London: Yesteryear Books, 1993.

13. For the VW 1500, see *The Autocar*, 26/5/61, pp. 838–839 and 849 (announcement); 22/9/61, pp. 433–437 and 465 (description); 6/10/61, pp. 546–549 (road test); 27/3/64, pp. 568–572 (test of 1500S); *The Field*, 29/4/65, p. 781; 4/7/63 (page unknown) (estate car); *The Motor*, 4/4/62, pp. 317–320; *Practical Motorist*, July 1962, pp. 1210–1211. For the VW 1600 fastback see, for example, *Autocar*, 6/8/65, pp. 259–261 (announcement); *Country Life*, 12/1/67, p. 73 (estate car); 20/6/68, p. 1694 (fastback).

14. For the career of Brooks Stevens see, for example, Mike McCarthy. "Design Intervention." *Classic and Sports Car*, December 1991, pp. 52–58. Stevens is well-known as having coined the phrase "planned obsolescence," which has been both interpreted and adopted to mean things that Stevens did not intend. "I was asked to talk to the Advertising Club of Minneapolis," recalled Stevens in 1991, "and was looking for a title. I eventually came up with the phrase 'Planned Obsolescence', meaning the desire to own something a little newer, a little better, a little sooner than is necessary. It did *not* mean organized waste, as Vance Packard called it in his book *The Hidden Persuaders*. The average American earns enough not to have to run a refrigerator or car until the thing just stops. The alternative is that everybody drives exactly the same car, or wears the same suit all his life.": *ibid.*, p. 58. In *The Hidden Persuaders*, however, Packard appears to offer a more tentative interpretation of the phrase: "In

1956 one of the largest makers of refrigerators was shaping a favourable trade-in formula so that housewives would be encouraged to seek the 'last word' in refrigerators. An executive said the company was committed to a programme of 'planned product obsolescence', presumably [*sic*] by creating new styles and features each year that would make appliance owners dissatisfied with the models they had": Vance Packard. *The Hidden Persuaders.* London: Penguin, 1991 [1957], p. 144. Others have used the phrase "dynamic obsolescence" to mean "planned obsolescence" in the sense intended by Stevens. In retrospect it could be argued that there is little practical difference between devising a philosophy that advocates waste as a means to a commercial end and devising one that requires such waste without advocating it openly.

15. *Motoring Which?* April 1971, pp. 42–55. For the 411 see also, for example, *Autocar*, 15/8/68, pp. 10–14 (detailed description); 14/11/68, pp. 12–17 (road test); *Country Life*, 17/4/69, p. 985 (test); *The Illustrated London News*, 24/8/68, p. 26 (announcement).

16. *Motoring Which?* July 1971, pp. 82–100.

17. J. Dewar McLintock. *Renault: The Cars and the Charisma.* Yeovil, Somerset: Patrick Stephens Ltd., 1983, p. 60. For the Dauphine and its rear-engined successors generally, see *ibid.*, pp. 58–85. McLintock writes as a long-time Renault enthusiast and Dauphine owner who road tested several examples.

18. Ralph Harris and Arthur Seldon. *Advertising in Action.* London: Hutchinson/Institute of Economic Affairs, 1962, pp. 242.

19. *Ibid.*, pp. 240–241.

20. *Ibid.*, p. 243.

21. Nick Larkin. "French Fancy." *Popular Classics*, September 1992, pp. 99–105. For the post-war Renaults generally, see Eric Dymock. *The Renault File: All Models Since 1898.* Yeovil, Somerset: G.T. Foulis/Haynes/Dove Publishing, 1998, pp. 190–409. See also Jon Pressnell. "Renault's Riches." *Classic and Sports Car*, August 2002, pp. 132–135 (Renault's collection of past products).

22. *Motor Trader*, 8/2/56, p. 116; 14/3/56, pp. 211–212.

23. See *Automobile Engineer*, April 1956, pp. 152–155 (description of Dauphine); April 1957, p. 165 (spare wheel tray).

24. For a description of the system, see *Automobile Engineer*, February 1955, pp. 81–83.

25. Richard E.V. Gomm: see *Motor Trader*, 8/3/61, p. 279.

26. *The Autocar*, 30/1/59, pp. 145–148; 28/4/61, p. 682 (Dauphine Gordini); *The Illustrated London News*, 6/7/57, p. 40 (standard Dauphine); *Motor Trader*, 26/4/61, p. 90 (Dauphine Gordini de luxe); *Practical Motorist*, March 1961, pp. 683–685 (Dauphine servicing); June 1962, p. 1090 (Ruddspeed conversion by K.N. Rudd (Engineers) Ltd. of Worthing, West Sussex). The "non-Gordini" Dauphine gained four forward gears in late 1960 with the Ondine variant.

27. Harris and Seldon, *Advertising in Action*, p. 243.

28. McLintock, *Renault*, p. 59.

29. *Ibid.*, p. 59.

30. *Ibid.*, p. 64. See also *Motor Trader*, 14/6/61, p. 310; 28/6/61, p. 370.

31. *Motor Trader*, 15/2/61, pp. 176–177.

32. *Motor Trader*, 10/1/62, p. 35 (Ordner was responding to Maurice Edelman, the Labour MP for Coventry North.)

33. *Motor Trader*, 19/9/62, p. 471.

34. For a rear view of the Floride see Dymock, *The Renault File*, p. 211. In their shape, though not in their inclination, the fins and tail-lights were quite similar to those of a 1957 Renault Dauphine fixed-head coupe by the Italian coachbuilder Allemano: see *Automobile Engineer*, May 1957, p. 187. The tail of the Floride was much neater overall, however, as was the design as a whole.

35. Most sources attribute the Floride, too, to Pietro Frua (1913–1983), working for Ghia: see, for example, Giles Chapman. "Frua: The Man and his Line." *Classic and Sports Car*, April 1987, pp. 118–122 (including interviews with many who knew Frua). The question remains controversial, however: see "Virgil M. Exner, Jr.: The Next Generation." *Collectible Automobile*, December 1994, p. 77 (summary of Virgil Exner Jr.'s career which includes the Floride/Caravelle among designs created for Ghia; this summary appears within John F. Katz. "Personality Profile: Virgil M. Exner, Sr.: Distinguished Designer." *Collectible Automobile*, December 1994, pp. 70–77, which includes interview material from Virgil Exner, Jr.). See also H. DeWayne Ashmead, PhD. "The History and Development of the Renault Caravelle." *www.renaultcaravelle.com/ashmead.html.* and Ashmead's attached bibliography, which includes a 2002 interview with Virgil Exner, Jr. Ashmead relates, in summary, that after preliminary sketches had been made at Renault, (1) Renault chief Pierre Dreyfus arranged to meet Ghia's managing director, Luigi Segre, to discuss the car. (2) Segre agreed to work on the car, and sought help from Virgil Exner, whom he had come to know while working on Ghia's Chrysler prototypes of a few years earlier. (3) Exner, as a Chrysler employee, could not help directly but suggested that Segre contact his son, Virgil Exner Jr. (4) Virgil Exner Jr., also an automotive designer but then serving with the USAF, became a consultant to Ghia and was given

Renault's existing sketches and design parameters. (5) Virgil Exner Jr. produced initial sketches for Segre, Renault approved the project, and Exner, still with the USAF, produced a formal design and sent his final drawings to Giovanni Savonuzzi, Ghia's chief in-house designer. (6) Savonuzzi made a clay model of the Exner design which was then approved by Renault. (7) Renault asked Ghia to build the prototype and Ghia sub-contracted the work to Frua. (8) Frua completed the prototype but did not receive payment from Ghia or further instructions from Renault, and so displayed the Dauphine GT, as it was then called, at the March 1958 Geneva Show as his own work. (9) Matters were then resolved sufficiently for the car to appear on the Renault stand as a Renault at the Paris Motor Show in October 1958, by which time it was called the Floride.

About points (6) and (7) above in particular there is controversy. Concerning (6), other sources state that Frua, one of a number of competitors for the project, presented a design on Ghia's behalf that was chosen as the winning proposal by the Renault board: see Chapman, "Frua," p. 120. Whether Frua ever saw the proposal from Exner described by Ashmead is not stated, and it would be interesting to know if Frua ever saw any Ghia documents or discussed the Floride's styling with anyone connected with Ghia before or during the development of the design. Jon Pressnell, who has written about many French cars, relates that Renault "asked Ghia to build a Renault equivalent [to the Karmann-Ghia]. The result, styled by Frua and built by Swiss Ghia offshoot Ghia-Aigle, was unveiled at the 1958 Geneva show as the Dauphine GT": Jon Pressnell. "Chic to Chic." *Classic and Sports Car*, February 1999, p. 123 (Caravelle compared with Simca Océane). Finally, Ashmead relates that Renault subsequently asked Frua directly to update the Floride to produce the 956cc 1962 Caravelle (distinguishable mainly by the deletion of the air intakes behind the doors and by a restyled hardtop for the fixed-head) and that Frua, having done so, claimed full credit for this design, prompting Ghia to commence legal proceedings against him as the design of the 1963–68 Caravelle was still essentially that of the Floride.

The picture is complicated (a) by questions of who of Frua and Ghia, if Frua styled the car for Ghia, actually carried out the design (as debate expressed in terms of responsibility and credit can inadvertently conceal or obscure who physically did what); and (b) by the early cars' being given different names in Europe and America. In Europe the name Caravelle first appeared in 1962 on the fixed-head coupe version of the updated Floride Speciale (with which a detachable hardtop was still available) before being adopted for both models (convertible with detachable hardtop and fixed-head coupe) when they were fitted with the 1108cc Renault R8 engine in September 1963. In the United States, where sales began in December 1959, all versions of the car were called Caravelle from the outset.

Ashmead also relates that, according to Virgil Exner Jr., Exner "designed the car while Ghia built the prototype as well as the first 1,000 cars…" The whole debate—like many design stories—is potentially further complicated by the fact that "built" can be used to mean "commissioned" or "ordered to be built," and "styled" can mean (i) "styled from scratch," (ii) "designed from existing parameters," (iii) "refined from a design already existing on paper or in clay," or (iv) "commissioned to be styled by an employee or sub-contractor in any sense of (i)-(iii) above." Rights to a design—including the right to claim it as one's own—are of course a further and different question, as if a firm says that it styled a car that may not in itself reveal who put pen to paper. Floride bodies were assembled by Chausson in the factory of the coachbuilders Brissonneau et Lotz.

For the story of the Caravelle generally, see Graham Robson. "1959–1968 Renault Caravelle: A Dream Car Come True." *Collectible Automobile*, October 1994, pp. 83–85. For Ghia, see David Burgess-Wise. "Ghia: The Dream Factory." *Classic and Sports Car*, April 1988, pp. 86–91.

36. The headlamp arrangement was anticipated in part by Pinin Farina's Lancia Florida of 1956 and by other Italian coachbuilders' designs in 1957, and appealed to MG's chief engineer Syd Enever who at the 1959 Geneva Show scribbled, on a press photograph of the Floride, "what would become the basis of the definitive MGB grille shape on the featureless front of the French car, [although] this was not really the origin of the MGB grille, for the body shape had already been developing in that direction. Don Hayter points out that by cutting off the longer front overhang of Jim O'Neill's original proposal, the flatter front face of the MGB more or less created itself": David Knowles. *MG: The Untold Story*. London: Windrow & Greene, 1997, p. 86. Asked about the resemblance in 1987, Enever's successor, Roy Brocklehurst, replied, "No comment.…Well, let's put it this way: it wasn't something you could ignore!": Jon Pressnell. "Twenty-Five Years of the MGB: Band Beyond." *Classic and Sports Car*, October 1987, p. 99.

37. McLintock, *Renault*, p. 68.

38. *The Autocar*, 5/11/65, pp. 970–974. See also *The Illustrated London News*, 28/4/62, p. 681 (956cc Caravelle); *The Motor*, 18/4/62, p. 405 (956cc Caravelle announcement); *Motor Trader*, 30/8/61, *Supplement: Service Data No. 373: Re-*

nault Floride (description of Floride); 14/3/62, p. 278–279 (announcement of 956cc Caravelle coupe and Floride S convertible).

39. *Small Car*, February 1964, pp. 54–57. See also *The Autocar*, 1/9/61, pp. 313–317 (description); *Country Life*, 19/4/62, p. 914; *The Field*, 11/1/62, p. 77; and Alastair Clements. "Starter Classic: Renault 4." *Classic and Sports Car*, May 2002, pp. 152–155.

40. See, for example, *Autocar*, 11/4/68, pp. 52–55 (16 TS); 15/5/69, pp. 10–14 (16 TS); *Country Life*, 10/3/66, p. 525; *The Field*, 12/5/66, p. 905; *The Illustrated London News*, 23/5/70, p. 39 (16 TS); *The Motor*, 10/6/67, pp. 35–40; 9/9/67, pp. 43–46 (24,000 mile assessment); *Small Car*, March 1965, pp. 28–31. For an American perspective see *Road & Track Road Test Annual 1969* [1968 tests], pp. 109–112.

41. See, for example, *Country Life*, 7/3/63, p. 482 (Renault R8); *The Field*, 12/12/63, p. 1221 (Renault R8); 26/8/65, p. 441 (Renault 1100); *The Motor*, 3/10/62, pp. 332–335 (Renault R8); *Small Car*, January 1965, pp. 52–59 (Renault R8 1100 with MG 1100). *Note*: In Britain the Renault R8–1100 has the bonnet of the R8 with sides that dip towards a shallow crease in the centre; the Renault 1100 (1965–69) has a longer nose and a flat bonnet; and the Renault R10 (1970–71) looks like a Renault 1100 but has a larger (1289cc rather than 1108cc) engine. Model designations differed in other markets.

42. John Reynolds with Jan de Lange. *Original Citroën DS*. Bideford, Devon. Bay View Books Ltd., 1996, p. 110. For Slough Citroëns generally, see John Reynolds. "Jewels from Slough." *Thoroughbred & Classic Cars*, November 1991, pp. 112–116. For the Citroën DS at Slough, see John Reynolds. "The Déesse that Slough Built." *Classic and Sports Car*, August 1993, pp. 64–69.

43. John Reynolds. *Citroën 2CV*. Stroud, Gloucestershire: Sutton Publishing Ltd., 1997, p. 122.

44. *Ibid.*, p. 122.

45. The sound is difficult to represent but was something like "Bbbbbbrrrrrr (rising note)—mmmmm (gradually falling note, as the gears were changed)—bbbbbrrrrr" (more slowly rising note as the car accelerated away). Quiet it was not.

46. *The Autocar*, 10/2/61, pp. 220–223. See also *Automobile Engineer*, December 1960, pp. 560–564 (design and manufacture); *The Field*, 13/7/61, p. 75 (test). In addition, see Peter Nunn. "Bijou Baby." *Classic and Sports Car*, October 1983, pp. 71–72; and Jon Pressnell. "Flawed Gem." *Classic and Sports Car*, February 2000, pp. 106–107.

47. Reynolds, *Citroën 2CV*, p. 131.

48. *Ibid.*, p. 90. For the Ami 6, see *Automobile Engineer*, June 1961, p. 221; *The Motor*, 3/1/62, pp. 885–888. (The Ami 6 of *The Motor* achieved 65 mph, 0–50 in 30.3 secs. and 43.6 mpg overall). For the Ami 8, see *Car*, February 1970, pp. 52–57 (with Fiat 500, Honda 600 and Renault 6).

49. By contrast, sales picked up in the late 1960s and 12,716 were sold in Britain during the design's last years of 1974–75: see Reynolds with De Lange, *Original Citroën DS*, pp. 120 and 135.

50. With thanks to my friend and DS owner Matthew Shiels for the opportunity for this experiment. Happily the Citroën DS and ID have been very thoroughly documented. In addition to recent sources and road tests in *The Autocar* and *The Motor*, see *Automobile Engineer*, August 1955, pp. 327–330 (description of suspension); *Country Life*, 3/8/61, p. 258 (Safari); 18/4/63, p. 864 (Safari); 9/6/66, p. 1512 (Safari); *The Field*, 4/5/61 (Safari); 3/8/61, p. 213 (DS 19); 26/3/64, p. 593 (Safari); 6/1/66, p. 33 (Pallas); *The Illustrated London News*, 5/8/61, p. 230 (Safari); 3/10/64, p. 522 (Safari); *Practical Motorist*, November 1963, p. 303 (performance conversion by Connaught Cars of Send, Nr. Woking in Surrey). See also Graham Robson. "1955–75 Citroën DS and ID Series: All Hail The Goddess." *Collectible Automobile*, August 1994, pp. 44–55. For a modern comparison of a 1960 DS with a 1957 Mercedes-Benz 190 and a 1959 Rover 90, see Jon Pressnell. "A Shark Among the Hippos." *Classic and Sports Car*, May 1990, pp. 72–77.

26. Alfa Romeo to Wartburg

1. For comparative advertising expenditures, see *Appendix 11A*, above.

2. It is sadly not possible to reproduce this advertisement without destroying the bound library volume used for reference here, of which the advertisement is a part.

3. In addition to the announcements and road tests in the motoring journals, see *Country Life*, 21/2/63, p. 376 (300SE); 29/10/64, p. 1148 (300SE lwb); 7/1/65, p. 28 (230SL sports); 9/9/65, p. 629 (200); 17/2/66, p. 368 (600 swb); 26/1/67, p. 186 (250SE); 19/6/69, p. 1619 (300 SEL 6.3); *The Field*, 3/10/63, p. 633 (300SE Coupe); 16/7/64, p. 149 (600 lwb—S.C.H. Davis); 26/5/66, p. 1025 (600 swb—Lord Strathcarron); *Illustrated London News*, 6/4/63, p. 522 (300SE).

4. For a dealer's view of the Lancia Beta and of the hugely exaggerated

media stories about its proneness to rust (it was claimed that Beta engines fell out of their cars, although this was mechanically impossible with front-wheel drive), see Geoff Owen. *Turning Back the Clock: The Life and Times of a Motor Trader.* Croydon: Motor Racing Publications Ltd., 2000, pp. 217–228 and 256.

5. See the quarterly *Advertising Statistical Review* for those years.

6. Lancia saloons were usually described as sedans in Britain.

7. *The Autocar*, 10/11/61, pp. 817–820. For the model generally, see Wim H.J. Oude Weernink. *Lancia Fulvia & Flavia: A Collector's Guide.* Croydon: Motor Racing Publications Ltd., 2000 [1984], pp. 19–60.

8. A standard Spitfire (Mk II) of the time cost £675 with a hardtop and could manage 92–94 mph on level ground, but would have to be running flat-out downhill to reach 100 mph. A tuned car could be faster. A Spitfire without overdrive cruised easily at 55–60 mph or, with overdrive, at 65–70 mph. Much of the car's noise, particularly apparent in a hardtop model, came from the suspension and drivetrain rather than from the engine alone.

9. In addition to the announcements and road tests in the motoring journals, see *Country Life*, 7/4/66, p. 808 (2600 Sprint); 10/10/68, p. 920 (1750 saloon); 3/7/69, p. 28 (1300 GT Junior); 24/7/69, p. 249 (Spider 1300 Junior); *The Field*, 19/12/57, p. 1158 (Giulietta coupe); 27/5/65, p. 991 (Giulia Super saloon); *The Illustrated London News*, 20/10/62, p. 625 (Giulia T.I. saloon); 1/4/67, p. 31 (Giulia saloon).

10. *Small Car*, September 1963, pp. 39–43. See also *Country Life*, 30/12/65, p. 1764; 12/9/68, p. 654 (2002) 2/10/69, p. 812 (2800 saloon); 6/8/70, p. 362 (1800); 17–24/12/70 (2800 CS Coupe); *The Illustrated London News*, 9/5/70, pp. 32–33 (2800 saloon).

11. As with Jaguar in the 1960s and 1970s, the marque eventually acquired a reputation for attracting aggressive drivers, and this limited its sales to certain social groups. But that was no reflection on the car itself, or on most owners.

12. These advertisements are reproduced in Michael Frostick. *Advertising and the Motor-car.* London: Lund Humphries, 1970, pp. 158–159. Frostick calls Fiat's the "cool, quiet approach. The antithesis of Ford in Morocco, Vauxhall in the dust": *ibid.*, p. 158.

13. *Motor*, 13/8/66, pp. 23–28.

14. *Ibid.*, p. 22.

15. Stuart Griffin. "Why Japan Matters." *Car*, July 1965, pp. 56–57. For the numbers of cars imported from Japan between 1958 and 1973, see *Appendix* 6, above.

16. Stuart Bladon. "First of the Millions." *Thoroughbred & Classic Cars*, January 1994, pp. 44–48 (test car restored). For the road test, see *Autocar*, 20/8/65, pp. 349–354.

17. Martin Lewis. "Advance Guard." *Autocar*, 6/11/85, pp. 100–102. For other assessments of the Corona, see *Car*, September 1967, pp. 54–59 (with Fiat 124); *Country Life*, 14/4/66, p. 882; *The Field*, 6/9/66, p. 1133; *Small Car*, June 1965, pp. 24–27 (with Isuzu Bellett, Ford Cortina Mk 1 and Morris 1100).

18. Lewis, "Advance Guard," p. 102.

Bibliography

Dates are given in the European form of day/month/year; i.e., 4/3/64 = March 4, 1964, rather than April 3, 1964.

Books and Individual Publications

Abbott, D., Marcantonio, A. and O'Driscoll, J. (eds.) *Remember Those Great Volkswagen Ads?* (Booth-Clibborn Editions, 1982)

Adeny, Martin. *The Motor Makers: The Turbulent History of Britain's Car Industry* (Collins, 1989)

Alder, Trevor. *Vauxhall: The Postwar Years* (GT Foulis/Haynes, 1991)

Allen, Michael. *Anglia, Prefect, Popular: From Ford Eight to 105E* (MRP, 1986)

Allen, Michael. *British Family Cars of the Fifties* (Foulis/Haynes, 1985)

Allen, Michael. *British Family Cars of the Early Sixties* (Foulis/Haynes, 1989)

Allen, Michael. *Consul, Zephyr, Zodiac, Executive: Fords Mark 1 to 4 (2nd ed.)* (MRP, 1990)

Anderson, Keith. *Jensen* (Foulis/Haynes, 1989)

Atkinson, Kevin. *The Singer Story* (Veloce, 1996)

Automobile Association. *Car Buyer's Guide* (AA, 1972)

Baldwin, Nick, Georgano, G.N., Sedgwick, Michael and Laban, Brian. *The World Guide to Automobiles: The Makers and their Marques* (Guild Publishing, 1987)

Bayley, Stephen. *Taste: The Secret Meaning of Things* (Faber and Faber, 1991)

Bayley, Stephen and Chapman, Giles (eds). *Moving Objects: 30 Years of Vehicle Design at the Royal College of Art* (Eye-Q Ltd./Ford, 1999)

Berger, Warren. *Advertising Today* (Phaidon, 2001)

Beynon, Huw. *Working for Ford (2nd ed.)* (Penguin, 1984)

Bobbitt, Malcolm. *Rover P4 60, 75, 80, 90, 95, 100, 105, 110* (Veloce, 1994)

Boddy, William. *VW Beetle: Type 1 & the New Generation (2nd ed.)* (Osprey, 1999)

Bonsall, Thomas E. *Disaster in Dearborn: The Story of the Edsel* (Stanford University Press, 2002)

Brandon, Ruth. *Auto Mobile: How the Car Changed Life* (Macmillan, 2002)

Broatch, Stuart. *Vauxhall* (Sutton, 1997)

Brown, S. and Whyley, D. *Austin: The Counties Years* (Arthur Southern Ltd./Austin Counties Car Club, 1992)

Browning, Peter and Needham, Les. *Healeys and Austin-Healeys (2nd ed.)* (Haynes, 1976)

Bullock, John. *Fast Women: The Drivers who Changed the Face of Motor Racing* (Robson Books, 2002)

Bullock, John. *The Rootes Brothers: Story of a Motoring Empire* (PSL, 1993)

Burgess-Wise, David. *Complete Catalogue of Ford Cars in Britain* (Bay View Books, 1991)

Burgess-Wise, David. *Ford at Dagenham: The Rise and Fall of Detroit in Europe* (Breedon Books, 2001)

Burgess-Wise, David. *Ghia: Ford's Carrozzeria* (Osprey, 1985)

Burgess-Wise, David. *Vauxhall: A Century in Motion* (Vauxhall Motors Ltd./CW Publishing, 2003)

Burton, Philip and Bowman Kreer, G. *Advertising Copywriting (2nd ed.)* (Prentice-Hall, Inc., 1962)

Cannon, Tom. *Advertising: The Economic Implications* (Intertext Books, 1974)

Chapman, Giles. *Cars That Time Forgot* (Parragon, 1997)

Chapman, Giles. *Mad Cars* (Sutton, 2002)

Chapman, Giles. *The Worst Cars Ever Sold in Britain* (Sutton, 2001)

Church, Roy. *The Rise and Decline of the British Motor Industry* (Macmillan, 1994)

Clarke, R.M. (ed) *Ford Consul, Zephyr, Zodiac Mk. 1 and 2 1950–1962* (Brooklands Books, 1990)

Clausager, Anders. *Complete Catalogue of Austin Cars since 1945* (Bay View Books, 1992)

Cook, Michael. *Triumph Cars in America* (MBI Publishing Co., 2001)

Costigan, Mike. *Complete Guide to Triumph Herald and Vitesse* (Bay View Books, 1992)

Covello, Mike (ed.). *Standard Catalog of Imported Cars 1946–2002* (Krause Publications, 2002)

Crocker, D. and Linden, T. (eds.). *Ethics of Consumption* (Rowman & Littlefield, 1998)

Daily Express. *Cars of the Early '60s: British and Imported Models 1960–64* (Daily Express/PRC, 1994)

Daily Express. *Cars of the Late '60s: British and Imported Models 1965–70* (Daily Express/PRC, 1995)

Daily Mail. *Ideal Home Book 1956* (Associated Newspapers Ltd., 1956)

Docker, Lady Norah. *Norah: The Autobiography of Lady Docker* (W.H. Allen, 1969)

Droste, Magdalena and Bauhaus Archiv. *Bauhaus 1919–1933* (Taschen, 1998)

Dymock, Eric. *The Ford in Britain File — Model by Model* (Dove Publishing, 2002)

Dymock, Eric. *The Renault File: All Models Since 1898* (Foulis/Haynes, 1998)

Earnshaw, Alan and Berry, Robert. *Vauxhall Cars 1945–1964* (Trans-Pennine Publishing Ltd., 2000)

Earnshaw, Alan and Berry, Robert. *Vauxhall Cars 1965–1984* (Vauxhall Heritage Services/Transpennine Publishing Ltd., 2001)

Edwards, Harry. *The Morris Motor Car 1913–1983* (Moorland, 1983)

Ensor, James. *The Motor Industry* (Financial Times/Longman, 1971)

Ewen, Stuart. *PR! A Social History of Spin* (BasicBooks, 1996)

Faith, Nicholas. *Crash: The Limits of Car Safety* (Boxtree, 1997)

Fox, Stephen. *The Mirror Makers* (Heinemann, 1990)

Freeman, Tony. *Humber: An Illustrated History 1868–1976* (Academy Books, 1991)

Frostick, Michael. *Advertising and the Motor-car* (Lund Humphries, 1970)

Galbraith, J. K. *The Affluent Society* (Penguin, 1999) [1958]

Georgano, Nick. *The Complete Encyclopaedia of Motorcars 1885 to the Present (3rd ed.)* (Ebury Press, 1982)

Geogano, Nick. *The Beaulieu Encyclopedia of the Automobile (Vols 1 & 2)* (The Stationery Office/Fitzroy Dearborn Publishers, 2000)

Georgano, N., Baldwin, N., Clausager, A. and Wood, J. *Britain's Motor Industry: The First Hundred Years* (Haynes, 1995)

Gloag, John. *Advertising in Modern Life* (Heinemann, 1959)

Green, Malcolm. *MG Sports Cars: An Illustrated History of the World-Famous Sporting Marque* (Bramley Books, 1997)

Groesbeck, Kenneth. *Advertising Agency Success: Principles, Management, Functions, Performance* (Harper & Brothers, 1958)

Haajanen, Lennart. *Illustrated Dictionary of Automobile Body Styles* (McFarland & Company, Inc., 2003)

Harris, Ralph and Seldon, Arthur. *Advertising in Action* (Institute of Economic Affairs, 1962)

Harris, Ralph and Seldon, Arthur. *Advertising in a Free Society* (Institute of Economic Affairs, 1959)

Harvey, Chris. *Jaguar Saloons: Grace, Space and Pace* (Oxford Illustrated Press/Haynes, 1991)

Harvey, Chris. *TR for Triumph* (Haynes, 1983)

Hege, John B. *The Wankel Rotary Engine: A History* (McFarland & Company, Inc., 2001)

Henry, Brian (ed.). *British Television Advertising: The First 30 Years* (Century Benham, Ltd., 1986)

Henshaw, David and Henshaw, Peter. *Apex: The Inside Story of the Hillman Imp (2nd ed.)* (Bookmarque, 1990)

Herndon, Booton. *Ford — An Unconventional Biography of the Men and Their Times* (Weybright and Tulley, 1969 (US ed.) and Cassell, 1970 (GB ed.)

Hill, Ken. *The Morgan: The Art of Selling a Unique Sports Car* (Blandford, 1996)

Holden, Len. *Vauxhall Motors and the Luton Economy, 1900–2002* (Bedfordshire Historical Record Society/The Boydell Press, 2003)

Holme, Bryan. *Advertising: Reflections of a Century* (Heinemann, 1982)

Hough, R. and Frostick, M. *A History of the World's High-Performance Cars* (George Allen & Unwin, 1967)

Hower, Ralph. *The History of an Advertising Agency: N.W. Ayer & Son at work 1869–1949* (Harvard University Press 1949)

Isaacs, Reginald. *Gropius: An Illustrated Biography of the Creator of the Bauhaus* (Bulfinch Press/Little Brown and Company (Inc.), 1991)

Knowles, David. *MG: The Untold Story* (Windrow & Greene, 1997)

Knowles, David. *MGB, MGC & MGB GT V8* (Bay View Books/MBI, 2000)

Kriegeskorte, Michael. *Automobilwerbung in Deutschland 1948–1968* (DuMont Buchverlag, 1994)

Kuch, Joachim. *Volkswagen Model History* (Haynes, 1999) [Note: published in the United States as *Volkswagen Model Documentation* (Robert Bentley Inc., 1999)]

Langworth, Richard. *Tiger, Alpine, Rapier: Sporting Cars from the Rootes Group* (Osprey, 1982)

Legate, Ray. *Salute the Victor: 40th Anniversary of the F Model* (Trinity Publications/Classic Car Mart, 1997)

Lindh, Bjorn-Eric. *Volvo: The Cars-From the 20s to the 80s (revd. ed.)* (Forlagshuset Norden AB, 1986)

Link House (pub). *Scooter & Three Wheeler Year Book 1962* (Link House, 1962)

Loewy, Raymond. *Never Leave Well Enough Alone (2002 ed.)* (Johns Hopkins University Press, 2002)

Logoz, Arthur (pub.). *International Automobile Parade/Auto Parade Vol II (1958 ed.)* (Arthur Logoz, 1958)

Long, Brian. *Daimler and Lanchester: A Century of Motoring History* (Longford International Publications, 1995)

Long, Brian. *Daimler V8 S.P. 250* (Veloce, 1994)

Long, Brian. *Standard: The Illustrated History* (Veloce, 1993)

Lovell, Bernard. *The Story of Jodrell Bank* (Oxford University Press, 1968)

Merlin, Didier. *Pininfarina 1930–1980: Prestige and Tradition* (Edita, 1980)

Moloney, James. *Bowties of the Fifties (2nd ed).* (Cars & Parts/Amos Press Inc., 2000)

Montagu of Beaulieu, Lord. *The British Motorist* (Macdonald, 1987)

Montagu of Beaulieu, Lord and Burgess-Wise, David. *Daimler Century* (PSL, 1995)

Manwaring, L.S. (ed). *The Observer's Book of Automobiles (1959, 1961, 1962, 1963, 1964, 1966, 1967, 1968 eds.)* (Warne, 1959–68)

Macartney, John. *In the Shadow of My Father* (John Macartney, 1998)

Mackenzie-Wintle, Hector. *Renault* (Sutton, 1998)

McLintock, J. Dewar. *Renault: The Cars and the Charisma* (PSL, 1983)

Munro, Bill. *Carbodies: The Complete Story* (Crowood, 1998)

Nader, Ralph. *Unsafe at Any Speed: The Designed-in Dangers of the American Automobile* (Grossman, 1965)

Nevett, T. *Advertising in Britain: A History* (Heinemann, 1982)

Newell, Ray. *Morris Minor: The First 50 Years* (Bay View Books, 1997)

Nutland, Martin. *Rolls-Royce Silver Wraith, Silver Dawn & Silver Cloud; Bentley Mk VI, R-Series & S-Series* (Veloce, 1997)

Ogilvy, David. *Confessions of an Advertising Man* (Atheneum, 1963)

Ogilvy, David. *Ogilvy on Advertising* (Orbis, 1983)

Ogilvy, David. *The Unpublished David Ogilvy* (Sidgwick & Jackson, 1988)

Owen, Geoff. *Turning Back the Clock: The Life and Times of a Motor Trader* (Fitzjames Press/MRP, 2000)

Packard, Vance. *The Hidden Persuaders (2nd ed.)* (Penguin, 1981) [1957]

Palmer, G. and Balfour, C. *Auto-Architect: The Autobiography of Gerald Palmer* (Magna Press, 1998)

Pagneux, Dominique. *Vedette: Le Grand Livre* (Editions E/P/A, 1996)

Piggott, Bill. *Triumph TR — TR2 to 6: The Last of the Traditional Sports Cars* (Haynes, 2003)

Platt, Maurice. *An Addiction to Automobiles* (Warne, 1980)

Pressnell, Jon. *Morris Minor: Exploring the Legend* (Haynes Publishing, 1998)

Price Williams, John. *Alvis: The Postwar Cars* (MRP, 1993)

Ramaciotti, Lorenzo. *Pininfarina Solitaires* (Automobilia, 1989)

Rawbone, Martin. *Ford in Britain: A History of the Company and the Cars* (Haynes Publishing, 2001)

Rees, Chris. *Complete Classic Mini 1959–2000* (MRP, 2003)

Rees, Chris. *Essential Ford Capri: The Cars and Their Story 1969–1987* (Bay View Books, 1997)

Rees, Chris. *Microcar Mania: The Definitive History of the Small Car* (Bookmarque, 1995)

Riden, Philip. *How to Trace the History of Your Car (2nd ed.)* (Merton Priory Press, 1998)

de la Rive Box, Rob. *Encyclopaedia of Classic Cars: Saloon Cars 1945–1975* (Rebo, 1999)

Reynolds, John with de Lange, Jan. *Original Citroën DS* (Bay View Books, 1996)

Richards, Patsy. *Inflation: The Value of the Pound (House of Commons Research Paper 02/44)* (House of Commons Library, 2002)

Roberts, Peter. *Any Color So Long as It's Black: The First Fifty Years of Automobile Advertising* (Willam Morrow & Company, 1976)

Roberts, Sam *Ford Model Y: Henry's Car for Europe* (Veloce, 2001)

Robson, Graham. *A-Z of Cars of the 1970s* (Bay View Books, 1990)

Robson, Graham. *Cars in the UK: A Survey of all British-built and officially imported cars available in the United Kingdom since 1945, Volume One: 1945 to 1970* (MRP, 1996)

Robson, Graham. *The Cars of BMC* (MRP, 1987)

Robson, Graham. *Cars of the Rootes Group: Hillman, Humber, Singer, Sunbeam, Sunbeam Talbot* (MRP, 1990)

Robson, Graham. *The Post War Touring Car* (Haynes, 1977)

Robson, Graham and Langworth, Richard. *Triumph Cars: The Complete 75-year History* (MRP, 1979)

Robson, Graham. *Triumph Herald and Vitesse: The Complete Story* (Crowood, 1997)

Robson, Graham. *Triumph Spitfire and GT6* (Osprey, 1982)

Robson, Graham. *Triumph 2000 and 2.5PI* (Crowood, 1995)

Ross, Alan and Mitford, Nancy et. al. *Noblesse Oblige: An Enquiry into the Identifiable Characteristics of the English Aristocracy* (Hamish Hamilton, 1956)

Ruiz, Marco. *The Complete History of the Japanese Car 1907 to the Present* (Foulis/Haynes, 1988)

Salmon, John and Ritchie, John (eds). *Inside Collett Dickenson Pearce* (B.T. Batsford, 2000)

Schönberger, Angela (ed.). *Raymond Loewy: Pioneer of American Industrial Design* (Prestel-Verlag, 1991)

Sedgwick, Michael. *Cars of the Fifties and Sixties* (Temple Press, 1983)

Sedgwick, Michael. *Vauxhall: A Pictorial Tribute* (Beaulieu Books, 1981)

Sedgwick, M. and Gillies, M. *A-Z of Cars 1945–1970 (2nd ed., revd. Jon Pressnell)* (Bay View Books, 1993)

Setright, L.J.K. *Drive On! A Social History of the Motor Car (2nd ed.)* (Granta Books, London, 2003).

Sharratt, Barney. *Men and Motors of 'The Austin': The Inside Story of a Century of Car Making at Longbridge* (Haynes, 2000)

Sharratt, Barney. *Post-War Baby Austins* (Osprey, 1988)

Skilleter, Paul. *Morris Minor: The World's Supreme Small Car (3rd ed.)* (Osprey, 1989)

Skilleter, Paul. *The XJ-Series Jaguars: A Collector's Guide* (MRP, 1984)

Skilleter, Paul and Simpson, Peter. *Vauxhall F Victor Restoration Briefing* (Kelsey Publishing Ltd., 1991)

Smith, Brian. *Daimler Days: A Celebration of 100 Years of Daimler Motor Cars (Vols. 1 & 2)* (Jaguar Daimler Heritage Trust, 1996)

Smith, Brian. *The Daimler Tradition* (Transport Bookman, 1972)

Smith, Brian. *Vanden Plas Coachbuilders* (Dalton Watson, 1979)

Society of Motor Manufacturers and Traders. *The Motor Industry of Britain Centenary Book, 1896–1996* (SMMT, 1996)

Society of Motor Manufacturers and Traders. *Motor Show Official Catalogue, 1964* (SMMT, 1964)

Springate, Lynda. *A Nostalgic Look at Riley Cars* (Silver Link, 1996)

Stein, Jonathan. *British Sports Cars in America* (Automobile Quarterly, Inc., 1993)

Stevenson, Heon. *Advertising British Cars of the '50s (2nd ed.)* (Magna Books, 1995)

Stevenson, Heon. *Selling the Dream: Advertising the American Automobile 1930—1980* (Academy Books, 1995)

Strathcarron, Lord. *Motoring for Pleasure* (Stanley Paul, 1963)

Taplin, Walter. *Advertising — A New Approach (revd. ed.)* (Hutchinson, 1963)

Taplin, Walter. *The Origin of Television Advertising in the United Kingdom* (Pitman, 1961)

Taylor, James. *Jaguar S-type and 420: The Complete Story* (Crowood, 1996)

Taylor, James. *The Post-War Rover P4 and P5 (revd. ed.)* (P4 Spares, 1990)

Taylor, James. *Rover P4: The Complete Story* (Crowood, 1998)

Taylor, James. *Rover P6 1963–1977* (MRP, 1993)

Taylor, Mike. *Ford Capri: 'The Car You Always Promised Yourself'* (Crowood, 1995)

Thoms, D. and Donnelly, T. *The Motor Car Industry in Coventry since the 1890s: Origins, Development and Structure* (Croom Helm, 1985)

Thoms, David, Holden, Len and Claydon, Tim (eds.). *The Motor Car and Popular Culture in the 20th Century* (Ashgate, 1998)

Thorley, Nigel. *Jaguar Mk I and Mk II: The Complete Companion* (Bay View Books, 1986)

Turner, Dave. *Ford Popular and the Small Sidevalves* (Osprey, 1984)

Turner, E.S. *The Shocking History of Advertising (2nd ed.)* (Penguin, 1965)

Turner, Graham. *The Leyland Papers* (Eyre & Spottiswoode, 1971)

Twitchell, James. *Adcult USA: The Triumph of Advertising in American Culture* (Columbia University Press, 1996)

Ullyett, Kenneth. *The Vauxhall Companion* (Stanley Paul, 1971)

Vauxhall Motors Ltd. *A History of Vauxhall* (Vauxhall Motors Ltd., 1980)

Vauxhall Motors Ltd. *Vauxhall Cars Since 1903 (revd. ed.)* (Vauxhall Motors Ltd., 1977)

Voller, David. (ed. Bart Vanderveen). *British Cars of the Late Fifties 1955–1959* (Warne, 1975)

Voller, David. *British Cars of the Late Sixties 1965–1969* (Warne, 1982)

Walker, Nick. *A-Z of British Coachbuilders 1919–1960* (Bay View Books, 1997)

Walker Hepner, Harry. *Advertising — Creative Communication with Consumers* (McGraw Hill, 1964)

Watson Dunn, S. *International Handbook of Advertising* (McGraw Hill, 1964)

Weernink, Wim. *Lancia Fulvia and Flavia: A Collector's Guide* (MRP, 1984)

Wildman, R. and Crawley, A. *Bedford's Motoring Heritage* (Sutton, 2003)

Williams, Jim. *Boulevard Photographic: The Art of Automobile Advertising* (Motorbooks International, 1997)

Wilson, A. *Advertising and the Community* (Manchester University Press, 1968)

Volkswagenwerk, Wolfsburg. *Volkswagen Instruction Manual: Sedan and Convertible* (Volkswagenwerk, 1962)

Wood, Jonathan. *Ford Cortina Mk I* (Osprey, 1984)

Wood, Jonathan. *Wheels of Misfortune: The Rise and Fall of the British Motor Industry* (Sidgwick & Jackson, 1988)

Wooton, Frank. *The Aviation Art of Frank Wootton (ed. David Larkin)* (Peacock Press/Bantam, 1976)

Wright, John and Warner, S. (eds.). *Speaking of Advertising* (McGraw Hill, 1963)

Zweiniger-Bargielowska, Ina. *Austerity in Britain: Rationing, Controls, and Consumption, 1939–1955* (Oxford University Press, 2000)

Newspapers and Periodicals — Contemporary

The Advertising Quarterly

Advertising World

Art and Industry

(The) Autocar

Automobile Engineer

Business

Campaign (Dublin)

Car (as Small Car to June 1965)

Car Mechanics

Country Life

The Field

Homes & Gardens

The Illustrated London News

Modern Publicity

(The) Motor

The Motor Industry of Great Britain (SMMT annual)

Motor Sport

Motor Trader
Motor Trend
Motoring Which?
Practical Classics
Practical Motorist
Punch
Road & Track
Statistical Review of Press Advertising, Statistical Review of Television
    Advertising (and successor titles: Statistical Review of Press and TV
    Advertising
Monthly Statistical Review of Press, TV Outdoor and Radio Adver-
    tising
Advertising with Stat. Review; and ASR — Advertising Statistical Re-
    view)
Time
The Times

Newspapers and Periodicals — Historical and Retrospective

The Automobile
British Car
Citropolis (Special Edition No. 2, 1998: The Citroën DS)
Classic Car Mart
Classic Car Weekly
Classic and Sportscar
Classics
Classic Van and Pick-Up
Collectible Automobile
The Daily Telegraph
Ford Heritage
Jaguar World
Jalopy
MG Enthusiast
Motoring Classics
Old Car
Popular Classics
Practical Classics
Restoring Classic Cars
Sports Car Monthly
Supercar & Classics
The Road Back
(Thoroughbred &) Classic Cars
Triumph World

Manufacturers' Brochures, Catalogues and Publicity Booklets

Austin — 50 Years of Car Progress, Pub. No. 1235 [1955]
Austin 1100, Pub. No. 2192/D
Austin 1100 Mk 2 and Austin 1300, Pub. No. 2440/B
Austin Car Prices, May 1968, Pub. No. 1168/BZ
Austin Healey Sprite Mk II, Pub. No. 1995 [c. 1961]
Austin Healey Sprite Mk Four, Pub. No. 2390/A [c. 1966]
[Ford] Outstanding Zephyr Six, Ref. D8109/1051EX [1951]
[Ford] Zephyr Six New Features, Ref. 1/J5677/153 [1955]
Ford Consul Cortina, Ref. T 5699/862/ENG./D [1962]
Ford Transit Bus, Ref. 177899/11/66 Dom [1966]
Hillman Super Minx, Ref 1025/H [c. 1961]
Hillman Super Minx, Ref. 2602/EX/LHD [c. 1962]
Superlative MGB, Pub. No. H & E 6242 [1962]
MG 1100, Pub. No. H & E 6230 [1962]
Morris 1100, Pub. No. H & E 6301/B [1963]
Morris J2 M16 16/18cwt Van, Pick-up & Minibus, Pub. No. H & E
    6542/A [1966]

Morris Colour Finishes, J2 M16 and J4 M10 Vehicles, Pub. No. H & E
    6488 [c.1966]
Morris Colour Finishes, Pub. No. H & E 6506 [1966]
Morris Price List (Home retail ex works prices), March 1963, Pub. No.
    H.6324
Morris Car Prices, May 1968, Pub. No. 2421/H
Nuffield Organization Price List, July 1963, Pub. No. H6355
Peugeot 204, Ref. 7–72 — PP 267 G.B. [1972]
Peugeot 504, Ref. 7–72 — PP 274 G.B. [1972]
Renault 8 [1100], Ref. 55 B 8620 [c. 1967]
Saab 96, Ref. B.50205 75.000.8.62 [1962]
Singer SM [1500] Series, Ref. 112 D/50 [1950]
Standard Vanguard Phase III, "IT makes history!" [1955]
Triumph Spitfire 4, Ref. No. 352/11/62/UK-25m [1962]
Triumph Spitfire Mk II, Ref. No. 352/365/UK [1965]
Triumph Spitfire Mk 2, Ref. No. 352/1066/UK [1966]
Triumph Spitfire Mk 3, Ref. 378/1268/EXP [1968]
Vauxhall Victor, Ref. V1076A/9/57 [1957]
Vauxhall News, Motor Show 1959 [unreferenced]
Vauxhall Velox & Cresta, Ref. V1379/4/63 [1963]
Vauxhall Victor, Ref. V1466 [c.1963]
[Vauxhall] Sleek, scorchy new Victor, Ref. V1783/12/67 [1967]
[Vauxhall] Victor, Ref. 1788/5/68 [1968]
[Vauxhall] New Victor Estates, Ref. V1834/6/68 [1968]
[Vauxhall] Victor, Ref. V1929/9/69 [1969]
Vauxhall Ventora II, Ref. VX 1936/9/69 [1969]
[Vauxhall] Return of the VX4/90, Ref. VX1934/10/69 [1969]
[Vauxhall] The Quality Story, for press release December 1, 1969
[Vauxhall] Ventora 2, Ref. V1981/9/70 [1970]
Vauxhall Cresta, Ref. V1982/9/70 [1970]
Vauxhall Viscount, Ref. V1982/9/70 [1970]
Vauxhall Victor, Ref. V1929/4/71 [1970]

Museums

The Museum of British Road Transport, Coventry
The National Motor Museum, Beaulieu, Hampshire
The Stondon Museum, Lower Stondon, Bedfordshire

Advertisements

Note: Advertising for a model was usually most lavish and concentrated at the beginning of its production run; when improvements were introduced; and occasionally when sales were declining towards the end of the model's life. Some advertisements continued to be published unchanged over many months, whilst others were current for long periods but appeared intermittently. This was particularly the case with a few colour pieces for relatively low-production, upmarket versions of family saloons. Some popular models were advertised quite sparsely, considering the numbers produced, by comparison with more specialized cars from the same manufacturers, for which advertising costs could represent a surprisingly high proportion of a car's factory price.

Very few advertisements referred to model years (beginning in September) in the American style, although new models would often be announced at Motor Show time in October. Most manufacturers advertised heavily during October, when advertisements would be seen for specialized and low-production models that received little or no conventional publicity during the rest of the year. Advertising themes were sometimes— although not always—carried over to the catalogues distributed, together with colour charts and manufacturers' price lists, by dealers. Prices were not always given as general inflation, changes of pricing policy and fluctuating rates of Purchase Tax could cause them to change at short notice. The tax component of a selling price was often stated separately.

In the 1960s, colour advertisements made up quite a small proportion of the total printed in any one year, as the majority of newspaper and magazine pages were printed in black and white. Most advertisements, particularly for family cars, were published in several magazines and papers at the same time, and many were produced in both colour and monochrome (black and white) versions. Where colour was too expensive or not possible in a particular publication, a colour illustration would often simply be reproduced in monochrome. Alternatively, a similar but not identical illustration would be used for black and white reproduction, although it might appear identical to the colour version at first glance (noted as "similar illustration" in entries below). In a few cases parallel colour advertisements in different magazines used illustrations that were almost, but not quite, identical (noted as "almost identical illustration" below). Here, the tunnel through which the car was speeding might change, or headlights would be on rather than off, or accompanying minor illustrations would be rearranged. Occasionally the headline and copy of an advertisement would be changed while the original picture remained, or *vice versa*, although this was relatively unusual.

Until the late 1960s, the arrangement of blocks of text and illustrations for a given advertisement could vary slightly from magazine to magazine, depending on the size and shape of the page available. Copy was sometimes shortened for smaller magazines. Some advertisements appeared in single-page format where the size of the magazine allowed, but were printed as double-page spreads in smaller magazines. In the early 1960s such spreads were uncommon, but in the last years of the decade they came to be used more freely. Advertisers often placed the car on one side of the spread and the text on the other, which reduced colour printing costs and ensured that the lines of the car, so carefully captured by the photographer, would not be broken up by the gutter between the pages. The question, "Small and clear or bigger but broken?" is still faced by advertisers today. Nowadays, where a picture is spread across the gutter, the car itself often appears on one page in its entirety.

The advertisements in non-motoring magazines referred to in the preparation of this book (which are the majority) are listed below by marque and model. Model names are given in the form in which they generally appeared in advertisements. Type designations used widely by enthusiasts and others, but which did not appear in advertisements, are added within square brackets. Manufacturers' model names sometimes changed in detail over time; for instance, a "Mark II" designation of a car might be used in early advertising and then abbreviated to "Mk II" or dropped, while nevertheless remaining correctly in use among owners and garages. Roman and arabic numerals for different Marks of a given car could be used inconsistently (see, for instance, the Triumph Spitfire brochures mentioned above). Retrospective appellations could take Roman or Arabic forms, either in parallel or successively with different Marks; where this is the case dominant usage or that adopted in recent specialist publications is followed. There were individual oddities, such as Singer's Vogue II, developed into what was variously described as the Vogue Series III or Vogue Mark III, although neither designation appeared often in advertising, if at all. Sometimes model names were not used in their complete form in advertisements: the Austin A60, for example, was not generally advertised as the Cambridge, even in its home market. (The name appeared prominently on the boot lid, however.) Marque and model names, particularly those of BMC, the Rootes Group and Standard-Triumph, frequently differed between home and export markets, and advertising reflected this. Some Ford and Vauxhall model names varied according to territory.

Different advertisements for a model are listed in the alphabetical order of the magazines in which they appeared except where an individual advertisement was published both in colour (C) and in black and white/monochrome (M) versions. In these cases the colour appearances are given first. Advertisements below which are illustrated in this book are marked with *asterisks after their entries. The advertisements listed represent perhaps between a fifth and a quarter of the different pieces placed by British car manufacturers and importers in non-motoring magazines during the 1960s.

The entries below include representative advertisements from the years 1955–59 for several cars which were produced (or were related to cars produced) after 1959, together with a few advertisements from 1970–74 for cars announced before 1970. Some British export advertisements for the general English speaking market are also included and are identified by [E] except, as with some BMC cars, where an advertisement was employed unchanged for home and export markets. Finally, for comparison, a few examples are given of American (US) advertising for British cars and for some continental models imported into both Britain and the United States.

Most of the advertisements shown in this book have been chosen from the much larger number which originally appeared, in 14" × 10" single-page format, in weekly issues of *The Field* between 1959 and 1970. They were superbly printed on high-quality paper and are among the best of their period. Many advertisements placed in general magazines and papers during the 1960s, including the majority of attractive colour pieces, were also published in the specialist motoring magazines, occasionally in expanded form in the case of announcement spreads. Although space does not allow appearances of advertisements in motoring magazines to be listed here, I hope that readers will find this bibliography useful in tracking down the advertisements from non-motoring sources which cannot always be found quickly through the usual enthusiast channels.

Researchers should note that some libraries removed advertising sections from magazines during binding.

Magazine source codes are as follows (w = weekly; f = fortnightly; m = monthly):

CF	Country Fair (m)
CL	Country Life (w)
CLA	Country Life Annual
E	Everybody's (Australia) (w)
ET	The Edinburgh Tatler (m)
F	The Field (w)
FC	Farm & Country (w)
G	The Geographical Magazine (m)
H	Holiday (US) (m)
HG	Homes and Gardens (m)
ILN	The Illustrated London News (w, later m)
NG	National Geographic (US) (m)
O	Outpost (Rhodesia) (m)
PM	Practical Motorist (m)
P	Punch (w)
RD	Reader's Digest (m)
S	The Sphere (w)
SA	Scientific American (US) (m)
SC	Sport & Country (f)
SK	The Sketch (w)
SM	The Scots Magazine (m)
SCM	Sussex County Magazine (m)
TA	Time (Atlantic Edition) (w)
U	Unknown
V	Vogue (m)
WW	The Wide World Magazine (m)

AC (AC Cars Ltd., Thames Ditton, Surrey)
428 Fastback: "There is only one motor car…" (M): CL 17/10/68; "…the Best of two continents" (M): CL 15/10/70; "British race-bred Chassis…" (M): F 19/10/72*.

• **ALFA ROMEO** (Imported by Alfa Romeo (GB) Ltd., 164 Sloane Street, London SW1)
Giulia 1600 TI Saloon: "We could…" (M): CL 6/2/64, F 23/1/64, ILN 14/12/63; "Four doors (and 105mph) are open…" (M): F 18/2/65.
Giulia 1600 Spider: "Why on earth…" (M): CL 2/4/64;
"News from Milan!…" (M): CL 9/4/64; "Game set match to Alfa Romeo…" (M): CL 20/5/65.
Giulia 1600 Sprint GT: "What is it that flies…" (M): CL 10/12/64, F 24/9/64; "From any angle…" (M): CL 22/4/65; "Take a test drive for two…" (M): CL 5/5/66, ILN 15/1/66, F 10/2/66, P 19/1/66.
Giulia Sprint GTC (dealer advertisement: Chipstead, London):

"...designed with a special touch of genius..." (M): F 21/10/65.

Giulia Super [saloon]: "Are all Alfas fabulously expensive?..." (M): CL 3/3/66, P 2/3/66.

Giulia SS: "Hand built..." (M): F [undated]*, P 13/1/65.

2600 Berlina: "Take a test drive..." (M): CL 24/10/63, ILN 26/10/63.

2600 Sprint: "You have probably promised yourself..." (M) F 31/10/63; "Test drive it..." (M): 22/10/64; "A very distinguished car..." (M): CL 12/11/64 & 8/4/65, P 17/3/65; "If you've never flown before..." (M): P 22/12/65; "Alas! It does 55mph more..." (M): CL 24/3/66, F 2/12/65 & 14/4/66, ILN 23/4/66, P 18/5/66; "Fast, bold and beautiful..." (dealer advertisement: Charles Garages, Liverpool) (M): F 21/10/65.

1300GT: "Prrroww!..." (M): ILN 10/6/67.

1750 GTV: "When the Sunday drivers..." (M): P 11/6/69.

1750 [saloon illustrated]: "The Italians are crazy about..." (M): P 3/12/69.

• ALVIS (Alvis Ltd., Holyhead Road, Coventry)

3 Litre [TD21]: "Styled by Graber..." (M): ILN 13/6/59 [illustrating Coupe] & ILN 24/10/59 [illustrating Saloon]; "Three Litre Saloon & Coupe; coachwork by Park Ward, styled by Graber" (M): CL 28/4/60 [illustrating Saloon], ILN 11/6/60 [illustrating Coupe] & 22/10/60 [illustrating Saloon]; "Alvis coachwork by Park Ward..." (M): CL 25/5/61; "Talk about Alvis..." (M): ILN 21/10/61.

3 Litre Series III [TE] "Alvis Three Litre Series III..." (M): CL 17/10/63; "The power of beauty..." (dealer advertisement: Henlys, London) (M): CL 24/3/66.

• ARMSTRONG SIDDELEY (Armstrong Siddeley Motors Ltd., Parkside, Coventry)

Star Sapphire: "The managing director's car..." (M): F 6/11/58 & 4/12/58; "In the top flight..." (C—two-tone green): CL 20/5/59, F 7/5/59, (M): CL 26/3/59, F 19/3/59; "Luxurious power, quiet comfort..." (C—two-tone cream over maroon): CL 22/10/59 & 12/11/59.

Armstrong-Siddeley marque: [E]: "...and Bristol Siddeley supply the power..." (M): T 9/5/60.

• ASTON MARTIN (Aston Martin Lagonda Ltd., Hanworth Park, Feltham, Middlesex; subsequently at Newport Pagnell, Buckinghamshire)

DB Mark III: "Elegance to gratify..." (dealer advertisement: Brooklands, London) (M): CL 19/3/59 [illustrating drophead coupe], CL 16/4/59 [illustrating saloon].

DB4: "The breathtaking DB 4..." (M): CL 2/11/60, ILN 12/11/60; "Choice of the perfectionist..." (M): F 24/5/62, ILN 26/5/62; [E]: "Choice of the perfectionist..." [copy as previous entry; different illustration] (M): T 8/6/62.

DB4 Vantage: "Body beautiful..." (M): CL 21/2/63 & 23/5/63, F 9/5/63 & 20/6/63*.

DB5: "The most exciting car of 1964..." (M): CL 17/10/63, F 24/10/63, P 16/10/63; "For you, a possession..." (C—silver): CL 3/12/64 & 10/6/65, ILN 20/3/65, P 3/2/65 & 19/5/65.

DB6: "Aston Martin—elegantly virile..." (M): ILN 20/7/68; "...so now you all know!..." (dealer advertisement: HR Owen Ltd., London) (C—maroon): CL 13/7/67 & 20/7/67; "When 'only the best is good enough'..." (C—silver): CL 4/4/68, ILN 30/3/68, P 15/5/68.

DBS: "Above all, make it an Aston..." (C—dark blue): CL 27/6/68, P 17/7/68; "Aston Martin—elegantly virile..." [copy as DB6 of ILN 20/7/68] (M): CL 15/8/68, P 4/9/68; "Aston Martin" [no copy] (M): G 2/69; "Aston Martin" [no copy, as previous entry with different photograph] (M): G 3/69*; "Lovely to look at..." (dealer advertisement: HR Owen Ltd., London) (M): CL 4/12/69.

• AUDI (Imported by Auto Union (G.B.) Ltd., Great West Road, Brentford, Middlesex)

100LS: "If you're in the market..." (M): CL 3/7/69; "Motor safer: own yourself the 100LS..." (M): CL 5/3/70; "Motor cooler: Own yourself the 100LS..." (M): CL 16/7/70; "Motor easier: own yourself the 100LS..." (M): CL 26/3-2&9/4/70 [single issue].

• AUSTIN and AUSTIN-HEALEY (Austin Motor Company Ltd., Longbridge, Birmingham)

Austin range: "This year's news is 9 new Austins..." (M): ILN 21/10/61.

A55 Cambridge [Mk I]: "The new Austin A55..." (M): WW 4/57; "Austin range makes headlines..." (M) CF 4/57; "Top car in the middle price bracket..." (M): CF 8/57; "For sheer enjoyment..." (C—two-tone cream over grey): S 8/2/58; "Home or away—it's the Austin A.55..." (C—two-tone cream over grey; same car as previous entry): F 6/3/58; "Contemporary travel—the A.55..." (C—two-tone cream over grey; same car as previous 2 entries): CL 17/4/58, (M): F 12/12/57; [E]: "The new Austin A55..." (M): T 27/1/58 & 28/4/58.

A95: "Look inside the Austin A 95 Saloon and you will find..." (M): SC 24/7/57; "Travel top flight—by Austin A.95" (C—blue): CL 20/2/58; "A beauty in any language..." (C—dark green with cream flash): F 29/5/58; [E]: "A beauty in any language..." [headline as previous entry; different copy and illustration] (M): T 24/11/58.

A95 Countryman [estate car]: "New powerful car does double duty..." (M): CF 2/57 & 4/57; "Doing two jobs beautifully..." (M): CF 10/57 & 12/57; "Wins its class on every point outright..." (M): F 3/7/58.

A105 Vanden Plas: "We stayed up to see your new A.105..." (C—light green): ILN 26/4/58; "Can we go to the carol service...?" (C—light green) [illustration as previous entry]: CLA 1959, ILN Christmas Number 1958.

A35: "Life's more fun with an Austin A.35..." (M): ILN 7/12/57; "You can't beat an Austin A.35..." (M): ILN 1/2/58; [E]: "You can't beat an Austin A.35..." (M): T 26/5/58.

Gipsy: "The 4-wheel drive Gipsy with sensational new suspension..." (M): CF 6/58, 9/58 & 4/59; "Godfrey Baseley tests the Austin Gipsy..." (M): CL 30/4/59, F 14/5/59*; "The go-anywhere Austin Gipsy..." (M): CF 6/59, 12/59 & 2/60; "How Austin helps with mountain rescue..." (M): CF 4/60 & 6/60; "The Austin Gipsy goes to market..." (M): CL 26/1/61 & 2/11/61; "The Austin Gipsy goes pigging..." (M): CL 27/12/62; "Game: the Austin Gipsy is ready..." (M): CL 3/6/65; "Know a motor car..." (M): CL 24/11/66; "An Austin Gipsy is as good as having a second horse..." (M): CL 25/11/65; [E]: "Aussie newsman Dvoretsky..." (M): T 1/9/58.

A40 [Farina]: "The new Austin A.40..." (M): CF 11/58; "The Austin A40 moves in dress circles" (C—pale blue with black roof): CL 19/2/59, ILN 14/3/59, (M): CF 2/59 & 10/59, F 19/2/59; "Every clever inch a beauty..." (C—red with black roof): CL 19/3/59, F 7/5/59; "Austin ahead..." [as second page of double spread also featuring A55 Cambridge—see below] (C—turquoise with black roof): ILN 12/3/60; "Austin looks years ahead..." (C—green): CL 21/7/60 [as second page of double spread also featuring A99—see below], P 13/7/60 [as second page of double spread also featuring Seven [Mini]—see below]; "You and your other self agree..." (C—red): CL 11/5/61, F 11/5/61, HG 7/61, ILN 6/5/61, P 15/5/61, (M) [E]: T 31/3/61.

A40 Mark II: "It's larger...." (C—red): CL 1/2/62, F 26/4/62 & 14/6/62, HG 3/62, (M) [similar illustration]: ILN 24/3/62; "This famous car..." (C—red): CL 14/6/62, P 2/5/62 & 23/5/62; "The new A40 has expanded inwards..." (C—red): P 4/7/62, (M) [E]: T 23/3/62; "The shape isn't just pretty to look at..." (C—red with black roof, tan interior): HG 3/63 & 5/63, P 27/2/63, RD 6/63; "The shape isn't just for fun..." (C—blue, blue interior): CL 7/3/73, F 14/3/63* & 16/5/63, HG 7/63 & 11/63, P 20/1/63; "If you can find a car..." (C—red with black roof): CL 16/4/64, F 19/3/64; "Some cars are rounded off at the corners..." (C—red with black roof): P 30/12/64, P 17/3/65; "You don't happen to own a cello yourself?..." (C—red with black roof): CL 23/9/65 & 10/3/66, HG 10/65, P 23/3/66.

Seven [Mini]: "Austin looks years ahead..." (C—white): HG 6/60 [as first page of double spread also featuring Austin-Healey 3000—see below], ILN 25/6/60 [as first page of double spread also featuring A55 Cambridge—see below], P 13/7/60 [as first page of double spread also featuring A40—see above], (M): [similar illustration] [E]: T 16/5/60; "We wish you a merry Christmas..." (C—red): ILN Christmas Number 1961; "Just try to find the 'ordinary' in an Austin Seven..." (C—blue): CL 16/3/61, F 9/3/61, ILN 18/3/61, P 22/3/61.

Super Seven [Mini]: "How luxurious can an Austin Seven get?..." (C—red): CL 26/10/61, F 19/10/61*, HG 12/61 & 1/62.

Austin 850 [Mini] [E]: "From Austin — a new breed of small car!..." (M): T 16/11/59 & 23/11/59.

Seven Countryman [Mini]: "Enormous..." (M): CF 10/60*.

Radford Mini de Ville: "Your town car Sir..." (M): F 2/5/63*.

A55 Cambridge Mk II: "New swift line...That's a nice car..." (C — two-tone red over white): CL 13/8/59, F 11/6/59, ILN 13/6/59, P 3/6/59*; "New swift line...'Satisfied?'..." (C — two-tone greenish-blue over white): CL 14/5/59, F 16/4/59, ILN 25/4/59, P 8/4/59; "Austin looks years ahead...Not many people know..." (C — blue): HG 4/60 [as second page of double spread also featuring Austin-Healey Sprite — see below], ILN 13/2/60 [as single advertisement], (M) [E]: T 4/4/60; "Austin looks years ahead...Kitzbühel. January 1960..." (C — two-tone turquoise over lilac, LHD car) [as first page of double spread also featuring A40 — see above]: ILN 12/3/60; "Austin looks years ahead...Nice to have friends..." (C — two-tone black over light grey): ILN 25/6/60 [as second page of double spread also featuring Seven [Mini] — see above], (M) [E]: T 6/6/60 & 13/6/60; "Get into an Austin...You won't mistake..." (C — turquoise): HG 4/61; "Get into an Austin..." (M): HG 11/60; [E]: "New swift line...Nice trim craft, that" (M): T 25/5/59, 22/6/59, 19/10/59 & 6/7/59; "Get into an Austin..." (M): T 12/12/60 & 6/1/61.

A60 [Cambridge]: "Get the power to go places..." (C — blue with white flash): CL 25/1/62, ILN 10/2/62, P 24/1/62; "Get the power to go places..." [copy as previous entry, almost identical illustration] (C — blue with white flash): ILN 19/5/62; "Get the style to go places..." (C — light blue with white flash): CL 1/3/62 & 10/5/62, HG 7/62, P 6/6/62, (M) [E]: T 13/4/62, 11/5/62, 29/6/62 & 27/7/62; "Austin send you Christmas Greetings..." (C — blue with white flash): ILN Christmas Number 1963; "Large families get a car as big..." (C — light blue with white flash): CL 13/12/62, P 16/1/63; "You get room to stretch your legs..." (C — blue with white flash, red interior): F 17/1/63, P 17/4/63, (M): ILN 18/5/63; "Which of today's family cars..." (C — blue with white flash): HG 9/64, ILN 15/2/64, P 3/6/64 & 22/4/64; "What do you value most in a car?..." (C — blue with white flash): HG 3/65; "How to make the pennies count..." (C — light blue with white flash): CL 2/12/65, F 6/1/66, HG 12/65, P 15/9/65 & 12/1/66; "Look sharp — there's an A60 behind you..." (M): O 6/63*.

A99 [Westminster]: "Austin looks years ahead...The wharves are silent..." (M): CF 5/60; "Austin looks years ahead...Beyond the glass doors..." (C — two-tone cream over light grey): HG 8/60 [as single advertisement], CL 21/7/60 [as first page of double spread also featuring A40 — see above], ILN 7/5/60 [as first page of double spread also featuring Austin-Healey 3000 — see below]; "Get into an Austin..." (C — two-tone light grey over dark blue): CL 12/1/61, F 12/1/61, ILN 14/1/61, P 25/1/61.

A110 [Westminster Mk I]: "This man gets power..." (C — maroon): F 11/1/62 & 17/5/62*, HG 5/62, P 28/2/62 & 18/4/62; "This man gets sports car response..." (C — light blue): F 15/3/62; "This man gets style..." (C — light blue): CL 19/7/62, HG 10/62, P 21/3/62; "Naturally, luxury like this..." (C — grey, red interior): F 21/2/63, P 29/5/63; "Of course, power such as this..." (C — main car maroon, upper car grey): CL 18/7/63, F 11/7/63, P 10/7/63; "If you want a car that can do 100mph..." (C — two-tone maroon over black): CL 13/2/64.

A110 Mark II [Westminster]: "Meet the new..." (C — grey): F 23/7/64; "Which is the car that's big and beautiful...?" (C — red): CL 4/3/65, F 17/12/64, HG 11/64, ILN 27/2/65; "If you're thinking of ferrying yourself..." (C — light grey over dark grey): F 14/10/65, HG 2/66.

Princess: see *Vanden Plas*, below.

1100: "Reindeer with front-wheel drive..." (C —cream): ILN Christmas Number 1965; "Discover the front-wheel-drive..." (C —cream): CL 9/6/66, F 14/4/66*.

1800: "There are two kinds of Security Express..." (C — white): HG 6/66, P 25/5/66 & 6/7/66.

3-Litre: "You can judge a car..." (C — red): ILN 30/8/69, P 10/9/69; "All the best thoroughbreds..." (C — green): ILN 9/8/69 & 13/9/69, P 27/8/69; "Possession is nine points of the law..." (C — black): CL 25/9/69, P 24/9/69; "OHMS..." (M): CL 23/4/70, ILN 25/4/70, P 29/4/70; "How far will you go...?" (M): ILN 30/5/70; "Liz Wilcox gained a lot..." (M): P 10/6/70.

Maxi: "Maxi. It goes with a way of life..." (C — sand): CL 20/6/74*.

Austin-Healey Sprite [Mk I]: "Austin looks years ahead..." (C — red): HG 4/60 [as first page in double spread also featuring A55 Cambridge — see above].

Austin-Healey 3000 [Mk I]: "Austin looks years ahead..." (C — two-tone black over red): CL 30/6/60* [as single advertisement], HG 6/60 [as second page of two page spread also featuring Seven [Mini] — see above], ILN 7/5/60 [as second page of two-page spread also featuring A99 — see above].

• BENTLEY (Bentley Motors (1931) Ltd., Crewe, Cheshire)

'S' Series [S1]: "Take a Bentley into partnership..." (M): F 4/10/56; "Power assisted steering..." (M): CF 6/57; "The latest Bentley..." (M): CF 10/57 & 3/58, F 10/10/57; "The Bentley 'S' Series saloon combines..." (M): F 13/3/58. [S2]: "The Eight Cylinder Bentley..." (M): CL 22/10/59; "I'll get a Bentley..." (M): 17/11/60* & 15/12/60.

• BMC [corporate prestige advertising] (British Motor Corporation Ltd., Birmingham and Oxford; incorporating Austin, MG, Morris, Riley, Wolseley, Vanden Plas)

"Buy your new BMC car now..." (C — Morris Oxford Series III in two-tone blue over white): F 27/3/58; "Order your new BMC car now..." (C — Austin A95 in two-tone green over white with green flash): F 15/5/58, S 3/5/58; "Order your new BMC car now..." [copy and backdrop as previous entry; different car outside house] (C — Riley Two-Point-Six in two-tone blue): CL 1/5/58; "BMC serves Canada...On the conclusion of the Royal visit to the land of the Beaver..." [celebrating exports worth over $194m since 1945] (C — various): ILN 22/8/59; "Reserved for sentimental journeys only..." (C — blue Morris Minor): CL 9/6/60; "A cure for Jose's headache..." (C — two-tone lilac over mauve Wolseley 6-99): CL 19/5/60, ILN 21/5/60, P 1/6/60; "BMC ready to meet..." (M) [E]: T 14/12/62; "BMC status quiz..." [4-page feature in Punch editorial style] (M): P 19/7/61; "BMC have the pull with front-wheel power..." (C — various) [5-page colour advertisement highlighting Morris 1100 and featuring BMC's Austin and Morris 1100 and Mini ranges]: P 16/10/63; "BMC makes a car for you..." (M): CL 17/10/63; "You have the pull..." (C — various): P 9/6/64; "Choosing your new car..." (M) [5-page advertisement showing 40 BMC models individually]: P 21/10/64; "BMC creative engineering..." (M): [9-page advertisement with pages in 2 groups near beginning and end of magazine]: P 30/8/67; "If you've got a big family..." [shows Austin 1800] (C — white): ILN Christmas Number 1967; "First choose BMC, then choose your BMC car..." (C — various): ILN 13/5/67.

• BMW (Imported by BMW Concessionaires England Ltd., Brighton)

700 LS: "Graduate to a..." (M): F 16/7/64.

1500 & 1800: "Graduate to a..." (M): F 6/8/64, 17/9/64 & 22/10/64.

1800 & 2000: "The new BMW 2-litre sports saloons..." (M): CL 1/5/69, ILN 24/5/69.

1800: "A symbol of engineering integrity..." (M): ILN 24/4/65.

1800TI: "Unbeatable BMW!.." (M): P 24/11/65.

1600 Coupe [2002 shape]: "Internationally acclaimed..." (M): CL 5/10/67 & 19/10/67, ILN 28/10/67; "Successful men choose..." (M): ILN 7/9/68; "The worst road..." (M): SA 4/68.

2002: "What's a 113 mph family coupe...?" (M): CL 23/1/69; "Move over..." (M): ILN 15/6/68, SC 10/71* (dealer advertisement: Seven Dials Motors, Brighton) [different copy].

2000 CS/CA Coupe: "The connoisseur's choice..." (M): CL 29/2/68 & 7/3/68, P 6/3/68 & 28/2/68.

2800CS [coupe]: "Experience..." (M): ILN 9/5/70.

2800 [saloon]: "The 125mph car that money alone can't buy..." (M): 5/3/70; "The 125mph dream car..." CL 8/10/70, ILN 9/5/70.

BMW range: "The BMW challenge..." (M): 8/5/70.

• BOND (Bond Cars Ltd., Preston, Lancashire; subsequently at Tamworth, Staffordshire)

Equipe GT: "Different! That's the Equipe G.T. ..." (M): CL 20/2/64 & 5/3/64, ILN 22/1/64 & 7/3/64; "Different! That's the Equipe G.T. ..." [as previous entry with different photograph] (M): CL 19/3/64 & 16/4/64.

Equipe GT4S: "The 1300cc shopping basket..." (M): CL 11/6/64, HG 11/69.

• BRISTOL (Bristol Cars Ltd., Filton, Bristol)
406: "Aero-engined precision..." (M): F 7/7/60.
407 5.2: "The new Bristol..." (M): ILN 21/10/61; "Bristol 407: 122mph plus..." (M): ILN 4/5/63.
408 5-Litre: "One of the world's few cars..." (M): ILN 24/10/64.
409: "The superb..." (M): CL 21/10/65.
410: "Inside the British built Bristol..." (M): ILN 19/10/68; "Bristol cars have been handbuilt..." (dealer advertisement: Anthony Crook Motors Ltd., London) (M): CL 19/10/67 & 17/10/68.
411: "The new Bristol type 411..." (M): F 16/10/69*.

• CHEVROLET (Imported by Lendrum & Hartman Ltd., Buick House, Albemarle St., Piccadilly, London W1)
Impala [1964 models; called Saloon, Convertible and Estate Car]: "The car that's so easy to drive..." (M): CL 16/1/64, 30/1/64, 13/2/64 & 19/3/64.

• CHRYSLER INTERNATIONAL (Imported by Warwick Wright, Ladbroke Hall, Barlby Road, London W10)
Plymouth [1965 Sport Fury hardtop]: "'65 Plymouth...spacious, gracious beauty..." (C — red with black roof): P 21/10/64.
Plymouth Barracuda [1969 model]: "The awkward customer's car..." (C — white with black stripe): P 9/4/69, 30/4/69 & 14/5/69, (M): P 15/10/69.
Dodge Challenger [1970 model]: "For those who think sports cars..." (M): P 18/2/70.

• CITROËN (assembled, and after February 1966 imported, by Citroën Cars Ltd., Slough, Buckinghamshire)
DS19: "Superlative Citroën..." (M): CL 24/4/58*.
ID19: "One new and brilliant..." (M): CL 23/10/58.
DS Safari: "Unique luxury estate car..." (M): CL 16/4/64, F 2/4/64; "If you want an estate car..." (M): CL 13/4/67 & 15/6/67, ILN 13/5/67*.
DS21 Pallas: "Why is this car such a snip...?" (M): ILN 1/4/67, P 19/4/67.
DS [cowled-headlamp type: copy covers all models]: "Advance and be recognised..." (C — dark blue): P 30/10/68 & 11/12/68; "There's safety in numbers..." (C — blue): P 13/11/68 & 19/2/69; "A few words about the new Citroën..." (C — blue, tan interior): P 16/4/69; "The advanced car at the retarded price..." (C — dark blue): P 19/3/69; "These are 12 important safety details..." (M): SA 6/68.
Citroën range: "A new generation..." (M): ILN 17/10/70.

• DAF (Imported by Automobile Distributors Ltd., Dutch House, 307–308 High Holborn, London WC1; subsequently by DAF Concessionaries Ltd., 10 Albemarle St., Piccadilly, London W1)
Variomatic: "The DAF was meant for YOU..." (M): CL 23/3/61; I thought he bought it for me"..." (M): F 10/6/65; "For the lady of the house..." (M): CL 24/3/66 & 19/5/66, HG 3/66.

• DAIHATSU (Imported by Dufay (Birmingham) Ltd., 175–177 Great Portland St., London W1)
[Compagno] Berlina: "The car with 'extras' that are fitted as 'standard'..." (M) CL 21/10/65, F21/10/65*.

• DAIMLER (The Daimler Company Ltd., Coventry)
One-O-Four: "Drive Daimler..." (C — grey): CL 18/10/56, F 18/10/56.
Majestic: "There's nothing to touch the Daimler Majestic..." (M): F 2/4/59; "The Daimler Majestic is all that its name implies..." (M): F 18/6/59, ILN 16/5/59 & 13/6/59; "The Daimler Majestic excites the critics..." (M): CL 16/4/59, F 23/4/59, ILN 18/4/59; [illustration as previous entry; different copy and headline]; "Know the pleasure of automatic motoring..." (M): CL 3/3/60; "High performance — high quality..." (M): ILN 28/5/60 & 9/7/60*, P 13/7/60; "High performance — high quality..." [copy identical to previous entry; different illustration] (C — two-tone maroon over silver): F 21/7/60, ILN 23/4/60 & 30/7/60.
SP250 V-8 Sports [Dart] [advertisement by W.D. & H.O. Wills for Capstan Medium cigarettes] (C — red dashboard): CL 12/7/62, 9/8/62, 13/9/62 & 4/10/62, F 12/7/62* & 4/10/62, P 11/7/62.
2½ Litre V8: "Presenting the..." (M): F 18/10/62, ILN 20/10/62, P 17/10/62; "Formula for prestige..." (M): CL 11/7/63 & 25/7/63, F 13/6/63, 4/7/63 & 21/5/64*.
V8–250: "Now the Daimler V8–250..." (M): P 18/10/67; "Step up your motoring enjoyment..." (M): ILN 27/4/68 & 8/6/68.
4.2 Litre Sovereign: "The new..." (M): CL 20/10/66, F 20/10/66*, ILN 22/10/66, P 19/10/66; "Prestige motoring in the modern manner..." (M): ILN 1/7/67; "Nobody has every been sold..." (M): ILN 22/3/69, 10/5/69 & 17/5/69.
Daimler range: "Prestige motoring..." [2½ Litre V8, Majestic Major, Majestic Major Limousine & SP250 Sports] (M): F 16/4/64, ILN 30/5/64, P 16/4/64; "The 1965 Daimler models..." [copy and illustration as previous entry but without SP250] (M): CL 15/10/64; "The utmost in prestige motoring..." [2½ Litre V8 & Majestic Major] (M): CL 27/5/65, ILN 27/3/65 & 8/5/65, F 17/6/65, P 31/3/65 & 19/5/65; "so much more than just a famous name..." [2½ Litre V8, Majestic Major saloon & Limousine] (M): CL 21/10/65, ILN 23/10/65; "The 1968 Daimler range..." [V8–250 & 4.2 Litre Sovereign] (M): CL 19/10/67, ILN 21/10/67; "Move up to Daimler for '69..." (M): F 14/11/68, P 20/11/68.

• DATSUN (Imported by Nissan-Datsun (U.K. Concessionaires) Ltd., 54–62 Regent Street, London W1; after 1968 at Harbour Way, Shoreham-by-Sea, Sussex)
1000: "If she's not a Penny Pincher..." (C—crimson): P 20/11/68; "Amazes the tough guys..." (C — white): P 30/4/69.
1000 & 1600: "Two rather remarkable family sedans..." (C — dark red 1000, light blue 1600): P 16/10/68.
1600 & 1300: "Love at first sight..." (C — light blue): P 11/12/68.
1600: "How come that lady's driving..." (C — light blue): P 10/9/69, 15/10/69, 26/11/69 & 24/12/69.

• FACEL VEGA (Imported by InterContinental Ltd., New Zealand Avenue, Walton-on-Thames, Surrey)
HK500: "Facel Vega is here..." (M): 16/4/60; "Take a good look at Facel Vega..." (M): ILN 22/10/60, P 19/10/60; "Out of the common market..." (M): P 18/10/61.
Facellia: "Now comes Facellia..." (M): CL 27/4/61, F 20/4/61*, P 19/4/61 & 17/5/61.
Facel Vega Mk II [Facel II]: "The quiet sensation..." (M): source unknown, c. 1961.

• FIAT (Imported by Fiat (England) Ltd., Northdale House, North Circular Road, London NW10)
[Note: Much British Fiat advertising during the 1960s was placed by the London distributor, Jack Barclay Ltd., at Berkeley Square, London W1 — identified by 'JB' below.]
2300 Estate Car & 1500 Estate Car [JB]: "Only your driving can improve a Fiat..." (M): CL 4/6/64, F 23/4/64.
2300S Coupe [JB]: "Only your driving..." (M): CL 9/4/64; "For grace, speed and individuality..." (M): CL 1/7/65.
2300N Coupe [JB]: "2300 series Fiats are intended..." (M): CL 19/5/65 & 7/4/66 & 8/12/66.
124 Saloon [JB]: "Voted 'car of the year'..." (M): CL 21/9/67.
125 [saloon] [JB]: "...fantastic new..." (M): CL 9/11/67.
Estate cars [2300 and 500 shown]: "We've sized up..." (M): CL 14/12/67 & 21/9/67, F 14/9/67.
128: "The biggest selling..." (M): SA 10/72.

• FORD (GB) (Ford Motor Company Ltd., Dagenham, Essex)
Ford range: "5-Star news at the Motor Show!..." (M): ILN 19/10/57; "Be first on the road with Ford..." (M): CL 29/10/59, F 29/10/59; "Ford shows the way!..." (C — various): ILN 22/10/60; "It's a Ford show..." (C — various): CL 19/10/61, F 19/10/61, ILN 21/10/61, P 18/10/61.
Anglia [100E]: "I've a Ford in mind...When I buy a car..." (M): ILN 20/7/57; "Scores every time!..." (M): F 4/9/58, ILN 6/9/58; [E] "New-look cars..." (M): T 24/2/58 & 24/3/58; "Anglia for power, comfort, style..." (M): T 14/4/58, 21/4/58 & 5/5/58; "We like that Anglia style..." (M): T 4/5/59; "I like that Anglia performance..." (M): T 15/6/59.
Thames [300E] [E]: "Thames vans for durability..." (M): T 8/12/58; "I like that Thames toughness..." (M): T 10/8/59.
Escort [100E]: "Now, more than ever..." (M): F 9/8/56; "Ford —

winning the light car team!..." (M): F 13/2/58; [E]: "Escort for durability..." (M): T 20/10/58.

Prefect [100E]: "Now, more than ever..." (M): F 20/9/56; "Now, more than ever..." [illustration and headline as previous entry; different copy] (M): F 22/11/56; "I've a Ford in mind...I've been casting about..." (M): ILN 22/6/57; "Perfect drive!..." (M): F 8/5/58, ILN 10/5/58.

Consul [Mk II saloon]: "I've a Ford in mind...The remedy for my 'travel-itis'..." (M): ILN 23/11/57; "Lengths ahead!... (M): F 3/4/58; "Beauty and balance..." (M): ILN 22/11/58; "Avant Garde?..." (M): CL 26/3/59, F 26/3/59; "Voyage of discovery..." (C—blue): F 8/12/60, HG 2/61; [E]: "Swifter—safer—roomier..." (M): T 17/2/58 & 17/3/58; "Consul for power..." (M): T 7/7/58; "Sun chasers!..." (C—light blue): T 24/10/60.

Consul Convertible [Mk II]: "Not all roads lead to Rome..." (C—white): CL 21/1/60, P 24/2/60.

Zephyr [Mk II saloon]: "I've a Ford in mind...I'll back a car..." (M): ILN 14/9/57; "Game, set and match!..." (M): F 5/6/58; "Meet the champion!..." (M): F 11/12/58; "Blended for the gourmet..." (M): ILN 31/10/59; "When experts meet..." (C—dark blue): CL 25/1/62, F 25/1/62*, P 31/1/62 [E]: "Presenting for '59..." (M): T 13/4/59.

Zephyr Convertible [Mk II]: "Have fun in the sun with Ford!..." (C—blue): CL 19/1/61, F 12/1/61, HG 3/61, P 1/3/61; [E]: "Summer airs!..." (C—light yellow): T 29/8/60.

Zodiac [Mk II saloon]: "Ford again sets the fashion..." (M): F 23/2/56; "Now, more than ever..." (M): F 18/10/56, ILN 20/10/56; "Ford sets the fashion in Coffee and Cream..." (C—monochrome photograph tinted in coffee and cream): V 2/58; "The light of cream satin..." [in same magazine issue as previous entry] (C—monochrome drawing tinted coffee brown on cream page): V 2/58; "Ford sets the fashion—everywhere..." (M): V 3/58; "Ford Automatically sets the fashion..." (M): V 7/58; "Ford Automatically sets the fashion..." [illustration almost identical to previous entry; different copy] (M): V 9/58; "Falling in love..." (M): 22/1/59, ILN 17/1/59; "Luxury becomes plain sailing..." (M): ILN 14/5/60; "White queen wins..." (C—two-tone white over green): CL [date unknown]; HG 4/60; "West-end safari..." (C—two-tone blue): F 22/9/60* & 10/11/60, P 7/12/60; "Gracing today's finest cars..." [Goodyear tyres] (C—two-tone yellow over olive green): CL 31/7/58; "Gracing today's finest cars..." [Goodyear tyres: copy as previous entry; illustration updated to show lowline model] (C—two-tone light over dark coffee): CL 3/9/59, ILN 1/6/60; "Zodiac for style..." (M): T 9/6/58, "Presenting for '59..." (M): T 27/4/59.

Zodiac Convertible [Mk II]: "Ford—Nationally Grand!..." (M) F 20/3/58; "Bracing as river breezes..." (M): CL 14/5/59, F 7/5/59.

Consul, Zephyr & Zodiac Mk II range [announcing lowline models]: "Now! The three new graces..." (M): F 5/3/59, ILN 28/2/59; [E]: "Presenting for '59..." (M): T 2/3/59.

Popular [100E]: "Singles win, double victory..." (C—green): CL 23/6/60, P 21/9/60.

Anglia [105E]: "The world's most exciting light car!..." (M): CL 1/10/59, ILN 3/10/59; "Where there's excitement..." (M): ILN Christmas Number 1960; "Sporting spirit..." (C—blue): F 23/3/61, HG 5/61, P 12/4/61; "The carriage awaits..." (C—yellow): P 31/5/61; "Eccitantissima!..." [LHD car] (C—red): F 21/4/61, P 10/5/61; "Exciting in, exciting out..." (C—maroon with light grey roof): F 18/5/61.

Anglia [105E] [E]: "The completely new Anglia..." (M): T 2/11/59; "Here's why..." (M): T 14/12/59; "How good life can taste!..." (C—magenta): T 25/4/60; "Light fantastic!..." (C—yellow with white roof and pillars): T 18/7/60, 12/9/60 & 21/4/61; "Leading light!..." (C—yellow): T 12/12/60 & 2/2/61; "You and your Anglia...Bravo!..." (C—red): T 8/9/61; "You and your Anglia...Prosit!..." (C—yellow with cream roof; light green roof): T 5/1/62; "Ole!..." (C—white): T 1/6/62.

Anglia Estate [105E]: "Enter the new shape of excitement!..." (C—blue): F 23/11/61*, P 15/11/61; "Ford estate cars..." (M): CL 2/2/67.

Consul Classic 315: "Set the style, make the pace..." (C—blue with white roof): F 6/7/61*; "Set the style, make the pace..." [copy as pre-

vious entry, different illustration] (C—white): ILN 24/6/61; "Set the style, make the pace..." [copy as previous entries, different illustration again] (C—white): P 19/7/61; "Family style..." (C—turquoise with white roof): ILN 23/9/61; "Go in style..." (C—turquoise with white roof): HG 11/61; "Go in style..." [illustration as previous entry, different copy]: ILN Christmas Number 1961; "Ford holidays are more so than others..." (C—white): CL 15/2/62, HG 3/62, P 14/2/62; "Getaway car for gadabout people..." (C—white): CL 29/3/62, F 22/3/62; "New Consul Classic 1½ Litre..." (C—white): F 8/11/62; "Pacemaker Plus!..." [copy and illustration as previous entry; different headline] (C—white): CL 8/11/62, HG 11/62.

Consul 315 [E]: "Long low luxury lines..." (C—white; blue): T 23/6/61, 21/7/61 & 15/9/61; "Presenting the new Consul 315..." (C—red): T 25/8/61; "Styled for the Autostrada..." (C—blue): T 11/5/02 & 7/9/02; "Make the pace on the Autobahn..." (C—red): T 29/6/62; "Highway or by-way..." (C—blue): T 20/7/62.

Consul Capri: "Let go with the new Consul Capri..." (C—white): CL 4/1/62, F 11/1/62, ILN 6/1/62; "Let go..." [copy as previous entry; different illustration] (C—yellow with white roof): P 24/1/62; "It is a little big for me..." (C—yellow with white roof): P 4/7/62 & 19/9/62; "On the first day of Christmas..." (C—white): ILN Christmas Number 1962.

Zephyr 4 & 6 [Mk III]: "Two new Zephyrs!..." [4-page advertisement using two illustrations] (C—red Zephyr 4, dark green Zephyr 6): P 13/6/62; "Two new Zephyrs..." [single page advertisement; two versions, both with copy as previous entry, each with one illustration from previous entry]: F 17/5/62 [Z 4 in foreground], HG 7/62, ILN 19/5/62 [Z 6 in foreground]; [E]: "Smartest cars you ever saw..." (C—red Zephyr 4, dark green Zephyr 6) [Z 4 in foreground]: T 8/6/62; "Go Zephyr..." (C—red Zephyr 4, dark green Zephyr 6) [copy as previous entry; different headline and illustration with Z 6 in foreground]: T 6/7/62; "Go Zephyr..." [copy as previous entry; different illustration with Z 4 only] (C—red): T 28/9/62; "Go Zephyr..." [copy as previous entry; different illustration with Z 6 only] (C—dark green): T 19/10/62.

Zephyr 6 [Mk III]: "Ignore the could-be-better!..." (C—maroon): F 18/4/63*.

Zephyr 4, Zephyr 6 and Zodiac Mk. III [E]: "Three new fabulous Fords..." (C—various): T 18/5/62; "Ford presents the totally new..." (C—white Zodiac, red Z 4): T 13/7/62.

Zodiac Mk III: "A new concept in Ford motoring..." (M): P 18/5/62; "Men who enjoy power..." (C—dark green): F 19/4/62, HG 6/62, ILN 21/4/62; "Shooting star..." (C—white): F 16/5/63*.

Zodiac Executive [Mk III, with Antler luggage]: "To match the luxury..." (C—black interior): CL 17/5/65*.

Consul Cortina [Mk I]: "New from Ford..." (C—maroon with light grey roof): CL 27/9/62, ILN 29/9/62, F 1/10/62*; "New from Ford..." [copy as shortened version of previous entry; monochrome illustration similar to previous entry but uses car in lighter colour] (M): RD 11/62; "Beautifully made—to go fast!..." (C—white): RD 6/63; "Big-car everything—at small-car costs!..." (C—blue): CL 21/2/63, F 21/2/63, HG 4/63, P 20/3/63; "Yearling with big promise..." (C—blue): P 25/9/63; [E]: "New from Ford..." (C—red with white roof): T 21/9/62; "Ford presents the big difference..." (C—olive green): T 23/11/62.

Consul Cortina Estate Car [Mk I]: "Largest in its class..." (C—blue with brown Di-Noc trim): F 21/3/63*; "Largest in its class..." [copy almost as previous entry, different illustration] (C—light blue with white flash): CL 28/3/63.

Consul Corsair: "Flair everywhere..." (C—white): CL 17/10/63, F 17/10/63, ILN 19/10/63, P 16/10/63; "Flair everywhere..." [copy almost as previous entry; different illustration] (C—white): CL 24/10/63, F 24/10/63*, HG 11/63, P 23/10/63; "Happy Christmas, beautiful Corsair..." (C—yellow): ILN Christmas Number 1963.   Corsair V4 G.T. Estate Car: "Ever seen a G.T. Estate Car?..." (M): F 7/4/66*; "Ever seen...." [copy as previous entry; different illustration] (M): CL 7/4/66.

Corsair [convertible by Crayford, advertised with Cortina convertible by Phillips Motors, London W1; following advertisements illustrate Corsair only]: "Exclusive motoring..." (M): CL 21/4/66; "Greet the sun..." (M): CL 6/10/66; "Fun in the sun..." (M): CL 20/10/66.

Zodiac and Zephyr [Mk IV]: "Mark of distinction..." [3-page advertisement] (C—silver): P 27/4/66; "Mark of distinction..." [single page version of previous entry; identical copy and illustration of car] (C—silver): CL 21/4/66 & 7/7/66, ILN 23/4/66, F 28/4/66*, P 22/6/66 & 13/7/66.

Zodiac [Mk IV]: "Mark of distinction..." [illustration as previous entry; different copy] (C—silver): P 21/9/66.

Zodiac Executive [Mk IV]: "Leather is as luxurious..." (M): CL 20/10/66, P 12/10/66; "Enter the distinguished world..." (C—olive green interior): P 19/10/66.

Cortina Estate [Mk 2]: "New Cortina Estate..." (M): CL 16/2/67*; "The 1967 Ford estate cars..." (M): CL 2/3/67; "A short history of the estate car..." (M): F 8/8/68.

Escort Estate [Mk I]: "The new Escort Estate..." (C—dark blue): CL 2/5/68; "We give you the elastic..." (C—light blue): CL 5/6/69 & 19/6/69.

Escort Mexico: "When it was first suggested..." (M): F 1972, undated*.

Capri [Mk I]: "Now what would a level-headed..." (C—orange with black roof): CL 17/5/73.

Capri 3000E [Mk I]: [no copy; lists prices of similarly performing cars] (C—silver-grey): CL 1972, undated*.

Capri GXL [Mk I]: "More than ever the car you promised yourself..." (C—blue): CL 22/2/73.

• FORD (US & Germany) (Imported by Lincoln Cars Ltd. (a subsidiary of Ford Motor Company Ltd.), Great West Road, Brentford, Middlesex; 1970–71 models listed imported by Lincoln Car Division, Dagenham Motors, 88 Regent St., London W1)

Galaxie [Canadian-built 1961 models]: "Reach for the stars..." (M): CL 14/9/61.

Fairlane 500 Station Wagon [Canadian-built 1964 model]: "Just right for all your needs in the country..." (M): CL 19/3/64, 16/4/64, 10/9/64 & 8/10/64, F 28/11/63, 5/4/64 & 24/9/64; [Canadian-built 1965 model]: "Just right for all your needs in the country..." [copy as 1964 model—see previous entry] (M): F 22/10/64.

Galaxie 500 Convertible [Canadian-built 1965 model,]: "Built for total performance..." [copy almost as previous entry] (M): F 1/7/65.

Galaxie 500 [Canadian-built 1966 hardtop sedan]: "Built for total performance..." (M): CL 19/5/66.

Mustang [1966 hardtop]: "Buy a Mustang for the fun of it..." (M): CL 21/4/66, F 21/4/66 & 12/5/66*.

Taunus estate car [17M]: "New and beautifully practical..." (M): F 1/6/61.

Mustang Mach 1 [1970 model]: "There's no substitute for cubic inches..." (M): P 29/4/70; [1971 model]: "Mustang Mach 1. Out on its own..." (M): CL 15/10/70, P 14/10/70.

Fairmont [Australian-built 1970 model]: "We offer the wide open spaces of Australia..." (M): CL 2/7/70, P 13/5/70 & 21/10/70.

20MXL: "Made in Germany..." (M): CL 8/10/70, P 28/10/70.

• GILBERN (Gilbern Cars Ltd., Llantwit Fardre, Nr. Pontypridd, Glamorgan, Wales)

Invader: "Cruise into the seventies..." (M): P 26/6/70; "More power to your elbow room..." (M): ILN 17/10/70, P 14/10/70.

• HILLMAN (Hillman Motor Car Co. Ltd., Division of Rootes Motors Ltd.; London Showrooms and Export Division: Rootes Ltd., Devonshire House, Piccadilly, London W1)

Minx [Series I]: "Safe on the 'stop', fast on the 'go'..." (C—two-tone white over blue): SC 3/10/56*; "Going far for Christmas?..." (C—two-tone white over light blue): F 22/11/56; [Series II]: "To commemorate 50 years of Hillman..." (C—cream over light blue); ILN c. 9/57; "Economy, comfort and reliability..." (C—two-tone cream over light green): V 1/58; "Hillman—A name for reliability in any language..." (C—two-tone off-white over greyish blue): ILN 7/6/58; "A la mode—on the road—Hillman..." (C—two-tone cream over light turquoise): V 7/58; [E]: "Here is Economy..." (M): T 26/5/58, 2/6/58 & 16/6/58; [Series III] [E]: "Here's how the American experts rate Hill-

man..." (M): T 26/1/59 & 9/2/59; "What a honey for the money..." (M): T 18/5/59; [Series IIIB]: "Be happy, go Hillman..." (C—two-tone light grey over blue): ILN Christmas Number 1960; [E]: "Take a Hillman into the family..." (M): T 17/2/61, 24/3/61 & 24/3/61; "Hillman gives you more for your money..." (M): T 16/6/61 [Series V de Luxe]: "Family showpiece..." (C—blue): ILN 6/2/65.

Husky [Series I]: "In with the load..." (C—red and green cars): S 14/11/58; [E]: "Longer, lower and huskier..." (M): T 28/4/58.

Minx Convertible [Series I]: "Go one better..." (C—light greyish blue): F 16/5/57.

Estate Car [Minx] [Series I]: "New 4-door Hillman Estate Car..." (C—light blue): F 27/6/57; [Series II]: "You're so right to choose Hillman..." (C—light blue): F 22/5/58; [Series III]: "The new Hillman Estate Car!..." (C—red): F 20/11/58; "The new low price Hillman Estate Car!..." [illustration as previous entry; different copy] (C—red): F 19/2/59; "The country car you can take to town!.." [illustration and copy as previous entry; different headline and layout] (C—red): CL 9/4/59; [Series IIIA]: "A town-bred car for country-size loads!..." (C—green): F 13/10/60*, ILN 29/10/60.

Super Minx: [Series I] "Rootes stands superb at the show..." (C—red): ILN 21/10/61; "International style setter..." (C—white with blue roof): F 28/6/62; [Series II]: "Super equipment..." (M): P 15/1/64 & 4/3/64; "Dear Sir and Madam..." (C—white with blue roof): HG 3/64; "Dear Sir and Madam..." [copy as previous entry, different layout and illustration] (C—white): ILN 11/4/64; [Series III]: "New sleek, stylish sweeping lines..." (C—blue with white flash): CL 22/10/64; "Every mile in style..." (C—white with black flash): CL 14/1/65; [Series IV]: "So much more of a car..." (C—blue): ILN 12/3/66 & 25/6/66.

Super Minx Estate Car [Series II]: "Loaded heavily in your favour..." (C—blue): CL 2/7/64, F 2/7/64; "International style setter, the sleek..." [E] (M): T 27/4/62 & 18/5/62; [Series III]: "Up country, down town..." (C—main car: blue): F 1/7/65 & 18/11/65; [Series IV]: "So much more from the start..." (C—main car: blue): CL 30/6/66, F 5/5/66 & 30/6/66*.

Imp: "An inspiration in light car design..." (M): P 2/12/63; "The power behind Imp..." (C—blue): ILN Christmas Number 1963; "Thank you darling!..." (M): P 20/5/64 & 10/6/64; "World-beater!..." (C—blue): F 20/10/64*, ILN 12/9/64; "Designed for this modern motoring world..." (C—red): ILN 24/10/64 & Christmas Number 1964; "Room for the crew..." (C—white): HG 3/65.

Super Imp: "Go for happy go luxury..." (C—blue): HG 3/66; "Clever people know all the best places..." (C—white): F 15/9/66*, ILN 10/9/66.

Imp Californian: "Hallo Beautiful!..." (C—white): ILN 11/2/67 & 6/5/67, P 21/6/67.

Hunter: "Call off the search..." (C—white): F 17/11/66; "New Hillman Hunter..." (C—white): CL 20/10/66 & 20/4/67, ILN 22/10/66; [Mark II]: "If you think £1,000 is about right..." (M): ILN 24/2/68.

New Minx [Hunter shape]: "New Minx is the big one!..." (C—white): ILN 1/7/67.

Estate Car [Hunter/New Minx]: "If the secret of a successful estate car..." (C—white): CL 7/9/67 & 19/10/67.

• HUMBER (Humber Ltd., Division of Rootes Motors Ltd.; London Showrooms and Export Division: Rootes Ltd., Devonshire House, Piccadilly, London W1)

Hawk [Series I]: "See the new Humber Hawk..." (C—two-tone lilac and maroon): ILN 6/7/57; "Drive the impressive Humber Hawk..." [illustration and copy as previous entry; different headline] (C—two-tone lilac and maroon): CL 17/10/57, ILN Christmas Number 1957, SC 16/10/57; "The incomparable..." (C—two-tone cream and maroon): F 21/5/59, ILN 13/6/59.

Hawk Estate Car [Series I]: "Humber luxury..." (C—two-tone cream and russet brown): F 21/11/57. "Humber luxury, performance, styling...New Humber Hawk..." [headline and copy as previous entry; different illustration] (C—two-tone green and beige): F 20/2/58 & 24/4/58, FC 27/11/57; "Humber luxury...The Humber Hawk..." [headline and copy almost as previous entry; identical illustration of car but with more people inside and different backdrop] (C—two tone green): CL 23/10/58, F 26/6/58, S 12/7/58.

Super Snipe [Series I]: "Now—the most luxurious...the aristocrat of cars..." (C—two-tone silver and black): F 23/10/58, S 25/10/58; "Now the most luxurious...New 2 1/2 litre..." [headline and illustration as previous entry; different copy] (C—two-tone silver and black): V 11/58; "The Humber Super Snipe..." [Copy almost as previous entry but one; different headline and illustration] (C—two-tone silver and black): F 23/4/59, (M): ILN 18/10/58; "Space...speed...beauty..." (C—two-tone grey): P 10/6/59; "Space...speed...beauty..." [copy as previous entry; different illustration] (C—two-tone grey): ILN 22/8/59; [Series II]: "Here is a car with a distinctive personality..." [copy as previous entry, different illustration showing Series II with Series I bonnet badge] (C—two-tone green): ILN Christmas Number 1959; "A magnificent possession..." [illustration as previous entry except for Series II bonnet badge added; different copy] (C—two-tone green): ILN 20/2/60; "A magnificent possession..." [copy as previous entry; different illustration] (C—two-tone green): CL 3/12/59; "A magnificent possession..." (C—two-tone green): ILN 20/2/60; [Series III]: "Luxury, power and safety combine..." (M): P 19/10/60; "Masterpiece...After driving..." (M—tinted maroon): ILN 18/3/61 & 19/4/61; "Masterpiece... A masterpiece in automobile engineering..." (C—two-tone blue): CL 29/6/61, ILN 17/6/61, P 24/5/61; "Masterpiece..." (M): [copy almost as previous entry, similar illustration]: P 28/6/61 & 19/7/61; "If your horizons have widened..." (C—dark blue with light blue roof): CL 7/12/61, F 25/11/61*, 29/3/62 & 17/5/62, ILN 28/4/62, (M) [similar illustration]: P 10/11/61, 7/3/62 & 23/5/62; "If your horizons have widened..." [copy as previous entry, different illustration] (C—dark blue with light roof): ILN 16/6/62; [Series IV]: "A magnificent car still further improved..." (C—main car: dark blue): CL 18/10/62, ILN 20/10/62, (M) [copy as previous entry, similar illustration]: F 18/10/62; "Perfection few other cars can claim..." (C—main car: dark blue): ILN Christmas Number 1962; "More than just another good British..." (M): P 16/1/63; "The greatest value today..." (C—main car: dark blue): CL 21/3/63, F 14/2/63; "Luxury with a capital H..." (C—dark blue): CL 5/12/63, F 17/10/63 & 13/2/64, ILN 8/2/64; "Leader in the world of lasting big car value..." (C—dark blue) [illustration as previous entry; different copy]: CL 19/3/64; "The greatest value today..." (C—dark blue) [illustration and copy as previous entry; different headline]: F 7/5/64, ILN 16/5/64; [Series V]: "Carriages at midnight..." (C—metallic light blue): CL 2/12/65, 13/1/66 & 21/10/66, F 16/9/65.

Super Snipe Estate Car: [Series I]: "Spacious, luxurious, powerful..." (C—two-tone red and cream): CL 22/10/59; [Series III]: "Finest in the country and the best in town..." (C—two-tone grey and black): F 24/11/60; "Finest in the country..." (C) [copy as previous entry, almost identical illustration]: CL 20/4/61, F 23/2/61, 30/3/61 & 11/5/61; "The Humber with a dual personality..." (C—green): F 9/5/63* & 27/6/63; "Luxury with a capital H..." [same headline as CL 5/12/63 for saloon (see above) but different copy & illustration] (C—green with light green roof): F 19/9/63.

Imperial: "Presenting the new Humber Imperial..." (C—dark blue with black roof): F 19/11/64*, ILN 23/1/65; "Every top man has his team..." (M): CL 10/3/66 & 23/6/66, F 24/2/66, 24/3/66 & 2/6/66, P 16/3/66 & 18/5/66.

Sceptre [Mk I]: "The inside story of out and out luxury..." (M): ILN 7/8/65, P 19/5/65; [Mk 2]: "For the man who wants to do more..." (M): P 13/7/66.

Sceptre [Mk 3: Hillman Hunter shape]: "The astonishing new...." (C—olive green): ILN 21/10/67; "What's the new deal to men...?" (C—dark blue): P 3/7/63, 24/8/68 & 25/9/68.

• Iso (Imported by InterContinental Cars Ltd., New Zealand Avenue, Walton-on-Thames, Surrey)

Rivolta: "Mailed fist...velvet glove..." (M): F 16/4/64, P 14/4/64.

Grifo: "At 163mph in the Iso Grifo..." (M): CL 20/4/67.

• JAGUAR (Jaguar Cars Ltd., Coventry)

Mark VIII: "A new luxury model now joins the Jaguar range..." (C—dark red): SC U/58; "A new luxury model..." [copy as previous

entry; identical illustration in different colours] (C—two-tone grey): F 18/10/56.

Mark IX: "With 3.8 litre 220b.h.p. engine..." (M): S 25/10/58.

3.4 Litre Mk 1: "The superlative new Jaguar now available in Britian..." (M): ILN 8/6/57.

3.4 Litre Mark 2: [Four advertisements with same copy, each with different illustration]: "A special kind of motoring..." (C—red): source unknown, c. 1960*; (C—light blue): P 19/7/61; (C—dark green): ILN Christmas Number 1961, P 18/10/61; (M): P 1/3/62.

2.4 Litre Mark 2 Saloon: "the joy of Jaguar motoring..." (M): P 24/5/67.

Mark X: "A completely new Jaguar..." (M): CL 19/10/61, F 19/10/61*, ILN 21/10/61.

'S' Type: "In addition to the famous..." (C—main car: red): CL 17/10/63, F 17/10/63*, P 23/10/63, (M): ILN Christmas Number 1963; "Can you afford not to own a Jaguar?..." (M): CL 6/4/67 & 15/6/67, ILN 29/4/67, P 26/4/67.

420: "A saloon, that for a combination..." (M): CL 4/7/68 & 18/7/68, ILN 5/5/68, P 29/5/68; "The 420 Jaguar sets the highest standard..." (M): ILN 13/5/67.

420 and 420 G: "Jaguar announce two outstanding new models..." (M): CL 20/10/66, F 20/10/66, ILN 22/10/66, P 19/10/66.

XJ6: "Creating an exciting new world..." (M): F 17/10/68*, P 16/10/68; "I'd forgive Jaguar anything..." (M): CL 10/7/69, ILN 5/7/69 & 19/7/69; "Don't blame him..." (M): CL 12/6/69 & 26/6/69, P 18/6/69.

Jaguar marque: "Sculpted grace..." (M—Le Mans trophy illustrated): ILN 5/3/60; [leaping cat mascot on bonnet]: "You enjoy..." (M): ILN 25/6/60; [leaping cat mascot alone]: "A special kind of motoring..." (M): F 13/10/60, ILN 22/10/60; "Superlatives..." (C): CL 21/10/65, F 21/10/65, ILN 23/10/65; "A long test mileage..." (C): CL 10/3/66, ILN 26/3/66, F 24/2/66 & 24/3/66, P 4/5/66; "Always a leap ahead..." (C): CL 9/6/66, F 26/5/66 & 30/6/66*, ILN 18/6/66, P 15/6/66.

Jaguar range ['three faces' series of advertisements]: "Grace, space, pace...Three basic models..." (M): CL 5/4/62, F 22/3/62*, ILN 23/6/62 & 5/5/62, P 14/3/62 & 30/5/62; "Grace, space, pace... A special kind..." (C—various): ILN Christmas Number 1962, P 17/10/62.

Jaguar range [conventional illustrations]: "Jaguar for 1958..." (M): F 17/10/57, SC 16/10/57; "Whatever Jaguar you choose..." (M): S 31/5/58; "Setting the pace..." (M): ILN 21/3/59; "Jaguar..a special kind of motoring..." [illustrations as previous entry; different copy] (M): ILN 22/8/59; "Jaguar—Grace...space...pace..." (M): CL 18/10/62, F 18/10/62, ILN 4/5/63, P 20/3/63, 29/5/63 & 3/7/63; "The sheer joy..." (M): F 4/6/64, P 3/6/64 & 1/7/64; "Jaguar announce two..." (M): F 22/10/64, P 21/10/64; "Jaguar offers the most complete..." (M): CL 21/10/67, F 19/10/67, ILN 21/10/67; "Jaguar proudly present..." (M): CL 16/10/69 & 13/11/69, P 12/11/69.

• JENSEN (Jensen Motors Ltd., West Bromwich, Staffordshire)

C-V8: "Very grand tourer...": CL 9/4/64; "Pianissimo power..." (C—bronze): F 25/6/64*; (M): [headline as previous entry; different copy and illustration]: 21/5/64; "If the going is rough..." (M—car; C—red interior): CL 28/5/64 & 18/6/64; "The Chairman's working late..." (M): F 1/7/65, 21/10/65 & 10/3/66.

Interceptor & FF: "The sleek new look..." (M): F 20/10/66*, ILN 22/10/66; "'Car of the year'..." (M) [illustration as previous entry; different copy]: CL 19/10/67, ILN 21/10/67, P 18/10/67.

• LAGONDA (Aston Martin Lagonda Ltd., London Showrooms: 96/97 Piccadilly, London W1)

Rapide (M): "...to serve with distinction..." (M): F 21/6/62*.

• LANCIA (Imported by Lancia Concessionaires Ltd., Lancia Works, Alperton, Middlesex)

Flavia 4-door Sedan [Berlina]: "Flavia 'con amore'..." (M): F 20/4/61*; "There are two kinds of motor car..." (M): CL 23/11/61 & 24/5/62; "If 401 people..." [illustration as previous entry; different copy] (M): CL 13/6/63, ILN 16/3/63; "What's that car, Proctor?..." (M): CL 31/10/63 & 4/6/64, ILN 14/3/64; "Why is the Lancia never at home?..." (M): ILN 26/9/64.

Flavia Convertible [Vignale]: "Lancia says no, it's for quattro..." (M): CL 11/4/63, ILN 4/5/63 & 1/6/63; "Lancia says no..." [illustration as previous entry; copy shortened]: CL 9/4/64, 7/5/64 & 23/7/64, ILN 10/4/64 & 16/5/64.

Flavia Coupe [Pininfarina]: "Grandissimo Turismo!…" (M): ILN 1/8/64.

Flaviasport [called Flavia Zagato in advertisement of 17/4/65]: "The very rich are different from you and me…" (M): CL 5/11/64; "You can do 100mph…" (M): ILN 17/4/65.

Fulvia Coupe: "If you ever felt like flirting…" (C — grey): CL 23/9/65.

Fulvia [2C Sedan] & Flaminia Coupe: "We can sell you…" (M): CL 8/4/65.

Flaminia [Berlina]: "This man could afford any car…" (M): F 8/11/62, ILN 20/10/62.

Lancia range: "The remarkable legacy of Signore Vincenzo Lancia…" [Lavish five page colour advertisement, in effect a catalogue in miniature, showing black Flavia Coupe; close-up details of Flaminia Superport, Flavia Vignale, Fulvia 2C Sedan and Flavia Zagato interior; grey Fulvia Coupe; and line-up of light gunmetal Flaminia Coupe, gunmetal Flavia 4-door Sedan, dark blue Flaminia 4-door Sedan, red Flavia Convertible, silver Flavia Coupe, grey Fulvia Coupe, white Fulvia 2C Sedan, lime green Flavia Zagato and black Flaminia Zagato GT]: (C — as above): CL 22/7/65.

• LEYLAND Motor Corporation (Leyland, Lancashire, including A.E.C. Ltd., Albion Motors Ltd., Scammell Lorries Ltd., Standard-Triumph International Ltd.)

Leyland range: "Mixing business with pleasure…" (M): ILN 12/2/66; "Mixing business with pleasure…" [headline as previous entry; different copy and illustrations] (M): ILN 12/3/66; "Moving fast — in a fast moving world." [showing Leyland bus and Triumph 2000] (M): P 8/6/66; "Moving fast…" [copy as previous entry; showing Leyland bus and Triumph Spitfire] (C — red car): P 7/9/66; "Moving fast…" [showing Scammell Tanker and Triumph 2000] (C — white car): P 21/12/66; "Moving fast…" [showing Leyland truck and Triumph Spitfire] (C — red car); "Moving fast…" [showing bus and Triumph 2000 estate car] (C — grey car): P 18/10/67; "Mixing business with pleasure…" [different series from previous entries; showing heavy tractor unit and Triumph GT6 Mk I] (M): P 31/1/68; "Mixing business…" [headline as previous entry; different copy and illustrations; showing flatbed truck and LHD Rover 2000] (C — white car): P 13/3/68.

• LOTUS (Lotus Cars Ltd., Delamare Road, Cheshunt, Hertfordshire)
Elan: "Naturally Lotus…" (M): CL 20/8/66, F 27/8/64*, ILN 8/8/64.
+2S/130: "Elegance breeds elegance…" (C — white): P 12/11/69; (M) [copy as previous entry, similar illustration]: P 8/10/69.
Sprint: "The Pace Setter…" (C — orange): [7" × 10" sheet, believed to be magazine insert, c. 1970].

• MASERATI (Maserati Concession Ltd., 142 Holland Park Avenue, London W11)
Mistral [spelt 'Mistrale' in this advertisement]: "Only a handful of motorists…" (M): F 20/10/66.

• MARTIN WALTER (Martin Walter Ltd., Dormobile Works, Folkstone, Kent.) [makers of motor-caravan conversions of popular light vans]
Bedford Dormobile Romany [CA]: "Roadside room-service…" (M): ILN 7/1/61; "We're a forward looking family…" (M): ILN 1/12/62; "For every occasion…" (M): ILN 4/5/63.
Morris J.4: "Enjoy Saturday & Sunday…" (M): P 9/5/62.
Ford Thames [400E]: "Wherever you're going you'll save £££…" (M): ILN 5/9/59.
Ford Transit [with small illustration of Bedford]: "You and the family — lingering a little longer…" (M): ILN 19/3/66.
Volkswagen Dormobile: "Best of both worlds…" (M): P 31/3/62; "Your key to new freedom…" (M): ILN 6/7/63; "The motor caravan with continental flair…" (M): P 18/9/63.

• MERCEDES-BENZ (Mercedes-Benz Great Britain Ltd., Great West Road, Brentford, Middlesex)
Mercedes-Benz range [showing 190 'Ponton' & 220S 'Fintail']: "A new chapter…" (C — blue 190 & beige 220S): ILN 3/10/59.
220S ['Ponton']: "Elegance for the Connoisseur…" (M): F 23/5/57,

ILN 27/7/57; "Famous for elegance and power…" (M): ILN 9/58 (week unknown); "Fair — fast — fashionable…" (M): F 16/4/59. (*Note:* An additional half-page monochrome advertisement was published in this series for the 220SE convertible in or around 1957; exact date unknown).
220SE ['Ponton']: "Lions on the track…" (C — red): ILN 11/4/59.
300SL [Roadster]: "A really fast answer…" (C — white): ILN 6/6/59.
300D [four-door hardtop]: "Through deserts and over mountains in luxury…" (C — blue): ILN 5/9/59.
190 ['Ponton']: "A small difference only…" (C — two-tone cream over turquoise): ILN 24/10/59.
190 ['Fintail']: "…of course, people just assume it's expensive…" (M): F 21/3/63.
220 ['Fintail']: "Mercedes-Benz advocates…" (US) (M): SA 6/65.
220S ['Fintail']: "People stop and whisper…" (C — grey): ILN 5/12/59; "Superb as a car…" (M): CL 20/4/61; "Superb as a car…" [headline as previous entry; different copy and illustration] (M): CL 15/6/61; "No other car gives motoring like this…" (M): CL 18/10/62 & 8/11/62, P 17/10/62; "In country or in town — incomparable…" (M): CL 8/10/84, F 24/6/64 & 15/10/64; "A pacemaker anywhere…" (M): F 1/10/66, P 21/10/64 & 4/11/64; "This is the way to see Europe…" (US) (C — olive green): NG 11/61; "Charming arrogance…" (US) (M): SA 4/65; "Ces roues vous meneront sûrement au but…" (French advertisement) (C — blue): source unknown, 8/62.
200 & 230 estate car ['Fintail']: "Smoothy…" (M): CL 21/10/65, F 21/10/65, "A new breed of Mercedes…" (M): CL 14/4/66, F 24/2/66 & 21/7/66.
300SE Convertible: "Luxury…" (M): F 21/2/63 & 9/5/63*; "Europe's most glamorous car…" (M): CL 17/10/63, P 16/10/63.
250S [saloon]: "Eighteen minutes after first light…" (C — white): P 13/7/66; "Eighteen minutes…" [headline and illustration as previous entry; different copy and layout] (C — white): P 7/9/66; "Buy the Mercedes-Benz 250S…" (US) (M): SA 3/67.
250SE [saloon]: "Imagine an engine with a built-in brain…" (C — black): CL 16/11/67, P 18/10/67 & 8/11/67.
300SEL [saloon]: "If you like people who deliver…" (C — black): CL 16/2/67.
600: "Imagine floating over the road…" (C — dark blue): CL 20/7/67, P 9/8/67 & 23/8/67.
280SL ['Pagoda' hardtop]: "Come glide with me…" (M): CL 15/2/68 & 21/3/68.
280SE [saloon]: "When you've reached the level…" (C — black): CL 8/8/68; "Steal a little thunder…" (C — white): CL 25/6/70, P 20/5/70 & 15/7/70.
250CE Coupe: "Steal a little thunder…" (C — maroon): CL 24/9/70, P 8/9/70 & 19/9/70.

• MG (MG Car Company Ltd., Sales Division, Cowley, Oxford)
Magnette [ZA]: "For my kind of motoring…I'm a keen motorist…" (M): F 26/7/56 & 15/11/56.
Magnette [ZB]: "For my kind of motoring…Whether you're rendezvous-ing at the Ritz…" (M): F 31/1/57; "For my kind of motoring…Everybody admires my M.G. Magnette…" (M): F 14/3/57; "Drive a Magnette — it brings out the expert in you…" (M): F 11/9/58; [Varitone]: "I have never driven a car with less vice…" (M): F 13/2/58 & 13/3/58.
Magnette Mark III: "Completely new…" (M): F 5/2/59; "Competely new…" [headline as previous entry; different copy and illustrations] (M): F 12/3/59 & 9/4/59; "More luxury…" (M): CL 11/6/59, F 14/5/59 & 18/6/59; "The car for the young…" (M): F 18/8/60, P 17/8/60; "Do look now — its pedigree is showing!…" (M): CL 7/4/60; "The car that recaptures…" (M): CL 30/3/61; "Streets ahead…miles ahead…" [showing Magnette and small illustration of MGA 1600] (M): CL 4/5/61, P 26/4/61 & 24/5/61; "Streets ahead…miles ahead…" [copy and illustration as previous entry; MGA omitted] (M): F 17/8/61, P 5/7/61; "Streets ahead…" [copy as previous entry, almost identical illustration; with MGA] (M): P 22/2/61; "Streets ahead…" [copy and illustration as previous entry; MGA omitted] (M): P 30/8/61.
Magnette Mk IV: "New Magnette Mk IV…" (M): CL 30/11/61, ILN

17/3/62, P 15/11/61; "Family motoring with sporting performance..." (M): F 1/2/62 & 29/3/62, ILN 21/4/62, P 7/2/62 & 7/3/62; "Relaxed motoring today..." (M): F 31/5/62, 26/7/62, 23/8/62 & 13/12/62; "Look! They've got an MG..." (M): F 4/4/63, ILN 16/3/63, P 13/2/63 & 1/5/63; "Look! They've got an MG..." [copy as previous entry; different illustration] (M): F 30/5/63 & 22/8/63, P 6/3/63 & 5/6/63; "An automatic choice..." (C — two-tone coffee over cream): ILN 4/5/63; "Breeding counts..." (C — red): ILN 22/1/64 & 7/3/64; "Breeding counts..." [copy as previous entry; small illustration of 1933 Magnette rather than TC] (C — red): CL 15/4/64 & 15/10/64, F 22/10/64*; "What's twice as good as owning an MG..." (C — two-tone cream over dark beige): ILN 10/4/65; "The spirit and joy of a true MG..." (C — two-tone dark green over cream): CL 17/2/66 & 14/10/66, F 20/1/66, ILN 11/6/65 & 20/11/65, P 20/10/65; "Rain and night falling..." (C — grey over cream): F 16/6/66.

MGA [E]: "For your biggest motoring thrill..." (M): T 7/4/58 & 5/5/58.

MGA Twin-Cam [E]: "Now — Twin-Cam MGA with disc brakes..." (M): T 15/12/58.

MGA Coupe; "Lovely, lively, luxurious..." (M): F, c. 1958.

MGA 1600 Mk II and Midget [Mk I]: "2 great performers..." (M): P 18/10/61.

Midget [Mk I]: "To own a Midget..." (M): P 20/6/62 & 18/7/62; "Not everyone can aspire to a Midget..." (M): P 3/4/63.

Mk II Sports Convertible: "Vintage year?..." (C — red): ILN 12/9/64; "No midget..." (C — blue, with white MG 1100): ILN 20/2/65, P 24/2/65; "Maybe you'll never race it..." (US): SA 4/65.

MGB: "Superlative MGB..." (C — cream): P 8/1/64 & 18/3/64; "First of the line..." (C — red): CL 20/8/64; "Proved on the track..." (C): ILN 21/1/64, P 28/10/64; "When you get a sudden, mad urge..." (C — red): CL 19/5/66, F 21/4/66*, P 27/4/66; "When you get a sudden..." [copy as previous entry, almost identical illustration] (C — red): ILN 9/4/66; "If you had the Octagon spirit..." (US) (M): SA 7/65; "If you want to know the kind of man he is..." (US) (M): SA 7/69; "People don't buy the MGB just because it's different..." (US) (M): SA 7/71.

MGB/GT (US): "Introducing...." (M): SA 5/66; "It's like the man who drives it..." (M): SA 5/50 & 7/70; "The thinking man's GT..." (M): SA 4/71.

MG 1100: "The most advanced MG of all time..." (M): F 18/10/62; "Who ever thought..." (C — red): F 21/10/65, P 23/2/66; (US) [as MG Sports Sedan]: "Paint a stripe..." (M): NG, undated, 1963*; "Popularity contest..." (M): SA 10/65; "Please don't drink the suspension system..." (M): SA 6/65.

Morgan (Morgan Motor Co., Malvern Link, Worcestershire)

Plus Four Plus: "Definitely a Morgan girl..." (M): CL 7/4/66.

Plus 4: [four-seater]: "Hands up all those..." (M): CL 14/7/66; [two-seater]: "Love affair..." (M): CL 20/10/66.

4/4 1600: "The birthday car..." (M): CL 15/10/70.

• Morris (Morris Motors Ltd., Cowley, Oxford; later Morris Motors Ltd. (Sales Division), Longbridge, Birmingham)

Minor: "Now it's a big car..." (M): CF 3/58, F 30/1/58, T 24/2/58; "I say, that's getaway..." (M): CF 7/58, T 20/10/59; "The gilt-edged security of family motoring..." (M): CL 12/2/59, F 29/1/59 & 30/4/59, ILN 17/1/59 & 11/4/59; "Almost as good as money in the bank..." (M): F 26/2/59; "Together...you'll choose a...Minor 1000..." (M): CF 1/59 & 3/59, WW 4/59; "Most motoring happiness for your money!..." (M): T 2/3/59; "Together...The moment 'Minor' owners meet..." (M): CL 31/12/59, F 31/12/59, T 1/2/60; "One in a million..." (M): T 24/2/61; "Over a million owners know..." (M): T 5/5/61.

Isis Series II: "Under £1000 and in the front rank..." (M): CF 3/57; "Now — with an unchallenged choice..." (M): ILN 24/8/57; "Move up to luxury motoring..." (M): CL 12/9/57, CF 9/57 & 11/57.

Oxford Series III: "Big styling advances!..." (M): F 18/10/56; "Exciting development of the brilliantly proved Morris Oxford..." (C — light blue): F 25/4/57; "Christmas coming up..." (C — two-tone light grey over crimson): F 21/11/57; "While his thoughts are under the bonnet..." (M): F 27/2/58, ILN 15/3/58; "While his thoughts..." [copy as previous entry; different illustration] (M): CF 9/58, F 24/4/58; "Two heads are best when buying a car..." (M): F 22/5/58; [E]: "Move up

to the motoring peaks!..." (M): T 20/1/58; "Most motoring happiness for your money..." (M): T 12/1/59.

Oxford [Series V]: "Who says dreams never come true!..." (M): CF 5/59, ILN 28/3/59, T 13/4/59; "All this — and Morris value too!..." (M): CF 7/59, F 21/5/59, ILN 16/5/59 & 6/6/59, T 5/10/59; "Who says..." [copy and illustration as previous entry; interior also illustrated] (M): ILN 16/5/59 & 6/6/59; "Trunks like this don't grow on trees..." (C — two-tone light blue and pinkish-cream): ILN Christmas Number 1959; "Together...when the car starts..." (M): CF 1/60* & 2/60, T 18/4/60; "Together... Many hands make bright work..." (M): CL 14/4/60, ILN 9/4/60; "Together...Saturday shopping..." (M): HG 9/60, ILN 4/6/60; "Christmas holidays are fun..." (C — pale blue over cream): ILN Christmas Number 1960; "Car for car..." (M): T 10/3/61; "We're going to have a beautiful Oxford..." (M): T 16/6/61.

Mini-Minor: "Wizardry on wheels!..." (M): CF 9/59*, ILN 5/9/59; "Together...No eight-hour day for you!..." CF 4/60*, CL 26/5/60, HG 7/60; "Sit in it..." (M): F 28/7/60; "Open on Christmas day..." (C — white): F 23/11/61.

850 [Mini] [E] "Wizardry on wheels!..." [export version of CF 5/59 for Mini-Minor above] (M): T 9/11/59; "Together...No eight-hour day for you!..." [export version of CF 4/60 for Mini-Minor above; illustration reversed to give LHD] (M): T 21/3/60; "Sit in it..." (M): T 12/9/60; "Sit in it..." [copy as previous entry; different illustration almost identical to Mini-Minor F 28/7/60 above] (M): T 10/10/60.

1100 Mk II: "If Morris ever better my old 1100..." (C — red): ILN Christmas Number 1968.

• Moskvich (Imported by Russian Cars, Thomson & Taylor House, 42 Portsmouth Road, Cobham, Surrey)

[408] Saloon: "Year's best family motoring bargain..." (M): 25/8/66.

• NSU (Imported by NSU (Great Britain) Ltd., 134 King Street, Hammersmith, London W6)

Prinz: "Wunder-buy!..." (US) (M): SA 9/59.

Ro80: "In 1978 the Ro80 may have a little competition..." (M): CL 17/10/68, 13/2/69 & 13/3/69, ILN 19/10/68 & 22/2/69; "Your very own piece of motoring history..." (C — brown): ILN 2/74*.

• Peugeot (Imported by Distributors Peugeot Ltd., Marshall House, Purley Way, Waddon, Surrey)

403 Station Wagon: "The Peugeot 403..." (dealer advertisement: Rosemex, London) (M): F 23/3/61 & 22/3/62.

404 Saloon: "The Peugeot 404..." (dealer advertisement: Rosemex, London) (M): F 28/6/62 & 2/5/63; "A car worthy of a trial..." (M): CL 28/5/64; "These are the cars..." (M): CL 22/10/64; "Call me indestructible..." (US) (M): SA 5/65; "This is one of the seven..." (US) (M): SA 10/65; "What's a beautiful car like you..." (US) (M): SA 2/66; "What are Peugeots made of?..." (US) (M): SA 5/66.

404 Station Wagon: "The car with so many hidden qualities..." (M): CL 29/4/65, F 6/5/65; "Cut round the dotted line..." (M): CL 11/4/68, 2/5/68 & 17/10/68.

404 Family Estate & Station Wagon [7/8 & 4/5 seats] and 204 Estate: "Peugeot Estates speak volumes..." (M): CL 8/6/67, F 14/4/66; "The times you wish you had a Peugeot..." (M): CL 22/5/69 & 16/10/69, F 16/10/69; "The car for the two car family..." [404 Station Wagon now called Estate Car] (M): CL 12/3/70, 16/4/70 & 7/5/70, ILN 21/2/70.

404 and 204: "Every year for seven years..." (M): CL 18/5/67.

204 Coupe: "What's fast, French and expensive?..." (M): CL 19/10/67.

504 [saloon]: "We've come a long way since 1889..." (M): CL 13/11/69, ILN 29/11/69 & 27/12/69; "Italian style..." (US) (M): SA 3/70; "For bones, backs and bottoms..." (US) (M): SA 10/70.

• Porsche (Imported by AFN (Frazer-Nash) Ltd., Isleworth, Middlesex)

356A [hardtop coupe]: "The most effortless fast car..." (M): CL 24/9/59.

356B: "The kind of motoring..." (M): F 23/11/61.

356C: "The Sunday Times..." (M): CL 19/8/65.

911 and 912: "A new generation of Porshes..." (M): CL 21/10/65; "Porsche in 1967..." (M): CL 20/10/66; "I have never driven a car which inspires..." (M): CL 17/11/66.

911: "Porsche driving…" (M): CL 7/9/67 & 19/10/67; "So far in 1968…" (M): CL 18/4/68; "In 1968…" (M): CL 19/9/68; "Porsche and ergonomics…" (M): CL 30/4/70; "Perhaps once in a generation…" (US) (M): SA 8/65; "This is the new Porsche…" (US) (M): SA 2/66; "…and you can almost hear it chuckling…" (US) (M): SA 2/67; "Some day, all convertibles…" [Targa] (US) (M): SA 11/67; "Porsche spent years…" (US) (M): SA 1/68; "Greetings…" (US) (M): SA 5/69; "I really am delighted…" (M): CL 19/4/73; "Throughout its 25 years as a car producer…" (M): CL 17/5/73.

911 T Sportomatic: "If any make of car…" (M): SL 18/3/71; "The Porsche 911T Lux Sportomatic…" (M): CL 29/4/71.

912: "Since the introduction…" (M): CL 31/7/69.

914: "The new 2-litre…" (M): CL 25/1/73.

Porsche range: "The Porsche programme…" (M): CL 15/10/70.

Princess (see *Vanden Plas*, below)

• (AMC) RAMBLER (Imported by Rambler Motors (AMC) Ltd., Chiswick Flyover, London W4)

770 4 door sedan: "Elegantly at home…" (M): F 19/8/65*; "1966 — Four superlative cars…" (M): CL 21/10/65.

770 Station Wagon: "Pack-up-and-go-anywhere car…" (M) CL 7/4/66 & 19/5/66.

770 Convertible: "Open Sesame!…" (M): CL 21/4/66.

Ambassador Convertible: "Sleek, sporty and spacious…" (M): CL 17/8/67.

Ambassador SST Station Wagon: "Seat eight, go anywhere…" (M): CL 4/12/69.

• RELIANT (Reliant Engineering Co. (Tamworth) Ltd., Dept. C.F., Two Gates, Tamworth, Staffordshire)

Regal Mk III: "Your second car…" (M): CF 11/57, ILN 27/7/57; "Relax in Reliant…" (M): ILN 22/2/58 & 19/4/58; "Relax in Reliant…" [headline and main illustration as previous entry; copy shortened and minor illustration omitted] (M): CF 7/58; "The small car that has everything…" (M): CL 26/2/59.

Regal Mk IV: "Years of exposure…" (M): CF 2/59; "The car with a dual personality…" (M): CF 4/59.

Regal Mk V: "New fibreglass body with rear opening boot…" (M): CL 13/8/59, CF 10/59; "Family motoring…Styled in the modern manner…" (M): CL 3/12/59, [with additional illustrations]: ILN 26/3/60 & 25/6/60; "Family motoring…The new…" (M): CF 2/60, 4/60, 6/60 & 10/60*.

[Regal] Mark VI: "What a difference…" (M): CL 30/3/61; "For your second car…" (M): CL 17/6/61.

Regal 3/25: "First choice for your second car…" (M): ILN 1/6/63; "Three wheeler with the most…" (M): ILN 21/12/63; "Britain's finest three wheeler…" (M): ILN 11/4/64; "It all adds up…" (M): ILN 19/12/64.

Sabre: [long nose]: "Swept motoring…" (M): CL 19/10/61, [version without copy]: ILN 21/10/61; "Exhilarating…" (M): CL 19/7/62; "Swept motoring…a new sports car experience…" (M): CL 16/10/62; [short nose]: "Reliant and rallies…" (M): ILN 4/5/63.

Sabra [for Israeli re-export market] [long nose] and Sabre Six G.T.: [no copy]: ILN 13/6/64.

Scimitar GT [coupe]: "Unique…" (M): ILN 9/4/66, 2/7/66, 10/9/66 & 1/10/66; "Astonishing value for money…" (M): HG 11/68.

Scimilar GTE: "Join the GTE set!…" (M): F 17/10/68*, ILN 19/10/68; "Now the Scimitar GTE goes automatic…" (M): ILN 19/10/68; "Load-swallower…" (M): CL 30/3/72; "When you own…" (M): ILN 3/73.

• RENAULT (imported and in some cases assembled by Renault Ltd., Western Avenue, London W3)

Dauphine: "Renault — The leader of the French Automobile Industry…" (M): ILN 20/4/57; "A first class reason…" (M): CL 19/9/57, ILN 17/8/57; "Her elegance, power and smoothness…" (C — red): CL 17/10/57; "So much extra…" (M): ILN 19/1057; "Recherchee (something rather special)…" (M): F 13/2/58 & 6/3/58, S 22/2/58 & V 4/58; "Sensationnelle (something rather superb)…" (M): F 12/6/58, V 10/58; "The 1959 Dauphine turns all heads!…" (M): S 25/10/58; "Have the lot, guv!…" (C — yellow): P 25/3/59*; "Newer-fangled than most…" (C — red): P 17/6/59; "Outright winner!…" (C — red): P 4/5/60.

Floride [convertible]: "Not for ordinary folk…" (C — bronze): F 8/6/51 & 22/6/51; [2+2 coupe]: "Not for ordinary folk…" (C — white): CL 13/7/61 & 3/8/61, F 29/6/61*; [Caravelle fixed head coupe]: "Caught in a rare moment of repose…" (C — yellow): CL 21/6/62 & 12/7/62; "Caught in a rare moment…" [copy as previous entry; different illustration] (C — colour of silhouette not apparent): CL 2/8/62.

8 Gordini: "Le Mans…" (M): CL 14/7/66, F 7/7/66.

[8] 1100: "There's a supple difference…" (C — maroon): CL 7/3/68; [as Renault 10]: "No more apologies…" (US) (M): SA 10/67; "Find another car…" (US) (M): SA 2/68; "How Renault scrimps…" (US) (M): SA 6/68 & 7/68; "Renault's wet sleeve philosophy…" (US) (M): SA 8/68; "Are you a man or woman?…" (US) (M): SA 2/69.

4: "Clan-carrier…" (C — maroon): CL 17/11/66 & 1/12/66, F 10/11/66*; "Country cousins!…" (C — white): CL 10/4/69 & 17/4/69, P 25/6/69; "Renault 4: for people who take a lot on…" (M): CL 8/1/70; "We bought our Renault 4…" (M): P 4/3/70 & 20/5/70; "At 10.30am on August 13th…" (M): P 11/11/70; "Owners of very large estates…" (M): P 30/9/70 & 2/12/70; "You can't mistake a Renault 4…" (M): CL 8/2/73.

16: "As if being voted best car of the year wasn't enough…" (M): CL 21/7/66, F 14/7/66, P 29/6/66; "What makes the big Renault 16…" (C — maroon): CL 10/11/66* & 24/11/66; "The shape of 2 cars in one…" (C — red): CL 4/4/68 & 2/5/68; "How the Renault 16 fell into shape…" (M): CL 18/12/69; "Few other estate cars…" (M): P 25/3/70; "Spend 15 minutes…" (M): P 21/10/70; "Chapter Two: the Renault 16 sedan-wagon…" (US) (M): SA 11/68; "In Volvoland…sold 65,000 Renaults…" (US) (M): SA 3/69; "The first alternative…" (US) (M): SA 6/69; "The only thing standing…" (US) (M): SA 8/70; "The road…" (US) (M): SA 12/70 & 2/71.

• RILEY (Riley Motors Ltd., Sales Division, Cowley, Oxford)

Two-Point-Six: "Magnificent six-cylinder motoring…" (M): F 5/9/57, ILN 7/9/57; "One of the most advanced cars you can buy today…" (M): F 10/4/58; "One of the most advanced…with fully Automatic Transmission…" [headline and illustration as previous entry; slightly different copy] (M): 19/6/58; "One of the most advanced…" [headline as previous entry; different copy and illustration]: (M): F 12/2/59, ILN 3/1/59; "One of the most advanced…" [headline as previous entry; different copy and illustration] (M): F 8/5/58.

One-Point-Five: "You'll like the winning ways of the new Riley One-Point-Five…" (M): ILN 4/1/58; "Everyone acclaims the new…." (M): F 17/7/58; "Everyone acclaims the lively…" [as previous entry except "lively" for "new"]; "You'll love the lively…" (M): CL 16/4/59, F 5/3/59 & 16/4/59, ILN 28/3/59 & 18/4/59; "For the motorist…" (M): F 12/4/62*; "So luxurious…" (M): CL 11/4/63, P 12/6/63; "The Riley world of magnificent motoring…" (C — blue): ILN 11/7/64 & 7/11/64.

4/Sixty Eight: "For the man who really cares…here's a superb…" (M): CL 30/4/59 & 24/9/59, F 23/4/59, ILN 23/5/59, 15/8/59 & 19/9/59; "For the man…The elegant styling…" (M): CL 19/5/60; "For the man…Are you three men in one…" (M): CL 5/11/59, ILN 2/1/60, 20/2/60, 19/3/60, 16/4/60 & 30/4/60; "You are really someone…" (M): ILN 11/6/60 & 9/7/60; "Riley for men who like…" (M): F 15/9/60*; "Take a close look…" (M): F 10/11/60; "For you who want high performance…" (M): CL 2/2/60 & 18/5/61, F 5/1/61 & 15/4/61; "For you who recognize true value…" (M): CL 13/4/61, F 2/3/61; "For you who like refinements…" (M): CL 9/3/61 & 22/6/61, F 9/2/61 & 14/9/61; "Riley for magnificent motoring…" (M): CL 19/10/61, F 9/11/61.

4/Seventy Two: "Three big new reasons…" (M): CL 12/4/62 & 24/5/62, F 1/3/62 & 24/5/62; "Riley elegance…" (M): CL 18/10/62; "Riley luxury, craftsmanship, performance…" (M): CL 14/3/63 & 30/5/63, F 18/4/63 & 12/9/63; "Riley world of magnificent motoring…" (C — two-tone coffee over cream): ILN 8/1/64 & 28/3/64; "Just imagine…" (C — two-tone coffee over cream): ILN 15/5/65; "We often sell this car…" (C — two-tone blue, blue interior): CL 18/8/66, 6/10/66, 1/12/66 & 23/2/67, F 6/7/67*.

Elf [Mk. 1]: "She's gay, she's safe…" (M): F 8/11/62*; "Most luxurious small car…" (M): F 10/1/63; "More power, more safety…" (M): CL 2/5/63, F 23/5/63, P 8/5/63 & 14/8/63.

Elf Mk. III: "The mini with the most…" (C — green with white roof): CL 13/4/67; "Travel 1st class…" (C — red with white roof): CL 26/10/67; "Mini-most…" (C — white): CL 6/2/69.

Kestrel: "Why do Riley owners…" (C — red): ILN 23/10/65 & 25/6/66; "Luxury car runs on water…" (C — white with green roof): CL 8/6/67, F 17/11/66.

Kestrel 1300: "Travel 1st class…" (C — yellow with green roof): CL 15/2/68 & 25/4/68.

• ROLLS-ROYCE (Rolls-Royce Motor Cars Ltd., Crewe, Cheshire [address not given in advertisements])

Silver Cloud [I]: "The best car in the world" [no copy] (M): CF 4/57, F 5/12/57; "Power-assisted steering…" (M): CF 12/57, F 18/4/57; "The best car in the world" [no copy] (M): F 8/5/58; "The best car in the world" [no copy; different illustration] (M): CL 16/10/58 & 12/5/60, F 16/10/58.

Silver Cloud II: "A new engine for the best…" (M): ILN Christmas Number 1959.

Touring Limousine [advertisement by coachbuilders James Young Ltd., a subsidiary of Jack Barclay Ltd., for coachwork on long wheelbase Silver Cloud II chassis; no copy]: (M): CL 20/10/60.

Countryman [advertisement by Harold Radford (Coachbuilders) Ltd. for specially equipped Silver Cloud II]: "Every luxury imaginable…" (M): CL 15/6/61.

Phantom V [advertisement by James Young Ltd. for coachwork on long wheelbase Phantom V chassis]: "Only the genius…" (M): CL 5/5/66.

Silver Shadow [I] [advertisement by James Young Ltd. for two-door adaptation of Silver Shadow saloon]: "What could possibly be added…" (M): CL 14/7/66 & 26/1/67.

Shadow [I] [saloon]: "Decisions…" (M): CL 2/5/68, P 9/10/68; "Workhorse…" (M): CL 11/9/69, P 23/4/69 & 3/9/69; "Apart from money…" (M): CL 29/5/69 & 2/10/69, P 21/5/69; "The decision you will take alone…" (M): CL 26/6/69*; "The easier you sit…" (M): CL 15/6/70, P 7/10/70; "The Rolls-Royce of cars…" (M): CL 29/7/71.

Silver Shadow [I] [convertible]: "The man who drives himself…" (M): CL 24/7/69, P 16/7/69; "Why doesn't every successful man…" (M): P 4/9/69; "And now, the Rolls-Royce of cars…" (M): CL 30/4/70; [Corniche Convertible]: "The whole is greater…" (M): CL 15/7/71*.

Silver Shadow [coupe, in style of convertible]: "What can you say…?" (M): CL 23/1/70.

• ROOTES GROUP (Rootes Motors Ltd., London Showrooms and Export Division: Devonshire House, Piccadilly, London W1)

"You get a touch of genius…" (C — various): CL 12/5/60 & 30/6/60, ILN 25/6/60, [copy as previous entry; similar illustrations] (M): P 13/7/60; "You get a touch…" [E] [copy slightly adapted from previous entry; identical illustrations] (M): T 16/5/60 & 13/6/60.

"One, two, three, Go!…" (C — tinted, various): P 13/7/66.

• ROVER (The Rover Company Ltd., Solihull, Warwickshire; London Office: Devonshire House, Piccadilly, London W1)

60 [P4]: "A remarkably economical 2-litre car…" (M): ILN 7/3/60.

90 [P4]: "The Rover 90…" (M): F 2/5/57; "Appreciation of Rover engineering…" (M): ILN 13/7/57; "Here, without fuss…" (M): P 18/3/59.

80 [P4]: "This — a more powerful…" (M): ILN 2/4/60.

100 [P4]: "The Rover 100 replaces…" (M): ILN 20/2/60.

105R [P4]: "Rover engineering…" (C — two-tone cream over fawn): F 13/2/58 & 27/3/58.

105S [P4]: "Pleasing behaviour is an inherent quality…" (M): F 24/4/58.

110 and 95: "…quietly, luxuriously, travel…" (C — dark blue): CL 14/6/63, F 25/4/63*, [two page version of previous entry with longer copy]: (C — dark blue and M): P 10/4/63.

Range [P4]: "The present successful specifications continue for 1958…" (M): ILN 19/10/57. [P4 & P5]: "The three Rover cars for 1960…" (M): ILN 24/10/59; "Rover 1963…" (C — cream and M): F 18/10/62.

3-Litre [P5]: "A new Rover…" (M): F 23/10/58; "A fine achievement…" (C — olive green): F 16/4/59, ILN 9/5/59; "A fine achievement…" [opening words as previous entry: different continuing copy

and illustration] (M): F 18/6/59; "In the standard of comfort…" (M): ILN 21/5/60; "In the standard…" [copy as previous entry; additional illustration] (M): P 6/7/60; "The Rover 3-Litre…" (C — black): F 13/10/60, P 19/10/60; "It was born…" (C — cream): CL 27/4/61, 1/6/61 & 13/7/61, F 8/6/61*, 13/4/61 & 1/5/61, ILN 27/5/61, P 12/4/61, 24/5/61 & 28/6/61, T 31/3/61; "The Rover 3-Litre is daunted by neither…" [illustration almost identical to that in as previous entry; different copy] (C — cream): P 18/10/61; "The New Series 3-Litre reflects…" (C — blue): CL 19/10/61, ILN 19/10/61; "One of the world's…" (C — dark blue): CL 26/4/62, F 22/2/62 & 5/4/62, ILN 24/3/62, P 28/3/62, 18/4/62 & 26/5/62; "One of the world's…" [copy as previous entry; different illustration] (C — light grey): CL 14/6/62, F 10/5/62, P 27/6/62; [E]: "Ninety years ago…" (C — black; two-tone olive green and dark green): T 7/11/60; "Ninety years ago…" [copy as previous entry; different illustration] (C — black; white): T 24/10/60.

3-Litre Mark II [P5]: "High performance, remarkable luxury…" (C — black): CL 18/4/63 & 30/5/63, F 23/5/63, ILN 22/6/63; "High performance…" [two-page version of previous entry with longer copy] (C — black and M): P 13/5/63.

3-Litre Mark III [P5]: "Don't let the comfort fool you…" (M): CL 21/10/65, F 21/10/65.

3-Litre [Mk II] Coupe [P5]: "100mph armchair comfort…" (C — dark blue): CL 26/3/64, F 26/3/64; "Silent power in complete luxury…" (C — olive green): F 7/5/64, P 26/2/64 & 15/4/64; "Relax — and leave the crowd behind!…" (C — olive green): CL 22/10/64, F 22/10/64*, ILN 24/10/64.

3.5 Litre V8 [P5B]: "Rover announce the incredibly smooth…" (C — maroon): CL 5/10/67, P 4/10/67.

2000 [P6]: "Rover engineering takes motoring years ahead…": (C — white and M): CL 10/10/63, F 17/10/63, ILN 12/10/63, P 16/10/63; "Individualist…" (C — cream): P 21/10/64; "Monte Carlo Rally 1965…" (M): P 3/3/65 & 17/3/65; "The Rover 2000…" (C — various): P 20/10/65.

2000 T.C. [P6]: "Some people buy this car…" (C — white): ILN 13/8/67*, P 18/1/67; "If you know…" (C — red): CL 22/6/67, (M): CL 20/7/67, F 6/6/67*, P 28/6/67; "When little things drop off…" (M): CL 14/3/68, P 28/2/68; "When you've moved on…" (C — tan interior): CL 22/2/68; "Are you driving a balloon?…" (C — red): ILN 22/2/69, ILN 1/3/69; "A Rover by any other name…" (C — blue): CL 10/4/69, ILN 21/6/69 & 6/9/69, P 7/5/69 & 25/6/69; "You can do it, but can your car?…" (C — brown): CL 12/3/70, 30/4/70 & 6/8/70, HG 4/70, ILN 18/4/70, P 22/4/70 & 6/5/70; "The new Rovers…" (C — white): ILN 24/10/70, P 30/9/70, [version identical except headline]: P 16/12/70.

2000 [P6] (US): "To whom it may concern…" (M): SA 8/65; "Why is the owner…" (M): SA 5/66; "For the same reason…" (M): SA 11/66; "Tell them how you had to walk…" (M): SA 1/67; "How to get your wife…" (M): SA 2/67; "How to get your husband…" (M): SA 3/67; "Heaven can wait…" (M): SA 4/68; "What makes a Rover worth…" (M): SA 6/68; "It costs a little over $4000…" (M): SA 8/68; "The best automobile advertisement…" (M): SA 9/68; "Revealing the Rover 2000…" (M): SA 11/68; "Rover Engineering vs. the Sandman…" (M): SA 2/69; "What women like about the Rover…" (M): SA 4/69; "Never mind our opinion…" (M): SA 5/69.

Three Thousand Five [P6]: "The first car…" (C — red): P 1/5/68.

3500S [P6] (US): "The new Rover V-8…" (M): 11/69; "American, European or Unique?…" (M): SA 1/70; "Baby V-8…" (M): SA 3/70; "America! Convert to Rover's Baby V-8…" (M): SA 5/70.

Land-Rover Series II: "New Series II Land-Rovers introduce…" (M): CF 7/58; "Only Land-Rover offers you…" (M): CF 11/58; "Only Land-Rover offers you…" [headline as previous entry; different copy and illustration] (M): CF 2/59; "Only Land-Rover offers you…" [Copy as previous entry; different illustration] (M): CF 4/59 & 7/59; "There's no substitute for experience…" (M): CF 8/59; "The world's most willing horsepower…" (M): CF 10/59, 1/60 & 4/60; "Game for anything…" (M): CF 3/60; "All on the winner…" (M): CF 5/60 & 6/60; "Leading in the winner…" (M): CF 10/60 & 11/60; "Farming in its blood…" (C — green): F 1/12/60; "Your best bet…" (C — green) F 23/2/61 & 30/11/61; "Who's always there on big dates?…" (C — green): F 2/7/64;

"Take a Land-Rover..." (M): F 19/5/66*; "Not a car but a fleet..." (M): CL 17/11/66 & 8/12/66; "Every Friday night..." (M): CL 26/6/69.

• SAAB (Imported by Saab (Gt. Britain) Ltd., 207/209 Regent St., London W1)

96 [2-stroke]: "Now in Britain!..." (M): CL 6/4/61; "Look what's new..." (M): CL 10/3/66; "You don't have to drive a Saab..." (M): CL 24/3/66.

96 [V4]: "Have Saab gone power mad?..." (M): ILN 13/4/68; "The plane-maker's contribution to safer driving..." (M): CL 26/3/70–2 & 9/4/70 [single issue], P 29/4/70.

99: "Big brother is here!..." (M): P 25/2/70; "There are two cars built in Sweden" (US) (M): SA 5/72; "Saab vs. Volvo..." (M): SA 10/72.

• SIMCA (Imported by Simca Motors [Great Britain] Ltd., Oxgate Lane, London NW2; formerly imported by Fiat (England) Ltd. of Wembley, Middlesex, up to around October 1960).

Range: "Change for the better..." (M): CL 19/10/67.

1100: "Simca 1100 is the star..." (M): CL 30/11/67; "From £759..." (M): CL 21/12/67.

1204: "As a second car..." (US) (M): SA 11/70.

1501 Estate: "Estate for sale..." (C — green): CL 15/1/70.

• SINGER (Singer Motors Ltd. (Division of Rootes Motors Ltd.), Coventry and Birmingham; London Showrooms & Export Division: Rootes Ltd., Devonshire House, Piccadilly, London W1)

Gazelle: [Mk I]: "Admired for elegance..." (M): F 27/9/56, ILN 29/9/56; "Acclaimed for economy..." (M): F 10/1/57 & 28/3/57; [Mk II]: "Now! A brilliant new..." (M): F 17/10/57; [Mk IIA]: "Elegance, comfort with the Singer Gazelle..." (C — two-tone green and white estate car; two-tone red and white convertible): CL 17/4/58, F 27/3/58 & 8/5/58, V 5/58, (M): F 27/2/58; [Mk III]: "Motoring's most elegant experience..." (C — maroon with cream flash): F 12/3/59 & 30/4/59, ILN 28/2/59 & 6/6/59, V 11/58, (M): F 16/10/58 & 28/5/59, ILN 28/2/59; [Mk IIIA]: "Foot loose and fancy free..." (M): CL 10/9/59; "You get a touch of genius..." (M): CL 26/5/60; [Mk IIIB]: "Singer looks ahead..." (M): CL 22/9/60; "Luxury, performance, economy..." (M): CL 13/4/61, ILN 8/4/61; [Mk IIIC]: "If you think he's proud..." (M): F 22/3/62*, P 28/2/62 & 18/4/62.

Vogue: [I]: "It's right in fashion..." (M): CL 27/7/61, F 27/7/61; [Series III]: "Announcing an exciting new model..." (C — olive green): CL 3/12/64, (M) [similar illustration]: ILN 20/2/65; "The Vogue is for luxury..." (C — lilac): CL 1/7/65, F 6/5/65; [Series IV]: "Ask any Vogue owner..." (M): F 3/3/66, ILN 7/5/66.

Vogue: [I] Estate Car: "It's loaded with luxury features..." (M): F 24/5/62*.

[New] Vogue [Arrow type]: "Step up in the world..." (C — green): CL 1/12/66 & 16/2/67, ILN 14/1/67; "Step up..." [illustration as previous entry; slightly different copy]: (C — green): ILN 13/5/67; "The '69 Swinger Vogue..." (C — bronze): P 23/10/68.

Vogue Estate: "Outstanding British estate..." (C — green): CL 28/3/68, F 19/10/67*.

Chamois [Mk I]: "The new luxury saloon in the light car class..." (C — dark green): ILN 12/12/64; "Luxury where it matters..." (M): F 18/3/65; [Mk. II]: "How to afford a luxury car..." (C — maroon): CL 19/5/66, HG 5/66, (M): F 7/4/66*.

• STANDARD (Standard-Triumph Group, Coventry)

Eight: "Time goes further with a Standard..." (M): F 18/7/57.

Ten: "Time goes further..." [copy as Eight above; different illustration] (M): F 15/8/57, ILN 27/7/57; "The day our Standard Ten arrived..." (M): ILN 8/3/58.

Companion: "We wouldn't be without our Standard Companion..." (M): F 26/6/58.

Pennant: "Standard-Triumph opens up a new world..." (M): F 5/3/59, ILN 21/2/60.

Ensign: "That extra look..." (M): F 6/3/58 & 17/4/58, S 22/3/58; "That extra satisfaction..." (M): F 15/5/58; "Those extra qualities..." (M): S 5/7/58; "The Standard Motor Company..." (C — crimson): ILN Christmas Number 1957.

Vanguard Phase III estate car: "Time goes further with a Standard..." (M): ILN 10/8/57.

Vignale Vanguard: "The Standard Motor Company..." (C — two-tone lilac and mauve): CLA 1959*, F 20/11/58, P 3/11/59, S 14/11/59; "The classic marriage..." (M): ILN 7/5/60; "The classic..." [copy and illustration as previous entry; small illustration of Ensign omitted] (M): CL 14/7/60.

Vanguard [Vignale] Estate Car: "There's a real V.I.P. car..." (M): F 21/7/60, ILN 2/7/60 & 20/8/60, P 6/7/60.

Vanguard Six: "Vanguard Six leads the £1000 class..." (M): P 31/5/61, 21/6/61 & 12/7/61.

Atlas: "Allways the best..." (M): F 2/6/60*.

Standard-Triumph [E] [corporate advertising for export markets] (Standard-Triumph Group, Coventry)

"In Denmark it's 'Det er Godt!'..." (M): T 7/4/58; "The cattleman in Australia..." (M): T 23/2/59; "It happened in Nigeria..." (M): T 29/2/60; "Floods in Malaya..." (M): T 8/8/60.

• SUNBEAM (Sunbeam-Talbot Ltd., Coventry; London Showrooms & Export Division: Rootes Motors Ltd., Devonshire House, Piccadilly, London W1)

Rapier: [Series 1]: "The car that has everything!..." (C — two-tone cream and brown): F 12/4/56; "The car that has everything!..." [headline as previous entry; different copy and illustration] (C — two-tone yellow and black): F 19/7/56; "Now! More power..." (M): F 14/3/57, SC 3/4/57; "More power...more zip!..." [as previous entry with 'Now'! of headline omitted] (M): F 14/3/57; "More than meets the eye..." [illustration as previous entry; different copy] (M): F 11/7/57, SC 21/8/57; "Now! More power, more zip!..." [headline as earlier entry; different copy and illustrations] (C — two-tone red and white/two-tone yellow and black): F 2/5/57; "We bought a Sunbeam Rapier..." (M): F 26/9/57; [Series II]: "The new..." (M): F 13/2/58, V 4/58; "The new..." [illustration and copy as previous entry; slightly different list of rally successes] (M): F 12/6/58, V 6/58; "The new..." [illustration and copy as previous entry; list of rally successes slightly different again] (M): F 1/5/58; "The new...sets a new standard in performance..." (M): ILN 27/9/58; "The new...sets a new standard in performance..." [illustration and copy as previous entry; slightly different list of rally successes] (M): F 9/10/58); "Record-breaking rally wins..." (M): CL 15/1/59 & 19/3/59, F 5/3/59, ILN 14/3/59; "Sunbeam Rapier gives you individuality..." (M): CL 7/5/59, ILN 16/5/59; [Series III]: "Built for people who prize individuality..." (M): ILN 23/4/60; "It pays to buy a winner..." (M): F 20/10/60 & 10/11/60, ILN 29/10/60, P 16/11/60; [Series IIIA]: "Rally or everyday driving..." (M): ILN 20/5/61; "For people with a zest for living...for people whose life..." (C — two-tone blue): CL 19/10/61, F 19/10/61; "For people...Not everyone..." (M): F 18/1/62; "For people...For some people..." (M): F 15/3/62; "For people...For the man..." (M): F 12/7/62; [Series IV]: "For people...Once again Sunbeam..." (M): F 12/11/64*, ILN 21/11/64.

Alpine: [Series II]: "It's a beaut..." (M): CL 19/1/61, F 12/1/61, P 18/1/61; "Sports Classic..." (M): P 26/4/61; "Pep, power, performance..." (M): P 7/6/61; [E]: "The car with winning ways..." [E] (M): T 22/6/62; [Series IV]: "Making the pace in the fast lane..." (M): CL 26/11/64; [Series V]: "68mph in second..." (M): CL 7/4/66; "This is the life!..." (M): P 8/6/66; "The trend is Alpine..." (M): ET 6/67*.

• TOYOTA (Imported by Motor Imports Co. Ltd., 7, Gresham Road, London SW9)

Corona [Mk 1]: "Flexibility, speed, power..." (M) F 9/6/66.

• TRIUMPH (Standard Triumph Group, Coventry)

Herald: [948cc]: "Away with the grease gun!..." (M): F 23/4/59; "Park with Pride!..." (M): CL 23/4/59, F 14/5/59, ILN 13/6/60; "Big insurance saving..." (M): CL 28/5/59; "Introducing the Twin-carb Triumph Herald saloon..." (M): ILN 12/3/60; "The safest family car..." (M): CL 12/5/60, HG 7/60; "Greetings from Standard Triumph..." (C — white): F 24/11/60, ILN Christmas Number 1960, P 7/11/60; [1200]: "For 60 years..." (C — two-tone red and white): ILN Christmas Number 1963; "The Triumph Herald is founded on steel girders..." (C — white): HG 6/65; [12/50]: "The Herald 12/50 has an opening for a smart dad..." (C — light yellow): HG 3/65; [13/60]: "The number one number two car…" (C—blue): CL 6/3/69, P 26/2/69; "The cosy parker…" (C—maroon): G 1/69 & 3/69*.

TR4A: "Cornering fast…" (C—white): P 13/4/66.

Spitfire [4] [Mk I]: "Black ties and Spitfire…" (C—white): CLA 1965*; [Mk 2]: "Hairpins never trouble…" (C—red): P 22/6/66; "Turn the new Triumph Mk II Spitfire inside out…" (AUS) (C—red): E 23/3/66*.

2000 [Mk I]: "When you realise that seating…" (C—light blue): P 30/11/66; "When you realise that all-round independent…" (C—light blue): ILN 4/2/67; "Today's most civilized car…" (C—red saloon and light blue estate car): ILN 13/5/67 & 27/5/67; "The Triumph 2000 has the fine points…" (C—white): ILN 30/12/67, P 3/1/68; "Lieutenant Commander Tim Hale…" (C—cream): ILN 8/6/68 & 22/6/68, P 26/6/68; "The hush-hush car…" (C—indistinct: photographed at dawn): ILN 3/5/69, P 30/4/69.

2000 Estate Car [Mk I]: "Guide for lovers of fine things…" (C—white): CL 28/4/66; "When you realise an estate car…" (C—green): CL 8/12/66*.

2.5 P.I. Mk2: "Our executive jet…" (C—green): CL 26/3/70, ILN 21/2/70, P 11/2/70 & 18/3/70.

1300: "If you can't get comfortable…" (C—green): CL 26/1/67; "The Triumph 1300 is the best small car…" (C—green): ILN 21/1/67, P 8/2/67 & 8/3/67; "Triumph 1300 has the built-in luxury…" (M): P 17/5/67; "One of the safest…" (C—light blue): CL 30/11/67, P 6/12/67, 20/12/67 & 24/1/68; "Car with the built-in everything…" (C—dark blue): ILN 6/1/68, P 17/7/68; "The car with the built-in everything…" [illustration and headline as previous entry; different copy and layout] (C—dark blue): CL 23/1/69, 20/2/69 & 4/12/69, ILN 18/1/69, 22/2/69 & 13/12/69, P 19/2/69; "The limousine with everything…" (C—dark blue): ILN 30/11/68, P 27/11/68 & 29/1/69; "The short answer to the limousine…" (C—light blue): CL 12/2/70, ILN 24/1/70, P 21/1/70 & 26/8/70.

1500: "Triumph have another success…" (C—blue): CL 17–24/12/70 [single issue] & 31/12/70, ILN 3/10/70, P 7/10/70 & 2/12/70.

XL90 [experimental design]: "The shape of Triumph to come…" (C—bronze): ILN 1/7/67.

• VANDEN PLAS (Vanden Plas (England) 1923 Ltd., Kingsbury Works, Kingsbury, London NW9)

[*Note*: During 1956–57, "Princess" became a marque name in advertisements and "Austin" was omitted from advertisements. The marque's connection with BMC was thereafter indicated by a small BMC rosette with the Corporation's address at the foot of advertisements. As Vanden Plas historian Brian Smith recalls, "Although in some instances the change had been anticipated, as from July 1960 the name 'Austin' was formally dropped from the title of Vanden Plas products which were thereafter marketed under the name of 'Princess' and, in consequence, Vanden Plas were able from 1960 onwards to exhibit at [motor shows] not as coachwork specialists but as motor manufacturers": Brian Smith, *Vanden Plas Coachbuilders*, p. 265. Graham Robson records the Austin Princess IV being badged simply as the Princess IV from the summer of 1957: see Graham Robson, *The Cars of BMC*, pp. 127–128.]

Princess IV: "The new Austin Princess…" (C—two-tone black over yellow): F 29/11/56; "The Austin Princess IV has power-operated steering…" (M): ILN 6/7/57; "Specially made for a well-defined group of people…" (M): F 28/11/57; "Specially made…" [copy as previous entry; different illustration] (M): F 17/10/57 & 6/2/58, ILN 19/10/57.

Princess [Limousine]: "Austin's Princess…it's the only name possible…" (C—two-tone black over yellow): F 28/3/57; "Why no other car has the prestige of a Princess…" (M): F 23/10/58 & 13/11/58; "The prestige of a Princess…" (M): CL 15/1/59 & 19/2/59, F 22/1/59, ILN 14/2/59; "The car in a thousand for the man…" (M): CL 22/10/59, 18/2/60 & 5/5/60.

4-litre [limousine]: "Princess outside, VIP inside!…" (M): F 8/3/62*, ILN 3/3/62, P 21/2/62 & 20/2/63.

3-litre: "The car in a thousand…Prestige…" (M): F 6/4/61, ILN 25/2/61 & 4/3/61, P 29/3/61.

3-litre Mark II: "I thought of 50,000 miles…" (C): CL 16/11/61, F 14/12/61, ILN 11/11/61; "I could only dream…" (M): CL 11/1/62, F 18/1/62, ILN 3/2/62, P 4/4/62; "What's he like?…" (M): ILN 8/12/62 & 9/3/63, P 21/11/62 & 20/11/63; "Think of a Princess…" (M): F 17/10/63; "Many luxury cars cost more…" (C—two-tone olive green over cream): CL 7/5/64, 28/5/64 & 18/6/64, F 2/5/64, 21/5/64, 11/6/64* & 25/6/64, ILN 9/5/64 & 30/5/64, P 29/4/64, 10/6/64 & 8/7/64, (M) [similar illustration]: CL 5/3/64 & 9/4/64, F 2/4/64, ILN 21/3/64 & 18/4/64.

4-litre R: "What did the perfectionist find…": (M): CL 2/9/64, 24/9/64, 8/10/64, 3/12/64, 6/1/65, 28/1/65, 11/3/65 & 15/4/65, F 24/9/64*, 15/10/64 & 18/2/65, ILN 3/10/64, 31/10/64, 11/12/64, 19/12/64, 23/1/65 & 24/4/65; "The man who drives everybody's car…" (M): CL 21/10/65, F 22/7/65; "Vanden Plas luxury…" (M): P 13/7/66; "Men who have arrived…" (C—black over lilac): CL 16/12/65, 17/3/66, 28/4/66, 26/5/66 & 16/6/66, ILN 5/3/66, 19/3/66 & 23/4/66, P 9/2/66, 16/3/66, 13/4/66, 4/5/66 & 1/6/66.

• VAUXHALL (Vauxhall Motors Ltd., Luton, Bedfordshire)

Victor [F-type]: [Series I]: "Salute the Victor…" (C—red): F 18/4/57, P 3/4/57, SC 3/4/57; "The success of the year…" (M): CL 19/9/57, F 5/9/57, SC 18/9/57; "Vauxhall leads again…" [with Cresta] (M): CL 17/10/57, F 17/10/57, SC 16/10/57; "See Britain in your own new Vauxhall…" (M): ILN Christmas Number 1957; "Nothing rivals the 1958 Vauxhalls for value!…" (M): F 16/1/58, S 25/1/58; "Nothing rivals the 1958 Vauxhalls for value…" [headline as previous entry; slightly different copy and illustration] (M): F 27/2/58; "You'll arrive in wonderful style…" (M) V 5/58; "Admired wherever you go…" (M): V 6/58; [Series 2]: "Marvellous new cars…" (M): CL 22/10/59; "Marvellous new cars…" [copy as previous entry; different illustration] (M): ILN 21/11/59; "See Britain in your own new Vauxhall…" (M): ILN Christmas Number 1959; "You may not know…but you recognise…" (M): CL 17/3/60, ILN 2/4/60; "You may not know…A Vauxhall, of course…" (M): ILN 9/4/60*; [Series 2, 5-bar grille model]: "Drive into the motorway age!…" (M): F 13/10/60, HG 12/60, ILN 22/10/60, P 19/10/60; "Own a wonderful world…" (M): F 16/2/61*, ILN 25/2/61; "Own a wonderful world…" [copy as previous entry; different illustration] (M): P 15/2/61.

Victor [F-type] and Cresta [PA]: "It all adds up to a Vauxhall!…" (M): F 23/10/58, S 25/10/58.

Victor Estate Car [F-type]: [Series I]: "The new Victor estate car…" (M): F 20/3/58 & 27/3/58, ILN 22/3/58, P 19/3/58; [Series 2]: "New low look…Always acknowledged…" (M): CL 30/4/59, CF 5/59, F 19/3/59; "New low look…City saloon…" (M): CL 3/9/59, CF 6/59, 7/59 & 9/59; "Space travel…" (M): CF 4/60; "Wide open space!…" (M): CF 5/60; "Goodness spacious!…" (M): CF 6/60 & 7/60; [Series 2, 5-bar grille model]: "Takes more, gives most!…" (M): CL 23/3/61.

Victor [FB]: "The car that says Yes!…" (C—two-tone pink): CL 19/10/61, HG 11/61, F 26/10/61*, 21/10/61, P 18/10/61 & 15/11/61; "The clean line…" (M): F 28/9/61, ILN 30/9/61, P 20/9/61; "A new Vauxhall…" (M): ILN Christmas Number 1961; "Good design…" (M) ILN 12/5/62; "Good design speaks for itself…" [illustration almost as previous entry; same headline; different copy]: (M): HG 6/62; "Hello stranger…" (M): P 30/1/63; "Nice day for a Victor…" (M): CL 7/2/63, F 31/1/63; "The Victor is just like…" (M): P 17/4/63; [1594cc model]: "Let's take my car!…" (M): F 19/3/64, ILN 21/3/64, P 8/4/64.

Victor Estate Car [FB]: "The clean line…and all the qualities…" (M): CL 7/6/62, F 7/12/61, 21/12/61 & 31/5/62; "This Vauxhall Victor likes…" (M): CL 5/7/62, F 12/7/62 & 18/8/62; "Estatecarmanship…" (M): F 17/1/63 & 4/4/63, ILN 17/1/63; "This Victor, they say…" (M): F 16/5/63, ILN 4/5/63.

VX4/90 [FB]: "Go on then—drive…" (M): CL 21/2/63, F 21/2/63*, P 27/2/63; "Vivid motoring…" (M): P 20/6/62 & 4/7/62.

Victor range [FB]: "These three Vauxhalls…" (M): F 20/9/62, P 19/9/62.

Victor 101 [FC]: "Victor 101—now with Powerglide…" (M): ILN 10/7/65, P 21/7/65; "Owning a Victor 101…" (M): CL 12/8/65, F 19/8/65*, ILN 14/8/65; "Zip up a 1-in-8 hill?…" (C—green): P 10/5/67, (M): HG 5/67; "You can pack…" [illustration as previous entry; different copy] (M): ILN 17/6/67.

Victor 101 Estate Car [FC]: "Space setter…" (M): CL 24/3/66, F

14/4/66 & 26/5/66; "It's yours. You can hardly believe it…" (M): CL 7/10/65, F 14/10/65; "How to improve on a winner: (M): CL 10/11/66.

VX4/90 [FC]: "A new VX4/90 — sleek, roomy, civilised…" (M): CL 21/1/65, F 21/1/65.

Victor [FD]: "The great '68 symbol…" (C — black): CL 30/11/67, HG 12/67 & 2/68, ILN 25/11/67 & 9/12/67, P 22/11/67; [2000]: "Victor's 54in. widetrack…" (C — light blue): P 12/6/68; "Victor sports an overhead camshaft…" (C — red): CL 19/12/68, P 27/11/68; "2 lively litres…" (C — maroon): CL 26/6/69, ILN 19/4/69, 7/6/69 & 19/7/69; P 11/6/69; [1600]: "Overhead cam power…" (C — white): CL 9/1/69, ILN 18/1/69, P 22/1/69, SM 3/69* & 4/69; [2000SL]: "Vauxhall use six kinds of make-up…" (C — white): G 4/70*; "Vauxhall: the long distance runner…" (C — metallic blue): G 7/70.

Victor Estate [FD]: "Pack up. Move out. In style…" (C — dark blue): CL 4/7/68, ILN 20/7/68 & 24/8/68, P 14/8/68. [3300]: "Victor 3300 estate. Big jetsmooth six…" (C — black): ILN 16/11/68 & 15/3/69.

Ventora [FD]: "The lazy fireball…" (C — dark red with black roof): HG 4/68 & 8/68, P 13/3/68, 27/3/68 & 17/4/68, (M): ILN Christmas Number 1968; "Mighty Ventora…" (C — blue with black roof): ILN 10/5/69, P 11/12/68, 19/3/69, 23/4/69 & 14/5/69.

Ventora II [FD]: "Something powerful…" (M): F 18/11/71.

Velox [PA]: ['one-piece rear window' model]: "V.e.l.o.x. — pronounced sensation!…" (M): ILN 21/5/60; [2.6 litre]: "Happier holidays…" (M): HG 2/61*; "As virile as they come…" (M): F 19/7/62, ILN 28/2/62, P 25/7/62.

Cresta [PA]: ['three-piece rear window' model]: "Vauxhall leads again…" [with Victor] (M): CL 17/10/57, F 17/10/57, SC 16/10/57; "Better looking than ever…" (C — two-tone grey over pink): F 25/9/58, ILN 6/9/58, P 1/10/58; "People going places…" (M): F 6/11/58 & 27/11/58, S 22/11/58; "People going places…" [headline as previous entry; different copy and illustration] (M): F 5/2/59, 26/2/59 & 16/4/59, ILN 14/2/59, 28/2/59 & 9/5/59; [Goodyear tyres]: "Gracing today's finest cars…" (C — two-tone grey over pink): CL 7/5/59, P 13/5/59; ['one-piece rear window' model]: [Goodyear tyres]: "Gracing today's finest cars…" (C — lilac and mauve): F 29/10/59, (M): CL 22/10/59; "Marvellous new cars…" (M): CF 11/59, ILN 24/10/59; "A new car ready and waiting…" (M): ILN Christmas Number 1960; [2.6 litre]: "Traffic…traffic…traffic…" (M): CL 26/1/61, F 26/1/61 & 16/3/61, P 1/2/61; "Own a wonderful world…" (M): P 22/3/61; "Traffic's no trouble…" (M): F 4/5/61 & 29/6/61, P 31/5/61 & 14/6/61; "Talk about weaving…" (M): CL 13/7/61; "The Big new Vauxhalls for '62…" (M): F 30/11/61 & 14/12/61, P 29/11/61 & 13/12/61; "Very distinguished motoring…" (M): CL 1/3/62, F 8/3/62, P 28/2/62; "Slave driver…" (M): CL 8/3/62*, HG 5/62; "Privileged pair!…" (M): CL 29/3/62, "Witch!…" (M): CL 12/4/62.

Velox and Cresta [PA]: "The new '61 Velox and Cresta…" (M): F 22/9/60.

Friary Estate Car [PA]: [Velox]: "Skittles anyone?…" (M): CL 26/5/60; [Cresta]: CL 5/4/62, F 5/4/62*.

Velox [PB]: "The new Velox takes it easy at 85mph…" (M): ILN 23/2/63, P 13/2/63; "This is the rugged, practical…" (M): F 21/3/63*, ILN 16/3/63, P 27/3/63.

Cresta [PB]: "Test-drive the magnificent…" (M): CL 5/3/64 & 4/6/64, F 12/3/64 & 11/6/64, ILN 7/3/64; "For successful men…" (M): CL 18/2/65, ILN 20/3/65, P 17/2/65 & 10/3/65; [3.3 litre]: "Most powerful car in the £1,000 bracket…" (M): ILN 1/5/65.

Cresta Estate Car [PB]: "Meet the newest estate car…" (M): F 14/5/64, ILN 30/5/64.

Velox and Cresta [PB]: "New Vauxhall (and friendly service everywhere)…" (M): (ILN Christmas Number 1962; "The looks will win your heart…" (M): F 12/9/63, P 11/9/63; "Admire the good looks…" [copy and illustration as previous entry; different headline]: (M): CL 17/10/63, P 16/10/63; [3.3 litre]: "New for '65: the 3.3-litre Vauxhalls…" (M): CL 1/10/64, ILN 3/10/64.

Vauxhall range, 1963: "These Vauxhalls are making history…" (M): CL 18/10/62, F 18/10/62, ILN 20/10/62, P 17/10/62; "From the new…to the big…" (M): F 24/10/63; "Visiting Britain?…" (M): ILN Christmas Number 1963.

Cresta [PC]: "If you want a car…" (M): F 9/12/65*, ILN 11/12/65, P 8/12/65; "Cresta by Vauxhall…" (M): F 10/2/66; "Escape!…" (M): CL 17/3/66, F 24/3/66, P 16/3/66; "There are times…" (M): CL 19/5/66, F 19/5/66, ILN 21/5/66; "Luxury Cruiser…" (M): CL 11/8/56, F 25/8/66; "It's five of the best cars…" (M): CL 20/10/66 & 24/11/66, P 26/10/66; "Cresta jets you to 50mph…" (C — bronze): P 5/7/67 & 4/10/67, (M): ILN 13/5/67; "One hundred and forty horsepower…" (C — black): CL 3/4/69 & 29/5/69, ILN 30/11/68, 22/2/69, 29/3/69 & 12/4/69, P 26/2/69 & 5/3/69; "For an easy life…" (M): CL 7/1/71 & 21/1/71; "3.3 litre big seater Cresta…" (M): SC 11/71.

Viscount [PC]: "The quiet world of powered luxury…" (M): CL 17/11/66*, ILN 5/11/66, P 2/11/66; "The safe, serene world of powered luxury…" (M): CL 27/10/66, P 19/10/66; "The whisper of 6 big cylinders…" (M): CL 12/12/68; "Vauxhall announce the new K cars…" (M): CL 29/7/71.

Viva [HA]: "The 1 litre car with the millionaire ride…" (M): CL 3/10/63, F 10/10/63*, ILN 5/10/63, P 2/10/63; "The brilliant Vauxhall Viva…" (M): P 18/3/64, "Look into the '65 Vauxhall Viva…" (M): ILN 10/10/64, P 14/10/64; "Great way to see the home country!.." (M): ILN Christmas Number 1964; "When you come to Britain, have a Vauxhall Viva meet you…" (M): ILN Christmas Number 1965; [90]: "Book your seats now…" (M): P 17/11/65; "You can get 2,568 copies of Punch in a Viva boot…" (M): P 4/5/66; "How to keep a back seat driver quiet…" (M): P 8/6/66; "Should a 125 year old comic…" (M): P 13/7/66.

Viva [HB]: "Viva goes automatic!…" (C — blue): CL 30/3/67 & 15/6/67, (M): HG 4/67, P 26/4/67; "Going automatic…." (C — blue): HG 11/67; "1-litre mile-eater…" (C — bronze): ILN 19/9/67, P 11/10/67 & 7/2/68; "Going Automatic…" (M): ILN Christmas Number 1967; "Look Dad. Four door…" (C — white): CL 17/10/68, F 14/11/68*, HG 11/68, ILN 26/10/68, P 6/11/68; "Four up and foot down…" (C — black): SM 6/69; [Brabham]: "Brabham breathed on it…" (C — white with black bonnet/side stripe): CL 21/9/67.

Viva Estate [HB]: "Viva's flaunting a fastback…" (C — light blue): P 16/8/67; "Flaunting a fastback…" [copy and illustration almost as previous entry] (C — pale blue): ILN 23/9/67.

• VOLKSWAGEN (Imported by VW Motors Ltd., 32–34 St. John's Wood Road, London NW8)

1200: "Now over 2,000,000 in use…" (M): F 20/3/58*; "For perfection to the smallest detail…" (M): S 22/3/58*; "For perfection reflected in every detail…" (M): F 24/4/58*; "The go-anywhere car…" (M): CL 19/2/59*.

• VOLVO (Imported by Volvo Concessionaires Ltd., 28 Albemarle Street, London W1)

[Amazon] 122S B18: "New for the fortunate few…" (M): CL 12/10/61; "Whispering power…" (M): CL 15/3/62; [131]: "Making the best even better!…" (M): CL 22/10/64 & 24/12/64.

[Amazon] 221 Estate Car: "Be sure…be fast…be safe…" (M): CL 27/2/64, 23/4/64 & 27/8/64; "The down to earth…" (M): F 20/7/67*.

144: "Created in Sweden…" (C — blue): P 3/5/67; "Who wants a car with engineered ashtrays?…" (C — red): P 7/6/67.

1800S: "Three's company…" (M): CL 25/3/65.

• WOLSELEY (Wolseley Motors Ltd., Cowley, Oxford)

Six-Ninety [Series II]: "Important occasion…" (M): F 18/10/56; "Wise indeed…" (M): F 21/2/57; [Series III]: "Kit for Kitzbuhel…" (M): 16/1/58; "Character plus the superlative quality…" (M): 20/2/58; "If I may say so, Sir…" (M): F 18/12/58, ILN 7/3/59.

Fifteen-Fifty [manumatic]: "Two-pedal motoring with Wolseley…" (M): F 24/1/57.

1500 [Mk. I]: "Sensational car…" (M): F 20/3/58; "Prove it for yourself!"… (M): 1/5/58; "Here's what the men who drive them all say…" (M): CL 4/6/59, F 4/6/59, ILN 4/4/59; "No better buy for business…" (M): ILN 2/4/60.

1500 [Mk. II]: "Compact…convenient…" (C — two-tone grey over dark blue): CL 23/2/61, F 4/5/61, P 10/5/61, (M): CL 23/2/61, ILN 11/3/61; "Social call…second car…" (M): CL 6/4/61, HG 5/61, P 21/6/61.

1500 [Mk. III]: "1 1/2 litre performance…." (C — cream): CL

22/3/62, F 22/3/62 & 10/5/62*, P 11/4/62; (M) [similar illustration]: CL 8/2/62, HG 9/62, ILN 10/3/62 & 7/4/62, P 14/2/62 & 28/3/62; "Compact, lively, economical, luxurious…" (M): F 14/2/63, P 6/2/63; "The compact, lively, economical Wolseley 1500…" (M): HG 8/62; "Power-to-weight. Luxury-to-size…" (C—dark blue): F 9/5/63, P 15/5/63, (M): CL 21/5/64, ILN 2/5/64, P 11/3/64.

15/60: "Farina links line with luxury for you…" (M): CL 8/1/59, F 15/1/59, ILN 10/1/59 & 9/5/59; "Fashioned for the fastidious" [main illustration as previous entry; different copy and small illustrations] (M): CL 26/2/59, F 19/2/59, ILN 31/1/59; "Just heavenly…" [main illustration as previous entries; different copy and small illustrations] (M): P 20/7/60; "Every inch a Wolseley…" (M): CL 7/1/60, F 14/7/60, ILN 9/1/60; "Lovely to look at…" (M): CL 28/4/60, ILN 30/1/60 & 28/5/60; "Line…luxury…" (C—two-tone cream over dark grey): CL 23/3/61, F 23/3/61, ILN 25/3/61, P 12/4/61; "White tie…first night…" (M): F 16/2/61, ILN 4/2/61; "Passport…two weeks…" (M): CL 1/6/61, F 8/6/61 & 6/7/61, HG 8/61, ILN 3/6/61.

16/60: "Surpassing all previous luxury value…" (M): CL 5/4/62, HG 12/61; "Luxuriously practical…" (C—two-tone light blue and white): "F 28/3/63, P 9/5/62 & 10/4/63, (M): HG 6/62, ILN 26/5/62; "Luxuriously practical…" [copy as previous entry; different illustration] (M): CL 4/4/63, F 7/3/63, P 13/3/63; "Family motoring at its most luxurious…" (C—two-tone maroon and beige): CL 19/3/64, F 26/3/64* & 7/5/64, ILN 14/3/64, P 8/4/64, (M): CL 2/4/64, HG 6/64 & 12/64, ILN 23/5/64; "If packing the family…" (C—two-tone cream and blue): CL 5/5/66, F 17/3/66 & 12/5/66, ILN 7/5/66, P 6/4/66; "If you want a car with effortless…" (M): ILN 1/5/65; "A world away from it all…" (C—two-tone cream and dark blue): CL 19/10/67, F 26/10/67, P 18/10/67 & 15/5/68.

6-99: "The most significant advance yet…" (M): ILN 5/3/60; "Amongst the world's high performance cars…" (M): F 2/6/60, ILN 2/7/60.

6/110: "Company car…incomparable value…" (M): F 12/7/62, G 7/62, P 30/5/62; "3 litre luxury for less than £1200…" (M): F 6/2/64 & 12/2/64, P 5/2/64.

6/110 Mk. II: "Now Wolseley luxury value…" [illustration as previous entry for 6/110, but in colour] (C—two-tone beige and chocolate): CL 9/7/64; "Now even more luxurious…" (M): F 9/7/64, P 17/6/64; "Combined operation…" (C—two-tone beige and chocolate): F 19/11/64*; "£1,179.13.9 inclusive of Purchase Tax…" (C—two-tone beige and chocolate): F 18/3/65, ILN 13/3/65, P 12/5/65, (M)

[different illustration]: F 8/7/65, HG 4/65; "Away from the clicking, clacking…" (C—two-tone beige and chocolate): CL 20/10/66, F 27/10/66, P U/3/67, (M): HG 7/66; "A world away from it all…" (C—two-tone black and cream): ILN 21/10/67.

Hornet [Mk. I]: "All the proved advantages…" (M): HG 2/62; "The new luxury-drive…" (M): CL 23/5/63, ILN 25/5/63, P 19/6/63; "Never before such luxury value…" (M): HG 12/62.

Hornet Mk. II: "Sure-footed, nimble and so luxurious…" [illustration as previous entry for Mk I; different copy] (M): HG 8/63, P 6/11/63; "A luxurious way of Mini motoring…" (C—green with cream roof): P 13/5/64, (M): HG 4/64; "Easy to handle…" (C—white with crimson roof): F 6/5/65, P 7/4/65; (M) [similar illustration]: F 3/6/65, HG 2/65, ILN 22/5/65; "In the hopping, shopping, bargain grabbing bustle…" (C—green with dark green roof): CL 24/2/66 & 21/4/66, F 10/2/66 & 31/3/66*, ILN 2/3/66, 11/5/66 & 8/2/67, ILN 12/3/66, 11/3/67 & 20/5/67.

Hornet [Mk. III]: "A world away from it all…" (C—light green with dark green roof): HG 4/68, ILN 16/3/68, P 12/6/68.

1100: "That's easy…" (M): HG 1/66; "If you're tired of all the thumping, bumping…" (C—two-tone green): CL 20/4/67, ILN 22/10/66, P 15/6/66 & 5/4/67;

1300: "A world away from it all…" (C—cream): CL 25/1/68, HG 6/68, ILN 27/1/68, P 31/1/68.

1300 Mk. II: "Take the high road…" (C—blue): HG 3/69, P 12/2/69; "Room to relax…" [illustration as previous entry; different copy] (C—blue): CL 27/2/69, 24/4/69, 8/5/69 & 19/6/69, HG 7/69, ILN 15/5/69, 24/5/69, 28/6/69, P 12/3/69, 9/4/69, 14/5/69 & 11/6/69; "Your first Wolseley is rarely your last…" (C—white): CL 18/9/69 & 31/7/69, ILN 26/7/69 & 20/9/69; "The Wolseley. The conservative business car…" (C—light blue): P 23/9/70.

18/85: "A world away from it all…" (C—metalic dark purple): CL 21/9/67, ILN 16/9/67, 30/3/68 & 25/5/68; "Retreat. Go now to your lakeside haven…" (C—dark metallic purple): CL 17/10/68, F 17/10/68*, ILN 19/10/68, P 16/10/68.

18/85 [Mk. II]: "The Wolseley. For dignified, unhurried…" (C—crimson): P 24/6/70; "The Wolseley. The ultimate in elegant…" (C—white): P 15/7/70 & 19/8/70; "The Wolseley. For the older man…" (C—red): P 12/8/70, 9/9/70 & 7/10/70.

Wolseley range: "Cars of distinction…" (M): ILN 19/10/63; "Buy wisely, buy Wolseley…" (M): ILN 20/10/62, P 7/11/62; "Motoring on a different plane…" (M): ILN 17/10/64.

Index

Numbers in **bold italics** indicate pages with illustrations.
Cars illustrated in the color section are identified by **C** after their model names.